IFIP – The International Federation for Information Processing

IFIP was founded in 1960 under the auspices of UNESCO, following the first World Computer Congress held in Paris the previous year. A federation for societies working in information processing, IFIP's aim is two-fold: to support information processing in the countries of its members and to encourage technology transfer to developing nations. As its mission statement clearly states:

IFIP is the global non-profit federation of societies of ICT professionals that aims at achieving a worldwide professional and socially responsible development and application of information and communication technologies.

IFIP is a non-profit-making organization, run almost solely by 2500 volunteers. It operates through a number of technical committees and working groups, which organize events and publications. IFIP's events range from large international open conferences to working conferences and local seminars.

The flagship event is the IFIP World Computer Congress, at which both invited and contributed papers are presented. Contributed papers are rigorously refereed and the rejection rate is high.

As with the Congress, participation in the open conferences is open to all and papers may be invited or submitted. Again, submitted papers are stringently refereed.

The working conferences are structured differently. They are usually run by a working group and attendance is generally smaller and occasionally by invitation only. Their purpose is to create an atmosphere conducive to innovation and development. Refereeing is also rigorous and papers are subjected to extensive group discussion.

Publications arising from IFIP events vary. The papers presented at the IFIP World Computer Congress and at open conferences are published as conference proceedings, while the results of the working conferences are often published as collections of selected and edited papers.

IFIP distinguishes three types of institutional membership: Country Representative Members, Members at Large, and Associate Members. The type of organization that can apply for membership is a wide variety and includes national or international societies of individual computer scientists/ICT professionals, associations or federations of such societies, government institutions/government related organizations, national or international research institutes or consortia, universities, academies of sciences, companies, national or international associations or federations of companies.

More information about this series at http://www.springer.com/series/6102

David Kreps · Charles Ess
Louise Leenen · Kai Kimppa (Eds.)

This Changes Everything – ICT and Climate Change: What Can We Do?

13th IFIP TC 9 International Conference
on Human Choice and Computers, HCC13 2018
Held at the 24th IFIP World Computer Congress, WCC 2018
Poznan, Poland, September 19–21, 2018
Proceedings

 Springer

Editors
David Kreps
University of Salford
Greater Manchester
UK

Charles Ess
University of Oslo
Oslo
Norway

Louise Leenen
CSIR, South Africa
Cape Town
South Africa

Kai Kimppa
University of Turku
Turku
Finland

ISSN 1868-4238   ISSN 1868-422X   (electronic)
IFIP Advances in Information and Communication Technology
ISBN 978-3-030-07615-3   ISBN 978-3-319-99605-9   (eBook)
https://doi.org/10.1007/978-3-319-99605-9

This Springer imprint is published by the registered company Springer Nature Switzerland AG
The registered company address is: Gewerbestrasse 11, 6330 Cham, Switzerland

Preface

This book contains the proceedings of the 13th International Human Choice and Computers (HCC13) Conference, held at Poznan University of Technology, Poznan, Poland, during September 19–21, 2018. The conference was held by the International Federation for Information Processing (IFIP) Technical Committee 9 (TC9): Information and Communication Technology (ICT) and Society, as part of the 2018 IFIP World Computer Congress (WCC).

The conference chairs, David Kreps, (Chair of Working Group, WG 9.5, and Chair of TC9), Charles Ess (Guest Program Chair), Kai Kimppa (Finland Representative, Vice Chair of SIG 9.2.2 and Vice Chair TC9), and Louise Leenen (Chair WG 9.10), chose the theme for this year's conference: "This Changes Everything." Tracks were advertised in the call for papers addressing a range of concerns across the working groups of TC9, and the accepted papers coalesced into six groups: History of Computing; ICT4D and Improvements of ICTs; ICTs and Sustainability; Gender; Ethical and Legal Considerations; and Philosophy.

The papers selected for this book are based on both academic research and the professional experience of information systems practitioners working in the field. It is the continued intention of TC9 that academics, practitioners, governments, and international organizations alike will benefit from the contributions of these proceedings.

The volume editors have, in addition, contributed an introductory paper "This Changes Everything," which is divided into two principle parts: the first looking at the nature and outcome of the call for this conference, and the second, subdivided into the six sections, introducing each individual paper in the volume.

Details of the activities of IFIP TC9 are posted at http://www.ifiptc9.org/.

July 2018

David Kreps
Charles Ess
Louise Leenen
Kai Kimppa

Organization

Program Chairs

David Kreps	University of Salford, UK
Charles Ess	University of Oslo, Norway
Kai Kimppa	University of Turku, Finland
Louise Leenen	CSIR, South Africa

Track Chairs

David Kreps	University of Salford, UK
Charles Ess	University of Oslo, Norway
Diane Whitehouse	The Castlegate Consultancy, UK
Chris Zielinski	University of Winchester, UK
Kai Kimppa	University of Turku, Finland
Penny Duquenoy	Middlesex University, UK
Petros Chamakiotis	University of Sussex, UK
Brad McKenna	University of East Anglia, UK
Chris Leslie	New York University, USA
Sisse Finken	IT University of Copenhagen, Denmark
Christina Mörtberg	Linnæus University, Sweden
Johanna Sefyrin	Linköping University, Sweden
Thomas Taro Lennerfors	Uppsala University, Sweden
Per Fors	Uppsala University, Sweden
Louise Leenen	CSIR, South Africa
Taro Komukai	Nihon University, Japan
Hossana Twinomurinzi	University of South Africa, South Africa
Jackie Phahlamohlaka	CSIR, South Africa

Program Committee

Njod Aljabr	University of Sussex, UK
Katerina Antonopoulou	University of Sussex, UK
Wenjie Cai	University of Greenwich, UK
Julie Cameron	Info.T.EC Solutions Pty Ltd., Australia
Paul Ceruzzi	Smithsonian Institution, USA
Petros Chamakiotis	University of Sussex, UK
Liezel Cilliers	University of Fort Hare, South Africa
Anna Croon	Umeå University, Sweden
Penny Duquenoy	Middlesex University, UK
Pirjo Elovaara	Blekinge Institute of Technology, Sweden
Charles Ess	University of Oslo, Norway

Sisse Finken	IT University of Copenhagen, Denmark
Gordon Fletcher	Salford Business School, UK
Per Fors	Uppsala University, Sweden
Marie Griffiths	University of Salford, UK
Marthie Grobler	CSIRO Data61, Australia
Vic Grout	Glyndwr University, UK
Wendy Gunther	VU Amsterdam, The Netherlands
Olli Heimo	University of Turku, Finland
Magda Hercheui	University College London, UK
Kaori Ishii	University of Tsukuba, Japan
Joey Jansen van Vuuren	CSIR, South Africa
Osden Jokonya	University of the Western Cape, South Africa
Billy Mathias Kalema	Tshwane University of Technology, South Africa
Kai Kimppa	University of Turku, Finland
Ela Klecun	London School of Economics and Political Science, UK
Taro Komukai	Nihon University, Japan
David Kreps	University of Salford, UK
Gloria H. W. Liu	National Central University, Taiwan
Mikael Laaksoharju	Uppsala University, Sweden
Louise Leenen	CSIR, South Africa
Thomas Taro Lennerfors	Uppsala University, Sweden
Chris Leslie	New York University, USA
Takashi Majima	Senshu University, Japan
John Martino	Victoria University, Australia
Tendani Mawela	UNISA, South Africa
Brad McKenna	University of East Anglia, UK
Mohammad Moeini Aghkariz	University of Sussex, UK
Kiyoshi Murata	Meiji University, Japan
Christina Mörtberg	Linnæus University, Sweden
James Njenga	University of the Western Cape, South Africa
Norberto Patrignani	Politecnico of Torino, Italy
Jackie Phahlamohlaka	CSIR, South Africa
Stavros Polykarpou	Judge Business School, UK
Trishana Ramluckan	University of KwaZulu-Natal, South Africa
Minna Rantanen	University of Turku, Finland
Mari Runardotter	Luleå tekniska universitet, Sweden
Purimprach Sangkaew	University of Surrey, Thailand
Johanna Sefyrin	Linköping University, Sweden
Peter Singleton	CHIL, UK
Bernd Stahl	De Montfort University, UK
Riana Steyn	University of Pretoria, South Africa
Gopal Tadepalli	Anna University, CEG Campus, India
Sam Takavarasha	University of Fort Hare, South Africa
Richard Taylor	IBO, UK

This Changes Everything
(Invited Paper)

David Kreps[1] ⓘ, Charles Ess[2] ⓘ, Louise Leenen[3] ⓘ,
and Kai Kimppa[4] ⓘ

[1] University of Salford, Greater Manchester, UK
d.g.kreps@salford.ac.uk
[2] University of Oslo, Norway
c.m.ess@media.uio.no
[3] CSIR, Pretoria, South Africa
lleenen@csir.co.za
[4] University of Turku, Finland
kakimppa@utu.fi

1 Existential Challenges

"I denied climate change for longer than I cared to admit. Not like Donald Trump and the Tea Partiers going on about how the continued existence of winter proves it's all a hoax.... I told myself the science was too complicated and the environmentalists were dealing with it.... A great many of us engage in this kind of climate change denial." Naomi Klein [1]

This Changes Everything. Many of us are likely to associate this phrase with Steve Jobs' introduction of the iPhone in 2007. To be sure, most of us are enthusiastic about information and communication technology (ICT) precisely because we believe and hope that it will change everything – for the better, we presume. But beyond the iPhone and ICTs more broadly, there are clearly other candidates for the "This." "This" may be the impact of the oncoming bioinformatics redesign of species - for example, chimeras supplying organ replacements and skin regeneration techniques. "This" could be the fourth industrial revolution of artificially intelligent robots set to upturn our economies with the automation of much un-skilled and semi-skilled work. But "This" is also, without question, the greatest challenge of our age: climate change.

Since 1974, the Human Choice and Computers conference series has consistently fostered innovative thinking about the interfaces between society and technology. Such thinking always reflects the social concerns of a specific time: Globalisation in 1998, Choice and Quality of Life in 2002, An Information Society for All in 2006, What Kind of Information Society in 2010, and Technology and Intimacy in 2016 are key examples. The number and range of challenges facing the world today at the interface between society and technology are not only mounting, but are increasingly doing so at the deepest levels of the existential – not simply in terms of meaning and justice, but, most fundamentally, in terms of the survival of different species and ecology generally.

With the awareness, in particular, that global leadership on the increasingly pressing issue of climate change is in short supply, Human Choice and Computers has turned - among other concerns - to the question: ICT and Climate Change - What Can We Do?

ICTs can play a fundamental role in the improvement of the education, understanding and explanation of climate change and issues of sustainability, the progress on gender equality, medical advances, and in addressing inequalities of access to the benefits of a highly technological society. It is also the site of challenges to individual rights, privacy, and accountability, and the means by which globalization has both spread and exacerbated inequalities. Awareness that the size of the share of the growing economic pie that the majority of us receive has long since stagnated - and even begun to shrink - has led to unfolding seismic shifts in the global order. Electorates (enfranchised and disenfranchised) in the Middle East, Europe and the US in recent years have punished those sections of society that had both benefited most from globalization and yet believed their own rhetoric that, as the pie got larger, everyone's share of it increased. The still more fundamental realization that it is simply not possible, on a finite Earth, to keep growing the pie, is an economics lesson that the planet is teaching us with increasing ferocity. A political economy of finite wants and non-growth, although it seems as far off as it was when Herman Daly wrote of it in 1973 [2], may yet impose itself – necessarily with the vital help of ICTs.

The challenges of climate change are indeed something no one, in any sector, can avoid, and the changes required to combat its effects will require all our efforts. The Chairs of 13th Human Choice and Computers Conference suggest that everyone in the information systems community should be working towards this end - or at the very least, not against it. How do these realizations manifest themselves in the ICT sector specifically, and what other challenges - which change everything - must we address?

Our call was as broad as one can possibly imagine for a set of fields that are essentially driven by precise and minute details (of engineering specifications, requirements of specific coding languages, OSs, information architectures, and so on). Not surprisingly the papers submitted to and accepted, through peer review and revision, by the Chairs of the conference, and gathered together in this volume, display a strong tension between our participants' training and experience in the specific and the precise, and the perhaps maximally broad demands of addressing our larger themes. The inherent difficulty of keeping one's eye upon the detail of means whilst retaining the vision of broader ends has gathered together a range of papers at various points along that spectrum. This volume, therefore, we believe, is successful in the primary aim of encouraging colleagues across the range of ICT concerns to take on these larger themes. We hope, further, that it inspires more – both in detail and breadth – across the fields and disciplines HCC represents.

There are many themes which we could pick out from the papers gathered in this volume, before addressing them more closely. In particular, however, we would like to highlight the occasional mention of the existential - as a way of pointing towards a resurgence of interest in existential philosophy as a framework for dealing with - well - existential questions in a world in which traditional religious frameworks have largely lost their purchase [3]. Of course, we are still faced with the multiple existential moments imposed upon us as still mortal beings, beginning with our vulnerability and mortality - both individual and, as the climate crisis foregrounds, collectively.

All of this leads to the larger point: part of the "everything" that "this" changes is precisely the traditional epistemological and thereby disciplinary assumptions that separated out the natural sciences and the humanities in the 19th century - the alleged "fact/value" distinction, among other examples. Consideration of how climate change affects ICTs, and ICTs' role within it, in fact promotes deep and searching questions about the very foundations of our field [4]. As Frantz Rowe, editor of the European Journal of Information Systems has said in a recent Editorial [5], critical and philosophical assessment of why as well as what we do in this field, is of increasingly paramount importance, and the boundaries of our disciplines must be questioned, and broadened, and many of our assumptions thereby irrevocably changed.

What we now know from over a century of post-positivist thought (including names familiar to IS scholars such as Latour, [6], Barad [7] and others; critical realist philosophers such as Roy Bhaskar [8] and process philosophers Henri Bergson [9] and Alfred North Whitehead [10]; feminist critiques of positivist science; and many others) is that many of the distinctions we have in the past taken for granted are, at best, heuristic and metaphorical. We can further point to examples of engineers, including computer scientists and network engineers (e.g. Bendert Zevenbergen [11]) who are now explicitly espousing virtue ethics and care ethics as required for the practices of engineering: with great power comes great responsibility - to care, to paraphrase him.

So the efforts in play in the conference, displayed in this volume, to likewise bridge these gaps, contribute to these broader developments - and these broader developments suggest that there is much more to be done, not only at the practical levels of designing new ICTs, etc., but at the more theoretical/foundational levels: our disciplines and their guiding assumptions have to be rethought - in particular, in order to take centrally on board the ethical and social responsibilities of those empowered and entrusted with the design of ICTs.

2 Summary of Papers

The conference was initially advertised in a Call for Papers with a wide series of different Tracks, reflecting the variety of concerns of the various Working Groups of Technical Committee 9. Each track called for papers that engaged somehow with the broader theme - what is 'changing everything' in the particular arena of focus for that Working Group? Gathered together, the papers therefore fall into a series of distinct groups focused not just, as described above, upon the detailed minutiae of solutions, but on a specific slant or aspect of the wide field of ICTs and Society. Nonetheless, as a whole, the main theme and grander concerns remain clear.

2.1 History of computing: 'This Changed Everything'

The papers in this category reflect on "where we came from" in terms of ICT developments that shaped our current interaction with computers. Ambrosetti and Cantamesse consider the "technological democratization" brought about by the introduction of PCs in the late nineteen-seventies and early eighties. The introduction of PCs to the general public marked "a watershed between a former, professional only (military, academic, or corporate) use of computers, and a later diffusion to a vast and not necessarily skilled public". The authors also analyze the gap between the skills of the average user and the expert user from the mainframe era through to the post-PC era.

Pyle narrates an example of a software development project in the mainframe era, a classified UK Defense project that ran from 1969 to 1973. This project established basic principles for Software Engineering but due to secrecy restrictions details could not be published. It brought about changes in the discipline by individuals who worked on the project and subsequently passed on the learning.

Tatnall narrates the Australian contribution to the building of computers, looking at the people who were involved in these projects, the culture that drove these developments and the resulting technologies.

2.2 ICT4D and Improvement of ICTs

Perhaps in no other area are the changes being wrought by ICTs so fast and so fundamental than in developing countries, where the 'leapfrog' phenomenon is bringing the advanced online economic activity of G7 economies to the furthest corners of the world. Takavarasha, Cilliers and Chinyamurindi investigate obstacles in developing countries for students in gaining access to technologies, while Steyn, de Villiers and Twinomurinzi consider the requirements for potential entrepreneurs to access and use ICTs. Van Biljon and Naude consider ICT4D from a research perspective. They give an overview of collaborative research patterns of South African ICT4D researchers with the aim of appealing for collaboration between researchers from different institutions as a mechanism of inclusion. Pathirana presents a digital merchant platform requiring only a smartphone and an internet connection. This allows merchants in developing countries easy access to the digital economy.

Our growing reliance on technology results in skills shortages. This issue is ad-dressed in papers by Hyrynsalmi, Rantanen & Hyrynsalmi as well as Jansen van Vuuren and Leenen. The first paper considers the harm that ICT skills shortages are likely to have on growth and innovation in Finnish ICT businesses. The latter paper focuses on how skills shortages in cybersecurity can be addressed in South Africa.

As a consequence of technological advances, virtual teams are becoming increasingly common in the modern workplace. Gomez et al. found that team composition in devising information strategies influences team cohesion in virtual environments. Such team cohesion has been shown to improve team learning.

2.3 ICTs and Sustainability

At the heart of the main conference theme, papers focused upon how ICTs can be developed and used sustainably address some the key issues of the transformations now underway.

Nyström and Mustaquim argue that the inclusive innovation framework (IIF) and strategies of open innovation can be helpful for designing a sustainable HCI system. Several papers address the dual roles ICTs play in terms of contributing to sustainability and contributing to entropy. Van der Velden investigates the relationship between sustainability and ICT by critically considering two sustainability frameworks. Patrignani & Kavathatzopolous reflect on the challenges of designing sustainable ICT systems from the perspective of the designers of these systems, specifically on their ethical competencies and how these competencies can be acquired. Junge and van der Velden analyze discourses on planned obsolescence of technology in the Norwegian media with the aim of finding the root causes for the "technology is neutral" perspective - a belief that can undermine policy and interventions to support sustainable technology.

Bednar & Spiekermann argue that the ICT community can only respond to the call for sustainable and value-based design of technologies if there is an understanding of how ICTs affect users. Their study on the changes ICTs have brought to a group of students' lives aims at providing a starting point for future value-based designs of ICTs.

2.4 Gender

The four papers in this category highlight different ways in which cognition of feminist approaches can benefit ICT development and design.

Sefyrin, Mörtberg and Elovaara describe a planned study that will explore how gender science, specifically feminist technoscience, can contribute to science practice challenges. This study will serve as a theoretical resource for the integration of gender equality in Swedish Higher education in IT.

Fiscarelli and Van Herck classify computer science conferences with the aim of identifying gender-based patterns for career length, collaboration, interdisciplinary research, and publication growth rates. Their findings provide insight into the participation of female authors in computer science research, and specifically consider the low percentage of female publishers in this discipline.

Male dominance in the ICT industry results in software and technologies that may not be representative of the wider population. Corneliussen, Herman and Gajjala analyze three case studies in different cultures to posit the benefit of a feminist gaze on ICT production.

Finken, Mörtberg and Elovaara argue for the inclusion of feminist technoscience in Participatory Design (PD) to benefit PD-based practices.

2.5 Ethical and Legal considerations

Five papers focus on the ethical development and use of ICTs. Heimo, Rantanen and Kimppa studied the effect of a Finnish school information system from a sociotechnical perspective. The system resulted in some unintended negative uses. The authors make recommendations for improvements that will promote values such as openness and fairness. Murata, Orito and Takubo explore the exploitation of social media users who openly and honestly share personal information. The authors propose policies to address and limit this exploitation. Kavathatzopoulos and Asai argue that the philosophical method of deliberative thinking, by focusing on the process of thinking, is the grounds on which to ensure ethical decision making for ICTs. Reijers et al. present a formal framework for the discussion of ethical issues that should be considered in the development of ICTs. Poulsen, Burmeister and Kreps study the ethical considerations of the elderly giving their trust to an untested robot. Although the study was based on a theoretical care robot model, the authors found that the robot inspired trust even when participants lacked an understanding of the model's ethical decision-making process.

Legislation to ensure ethical behavior of data is the focus of two papers. Komukai and Ozaki present an approach to improve cross-border investigation by considering the rights of states that control the data as well as individuals in the context of international law and human rights. Ishii explores legal issues regarding portability.

2.6 Philosophy

Philosophy - as we saw at the beginning of this editorial - is becoming an increasingly important arena in the Information Systems community, and the wider consideration of the creation and use of ICTs. Galanos argues that terms such as "AI" (artificial intelligence) and "robot" are not well defined, at least not when used in the media or public discourses. The consequence of this is that it "…appears that propositions about AI are neither right nor wrong: they are meaningless". The author calls for researchers in this field to work towards the improvement of public understanding in this field.

Rantanen and Koskinen also focus on the importance of a shared understanding of terminology; they discuss different definitions of the term "Public Health Record." This brings about challenges in having a rational discourse between patients, citizens, health care providers, system developers and policy makers.

Kajtazi and Haftor raise the need for a coherent theory of information inadequacy by analyzing 50 instances of information inadequacy.

3 Conclusion

In sum, the papers presented in this volume each – in their own specific and detailed focus – and collectively, represent what the editors believe to be a turning point in the research community around ICTs: the multiple challenges facing society in 2018 are so broad, profound, and pressing, that *this really changes everything*.

References

1. Klein, N.: This Changes Everything. London, Penguin (2014)
2. Daly, H.: Economics, Ecology, Ethics. Freeman, San Francisco (1973)
3. Lagerkvist, A.: Digital Existence. Routledge, London (2018)

4. Kreps, D.: Against Nature: The Metaphysics of Information Systems. Routledge, London (2018)
5. Rowe, F.: Being critical is good, but better with philosophy! From digital transformation and values to the future of IS research. Eur. J. Inform. Syst. **27**(3), 380–393 (2018)
6. Latour, B.: We have Never been Modern. Pearson, Harlow (1993)
7. Barad, K.: Meeting the Universe Halfway (2007)
8. Bhaskar, R.: The Philosophy of Metareality. Routledge, London (2002)
9. Bergson, H.: Matter and Memory. Dover, New York (1908[2004])
10. Whitehead, A.N.: Process and Reality. Free Press, New York (1978)
11. Zevenbergen, B., Brown, I., Wright, J., Erdos, D.: Ethical privacy guidelines for mobile connectivity measurements (2013). http://dx.doi.org/10.2139/ssrn.2356824

Contents

ICTs and Sustainability

Gender

Ethical and Legal Considerations

Philosophy

History of Computing: 'This Changed Everything'

The Basic Dream of the PC, or "Did You Ever Play Tic-Tac-Toe"?

Nadia Ambrosetti[1]([✉])[ID] and Matteo Cantamesse[2][ID]

[1] Università degli Studi, Milan, Italy
nadia.ambrosetti@unimi.it
[2] Università Cattolica del Sacro Cuore, Milan, Italy

Abstract. In the late Seventies-early Eighties of the 20th century, the diffusion of the PC marked a watershed between the strictly professional use of computers, and their diffusion to a huge public. It represented the democratization of a powerful and remarkable technology, a first stage in a never-ending and pervasive process of independence and freedom of the individuals. This revolution, however, placed in the historical perspective of the last century, proves to be a fundamental step (but still a single step) in the evolution of the users' digital skills and in the transformation of their experience and life.

Keywords: PC · Skills · Cloud · Main frame · Computing · Digital divide
Digital literacy

1 The Dawn of a New Era of Computing

A difficult goal for historians is to faithfully represent daily life of a past period. It is also particularly hard to imagine our lives with the ancestors of PC, and the struggle doubles, if you try to combine the two.

What computers actually were and were perceived in collective imaginary, before the spread of PC, is well represented in the episode of the popular TV-series "Columbo", entitled "A Deadly State of Mind", starring Peter Falk and George Hamilton, which first aired in 1975.

In a scene, the protagonist faces the murderer in a research data center room where they enter to talk in peace. In fact, computers are running, as you can argue from the continuous flashing of different lights, and by the movement of the magnetic tape reels, but the lab is silent and empty: nobody is performing queries on the site, as jobs are launched by users on terminals placed in other rooms or buildings, and results will be available after a possibly very long time of computation. Columbo himself learns this lesson in another episode of the series, when, while waiting for an address at the city data center in Los Angeles, he haunts the employee with continuous requests to speed up.

This last example displays very well the typical, necessarily mediated interaction between an end user and a computer, in the centralized time-sharing computer model.

When, at the turn of the seventies and eighties, the PC appeared on the world scene, it became a widespread device, potentially (and hopefully for the manufacturers) present in every home, an exciting tool for smart people, like the protagonist of the

D. Kreps et al. (Eds.): HCC13 2018, IFIP AICT 537, pp. 3–15, 2018.
https://doi.org/10.1007/978-3-319-99605-9_1

Fig. 1. The scene taken from "A Deadly State of Mind"

1983 movie "War Games". This young, skilled and promising hacker, while attempting to enter the computer of a well-known video game company, manages to reach, with his PC, a military supercomputer designed to respond to a missile attack, and plays Tic-tac-toe against the mainframe.

Individuals and (personal) computers had a brand-new interaction model: end users could finally learn to code, because programming was not only feasible, but also one of the main activity on a PC and, most of all, a great challenge (Fig. 2).

Fig. 2. A scene taken from "WarGames"

In 1990, in an interview about the digitalization of libraries, in the movie "Memory and Imagination", Steve Jobs [1] defines the computer as "the most remarkable tool that we've ever come up with". The main benefits imagined by Jobs for the immediate future were that the computer would allow people to access huge amounts of data by a click, and could also reshape the way of learning, by means of simulation.

Even Ceruzzi [2], while telling the history of modern computing, entitles his chapter "Augmenting Human Intellect, 1975–1985", meaning that the PCs acted as an actual driver of paradigm change and innovation, in the industrial market design: "When the established computer companies saw personal computer appear, they, too, entered a period of creativity and advance".

In just over a decade, the spread of the PC could be imagined as a restyling of the access to knowledge for a large amount of people, thanks to its small size, and affordable price. Multi-purpose, and suitable for individual use, PCs were designed to be operated directly by end users, without the mediation of computer scientists, or technicians, as the film "War Games" shows.

Therefore, the advent of the PC marked a watershed between a former, professional-only (military, academic, or corporate) use of computers, and a later diffusion to a vast and not necessarily skilled public.

2   The Individual Machine

The wide presence of the PC can be considered as an evidence of the technological democratization, a first footstep in an irresistible process of independence and freedom of the individuals: during the Seventies, technologists and computer scientists were already looking forward to such future.

As quoted by Rogers and Larsen [3], in 1976 at a convention of government officials, Ted Nelson, who authored relevant books about the link between computers and freedom [4, 5], concluded his presentation by yelling, on the notes of "2001: A Space Odyssey" theme: "Demystify computers! Computers belong to all mankind!".

He was urging to disrupt the prevailing computer order and bringing about a conception of the computer as a personal device, accessible by everybody, included the elderly, women, children, minorities, and blue-collar workers. He was also meaning that the adversary to beat was Central Processing, under any commercial, ethical, political, and socio-economic point of view (Fig. 3).

Fig. 3. The front cover of Ted Nelson's manifesto "Computer Lib"

Apart from philosophical considerations, new opportunities and advantages were evident and undeniable: users could rely on free access to digital calculation at any time, at home, each at their own pace; understand the computer science principles by learning to code; play and create video games, new media, and art (ASCII art), just to quote the most amazing ones.

The skills involved in this phase were not only hard, linked to the knowledge domain the users were working in, but also soft, as the users could implement their own solutions to problems, even creating algorithms, or new field of research: "the more you know about computers […], the better your imagination can flow between the technicalities, can slide the parts together, can discern the shapes of what you would have these things do" [5].

In the following years, the evolution of hardware and, consequently, of software led to the design of more user-friendly devices, featured by GUI; computers could still be programmed, but common users had ready-to-use software packets available for most common tasks, with no need to program. Starting from that moment, skills needed for common users included digital literacy. This marked the beginning of what Andrew Odlyzko [6] calls the "unavoidable tradeoff between flexibility and ease of use".

Until the diffusion of Internet access, personal computers were mostly stand-alone systems, upgraded (and updated) via local procedures: this only partially limited the possibility to share documents and programs, as floppy disks and later CDs or DVDs, due to their small size and weight, worked perfectly as a ubiquitous form of data storage and exchange, at least for users' files.

Nonetheless, the opportunity to have immediate access to information, data, and resources changed drastically the PC, as technologists and computer scientists pointed out, in the late Nineties, by opening the quarrel about the death of the PC.

On the one hand, Donald Norman in 1998, in his "The Invisible Computer" [7], presents his visions of the future: a skeptical one about the PC, and an optimistic one as for information appliance; entering the new age of ubiquitous computing implies the use of far simpler devices than the personal computer, designed for the mass market and not for early adopters. Therefore, he underlines the importance of user-centered design, so that "the technology of the computer disappears behind the scenes into task-specific devices that maintain all the power without the difficulties".

One the other hand, in 1999, Bill Gates, for instance, [8] clearly states that the PC is not destined to die, replaced by other devices, but to evolve, working together with other devices: the user experience and interaction will become more reliable and simpler, disregarding the complexity of the underlying technology, and, on this idea, he was ready to bet the future of his company.

The quarrel was still not over in our century, but changed partially form, due to the collapse of desktop sales: in 2011, Roger Kay [9], discussed about the role remaining to desktop PCs, compared with laptops and smart devices, which were lapping desk-top units. He had noticed that desktop PCs would survive at least for a bedrock market segment, composed by users who didn't want to or could not switch to another device: "the anti-mobility crowd (operators of desktop pools for task workers), those who wanted the modularity of desktops (the white box builders, who buy parts opportunistically and jerry-rig systems together), a "comfort" segment, who liked a desktop for its better ergonomics (although notebook users could pony up for a docking station with spacious keyboard, large monitor, and ergo mouse), and the performance folks, who wanted a big heat envelope to house the hottest, fastest components (graphical workstation users and PC gamers)". In 2017 the reasons of the survival of desktop PCs appear still the same: despite lack of mobility, they are still preferred to laptops and tablets as home servers, gaming systems, media centers, and for video editing, due to their higher computational resources, bigger mass storage capacity, smarter time of reaction on heavy workload, running multiple operating systems [10], and better performance of IO peripheral set (i.e., screen dimensions and resolution, refresh frequency, quality of sound).

3 Was It a Revolution?

Trying to answer this question is very challenging, mainly because it can be considered under many respects, and the different starting point can lead to very different conclusions.

From an industrial point of view, Peled [11], in 1987, after describing how pervasive is the presence of computers in industry and in research, welcomes the next revolution, which would be supported by parallel processing, and miniaturization, and would transform the computer in a "ubiquitous intellectual utility", taking for granted that one revolution has already happened.

As for a sociological interpretation, in 1988, Pfaffenberger [12] raised the question about the mythology of personal computer: for vendors, it would have been a crucial factor to sell millions of computers to people who "in reality had very little practical need for them, and most of the machines wound up in closet". Nonetheless, the social change implied in the spread of personal computer can't pass in silence: the computer industry founders needed such an epic narration, that "may have been as important to an emergent industry as its technical achievements", because "investors must construct a meaning-framework for their artifacts to create a need that did not previously exist". According to the author, in the early personal computer era, the dynamics of social behavior were determined by the interaction among three factors: a dominant ideology represented by the centralized, administrative authority in large organizations; the adjustment strategy, typical of hackers and home users, who wanted to change their low rank, without openly refusing the underlying ideology of the system; and the reconstitution strategy, endorsed by the computer industry founders and embraced by many users, aimed to replace the existent dogmatic value system with a new one, that would encourage decentralization. In a sense, a warm, controlled revolution.

In 1992, Pool [13] gives an overview of the innovations introduced in the world of research starting from the introduction of personal computers: ranging from the greater ease of communication, to the help in carrying out experiments, to data collection, to the execution of calculations, and to the drafting of a manuscript, or a grant proposal, PCs paved the way to a revolution in teaching and disseminating science.

Six years later, in 1998, one more sociological reading displays the changes introduced in everyday family life both by PCs, and the Internet. Hood [14] points out the main benefits of "entrepreneurial freedom" owed to what he calls without compromise "The PC Revolution": a better control on family finances; the growth of schooling in the previous years; a boom of home start-up businesses; a new market in the field of education; easier access to retail goods and services; a drastic cut in phone bills. In other words, a burst of energy for the American society, depending on both the private individuals' and the government's initiative.

Such energy is still considered as an innovation driver in a later (2005) socio-technological study by Gershenfeld [15], who takes the PC revolution for granted, and considers it as a prerequisite. The "coming revolution" will be the personal fabrication, i.e. the ability (for everybody) of designing and producing objects, with devices combining consumer electronics, and industrial tools.

Another interesting point of view to observe the spread of the PC and to evaluate its revolutionary potential, is knowledge. Beaudry [16] has used U.S. metropolitan area-level data, referred to the period 1980–2000, the PC diffusion era, to test "whether the recent patterns of PC adoption and the increase in the return to education across U.S. metropolitan areas conform to the predictions of a model of endogenous technology adoption describing such revolutions." In other words, the authors try to verify with an econometric analysis if the diffusion of the PC, a new, skill-requiring technology, can be considered as a revolution (and not a change in the long term). If so, then some conditions that have established with their model, must be valid. The research analysis of data highlights the presence in the period considered of distinctive implications of technological revolutions, according to a neoclassical model of technology adoption. For example, data shows a greater return in the US areas where the presence of skilled workers was relevant and therefore technology spread was more rapid: this is coherent with a model of revolution and its speed of diffusion.

Under an economical respect, in 2011, Sichel [17] presents an economic framework for evaluating the aggregate impact of computers: the conclusion of his quantitative and historical analysis is that the contribution of computers (included PCs) to the American economic growth has been modest. In 2015, Berger and Frey [18] offered a very different interpretation of the impact of the PC revolution, showing "how a previously undocumented shift in the skill content of new jobs, following the Computer Revolution of the 1980s, has altered patterns of new job creation across U.S. cities".

To conclude, we can say that the ordinary people's perception of a revolution, finds an overall confirmation in important studies in different fields of research.

4   Extending the Historical Landscape

The introduction and spread of PCs changed everything, or, at least, determined a significant technology revolution: starting from this idea and under the influence of some of the studies mentioned above [16, 18], a small set of indexes has been identified, useful for comparatively describing the relationship with the available devices.

The goal was to point out how users' skills, and consequently their experience, changed over the decades, before and after such a turning point.

The three indexes are the following:

1. Skills: a list of competences, required or recommended to operate the device.
2. Divide: it compares the difference between average and expert users' skills.

3. Locus of control: it labels the distance between the users and the actual control on their operations. It can be local, if the user can operate the device autonomously; remote, if device operation depends on the access to a facility or a service [19].

4.1   Before the Digital

At the beginning of the 20th century, the ancestors of the PCs available to users were mechanical and later electromechanical devices, mainly intended for typewriting and accurate calculation.

The results (either documents, or calculations), unless printed or written on paper, were volatile, and could not be stored in a memory to be retrieved or shared.

The average users were therefore professionals (employees, journalists, writers, accountants, bookkeepers, engineers, scientists) in need of reliable devices, at a reasonable price.

Only a faster execution made expert users stand out, as devices were not programmable, and allowed a limited set of operations. Therefore, besides skills closely linked to a specific domain of knowledge, users really needed only literacy and numeracy (Table 1).

Table 1. Pre-digital

Skills	Divide	Locus of control
Literacy, numeracy, users' domain skills	Average and expert users share the same core skills	Local

4.2   The Age of Gods, or Main Frame Age

In the main frame era, access to computer was limited, because of their cost and value as strategic tool; main frames were typically housed in university campuses, or corporate buildings, or in government facilities, in large inaccessible rooms, like the one in Fig. 1.

Like before, users were mainly professionals, but, as for their skills, they can be split into two different and not overlapping sets.

One the one hand, expert users, such as engineers, programmers, and computer scientists, needed to be both hard- and soft-skilled users, in order to design software useful for specific requirements of large institutions or businesses, in the fields of research, national security, administration, and so forth. They had direct access to the mainframe and to institutional or corporate databases.

Average users, though professionals, didn't need specific device-related skills, but acquaintance with its interface was enough, as they could only use some predefined procedures, in order to find mostly printed answers to their time-consuming queries.

For average users, interaction with computers was quite comparable to consulting an oracle in ancient times: the question was asked to an intermediary, the answer (job result) was given to the consultant (printed on continuous forms, striped on one side, to facilitate the reading of long series of data); if the question had been for some reason not accurate or uncomplete or if a new question was suggested by results, the whole procedure had to be repeated from the beginning, because any further query required a brand-new job to be executed.

In addition to the previous skills, users therefore needed (Table 2):

Table 2. Main frame

Skills	Divide	Locus of control
Digital literacy, digital numeracy, programming, querying, problem solving, algorithm design	**Average:** digital literacy	**Average:** remote
	Expert: digital literacy, digital numeracy, programming, querying, problem solving, algorithm design	**Expert:** local

4.3   The PC Age

The appearance of the PC in the late 1970s was noticed above all by professionals and by a category of digital enthusiasts, who could not wait to put their hands on it: the proto-nerds, already described above.

The Heroic Age. Young proto-nerds devoted themselves to programming, typically in a garage or in a cellar, where they could work in peace, and store old cards, cables, peripherals, monitors to be assembled, without cluttering their room, and being scolded by their mother. The protagonist of the TV series "Whiz Kids", aired in 1983–1984, perfectly embodies this figure; Richie Adler has become an expert computer user thanks to Ralf, a PC he has assembled with the equipment received from his father, a telecommunication engineer, who acquires obsolete used devices. This explains why a teenager can afford a personal computer in the early 1980s. Richie's skills range from assembling the hardware, to programming, applied to both simple computer graphics, and robotics. Besides this mythical figure of owner, many professionals began to use a PC to have access to a modern device in an exclusive way. Their competence was mainly linked to their field of expertise and to software designed to support them: in any case, they needed to have acquaintance with both hardware and software (Table 3).

Table 3. Heroic PC age

Skills	Divide	Locus of control
Digital literacy (OS), digital numeracy (spreadsheet), computer architecture principles, computer graphics, programming, problem solving, algorithm design, robotics	Rare average users	Local

The Human Age. the decrease in the prices of computers and their greater usability, due to the introduction of visual interfaces and the mouse, made computers become mainstream. The metaphor of the desktop made a significant contribution to reducing learning times, determining the perception of a reduced distance between the computer and real life. Internet access led to further growth of interest for PCs, and, finally, laptops gave users the ability to take their computers with them.

Non-specialist users became the majority: for them digital literacy and numeracy (including skills like using the main features of an operating system, writing a document, calculating with a spreadsheet, surfing the internet or sending an email) were quite enough, while expert users' skills could range from creating and querying DBMS, to designing in computer graphics, to object-oriented programming, to modeling, to neural networking and lastly to robotics. The gap between the two begins to be remarkable.

As for the locus of control, the PC is still the center of any operation (Table 4).

Table 4. Human PC age

Skills	Divide	Locus of control
Digital literacy (OS and Internet connection), digital numeracy (suites SOHO), DBMS, computer graphics, OO-programming, modeling, neural networking, robotics	**Average:** Digital literacy, digital numeracy **Expert:** DBMS, computer graphics, OO-programming, modeling, VR, neural networking, robotics	Local

4.4   The Post-PC Era

This change has been very effectively represented in an advertisement by Apple launched in 2017: a young girl starts his day with his tablet, then she video-chats with her friends, takes photos for a research, reads comics on the bus, and finally writes her research work, lying on the lawn in the back garden; a neighbor asks her what she is doing on her computer and the girl asks: "what's a computer?" [20]. The post-PC era has featured everyday life.

Handheld devices, such as tablets or smartphones, have completely transformed the user's relationship with the computer: very small size, portability, Internet connection always active, more and more simplified interaction, and voice activated functions make these devices the ideal companion for everybody, either professional or not. Even very young children can learn in few minutes taking pictures, texting (by dictating or sending a vocal message), drawing, and playing games on a smartphone.

Based on the 2017 U.S. Mobile App Report by comSCORE, app users spend 77% of their time on their top 3 app, and 96% on their top 10, meaning that the features really used are extremely limited and possibly users' skills are limited too.

Complex software systems are not designed for mobile devices for a lot of reasons: insufficient computational power, lack of specific libraries or frameworks, usability limitations, such as the small screen size or the impossibility to display a multipart interface. However, as users do need to read a document, to check their data in a spreadsheet, or to revise a presentation while in mobility, software and storage are also offered as a service by a provider: the cloud computing is the current actual shift.

PCs (or laptops) are still in use for working in offices, for programming and for resource demanding software, but they also can run web and cloud applications.

The locus of control is becoming more and more remote, so that the users don't even know (and they don't need to) where their data are actually stored, or which server is performing their queries.

Skills have drastically changed and consequently the divide between average and expert users, who are required to have more and more a cross-disciplinary expertise, for dealing with increasingly complex problems (Table 5).

Table 5. Post-PC age

Skills	Divide	Locus of control
Decreasing importance of literacy Digital literacy	**Average:** no significant differences **Expert:** data mining, big data science, networking for IoT	Remote

4.5 Continuity and Discontinuity

The PC revolution reveals strong discontinuities both with the previous and the following times. They appear even more evident by summarizing in charts the considerations made so far under the three points of view.

In Fig. 4, users' skills are represented like heaps: as average and expert users, in pre-digital and heroic PC age, substantially coincide, they are considered as one. In addition, the incipient reduction of need for literacy, due to assistive technologies like spell checker, speech recognition and synthesis, has been represented as a partially faded bar.

As for average users, we can remark that the skills they do need, are mainly limited to a small number of basic competences, such as literacy and numeracy, either digital or not. Expert users, on the contrary, benefit of the huge variety of available applications.

If we consider separately the two sets of heaps, it appears that average users' skills reached a peak during the heroic PC age, when much more skills were required to operate computers. Then we assist to the drop to a defined and limited set of skills. On the contrary, expert users' skills continue to grow and become more and more complex, requiring also a significant technical expertise (Fig. 5).

Again, if we look at the locus of control, we can spot a kind of periodicity along time, as it moves from local to remote during main frame age and post-PC age, needing an always-on Internet connection. While the first shift (from pre-digital to main frame age) involved a drastic change of device type, the second one was determined by the progressive introduction of cloud computing services, such as file storage, office suites, shared repositories for collaborative projects, online code editors and compilers and many more (Fig. 6).

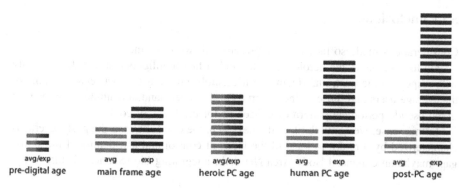

Fig. 4. The users' skills heap

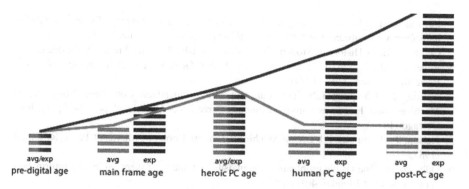

Fig. 5. The average vs. expert user skills divide

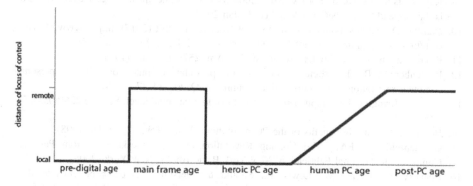

Fig. 6. The locus of control

5 Conclusions

Considerations made so far show the presence of two dynamics.

On the one hand, the heroic era of the PC in fact highlights a strong discontinuity with respect to the past, introducing an irresistibly growing gap between the skills of the average users and those of the experts. On the other hand, a continuity can be spot in the pseudo-periodical pattern evidenced as for the locus of control.

In this sense, we could think to the next step, the one following the post-PC era, as characterized by a return to local of the locus of control and a widening of the skills' gap: maybe an enhanced Body Area Network, integrating bio-technical features?

References

1. Lawrence, M.: Memory & Imagination: New Pathways to the Library of Congress (1990). https://www.youtube.com/watch?v=6kalMB8jDnY. Accessed 31 Jan 2018
2. Ceruzzi, P.E.: A History of Modern Computing, 2nd edn. The MIT Press, Cambridge (2003)
3. Rogers, E.M., Larsen, J.K.: Silicon Valley Fever: Growth of High-Technology Culture. Basic Books, New York (1984)
4. Nelson, T.: Computer Lib: You Can and Must Understand Computers Now; Dream Machines: New Freedoms Through Computer Screens - A Minority Report. Self-published, Chicago (1974)
5. Nelson, T.: Computer Lib/Dream Machines. Tempus Books of Microsoft Press, Redmond (1987)
6. Odlyzko, A.: The visible problems of the invisible computer: a skeptical look at information appliances. First Monday 4(9) (2016)
7. Norman, D.A.: The Invisible Computer. MIT Press, Cambridge (1998)
8. Gates, B.: Why computers will not die. Newsweek 133(22), 64 (1999)
9. Kay, R.: Is the PC Dead? Forbes (2011). https://www.forbes.com/sites/rogerkay/2011/02/28/is-the-pc-dead/#33ff6ebe6f31. Accessed 31 Jan 2018
10. Nations, D.: Things Your PC Can Do That Your iPad Can't (2017). https://www.lifewire.com/things-pc-can-do-ipad-cant-1994090. Accessed 31 Jan 2018
11. Peled, A.: The next computer revolution. Sci. Am. 257(4), 57–65 (1987)
12. Pfaffenberger, B.: The social meaning of the personal computer: or, why the personal computer revolution was no revolution. Anthropol. Q. 61, 39–47 (1988)
13. Pool, R.: Bringing the computer revolution down to a personal level. Science 256(5053), 55 (1992)
14. Hood, J.: The family benefits of the PC revolution. Policy Rev. 87, 15–16 (1998)
15. Gershenfeld, N.: FAB: The Coming Revolution on Your Desktop – From Personal Computers to Personal Fabrication. New York Basic Books, New York (2005)
16. Beaudry, P., Doms, M., Lewis, E.: Should the personal computer be considered a technological revolution? Evidence from U.S. metropolitan areas. J. Polit. Econ. 118(5), 988–1036 (2010)
17. Sichel, D.E.: The Computer Revolution: An Economic Perspective. Brookings Institution Press, Washington, DC (2001)
18. Berger, T., Frey, C.B.: Did the computer revolution shift the fortunes of U.S. cities? technology shocks and the geography of new jobs. Reg. Sci. Urban Econ. 57, 38–45 (2015)

19. Beniger, J.: The Control Revolution: Technological and Economic Origins of the Information Society. Harvard University Press, Cambridge (2009)
20. Apple. iPad Pro Anything you can do, you can do better. https://www.apple.com/ipad/?cid= www-us%E2%88%92yt%E2%88%92pad%E2%88%92sct%E2%88%92sco%E2%88% 921116. Accessed 31 Jan 2018

Software Engineering in a British Defence Project in 1970

Ian Pyle$^{(\boxtimes)}$ (iD)

York, UK

Abstract. This software development project took five years from 1968, and engaged 50, rising to 130, people. They were programmers from a commercial company, together with scientists from a government laboratory. In the infancy of software engineering, completely new techniques were established to carry out the task, based on system theory, which are described here. The project was completed in 1973.

Keywords: Historical · Multi-computer · Radar · Linesman

1 Introduction

Linesman was the UK's Air Defence System for the 1970s. After all the hardware had been installed, including all the radars and about 10 specially-designed computers at the building called L1 at West Drayton (near Heathrow airport), it was found in about 1967 that the contractor could not make the software for the computers, called the Radar Data Processing System (RDPS). This is the story of how that software was developed. It explains the software engineering approach and techniques used to design and produce the software for the RDPS.

A team from Harwell was assigned to assist the contractor, and subsequently (after a major review) to lead the software development. Stimulated by the dramatic publication of the report [1] of the NATO conference at Garmisch, "Software Engineering", we decided to apply the principles of systems engineering to the development of the software for the RDPS.

1.1 Classification

Because it was essentially military, all work on the project was subject to the United Kingdom's Official Secrets Act, which meant that everything about it had to be treated carefully to prevent disclosure. Some of the rules were ridiculous (for example, the order code of the computers used was classified!) and the general limitation of information made it extremely difficult at the beginning to find out what the project was about and what the problems were. When there was a public crisis about it, we discovered more from the daily newspapers that we had from the internal documents.

I. Pyle—Formerly of AERE Harwell.

Published by Springer Nature Switzerland AG 2018. All Rights Reserved
D. Kreps et al. (Eds.): HCC13 2018, IFIP AICT 537, pp. 16–30, 2018.
https://doi.org/10.1007/978-3-319-99605-9_2

Specifically, the Software Engineering approach and techniques had to be classified ("Restricted"), and the present paper, over thirty years after the documents were written, is probably the first public exposure of the details. (Earlier publications [2, 3] about techniques used had to be guardedly disguised to avoid disclosure).

1.2   Contractual Relationships

In common with most British Defence Procurement projects at the time, Linesman was carried out as a "cost-plus" contract, involving two principal parties: the Design Authority (a private company, in this case The Plessey Company) who had to develop and install the equipment, and the R&D Authority (a government laboratory, in the case the Royal Radar Establishment: RRE, Malvern) who had to monitor the technical work being done by the Design Authority, and confirm that it was appropriate for the situation. In addition, the prospective end-user (a military body, in this case the Royal Air Force) was involved in negotiations, particularly for training and eventual hand-over.

Harwell only became involved at a late stage in the project, initially in support of RRE, and with increasing despair as we discovered the inadequacy of the monitoring and software engineering, in spite of increasing the numbers of people involved. After a full review of the project, it was decided that Harwell should also take a leading part in the work of the Design Authority, as well as continuing to support the R&D Authority. The present paper is about the approach we took within the Design Authority to achieve the required behaviour of the RDPS.

2   Background

Previous attempts to make the software for the RDPS had been overwhelmed by the complexity of the requirements. In evidence to a parliamentary enquiry [4], a representative of Plessey said "The software task involves the writing of more than a quarter of a million 48-bit words and there existed nowhere any previous experience of the programming of so large and complex an on-line real time system for air defence purposes." The company specialised in electronics and telephone exchanges, and they recruited programmers who were only familiar with sequential programming. There were no system programmers.

"An unsuccessful attempt was made by the Company in 1967 to obtain assistance from software houses, but experience relevant to the Linesman task did not exist anywhere. It was only from AERE that it was found possible to obtain a substantial element of high grade programming effort." Staff from A.E.R.E. Harwell (particularly nuclear physicists, but initially from the computing group) were well experienced in using computers for data gathering and control of experimental apparatus with extensive electronics. A small team was allocated to the project in 1968, and we proposed a novel approach, which was strongly influenced by the NATO Software Engineering report; the style was essentially what was later described as the V-model.

The fully structured software system design applied System Theory to this problem, by insisting on well defined components and interactions between them, at each element in a hierarchy. This brought out the importance of documentation for the project, and led to the specification of a documentation structure to describe the software, from design through implementation and testing to handover. A document called the Software Standard [5], was written to define the rules of operation for the software development, including comprehensive authorisation and change control. There were no software tools to support the development, so all the documentation was produced in a form that could be properly checked by human readers. Essentially, all the information needed to ensure consistency on each item was included in a single document. Between one document and another, relevant sections of text were identical.

3 Systems

From the totality of the RDPS, down to individual software modules, everything was treated as a "system" having two aspects: (a) the whole, with specific behaviour and specific allocated resources; and (b) a set of components, each of which could be a smaller system, which interacted to provide the behaviour of the whole.

The Software Standard introduced nomenclature for the significant kinds of software items in this project: "suites" for software involving several computers, concerned with a particular function; "packages" for software within a single computer dealing with a particular function; and "modules" as software components that are actually compiled. Completed working software (as it became produced, and on which other software would be built), was called a "presystem".

The review of the system requirements identified three major areas: primary (relating to the maintenance of a recognised air picture of the UK air space), secondary (relating to maintaining the computer system and intercommunication between its physical components in the presence of all possible failures), and tertiary (providing facilities for program production and maintenance). The software staff were accordingly divided into three departments to cover these areas.

The standard recognised that the requirements could not be stated in full before the design of the system began; the design had to be undertaken with the assumption that the requirements (particularly the primary requirements) would change in detail, although the secondary and tertiary requirements would be more stable.

4 Structure and Content of the Software Standard

Because the intended users of the software standard were experienced programmers with little knowledge of higher level software design or software engineering, the standard was written with great detail specific to the Linesman Radar Data Processing System. There were seven parts, covering different aspects of the process of software development (see Appendix A for the list of contents, showing the sizes of each section, and the date when the version was issued). The introduction explained the purpose of the standard, specifically identifying the particular objectives, as

(a) to assist individual programmers to produce programs which properly interface with others to make a coherent working whole;

(b) to provide tangible output for other designers and management before implementation;

(c) to become the reference basis for the final implementation;

(d) to provide the information needed for debugging and testing, and for training the eventual users about the total design of the system; and

(e) to accumulate information about effort for future estimation.

For the three main parts (Requirements, Design, Implementation) there are a number of sections, in each of which the standard explains the scope of the section, the activities to be done, the products that would result, the criteria for completion, and the possible need for repetition.

4.1   Requirements

Originally, the requirements for the RDPS had been expressed from the point of view of the operators, with detailed descriptions of their consoles, the messages they might receive, and the responses they might give to them.

Following the appointment of Harwell staff to oversee the project, the point of view was shifted to the computer system, and the requirements were re-cast in terms of the data that had to be held, and the processes that were to be applied to these data. Specifically, the standard called for detailed specification of the observed objects (which we called the "World Model"), historical background to be taken into account, the monitoring, assessment and control procedures, outline specification of the computing system, specification of operational events, and specification of transactions. For each of these, the standard explained the scope of the particular requirement, the activities to be carried out to write the relevant text, the document to be produced (and by whom it was to be checked), the criterion for completion of the work, and conditions under which some repetition of the work may have been necessary.

4.2   Design

The design of the RDPS software was explained in a sequence of sections, descending top-down in detail from the overall software system design, through presystems, suites and packages, to individual modules. For each level, the standard gave the issues to be taken into account, the decisions to be made, and the outputs to be produced. A co-ordinator had to be appointed to take continuing responsibility for the design through all the development. For example, for suite design, the design team had to decide how to distribute the suite's functionality between packages in different computers, and what communication was needed between these. They had to decide how the resources allocated for the suite were to be distributed among its constituent packages. At the bottom level, the module designer had to give identifiers for the module parameters, define the data structures needed, prepare a module algorithm including debug points, and prepare an outline test plan.

When each design document had been written to part 3 (see "Planning and Progress measurement" below), and approved by the appropriate authority, the design team had completed that stage of the work, and was assigned another item of work.

4.3 Implementation and Testing

Implementation was bottom-up, with section dealing with ascending levels of complexity, from modules to packages, suites, presystems and the whole system. For each, the standard identified the focus of the work, as the element was assembled from its constituents and tested to show that it conformed to its specification. For example, for a package, the activities included deciding the sequence of modules to be assembled, describing the test environment for off-line and on-line testing, labelling of all test points with in the package, preparation of test data and expected trace points; the results included corresponding output values, package execution times and module use counts, together with the overall package size. A log was produced recording all significant activities.

Presystem implementation and testing formed a significant part of the overall demonstration of progress of the development project.

4.4 Resources

The standard recognised that the utilisation of resources and maintenance of records was vital for successful engineering, and defined the duties of a specific group that had responsibility for this work; they were called the System Keepers. Their work involved both clerical and analytical activities. Records were kept of the system, the presystems, and the various computer roles, including lists and software logs. The system keepers were also responsible for the preservation and maintenance of paper tapes and magnetic tapes for the system.

They also monitored, analysed and assessed the utilisation of resources within the system; specifically, for the use of core stores, CPUs, and the inter-computer communication highways. The system keepers had to liaise with coordinators for each element of the design.

4.5 Approval of Documents

Every document had to be approved in some way before it was considered to be satisfactory. There were several levels of approval, depending on the kind of document. Every document began as "Draft," when its author could modify it arbitrarily. Other levels were "Edition," "Issue," and "Certified," following checking and approval by appropriate bodies, including an Internal Approval Authority and an External Approval Authority. The standard laid down the criteria (depending on the type of the document) and corresponding approval authorities.

4.6   Appraisal and Preparation for Handover

In preparation for handover of the developed system to the intended users, particular documents had to be prepared and checked, covering manuals and software details for subsequent use and maintenance of the system. The standard specified what these must contain, and how they were to be checked. For example, the final part (part 7) of each document defining a software item had to be prepared by the System Keepers based on material from periodic appraisals, including a summary of the usage of the item, the faults attributed to it, details of amendments to it, together with an appraisal of the item's effectiveness and notes on any foreseen modifications or extensions.

5   Results

The application of the software standard resulted in the production of a very large number of documents, of which only a few can be mentioned here.

5.1   Requirements

The first and most significant challenge was to find a form of words which everyone would agree was the purpose of the RDPS. What was agreed was very different from anything written previously (although the words had been spoken). This was Part 1 of the top-level design document [6]. The text is given in Appendix B. Notice that the overall purpose was developed there into layers of facilities, called primary (Application Software), secondary (System Foundation) and tertiary (Program Preparation). By analysing the dependencies between these layers, it became clear that, in contrast with earlier priorities, the development of the RDPS software had to focus first on Program Preparation, then on the System Foundation, and, only after those had been designed, on the Application Software. Until then, effort had been concentrated on the sequence of primary facilities needed, and got nowhere.

5.2   Planning and Progress Measurement

The documentation structure identified in the Software Standard provided the basis for planning the development, and for measuring progress, by the stages of parts of the various documents.

For each item, whatever its size, the documentation was produced as a sequence of parts, with time-gaps between the writing of specific stages. In general, Part 1 specified the behaviour of the item and the resources allocated for it. Part 2 specified the constituents of the item, defining the behaviour and resources for each constituent. Part 3 described the interactions between the constituents, explaining how they jointly produced the behaviour given in Part 1. On completion of Part 3, the document was checked and then distributed for use as a basis for the design of the constituent systems. In parallel, Part 4 was written to specify the order of assembly of the constituents, with the rationale. Part 5 specified the tests to be carried out (after the constituents had been produced) which confirm that the interactions of Part 3, and the behaviour of Part 1, were achieved. When the constituents had been produced, Part 6 was written to record the results of the tests identified in Part 4. Part 7 recorded the handover of this item as a constituent of the next higher system.

A different principle was used for large-scale progress measurement, in terms of demonstrated facilities on the computers; these were called "Presystems" (see below).

6 Presystems

Seven presystems were defined, mostly chronological, but for the infrastructure distinguishing between "basic" facilities need to progress, and "advanced" facilities to give additional functionality.

6.1 Programming Support

Presystem 1 provided the Basic Programming Support, i.e. compilation and assembly of modules, preparation of magnetic tapes for loading into on-line computers, on-line debugging aids, and simple reporting from post mortem dumps. This used an XL4 computer with an operating system called OS090.

Presystem 2 provided additional power for the workload of developing the RDPS software, as a computer bureau, using an additional computer, an ICL 1902A, with disk files and fast input/output. The operating system was called XANOS.

6.2 Foundation

Presystem 3 was the Basic System Foundation, providing scheduling of tasks on the on-line computers, communication between them, loading of software from magnetic tapes, control of the allocation of computers to specific rôles, on-line debugging facilities, peripheral handling and regular checking for faults.

Presystem 4 was for Advanced System Foundation, for responding to detected faults and making appropriate changes to allocations, for reconstituting data after a reconfiguration, for diagnosing reported faults, and for driving special equipment to investigate faulty electronic units. Subsequently, Presystem 4 was split, because a major hardware upgrade to the computers affected testing. The revised Presystem 4 contained the facilities independent of the upgrade, and a further presystem, called 4T, was defined to contain the additional facilities dependent on the upgrade.

6.3 Applications

Presystem 5 handled the various kinds of buttons and lamps at operators' consoles, including a command language interpreter for recognising operators' key sequences and taking appropriate actions.

Presystem 6 dealt with autonomous processes (detecting relevant changes) and maintaining the world model (both live and simulated).

Presystem 7 handled height finder equipment and secondary radar interactions.

7 Management

During the early period, before the design had made much progress, the management were extremely uncomfortable, because there was no way of estimating the amount of effort or time that would be required. However, once the structure in terms of presystems and suites had been identified, an overall plan could be prepared, and priorities identified for the allocation of staff and computer resources. Then as work on implementation progressed, confidence increased, although there were still problems of interaction between the hardware changes found necessary and the availability of the computers for debugging.

8 Quality

Surprisingly, the Software Standard did not mention quality: there was nothing about Quality Control or Quality Assurance, and I been unable to find any occurrence of the word "quality" in the document.

In retrospect, I think that the reason was that we considered quality to be intrinsic to the structure and procedures in the standard, not an "add-on": by having text copied verbatim from one document to another, and by insisting that each document had a clearly-defined focus, with well-structured contents and checking by all relevant parties, we presumed that the quality would automatically be there.

In practice, we did set up a quality control unit (a good management decision!), but its responsibilities were administrative rather than technical: they had to confirm that each document had been written and checked in accordance with the rules set down in the Software Standard, according to the type of the document.

9 Education

No-one in the project was a software engineer as we now understand the term. We were working from first principles, and disseminating our experience and insights as the project progressed. Some of the ideas of software structure were unfamiliar to the programmers, who were experienced mainly in a dialect of Coral 66 [7]: supposedly for real-time programming, but with no features (such as multi-programming, or interrupt handling) that are now known to be required for that field (see Jackson [8]). The ideas of the software standard were spread by example and mentoring. (I ordered fifty copies of the NATO Software Engineering report for distribution to staff and management).

9.1 Tasks

A particular problem was that most programmers did not understand the concept of a task, or process, in a multiprogramming environment. (The seminal description by Wirth [9] was still years ahead). Only after the successful implementation of the OLOS suite (On-Line Operating System) were most staff convinced that this was a viable and essential feature of the software.

10 Handover

The RDPS was handed over to the Royal Air Force in July 1973, at a formal meeting which reviewed all the software according to the structure and terminology of the Software Standard. The R.A.F. gave a demonstration of the completed system to invited guests on 18th December 1973.

11 Origin of Software Standard

The ideas behind the document were largely derived from experience in the design of software at Harwell (e.g. the Fortran compiler for the Atlas computer, and the HUW system [10]) and "systems" thinking, helped by the NATO report on Software Engineering. However, for the context of the Linesman RDPS, it was recognized that principles were not enough, and great care was needed to express the ideas in concrete form for this project.

A group of three people: myself, J.R. Taylor (Harwell), and D.M. England (Plessey), spent about three months in the spring of 1970 carefully writing the document, in preparation for the eventual decision to change the direction of the software development to the method explained here. The edition of the document that I preserved is dated July–November 1970.

12 Conclusion

This was an innovative software engineering project, on a larger scale than had previously been encountered in the U.K. Over a hundred people were employed on the development of software for a major defence requirement. The software engineering principles used were simple (and, some said, boring!), without any particular "method" or silver bullet: just carefully-focussed well-structured writing, with extensive appropriate checking. The constraints were severe, yet a system was produced which was handed over and accepted by the military. Because of its military nature, little has been published about it hitherto.

'This changed everything' because the work reported here established basic principles for Software Engineering: in System Theory. The idea of a system as a set of interacting components, whose properties exceeded those of the individual components, was reified here to provide an effective method of developing software. The success of the project was attributable to the many people involved in the development of the ideas as well as in the actual software development. The pressure on us all was immense, conscious of the political and military implications of the project. This was a major team effort, and the experiences of those involved enabled them to carry out subsequent (classified) projects with great success. The major failure was the consequence of the Official Secrets Act: details about the method could not be widely disseminated. The learning was passed on to other developments only by the people who had been involved (from Harwell and Plessey, and, to a lesser extent, the Royal Air Force). I recognised that that the resulting system would be unlikely to be fully satisfactory, and (as a result of experience with implementing this approach to software engineering) in an Infotech State of the Art lecture [11], I proposed the acronym "DITHER" to express the overall process: Design, Implement, Test, Evaluate, Replace. Thus hoped that this work would enable the commissioning authority (i.e. the British Ministry of Defence) to do a better job next time. Unfortunately it did not. After Linesman, the United Kingdom Air Defence Ground Environment (UKADGE) was out-sourced to a different company which encountered problems that were different but with no significant improvement in outcome. But Harwell continued to develop software systems for sensitive projects, with great success.

What had previously been a failing project, severely criticised in the press and the subject of parliamentary questioning [12], dropped out of the news. It was working.

13 About This Document

Although the work described here was carried out in the years around 1970, it could not be published then. The present document was started in 2010, as a "memoir" recording my recollections about the project. Because it referred to classified information, it was submitted for security clearance in May 2017, and was cleared for publication. Further details are available from the author at <ian.pyle@cantab.net>.

Appendix A – Contents of the Software Standard

			Date	Pages
1	INTRODUCTION		24.7.70	4 pp
	1	Function of Document		1/1
	2	Design Environment		1/1
	3	Objectives of Documentation		1/1
	4	Structure of the Standard		1/1
	5	Designation and Approval of Documents		1/4
	6	Status of Standard and Revision Procedures		1/4
2	SPECIFICATION OF OPERATIONAL REQUIREMENTS		26.10.70	10 pp
	1	Introduction		2/1
	2	Outline Requirements		2/1
	3	Detailed Specification of Observed Objects		2/2
	4	Historical Assessment		2/3
	5	Specification of Monitoring, Assessment and Control Procedures		2/3
	6	Outline Specification of Computing System		2/5
	7	Specification of Operational Events		2/7
	8	Specification of Transactions		2/8
3	DESIGN		24.7.70	14 pp
	1	Introduction		3/1
	2	Overall Software System Design		3/2
	3	Presystem Design		3/5
	4	Suite Design		3/6
	5	Package Design		3/8
	6	Module Design		3/13

(*continued*)

(*continued*)

			Date	Pages
4		IMPLEMENTATION AND TESTING	24.7.70	14 pp
	1	Introduction		4/1
	2	Module Implementation and Testing		4/1
	3	Package Assembly and Testing		4/3
	4	Suite Assembly and Testing		4/7
	5	Presystem Assembly and Testing		4/9
	6	System Assembly and Testing		4/12
5		UTILISATION OF SYSTEM RESOURCES AND MAINTENANCE OF RECORDS	26.10.70	10pp
	1	Introduction		5/1
	2	Maintenance of Records		5/2
	3	Monitoring, Analysis, and Assessment of Resource Utilisation		5/6
6		APPROVAL of DOCUMENTS	26.10.70	4 pp
	1	Introduction		6/1
	2	Levels of Approval		6/1
	3	The Internal Approval Authority		6/3
	4	Technical Editing		6/4
7		APPRAISAL AND PREPARATION FOR HANDOVER	27.11.70	5pp
	1	Introduction		7/1
	2	User Manuals and User Guides		7/1
	3	Maintenance		7/3
	4	Appraisal		7/4
Appendices			Date	Pages
A		DOCUMENT DESIGNATION, STATUS AND HANDLING	24.7.70	17 pp
	A1	Document Designation		11
	A2	Document Status and Handling		5
	A3	Integration of Existing Documents into the Document Structure		1
B		DOCUMENT PREPARATION	24.7.70	40 pp
	B1	Document Style and Layout		11
	B2	Design Document Formats		29
C		DIAGRAMMATIC AIDS	31.8.70	40 pp
	C1	Flowcharts		19
	C2	Decision Tables		2
	C3	Hierarchy Diagrams and Matrices		6
	C4	Communication Diagrams and Matrices		5
	C5	Data Structure Diagrams		3
	C6	Timing and Sequence Charts		2
	C7	Core Maps		
D		RECORD PREPARATION		
	D1	Lists, Indexes, and Glossaries		
	D2	Load Lists		
	D3	Data Lists		
	D4	Software Logs		

(*continued*)

(*continued*)

Appendices			Date	Pages
E	TECHNIQUES			
	E1	Programming in Minicoral		
	E2	Programming in XAL		
	E3	Off-line Testing		
	E4	On-line Testing and Field Trials		
F	REFERENCE MATERIAL			
	F1	Glossary		
	F2	Bibliography		

Appendix B – The RDPS Software System: Overall Requirements

The following is the text of Part 1, Sect. 1, of SDA 000000/3, edition 5, which was distributed for review, with the intent of raising its status to Issue 2 on 6th September 1971.

1. FUNCTION

The Radar Data Processing System (RDPS) provides the information for the central co-ordination and controlling element of the Linesman U.K. Air Defence System. Its function is to maintain and display representations of the airspace activity of defence interest in the U.K. Air Defence Region and approaches (both live and simulated) as a 'Recognised Air Picture', on the basis of information received from radar, data links, operator injections, and an environment simulator. The information is to be displayed on equipment in the L1 building, and transmitted over data links for use elsewhere, especially to Continental Early Warning Stations.

1.1 PRIMARY FACILITIES

The facilities to be provided by the RDPS (Hardware and Software) are defined in document SRA 000099. The following list summarises the primary facilities that are required to fulfil the function defined above.

Automatic input/output of information over data links from and to equipments external to the RDPS, in locations outside the L1 building, with some checking of content.

- Input of information from operators by means of keys and rolling balls at their consoles, using displays to assist the construction of data fields and assist in checking prior to injection.
- Output of information to operators by means of various displays: Electronic Data Display (EDD), Marked Radar Display (MRD), Label Plan Display (LPD), Higher Formation Display (HFD), General Situation Display (GSD) and Totes,

The information processing needed to provide these facilities calls for:

- construction, maintenance and updating of a world model, including transformation and vetting of inputs;
- periodic checks to determine whether significant or critical conditions have developed in the world model;
- messages played out by the system indicating condition known to be of interest;
- routine playout of data from the world model for display or transmission to another system;
- playout of specific data from the world model to console operators on demand;
- computations performed on the world model on request from console operators.

The software which provides these primary facilities is called Applications Software (or functional suites).

1.2 SECONDARY FACILITIES

In order that the primary facilities of the RDPS may be fulfilled, there is a secondary function, namely to enable the RDPS to operate continuously; giving service in the face of the inevitable faults (or other anomalous occurrences) to hardware and software, informing the system controller when any malfunction is suspected, and taking such automatic recovery procedures as are possible.

A discussion of the availability to be expected is given in Part 3. The secondary facilities therefore are:

(a) detecting and reporting suspected faults,
(b) degrading gracefully and recovering rapidly in the event of a fault occurring,
(c) assisting engineers in the investigation and cure of faults,
(d) reacting to instructions from the system controller concerning the hardware of the RDPS.

The information processing needed to provide these secondary facilities calls for:

- construction, maintenance and updating of system records of the hardware state and the roles occupied;
- reloading of programs into computers when needed;
- reconstitution of data for programs between loading and use;
- using a healthy computer to obtain information for diagnosis of hardware faults;
- checking hardware for presence and correct functioning;
- communication with system controller about suspicious events;
- providing an on-line debugging environment.

The software which provides these secondary facilities is called Foundation Software (or system foundation).

1.3 TERTIARY FUNCTION AND FACILITIES

The tertiary function needed is to prepare information to be transferred into the main system, and post process information transferred out of it. During the development stages, the tertiary function is very important, as it calls for program preparation facilities. The same facilities are also needed during the operational use of the RDPS, in order to repair software errors and make enhancements, although the level of activity will be lower. This function calls for a general sequential job execution facility, which is defined in Appendix D.

1.4 OTHER FUNCTIONS AND FACILITIES

Finally there are number of administrative and documentation tasks which will be processed by computer in the interests of accuracy and efficiency. These include planning and maintaining: resource utilisation records, document numbering schemes, and indexes.

References

1. Naur, P., Randell, B. (eds.): 1968 NATO Conference, "Software Engineering", Report on a Conference Sponsored by the NATO SCIENCE COMMITTEE, Garmisch, Germany, 7–11 October 1968. Scientific Affairs Division NATO, Brussels, Belgium (1968). http://homepages.cs.ncl.ac.uk/brian.randell/NATO/nato1968.PDF
2. Pyle, I.C.: Some techniques in multi-computer system software design. Softw. Pract. Experience **2**, 43–54 (1972)
3. Stenson, J.: Reconfiguration of computers in critical systems. In: Computing with Real Time Systems: Proceedings of First European Seminar on Real-Time Programming, A.E.R.E. Harwell, 5–7 April 1971. Transcripta Books (1972)
4. Fourth report from the Select Committee on Science and Technology, Session 1970–71: The prospects for the United Kingdom Computer Industry in the 1970's, vol. 3: Appendix 42: The Linesman and Mediator Projects (Plessey). HMSO 621-III (1971)
5. Plessey document ("Restricted"): "Software Standard", reference number SSJ 000001 of 27.11.70, later changed to MSJ 000001 (1970)
6. Plessey document ("Restricted"): "The RDPS Software System" reference number SDA 000000 (1971)
7. Woodward, P.M.: Official Definition of CORAL 66. HMSO, November 1970. (ISBN 0114702217)
8. Jackson, K.: Adding real-time features to CORAL 66 via the operating system. In: Computing with Real Time Systems: Proceedings of First European Seminar on Real-Time Programming, A.E.R.E. Harwell, 5–7 April 1971. Transcripta Books (1972)
9. Wirth, N.: Toward a discipline of real-time programming. Commun. ACM **20**(8), 577–583 (1977). (ISSN: 0001-0782)

10. McLatchie, R.C.F.: HUW, an interactive computer system on IBM System 360/65. In: SEAS XIV, Conference, Grenoble (1969)
11. Pyle, I.C.: Hierarchies: an ordered approach to software design. Infotech State of the Art lecture 15 June 1971, in Infotech State of the Art report, Software Engineering, pp. 255–268 (1972)
12. Select committee on Science and Technology (Subcommittee A) Minutes of evidence: Wednesday 31st March 1971; Annex E: Question 5. Military/Civilian systems for Air Defence and Air Traffic Control (Linesman/Mediator)

History of Early Australian-Designed Computers

Arthur Tatnall[✉] [ORCID]

Victoria University, Melbourne, Australia
Arthur.Tatnall@vu.edu.au

Abstract. This paper examines the development of a number of computers designed and built in Australia that really changed everything! Australia designed and built CSIRAC, the fourth stored program computer in the world. Prior to this however, in 1913 the Automatic Totalisator, although not a computer, performed many of the calculations later done by computers. SILLIAC, based on the ILLIAC was built in Australia. UTCOM and WREDAC, although built in the UK, were extensively modified in Australia. In the early microcomputer era the Australian designed and built Microbee computer was used extensively in homes and schools. The paper then discusses the ill-fated project to design and built an Australian Educational Computer. These computers were each designed and built for a purpose and the paper looks at the people, technologies and events that propelled this process. Actor-network theory is used as a lens for understanding the human and non-human elements of these historical developments.

Keywords: Computers · Design · Manufacture · Uses · Australia
History · Actor-Network theory

1 Introduction

Although Australia is rather different to Eastern European countries, there are some commonalities in the need to develop their own computers and ICT industries rather than relying on those of the large developers elsewhere. Australia is not currently well known for designing and manufacturing its own computers, but has an important history in this regard.

Although not in any way what we would regard as a stored program digital computer, the Automatic Totalisator (1913) used many computing concepts in performing mathematical calculations to determine the betting odds in horse racing. Arguably the world's fourth of fifth stored program digital computer, CSIRAC was designed and built in Australia in the late 1940s. SILLAC (based on the ILLIAC computer), but not an exact copy, was built in Australia and became operational in 1956 as one of the most advanced computers in the world at that time. Although not designed and built locally, UTECOM and WREDAC (1956) were significantly modified for Australian use.

Moving to the 1980s and microcomputers, the Microbee which was designed and built in Australia for both home and education markets sold 70,000 to over 3,000

D. Kreps et al. (Eds.): HCC13 2018, IFIP AICT 537, pp. 31–41, 2018.
https://doi.org/10.1007/978-3-319-99605-9_3

Australian schools as well as schools in Scandinavia, Asia and Russia. In the mid-1980s an attempt was made by the Commonwealth Government to design an Australian Educational Computer. Initial design work was done but this did not proceed to construction.

In studying the history of technological innovation, in addition to history methodology [1, 2] actor-network theory (ANT) [3–6] can provide a useful lens [7]. ANT was designed to give a socio-technical account in which neither social nor technical positions are privileged, a significant voice is given to technological artefacts, and nothing is purely social or purely technical. Innovation Translation, informed by ANT provides a way to examine the adoption and implementation of these innovations [8]. 'Translation', in this context, can be regarded as a means of obliging some entity to consent to a 'detour' that takes it along a path determined by some other entity. Callon [4] proposes a process of translation with four aspects or 'moments'.

- Problematisation involves defining the nature of the problem in such a way as to be seen by other actors as being the answer [9].
- Interessement involves interesting and attracting an entity by coming between it and some other opposing entity [10].
- Enrolment then occurs through a process of 'coercion, seduction, or consent' [11] and, if all goes well, leads to the establishment of a solid, stable network of alliances [34].
- Mobilisation locks in as the proposed solution gains wider acceptance [9] through some actors working to convince others.

2   The Automatic Totalisator, 1913

By far the most important early development in the history of Australian computing was George Julius's invention of the automatic totalisator as this device used many of the concepts later found in electronic computers [12]. Although far from being a stored program digital computer, this electro-mechanical device performed mathematical calculations to determine the betting odds in horse racing. In totalisator betting systems, also known as Parimutuel betting systems, all the money wagered on an event is pooled together with dividends being calculated from the weight of money bet on each competitor. The competitor that has attracted the most money will return the smallest dividend, while the least supported horse will return the highest dividend [13, 14].

George Julius, who was born in England but migrated to Australia, invented the world's first automatic totalisator. The 'Julius' as it became known, was first used at a racetrack in New Zealand before being adopted in many countries around the world. Julius did not, however, originally conceive the automatic totalisator as a betting machine, but as a mechanical vote-counting machine [15].

Julius reported: "A friend in the west conceived the idea of getting me to make a machine to register votes, and so to expedite elections by giving the result without any human intervention. I invented one that aroused some interest, and it was submitted to the Commonwealth Government." [15]. When the Australian Government rejected the voting machine, Julius adapted it as a racecourse totalisator. Swade [14] described how the Julius totalisator, with its automatic odds machine, was the "earliest on-line, real-time data processing and computation system" as other data processing systems of the time "required operators to prepare batches of punched cards which were then processed en mass" [14] (Fig. 1).

Fig. 1. The world's first automatic totalisator (From Conlon, B. (2017). "Totalisator History")

3 CSIRAC: Australia's Stored-Program Computer, 1949

In the 1940s Australia was well placed to enter the computer age as it had a manufacturing base for the high technology of the day: the vacuum tube [16]. Pearcey [17] describes the transition from analogue type instruments like the slide-rule and the simple desk-calculator, along with books of mathematical tables to the digital computer, and how it was made possible by the prior development of a large scale domestic radio industry during the 1920s and 1930s in this country which was served by a reliable vacuum tube-based radio technology. All that was now missing, technically, was some of the expertise in television and radar (again based on the vacuum tube) developed in Britain during the 1930s and 1940s. The close relationship between Australia and the UK at that time, and the fact that Pearcey and others who were to become involved in computing in Australia had worked on radar in the UK during the war, provided this last technical ingredient [16, 18] (Fig. 2).

> "Further, by the end of WW2 the techniques of the early high-definition television developed by EMI and L Baird in the UK during the 1930s and the radar technology which stemmed from it by 1945 provided all the technology needed to create the electronic computer." [17:6]

Working at the Radiophysics Laboratory of the Council for Scientific and Industrial Research (now known as the CSIRO[1]), in 1947 Trevor Pearcey and Maston Beard began working on the development of an electronic computer [19]. The CSIR Mk1

---

[1] Commonwealth Scientific and Industrial Research Organisation (CSIRO).

(CSIRAC[2]) was built by Pearcey and Beard and became operational in 1949. It was Australia's first stored-program electronic digital computer, and (arguably) the world's fourth or fifth, being used at the CSIRO Division of Radiophysics in the Universities of Sydney and Melbourne until 1964 [17]. It is currently on display in Museum Victoria in Melbourne as the only surviving intact first generation computer [20, 21].

According to Maynard [22], Pearcey got his ideas on computing from two physiologists who had described how they thought the human brain worked. Beard had the technical skills and the knowledge and together they built CSIR Mk1 up from first principles, not greatly influenced by overseas developments [22].

"The construction of the CSIR Mk.1 as it was first called was of standard components available from a well-developed radio industry, but no miniaturisation or circuit packaging was then possible. Only the bank of up to 32 sonic delay lines, each five feet long and filled with mercury to carry the stored pulses corresponding to the data and the instructions, together with cabinets and electronic chassis, were fabricated on site... The Mk.1 was one of the earliest, truly automatic, stored program computers." [17:15]

Fig. 2. CSIRAC, Museum Victoria in Melbourne (Photo courtesy of Museum Victoria)

CSIRAC was what we would now call a first generation computer with over 2,000 thermionic (radio) valves that required a one-hour warm-up period each morning. It was a large and complex machine covering over 40 m^2, consuming around 30 kW of power [21]. It required its own maintenance and programming technicians and used mercury delay line storage with a total capacity of 1024 words and an access time of 10 ms [19]. Programs were stored and loaded on wide paper tape and the operator, who was often actually the programmer, commanded a bank of a hundred or so switches which had to be manipulated during program execution. It was essential for efficient

---

[2] It was later renamed CSIRAC (Commonwealth Scientific and Industrial Research Organisation Automatic Computer).

operation that the power supply be kept stable, and the story is related that on one occasion the computer was overloaded and crashed when someone turned on an electric jug in a nearby tearoom causing a power fluctuation [21].

Unlike a number of other computing developments around world at the time, CSIR Mk1 was not built for military purposes but as a research machine to perform calculations for agricultural issues such as animal health and plant growth but later extended its interests into manufacturing [23]. Later, the newly formed CSIRO developed new interests in radiophysics, radio-astronomy and industrial chemistry. Australia is a very dry continent and the Commonwealth Government was, at the time, interested in the possibility of inducing rain over important agricultural areas by cloud seeding. If it could have been achieved this would have revolutionised agricultural production in Australia [20], and CSIRO was thus interested in researching the related physics. (It is interesting to reflect that in retrospect, radio-astronomy in Australia turned out to be highly successful while the rain-making project did not).

4 SILLIAC, 1956

Built in 1956 by the University of Sydney as a tool for theoretical physics, SILLAC (Sydney version of the Illinois Automatic Computer) was based on the ILLIAC computer, developed at the University of Illinois and not an entirely Australian invention like CSIRAC, and it was not an exact copy of ILLIAC. As one of the most advanced computers in the world, SILLIAC was one of the first to be dubbed a 'supercomputer', and was much more powerful than Pearcey's CSIR Mark 1 [12]. SILLIAC was the size of a double-decker bus, contained 2,800 vacuum tubes and was programmed with paper tape [24]. Its chassis and wiring was built by the Australian subsidiary of British company STC but the Government Aeronautical Research Labs was responsible for the project as a whole [12]. SILLIAC became operational in 1956.

Nuclear physics was very important at the time with laboratories around the world producing results. Using SILLIAC, the University of Sydney were the first to synthesise all these experimental results into a theoretical model: into a picture of what a nucleus must look like. The biggest user after the School of Physics itself was the Snowy Mountains Hydro-Electric Authority where it was used in designing the major scheme for hydroelectricity and irrigation in south-east Australia. SILLIAC was used to design dams, tunnels and many other aspects of the project. It considerably reduced the time taken for all the design work. Finally, when spare parts could no longer be found SILLIAC was dismantled in 1968.

5 UTECOM and WREDAC, 1956

These two early computers were commissioned and used, but not built in Australia. Both were commercial models (highly modified in the case of WREDAC), built in England and shipped to Australia by the manufacturers [12].

5.1   UTECOM at the NSW University of Technology

In response to a shortage of scientists and engineers the New South Wales Government established an Institute of Nuclear Engineering at the NSW University of Technology with the intention of examining the use of nuclear power. For this purpose an electronic computer was regarded as essential and the university decided on DEUCE[3], manufactured by British computer company English Electric. The computer was built at the English Electric manufacturing and research facility in Staffordshire where it was tested, disassembled and shipped to Australia where it became UTCOM[4] [25].

5.2   WREDAC at the Weapons Research Establishment in South Australia

This computer was unusual for Australia as being the only early computer used for military purposes. It was located in Woomera, a town in South Australia built by the British to develop atomic weapons and with the Woomera Rocket Range to test them. The Weapons Research Establishment (WRE) was populated largely by British scientists, and was incorporated with other Australian Department of Defence research laboratories. Their weapons testing activities involved detailed mathematical calculations and by the early 1950s the WRE became interested in the 'new electronic computers'.

The Elliott 402 looked promising but it was the enhanced Elliott 403 that seemed to satisfy the WRE's requirements. The modified machine was called WREDAC[5] and was special in taking input from locally built analogue to digital conversion of missile range data, processing this with locally written software, and producing off-line performance reports on Australia's first line printer and the world's first digital plotters [26].

6   The Microbee, 1982

The Microbee computer was designed in Australia by Owen Hill and Matthew Starr from Applied Technology Pty Ltd who, in 1982, developed kit sets for the electronics enthusiasts market, complete with assembly instructions [27]. It was based on a Z80 microprocessor S-100 system. These sold for $399. Fully assembled Microbees with higher specifications soon followed, and by August 1982 almost a thousand computers were being made a month [28] (Fig. 3).

The Microbee designers were thinking of both home and education markets and it wasn't long before the first Microbee contract was let for New South Wales schools. This was soon followed by Western Australia, South Australia, Queensland and

---

[3] Digital Electronic Universal Computing Engine (DEUCE) was an improved version of the ACE (Automatic Computing Engine) designed by Alan Turing.

[4] University of Technology Electronic Computer (UTECOM).

[5] WRE Digital Automatic Computer (WREDAC).

Fig. 3. Microbee advertisement

Victoria. Some were also sold in Scandinavia, Asia and Russia [27]. By the mid-1980s more than 70,000 Microbees had been sold and over 3,000 Australian schools, including many secondary schools, were using Microbees. In the later 1980s, however, the rise of Apple and IBM meant that Microbee disappeared from the market.

7 The Australian Educational Computer, 1986

In 1983 the Australian Government's Commonwealth Schools Commission set up a 'National Advisory Committee on Computers in Schools' (NACCS) to plan the National Computer Education Program [29]. The terms of reference of this committee were to provide advice on professional development, curriculum development, software/courseware, hardware, evaluation and support services [23, 30].

At the time, software from organisations like the Minnesota Educational Computing Consortium was utilised in Australian schools but this software typically had an American outlook, leading to cultural problems. One example of this was the Apple // simulation game 'Lemonade' which was based on making and selling lemonade from a street stall. The only problem was that lemonade stands are almost unknown in Australia. The BBC Computer simulation program 'Suburban Fox' where the student has to take the part of a fox finding its prey and avoiding cars and the fox hunt is another example. The problem was that fox hunting was quite foreign to Australian students [30].

A number of other countries had developed their own educational computers: Acorn BBC Computer (UK), Compis (Sweden), ICON (Canada) and Poly (New Zealand). NACS thus saw an opportunity for Australia to develop an educational computer system of its own. It was also recognised that this project would have had the added advantage of the new computer being built in Australia by an Australian company.

The idea was that the Commonwealth Schools Commission be responsible for the production of an Educational User Requirement and an Educational Technical Requirement, while the Department of Science and Technology would take charge of a Systems Concept Study. If no existing computers were to satisfy this then the they would draw up an Australian Design Specifications and arrange for the manufacture of pilot and prototype systems [29].

An Educational User Requirement Working Party was appointed early in 1985, consisting of educators at all levels from around Australia and produced a report [31] outlining the many and varied potential educational needs of computer users in schools, and the need for integration of information technology concepts into the curriculum. In summary, its report highlighted several critical user requirement issues to be taken into consideration by the Educational Technical Requirement working party:

- The needs of various different types of users at both primary and secondary schools.
- The nature of the physical, school and classroom environment.
- The variety of applications.
- A consideration of modularity, expandability, entry cost, user interface, robustness, reliability, portability, compatibility and adoption of current recognised standards.

The Technical Requirements Working Party was set up later in 1985 as an 'expert' committee with membership reflecting the range of relevant groups and interests from each Australian educational sector, state and territory[6]. Its report was published in March 1986 and contained two main sections [32]:

- A Technical Requirement, which gave detailed coverage to: user interface, input devices, output devices, processing resources, networks, telecommunications and system requirements.
- A section dealing with possible implementations of these requirements to satisfy at least three envisaged types of use: Personal Systems, Classroom Systems and School Network Systems.

The next steps should have been setting up a System Concept Study to be followed by a Development Proposal, but at this stage the project stopped [23, 30]. The three year Government initiative for the National Computer Education Project was at an end and so was its funding. Further development funds from the Department of Science and Technology were not made available and so work on the Australian Educational Computer ceased [33]. Although this was disappointing at the time, in the light of later developments it was perhaps a relief not to have created a white elephant like the ICON in Canada, as within a few years the Apple Macintosh and MS-DOS (- later Windows) PC had become dominant.

8 An Actor-Network Analysis

Any study of these matters needs to be a socio-technical one and actor-network theory is thus a useful way to frame this. ANT involves looking for actors (both human and non-human) and how they interact with each other to produce the observed result (or in some cases not to produce any result at all).

The initial idea for building CSIR Mk1 came from a need to provide the computing power for calculations related to research work in radio-astronomy and rain-physics, and the Commonwealth Government's goal of assisting Australian agriculture by cloud

---

[6] Arthur Tatnall was a member of this committee.

seeding to produce rain. The problematisation [4] proposed was thus to find a means to assist with the huge number of complex calculations required for these purposes. The actors that contributed to the conception, design and construction of CSIRAC included: Pearcey, Beard, radar technology, the Australian radio industry, radio-physics, rain-physics, the Commonwealth Government, Australian agriculture and the CSIRO [23]. The essential need was for a means of handling complex calculations, and the actors that created this need were CSIRO researchers in radio-astronomy and agriculture. Their interactions with the Commonwealth Government along with those of the Australian radio industry, radar technology, Pearcey and Beard became the means. CSIRAC itself was an important actor that needed constant attention. Constant room temperature through air conditioning was essential and radio valves continually blew.

The mobilisation [4] resulting from this led to the subsequent building in Australia of several other first generation computers: SILLIAC at Sydney University, UTECOM at the University of NSW and WREDAC at the Weapons Research Establishment. With SILLIAC, UTECOM and WREDAC a variety of human actors, governments, universities, overseas computer companies, technologies and applications were involved. Understanding the development and use of these computers needs an understanding of the complex interactions of all these actors[7].

When CSIRAC's useful life at CSIRO and universities came to an end, new actors began to enter the picture with its final translation involving display in Museum Victoria. With another set of human actors and a new physical location CSIRAC took on a new role as a means of showing school children and the public Australia's first computer, how it worked and also how much computers have changed over the 70 year lifespan of the stored-program electronic digital computer.

Development of the Microbee had little to do with CSIRAC, except perhaps as an inspiration of what Australia could do, but required: the advent of the microprocessor, Microbee's human designers, the absence of any dominating microcomputer competitors at the time and the desire by many homes and schools to have their own low price computers. Microbee's human designers worked on producing a computer that these potential users could afford and relate to.

The project to build the Australian Educational Computer involved the Commonwealth Government, State and Territory Governments, Commonwealth Schools Commission, Department of Science and Technology, other State and Commonwealth education authorities, committee members, reports, specifications documents, the computer industry and changes in funding priorities. Various interactions between these actors led to the development of the specifications for this computer, but not to its construction [30]. Getting a technological innovation adopted, or in this case even manufactured, involves convincing people of its value, of interessement. Convincing people was almost impossible in this case as outside the committees and the government very few people knew about it. Perhaps this was a factor in its demise.

---

[7] Doing so is, however, not within the scope of a paper of this length.

9   Conclusion

In considering the history of the design of early computers in Australia it is necessary to look at the purpose for which they were built, the people involved, current culture and not just characteristics of the technology itself. This involves understanding both the human and non-human elements of these historical developments.

References

1. Howell, M.C., Prevenier, W.: From Reliable Sources, an Introduction to Historical Methods. Cornell University Press, Ithaca (2001)
2. Mahoney, J., Rueschemeyer, D.: Comparative Historical Analysis in the Social Sciences. Cambridge University Press, Cambridge (2003)
3. Callon, M., Latour, B.: Unscrewing the Big Leviathan: how actors macro-structure reality and how sociologists help them to do so, in advances in social theory and methodology. In: Knorr-Cetina, K., Cicourel, A.V. (eds.) Toward an Integration of Micro and Macro-Sociologies, pp. 277–303. Routledge & Kegan Paul, London (1981)
4. Callon, M.: Some elements of a sociology of translation: domestication of the scallops and the fishermen of St Brieuc Bay, in power, action and belief: a new sociology of knowledge? In: Law, J. (ed.) Routledge & Kegan Paul, London, pp. 196–229 (1986)
5. Latour, B.: The powers of association, in power, action and belief: a new sociology of knowledge? Sociological review monograph 32. In: Law, J. (ed.) Routledge & Kegan Paul, London, pp. 264–280 (1986)
6. Latour, B.: Aramis or the Love of Technology. Harvard University Press, Cambridge (1996)
7. Tatnall, A.: Actor-network theory as a socio-technical approach to information systems research, in socio-technical and human cognition elements of information systems. In: Clarke, S., et al., (eds.) Information Science Publishing, Hershey, pp. 266–283 (2003)
8. Tatnall, A.: Computer education and societal change: history of early courses in computing in universities and schools in Victoria. Inf. Technol. People **28**(4), 742–757 (2015)
9. McMaster, T., Vidgen, R.T., Wastell, D.G.: Towards an understanding of technology in transition. Two conflicting theories. In: Information Systems Research in Scandinavia, IRIS20 Conference, University of Oslo, Hanko, Norway (1997)
10. Law, J.: The heterogeneity of texts, in mapping the dynamics of science and technology. In: Callon, M., Law, J., Rip, A. (eds.) Macmillan Press, UK, pp. 67–83 (1986)
11. Grint, K., Woolgar, S.: The Machine at Work – Technology, Work and Organisation. Polity Press, Cambridge (1997)
12. Philipson, G.: A Vision Splendid - The History of Australian Computing. Australian Computer Society, Sydney (2017)
13. Punters. What is Tote Betting? (2017). https://www.punters.com.au/betting/products/totes/
14. Swade, D.: A sure bet for understanding computers. New Sci. **116**, 49–51 (1987)
15. Conlon, B.: Totalisator History, December 2017. http://members.ozemail.com.au/∼bconlon/julius.htm
16. Tatnall, A.: History of computers: hardware and software development. In: Encyclopedia of Life Support Systems 2012, UNESCO - Eolss Publishers Co Ltd, Ramsey, Isle of Man, UK (2012)
17. Pearcey, T.: A History of Australian Computing. Chisholm Institute of Technology, Melbourne (1988)

18. Tatnall, A., Davey, W., Burgess, S., Davison, A., Wenn, A.: Management Information Systems - Concepts, Issues, Tools and Applications, 3rd edn. Data Publishing, Melbourne (2002)
19. University of Melbourne. CSIRAC: Our First Computer (2012). http://www.csse.unimelb. edu.au/dept/about/csirac/. Accessed Feb 2013
20. McCann, D., Thorne, P.: The Last of the First - CSIRAC: Australia's First Computer. The University of Melbourne, Melbourne (2000)
21. Museum Victoria. CSIRAC (2012). http://museumvictoria.com.au/discoverycentre/ infosheets/csirac/. Accessed Feb 2013
22. Maynard, G.: Interview on the History of Business Computing, Melbourne (1990)
23. Tatnall, A.: Aspects of the history of computing - an actor-network perspective. In: Kapriev, G., Roussel, M., Tchalakov, I. (eds.) Le Sujet De L'Acteur - An Anthropological Outlook on Actor-Network Theory, pp. 145–162. Wilhelm Fink (2014)
24. Williams, R.: SILLIAC - Australia's first supercomputer built 50 years ago (2007). http://www. abc.net.au/radionational/programs/scienceshow/silliac—australias-first-supercomputer-built-50/3384532#transcript. Accessed Jan 2018
25. Vowels, R.A.: UTECOM: An English Electric DEUCE. Vowels, Victoria (1993)
26. Deane, J.: Australia's WREDAC – It*Was* rocket science. In: Tatnall, A. (ed.) Reflections on the History of Computing. IAICT, vol. 387, pp. 1–21. Springer, Heidelberg (2012). https:// doi.org/10.1007/978-3-642-33899-1_1
27. Wordsworth, E.J.: Microbee Technology: About Us/History (2016). https://www. microbeetechnology.com.au/aboutus.htm. Accessed Jan 2018
28. Laing, G.: Secret of Project Granny Smith, in the Age. Fairfax, Melbourne (2005)
29. Commonwealth Schools Commission, Teaching, Learning and Computers. Report of the National Advisory Committee on Computers in Schools. Commonwealth Schools Commission, Canberra (1983)
30. Tatnall, A.: The australian educational computer that never was. IEEE Ann. Hist. Comput. 35(1), 35–47 (2013)
31. Commonwealth Schools Commission: Australian School Computer Systems: Educational User Requirements. Commonwealth Schools Commission, Canberra (1986)
32. Commonwealth Schools Commission: Australian School Computer Systems: Technical Requirements. Commonwealth Schools Commission, Canberra (1986)
33. Tatnall, A., Leonard, R.: Purpose-built educational computers in the 1980s: the australian experience. In: Tatnall, A. (ed.) HC 2010. IAICT, vol. 325, pp. 101–111. Springer, Heidelberg (2010). https://doi.org/10.1007/978-3-642-15199-6_11
34. Singleton, V., Michael, M.: Actor-networks and ambivalence: General practitioners in the UK cervical screening programme. Soc. Stud. Sci. 23(2), 227–264 (1993)

ICT4D and Improvement of ICTs

Assessing ICT Access Disparities Between the Institutional and Home Front: A Case of University Students in South Africa's Eastern Cape

Sam Takavarasha Jr.[ID], Liezel Cilliers[(⊠)][ID],
and Willie Chinyamurindi[ID]

University of Fort Hare, Alice, South Africa
{Stakavarasha, Lcilliers, WChinyamurindi}@ufh.ac.za

Abstract. Information and Communication Technologies (ICTs) have been used to promote equality and inclusivity, foster human development, enhance opportunity and fight poverty in developing countries. In spite of this effort, inequality to ICT access persists in developing countries like post-apartheid South Africa. This paper contributes to the ICT4D discourse by investigating ICT access disparities between various actors within a country. The theoretical foundation adopts elements of Engeström's [1] activity theory as a conceptual lens for examining the access disparities experienced by users at home and within a formal institutional activity system, such as a university. Fifteen in-depth interviews were conducted with university students at two campuses of a previously disadvantaged university in the Eastern Cape province of South Africa. The study shows that the reason for different access, limited access on the home front and unlimited access on the institutional front, was due to access cost, lack of devices, inadequate skills and lack of awareness of the value of internet access. We conclude that these factors worsen poverty by limiting access to opportunities for the majority of the population that lacks institutional access.

Keywords: ICT access disparities · Activity theory · South africa
Social exclusion

1 Introduction

Several Information Systems scholars have presented Information and Communication Technologies (ICTs) as effective tools to improve inequality [2–4]. ICTs can be used to fight poverty, foster development and reducing inequalities to economic access in the information age [5]. While acknowledging the usefulness of other social, economic and technical imperatives, the importance of sustainable and affordable ICT access has been urged in literature as a critical driver of inclusivity in the information age [6].

Some key applications of ICT include agriculture, remittance economy, education and healthcare [7, 8]. The usefulness of ICTs in supporting these essential sectors of the economy has compelled information systems scholars to promote universal access.

© IFIP International Federation for Information Processing 2018
Published by Springer Nature Switzerland AG 2018. All Rights Reserved
D. Kreps et al. (Eds.): HCC13 2018, IFIP AICT 537, pp. 45–59, 2018.
https://doi.org/10.1007/978-3-319-99605-9_4

The strategic nature of ICT enabled applications suggests that unequal access to ICTs will inevitably worsen social exclusion as well as economic inequalities between communities in the proximate future. Social exclusion refers to the whole or partial exclusion of individuals and population segments from the opportunities available to the society they live in [9]. To mitigate against social exclusion, several measures have been employed to ensure sustainable and affordable access by disadvantaged communities. These measures include the use of free basics [10] community networks [6]; telecentres [11] and infrastructure sharing [12].

Studies on the digital divide have often focused on the availability and unavailability of Internet access between and within countries [13]. This is in spite of the growing number of IS scholars that call for a shift beyond the elementary idea of binary access or lack thereof [14, 15]. Socio-technical scholars of IS advocate for an understanding of both the technical and the social imperatives that affect the usage of ICTs. They view the usage of IS and ICTs as dependent on social phenomena that influence the users' ability to access and effectively use ICTs as articulated by Bednar and Welch [16]. This is supported by the United Nations [17] that also posits that the realization of ICT capabilities depends on the interface between technological and human factors.

Against this background, this study endeavours to analyze the inclusivity of ICT access within a country by comparing the home and institutional platforms. The home platform, hereafter operationalized as the home activity system, is used as a proxy for ordinary citizens' access. Likewise, the university activity system represents the ideal quality of access that institutions achieve with the same ICT penetration. These two activity systems were chosen to expose the difference in access to use ICT as a tool for development and opportunity enhancing access to information. In developing countries, like South Africa, where enclaves of affluence exist alongside expanses of extreme poverty, the reasons why one segment of the population fail to exploit the available opportunities that ICT provides are often not well understood. South Africa was chosen for the historical and political profile that are believed to have shaped people's social relations into structural exclusion that affects these previously marginalized groups [18].

Third generation activity theory (also called, cultural-historical activity theory) was adopted as a theoretical lens for this study. The theory can conceptualize the interaction between a subject and an object using a tool for achieving a particular outcome. Activity theory conceptualizes this interaction in a way that considers social, cultural and historical contexts of the unit of analysis. Unlike the earlier generations that only analyze the subject-tool-object interaction, the third generation also enables such an investigation in the contexts of two activity systems as discussed in Sect. 2. It enables contextualism by investigating the Rules, Community and Division of labour that shape the use of Tools (i.e. ICTs) by Human subjects (students) in their endeavour to pursue ICT enabled opportunities.

The study uses 15 in-depth interviews conducted at a previously disadvantaged university in South Africa's Eastern Cape province. University students were chosen as the research population because of their access to the internet in both the home and institutional activity systems. The objective of this study is achieved by answering the following research question: What are the factors that influence the disparities in ICT access between the home and the institutional front if any?

2 Literature Review

The challenge of inclusive ICT access has been situated at the centre of The Information and Communication for Development (ICT4D) policymaking debate. This is because of the importance of ICT capabilities such as more efficient in economic and social processes, improving the effectiveness of cooperation between various stakeholders, and increasing the amount of information available to people, businesses and governments [17]. UNESCO [19] also draws parallels between digital inclusion and poverty reduction. They propose that ICT can provide a voice to marginalized communities through interventions in a context-specific manner that respects local socio-political and socio-economic processes, meaning making, autonomy and expression.

Zavaleta et al. [20] posit that social isolation or deprivation of social connectedness is a core impediment to the achievement of well-being. Social exclusion studies have also focused on the potential of ICTs to foster inclusive services to disadvantaged groups. This includes inclusive health care access [21, 22] and inclusive education by disadvantaged groups like the disabled [23], among other subjects. The body of literature on inclusive education provides insights that advocates of ICT access can use. The merits of inclusivity access as an approach to developing digital skills and access to opportunities to previously disadvantaged communities in developing countries cannot be overestimated. For instance, many communities that are still affected by social exclusion challenges several years after the democratic dispensation in South Africa cannot escape their plight without inclusive interventions. They suffer under-investment in rural areas, inadequate access to markets and unfair market conditions, inadequate access to advanced technologies, weak infrastructure, high production and transport costs, gender asymmetry in access to assets and services, conflicts, HIV/AIDS, natural disasters, deforestation, environmental degradation and loss of biodiversity, and dependency on foreign aid [7]. This challenges both a result and a cause of previous and ongoing poverty traps as articulated by Sachs [24].

Literature shows that marginalized groups lag behind in the adoption and acceptance of new technologies. We argue that this applies to marginalized groups on the home activity system in comparison with the unlimited access on the institutional front. For instance, Roupa et al. [25] found that elderly citizens make less extensive use of services and opportunities offered by mobile phone technologies. They were mainly using mobile phones for making phone calls yet the few of them that used advanced technologies reported high satisfaction with the way that these technologies improved their lives. This shows that access to technologies is not synonymous with effective usage that supports the benefits of ICT enabled opportunities.

There has been some effort to promote universal access to ICTs [26]. Some of these efforts have focused on technologically oriented solutions while others have been socially embedded [27, 28]. The technological approach has been criticized for assuming that availing technologies to under privileged people would result in the adoption of ICT to improve livelihoods [29, 30]. On the other hands, the social embeddedness approach sought to align technologies to the social imperatives that determine livelihood choices in a community. Given the underutilization of interventions that employed adequate technologies like telecentres [31], this study suggests that an appreciation of the socio-economic and socio-political context is necessary for understanding the ICT adoption by a community.

Consequently, this study is situated on at the intersection of activity theory's application in ICT4D [32, 33], education [34, 35], and IS research [36]. Vygotsky's [37] Activity Theory (AT) is an analytical technique for identifying tensions and contradictions that exist among issues and problems that can arise in an activity. There are three generations of AT namely the first, second and third generations. The first generation AT simply consists of a subject and object that are mediated by tools [34]. The second generation AT situates the interaction of a subject and object in a contextual setting of a community that is governed by rules and division of labour which affect the undertaking of the activity [1].

Finally, the third generation AT expands on the seconds by including connected activities (Fig. 1). The dual-activity system depicts the outcome of the interaction of two activities when activities come into contact with each other to produce an outcome [1]. This study, therefore, adopts the third generation AT to compare the difference between two digital exposure activity systems. These are the school system and the home system. The university student is the subject, and the usage of ICTs is the object. See Fig. 2 for a representation of the application of AT in this study.

The Research Context: This study was conducted at an institution of higher learning in the Eastern Cape of South Africa. South Africa is a sub-Saharan African country. South Africa has a Gini-coefficient of 0.66 to 0.7 which makes it one of the countries with the most inequality in the world [38]. The institution under study is a previously disadvantaged university, and most of the students are from impoverished rural areas in the Eastern Cape. The Eastern Cape has been reported to have the second lowest Internet access at 37% in South Africa. At least 11.3% of the population access the Internet through educational institutions and Internet cafes, while in 2014 the majority of the population (80%) accessed the Internet through mobile devices [39]. While the institution has three campuses, this study was conducted at the two biggest campuses. Most of the students that are enrolled at these two campuses are below the age of 23, unlike the third campus where the student profile tends to lean towards more mature, working adults which was not the population chosen for this study.

3   Methods and Approach

This study adopts an interpretive paradigm for conducting case studies as articulated by Klein and Myers [40]. Of the seven principles for interpretive case studies, principle of Dialogical Reasoning which requires 'sensitivity to possible contradictions between the theoretical preconceptions guiding the research design and actual findings.' We also adopted the principles of Contextualization which calls for 'critical reflection of the social and historical background of the research setting.'[1]. While activity theory is often

---

[1] [40] p. 72.

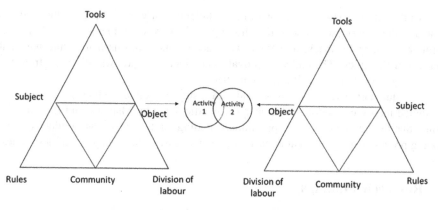

Fig. 1. Third generation activity theory [34]

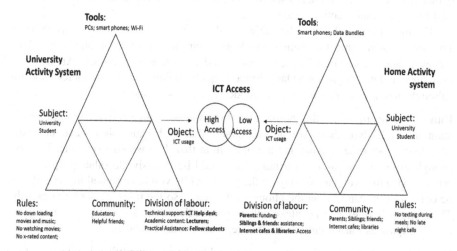

Fig. 2. Interaction between the university and home activity system

considered to be a paradigm, we adopted these principles of interpretivism because they complement activity theory's quest for both contradictions and contextualization.

In-depth interviews were conducted with students from two campuses of a university in South Africa's Eastern Cape Province. The combined student population from these two campuses are approximately 15 000. The study participants were selected making use of a convenient sampling allowing for gender and year of study. The interview process reached the saturation point after 15 interviews were conducted.

The interview guide was designed after a literature review was conducted to ascertain the reasons why ICT access are limited in developing countries. This allowed the researchers to have a deeper understanding of the reasons behind the differences in Internet access between the two activity systems. The researchers also attempted to conduct both exploratory and confirmatory research on the themes identified from literature as well as the theoretical framework.

A pilot study was conducted with three students that were not part of the study to validate the interview guide's user-friendliness. A few problems were identified through the user feedback, and these were documented and used to refine the final version of the guide. The ethical approval to conduct the study was obtained from the University's Research and Ethics Committee.

The qualitative evidence was analyzed using selective coding [41] from the grounded theory methodology for analysis as articulated by Matavire and Brown [42]. After the first two interviews, preliminary coding of the data was conducted. The coding process was repeated after each interview to assess the emergence of new codes.

4 Research Findings

This section presents a summary of the results of the in-depth interviews. Selected quotes from the in-depth interviews are categorized by the components of Engeström's [43] third-generation activity theory.

The university student are the subject of the home and university activity systems. The study shows that the millennials learn their digital skills at university. They however lack information literacy training and e-commerce exposure. At the home front they are late adopters who lack digital etiquette training and e-commerce exposure although they are warned to exercise modesty with social media.

Rules: The results show that home rules do not affect online activity. As one participant advised, 'No, there are no rules, and that is because they have no much knowledge about the internet and the only thing that they would say is that I am old enough to know not to do something that would be offensive to other people or too private. Also that you cannot stay on the phone while you have something you should be doing or you can't be on the phone while eating, so the rules are such things only' These extrinsic rules are in contrast with intrinsic rules in the university system, e.g. not using cellphones during class time, that regulate access to content.

Community: The same disparities were found in the community's role players, which also differ in ICT capacity and scale of influence. Unlike the university, which had an ICT help desk, lecturers and peers the home had inadequate funding from parents and little technical help from internet cafes. Participant Mi2 'Specifically using the internet I was never taught at home, using Microsoft I was taught that at a community centre but unfortunately they didn't have internet, they were just teaching basic Microsoft Word and Excel. Accessing internet there was no one to teach, you would go to the internet café and get someone to assist you by connection, how you do it is your struggle, no one teaches you'.

Division of Labour: There is also a sharp contrast between the divisions of labour, which was found to be less diverse and less effective in the home activity system. For instance, very few participants had any influence from friends, neighbours and libraries when they are at home. Participant Si10 was exceptional 'I had a neighbour who was studying engineering at Ibika. He was advanced in technology, so I used to follow him. He owned a computer and a smart phone, and I was always with him. However, I was young then, and all I knew about technology was watching movies on his laptop. He was the person who motivated me to get an interest in the computer world.' Other participants only reported lack of actors who should otherwise play role that support ICT access. This is due to lack of capacity on the part of these actors involved in the home activity system.

Tools: These ICT tools on the university system are more in variety and effectiveness that those at home. A key difference is lack of WIFI which restricts access to the home system as participant Ai1 puts it, 'At home [access] is a struggle with expensive data as you know... I can't even use my laptop because to connect it to internet is very expensive at home, so I use my phone'.

Based on the interview results presented in Tables 1, 2, 3, 4, 5 and Fig. 2 shows how the components of third generation activity theory reveal the differences in ICT access, capacity and scope between the home and the university systems. See Fig. 2. For the graphical representation of the activity systems.

Table 1. Interview results of the experience of subjects at University and home

	University	Home (Rural & City)
Subject	• I am from a very small town called Flagstaff, I grew up in rural areas, and I came here when I was 19 years, and there was a course for computer in my first year, and that was the first time I learned to use a computer. Ai1 • "I was 19 years in 2012, and I learned for the first time in university. There was an orientation day, and we were supposed to write a test during registration first year, I wrote the test and failed, but then it was just a test to check if I can use the internet and computer, and then I leaned by myself." Ti4 • "I haven't been formally trained, but just from my general knowledge I can identify valuable information just by looking at the source of the information and the content of the information," Si8 • "No I have never been taught on how to buy online or how to treat others, I have bought something online, and I wouldn't really say I have been taught. On how to protect myself or my own privacy because I think for me it comes with what you want to be exposed to on the internet and I just limit the information I put on the internet especially about myself, so I would say for me it has always been a self-taught skill." Si5	• "...No, I got my first smartphone this year and at home, I had my first phone when I was doing grade-10 called V360 for calls and text-messages." Ai1 • "There is a huge gap and need for training. If I can give you an example of my Dj career, some other things that DJs write are too offensive...because those guys are illiterate' They just know how to play music and they can't really deal with criticisms from social media and other people. It's like you are running a business and so some people will always complain that they don't like this and that...and these guys would take it negatively but me I would always take it differently because I have got those skills." Mi3 • I have never used internet to buy anything, you know when you not used to these digital things and you hear people saying there are scams in buying things online, and then you become scared even when you want to buy, • Yes, she did teach me and even at school, we were taught that we must not just use the internet anyhow because one day you going to get a job and they will check your character on the internet and even Facebook. Then it will be difficult for you if they find something negative to be hired for certain job position or even at all because of what you once posted on the internet
	• Learned internet at university • No e-commerce exposure • No information literacy training	• Late smart phone adopter • No digital etiquette training • No e-commerce exposure • Warned to be modest on social media

Table 2. The rules that control the conduct of subjects the home and university activity system

	University	Home (Rural & City)
Rules	• …they restricted us to not download movies or listening to music online. Well it's good for the institution, but for us, it's not because sometimes when studying we need to take a break and listen to music or watch something to refresh Ki14 •..there are rules which one has to agree to when logging in to the university networks and these rules govern what you can do here. The rules state that you can't do things like visit porn sites, downloading movies and other stuff. Pi15 • We are allowed to use our devices in class as long they don't disturb lectures, Mi3 • …we are only allowed to do things that are regarded as part of school work and doing things like watching movies online is forbidden. SI9 • I think the Wi-Fi needs to be improved; the software needs to be updated to the current versions. Also, they should allow us to use some services like torrents. We should be allowed to enter the labs with our own laptops as currently, they won't allow us because they don't want people stealing the laptops in the labs	• No there are no rules, and that is because they have no much knowledge about the internet and the only thing that they would say is that I am old enough to know not to do something that would be offensive to other people or too private. Also that you can stay on the phone while you have something you should be doing or you can't be on the phone while eating, so the rules are such things only • Yes, I think there are rules [home] because you can't really do those things, you have to ask permission to use the internet for academic purposes only, and maybe you can use them when they are not around do your other stuff but you can't access the internet for anything other than academic. Mi3 • It depends because we are not allowed to be on our phone while dining as a family or during the sleeping time but our parents don't really have much control on that, so there are no rules I can say. Ti3 • ….not rules but WhatsApp is always an issue with parents when you always on it but then when they refuse me WhatsApp I can always go out and be with my friends and do my WhatsApp, as long as I have done all my duties and back in the house at the right time. Ai1
	• Access to bad sites is blocked • Not allowed to download drama series • allowed to use own devices	• No parental rules about internet use • No excessive use mobile and use during diner

Table 3. The influence of the home and university community on students' digital access

	University	Home (Rural & City)
Community	• No, I don't have friends who know better than me in using the internet.... Yes, they [Lecturers] do give me enough information I need because most of the things I know is because of them • I leaned here a lot from my friends; I didn't learn anything from ICT and lecturers because even though there is a computer lab in my department, we were told to do books when we want to access it. Ai1 • Yes, I had two friends one doing a B. Comm General and the other Economics we used to do CLT practical together, and since I was struggling with computers a lot, they helped me a lot. Ki14 • ..... but I have friends who still post their nude pictures online or share derogatory statement online which are things that may cost them in the future because I heard employers look at your online activities. I think they need to be taught more about avoiding things like that. Pi15 • Yes, I remember very well the lecturer was by Dr N. She spoke an about cyber bullying and that we should respect others. She also spoke about restricting the amount of information you give out online and on social media to avoid cyber bullies	• Specifically using the internet, I was never taught at home, using Microsoft I was taught that at a community centre but unfortunately they didn't have internet, they were just teaching basic Microsoft word and excel. Accessing internet there was no one to teach, you would go to the internet café and get someone to assist you by connection, how you do it is your struggle, no one teaches you. Mi2 • In rural areas one thing is that people who have already acquired skills that they would be able to teach those who don't have move out of the village to better city and we are left alone to hustle the skills on our own, when they come back we have already got the skills on our own and some of them become very interested to assist there and there in improving what we already have. Mi2 • In the rural areas side there really nothing much you can learn there, there's not much support they can give you like in my rural community most people are illiterate, and even my own parents are not educated, so they don't really know much about those things to be able to offer any support. Mi3 • In my township community some of my friends have access to these things, and I can go to their homes and be able to access the internet as much as I want unlike at my home where it is limited and restricted by rules, and I can also get skills and knowledge from them by asking of what I don't know, and they tell me because they are much informed." Mi3
	• Educators; • Friends/fellow students	• Parents; Siblings; friends; • Internet cafes; libraries

Table 4. The effect of division of labour on students' digital access

	University	Home (Rural & City)
Division of labour	• They [ICT support] give me support like ICT when I have a problem with my laptop I do go to them, and they fix it for me so that I can be able to use it and also access the internet. Ni6 • [ICT support] they do not assist us with the learning, but they help with setting up our login profiles, our emails and printing our student cards. Si9 • Lecturers also do support as they give us support on how to access information especially about certain projects that they give us." • "The tutors move around helping the struggling students but often we are taught as a group and some people can't understand things quickly and the class may even end and they still do not understand what we were learning" Si9	• "[Siblings] my sister who is 5 years older than me taught me most of the things about technology, how to use a phone and most of the things I know now I learned from her." Si8 • "[Friend] I can't say I learned something (from friends) because the community I come from is a bit behind, in fact, I had to be the one teaching them when I went home" Si15 • "[Neighbours] I had a neighbour who was studying engineering at Ibika. He was advanced in technology so I used to follow him. He owned a computer and a smart phone and I was always with him. However, I was young then and all I knew about technology was watching movies on his laptop. He was the person who motivated me to get an interest in the computer world." Si10 • "[Parents] at my home there is no one to help me with the money to buy bundles because no one has it." Oi6
	• Technical support from ICT Help desk; • Academic content from Lecturers; • Practical Assistance from Fellow students	• Parents provide funding; • Siblings & friends assist; • Internet cafes & libraries provide Access

Table 5. How digital tools are being used by students at home and university activity systems

	University	Home (Rural & City)
Tools	• ".. here at school I have free Wi-Fi all the time. ... So on a daily basis, I would say I get about 9–10 h of internet access." Si8 • ".... almost 90% of my classmates have laptops, and 99,5% have smartphones." Ai1	• 'At home [access] is a struggle with expensive data as you know... I can't even use my laptop because to connect it to internet is very expensive at home, so I use my phone' Ai1 • "Flexibility is serious caution and the fact that you can't compare desktop with the phone then you can't really be flexible on the phone as you would do on a desktop." Mi2 • "we have limited resources when it comes to technology in the Eastern Cape, and the teachers seem not to take

(continued)

Table 5. (*continued*)

University	Home (Rural & City)
	technology serious, and they do not dedicate time to teach students how to use computers. There is also a lack of internet connectivity. I started to hear about Wi-Fi when I got to university."Ki14
• Computers; • Smart phones; • Free Wi-Fi	• Smart phones; • Data Bundles;

5 Discussion

This paper has attempted to promote inclusive ICT assess by investigating the disparities between access at the home and institutional levels and discussing how to address them. It used university students operationalized as subjects for assessing the two activity systems as articulated by Engeström's [1] third generation activity theory. The university (operationalized as activity system (1) was presented as a proxy of institutions that provides access to its patrons. It was selected because educational institutions provide about 11.3% of Internet access in the Eastern Cape. The home activity system (operationalized as activity system (2) represents students' rural and city homes where they reside during the holidays and after they complete their studies. The internet access in the home activity system was found to be mainly through mobile data bundles. Mobile access amounts to 80% of internet access in the Eastern Cape of South Africa [39]. This does not suggest that the entire 80% of mobile access in the province is used on the home activity system, the researchers observed that a majority of institutional internet users in the Eastern Cape also use mobile access.

Our findings show that Internet access is limited on the home front yet it is unlimited at the institutional activity system. The informants claim that their internet access drops from 100% at university to about 30% when they go home. Participant Si8 advised, '.. here at school I have free Wi-Fi all the time. … So on a daily basis, I would say I get about 9–10 h of internet access.' This disparity is expected to also occur between the home and other institutional fronts like the workplace. This is mainly because of the access costs, which discourage many domestic users from subscribing to conventional broadband access. As participant Ai1 advised, 'At home [access] is a struggle with expensive data as you know… I can't even use my laptop because to connect it to internet is very expensive at home, so I use my phone.' The home activity system also lacks ICT devices that are necessary for connecting to the internet. ICT devices are operationalized in this study as tools that mediate between subject and object to produce the outcome of ICT enable opportunities. Very few rural and high-density suburb inhabitants have personal computers and smartphones.

While this may be due to lack of awareness of the need for Internet access, we found that it is also due to lack of financial resources. There is a need to address the socio-economic inequalities and socio-political issues that cause these disparities. Both lack awareness, and low income are linked to the socio-historical contours of the social exclusionary policies of the apartheid Era as articulated by Kruger et al. [44].

The study found some regulatory and ethical rules that govern the usage of ICTs at university yet on the home activity system these rules were rather insignificant. This is arguably because of the need to address the misconduct that accompanies high usage at the university while the insignificant online activity at home hardly warrants the intervention of parents and guardians. As interviewee Ki14 put it, '..at home, there are no rules they don't mind if I'm using my laptop.' We found that part of their lack of involvement emanates from their lack of digital skills.

The exclusion from the digital economy is so widespread that the participants reported that in their home communities, the students have very little to no contact with anyone who can help them to develop digital skills. As stated by one participant, '... [in] my home town Bizana most people know nothing about using mobile devices or the internet.' This suggests that the young people that are not enrolled in universities or employed by any institution have limited contact and scope to develop the digital skills that are necessary for exploiting ICT enabled opportunities that are getting more important in the information age.

There is also a difference in the division of labour. The university system has technical skill and assistance from lecturers, fellow students and ICT helpdesk knowledge support, yet the home can only provide limited financial assistance and almost no digital skills at all. Participant Si15 said, 'I can't say I learned something (from friends) because the community I come from is a bit behind, in fact, I had to be the one teaching them when I went home.' Participant Oi6 added '[Parents] at my home there is no one to help me with the money to buy bundles because no one has it.' Another participant suggested that poor support is due to lack of knowledge of the usefulness of the internet. In her own words, '... [in] my home town Bizana most people know nothing about using mobile devices or the internet. As a result, even when I asked for money to go to the library they would not understand why I need to go to the library.' This is a serious disadvantage for young people growing up in the digital era where more and more government and business to citizens' information is migrating to online platforms.

Since activity theory assists use to unearth the contradictions in the phenomena under investigation [45], we found different levels of access between activity systems that enjoy the same coverage yet there are no rules or actors that inhibit use of ICTs by the marginalized people. The home and institutional activity systems have roughly the same 3G, 4G and LTE mobile coverage in the Eastern Cape. The same applies to fixed internet infrastructure within city limits yet the home activity system has less access. As a result, the disparities in access and usage cannot be conceptualized as a spatially determined anomaly but rather as socio-economic and socio-culturally defined one. For that reason, the ICT infrastructure and mobile operator companies may claim to be serving the nation equally yet the end users face different levels of access. There is, however, a discernible co-existence of being previously disadvantaged and being currently uninvolved in the digital world as typified by the home activity system.

According to Hickey and du Toit, [46] social exclusion can be associated with political, economic, socio-cultural and spatial imperative and these are said to be closely related to long-term historical processes. Such a situation represents adverse incorporation on the part of the users on the home front [46].

6 Limitations and Conclusion

This study made its contribution to inclusive access by identifying the factors that shape the access disparities between the home and institution activity systems. While it has revealed the of glaring disparities in access between the two activity systems, the paper faces limitations in attempting to assess the socio-historically determined factors and effects of exclusion thorough the eyes of students since they did not experience the causal influence of apartheid. We conclude that there is evidence of socio-demographically shaped patterns of social exclusion within the Eastern Cape Province. While we found no deliberate effort to perpetuate exclusion by social status, this study shows that it is inadequate to ensure uniform investment in ICT infrastructure between the home and the institution. There is a desperate to address the socio-political and socio-economic factors before equal opportunities in the digital front can be realized. We confirm that ICT access disparities require no technological deterministic solution. Future research must consider the using adverse incorporation theory for assessing access inequalities because it enables an assessment of the effect of localized livelihood strategies over both time and space.

Acknowledgement. This research project was jointly funded by the South African Medical Research Council (SAMRC) and Forte, the Swedish Research Council for Welfare, Working Life and Welfare.

References

1. Engeström, Y.: Expansive learning at work: toward an activity-theoretical reconceptualization. J. Educ. Work **14**(1), 133–156 (2001)
2. Walsham, G.: Are we making a better world with ICTs? reflections on a future agenda for the IS field. J. Inf. Technol. **27**(2), 87–93 (2012)
3. Qureshi, S.: Are we making a better world with information and communication technology for development (ICT4D) research? findings from the field and theory building. Inf. Technol. Dev. **21**(4), 511–522 (2015)
4. Sahay, S.: Are we building a better world with ICTs? empirically examining this question in the domain of public health in India. Inf. Technol. Dev. **22**(1), 168–176 (2016)
5. Khaliq, I.H., Naeem, B., Abbas, Q., Khalid, S.: Contribution of ICT to poverty reduction among women in Kilosa district. J. Bus. Fin. Aff. **6**(1), 238 (2016)
6. Takavarasha Jr., S., Adams, C., Cilliers, L.: Community networks for addressing affordability of ICT access in african rural areas: a case study of Zenzeleni, Makhosi, South Africa. In: Takavarasha Jr, S., Adams, C. (eds.) Affordability Issues Surrounding the Use of ICT for Development and Poverty Reduction. IGI Global, Hershey (2018)

7. Van Zyl, O., Alexander, T., De Graaf, L., Mukherjee, K.: ICT for agriculture in Africa. In: Yonazi, E., Kelly, T., Halewood, N., Blackman, C. (eds.) E-transform Africa: The Transformational Use of ICT in Africa (2012)

8. Al-Zahrani, A.: Toward digital citizenship: examining factors affecting participation and involvement in the internet society among higher education. Int. Educ. Stud. **8**(12), 203–217 (2015)

9. de Haan, A., Maxwell, S.: Editorial: poverty and social exclusion in North and South. IDS Bull. **29**(1), 1–9 (1998)

10. Cilliers, L., Samarthya-Howard, A.: Everyone will be connected': free basics in Africa to support ICT4D. In: Takavarasha Jr, S., Adams, C. (eds.) Affordability Issues Surrounding the Use of ICT for Development and Poverty Reduction. IGI Global, Hershey (2018)

11. Van Der Vyver, A.G.: A model for economic development with telecentres and the social media: overcoming affordability constraints. In: Takavarasha Jr, S., Adams, C. (eds.) Affordability Issues Surrounding the Use of ICT for Development and Poverty Reduction. IGI Global, Hershey (2018)

12. Zanamwe, N., Rupere, T., Mapako, B., Nyambo, B.: Fostering affordability of ICT access in developing countries through infrastructure sharing: the devil is in the detail. In: Takavarasha Jr, S., Adams, C. (eds.) Affordability Issues Surrounding the Use of ICT for Development and Poverty Reduction. IGI Global, Hershey (2018)

13. Skaletsky, M., Soremekun, O., Galliers, R.D.: Information technology for development: The Changing – and Unchanging – Face of the Digital Divide: an Application of Kohonen Self-Organizing Maps, Information Technology for Development (2013)

14. Gilwald, A.: Beyond access. Addressing digital inequality in Africa. PAPER SERIES: NO. 48, March 2017. https://www.cigionline.org/sites/default/files/documents/GCIG%20no.48_0.pdf

15. Vengerfeldt, P.: Digital divide - questions beyond access. In: Silverstone, R. (ed.) EMTEL Conference in London, 23rd–26th April 2003 (2003)

16. Bednar, P., Welch, C.: The innovation-diffusion cycle: time for a sociotechnical agenda. In: Twenty-Fifth European Conference on Information Systems (ECIS), Guimarães, Portugal (2017)

17. United Nations, Information and communications technologies for inclusive social and economic development. Commission on Science and Technology for Development Seventeenth session Geneva, 12–16 May 2014 (2014)

18. Du Toit, A., Neves, D.: 'In Search of South Africa's second economy: reflections on chronic poverty, vulnerability and adverse incorporation in Mt Frere and Khayelitsha. Paper prepared for the conference on Living on the Margins: Vulnerability, social exclusion and the state in the informal economy; Cape Town, 26–28 March 2007. PLAAS and CPRC (2007a, forthcoming)

19. UNESCO: Poverty and Digital Inclusion: Preliminary Findings of Finding a Voice Project. The United Nations Educational Scientific & Cultural Organization, New Deli, India (2007)

20. Zavaleta, D., Samuel, K., Mills, C.: Social isolation: a conceptual and measurement proposal. OPHI WORKING PAPER, NO. 67 (2014)

21. MacLachlan, M., Khasnabis, C., Mannan, H.: Inclusive health. Trop. Med. Int. Health **17**(1), 139–141 (2012)

22. Angeli, F., Jaiswal, A.K.: Business model innovation for inclusive health care delivery at the bottom of the pyramid. Organ. Environ. **29**(4), 486–507 (2016)

23. Palomino, M.C.P.: Future teachers to use ICT for inclusive education. Dig. Educ. Rev. (2017)

24. Sachs, J.: The End of Poverty. Penguin Press, New York (2005)

25. Roupa, Z., Nikas, M., Gerasimou, E., Zafeiri, V., Giasyrani, L., Kazitori, E., Sotiropoulou, P.: The use of technology by the elderly. Health Sci. J. **4**(2), 118–126 (2010)
26. Abascal, J., Civit, A., Nicolle, C.: Universal accessibility and the digital divide. In: Kotzé, P. (eds.)
27. Kotzé, P., Marsden, G., Lindgaard, G., Wesson, J., Winckler, M. (eds.): INTERACT 2013. LNCS, vol. 8118. Springer, Heidelberg (2013). https://doi.org/10.1007/978-3-642-40480-1
28. Avgerou, C.: Information systems in developing countries: a critical research review. J. Inf. Technol. **23**(3), 133–146 (2008)
29. Avgerou, C.: Discourses on ICT and development. Inf. Technol. Int. Dev. **6**(3), 1–18 (2010)
30. Mhlanga, B.: Information and communication Technologies (ICTs), policy for change and the mask for development: a critical analysis of Zimbabwe's E-readiness survey report. IJISDC **28**(1), 1–16 (2006)
31. Dusek, V.: Philosophy of Technology: An Introduction. Blackwell, Oxford (2007)
32. Best, L.M., Rajendra, K.: Sustainability failures of rural telecenters: challenges from the Sustainable Access in Rural India (SARI) project. Inf. Technol. Int. Dev. **4**, 31–45 (2008)
33. Karanasios, S.: Framing ICT4D research using activity theory: a match between the ICT4D field and theory? Inf. Technol. Int. Dev. **10**(2), 1–17 (2014)
34. Slavova, M., Karanasios, S.: When institutional logics meet information and communication technologies: examining hybrid information practices in ghanaian agriculture. J. Assoc. Inf. Syst. (Forthcoming)
35. Robertson, I.: Sustainable e-learning, activity theory and professional development. In: Atkinson, R., McBeath, C. (eds.) Hello! Where Are You in the Landscape of Educational Technology? Proceedings Ascilite, Melbourne (2008)
36. Bennett, E.: Activity theory: what does it offer elearning research? In: Yeats, W.B. (eds.) ALT-C 2009 in Dreams Begins Responsibility, 8–10 September 2010, Manchester (2010)
37. Karanasios, S.: Toward a unified view of technology and activity: the contribution of activity theory to information systems research. Inf. Technol. People (2017)
38. Vygotsky, L.: Mind in Society: The Development of Higher Psychological Processes. Harvard University Press, Cambridge (1978)
39. Mail & Guardian: Is South Africa the unequal society in the world? (2018). https://mg.co.za/article/2015-09-30-is-south-africa-the-most-unequal-society-in-the-world
40. My Broadband (2015). https://mybroadband.co.za/news/telecoms/127450-internet-access-in-south-africa-best-and-worst-provinces.html
41. Klein, H., Myres, D.: A set of principles for conducting and evaluating interpretive field studies in information systems. MIS Q. **23**(1), 67–94 (1999)
42. Glaser, B.G.: Basics of Grounded Theory Analysis. Sociology Press, MillValley (1992)
43. Matavire, R., Brown, I.: Profiling Grounded theory approaches in information systems research. Eur. J. Inf. Syst. **22**(1), 119–129 (2011)
44. Engeström, Y.: Learning By Expanding: An Activity Theoretical Approach to Developmental Research. Orienta-Konsultit, Helsinki (1987)
45. Kruger, S., du Toit, A., Ponte, S.: De-racialising exploitation: 'black economic empowerment' in the South African Wine sector. DIIS working Paper no 2006/34. Danish Institute for International Studies, Copenhagen (2006)
46. Engeström, Y., Sannino, A.: Discursive manifestations of contradictions in organizational change efforts a methodological framework. J. Organ. Change Manag. **24**(3), 368–387 (2011)
47. Hickey, S., du Toit, A.: Adverse incorporation, social exclusion and chronic poverty. CPRC Working paper 81 (2007). http://www.chronicpoverty.org/uploads/publication_files/WP81_Hickey_duToit.pdf
48. Du Toit, A.: Forgotten by the Highway: Globalization and Chronic Poverty in Ceres
49. South Africa: PLAAS Research paper, Bellville (2004)

Creating an ICT Skills Enhancement Environment for Entrepreneurs

Riana Steyn[1]([⊠]) [iD], Carina de Villiers[1], and Hossana Twinomurinzi[2]

[1] Department of Informatics, University of Pretoria, Pretoria, South Africa
Riana.steyn@up.ac.za
[2] School of Computing, University of South Africa, Pretoria, South Africa

Abstract. Entrepreneurship is seen as a primary tool in the fight against unemployment, poverty and social inequality. Although various entrepreneurial training models exist, many of these have not considered the influence of current information and communication technology (ICT), even though ICT is a contemporary tool that entrepreneurs can leverage to increase the likelihood of a successful and sustainable business. This study therefore considered one entrepreneurship model that has been successful in entrepreneurial training in South Africa, the "content model for entrepreneurship education" (E/P), and investigated how ICT could be incorporated into this. The findings of 33 participants, who had been trained using the E/P model, suggest that, while many are familiar with most of the proposed ICT software programs, they do not necessarily incorporate them in practice. Linking ICT to the business skills section of entrepreneurial training seems to be an appropriate way of making the training practically feasible for participants. However, most of the participants highlighted the need for further guidance through a mentorship programme, for example. Guidance can also take the form of graduate programmes or learnerships. The results of the study clearly show how ICT can be linked to entrepreneurial training interventions, as well as the practical aspects of such a course. They also show that entrepreneurial interventions with high-tech equipment should perhaps not be overlooked, and that the basics first should be mastered.

Keywords: Entrepreneurs · ICT · Entrepreneurship education
Content model for entrepreneurship · Skills development

1 Introduction

A need to improve multisectoral issues, such as e-skilling, was identified as a means to uplift the people of South Africa in an attempt to decrease social issues like unemployment and crime. Unemployment is one of the largest concerns relating to South Africa's economic growth [1]. As many countries realise the importance of entrepreneurs and small firms in relation to their contribution to the economy [2, 3], it is not surprising that one of the focus areas identified by the South African government is entrepreneurs, or more specifically, micro-enterprises, and their capability to adopt information and communication technology (ICT) innovatively. Primarily, entrepreneurs have rarely undergone any form of training or received any assistance that can

© IFIP International Federation for Information Processing 2018
Published by Springer Nature Switzerland AG 2018. All Rights Reserved
D. Kreps et al. (Eds.): HCC13 2018, IFIP AICT 537, pp. 60–81, 2018.
https://doi.org/10.1007/978-3-319-99605-9_5

help them improve their businesses. This is confirmed when Pretorius, Nieman and Van Vuuren [4] state that there is an "absence of entrepreneurial education in general". Many scholars have emphasised that entrepreneurs are the engines that drive a country's economy [4–6]. Mutula and Van Brakel [5] mention that small and medium enterprises (SMEs) contribute to 60% of Europe's economic activity, and that 99% of the total number of companies in Turkey are SMEs. That SMEs are important for the country's economy is not a new phenomenon. From 1990 to 1995, 77% of all new jobs created in the United States were created as a result of small businesses [7]. As early as the 1980s, it was noted that most European governments provided support to see how entrepreneurship could be stimulated among young people [8]. Closer to home, Barkhuizen and Bennett [9] note that, in Namibia, 20% of employment is attributed to SMEs. Linking up with these figures and bringing the context of this paper into perspective is a study conducted by Antonites and Van Vuuren [1] in 2005, which pointed out that, in South Africa, small firms contributed 47% to job creation, which shows that small businesses were already playing a large role in the country in 2005, and that this role is expanding as time goes by.

The importance of these entrepreneurs successfully engaging with technology is increasing in the globally connected world in which we live. During investigations into ICT skills readiness in Botswana, it was discovered that one of the reasons for some companies not adopting ICT as they should is the limited resources available to hire and retain these skilled workers [5]. Reimenschneider et al. [7] also mention that a reason for small businesses not adopting ICT is that they immediately want to see a return on their investment and anticipated benefits; benefits that are not necessarily clear up front. The lack of education received by SMEs on the importance and benefits of computers emerged as a factor for ICT not being used in small businesses [3]. These benefits might take years before they can truly become evident, and smaller businesses cannot afford to wait so long to see if something has worked or not. Bhattacherjee and Sanford [10] mention that adoption is viewed as a one-time decision, while the long-term effects or post-adoption effects are ignored. This means that SMEs that do not raise their technology skills level will be left behind. This implies no growth for their businesses and, in many cases, no food on the table. As mentioned before, entrepreneurship is seen as a suggested solution to combat issues such as unemployment, poverty and low economic growth across the world [11]. However, what exactly entrepreneurs need to do to become successful from an ICT point of view is not very clear. This lack of skills will lead to more informal entrepreneurs or survivalists (people who work from the perspective of "what I make today puts food on my table tonight") being excluded from society in general.

The "content model for entrepreneurship education" (E/P) was analysed to see what is currently being taught in entrepreneurship. This discussion highlights the gap that exists in the training of entrepreneurs, identified as the absence of ICT training. It will be helpful to see how ICT can be incorporated into entrepreneurial training to assist in its effective adoption [8].

This paper will firstly discuss literature related to entrepreneurs and entrepreneurship training, followed by a discussion of the chosen methodology for the study. Findings from the data that is gathered will be analysed and discussed, before a conclusion is reached.

2 Literature Review

2.1 Entrepreneurs

There does not seem to be a common definition of an entrepreneur [4]. This creates a problem, since one has to agree on a standard definition of what an entrepreneur is before one can truly conduct any entrepreneurial studies. Even though it is not a clear definition, Dhliwayo and Van Vuuren [12] make the following statement about the entrepreneurial mindset: "It denotes a way of thinking and action about business and its opportunities that captures the benefits of uncertainty". Entrepreneurship is sometimes seen as a form of creativity as "new businesses are original and useful" [13]. Antonites and Van Vuuren [1] set out to determine a general definition for an entrepreneur, and, after reviewing various authors, suggest the following definition: "An individual with the potential of creating a vision from virtually nothing". They continue to acknowledge that "the entrepreneur is able to identify an opportunity where the regular man on the street would see chaos, contradictions, ambivalence and confusion". This paper will adopt the definition by Antonites and Van Vuuren [1].

Various classifications of entrepreneurs exist according to Esselaar et al. [3], who conducted a study in 13 countries to determine ICT usage and whether it had an impact on the profitability of SMEs. They distinguish between survivalists, or informal operators, and actual small businesses. The survivalists or informal operators are the ones who try to live day by day. Thus, survivalists do not distinguish between their personal finances and their business finances. They normally consume all income generated by sales immediately and do not necessarily keep record of their actual revenue. These are the entrepreneurs who try to improve their lives and the lives of their family members, or who merely try to survive as an alternative to unemployment. These entrepreneurs are the focus of this paper, as they are the ones who will assist in uplifting people in their communities, reduce unemployment and hopefully contribute to reducing poverty.

2.2 Content Model of Entrepreneurship Education

There are a number of debates around entrepreneurial education, with the main question being whether or not entrepreneurship can be taught [14]. Entrepreneurs are sometimes introduced as having "extraordinary genetic endowment" [15]. Even though this may be the case, there is a demand and call for contributions to train entrepreneurs across the world. Firstly, one has to understand that there is a difference in terminology used throughout the world. This is noted by Gibb [8], who explains that entrepreneurship education is labelled "enterprise" within the United Kingdom educational system. This "enterprise" focuses more on individual development and not necessarily on making a profit.

Another key factor to be considered when looking at entrepreneurial training and curriculum design that incorporates ICT is the entrepreneur's belief in his or her own ability to become a successful entrepreneur [16]. This belief is the result of the entrepreneur's motivation to succeed in business. Ndubisi and Kahraman [17] point out the correlation between personality traits, such as innovation and the ability or willingness to take risks, and actual ICT usage.

The demands for entrepreneurship training are increasing and have led to various training models being developed. Various authors' viewpoints of the business skills required by an entrepreneur can be viewed in Table 1.

Table 1. Business skills required per entrepreneur

Skills list	Authors
• Business plan • Financial management • Marketing • Operational skills • Human resources • Legal skills • Communication • Management	Van Vuuren and Nieman [18]
• General management • Legal skills • Cash flow management	Pretorius et al. [4]
• General management • Marketing management • Financial management • Human resource management • Production and operations management • Corporate communications management • Information management and e-business • Purchasing and materials management	Van Vuuren and Botha [16] Nieman and Bennet [19] Pretorius et al. [4]
• Legal skills • Business plan compilation • Cash flow management	Van Vuuren and Botha [16]

Various entrepreneurial training models in South Africa and the rest of the world were investigated to determine the real skills needs of the entrepreneurs [4, 8, 11, 16, 18, 20, 21]. Additional searches into entrepreneurship education training programmes led to a literature survey recently conducted by Azim and Al-Kahtani [14], based on entrepreneurship education and training, in which they summarise the content that various authors identified as required in entrepreneurship education and training (EET) programmes; they are shown in Table 2.

Throughout all these investigations, the one gap that stills exists is which ICT is required, and to effectively incorporate these required skills into the training interventions from a more practical point of view.

Table 2. Summary of the content of an EET programme [14]

Study	Contents
Timmons et al. [22]	• Business plan
Johannisson [23]	• The know-why (attitudes, values, motivations)
	• The know-how (abilities)
	• The know-who (short- and long-term social skills)
	• The know-when (intuition)
	• The know-what (knowledge)
Noll [24]	• By researching customer insights, conducting a self-assessment of personal creativity, conducting a feasibility study and identifying various business entry strategies
	• By assessing personal resources and financial status, researching and evaluating the risks necessary to get started, writing a working business plan, and approaching others for money and other resources
	• By learning to allocate resources, using various marketing strategies and managing money and personnel
Garavan and O'Cinneide [15]	• The formation stage: Emphasis: General business knowledge content: The business world, the nature of entrepreneurship, the characteristics of effective teams and the nature of business transactions and activities
	• The development stage: Emphasis: Skills and attitude • Content: Business planning, market selection, financial planning, product identification and making financial presentations
	• Implementation stage: Emphasis: General knowledge and attitude. Content: Financial planning, managing company growth, management functions and attitudes and making the transition from entrepreneur to manager
Kourilsky [25]	• Opportunity recognition: The identification of unfulfilled needs in the marketplace and the creation of business ideas. Observation of the market, insight into customer needs, invention and innovation
	• Marshalling and commitment of resources: Willingness to take risks as well as skills in securing outside investment
	• The creation of an operating business: Financing, marketing and management skills
Rae [26]	• Communication skills, especially persuasion
	• Creativity skills
	• Critical thinking and assessment skills
	• Leadership skills
	• Negotiation skills
	• Problem-solving skills
	• Social networking skills
	• Time management skills
Hisrich and Peters [27]	• Technical skills: Include written and oral communication, technical management and organising skills
	• Business management skills: Include planning, decision making, marketing and accounting skills
	• Personal entrepreneurial skills: Include inner control, innovation, risk taking and innovation

(*continued*)

Table 2. (*continued*)

Study	Contents
Vesper and Gartner [28]	• Concept of entrepreneurship
	• Characteristics of an entrepreneur
	• Value of entrepreneurship
	• Creativity and innovation skills
	• Entrepreneurial and ethical self-assessment
	• Networking, negotiating and deal making
	• Identifying and evaluating opportunities
	• Commercialising a concept
	• Developing entry strategies
	• Constructing a business plan
	• Finding capital
	• Initiating the business
	• Growing the business
	• Harvesting strategies
Onstenk [29]	• Motivation, need for autonomy and independence, creativity and originality, taking initiative, risk taking, looking for possibilities, posing challenging objectives, self-confidence, internal locus of control and endurance
	• Operational management, personnel and organisation, financial administration, marketing, financial management and making a business plan
	• Recognising business opportunities, interpretation of market information and the development of customer orientation to the development and effective operation of relation networks and the building of an innovative organisation

2.3 Content Model of Entrepreneurship Education

One initiative currently running implements one of these training models in both short courses and degree programmes at an academic institution in South Africa. This training is based on the model proposed by Van Vuuren and Nieman [18] called the content model for entrepreneurship education:

$$E/P = a + bM[(cE/S \times dB/S)]$$

Where:

E/P   = Entrepreneurial performance
M   = Motivation
E/S   = Entrepreneurial skills
B/S   = Business skills

a, b, c and d are co-coefficients

As the main focus of this paper is not necessarily on entrepreneurship training per se, but rather on how ICT can be integrated, it will not go into detail on the equation above and will only engage in a high-level discussion of what each construct of the equation means. The co-coefficients mean that, for each construct, some basic skills exist, and thus the assumption is that these skills will feature on various levels and will have a direct influence on the construct under discussion.

The background of E/P model is supported by the expectancy theory of the motivation model that was developed in 1964 by Vroom [18]. Van Vuuren and Botha [16] state that the E/P model "is concerned with elements that drive entrepreneurial performance and was developed to guide syllabi and curriculum development". Van Vuuren and Botha [16] mention that E/P can be presented in the following way:

- Increase in productivity
- Increase in the number of employees employed
- Net value of the business
- Increase in profitability
- Completion of the first market-related transaction.

Personality and work environment can increase the performance of the entrepreneur.

Motivation is believed to be the way in which one believes that a specific system or ICT will benefit one in one's day-to-day activities [30]. Van Vuuren and Nieman [18] point out that the relationship between motivation and performance is the desire to be successful. "Motivation is seen as the entrepreneurs' level of need for achievement" [31].

Entrepreneurial skill constitutes the distinction between an entrepreneur and a manager, as these are two different things. One can train someone in a specific work domain with the relevant knowledge and skills required to perform certain tasks, such as an accountant. Life in the entrepreneurial domain cannot be taught, as there are no actual theories that can be tested. One can teach an entrepreneur fundamental knowledge, but there are no theories to assist in the everyday uncertainties that entrepreneurship will bring about [18].

Van Vuuren and Nieman [18] list a number of business skills that are required for an entrepreneur. It seems that these business skills are the more practical aspects of the entrepreneurial training model:

- Business plan.
- Financial management: Van Vuuren and Nieman [18] note a number of financial management skills. These are "keeping financial records, understanding taxes, as well as cash flow management, including knowledge regarding a cash budget, ratio analysis, interpreting business ratios and understanding financial statements". Although the curriculum will not ensure that whoever completes the course is a financial expert or accountant, the fundamental financial principles are important to understand.

- Marketing: A successful entrepreneur is one who knows the target market and customers' needs and can address those needs. ICT can be used to assist entrepreneurs in creating their own website, or even a presence on a social media platform, such as Facebook, which can, in turn, assist them in connecting with a much larger target audience than before.
- Operational skills.
- Human resources skills.
- Legal skills: It is not necessary for an entrepreneur to become a legal expert, but understanding basic legal aspects and terms can help them when setting up and managing various contracts, such as employment contracts, sales contracts and lease agreements. It is also beneficial to be able to draft a contract through the use of a tool, such as Microsoft Word, in order to structure documentation effectively.
- Communication: An entrepreneur must have good writing and listening skills, and must be able to talk to anybody. One way in which ICT can be used to assist entrepreneurs in enhancing their communication is by not only ensuring access to a mobile device, but also to an email account and proper email ethics, which is another gap identified in training programmes.
- Management: Leadership is one of the key aspects for an entrepreneur, as this assists entrepreneurs to maintain control over their businesses.

It is clear at this stage that the training focuses on business needs, but there is no link to ICT. The authors did a basic mapping exercise to assist the entrepreneur in deciding which ICT training to undergo. The emerging need for ICT training includes the following:

- Business plan – Microsoft Word
- Financial management – Microsoft Excel
- Marketing – website design from a template, social media
- Legal skills – Microsoft Word
- Communication – mobile device, email account

These ICT skills are explored in this paper to determine their relevance.

3 Methodology

This research followed an interpretivist approach, and employed questionnaires, as well as focus groups and interviews in its survey strategy to gather data.

A course called "e-Skills for entrepreneurs", presented at an urban university, attracted 33 participants in July 2017. The authors had research funds available and subsidised a portion of the course fee, which meant that the two-day course only cost each delegate ZAR200, and included full use of the computer laboratories, as well as lunch. Although the course was initially designed for entrepreneurs who had already started their own small businesses, the authors quickly realised that there was a need for other citizens to attend such a course, as they had ideas for businesses, but they did not yet know how to realise these or how to obtain funding. During the first day of the course, the delegates were asked to complete a questionnaire to determine their skills levels, as well as the real need for technology. Throughout the two-day training, various discussions were held with these attendees and their responses were recorded as they formed part of the data analysis in the next section.

Although it seems as if the delegates could have been small business owners and not entrepreneurs, the definition introduced earlier (that an entrepreneur is able to identify an opportunity where the regular man on the street would see chaos, contradictions, ambivalence and confusion) was still the focus. The ideas identified by these potential entrepreneurs clearly showed that they could be defined as entrepreneurs.

Linking it back to the E/P, the technology that was added to the business skills construct was taught practically in the following way:

- Microsoft Excel – setting up a basic budget, and understanding basic formulas and graphs for your business
- Microsoft Word – creating a business plan that can be presented to a financial institution for possible funding, understanding basic Microsoft Word functions to allow for any documents to be drafted, writing a vision, mission and goals, and defining a basic marketing plan
- Gmail – setting up and managing an email account (including proper email ethics and responding to business requests)
- Social media as part of a marketing campaign – creating a Facebook page, managing advertising through social media, linking social media marketing to the business plan
- Free website development tools – using tools such as Weebly to create a website for the business

Except for the specific applications mentioned above, it is important to understand the participants' access to ICT and their needs in this regard.

The data was analysed using a thematic analysis approach. This approach allowed for classification into themes to see what had been left out [32]. Aronson [33] says that thematic analysis "focuses on identifiable themes and patterns of living and/or behaviour", which is similarly defined by Vaismoradi, Turunen and Bondas [34]. However, they continue to state that thematic analysis is a flexible tool that provides for a richer and more detailed analysis of the data, and focuses on the context being studied. The context for this paper is the survivalist entrepreneurs' access to ICT, and their ability to successfully implement it. Aronson [33] and Vaismoradi et al. [34] mention the steps involved in thematic analysis. These were compared and mapped accordingly:

- Collect data and transcribe the conversations, after which patterns can be identified [33].
- Familiarise yourself with the data [34].
- Identify all data relating to each pattern already identified [33].
- Generate initial codes [34].
- Combine and catalogue these patterns into sub-themes, thus bringing together pieces of data to form a bigger picture [33].
- Search for themes [34].
- Use emerging patterns from the themes in further discussions with the participants if needed [33].

- Review themes.
- Check if the themes work with the codes and the entire data set [34].
- Build a valid argument around the selected themes, which will develop a themed storyline in the end. This "helps the reader comprehend the process, understanding and motivation" of the participants. One should also refer to the literature to understand the context and thus incorporate the literature into the findings or themes [33].
- Define and name the themes.
- Refine the themes and the overall story [34].
- Produce the report [34].

In a thematic analysis, the importance of the theme does not necessary depend on quantifiable measures, but rather on whether the theme captures something important in relation to the overall research question [34]; in this case: What should entrepreneurs know about technology?

This research applied the thematic analysis approach based on the steps listed above. However, it is important to note that the content of the course was designed based on the initial literature review. The first three steps comprised the following:

1. Collect data and transcribe this according to patterns. Throughout the two-day course, the authors interacted with all the participants, facilitated focus group discussions and interviews, and distributed a questionnaire to ask a set of basic questions. All the questionnaires were captured and analysed, along with the focus group and interview notes.
2. Generate initial codes.
3. Combine and catalogue these patterns into sub-themes. Due to the fact that the initial questionnaire was based on the literature, the questionnaire was set up according to certain codes that had already been defined.

Emerging patterns from the themes will be discussed in the section below, which will be followed by the conclusion.

This research paper forms part of the last step, which constitutes reporting on the findings.

4 Findings

Although this course was initially designed for businesses that already existed, the authors realised that potential entrepreneurs could also benefit from it. Of the 33 participants, only six already had successful businesses. However, all the others could provide a business idea. Only 12 did not specify their business ideas. The ideas, which can be seen below, prove that an entrepreneurial culture exists (Table 3):

The categories for the types of businesses can be viewed in Table 4. These results give context to understand the types of entrepreneurs interviewed so that one can determine their relevance to the study.

From a gender perspective, 27 participants were female and six were male, which indicates that more women seem to be interested in entrepreneurial ventures.

Table 3. Business ideas

Briefly explain what your business or business idea is about:	Type
My business is going to be selling African food, for example, home-cooked meals	Catering
Catering business	Catering
Chicken farming	Farming and agriculture
Planning to do an internet café	ICT
I have registered with law to start a business. I want to buy a franchise, then I need a business plan	General
Farming, growing vegetables and chickens	Farming and agriculture
Fast food for everyone, we are five partners and we wish our business to become a big restaurant	Catering
I want to own a filling station	Automotive
Hairdresser	Cosmetics
I buy mangos and spices. I make atchar (a South African pickle) and sell it to people who own tuck shops and to households	Catering
I do catering and decor for parties and weddings and other special events	Events and catering
I am still planning to start a beauty salon that specialises in nails and eyelashes	Cosmetics
Fast food and car wash, serving my customers while their cars are being washed	Automotive and catering
Mechanical engineer, engine mechanics and tyre repair	Automotive
My business is a fashion designer	Cosmetics
My business is an NGO. I want to help the community, especially the children who cannot afford to go to the school, to get bursaries	Social services
Network and marketing business that sells healthcare products and cosmetics	Network marketing
Rental room	Accommodation
Selling fast food	Catering
We sell home-cooked meals during weekends	Catering

Five participants did not state their age. The average age of the participants who answered the question relating to their age was 24 years, where the oldest participant was 42 years old and the youngest participant was only 15 years old.

To understand the basic availability of facilities, the participants were asked if they had electricity at home, as technology without electricity means nothing. Only one participant did not specify whether he or she had electricity. The rest of the participants indicated that they had electricity at home. This is a major benefit for ICT training.

The responses to the question prompting participants to indicate whether or not they owned a computer can be seen in Table 5, followed by an indication of the participants' access to computers in Table 6.

Table 4. Business categories

Type of business	Number
Catering	5
General	1
Social services	1
Network marketing	1
Automotive	3
Events	1
Farming and agriculture	2
ICT	1
Cosmetics	3
Accommodation	1

Table 5. Computer ownership

Ownership of a computer	Number of responses
I have my own computer	8
My family owns a computer	7
None of the above	17
Not specified	1

Table 6. Access to a computer

Access to a computer	Number of responses
I have easy access to a computer	16
I have limited access to a computer	10
I have no access to a computer	6
Not specified	1

It is clear from Tables 5 and 6 that most of the participants had access to a computer, although not many of them owned their own computers. Six participants did not have access to a computer, which meant that the training interventions could not focus on computers only, but also had to focus on using a mobile device for their businesses, if they had access to such a device.

This question was raised during the focus group discussion, after which participants were asked if they at least had access to a nearby internet café. Three participants indicated that they did not have access to a nearby internet café, thus implying that they had absolutely no access to a computer. One participant mentioned that receiving training in computer skills was valuable, but that the lack of access to computers afterwards was problematic, since it was difficult to continue with the skills development on an individual level after the completion of the training. It was also mentioned that if participants had access to computer facilities, they could assist other members of their communities to grow their levels of skills and knowledge.

Focusing on their mobility and connectivity, the participants were asked if they owned a mobile phone or a tablet. Only one delegate said "no", but two participants did not answer this question. Of the participants who indicated that they had mobile devices, only four had contracts with service providers, which meant that the other participants all used prepaid services to gain connectivity. If their money runs out, they will have no connectivity at all. For survivalists, this could be a major problem, as they would rather put food on the table than buy airtime. The participants who indicated that they had a mobile device were asked how many phones they were using. Eight of the participants said that they had two phones. During the focus group discussion, the participants said that they had more than one device, as it depended on who they needed to contact. The reason for this was that certain service providers' rates are cheaper if one contacts a number using the same service provider. When asked whether their device could connect to the internet, four participants said "no", two said that they could connect to the internet, one did not specify, and the other 27 participants indicated that they could access both the internet and their emails via their phones.

Table 7 shows the responses to questions relating to when participants were first introduced to computers as a means to understand what their background knowledge of technology was, and if they had equal opportunities for using technology.

Table 7. Introduction to technology

When were you introduced to technology for the first time?	Number of responses
During my studies after school	10
Today is the first time I am going to work on a computer	3
When I grew up at my school	10
When I grew up in my home	6
When I started to work for the first time after school	4

It was interesting to see that there was an equal split: ten participants said that they came into contact with computers during their years at school, ten participants said that they came into contact with computers during their studies, six participants said that they had computers at their homes while growing up, and four participants said that they came into contact with computers when they started working for the first time. Three participants indicated that the day of the training was the first time they had ever worked on a computer. This was alarming, as one tends to think that everybody has access to a computer.

Table 8 represents the participants' answers when asked how long they have been using computers. The majority of the participants were fairly new to the use of computers, where 63% said that they had either been using computers for less than one year or between one and two years. Only one participant did not specify the duration.

Table 9 indicates the specific software or technology tools that participants have either used before, or that they have seen, but might not be able to use comfortably.

It is important to note that, of the seven participants who had never used the internet before, only four had never used email. The remaining three participants had email, but had never accessed the internet before.

Table 8. Duration of previous computer usage

How long have you been using a computer?	Number of responses
1–2 years	5
2–3 years	4
3-4 years	3
Less than one year	15
More than four years	5
Not specified	1

Table 9. Software tools or technology

Software/Technology/Tools	Number of participants using or who have seen software before
Email	26
Internet	26
Facebook	29
Twitter	14
Skype	11
Online shopping	9
Microsoft Word	23
Microsoft Excel	24
Presentation software	22
Accounting software	10

When considering their social media usage, only four participants did not have Facebook, but 19 participants did not have or use Twitter.

It was evident that these participants were familiar with some of the proposed technology for this course.

When the participants were asked: "Do you believe that you were given opportunities to become computer literate?", only one delegate did not specify. The rest all answered "yes". When asked to elaborate on when or where they were given these opportunities, the answers included the following:

"Teachers at my primary and high school. I was given weekly computer classes."
"I got a learnership sponsored by XXX Company."
"SAQA gave me this opportunity at the University of Pretoria."
"High school."
"Jale College at Themba, Hammanskraal, 2016 and 2017. To study IT (Information Technology)."

The rest of the respondents (13) all said that the opportunity to attend the e-skills course was their first opportunity in this regard.

The participants were asked if they thought that digital literacy could help one grow as a human being. Two participants did not specify and the rest all said that they believed so.

Except for two participants who did not respond, all the other participants thought that digital literacy should be made available to all people, thus advocating equal opportunities for all.

When the participants were asked if they felt that there were opportunities for them to explore and expand on their digital literacy skills, five said "no", one did not specify, and the rest all said "yes".

The responses from those who said "yes" included the following:

"Many people may have greater chances of becoming employed, as digital literacy seems to now be an essential in a potential employee."

"Digital literacy makes life easy, is user friendly, accurate and saves time."

"I can further my skills in computer skills centres located in my community."

"I can open up an afternoon programme where we can offer people computer skills and more."

"I can work at many places like become a receptionist and work at any office."

"Make advertisement (digital)."

"Opportunities to get work and to have more knowledge about computers."

"If I can explore and expand my digital literacy computer skills, I will be able to run my business very well."

"I will be able to be employed in an office such as typist, PA or receptionist."

It is interesting to note that most of the participants see some kind of digital literacy skills as their "access point" to finding employment, but most of them still focus on finding a job opportunity. It is clear that unemployment is still one of the biggest concerns relating to South Africa's economic growth, as mentioned by Antionites and van Vuuren [1]. Not many of the participants stated that it could actually grow their businesses or allow them to implement their business ideas.

Through the last question, the participants were asked if they thought it was important to be digitally literate in today's world, and why. Their responses to this question were as follows:

"Yes, because computers help us with a lot of things like researching for available jobs and getting information that you need about something."

"Yes, because it makes people access information quickly, it saves time, since, well, time is money."

"Yes, everything we do today is using technology."

Seventeen participants had similar responses.

The main outcome of the course was for the participants to each have a proper business plan, marketing plan and a basic budget, which all of them had before they left the training venue. This meant that adding the technology training to the business skills section of E/P made sense. The participants could use this to either start their businesses or apply for funding. In the two weeks following the completion of the course, the authors provided many of the participants with guidance and feedback on their business plans, as they continued to work on them via email. The authors thus became mentors for these entrepreneurs to help them finalise their business plans; a need that clearly existed in the group. This is similar to the implementation of E/P, where a ten-week mentorship programme runs after the course has been completed.

Besides the need for training participants during the two-day course, there is also a need for an extended mentorship programme to assist participants individually in order to ensure that their businesses are structured in such a way that they can apply for funding.

During the focus group discussion, participants discussed how they felt about technology and the opportunities that it held for them. The following question was asked: "Do you feel there are opportunities?"

The biggest obstacle that most of the participants noted was the current lack of employment in the country, and the subsequent need for them to start something themselves in order to survive, and to contribute to the growth of the economy.

Another problem that was raised by many of the participants was that they felt that there were some employment opportunities, but that many people were unskilled and thus could not meet the requirements for the vacancies that were available.

Concept	Theme
Clear indication of business idea	Business idea
Business not already functioning	
"If I can explore and expand my digital literacy computer skills I will be able to run my business very well."	
Average age is 24	Gender and age
Youngest was 15	
Oldest was 42, thus need for a better life	
Some 52% do not own a computer	Ownership of and access to computers
Most have access to a computer	
Getting trained means nothing without access	
Access can assist them to train other community members	
Only two did not own a phone	Mobility and connectivity
Prefer prepaid services	
Cheaper rates determine number of phones	
Devices can connect to the internet	
Four cannot connect to the internet	
Majority have internet and email	
Ten were introduced to computers during their school years	Background, experience and skills (co-coefficients = e)
"Teachers at my primary school and high school. I was given weekly computer classes."	
Ten were introduced during their studies	
The majority had experience	
The majority had less than one years' experience	
Some 60% has two years' experience or less	
High school	
Learnership	
E-skills course was the first opportunity	

(*continued*)

(*continued*)

Concept	Theme
Make available to all, create equal opportunity	
"Digital literacy makes life easy, is user friendly, accurate and saves time."	
"I can further my skills in computer skills centres located in my community."	
Email	Specific software, applications and tools
Internet	
Facebook	
Microsoft Word	
Microsoft Excel	
Presentation software	
Accounting software	
Mobile devices	
Computers	
"Make advertisement (digital)."	
"Yes, everything we do today is using technology."	
"Offer tablets so that we have something to work on afterwards."	Technology or providing them with some type of resource such as a tablet
"Yes, because it makes people access information quickly, it saves time, since, well, time is money."	Opportunity, learnerships or mentorships
They feel that more learnership and internship programmes should be developed to allow one to gain experience.	
Employment opportunities: many people are unskilled and thus cannot meet the requirements for the vacancies available.	
"Send regular updates on new features."	
"Many people may have greater chances of becoming employed as digital literacy seems to now be an essential in a potential employee."	Employment
"I can open up an afternoon programme where we offer people computer skills and more."	
"I can work at many places like become a receptionist and work at any office."	
"Opportunities to get work and to have more knowledge about computers."	
"I will be able to be employed in an office such as typist, PA or receptionist."	
"Yes, because computers help us with a lot of things like researching for available jobs and	

(*continued*)

(*continued*)

Concept	Theme
getting information that one needs about something."	
"Lack of employment in the country."	

They also mentioned that, for some employment opportunities, the employment sector required experience even after skills had been obtained. These people did not have experience, which meant that they could not grab these opportunities. They felt that more learnership and internship programmes should be developed to allow one to gain experience.

The participants were asked if it would help them to bridge the technology skills gap if they were given mobile devices or tablets. They felt that this would definitely help bridge the gap, although they felt that it would expose them to a security risk. However, the participants were willing to take the risk of carrying a smart phone or tablet around with them if it could help them to enhance their skills and grab opportunities.

When asked if there was anything that could be done to improve the course, the participants responded in the following way:

"Offer tablets so that we have something to work on afterwards."
"Send regular updates on new features." – linking to the mentorship programme mentioned before.
"Making presentations for my business."

It emerged that most of the participants were trying to find employment. It was clear to the authors that the participants needed guidance. When asked how they searched for jobs, the participants responded almost in a choir with: "We Google". They were then asked what they inserted into the Google search engine, to which they responded: "Position available for jobs". This was clearly a mistake. A general discussion on how to properly look for employment opportunities was started. They were also introduced to LinkedIn and were assisted to create accounts for themselves.

As the need for employment emerged, the authors thought that perhaps one should guide them in creating their CVs as well. However, the response was a surprise. They all said that they preferred to compile a business plan to start their own businesses so that they could create their own employment opportunities.

As part of the thematic analysis, the following mapping was completed.

5   Discussion

It seems as if all the participants preferred the structure of the course, and could see the benefit of each topic as it related to their businesses or their business ideas. From the thematic analysis, a number of main themes emerged. These can be considered or perhaps incorporated into the course. The main themes comprised the following:

- Ownership of and access to computers
- Mobility and connectivity
- Background, experience and skills
- Technology or providing them with some type of resource, such as a tablet
- Opportunities, learnerships or mentorship
- Employment or the lack thereof

The need for mentorship or some kind of guidance to successfully implement business ideas emerged. This is a similar need identified by the E/P model of Van Vuuren and Nieman [18]. In this regard, these authors have introduced a ten-week mentoring programme. However, there is still no focus on the ICT leg of the training.

Through this study, the need for ICT skills has become clear. As one delegate rightfully said: "Because in these days, technology is useful, and if you are not familiar with it, you won't make it". However, there still seems to be a lack of opportunities for these entrepreneurs to be included in a programme in which they feel safe asking questions and confident that someone will help them. They want to take ownership of their futures and start their own businesses, but they need some guidance on how to formally go about this and how to use technology effectively in order to grow their businesses.

What is evident from the results is that one should stick to the basics when planning entrepreneurial interventions. There is no need to overcomplicate interventions with high-tech solutions, but rather to give delegates something practical that they can use to grow themselves and their businesses, and to become part of an inclusive society.

Although these entrepreneurs should be taught the basics first, the subsequent mentorship programme must ensure that these basic features are working. The sections in bold below are the additional recommendations that emerged as needs after the training intervention:

- Microsoft Excel – setting up a basic budget, and understanding basic formulas and graphs for your business
- Microsoft Word – creating a business plan that can be presented to a financial institution for possible funding, understanding basic Microsoft Word functions to allow for any documents to be drafted, writing a vision, mission and goals, defining a basic marketing plan, providing a CV template for delegates to complete in their own time
- Gmail – setting up and managing an email account (including proper email ethics and responding to business requests)
- Social media as part of a marketing campaign, creating a Facebook page, managing advertising through social media, linking social media marketing to the business plan
- Free website development tools – using tools such as Weebly to create a website for the business
- Google search – using the Google search engine more effectively to look for opportunities
- LinkedIn – understanding LinkedIn, not only from a personal perspective, but from a business perspective as well
- Microsoft PowerPoint – Creating a presentation based on the business plan
- Assistance in getting access to either a tablet or a smart phone – finding a sponsorship.

6 Conclusion

Many training interventions currently exist, and many of them are exceptional. However, not many of them focus on the ICT needs of entrepreneurs with smaller businesses, or of survivalists. One also tends to think high-tech when one starts to explore available technology opportunities, and often the basics are not even right. This paper identified the training needs of entrepreneurs from a more practical point of view, and showed the real needs of these entrepreneurs.

When looking back at E/P after incorporating technology into the business skills part of the model, it seems as if the technology and/or software tools identified make sense for the entrepreneurs. It is also clear that there is a need not only for being taught the skills, but also for getting some sort of access to resources that could help one grow one's business.

Another thing that should be considered, not necessarily as part of ICT training, but rather as part of general entrepreneurial training, is to find a way in which entrepreneurs can become learners in their specific industries for a period of time, to truly understand how their businesses should work, and then to take that knowledge and apply it to grow their own businesses.

It is still evident, though, that unemployment is the main reason for these entrepreneurs trying to find an alternative solution or a way out of their current circumstances so that they can provide a better future for their families. Although entrepreneurship could be the answer to many unemployment and poverty issues, access to these training interventions and resources remains a problem.

References

1. Antionites, A.J., van Vuuren, J.J.: Inducing entrepreneurial creativity, innovation and opportunity-finding skills. SAJEMS 8(3), 255–271 (2005)
2. Oke, A., Burke, G., Myers, A.: Innovation types and performance in growing UK SMEs. Int. J. Oper. Prod. Manage. 27(7), 735–753 (2007)
3. Esselaar, S., Stork, C., Ndiwalana, A., Deen-Swarray, M.: ICT usage and its impact on profitability of SMEs in 13 African Countries. In: Information and Communication Technologies and Development, Berkeley, CA, pp. 40–47 (2006)
4. Pretorius, M., Nieman, G., Van Vuuren, J.J.: Critical evaluation of two models for entrepreneurial education: an improved model through integration. Int. J. Educ. Manage. 19 (5), 413–427 (2005)
5. Mutula, S.M., van Brakel, P.: ICT skills readiness for the emerging global digital economy among small business in developing countries: case study of Botswana. Libr. Hi. Tech. 25 (2), 231–245 (2007)
6. Burn, J.M.: The impact of Information technology on organisational structures. Inf. Manag. 16, 1–10 (1989)
7. Reimenschneider, C.K., Harrison, D.A., Mykytyn, P.P.: Understanding it adoption in small business: integrating current theories. Inf. Manag. 40, 269–285 (2003)
8. Gibb, A.A.: The enterprise culture and education: understanding enterprise education and its links with small business, entrepreneurship and wider educational goals. Int. Small Bus. J. 11 (3), 11–34 (1993)

9. Barkhuizen, N., Bennett, M.: Training adult entrepreneurs in an emerging economy: the case of namibia. Mediterr. J. Soc. Sci. **5**(3), 298–306 (2014)
10. Bhattacherjee, A., Sanford, C.: Influence processes for information technology acceptance: an elaboration likelihood model. MIS Q. **30**(4), 805–825 (2006)
11. Botha, M., Nieman, G., van Vuuren, J.J.: Measuring the effectiveness of the women entrepreneurship programme on potential, start-up and established women entrepreneurs in south africa. S Afr. J. Econ. Manag. Sci. **10**(2), 163–183 (2007)
12. Dhliwayo, S., van Vuuren, J.J.: The strategic entrepreneurial thinking imperative. Acta Commercii, 123–134 (2007)
13. Sarri, K.K., Bakouros, I.L., Petridou, E.: Entrepreneur training for creativity and innovation. J. Eur. Ind. Training **34**(3), 270–288 (2009)
14. Azim, M.T., Al-Kahtani, A.H.: Entrepreneurship education and training: a Survey of Literature. Life Sci. J. **11**(1), 127–135 (2014)
15. Garavan, T., O'Cinneide, B.: Entrepreneurship education and training programmes: a review and evaluation, part-1. J. Eur. Ind. Training **18**(8), 3–12 (1994)
16. van Vuuren, J.J., Botha, M.: The practical application of an entrepreneurial performance training model in South Africa. J. Small Bus. Enterp. Dev. **17**(4), 607–625 (2010)
17. Ndubisi, N.O., Kahraman, C.: Malaysian women entrepreneurs: understanding the ICT usage behaviors and drivers. J. Enterp. Inf. Manag. **18**(6), 721–738 (2005)
18. van Vuuren, J.J., Nieman, G.: Entrepreneurship education and training: a model for syllabi/curriculum development. In: 1999 International Council For Small Business Naples Conference Proceedings. Naples (1999)
19. Nieman, G.H., Bennet, A. (eds.): Business Management: A Value Chain Approach. 2nd ed. Van Schaik Publishers, Pretoria (2006)
20. Kunene, T.R.: A critical analysis of entrepreneurial and business skills in SMEs in the textile and clothing industry in Johannesburg. University or Pretoria, South Africa (2008)
21. Hynes, B.: Entrepreneurship education and training - introducing entrepreneurship into non-business disciplines. J. Eur. Ind. Training **20**(8), 10–17 (1996)
22. Timmons, J.A., Muzyka, D.F., Stevenson, H.M., Bygrave, W.D.: Opportunity recognition: the core of entrepreneurship. In: Churchill, N. (ed.) Frontiers of Entrepreneurial Research. Babson College, Babson Park, MA (1987)
23. Johannisson, B.: University training for entrepreneurship: a Swedish approach. Entrepreneurship Reg. Dev. **3**(1), 67–82 (1991)
24. Noll, C.L.: Planning curriculum for entrepreneurship education. Bus. Educ. Forum **47**(3) 1993
25. Kourilsky, M.L., Entrepreneurship Education: Opportunity in Search of Curriculum, in Ewing Marion Kaufmann Foundation. Center for Entrepreneurial Leadership, Kansas City, MO. Ewing Marion Kaufmann Foundation. Center for Entrepreneurial Leadership, Kansas City, MO (1995)
26. Rae, D.M.: Teaching entrepreneurship in Asia: impact of a pedagogical innovation. Entrepreneurship Innov. Change **6**(3), 193–227 (1997)
27. Hisrich, R.D., Peters, M.P.: Entrepreneurship, 4th ed. Irwin McGraw-Hill, Boston (1998)
28. Vesper, K.H., Gartner, W.B.: University entrepreneurship programs. Lloyd Grief Center for Entrepreneurial Studies, Marshal School of Business, University of Southern California, Los Angeles (2001)
29. Onstenk, J.: Entrepreneurship and vocational education. Eur. Educ. Res. J. **2**(1), 74–89 (2003)
30. Venkatesh, V., Morris, M.G., Davis, G.B., Davis, F.D.: User acceptance of information technology: toward a unified view. MIS Q. **27**(3), 425–478 (2003)

31. Ladzani, W.M., van Vuuren, J.J.: Entrepreneurship training for emerging SMEs in South Africa. J. Small Bus. Manage. **40**(2), 154–161 (2002)
32. Myers, M.D.: Qualitative Research in Business and Management. SAGE Publications Ltd., London EC1Y 1SP, p. 284 (2009)
33. Aronson, J.: A pragmatic view of thematic analysis. The qualitative report **2**(1) (1994)
34. Vaismoradi, M., Turunen, H., Bondas, T.: Content analysis and thematic analysis: implications for conducting a qualitative descriptive study. Nursing Health Sci. **15**, 398–405 (2013)

Collaboration Towards a More Inclusive Society: The Case of South African ICT4D Researchers

Judy van Biljon[(⊠)][iD] and Filistea Naude[iD]

University of South Africa, Pretoria, South Africa
{vbiljja, fnaude}@unisa.ac.za

Abstract. In this study, research collaboration in the context of South African Information and Communication for Development (ICT4D) researchers was investigated using a mixed methods approach. South Africa, a country with stark development challenges and on the other hand a well-established ICT infrastructure, provides an appropriate context for ICT4D research. Firstly, a quantitative analysis of South African research collaboration between 2003 and 2016 was conducted to determine the existing research collaboration patterns of South African ICT4D researchers. This is based on the publications in three top ICT4D journals namely the Electronic Journal of Information Systems in Developing Countries (EJISDC), Information Technologies & International Development (ITID), and Information Technology for Development (ITD). The results show that most co-authored papers were intra-institutional collaborations, with limited inter-institutional collaboration between South African authors or between South African and other African authors. Secondly, interviews were conducted with South African researchers who emerged as inter- and intra-institutional collaborators to gain insight into the technology, drivers and barriers affecting South African research collaboration. We report our findings and discuss the implications for employing research collaboration as a mechanism for addressing inequality and supporting inclusion.

Keywords: ICT4D · Research collaboration · Co-authoring
Research cooperation · South Africa

1 Introduction

There is a global trend towards multidisciplinary teams conducting collaborative research to address complex challenges and achieve objectives not feasible for independent entities working unaided [1]. The nature of technologies being used in development projects is dynamically evolving and ICT4D research needs to become more multidisciplinary than before [2]. National and international research collaboration and the inclusion of novice researchers is advocated for knowledge development, exchange and incentivized by government and agency funding. However, practical constraints such as time and funding, intellectual property rights and competition among researchers can inhibit collaboration [3, 4]. Collaboration has been defined as a mutually beneficial, well-defined relationship entered into by two or more individuals

© IFIP International Federation for Information Processing 2018
Published by Springer Nature Switzerland AG 2018. All Rights Reserved
D. Kreps et al. (Eds.): HCC13 2018, IFIP AICT 537, pp. 82–94, 2018.
https://doi.org/10.1007/978-3-319-99605-9_6

or organisations to achieve common goals [5, 6]. Research collaboration can be defined as a two-way process where individuals and/or organizations share learning, ideas and experiences to produce joint scientific outcomes [7].

The political system of apartheid in South Africa (1948–1993) caused internal division and international isolation. Apartheid ended with democratic elections in 1994, and there has been many initiatives since to overcome the consequences of apartheid towards building a more equitable, inclusive society. Research collaboration including inter-institutional collaboration and international collaboration has potential for bridging divides and building national research capacity.

This paper investigates research collaboration in the context of ICT4D research in South Africa. The purpose of this study is to describe researcher collaboration by considering the drivers and barriers related to scholarly collaboration from the researchers' perspective, the patterns of collaborating and the uniquely South African characteristics that influence research collaboration. The research was conducted as a two phased, mixed method study involving a sequential quantitative–qualitative design. The first phase involved a review of South African ICT4D research collaboration based on the publications in EJISDC, ITD and ITID in the period 2003 to 2016. The second phase comprise interviews with researchers who were involved in the inter-institutional collaborations identified in phase one. Co-authoring is used as a proxy for research collaboration since most research collaborations involve co-authored publications. The contribution is to provide unique insights from the perspective of South African ICT4D researchers that could be generalized towards an improved understanding of South African research collaboration. The findings should be useful to individual researchers, research organizations, governments and international funding organizations.

2 Research Collaboration in Context

Research collaboration is advocated towards improving impact where research impact includes a range of impacts of different types, which may be of different levels of importance to various stakeholders [8]. This impact is measured by a number of criteria, including the quality of the research outputs, the funding associated with the research outputs and the related citations [9]. Research outputs, including publications, postgraduate qualifications or funding proposals are evaluated through a peer-review system of which the integrity relies on a social network of informed yet unbiased researchers. This suggests duel imperatives, a knowledge generation and dissemination imperative where close collaboration is necessary but also a collaboration aspect where the other researcher is proposed as an impartial examiner or referee of papers and funding proposals. The need for and importance of inter-institutional collaboration in South Africa (RSA) has been highlighted in a number of national documents.

Onyancha and Maluleka [10] investigated co-authorship and collaborative research in sub-Saharan Africa. Using the Clarivate Analytics Web of Science citation indexes, the fifteen most productive countries in terms of number of publications in the period 1995 to 2008, were selected. Continental collaboration among sub-Saharan African country researchers was found to be minimal, compared to international collaboration between foreign country researchers and sub-Saharan African country researchers.

Tiovanen and Ponomariov [11] investigated the structure of African research collaboration. Research papers with an African address published between 2005 and 2009 were retrieved using Clarivate Analytics Web of Science database and text mined with the Vantage Point software. Social Network analyses software UCINET was used to analyse the research collaboration networks. The co-authorship links data showed three distinct African collaborative research regions, i.e. Southern-Eastern, Western and Northern. Collaboration between African countries are weak and there is an absence of regional integration of collaborative research networks. In terms of international collaboration, Europe is the largest collaboration partner for Africa, followed by North Africa. South Africa and Nigeria were the strongest research countries and integrative hubs in their regions.

Pouris and Ho [12] investigated research collaboration in Africa by analysing co-authorship data from articles published between 2007 and 2011 and retrieved from Clarivate Analytics Web of Science database. Internationally collaborative articles increased from 52% to 58% for the period investigated. Collaborative authorship in Africa is substantially higher than the rest of the world with medical and natural resources being the main research focus areas of African research.

Sooryamoorthy [13] investigated collaboration of South African Scientists using South African science publications data from Clarivate Analytics Web of Science database for the years 2000, 2003 and 2005. A number of variables had an impact on the number of citations that a South African scientist receives, such as number of authors, number of foreign authors, collaboration type as well as the discipline and sector of the author. Citation rates were higher for publications that were co-authored. The publications with international collaboration and external-institutional collaboration had higher visibility and received more citations than internal institutional collaboration. For South African publications, the number of citations increased as the number of collaborators increased. International collaboration received more than double the citations that domestic collaborations received. About 80% of the publications came from the top seven universities in South Africa.

Sooryamoorthy [14] studied the relationship between publication productivity and collaboration of 204 South African Science academics and researchers at two KwaZulu-Natal higher education institutions during 2007 to 2008 using face-to-face interviews. Results showed that the number of research projects, the number of international collaborative projects, the duration of the collaborative projects, the number of the collaborators and the length of the collaboration had an impact on research productivity. Respondents preferred collaboration rather than working individually in the production of international research papers. International collaboration increased the chances of publication. The South African research funding and incentive system have an impact on collaboration, because the subsidies due to the non-South African collaborators are not paid (unless formal associations are recorded). Therefore, single authored papers are beneficial from a South African funding perspective.

Sooryamoorthy [15] studied the collaboration patterns of South African Scientists using data from the Clarivate Analytics Web of Science database for the period 2000, 2003 and 2005. Results indicate that collaborative research is a growing phenomenon among South African scientists, with scientists showing a preference for collaboration over single authored research. International collaboration is preferred over domestic collaboration. The productivity of South African Scientists were improved through collaboration. Factors such as the number of authors and the number of countries involved had an impact on collaboration. Authors from Europe and secondly North America were the preferred collaborators for South African Scientists.

Boshoff [16] studied collaboration among the 15 countries of the Southern African Development Community (SADC) as well as between SADC and the rest of Africa for the period 2005 to 2008. SADC researchers collaborate more with international high-income developed countries (47% of SADC papers) than with African researchers. Only 3% of SADC papers were jointly authored by researchers from two or more SADC countries and only 5% of SADC papers were a collaboration with researchers from African countries outside SADC. South Africa is the leading country in terms of research output (81% papers), with the highest publication productivity of the SADC countries, and 78% of intra-regional co-authored papers.

The collaboration patterns of 50 African countries were studied for the period 2000–2012 using data from the Clarivate Analytics InCites Research Performance profiles database [17]. Finding indicate that South Africa is the research hub of Africa. The USA is the country that collaborated the most with Africa while the UK, Germany and France are the European countries that African countries collaborate with the most.

An ICT4D scholarly research collaboration study [18] revealed that 66% of the articles published in the EJISDC between 2000 and 2013 were co-authored articles. The collaboration patterns of the EJISDC showed that 32% of articles were intra-institutional collaboration, 45% were national collaboration and 20% were international collaboration. Most of the EJISDC authors were from Africa, followed by Asia, North America and Europe. Most of the African authors, were from South Africa (37%).

The effectivity of South African researchers in converting ICT4D research activity into significant research outputs were investigated by Turpin [19], who concluded that South Africa has a prominent presence in ICT4D journals, but this prominence is concentrated in one research institution and one ICT4D journal.

A study mapping the research collaboration networks in computer science for the UbuntuNet region (central, eastern and southern African Countries) identified the top five countries based on the number of publications as South Africa (77.64%), Kenya (6.9%), Ethiopia (3.8%), Tanzania (3.32%) and Uganda (3.14%) respectively [20]. The results showed a high degree of collaboration with 88% of the publications multi-authored. However, collaboration with intra-collaboration of research within Ubuntu-Net region is low if compared to the inter-collaboration between countries in UbuntuNet region and other countries outside Africa [20].

In summary, the findings from the studies on research collaboration in Africa concur that South Africa is a key player on the African research landscape; there is a high degree of collaboration but the collaborations are mostly intra-institutional or with countries outside Africa. There is evidence supporting research collaboration as a factor improving productivity and increasing researchers' visibility in terms of citations. Notably, the top 7 universities in South Africa contributed 80% of the African research [13]; this underlines the importance of inter-institutional research for building South African research capacity.

3 Research Design

Mixed methods research is a methodology framed around the idea of gathering and analysing both quantitative and qualitative data and integrating or combining the two datasets for further analysis [21]. This methodology was considered appropriate for this study since we needed to present the current research collaboration and gain insight on the drivers of collaboration behavior. A bibliometric analysis was used to quantify the existing research collaboration and we then aimed to explain that through insights gained from interviews (guided by structured, open-ended questions) with selected ICT4D researchers. The procedures followed are outlined in more detail below.

3.1 Study 1: Quantification of South African Research Collaboration

Data were collected from the top three ICT4D journals as identified by Heeks [22] namely: Electronic Journal of Information Systems in Developing Countries (EJISDC), Information Technologies & International Development (ITID), and Information Technology for Development (ITD). The journal details and publishing information are depicted Table 1. The starting years of the three journals differ, and therefore only papers published between 2003 and 2016 were selected.

Table 1. Journal information

Journal	Electronic Journal of Information Systems in Developing Countries (EJISDC)	Information Technologies & International Development (ITID)	Information Technology for Development (ITD)
Journal webpage	http://www.ejisdc.org	http://itidjournal.org/	http://www. tandfonline.com/ loi/titd20
Volume	11–77	1–12	10–22 (Zero articles published in 2004)
Start year	2000	2003	1986
ISSN	ISSN: 1681-4835	ISSN: 1544-7529	ISSN: 0268-1102
Open access	Open Access	Open Access	Not Open Access
Publisher	City University of Hong Kong	USC Annenberg School for Communication	Taylor & Francis

Naude [23] maintains that the coverage and indexing of ICT4D journals in the citation enhanced databases Web of Science and Scopus are inadequate, and coverage in commercial subject databases limited. Bibliometric, citation and South African authorship data for the selected the ICT4D journals listed in Table 1 were not available (or only partially available) in the traditional citation-enhanced platforms Web of

Science and Scopus. The bibliographic data for EJISDC and ITD were exported from the Inspec database (IET) and the ITID data from EBSCOhost Business Source Complete database. The data for the three journals were exported into MS Excel format for analysis. The bibliographic data for the three journals combined comprised 1064 items. The data was collected in July 2017. The contents pages of the published journals were compared to the bibliographic data downloaded from the Inspec and EBSCOhost Business Source databases. Only research articles were included, and other article types such as editorial introductions, book reviews, etc. were omitted.

The data extracted from the databases provided the following information for each journal: title of paper, authors, year, volume, issue, author affiliation. The following information was added manually on the spreadsheet: total number of authors, number of countries involved in each paper, country affiliation of the authors and collaboration type.

The author affiliation data was used to identify the South African authored papers. A paper was classified as South African if there was at least one South African author. In cases where authors had more than one affiliation, the South African affiliation was used as the primary affiliation. After the data was collected per journal, the total number of volumes, issues, number of articles, number of South African authored articles and number of South African authors were calculated per annum as shown in tables 2 to 4 [24]. A list of the 103 South African authored papers published in the EJISDC, ITID and ITD can be viewed at [24].

Articles with South African authors were categorized into the three collaboration types: Intra-institutional (authors from the same institution collaborating), Inter-institutional (authors from different institutions collaborating) and International collaboration (authors from different countries collaborating).

3.2   Study 2: Qualitative Investigation into the Drivers, Barriers and Incentives

During the months of September to December 2017, interviews were conducted with 10 South African researchers involved in inter- and intra-collaborative research. Ethical clearance for this research was obtained from the Research and Ethics Committee in the School of Computing at the University of South Africa. The interview was structured according to the questionnaire provided as Appendix B [24]. The aim of the interview was to gain insight about the drivers of and barriers to collaboration as well as what would be perceived as useful incentives.

4   Results and Findings

4.1   Study 1: South African Research Collaboration

To contextualize South African ICT4D research, Tables 2, 3 and 4 (see Appendix A - can be viewed at [24]) provide the number of South African papers (based on South African author affiliation), compared to the total number of papers. Despite the limitations inherent in any snapshot, this provides evidence of an increasingly active

ICT4D research community in South Africa, which justifies the selection of this community for analyzing research collaboration. The results provide a profile of South African ICT4D research and shows initial low participation of South African researchers with a steady growth of South African authored papers in the last 6 years (2010 to 2016).

- Table 2 depicts the results for EJISDC. Of the 468 articles published between 2003 and 2016, 62 (13.24%) articles were contributed by 128 South African authors [24].
- Table 3 shows the results for ITD. Notably of the 271 articles published between 2003 and 2016, 24 (8.85%) articles were contributed by 42 South African authors [24].
- Table 4 depicts the results for the ITID. Of the 325 articles published between 2003 and 2016, 17 (5.23%) articles were contributed by 23 South African authors [24].

Table 2 shows the collaboration patterns of South African authors in the three selected ICT4D journals. The results indicate that for the EJISDC, only 10 (16.13%) of the 62 articles were single authored, compared to 52 (83.88%) that were multi authored. The South African EJISDC collaboration patterns show that of the 52 articles, intra-institutional collaboration was the highest with 30 (48.38%) articles, followed by international collaboration with 13 (20.97%) articles and inter-institutional with 9 (14.52%) articles. Of the 13 internationally collaborated articles, South African authors were first authors in 6 of the articles.

Table 2. Collaboration patterns of South African (RSA) ICT4D authors

Collaboration type	EJISDC no of RSA articles	%	ITID no of RSA articles	%	ITD no of RSA articles	%
Single author	10	16.13	8	47.05	5	20.83
Intra-institutional	30	48.38	3	17.64	8	33.33
Inter-institutional	9	14.52	1	5.88	1	4.18
International	13	20.97	5	29.43	10	41.66
Total	**62**	**100**	**17**	**100**	**24**	**100**

For the ITID, 8 (47.05%) of the 17 articles were single authored, compared to 9 (52.95%) that were multi authored. Of the South African ITID collaborated articles, international collaboration was the highest with 5 (29.43%) articles, followed by intra-institutional collaboration with 3 (17.64%) articles and inter-institutional with 1 (5.88%) article. Of the 5 internationally collaborated articles, South African authors were first authors in 4 of the articles.

For the ITD, 5 (20.83%) of the 24 articles were single authored, compared to 19 (79.17%) that were multi authored. Of the South African ITD collaborated articles, international collaboration was the highest with 10 (41.66%) articles, followed by intra-institutional collaboration with 8 (33.33%) articles and inter-institutional with 1

(4.18%) article. Of the 10 internationally collaborated articles, South African authors were first authors in 7 of the articles.

Collectively, looking at the EJISDC, ITD and ITID combined; of the 1064 articles published between 2003 and 2016, 103 (9.68%) articles were contributed by 193 South African authors. Of the 103 South African authored articles, 23 (22.33%) articles were single authored and 80 (77.67%) multi authored. Of the 80 collaboratively authored South African articles, 41 (51.25%) were intra-institutional collaboration, 28 (35%) were international collaboration and 11 (13.75%) were inter-institutional collaboration. Of the 28 internationally collaboratively authored South African articles, South African authors were first authors in 17 (60.71%) of the articles.

Table 3 compares the South African authorship patterns of the three journals in this study. The data from the EJISDC and ITD show that the most common collaboration is between two South African authors, followed by 3 authors and then single authorship. In contrast the ITID journal analysis indicates that single authorship is the most popular followed by two authors collaborating.

Table 3. Authorship patterns of South African (RSA) ICT4D authors

Authorship	EJISDC no of RSA articles	%	ITID no of RSA articles	%	ITD no of RSA articles	%
1 author	10	16.14	8	47.07	5	20.83
2 authors	30	48.39	6	35.29	8	33.33
3 authors	15	24.19			8	33.33
4 authors	5	8.06	2	11.76	2	8.33
5 authors	1	1.61	1	5.88		
6 authors	1	1.61				
7 authors					1	4.18
Total	**62**	**100**	**17**	**100**	**24**	**100**

Collectively, when EJISDC, ITD and ITID are combined; of the 103 authored South African articles published between 2003 and 2016, there were 23 single authorship articles, 44 articles with 2 authors, 23 articles with 3 authors, 9 articles with 4 authors, 2 articles with 5 authors, 1 articles with 6 authors and 1 article with 7 authors. This shows that the most common authorship pattern is collaboration between 2 South African authors.

An analysis of the countries that South African ICT4D researchers collaborated with in the period 2003 to 2016, are depicted in Table 4. South Africa collaborated internationally on 28 articles. South Africa collaborated the most with other authors from the African region, showing the 7 African countries below. The second biggest regional collaboration partner for South African was Europe, with 6 European countries co-authoring articles with South African researchers. South African researchers also collaborated with North America (USA and Canada) as well as Oceania (New Zealand and Australia). The lowest collaboration was in the regions Asia (India) and Latin America (Brasil). There was no collaboration between South Africa and the Middle East region.

Table 4. Country Collaboration patterns of South African ICT4D authors

Country	EJISDC no of articles	EJISDC no of authors	ITID no of articles	ITID no of authors	ITD no of articles	ITD no of authors
Region: Africa						
Namibia	2	2	1	1		
Nigeria	1	2				
Uganda			1	1		
Tunisia					1	1
Ghana					1	2
Malawi					1	2
Zimbabwe	1	1				
Region: Europe						
Finland	1	1				
Norway					2	2
Italy					1	1
Ireland					1	1
Netherlands					1	1
UK	1	1	1	1	3	5
Region: North America						
USA	2	3	3	5	3	3
Canada	1	1				
Region: Oceania						
New Zealand	1	1				
Australia	2	2				
Region: Asia						
India	1	1	1	1		
Region: Latin America						
Brasil					1	1

Based on the inter and intra-institutional publications identified in EJISDC, ITD and ITID respectively, 10 of the authors involved in inter-institutional collaborative publications were interviewed. The questionnaire is available in Appendix B [24]. The next section presents the findings from the interviews providing some insights towards understanding research collaboration drivers and barriers.

4.2   Study 2: Explaining South African Research Collaboration

The interviews were conducted telephonically or via online digital communication (Skype voice only). All of the 10 South African interviewees had doctoral degrees and have been involved in inter- and intra-collaborative research. Four of the authors were no longer involved in inter-institutional collaborations due to one or more of the following barriers mentioned by the interviewees: Lack of funding, lack of awareness of opportunities or access to suitable collaborators, administrative procedures and lack of administrative support. Researcher assessment focuses on the numbers (quantity rather than the quality of the outputs) [25]. In the South African funding model, research credit is divided by the number of authors. In the case of foreign researchers, the money related to the credit is not paid to them or transferred to the collaborating South African researchers. Additional factors include cultural differences in terms of time management, attitudes, work ethic and practices, competition and the lack of overarching, longer-term projects.

Interviewees mentioned the following drivers of research collaboration: Access to funding, complementary skills (strategic, technical or methodological), access to new collaboration networks and data, personal connections, similar work ethics and willingness to compromise. Usefulness in terms of career and profile building (CV).

Based on studies in the fields of health, social science, education and public affairs, 19 factors that influence the success of research collaborations were identified and grouped those into six categories, namely environment, membership, process/structure, communication, purpose and resources [6]. Considering the results in terms of these categories it becomes clear that the drivers and barriers often depict different aspects of the same factor. The interview data will now be unpacked in terms of these categories. The participants did not mention all of the 19 issues identified previously. That does not detract from their relevance since participants may simply not have thought about that at the time. Therefore all 19 issues were retained while those that emerged from the interviews are now discussed in more detail.

Environment (geographic location and social context): The factors previously identified as conducive were a *history of collaboration*, the collaborators being seen as *leaders in the research community* and a *favorable political/social climate*.

- Participants#2, 3, 7 and 9 confirmed the necessity for a favorable political and social climate.
- Participant#9 mentioned that lip-service was being paid to collaboration while the administrative and financial support was lacking.
- Due to the isolation caused by apartheid there was no history of collaboration and that accounts for the responses indicating a lack of awareness on where to start collaborations (Participant#6).

Membership

- Participants#1, 6 and 11 mentioned mutual respect, understanding and trust,
- Participants#1, 4, 5 mentioned the need for an *appropriate cross section of members,*
- Participant#10, mentioned the need to see collaboration as *in the individual's self-interest*) and personally felt that collaboration was not worth the effort so the individual stopped collaborating,
- Participant#7 mentioned the individual's ability to *compromise*
- Participant#8 mentioned *feelings of inferiority* towards researchers from developed countries that was intensified by their behavior

Process/structure

- Participant#1 mentioned administration but none of the participants unpacked the details in terms of the other factors including *members share a stake in both process and outcome, multiple layers of decision-making, flexibility, development of clear roles and policy guidelines and adaptability.*
- Participant#5 mentioned the need for longer term projects needed to address complex problems that attract multi-disciplinary and highly rated researchers.

Communication

None of the participants specifically mentioned open and frequent communication or established informal and formal communication links but language was mentioned as a barrier for those who were not first language English speakers (Participant#6).

Purpose

Participant#2 mentioned a shared vision and context. Concrete, attainable goals and objectives and a unique purpose were implicit in the drivers but not formulated as such.

Resources

All the participants mentioned funding, either as a driver of research collaboration or lack thereof as a barrier. Furthermore, Participants#4 and 8 mentioned access to data, infrastructure and collaboration networks as drivers. The researchers used the Internet, email, text messages and Voice-over-Internet technologies for their collaboration. Citation management systems and software packages for quantitative and qualitative analysis were also used with a preference for open source systems.

In summary, the unique South African collaboration factor that emerged pertain to the lack of a collaboration history. This manifests in terms of a lack of personal collaboration goals, lack of awareness of collaboration opportunities, lack of collaboration skills and perceptions of inferiority towards researchers from developed countries. The latter may be unintentionally strengthened by cultural differences. Another important issue is that the South African funding model incentivizes single authored papers. Personality and cultural factors are subjective, but notably more than one researcher mentioned openness and a 'can do' attitude as South African traits.

5 Conclusion

Our results show that most of the South African authored ICT4D articles were co-authored EJISDC (83.87%), ITID (52.95%) and ITD (79.17%). Most of the collaborations (65%) were national collaboration (i.e. between South Africans), most of those were with authors in the same institution (51.25% intra-institutional) with the number of inter-institutional collaborations (13.75%) being very low. This suggests that inter-institutional collaboration on the South African authored articles is limited. These findings on ICT4D collaboration corresponds with previous research on collaboration patterns for South African authors and signals a potential research capacity building barrier. Due to historical segregation there are large discrepancies between the research capacities of the different South African institutions; therefore promoting research collaboration as a mechanism of inclusion is important. Considering the drivers of collaboration, access to funding and resources, knowledge gains and building an international profile was found to be important. The main barriers were reported to be funding, time and lack of administrative support in managing grants. The fact that these were all established researchers could influence the responses but it was necessary to interview researchers with proven experience in collaborating. The findings corroborate the relevance of most of the collaboration factors previously identified. The contribution of this paper is to confirm that the general findings on collaboration patterns apply to ICT4D researchers; thus their perceptions on research collaboration can be considered as a point of departure in explaining South African research collaboration. The second contribution is to provide insights on the uniquely South African factors that influence collaboration from the ICT4D researcher's perspective. More research is needed to include the views of emerging researchers and to compare the findings with research collaboration patterns in other African countries.

References

1. Anandarajan, A., Anandarajan, M.: An overview of e-Research collaboration. In: Anandarajan, A., Anandarajan, M. (eds.) e-Research Collaboration, pp. 3–13. Springer, Heidelberg (2010). https://doi.org/10.1007/978-3-642-12257-6_1
2. Zheng, Y., Hatakka, M., Sahay, S., Andersson, A.: Conceptualizing development in information and communication technology for development (ICT4D). Inf. Technol. Dev. **24**, 1–14 (2017)
3. Sonnenwald, D.H.: Scientific collaboration. Ann. Rev. Inf. Sci. Technol. **41**, 643–681 (2007)
4. Wagner, C.: International collaboration in science and technology: promises and pitfalls. In: Science and Technology Policy for Development. Dialogues at the Interface, pp. 165–176 (2006)
5. Sooryamoorthy, R.: Scientific collaboration in South Africa. S. Afr. J. Sci. **109**, 1–5 (2013)
6. Mattessich, P., Murray-Close, M., Monsey, B.: Collaboration: What Makes It Work: A Review of Research Literature on Factors Influencing Successful Collaboration, 2nd edn. Amherst H. Wilder Foundation, Saint Paul (2001)
7. Cataldi, M., Di Caro, L., Schifanella, C.: Ranking researchers through collaboration pattern analysis. In: Berendt, B., et al. (eds.) ECML PKDD 2016. LNCS (LNAI), vol. 9853, pp. 50–54. Springer, Cham (2016). https://doi.org/10.1007/978-3-319-46131-1_11
8. Neylon, C., Willmers, M., King, T.: Rethinking impact: applying altmetrics to Southern African research. Scholarly Communication in Africa Programme, pp. 1–20 (2013)
9. Von Solms, R., Von Solms, B.: Publish or perish … but where? S. Afr. Comput. J. **28**, 1–11 (2010)
10. Onyancha, O.B., Maluleka, J.R.: Knowledge production through collaborative research in sub-Saharan Africa: how much do countries contribute to each other's knowledge output and citation impact? Scientometrics **87**, 315–336 (2011)
11. Toivanen, H., Ponomariov, B.: African regional innovation systems: bibliometric analysis of research collaboration patterns 2005–2009. Scientometrics **88**, 471–493 (2011)
12. Pouris, A., Ho, Y.-S.: Research emphasis and collaboration in Africa. Scientometrics **98**, 2169–2184 (2014)
13. Sooryamoorthy, R.: Do types of collaboration change citation? Collaboration and citation patterns of South African science publications. Scientometrics **81**, 177–193 (2009)

14. Sooryamoorthy, R.: Publication productivity and collaboration of researchers in South Africa: new empirical evidence. Scientometrics **98**, 1–15 (2014)
15. Sooryamoorthy, R.: Collaboration and publication: how collaborative are scientists in South Africa? Scientometrics **80**, 419–439 (2009)
16. Boshoff, N.: South-South research collaboration of countries in the Southern African Development Community (SADC). Scientometrics **84**, 481–503 (2010)
17. Adams, J., Gurney, K., Hook, D., Leydesdorff, L.: International collaboration clusters in Africa. Scientometrics **98**, 547–556 (2014)
18. Naude, F.: Country trends and scholarly collaboration in the ICT4D research community 2000–2013: a single journal study. Electron. J. Inf. Syst. Dev. Ctries. **72**, 1–26 (2016)
19. Turpin, M.: Assessing South African ICT4D research outputs: a journal review. S. Afr. Comput. J. **30**, 108–127 (2018)
20. Marwa, C.W., Sangeda, R.Z., Lwoga, E.T.: Mapping the research collaboration networks in computer science: the case of central, eastern and southern African Countries. In: UbuntuNet Connect 2017, Addis Ababa (2017)
21. Creswell, J.W., Clark, V.L.P.: Designing and Conducting Mixed Methods Research. Sage Publications Ltd., Washington, D.C. (2011)
22. Heeks, R.: Theorizing ICT4D research. Inf. Technol. Int. Dev. **3**, 1–4 (2007)
23. Naude, F.: Electronic journal of information systems in developing countries (2000–2013): a bibliometric study. Electron. J. Inf. Syst. Dev. Ctries. **72**, 1–23 (2016)
24. Naude, F., van Biljon, J.: South African ICT4D papers 2003–2016. https://figshare.com/articles/South_African_ICT4D_papers_2003_-_2016/5769099
25. Visser, G.: On citations, rating games and other pesky animals: which zoo for South African human geography? S. Afr. Geogr. J. **89**, 135–144 (2007)

iPay.lk – A Digital Merchant Platform from Sri Lanka

Parakum Pathirana[✉], Conrad Dias, Thisan Samarasinghe,
and Shanmugarajah Sinnathamby

iPay (Pvt) Limited, Colombo, Sri Lanka
{amaranga, shanmugarajahs}@gmail.com,
{conraddias, thisans}@lolctech.com

Abstract. Mobile device ownership has increased across the globe making it the highest adopted platform. With the rapid technology advancements on the smartphones, improvements on the telecommunication networks, falling handset prices and reducing connectivity costs has resulted in mobile devices becoming the primary instrument which our daily lives revolve around transforming how consumers search, evaluate and procure goods or services. Payments are rapidly moving towards mobile while the commerce been transitioning to mobile. The recent developments in information communication technology has played a pivotal role in facilitating the modern digital businesses by reducing time required to perform transactions between buyers and sellers thus creating different customer behaviours. This new digital business paradigm has also resulted in making physical barriers such as distance and time irrelevant.

This paper presents an innovative digital merchant platform (including payments) currently been deployed in Sri Lanka. iPay is a novel solution that operates on the comparatively low cost of mobile devices to increase financial inclusivity in developing economies. One of the key challenges faced in such economies is that only a comparatively small population, concentrated in urban areas have access to banking facilities. There exists a vast potential in the much greater proportion of the population who are primarily engaged in agrarian based activities and cottage industries. The simplified nature of iPay allows this segment to be part of the banking system. iPay also enables the complete 'digitalisation' of merchants, with just a smartphone and an internet connection. This allows merchants to become part of a growing digital economy, and enabling other digital 'strategies' such as marketing campaigns to improve stock control and management, aiding merchants dealing with perishable goods. Cash accounts for bulk of financial transactions in Sri Lanka, which is primarily due to individuals' not been able to access money in the banking system. iPay solves this problem by enabling access to funds 'on-the-go' which eases the burden of cash management on the economy as well as greatly reduces the risk of cash losses.

The nature of the iPay increases financial inclusivity, and helps to alleviate poverty by increasing employment opportunities across the economy. Major percentage of the population in developing countries have limited reach to credit, hindering their growth potential. Banks and financial institutes are unable to grant credit facilities, as they are not operating in the banking system, resulting-in the inability to make a concrete assessment of a person's credit

© IFIP International Federation for Information Processing 2018
Published by Springer Nature Switzerland AG 2018. All Rights Reserved
D. Kreps et al. (Eds.): HCC13 2018, IFIP AICT 537, pp. 95–110, 2018.
https://doi.org/10.1007/978-3-319-99605-9_7

worthiness. iPay will be able to solve this by performing complex analytics on individuals' payment patterns in order to assist financial institutions calculate a 'credit index'. This availability of credit would greatly assist the rural population in developing cottage industries, which would in-turn provide employment as well as earn foreign exchange.

Keywords: Mobile payment platforms · Digital merchant · m-payments Mobile money

1   Introduction

With the rapid growth of mobile telephone ownership, improvements on mobile phone hardware and increasing Internet connectivity has made mobile phones a vital part of our everyday lives. In this process, mobile phones have already replaced certain devices such as cameras, Satellite Navigation systems, music players, etc. Thus, mobile phones have reduced the need for people to carry multiple devices resulting in greater convenience and cost savings. The immediate reachability of the mobile phone has made it a commercially viable tool to carry out financial transactions [1]. Digitisation and automation of financial services resulting as proliferation of mobile telephony has been cited as one of the most significant developments during last two decades [2].

In early 2000, many enterprises expected their internet business to do well. However, they started to collapse due to shrinking profit margins and extremely competitive market forces [3]. With the learnings from the 'dot.com' bubble, businesses such as Amazon.com started selling electronic books, Blockbuster.com started selling digital movies to increase their profit margins by introducing digital business goods [4]. The creation of digital business goods has resulted in a paradigm shift changing merchants' business processes and customers' purchase activities while decreasing number of intermediaries involved greatly [4, 5]. Further, proliferation of mobile devices and social media has also contributed to the expansion of digital business goods market [6].

A white paper published by the European Commission in early 2000 has highlighted three key factors aiding in proliferation of new payments platforms [7].

1. Rethinking the product proposition from both marketing and technical perspectives
2. Staying away from creating a culture of fierce competition and creating the proper infrastructure at an acceptable cost for all the players
3. Creating predictable and efficient regulatory frameworks

In 2010, 'FinTechs' joined the competition as an emerging paradigm for providing efficient financial solutions [8]. FinTechs provide new financial service models and software applications implementing the new and efficient processes running on cutting-edge IT technologies thus competing with the traditional banking system [9]. Payment services offered by FinTechs encompasses the traditional banking services with added convenience, usability, security and higher efficiency.

Cash accounts for a staggering 85% of all financial transactions that take place across the world [41]. In the backdrop of these numbers, cashless payment methods are being increasingly encouraged and adopted across the island [42]. This includes the use of debit/credit cards as well as the enablement of online payments for most utility services and fund transfers. The internet and smartphones are key driving forces behind iPay (the digital merchant solution/payment platform explained in detail in Sect. 4). These are two domains with a rapid growth in the recent past, both in Sri Lanka as well as across the world. Broadband penetration increased by 10%, whilst Mobile telephone connections increased by 10.2%, raising the islands' mobile penetration to 116.3% (end 2015). Total internet connections grew by 20.5% during 2015, largely supported by the rapid growth of 22.2% in mobile internet connections. Government initiatives also provided over 200 public Wi-Fi locations providing free internet access [42]. Further, Sri Lanka has been ranked as the cheapest country to own a mobile phone by the ITU [44] in terms of value, as per the Measuring the Information Society Report of 2015. ITU has also ranked Sri Lanka among the top five for all forms of the cheapest internet broadband prices.

These factors presents a completely new variety of opportunities to ensure the success of a product such as iPay. Financial inclusivity and Digital Payment enablement are some of the key concerns which iPay seeks to address. A considerable volume of Sri Lankan consumers and merchants reside outside the banking system, especially in rural areas. Most consumers and merchants still prefer to use cash for financial transactions. This results in the Central Bank of Sri Lanka annually spending millions of rupees to maintain the country's supply of physical currency. Adding to this burden are the problems in getting consumers to go 'cash-less'. Credit cards still require manual swiping and signatures. Non-cash transactions usually involve a nominal, but additional fee, which is ultimately passed on to the customer. All this combined with the risk-averse psychology of consumers have all become barriers in the journey towards a truly cashless society.

2 Mobile Payment Platforms Evolution

In the section, a summary of mobile payment platforms covering pure SMS based payments platforms, USSD based payment platforms, WAP/GPRS payment platforms, Mobile Application based payment platforms, SIM based application payment platforms, Samsung Pay payment Platform, Android Pay Payment Platform, Apple Pay Payment platform are discussed in order illustrate how payment platforms evolved over the years.

2.1 Pure SMS Based Payment Platform

Pure SMS based payment platforms allows to pay for goods or services by sending a text message from a mobile phone. The purchaser sends a text message via his/her phone and the service provider clears the transaction between the purchaser and the vendor (Fig. 1).

As depicted in the diagram the transaction completes when the mobile user sends a standard text message containing the timestamp, random number, source account, destination account, amount, currency and the target mobile phone number to the

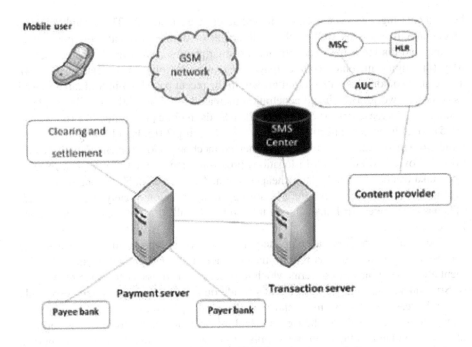

Fig. 1. Overview of the pure SMS based payment platform

payment platform [15]. The pure SMS mobile payment platform offers convenience features to customers including quick and easy use, absence of the need to remember passwords or install special applications. The platform connects millions or billions of new customers with the merchant at virtually zero cost.

2.2   USSD Based Payment Platform

USSD is a protocol in GSM networks, which allows the transfer of information between the user mobile phone and the payment platform. This is facilitated by user entering a special code on his/her mobile phone.

As depicted in Fig. 2, the mobile user sends a USSD request to the USSD gateway, which spawns a session and re-route the session info to a specific application. The application forwards this info to the USSD gateway, which makes USSD messages and routes back to the mobile phone user. Bank interactions are done via the payments server with the facilitating banks [16]. Further, many telecom operators deployed USSD services to offer services such as free air time top-ups, thus incremental costs of adopting the same platform for mobile payments is greatly reduced [17].

2.3   WAP/GPRS Based Payment Platform

As illustrated in Fig. 3, the communications occur via the GPRS network through the user's WAP enabled mobile phone. The WAP gateway routes the user request to the

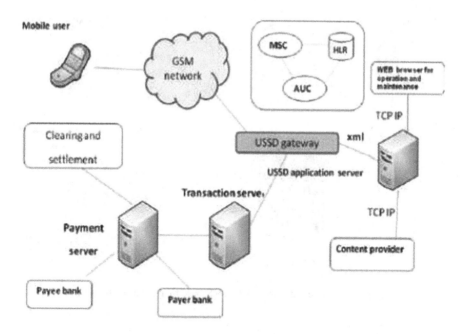

Fig. 2. Overview of the USSD based payment platform

content server. Similar to the USSD based platform, Bank interactions are done via the payments server with the facilitating banks. The mobile user is authenticated via a digital certificate [18].

Services provided by WAP/GPRS based payment platforms include web store purchases such buying mobile entertainment content such as videos, audio, wall papers, games or ringtones which are generally charged to the mobile phone bill [18].

2.4   Mobile Phone Application Based Platform

As depicted in the Fig. 4, a special software is installed on users' mobile phone the payments will be carried through this.

Once the user initiates the payment via the software installed on the phone, those instructions are transferred through a communication channel (SMS, USSD or WAP/GPRS) to the transaction server [19]. Security, cost and services available is correlated with the type of communication channel used [20].

2.5   SIM Based Application Platforms

In contrast to the mobile application based payment platform, in the SIM based payment platform the application is stored in the SIM, instead of the mobile phone.

As illustrated in Fig. 5, the user receives the application via the OTA server. This platform enables the user to send encrypted messages to the OTA server, which then

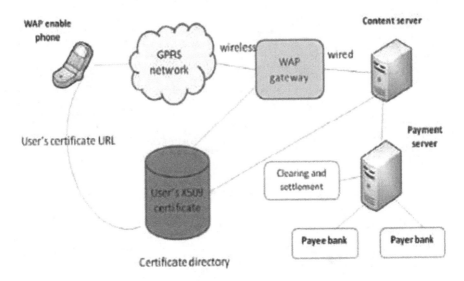

Fig. 3. Overview of the WAP/GPRS based payment platform

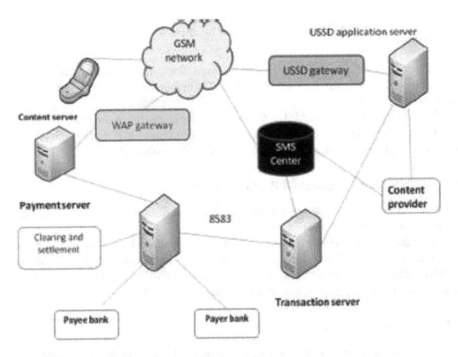

Fig. 4. Overview of the Mobile Application based payment platform

decrypts them using the HSM module. Bank interactions are facilitated via the pay-ments server with the participating banks [21, 22].

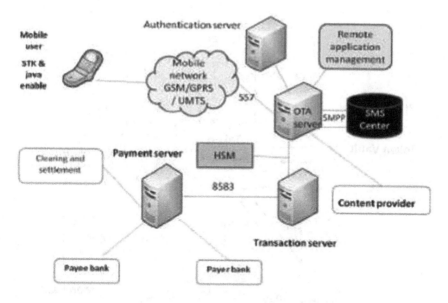

Fig. 5. Overview of the SIM based payment platform

2.6 Samsung Pay Payment Platform

Samsung Pay offers tokenized transactions through NFC technology with tap-to-pay terminals and other magnetic stripe based terminals [32]. Samsung Pay uses a technology known as Magnetic Secure Transmission (MST), which emits a signal when a mobile phone is held against a compatible PoS machine simulating the magnetic stripe found on credit/debit cards.

As illustrated in Fig. 6, when a user registers the card information, it is routed to the Token Service Provider in an encrypted form. After the card details are verified by the card company, the platform generates a token encompassing account data, which is sent to the users' mobile phone. This token is a one-time key, which cannot be reused if it is lost or stolen [32].

2.7 Android Pay Payment Platform

Android Pay also uses tokenization. Tokens are generated in the cloud. Android Pay uses NFC to transmit payment instructions between the mobile phone and the PoS machine thus facilitating the contactless transactions [36].

2.8 Apple Pay Payment Platform

Apple Pay allows users to make payments over the web, via apps or physically in person. Similar to Samsung Pay, Apple Pay also facilitates the user to make contactless payments with the addition of two-factor authentication (Fig. 7).

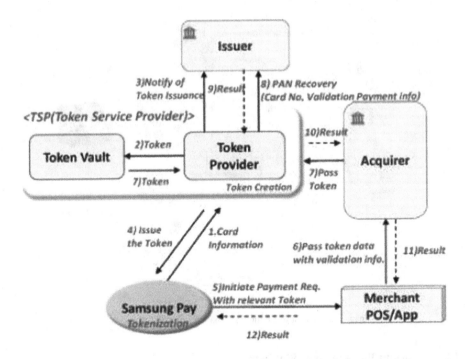

Fig. 6. Overview of the Samsung Pay payment platform

Either, the user can manually enter the card details into the Apple Pay or he can scan the card. No card related information is saved on the phone, and it is encrypted and sent to the token provider. This is decrypted to determine the card issuer, and then it is re-encrypted with a key only a specific payment network can unlock. This information along with users' iTunes activity and device data is sent to the bank. Based on this, bank will either approve or reject the new card addition to the Apple Pay [31].

3   Mobile Payments

3.1   Solving a Problem that Does not Exist?

The thought of paying for goods and services via the mobile is not a recent thought process [23]. Thus, many corporates realising the commercial potential launched commercial mobile payment platforms decades ago [8]. Mobile network operators envisioned this as means of generating additional revenue by providing value added services while banks (and other financial establishments) envisioned the potential of mobile payments to increase the use of electronic transactions enabling greater cost savings and new efficiencies [8]. Some researchers have gone into the depth of declaring mobile payment applications as the next killer-applications [24, 25, 45, 46]. However, certain researchers have been more sceptical about mobile payments applications and argued that mobile applications are trying to solve a problem that does not

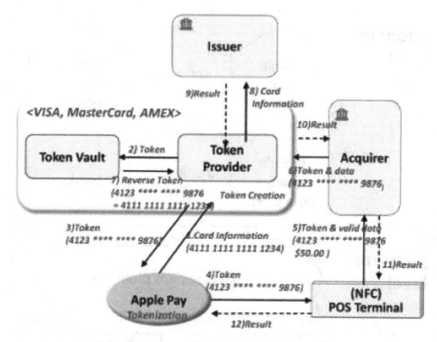

Fig. 7. Overview of the Apple Pay payment platform

exist [26, 27]. Number of new mobile payment initiatives increased during 2000 with the introduction of Near Field Communicate (NFC), yet most mobile initiatives have failed despite few cases such as Osaifu-Keitai in Japan [28].

3.2   Engineering a Successful Mobile Platform

There are multiple actors involved in a successful mobile platform. This is evident in modern successful payment platforms such as Alipay [29, 30], Apple Pay [31], Samsung Pay [32] and Android Pay [33]. The mobile payment platform can be visualized as a multisided platform as it involve more than one group of users: namely the consumers and merchants.

As illustrated in Fig. 8, the mobile payment platform has number of actors (consumers, merchants, mobile network operators, financial institutions including banks, payment networks and service providers, mobile and PoS terminal manufacturers and other third parties such as trusted service managers) who are performing complex coordination's between different tiers (user level, platform level and sponsor level) [34]. The sponsor level exercises the property rights, determines the participants and develop the underlying technology stack while focussing on standardization and economics. The platform level functions as the primary point of contact of the users (covering both consumers and merchants).

The chicken-and-egg problem is one of the most crucial concerns for the mobile payments platforms [35]. The chicken-and-egg problem is simply the consumers may

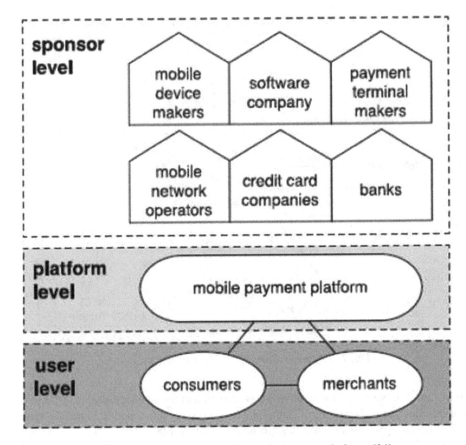

Fig. 8. Multisided architecture of mobile payment platforms [34]

not wanting to join a platform without enough merchants and vice versa. This can be addressed by offering discounts to one or both sides or by leveraging on existing associations with other actors such as consumers who are already customers of mobile network operators and merchants who are already banking with existing financial institutions.

A research carried out in 2015 among four mobile payment platforms including Paybox, Mobipay, Postfinance and Moneta has listed following reasons as to why they failed [34].

- Malfunctioning collaboration
- No win-win business model
- Lack of support and promotion
- Inadequate technology and standards
- Low value compared to existing solutions

One of the biggest challenges faced by the mobile payment platforms is diverse industries with different views collaborating successfully and efficiently. The best example is the difference of opinion between the financial institutes and the mobile network operators. Establishing a win-win business model for all actors involved is further challenging, thus resulting in lack of support and promotion. Financial institutes do not want the mobile network operators to drive the lucrative mobile payments market, and they join only to keep some controls over the market. Another challenge is on the technology and standardization front: where consumers may not own a sophisticated device facilitating NFC enabled payment services and merchants may require new terminals for accepting payments. Further, users and merchants needs to be enticed to the switch to the new mobile payment platform. In order to do this successfully, key value added features should be there changing consumer behaviour in a positive way while encouraging the merchants to adopt the new payment infrastructure.

4 Proposed Digital Merchant Platform

This section provides an overview of the payment ecosystems in Sri Lanka, and detailed account of iPay platform including how it delivers the intended benefits.

4.1 Payment Market in Sri Lanka

Sri Lanka traditionally has been a cash based economy with some card-based transactions. The payments landscape is currently undergoing a slow transformation in Sri Lanka [37]. According to Master Card Survey Cash accounts for about 85% of global consumer transactions. Even in developed economies, still cash accounts for more than 50% of payments except in USA, which is around 35–40% [38]. Cash transactions accounts for 80%-90% in Sri Lanka and other Asian economies [39]. This is despite availability of debit cards, credit cards and POS's. Physical cash handling and cash management is a huge cost for the central banks and governments and Sri Lanka spends 5% of the GDP for the same [14]. Recently, the Indian government took steps to reduce physical cash by demonetising and promoting cashless digital payments. Sri Lanka has a population of over 21 million and the working population (above the age of 20 years) is around 7.9 million [37]. Further, the Sri Lankan banking system has over 18.4 million credit and debit cards as at 2016. Out of this, 17.1 million are debit cards and the rest are credit cards.

Sri Lanka has 1,019,681 registered business establishments (or merchants), out of which only 41,283 merchants accept credit/debit cards. The implication is that only 4% of the merchants can accept cashless payments via 18.4 million credit/debit cards in circulation. Thus, creating a mismatch in the use of debit cards as a payment mechanism. The iPay platform intends to address this shortcoming while fulfilling the cashless transaction ecosystem the government intends to have in 2025 [41, 44]. iPay is a platform that replaces the physical cash usage and brings frictionless transacting convenience to customer and bringing efficiencies to merchants and the entire banking eco system. Creating customer convenience by saving time spent on completing a certain task (such as making a payment) has become an overwhelmingly important consideration in mobile payment platform design [44].

4.2 iPay Architecture

"iPay" is a mobile application which enables a user to link his credit cards/debit cards/savings accounts and current accounts, in a mobile application and securely make payments or facilitate other transactions. As opposed to traditional cash and card transactions, users simply "approve" the transaction on their mobile devices, from anywhere in the world, avoiding the hassle of counting cash and swiping cards.

The iPay technology is built to facilitate JustPay enabled services of LankaClear – the central cheque clearing house in Sri Lanka. An initiative that is aptly supported by the Central Bank and all the member banks of LankaPay Common Electronic Fund Transfer (CEFTS) to facilitate secure real-time retail payments below Rs. 10,000 under an extremely low tariff scheme. iPay is a robust solution built on a highly scalable architecture using state of the art technology, which would allow any type of merchant to offer iPay services, from Pavement Hawkers to Corner Stores, Coffee Shops to Super Markets and Super Stores to Department Stores. Anyone with a bank account, computer or smartphone and an internet connection can experience the frictionless transactions via iPay. The high-level architecture of the iPay platform is illustrated below.

As illustrated in Fig. 9, multiple acquiring banks are integrated with a single SDK in the mobile App and transactions occurring at each acquiring bank are routed to the Lanka Clears' JustPay network via the respective iPay banking module.

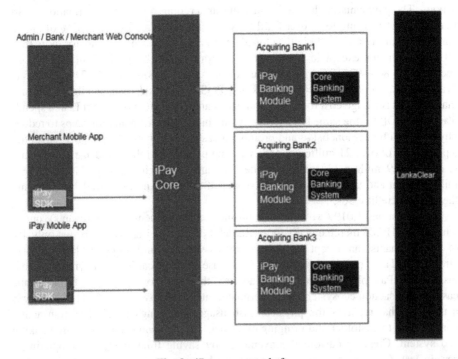

Fig. 9. iPay payment platform

The world of physical cashless payments has been dominated by companies like Visa, Master and PayPal. Further, there are FinTech solutions such as Apple Pay, Android Pay, Stripe and so on. All these platforms are based on the existing payment ecosystem of Visa or Master Network. They add more layers of complexity and friction to the existing layers, resulting in increased transaction cost to the consumer. In comparison, iPay brings frictionless transaction capability at a fraction of the cost. The iPay platform reduces complexity to all stakeholders including customers, merchants and acquiring or partner bank, while allowing customers to register online with their existing bank account. Merchants do not require any special equipment nor complex process to register. Merchants receive their money to the account online real-time basis, with transactions fee amounting to 1–1.5%. Further, Real-time credit eliminates the reconciliation process. Banks can introduce credit without having to manage an ecosystem of plastic cards, but only having a current account with credit facility, which could be facilitated by the iPay platform without any other intermediary software.

The iPay platform cater to all types of merchant from traditional pavement hawkers, in-store merchants, e-commerce merchants to digital merchants with InApp purchase experience. The platform further supports peer-to-peer payments for registered customers. The customer experience has been simplified through the multiple payment interaction options. The simplest and most cost effective being the 'Scan & Pay' through merchant QR Code scanning. The platform further facilitates 'Tap & Pay' via integrated NFC cards and 'Discover & Pay' via BLE beacons. Further, the platforms also support searching for merchants, adding as a favourite or locating based on the GPS location

5 Discussion

One of biggest issues in providing credit to poor is the lack of documented credit histories [45]. The iPay platform can solve this problem by means of analysing existing data about consumers and promoting alternative credit evaluations mechanisms. Traditional credit evaluations mechanisms such as reference checks via credit bureaus or relying on monthly income statements is not viable options when assessing the credit worthiness of rural communities who have not been part of the formal banking system. Thus, new credit evaluations techniques such as analysing utility bill payment cycles, and his other expenditure patterns available on iPay platform can be used to carry out the credit evaluation. This will enable the banks to provide credit to poor at a much lower cost. iPay is aimed at facilitating transactions less than 10,000 LKR. Further, iPay can be used by merchants of various sizes, and industries. Even a pavement hawker can become a part of the iPay platform at nearly zero cost (the platform will provide him a smartphone free of charge, or he can even use non-smart phone also) enabling him to advertise his products or services on the iPay platform at no cost with very little technical know-how. Thus, the iPay platform can be used for digital enablement of conventional merchants. Since, there is no physical transfer of cash, the security aspects are covered. This is especially beneficial for small pavement hawkers/shop owners/fuel pumps who operate during night-time with inherent risks and challenges.

Another challenge for entrepreneurs/start-ups in Sri Lanka is the lack of ability to accept electronic payments. The iPay payment platform can be seamlessly integrated with any of the existing mobile apps, websites with limited technical knowledge in matter of hours while giving better user experience to the consumer when making mobile payments (the iPay platform uses similar transition present in Facebook app, and Facebook messenger app). Thus, the consumer does not need to reveal his banking details to a generic app, providing him/her better assurance on data. Similar to other countries, telecommunications and electricity infrastructure has penetrated further in the rural areas compared to the banks. The cost of transactions can also be lowered by adopting iPay platform. Hence, banking institutions can also leverage on iPay platform to reach out to rural areas at virtually zero cost. Thus, banks can utilise the iPay platform to extend previously unbanked and low-income rural communities.

The iPay platform can also solve another common issue applicable to most of the banking institutions – how to keep the customers active. Compared to a traditional banking app, iPay is an eco-system comprising of various merchants and their portals. Merchants will push new offers, discounts via the platform, and based on the expenditure consumers will also earn reward points which can be redeemable via merchants. Thus, banks can use the platform to keep the customer engaged.

Another goal of iPay is to increase Digitalisation among Sri Lankan merchants. Since most merchants prefer to carry out cash transactions, this imposes a certain burden on the economy. Digital enablement would help reduce this overhead whilst facilitating real-time as well as easy cash management. This is not limited to payments, but merchants will be presented with a completely new range of digital 'opportunities' to promote and develop their businesses. These include awareness on special promotions, digital marketing campaigns and trend analysis as an input to business strategy. In addition, iPay can address challenges such as theft or robbery associated with collecting physical cash, especially in places such as fuel stations operating 24/7.

References

1. Batchelor, S.: Mobile phone-enabled payment systems transformation 2008. Enterp. Dev. Microfinance **19**(1), 13–30 (2008). https://doi.org/10.3362/1755-1986.2008.003
2. Shaikh, A.A., Karjaluoto, H.: On some misconceptions concerning digital banking and alternative delivery channels. Int. J. E Bus. Res. (IJEBR) **12**(3), 1–16 (2016)
3. Kim, C., Kim, J., Lee, I.: Toward an evolution strategy for the digital goods business. Manage. Decis. **50**(2), 234–252 (2012)
4. Lang, K.R., Shang, R.D., Vragov, R.: Designing markets for co-production of digital culture goods. Decis. Support Syst. **48**, 33–45 (2009)
5. Williams, K., Chattergee, S., Rossi, M.: Design of emerging digital services: a taxnomy. Eur. J. Inf. Syst. **17**, 505–517 (2008)
6. Pathirana, P.A., Azam, S.M.F.: Behavoiral intention to use social media among the banking consumers in Sri Lanka – an emperical study. Eur. J. Soc. Sci. **54**(2), 123–133 (2017)
7. Lefebvre, P.J.: Digital money – a view from the European commission. Eur. Bus. Rev. **99–4**, 242–256 (2000)

8. Mark, D.R., Verschur, E., Nikayin, F., Cerpa, N., Bouman, H.: Collective action for mobile payment platforms: a case study on collaboration issues between banks and telecom operators. Electron. Commer. Res. Appl. **14**(5), 331–344 (2015)
9. Moon, W.Y., Kim, S.D.: A payment mediation platform for heterogeneous FinTech schemes. In: Advanced Information Management, Communicates, Electronic and Automation Control Conference (IMCEC), pp. 511–516. IEEE, October 2016
10. Investopedia. https://www.investopedia.com/terms/m/mobile-payment.asp. Accessed 28 Dec 2017
11. Fan, T.S., Beng, L.Y., Roslan, R.: Privacy in new mobile payment protocal. World Acad. Sci. Eng. Technol. **2**, 198–202 (2008)
12. Tehrani, M.A., Amidian, A.A., Muhammadi, J., Rabiee, H.R.: A survey of system platforms for mobile payment. In: International Conference on Management of e-Commerce and e-Government, pp. 376–381. IEEE Computer Society (2010)
13. MasterCard. https://www.mastercard.com/gateway/processing.html. Accessed 10 Jan 2018
14. Pathirana, P.A., Azam, S.M.F.: Factors influencing the use of mobile payments - a conceptual model. In: 35th National Information Technology Conference, Sri Lanka/IEEE Xplore Digital Library (2017)
15. Kim, C., Choe, S., Choi, C.: A systematic approach to new mobile service creation. Expert Syst. Appl. **35**, 762–771 (2008)
16. David, M., Dawling, J.: State of the art review of mobile payment technology, Trinity College Dublin, Department of Computer Science (2003)
17. Bourreau, M., Valetti, T.: Competition and interoperability in mobile money platform markets: what works and what doesn't? (2015)
18. Ho, H., Fong, S., Yan, Z.: User acceptance testing of mobile payment in various scenario. In: IEEE International Conference on e-Business Engineering. IEEE Computer Society (2008)
19. Mckitterick, D.A.: A web services framework for mobile payment services, Master thesis in University of Dublin (2003)
20. Kaplan, M., Rand, C.: U.S. Patent Application No. 11/125,833 (2005)
21. Trichina, E., Hyppönen, K., Hassinen, M.: SIM-enabled open mobile payment system based on nation-wide PKI. In: Pohlmann, N., Reimer, H., Schneider, W. (eds.) ISSE, pp. 355–366. Vieweg, Heidelberg (2007). https://doi.org/10.1007/978-3-8348-9418-2_38
22. Zou, J., Zhang, C., Dong, C., Fan, C., Wen, Z.: Mobile payment based on RFID-SIM card. In: 2010 IEEE 10th International Conference on Computer and Information Technology (CIT), pp. 2052–2054. IEEE (2010)
23. Karnouskos, S.: Mobile payment: a journey through existing procedures and standardization initiatives. IEEE Commun. Surv. Tutor. **6**(4), 44–66 (2004)
24. Rosingh, W., Seale, A., Osborn, D.: Why banks and telecoms must merge to surge. Strat. Bus. **23**, 48–59 (2001)
25. Zheng, X., Chen, D.: Study of mobile payments systems. In: IEEE International Conference on E-Commerce, pp. 24–27 (2003)
26. Alliance, S.C.: Contactless payment and the retail point of sale applications, technologies and transaction models (2003)
27. TechCrunch. NFC is great, but mobile payments solve a problem that doesn't exist (2012). https://techcrunch.com/2012/06/30/nfc-is-great-but-mobile-payments-solve-a-problem-that-doesnt-exist/
28. Flood, D., West, T., Wheadon, D.: Trends in mobile payments in developing and advanced economies. In: RBA Bulletin, pp. 71–80 (2013)
29. Guo, J., Guo, J., Bouwman, H., Bouwman, H.: An ecosystem view on third party mobile payment providers: a case study of Alipay wallet. Info **18**(5), 56–78 (2016)

30. Wee, W.: China's Alipay has 700 million registered accounts, beats PayPal? TechinAsia (2012).   www.techinasia.com/chinas-alipay-700-million-registered-accounts-beatspaypal/. Accessed 20 Jan 2013
31. Hargrave, S.: Apple pay and iBeacons—a digital marketing revolution could be on its way. London Media Advertising Daily (2014). http://www.mediapost.com/publications/article/233982/apple-pay-and-ibeacons-a-digital-marketing-revo.htlm
32. Kim, J.W.: What is Samsung Pay. Daum Cafe (2015)
33. Bhat, P., Ramaswamy, S.: Android Pay: the next generation of payments on Android. Talk at Google I/O (2015)
34. Gannamaneni, A., Ondrus, J., Lyytinen, K.: A post-failure analysis of mobile payment platforms. In: 2015 48th Hawaii International Conference on System Sciences (HICSS), pp. 1159–1168. IEEE (2015)
35. Caillaud, B., Jullien, B.: Chicken & egg: competition among intermediation service providers. RAND J. Econ. **34**, 309–328 (2003)
36. Andriod. Andriod Pay – it's not exactly magic. https://www.android.com/pay/. Accessed 12 Jan 2018
37. Central Bank of Sri Lanka. Annual Report 2016 (2017)
38. Master Card Survey. Most cashless nations of the world, where consumers still prefer cash despite heavy fines (2017). https://worldcore.eu/blog/cashless-nations-world-consumers-still-prefer-cash-despite-heavy-fines/
39. Central Bank of Sri Lanka Road Map. Monetary and Financial Sector Policies for 2018 and Beyond (2018)
40. BBC. India rupee: Illegal cash crackdown failed - bank report (2017). http://www.bbc.com/news/world-asia-india-41100613. Accessed 10 Jan 2018
41. Business Times. 18.4 mln credit/debit cards in use, vol. 25, no. 20, pp I, 27 August 2017 (2017)
42. Central Bank of Sri Lanka. Payments Bulletin Third Quarter 2016 (2016). http://www.cbsl.gov.lk/pics_n_docs/10_pub/_docs/periodicals/payment_bulletin/2016/Payments_Bulletin_3Q2016.pdf
43. PM's Office. V2025 A Country Enriched (2017). http://www.pmoffice.gov.lk/download/press/D00000000061_EN.pdf. Accessed 10 Jan 2018
44. ITU. ITU releases annual global ICT data and ICT Development Index country rankings, 22 November 2016. https://www.itu.int/en/mediacentre/Pages/2016-PR53.aspx. Accessed 10 Jan 2018
45. Liébana-Cabanillas, F., Lara-Rubio, J.: Predictive and explanatory modeling regarding adoption of mobile payment systems. Technol. Forecast. Soc. Chang. **120**, 32–40 (2017)
46. de Luna, I.R., Montoro-Ríos, F., Liébana-Cabanillas, F.J.: New perspectives on payment systems: near field communication (NFC) payments through mobile phones. In: Mobile Commerce: Concepts, Methodologies, Tools, and Applications, pp. 1487–1507. IGI Global (2018)

Do We Have What Is Needed to Change Everything?
A Survey of Finnish Software Businesses on Labour Shortage and Its Potential Impacts

Sonja M. Hyrynsalmi[1], Minna M. Rantanen[2], and Sami Hyrynsalmi[3(✉)]

[1] Department of Future Technologies, University of Turku, Turku, Finland
{smnyla,minna.m.rantanen}@utu.fi
[2] Turku School of Economics, University of Turku, Turku, Finland
[3] Tampere University of Technology, Pervasive Computing, Pori, Finland
sami.hyrynsalmi@tut.fi

Abstract. The fourth industrial revolution is expected to bring major changes both in society as well as in the modern industry. Naturally, it will also shake the labour market—however, not only by replacing blue collar duties by robots, but also by renewing the set of skills and competencies needed in new kinds of work duties. In this study, we use a data (n = 160) from a survey to the Finnish software businesses to evaluate how software companies perceive the labour shortage and its implications in the verge of the new industrial revolution. The results show that already now there are signs that the labour shortage might harm the growth and innovations in the ICT field. This study presents the results from the survey and discusses whether there are enough competent resources to support the industrial revolution.

Keywords: Fourth industrial revolution · Skills · Competence
Software business

1 Introduction

Nowadays, a common interpretation is that we are right now on the edge of the fourth industrial revolution. New technologies and innovations are arising from areas such as robotics, artificial intelligence, machine learning, nanotechnology and biotechnology. Together, they are forming new kinds of possibilities for humankind [1,2].

The history already identifies three different industrial revolutions. The first industrial revolution was characterised by the industry's utilisation of steam power. The second industrial revolution was full of innovations powered by electricity and the third industrial revolution was the time of digitalisation. Now, the fourth industrial revolution is seen as a fusion of physical, digital and life-science technologies [3].

© IFIP International Federation for Information Processing 2018
Published by Springer Nature Switzerland AG 2018. All Rights Reserved
D. Kreps et al. (Eds.): HCC13 2018, IFIP AICT 537, pp. 111–122, 2018.
https://doi.org/10.1007/978-3-319-99605-9_8

However, the differentiating factor between previous industrial revolutions and the current one is the speed of current breakthroughs [4]. It has been evaluated, that the fourth industrial revolution is evolving at an exponential pace rather than a linear. It is also notable, that the new revolution is disrupting almost all sectors of the modern industry in every country at the same time [1].

Major technological innovations in all industrial revolutions have been shown to be accompanied by large-scale transformations in the labour market [5,6]. In addition, it is also said that all of them has always been a race between education and technology [7]. This ongoing technological change has already shown that Robotic Process Automation (RPA) made computing more affordable and at the same time educated software workers with cognitive problem-solving and project skills are becoming highly recognised [8].

In a recent report, the World Economic Forum [9] points out that the fourth industrial revolution will influence the skill sets required in both old and new occupations. Those new skills and competences will change in most industries, and most notably in the field of information and communication technology (ICT). It may also affect male and female workers differently, and transform the dynamics of the industry gender gap.

As an early signal for the new industrial revolution, the need for new skills and competences has arisen among software companies. Already now, various ICT specialist jobs have been among the most dynamic occupations in the past few years [10]. Furtermore, several forecasts have suggested that the demand for ICT professionals with different skills and competences will continue grow, and it is expected that the growth rate, in a shortcoming future, is likely to be even faster. In 2014, ICT specialists accounted for 3.6% of all workers in Organisation for Economic Cooperation and Development (OECD) countries [11], and in the European Union (EU), nearly 8 million persons were employed as ICT experts, representing 3.7% of total employment in 2014 [12]. According to, e.g., World Economic Forum, ICT specialist open vacancies are going to be harder to fill and the fourth industrial revolution is also changing the skills that employers need and shortening the applicability time of employees' existing skill sets in the process [9].

The ICT industry has an important role to play in creating the foundation for the new business from the fourth industrial revolution. The lack of ICT labour is not only the problem of software industry, because ICT is nowadays cross-disciplinary — more new talents and innovators are needed in the all industrial sectors. If there is not enough labour for the new business, there will be a shortage of new innovations and new jobs [12]. Thus, it is important to acknowledge how labour shortage could impact on outcome of the fourth industrial revolution.

This study does not focus on the often-seen argument for robots 'stealing' people jobs. On the contrary, this study focuses how demands of the fourth industrial revolution are changing the software industry jobs and how companies, universities and ICT professionals can cope with ever-increasing and fast change. On the other way around, this study concern humans, their skills and position in an ever-changing environment.

In this study, we focus on the following research question:

RQ How do software companies perceive labour shortage and how does it influence into companies?

To answer the presented question, we use a survey of Finnish software companies regarding the labour shortage in ICT industry. In total, the survey received 160 responses (i.e., n = 160). We are interested to study is there really a lack of competence in the field of software industry.

The remaining of this work is structured as follows. Section 2 shortly discusses related work while Sect. 3 presents the acquisition of empirical material for this study. Section 4 presents the results and it is followed by the discussion of implications as well as limitations in Sect. 5. The last section concludes the study.

2   Background

Industrial revolutions have had different kinds of needs from the workforce. First, steam power and factories took over artisan handwork and after that, machines and more efficient manufacturing chains changed demand for the workforce at the second industrial revolution. The third industrial revolution, the so called digital revolution, generated demand for a new kind of white-collar, the non-production, workers [3,6].

In the academic research field the skill-biased technical change (also known as unskilled labor-saving) has been at the eye of debate years [13,14]. According to Goldin and Katz [7], skill-biased technical change was a characteristic for the twentieth century. The demand for skilled labour, despite unskilled labour, growth in every decade of twentieth century [15]. In software business 'soft skills', such as self-direction, information-processing, problem-solving and communication, become more important [16].

'The Future of Jobs' -survey by the World Economic Forum shows that there is a growing demand on technical and social skills as well as cognitive abilities in the field of information and communication technology. According to the report, the main job families which are going to have difficulties of recruitment are database and network professionals, software and applications developers and analysts, electrotechnology engineers and architects and surveyors [9].

The fourth industrial revolution will also shake not only the jobs and required skills but also the business field of information and communication technology. For instance, a study by Roland Berger Strategy Consultant [17], commissioned by the Federation of German Industries (BDI), shows that Europe has a great potential at the field of new business opportunities in ICT. They suggest that the new digital transformation of the industries could add as much as EUR 1.25 trillion to the overall Europe's industrial value creation by 2025; however, if Europe misses the change to the new markets, that value will diminish it by EUR 605 billion.

European Union has also investigated the business potential in ICT industry and estimated that new business from digital economy could contribute EUR 415 billion per year to the EU economy. Furthermore, this kind of development would create hundreds of thousands new jobs in the EU [18]. However, for fulfilling the new business potential, new skills and more labour is needed. Nevertheless, finding the skilled labour is going to be even harder: European Commission [18] has studied that by 2020 there will be 756,000 unfilled vacancies for ICT professionals in the whole economy. The European Union's e-skills report for the year 2020 has predicted that demand for new skills ranges at every skill level, but in the next decades there is going to be growing demand especially for more advanced digital skills [19].

For instance in Finland, estimations of needed ICT labour varies from 7,000 to 15,000 and the estimated need is growing yearly by 3,800 persons when only 1,100 students graduate from the field of computer science and technology [20]. That is alarming number which fosters debate about Finland losing it opportunity to be one of the world's leading countries in digitalisation. More political focus and actions are demanded from government to the technological education [21].

Past few years there has been shown strong growth in the Finland software industry and companies really are ready to expand to the international markets [22,23]. That is a good sign because export of ICT industry is already crucial to the Finnish national economy. It is already the second largest industry group after paper and pulp industry and covering 11.4% of national export yearly [24].

However, there is a danger that Finland is not using it full potential from fourth industrial revolution. World Economic Forum has stated that Finland is one of the top 5 countries which enjoy a high state of digital advancement while there are signs of a slowing momentum. These top countries (i.e., Finland, Denmark, Norway, Sweden, and Switzerland) are all leading countries in digital technology right now. However, they all face challenges with sustaining growth and reinventing themselves [25].

Like in all technological competences in every industrial revolution, there will be winners and losers in the fourth industrial revolution. Those countries who will adapt new technologies and skills more agile than others countries are more likely to be winners in this revolution. Furthermore, it is also the race between continentals because the availability of a large talent pool would contribute to make Europe a better place to invest and do business [26]. Luckily, already now the European Union, OECD and the World Economic Forum among other actors have done a lot of strategy implications and cleared pathway to countries really take advance from the fourth industrial revolution.

3   Research Process

The primary data for this study was collected with a questionnaire survey targeted to the owners of Finnish software businesses. The survey was sent via e-mail to the member companies of Finnish Software Industry & Entrepreneurs Association by the association on the requested of Helsingin Sanomat[1], the largest national newspaper in Finland. The association acts as an advocate of software industry in Finland and a community for software business executives. It promotes growth and internationalisation of the industry. The association has approximately 600–700 members.

The survey's questions considered labour shortage in software business. The survey has two parts: First, the future development of the responding company were asked. Second, questions regarding the impact of labour shortage as well as the language used in the workplace and the percentage of non-Finnish workers were inquered. Overall, the survey consisted of 11 questions, varying from open-ended to multiple choice and scale questions using Likert scale. The survey was done in Finnish.

The survey was conducted in the beginning of fall 2017. In total, 160 top level managers answered to the questionnaire. Thus, the approximate response rate for the survey is around 23–26%. The respondents are from different areas of software business, ranging from consultancy to product and service business. A clear majority of the respondents' companies belong to business-to-business markets.

For the scale questions, the averages and median values were calculated. An equal interest is on the open-ended questions. Those questions were analysed by using qualitative approach. In the analysis, we followed the general guidelines given by Robinson et al. [27].

Each answer was analysed and coded by a researcher. The codes were not predefined; on the contrary, they were created based on the repeating themes in the answers. After all answers were coded, the codes were reviewed and similar codes were combined. All answers given by the respondents were written in Finnish. Therefore, all quotations presented in this study are translated by the researchers.

4   Results

In the following, we will first present the results of quantitative questions. It is followed by the analysis of responses to the open-ended questions.

4.1   Quantitative Responses

In total, 160 answers were gathered to the survey. In the first part of the survey, companies' expectations for the near future were asked. Overall, the respondents are feeling optimistic towards the future: Only 3.1% of the respondents predicted that the turnover would decrease in the forthcoming six months while 90.0% believed it would grow either moderately or considerably. However, responding

---

[1] Kempas, K. "Koodareita haetaan yhä useammin ulkomailta, koska Suomessa ei riitä osaajia – jotkut yritykset haluavat olla'sataprosenttisesti suomalaisia'". Helsingin Sanomat, October 5th, 2017.

companies were more critical regarding development of their profitability. As many as 6.3% evaluated that the profitability will worsen a little during the next six months, 31.9% claimed it will stay same. Again, a majority of 43.8% claimed that the profitability will grow better a little and 18.1% of the respondents answered that it will grow remarkably.

Altogether, these results reveal that a clear majority of the companies forecast remarkable growth in near future. A reasonable share of companies believed that both turnover (34.4%) and profitability (18.1%) will increase significantly during the next six months. These can be read as weak signals of growing economy. Moving forward to need of new staff, only two companies (1.3%) believes that the total number of staff in the company is likely to decrease. At the same time, approximately one fourth (23.8%) is not expecting any changes in six months. However, more than a half of respondents (56.9%) are willingly and expecting to recruit new personnel. Furthermore, from all responding companies, 29 (18.1%) are interest to recruit several new people and increase the size of personnel significantly.

Also the working language of the companies was asked. From all respondents, 78.8% announced using either only English or some combination of English, Finnish and Swedish. Only 21.3% revealed using only Finnish as working language. In addition, the percentage of foreign workers were inquired and the results are shown in Table 1. While more than one third of responding companies does not have foreign staff at all, 41.9% of companies have from 1 to 20% of workers from abroad.

Table 1. The percentage of foreign workers in responding companies (n = 160).

Foreign workers	Share of answers
None	36.9%
1–20%	41.9%
21–40%	14.4%
41–60%	4.4%
61–80%	0.6%
81–100%	1.0%

In the second part of the survey, companies were inquired opinions regarding the labour shortage. In a Likert scale question, an opinion was asked on the statement that there are not enough information and communication technology labour in Finland. As shown in Fig. 1(a), 38.8% respondents are confident that there is not enough information and communication competence in Finland for their need and 28.8% respondents are positively sure about that. The average value for the question is 3.79 and median value is 4.

In the second Likert scale question, an opinion was asked on the statement that the lack of information and communication competent labour is influencing to a company's growth potential. Figure 1(b) shows that 30.6% of the

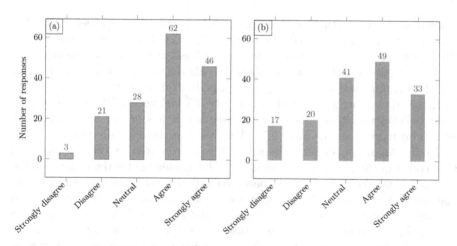

Fig. 1. Distribution of answers for (a) 'There are not enough information and communication technology labour in Finland', and (b) 'Lack of information and communication competent labour is influencing to a company's growth potential' (n = 160).

respondents agrees that lack of competence is effecting their company's growth potential and 20.6% strongly agrees with the statement. The average value of the responses is 3.38 and median value is 4.

In addition, it was whether the company is looking for new employees also from abroad or mainly in abroad. From all companies, 42.5% stated that they are looking new employees mainly from Finland while also 42.5% stated that they are looking from Finland and abroad. Only 6.9% of companies stated that they are looking new employees primarily from abroad.

To summarise quantitative responses, the responding companies are seeing the forthcoming future as bright – a clear majority of the respondents were expecting growth in all three aspects: turnover, profitability and size of personnel. From all respondents, 63.2% have already non-Finnish staff members. Furthermore, the number of companies using English as their working language is higher than the number of companies having foreign staff. Thus, this might be seen as an indication that there are companies that would be able easily to take foreign workers, but have not yet done so. Furthermore, nearly half of the companies were looking for new candidates also from abroad while only a small portion was looking only candidates from abroad.

Finally, the results also show that the companies' have identified labour shortage problem. As reported by Fig. 1, there seems to be a lack of competent labour in Finland. Furthermore, a majority of companies see the lack of competent workforce—whether from Finland or from abroad—as a drag for the growth.

4.2   Qualitative Responses

Out of the all, 90 respondents (56.3%) answered to the open-ended question *how labour shortage affects your company*. In total, there are nearly 3,000 words written as answers to the question. The lengths of the answers varied from a few dozens of words to a hundred. As described in Sect. 3, all answers were coded. The following observations were made on the basis of the finalised coding.

First, there is a clear division between whether there are labour shortage and does it influence on the companies growth strategy. One answer could not be classified in either group. A clear majority (65 companies, 73%) of the respondents believes that there is labour shortage and it has or will have an impact. Still, a bit more than one fifth (27%) believes that there are no influence.

In the following, different issues that were repeated in the answers, and thus coded in the analysis, are discussed. The arguments for the negative influence of labour shortage are often based on experienced problems. For example, one respondent states *"Recruiting processes are long and require lots our own resources. Our own experts are every now and then overburdened, [...]"*, thus illustrating the common problems caused by the labour shortage. This quote also emphasises another problem often occurring in the answers: the recruiting processes are long and arduous. Furthermore, there are both respondents that say the recruitment is hard in the capital area as well as those stating that recruitment is hard outside of the capital area.

Another aspect frequently occurring in the answers are the effects caused by the labour shortage. For example, a respondent stated that *"We cannot offer as much services as our clients would need. We cannot get enough competency for the projects, which is the reason why the projects are expensive, slow and risky. [...] The workers are able to survive from the projects, by the hard way, but there are not enough skilled workers who could help to avoid pitfalls or be able to take modern alternatives in the use."* Thus, underlining that more competent labour would be able to work more efficiency and be able to learn and utilise the newest tools and frameworks.

In addition, one company told that *"Due to the labour shortage of software business, we cannot respond to the demand and we are forced to answer 'no-can-do'. Furthermore, we cannot develop our product to international markets because the domestic demand already uses all of our resources. We could grow remarkably faster if there would be more competent workforce available."* Similar reasoning for the influences of the labour shortage were present also in other responses.

On the contrary to aforementioned perceptions, there are roughly two different kinds of answers that disagree with the labour shortage causing problems to the industry. However, only 27% of the answers did not see the labour shortage influencing to the company's growth. In the first group, the respondents do not see the labour shortage influencing the companies or their growth in any way. For example, one respondent explained that *"It [the labour shortage] does not have influence. There are thousands of educated people unemployed in the software field. The problems is that the companies wish to have the top experts with a small salary and there is a lack of that kind of workforce in all fields. The special problem in the software field is that knowledge expires mostly in five years."*

In the latter group, the respondents do not have had problems caused by the labour shortage either due to the use foreign workforce and offices abroad, or they have not have any problems yet, but are doubtful that in the future there might be. As an example of the former, a respondent stated that *"We have recruited foreign workers so there are no influence [of the labour shortage]. It is actually a good thing that there are no Finnish workers anymore so teams' diversity grows naturally."* Also, other respondent stated that *"No influence, we have found top experts. Today, one arrived in Helsinki from [a city in USA] with his vanload."* As an instance of the latter, one of the respondents told that *"Currently, there are no labour shortage, the problems are in somewhere else. However, if the problems can be fixed, getting new staff, and possibly the labour shortage, become more relevant issue."* Nevertheless, this can be seen as an indication that there are no enough competent workforce available in Finland.

To summarise qualitative results, there are arguments for and against that the labour shortage influences negatively on firms and their growth. However, around three-fourths of the respondent agreed in their open-end answers that the labour shortage influences in their companies. The main themes arisen from the data are (i) the problems in recruiting new staff both in the capital area as well outside the capital area, (ii) the lack of top experts prevents adoption of new tools and frameworks, and (iii) due to the lack of competent labour, companies are not able to grow as fast as they would hope to.

Yet, there are also opposite views and observations that the labour shortage problem does not influence on the growth of the firms. Often the respondents refer to being able to either outsource work to another countries or by hiring foreign staff. However, also companies having foreign workers and actively recruiting those report problems in acquiring new staff.

5   Discussion

In the following, we will first discuss the key findings of this survey and their implications. This sections ends with limitations of the study and some proposals for future work.

5.1   Findings and Implications

This paper sought to study how do Finnish software companies perceive the labour shortage and whether it has an impact on the companies or not. Based on the survey, it seems that a majority of software companies have already experienced problems in recruiting competent workforce. Furthermore, several respondent explained how the lack of competent workforce influence to the quality of products, project timetables, and even in the potential growth of the company. These lead to the question presented in the title of this study: *Do we actually have what is needed to change everything with the fourth industrial revolution?* Otherwise, the fourth industrial revolution, that is expected to be a major disruption in several industrial fields, could become only a disrupted disruption.

In this study, we have noted that right kind of skills in the software industry are already hard to find. We also expect that it will become even more harder in the next couple of years. This has a lot to do with national prosperity — if there is not enough right kind of workforce, there will be no new business and from that no new jobs. As a result, the society will not be renewed at the same pace than other countries and the whole fourth industrial revolution will not fully implement to that specific country. Thus, this is a matter of national development and should not be left solely on the shoulders of entrepreneurs.

European Union and OECD have, for years, promoted skills strategies. For instance, OECD has developed a comprehensive skills strategy that help countries to analyse their national skill systems and identify its strengths and weaknesses. The strategy helps a country to benchmark itself internationally and develop policies that can transform better skills into better jobs, economic growth and social inclusion [11]. However, it must be noted that strategies alone do not create change — political commitment is needed as well as meaningful development of strategies and actions based on them.

Nevertheless, there is always risk when skill policies are developed based on trends and current task demands [11]. Economic history has shown to us, economies have continued to create enough jobs for their workforce after periods of disruption, However, digital revolution is more difficult to foresee due its unique characteristics [5].

It is worthy to note, that when we are considering skills, we should not focus only for problems of filling the open vacancies. The new industrial revolution will acquire new skills also from the old workers. Investing in re-skilling current employees will more likely rise more and more common in next few years.

In the fourth digital revolution, the possibilities are likely unlimited. This new revolution will combine the physical, biological and digital worlds — and in the unskilled hands, there is a change that it could bring more harm than good. This is reason why a high educated competence is needed with multidisciplinary skills.

Altogether, the fourth industrial revolution is expected to shake all known industries. Information and communication technology is a a cross-cutting field and therefore the lack of right kind of skills and competences will effect not only for software business but also to the fields of art, life science, economics and others. That is, to be able to *change everything*, we have to get our focus on the right skills for the new era.

5.2   Limitations and Future Work

Naturally, this study has certain limitations that should be acknowledged. First, the study is based on a survey sent to the members of the software entrepreneurship association. The association and its members represent only a fraction of the whole software industry in Finland; however, the member companies are well-doing companies in Finland and they are represent well the whole industry. However, this might bias the results.

Second, the whole survey was implemented in Finland and the generalisation of results in other western countries is questionable. While Finland shares remarkable similarities with other European and western countries, it is located in the northern end of the Europe and might not be able to lure competent workforce as well as the central European countries.

Nevertheless, this study opens avenues for future research. First, a qualitative survey to both job seekers and companies would reveal more insights on the phenomena. Second, it seems that the governments, such as Finland, need more detailed skills and competency strategy to respond to the changes bring by the fourth industrial revolution. Thirdly, education and re-education in the field of ICT should be studied more in relation to this change.

6 Conclusion

This paper surveyed how software businesses in Finland perceive labour shortage. From the 160 responses, a clear majority is stating that the labour shortage will slow down the growth potential. The companies revealed, e.g., that recruiting processes took long time and too much companies resources and it is hard to find competent workforce for senior level positions. Therefore, the companies are not able to grow their business as they would like to.

The title of this study asked whether we have all that is needed to change everything. As the new industrial revolution is expected to have, again, a massive impact on our society and living, the companies thriving the revolution need competent workforce to do so. Based on the results achieved in the empirical inquiry of this study, we have to state that we might not have all that is needed for the change.

Acknowledgements. The authors wish to thanks Managing Director *Rasmus Roiha* and Finnish Software Industry & Entrepreneurs Association for sharing the dataset used in this study.

References

1. Schwab, K.: The Fourth Industrial Revolution. Foreign Affairs (2018). https://www.foreignaffairs.com/articles/2015-12-12/fourth-industrial-revolution. Accessed 23 Jan 2018
2. Hermann, M., Pentek, T., Otto, B.: Design principles for industrie 4.0 scenarios. In: 2016 49th Hawaii International Conference on System Sciences (HICSS), pp. 3928–3937 (2016)
3. Katz, L.F., Margo, R.A.: Technical change and the relative demand for skilled labor: The united states in historical perspective. Working Paper 18752, National Bureau of Economic Research (2013)
4. Frey, C.B., Osborne, M.: Technology at Work: The Future of Innovation and Employment. Oxford Martin School and Citi GPS, Oxford (2015)
5. OECD: New Markets and New Jobs. Number 255 in OECD Digital Economy Papers. OECD Publishing (2016)
6. Frey, C.B., Osborne, M.A.: The future of employment: How susceptible are jobs to computerisation? Technol. Forecast. Soc. Chang. **114**, 254–280 (2017)

7. Goldin, C., Katz, L.: The Race Between Education and Technology. Harvard University Press, Cambridge (2009)
8. Autor, D.H., Levy, F., Murnane, R.J.: The skill content of recent technological change: an empirical exploration. Q. J. Econ. **118**(4), 1279–1333 (2003)
9. World Economic Forum: The Future of Jobs: Employment, Skills and Workforce Strategy for Fourth Industrial Revolution. Global Challenge Insight Report. World Economic Forum, Geneva, Switzerland (2016)
10. Lehner, F., Sundby, M.W.: ICT skills and competencies for SMEs: results from a structured literature analysis on the individual level. In: Harteis, C. (ed.) The Impact of Digitalization in the Workplace. PPL, vol. 21, pp. 55–69. Springer, Cham (2018). https://doi.org/10.1007/978-3-319-63257-5_5
11. OECD: Skills for a digital world. Policy brief on the future of work. OECD Publishing, Paris (2016)
12. Eurostat: ICT specialists in employment. Technical report, European Union (2017)
13. Berman, E., Bound, J., Machin, S.: Implications of skill-biased technological change: international evidence. Q. J. Econ. **113**(4), 1245–1279 (1998)
14. Autor, D.H., Katz, L.F., Krueger, A.B.: Computing inequality: have computers changed the labor market? Technical report 5956. National Bureau of Economic Research, Cambridge, MA (1997)
15. Falk, M., Biagi, F.: Relative demand for highly skilled workers and use of different ICT technologies. Appl. Econ. **49**(9), 903–914 (2017)
16. Spiezia, V.: Jobs and skills in the digital economy. OECD Observer (2016)
17. Roland Berger Strategy Consultants: The digital transformation of industry: How important is it? Who are the winners? What must be done now? A European study commissioned by the Federation of German Industries (BDI) and conducted by Roland Berger Strategy Consultants (2015)
18. European Comission: The Digital Single Market - State of Play. European Union (2017)
19. Berger, T., Frey, C.B.: Digitalization, jobs and convergence in Europe: strategies for closing the skills gap. Technical report, University of Oxford (2016)
20. Tieto- ja viestintätekniikan ammattilaiset TIVIA ry: Ohjelmisto-osaaminen Suomen talouskasvun ja uudistumisen jarruna – vuonna 2020 Suomesta puuttuu 15 000 ohjelmistoammattilaista (2017). Press release
21. Naumanen, M., et al.: Tekbaro 2017. Tekniikan akateemiset TEK, Helsinki, Finland (2017)
22. Luoma, E., Rönkkö, M., Tahvanainen, S.: Finnish software industry survey 2017 (In Finnish Ohjelmistoyrityskartoitus 2017) (2017). http://www.softwareindustrysurvey.fi/wp-content/uploads/2017/10/Oskari2017-vfinal.pdf. Accessed 23 Jan 2018
23. Rönkkö, M., et al.: National software industry survey 2008: The finnish software industry in 2007. Technical report, Helsinki University of Technology (2008)
24. Haaparanta, P., et al.: 100 vuotta pientä avotaloutta - Suomen ulkomaankaupan kehitys, merkitys ja näkymät. Technical report, Valtioneuvoston selvitys- tutkimustoiminta (2017)
25. Chakravorti, B., Bhalla, A., Chaturvedi, R.S.: 60 countries' digital competitiveness, indexed. Harvard Business Review (2017)
26. Korte, W.B., Hüsing, T., Dashja, E.: High-Tech Leadership Skills for Europe - Towards an Agenda for 2020 and beyond. European Communities (2017)
27. Robinson, H., Segal, J., Sharp, H.: Ethnographically-informed empirical studies of software practice. Inf. Softw. Technol. **49**(6), 540–551 (2007)

Cybersecurity Capability and Capacity Building for South Africa

Joey Jansen van Vuuren[1] and Louise Leenen[2(✉)]

[1] Tshwane University of Technology, Pretoria, South Africa
jansenvanvuurenjc@tut.ac.za
[2] Council for Scientific and Industrial Research, Pretoria, South Africa
lleenen@csir.co.za

Abstract. Cybersecurity capability and innovation cannot be attained by a single party; researchers, government, private industry and academia should join hands and create public-private partnerships to share their knowledge and create solutions. If South Africa wants to be sufficiently equipped to respond to cyber-threats and to ensure growth in the cybersecurity sector, the country needs to strengthen the pipeline of cyber talent and support the development of a cybersecurity workforce. These requirements provide an opportunity for industry, in collaboration with government and academia, to initiate innovative and exciting approaches to establish cybersecurity and a cybersecurity work-force in South Africa. This paper considers measures for governments, business and academia to alleviate the cyber skills shortage, and pay particular attention to the South African case.

Keywords: Cybersecurity workforce · Cybersecurity training
Cybersecurity skills shortage

1 Introduction

A secure cybersecurity environment requires a robust workforce [1]. The current shortage of cybersecurity capability is a worldwide phenomenon resulting in companies and citizens being vulnerable to cyber-threats due to a lack of cybersecurity skills. Cybersecurity attacks are an inevitability [2] and the increasingly complicated threats that change on a daily basis, result in an inability of the insufficient number of qualified cybersecurity professionals to maintain security [3]. Christos Dimitriadis, Systems Audit and Control Association (ISACA) board chair and group director of Information Security for INTRALOT, confirms that due to the increase in cyber-attacks, enterprises need more resources to protect data and are facing a challenge in finding top-flight security practitioners with the necessary skills to do the job [2]. Jim Michaud, director of Human Resources and Business Development at the SysAdmin, Audit, Networking, Security (SANS) Institute, already emphasised this fact in 2015 by stating "Cyberse-curity is the single most important business issue for so many CIOs right now, and the situation is going to get worse before it gets better" [4]. The 2015 Global Cybersecurity Status report, published by ISACA in 2015, indicated that there were already 300 000 unfilled cybersecurity jobs in the US alone and estimated this figure would increase to

1.5 million by 2020 [4]. According to the US Bureau of Labor Statistics, the demand for cybersecurity professionals will grow by 53% during 2018. Industry, governments, academia and non-profit organisations need to work together and focus aggressively on meeting this need [3]. Speculation is that the market for cybersecurity professionals may be growing 12 times faster than the U.S. job market as a whole [5].

The broad scope of the cybersecurity includes policies, standards that requires compliance from the perspective of software engineering and application security, and this is also a contributing factor to the skills shortage as indicated by Jenn Henley, Director of Security for Facebook. [6]. South Africa is still in their infancy in this process; although the National Cybersecurity Policy (NCPF) was approved in 2012 very few of the regulatory frameworks are in place. Cybersecurity education in the country is mostly limited to short courses or specialisation modules in a Masters Degrees.

2   Cybersecurity Skills

2.1   Cybersecurity Skills Shortage

A cybersecurity workforce study by ISACA's Cybersecurity Nexus (CSX) in 2017 showed in cases where companies normally receive between 60 to 250 applications for advertisements for non-cybersecurity positions, only 3% of the surveyed organisations received more than 20 applications for each cybersecurity opening, while 59% received an average of only five applications for each cybersecurity opening. This application rate is even worse if taken into account that 37% of respondents stated fewer than one in four candidates have the qualifications to keep the company secure. It mostly takes six months or longer to fill the advertised position resulting in Europe having one third of their cybersecurity jobs unfilled. Most employers indicated they need candidates with technical skills and practical hands-on experience, resulting in the current emphasis on security certifications [2, 7]. The most difficult jobs to fill are those with additional requirements such as financial skills, and job requiring a security classification take more than 10% to fill [8].

Trevor Halstead of Cybrary (online education and training provider), sums up the critical situation: "We really screwed things up this time. Somehow, we are in a situation where the sector of technology with the greatest potential negative impact on our lives, businesses, governments, peace, safety and security happens to have a severe deficiency of qualified people to fill its jobs," [4].

A lack of awareness of cybersecurity careers contributes to this critical shortage phenomenon; a study by Raytheon and the National Cybersecurity Alliance published in October 2015 indicated 67% of men and 77% of woman in the US and 62% of men and 75% of woman globally, did not receive any counselling in high school or secondary schools on careers in cybersecurity [4]. Jim Michaud from SANS highlights the fact that there is also an underrepresentation of woman in this field [4].

2.2   Cybersecurity Careers

Cybersecurity is a very broad field and can be classified in different categories according to the roles in the corporate environment. For each of these categories different skills, tools and techniques must be identified to advance career paths [6]. The Cybersecurity Skills Gap Analysis (CSGA) report, prepared by the Workforce Intelligence Network for South Michigan, defines four broad cybersecurity occupation categories, each associated with distinct aspects of cybersecurity; frontline cybersecurity, cyber-sensitive service, physical security and access, and indirect cyber-related workers [9].

The framework used by most companies in the US was established by the National Initiative for Cybersecurity Education (NICE), created by the National Institute for Standards and Technology (NIST). This framework provides a common, consistent lexicon that categorises and describes cybersecurity work in terms of seven categories: [9, 10]: Securely Provision, Operate and Maintain, Oversee and Govern, Protect and Defend, Analyse, Operate and Collect, and Investigate.

The CSGA report indicates the top cybersecurity occupations in demand in the US are cybersecurity analyst/specialists, cybersecurity engineer, auditors, network engineers/architects, and software developers [9, 10]. These occupations include the high-value skills that are in critically short supply, with the most scarce being intrusion detection, secure software development, and attack mitigation [1]. The largest number of postings (232,552) were part of the "Operate and maintain" category. The importance of the conceptualisation and the design of secure systems is reflected in the listings for "Securely Provision". The third most in demand skills are in the "Analyse" category [9, 10].

The majority (89%) of cybersecurity job positions require a bachelor's degree or higher [9]. The report of Intel Security, in partnership with McAfee, indicated that about half of the surveyed companies prefer at least a bachelor's degree in a relevant technical area to enter the cybersecurity field [1]. Computer science, engineering, management information systems, information technology, and business administration were the most prominent fields of study. The most common certifications required for frontline cybersecurity workers were Certified Information Systems Security Professional (CISSP), SANS/GIAC certification, and certified systems auditor. There is also a high demand for cybersecurity in the defence industry (more than 10% of advertised position [11]) and therefore many postings required a security clearance [9].

2.3   Cybersecurity Professionals Requirements

Van Zadelhoff, [12] argues one of the main reasons for the critical shortage is that security businesses tend to recruit job candidates with traditional technology credentials, for example, college degrees. IBM's response to the shortage is to create "new collar jobs" where skills, knowledge and a willingness to learn is given priority over degrees. Cutting-edge technology, such as Artificial Intelligence (AI), is core in these jobs. AI not only provides a way to help overcome the skills shortage, but is also a step forward in the way employees will work and companies will defend themselves. AI is currently used to gather and correlate the insights from a huge number of sources which can be used by security professionals to extract relevant information. Companies are already using IBM's Watson for Cyber Security to connect obscure data points humans cannot possibly identify on their own, enabling employees to find security threats 60 times faster than manual investigations [12].

The National Initiative for Cybersecurity Education for cybersecurity professionals identify cybersecurity workload and workforce requirements [13]. The best candidates and professionals possess a solid mix of business, communication and technical skills [3]. Loeb also suggests new pathways, other than degrees, to widen the talent pipeline. Soft and technical skills are equally important for the cybersecurity practitioner; the inadequacy of the normal science and engineering training has been expressed and there is presently an impetus to expand cybersecurity education. Cybersecurity education must be addressed and deployed more rapidly and more widely than Science, Engineering and Technology Education [14].

3 Cybersecurity Capability and Capacity Building

3.1 Government and Education

The International Telecommunications Union (ITU) conducted a survey, the Global Cybersecurity Index (GCI), providing insight into the cybersecurity engagement of sovereign nation states and showing the commitment of countries towards cybersecurity. Their methodology uses a cyber maturity metric to assess the various facets of nations' cyber capabilities [15, 16].

According to the GCI, the five most advanced countries are those listed in Table 1, and the top five African countries are listed in Table 2. Detailed information on Tunisia is not provided in the report, and Egypt and Tunisia were included in the Arab region.

Table 1. Global security index 2017. Top five most committed countries [16]

Country	GCI Score	Legal	Technical	Organi-zational	Capacity Building	Cooper-ation
Singapore	0.92	0.95	0.96	0.88	**0.97**	0.87
United States	0.91	1	0.96	0.92	1	0.73
Malaysia	0.89	0.87	0.96	0.77	1	0.87
Oman	0.87	0.98	0.82	0.85	0.95	0.75
Mauritius	0.82	0.85	0.96	0.74	0.91	0.70

Table 2. Global cybersecurity index 2017 top five most committed african countries [16]

Country	GCI Score	Legal	Technical	Organi-zational	Capacity Building	Cooper-ation
Mauritius	0.83	0.85	0.96	0.74	0.91	0.7
Egypt	0.77	0.92	0.92	0.4	0.92	0.7
Rwanda	0.6	0.6	0.71	0.79	0.66	0.28
Tunisia	0.59					
Kenya	0.57	0.75	0.73	0.36	0.41	0.6

To determine the Capacity Building measurements, countries were evaluated on standardisation bodies, cybersecurity good practices, R&D programs, public awareness campaigns. professional training courses, national education programs and academic curricula, incentive mechanisms and the home grown cybersecurity industry [16]. These results are given in Tables 3 and 4 - the level of commitment ranges from the highest (green/dark grey) to the lowest (light red/grey).

Table 3. Top five countries in the World - Global Cybersecurity Index for Capacity building,

	Score	Global Rank	Standardisation bodies	Cyber-security good practices	R&D programmes	Public Awareness campaigns	Professional Training Courses	Educational pro-grammes	Incentive mecha-nisms	Home-Grown in-dustry	CAPACITY BUILDING
Singapore	0.078	145									
United States	0.432	67									
Malaysia	0.069	148									
Oman	0.430	68									
Mauritius	0.83	6									

The CGI shows governments across the globe initiated several programs to alleviate cybersecurity shortages. However, in a study by the research firm Vanson Bourne, all 775 respondents indicated cybersecurity education was deficient and 76% indicated that their government was not investing enough in cybersecurity talent [1]. The key

Table 4. Top five countries in Africa - Global Cybersecurity Index for Capacity building

	Score	Global Rank	Standardisation bodies	Cyber-security good practices	R&D programmes	Public Awareness campaigns	Professional Training Courses	Educational programmes	Incentive mechanisms	Home-Grown industry	CAPACITY BUILDING
Mauritius	0.83	6									
Egypt	0.772	14									
Rwanda	0.602	36									
Tunisia	0.591	40									
Kenya	0.574	45									

success factor is the availability of cybersecurity education for individuals in the pipeline and the workforce; therefore the adaptation of training programs to include cybersecurity content and the development of new cybersecurity qualifications are vital factors. The Australian minister of education announced that the government will invest $4.5 million in Cybersecurity education centres to enhance cybersecurity careers. Theses Academic Centres of Cybersecurity in Australia have the aim to enhance cybersecurity research and produce work-ready graduates. Survey results in Australia has shown that two thirds of Australian young adults have never discussed a career in cybersecurity in the high school [17]. The Department of Energy in the US indicated that they will also provide $25 million for cybersecurity education.

Current research shows that most educational institutions do not prepare students for a career in cybersecurity [1, 17, 18]. Exposure to cybersecurity careers is crucial for the development of interest in the field. Education, including practical hands-on training in cybersecurity, must start at an early age (in school) and target a diverse range of students. These programs, which should also be available at universities, will create awareness of potential cybersecurity careers and can also identify promising recruits for cybersecurity professions. It is important to generate interest and enthusiasm among people with the skills, knowledge, and aptitude to fill cyber positions [14]. Currently curricula is not updated fast enough due to staffing difficulties, lack of budget and politics. Universities must be enabled to set up their students with tools to be successful Cybersecurity practitioners [18]. Universities must work with industry and government to tailor curricula that include practical training. These potential partnerships can leverage private sector talent in training teachers, enhancing curricula, and in offering internship and training opportunities to talented high school and university students, and can be mutually beneficial [1]. Cybersecurity curricula have to follow an integrated and multidisciplinary approach with emphasis not only on technology but also on the role of humans, processes, organisations and governance. Curricula for cross-cutting cybersecurity curricula must be developed that will introduce core principles, such as threat awareness and planning; cybercrime and computer forensics; security practices and principles; safety, privacy and ethics; and online interaction.

Although university degrees are necessary, additional pathways are required to widen the pipeline [1]. Businesses to start investing in both short courses and formal qualifications for the development of cybersecurity skills.

Research is an essential part of the cyber environment. Collaboration between industry, research institutions and universities can establish interdisciplinary faculty teams to conduct projects with the goal of developing university-industry relationships and create a platform to access larger-scale industry and government research funding. It can initiate dialogue between industry members and academic members about future cyber security threats and workforce requirements in order to develop new content for cyber security education.

Competitions are a critical part of cyber education. Companies expect proof of cybersecurity skills; in the case of cyber, skills are best built in lab environments where individuals can respond to real threat scenarios. "When you're protecting the data for thousands, or perhaps millions, of individuals, "learning on the job" just won't cut it anymore" [3]. The social and gaming aspects of cyber competitions are particularly compelling to the youth and is a valuable tool in cyber workforce development. During these games, both offensive and defensive skills are used in a sandboxed environment (real world) with no influence on the company or online systems. In addition, participants learn the soft skills of leadership, communication, critical/analytic thinking, teamwork, and creativity that are desirable characteristics in a cybersecurity role. Recruiters sometimes observe candidates during these games and candidates with these skills often get job during the competitions [14]. Jessica Gulick, CEO of Katzcy Consulting, emphasised this point by stating: "Cyber games train us to know what we're looking for, as well as how best to respond. By developing cyber teams that compete in games like sports teams do, we can establish a code of ethics and a non-military approach focused on collaboration and strategy that will create the workforce we need for the future." [6].

Imprecise job descriptions and the lack of metrics to assess skills complicate the recruitment process for cybersecurity jobs. There is often a mismatch between job descriptions and actual duties that creates unhappiness in the workforce [1]. Although the US has provided the NIST Cybersecurity Workforce Framework, most job descriptions in other countries are not yet standardised across the public and private sectors [1].

Government should consider collaboration with the private sector to enhance training opportunities for students. These programs include bursaries for potential students, private sector internships, and co-operative education programs for university students studying in science and technology [1]. Raising awareness and formal studies will increase the number of trained people, but it will take some time to have an effect. People in mid-career from other fields can be converted through assessment tools and offered training [14]. Training programs must be developed on a national level to address the need, and they should engage a diverse workforce, including women and veterans, and offer flexible working conditions [14]. The CSIS study has shown the lack of minorities in cybersecurity occupations. The workforce can also be expanded by increasing the number of working visas in this field [1].

3.2 Business

In a future world where cutting-edge technology is at its core, businesses need to change their approach in order to accommodate the new cyber-related jobs. Companies need to be strategic in deciding what skills will be needed to combat future cybersecurity threats and how new technologies can offset workforce shortages. To accomplish the shift from knowledge-based learning to skills-based training, organisations need to invest in their workforce. Although this type of training is expensive, the outcome of such investment will be experienced cybersecurity professionals [3]. Companies interested in adopting a "new collar" approach to fill security positions should consider the following:

- Re-examine their workforce strategy, identify the skills needed, and where those skills can be sourced from. This will also influence future recruitment processes [12].
- Start robust support programs for new employees that can include mentorships and the shadowing of experienced cybersecurity employees. Expose new employees to varied projects to broaden their cybersecurity knowledge. This support can include advice about expectations in the industry, cybersecurity roles, work shadowing skills requirements and other training opportunities [12].
- Groom employees with tangential skills—such as application specialists and network specialists—to move into cybersecurity positions. Creating such career paths can be a solid investment, as it can be cheaper to fill the gaps and enhance employee morale [2].
- Redefine minimum credentials for entry-level cybersecurity jobs by relaxing degree qualification requirements and accept non-traditional types of education (certifications) since universities do not currently offer sufficient cybersecurity programs [1]. Open additional pathways to cybersecurity careers to widen the talent. Despite the stigma attached to hacking, employers can consider employing previous hackers [1].
- Focus on continuous learning and upskilling the current workforce because cybersecurity is a highly dynamic field that requires ongoing education and exploration. Many new professionals lack the necessary skills and even proficient workers will require continuous skill development. Employers are increasingly providing on-the-job training [1].
- Retain employees by keeping them informed through classes, certifications, and conferences. Employees may reluctant to enroll employees for expensive training courses because they may be recruited by other companies. However, the absence of training is often a significant factor in a decision to seek alternative employment [1]. Studies show substantially more women leave the field early than men [3]. Create a culture of talent maximisation to retain staff. Even when budgets are tight, initiatives such as alternative work arrangements, investment in personnel growth and technical competency, and job rotation help to round out skills and minimise frustration with repetitive (but necessary) tasks. Invest in performance-based mechanisms for hiring and retention processes [2].

- Employers should grow skills in response to anticipated needs, including automation of some functions from "human in the loop" to "human on the loop" processes, to reduce the current the burden on existing cybersecurity staff. Although automation cannot replace the human judgement, cybersecurity staff must adapt their skills to this increasing automated environments and focus their time and talent on the more advanced threats that require human intervention [1]. Automation of operational security tasks can decrease the overall burden on staff. AI provides employees with more intelligence and contextual recommendations at a speed and scale previously unimagined, so upskilling your workforce is now a completely different ballgame [12].
- Practical skills for cybersecurity can be enhanced through cybersecurity exercises. These exercises can be developed to simulate real-life cyber situations where participants will gain insight into the causes of the cyber-attacks and the effects and recovery after a cyber-attack.
- Business can support cybersecurity career development by building a local cybersecurity ecosystem and influencing early career thinking of young cybersecurity talent. Business must connect with government organisations, educational institutions, and other groups; they can contribute ideas to teachers about topics and activities to include in the curriculum, sponsor Capture the Flag security events, and work with schools to generate interest in the field. These groups are always looking for willing experts and mentors [12]. Engagement with and cultivation of students and career changers are encouraged and can done through university outreach or internship programs [2].

There are many benefits for business to become involved in cybersecurity career development, even from efforts focused on the development of national Capabilities and capacity:

- Employers that participate in cybersecurity collaborations will have increased visibility and enhance their profile and reputation amongst learners and parents. Their interactions with educational institutions will promote cybersecurity as a socially responsible profession. Investment in new talent will also contribute to the building of links between businesses and universities.
- During the development of young peoples' skills, knowledge and understanding of applications in the real world, business can tap into the creative thinking of young people.
- Employers can get early access to promising technology graduates with the required skills by engaging with potential recruits early in their degrees and potentially save on graduate recruitment costs.
- Engagement in outreach activities will provide career development opportunities for their cybersecurity employees e.g. communication, planning and presentation skills.
- By providing internships, cybersecurity employers can help shape the skill of future cybersecurity professionals, get a head start in recruiting the most motivated students, bring enthusiasm and a fresh approach to their business, and create a cost effective way to add additional resources to a team. After the internship period, employers can recruit interns for who are already up-to-speed with the business.

3.3   South Africa

South Africa is not an exception in this skills shortage phenomenon; there is only a small pool of experienced cybersecurity professionals and local businesses compete for those skills. If the country aims to be equipped to respond to cyber-threats and have a growing cybersecurity sector, it needs to strengthen the pipeline of cyber talent and help to prepare students for entry-level security career opportunities. This a specific opportunity for industry to work with the education sector and the government in order to adopt an innovative and exciting approach to teaching cybersecurity skills and creating learning materials on topics such as developing safe and secure software.

The Cybersecurity Centre of Innovation (CCOI), recently established by the Council of Scientific and Industrial Research (CSIR) follows an integrated and multidisciplinary approach to the challenge of cybersecurity capability and capacity building, with an emphasis not only on technology but also on the role of humans, processes, organisations and governance. Several workshops were held to support higher education institutions to develop new cybersecurity qualifications. However, the development of a cybersecurity capability for South Africa cannot be attained by a single party. Researchers, government, industry, the private sector and academia should join forces and create public-private partnerships to share their knowledge and support the development.

Schools

Government and business can influence the early career thinking of potential young cybersecurity talent and learning in schools. School children should be inspired to follow cybersecurity careers to contribute to a robust pipeline for universities, Technical and Vocational Education and Training (TVET) colleges and new entrants to the industry. Cyber professional can influence learners and challenge stereotypes about the cybersecurity career paths of skilled people. Curricula for cyber science that introduce the core principles such as threat awareness and planning, cybercrime and computer forensics, security practices and principles, safety, privacy and ethics, and online interaction, must be developed.

Business can support workshops or cyber camps for school learners where cybersecurity experts can teach students about cybersecurity threats and defences. These workshops should include cross curricular concepts e.g. the law and use resources such as board games, mobile apps and online games to maintain excitement. Cybersecurity exercises can be developed to simulate real life cyber situations where practical experience can be gained on the causes of the cyber-attacks, and the effects and recovery after a cyber-attack, and professionals can support the content with examples of real-life scenarios. The CSIR is already collaborating with universities on conducting cybersecurity games.

Cybersecurity professionals and employers can also support mentoring programs for teachers and the development of teaching resources. In addition, a cyber-aware accreditation pathway can be created for teachers and children. Information on the role of cybersecurity professionals in an organisations, the remuneration for these careers and both technical and non-technical career paths can be included.

Higher Education

Currently, Information Security in South Africa are mostly offered via short courses, or specialisation modules in Masters Degrees. New cybersecurity education opportunities must be created in the higher education sector to develop capacity and capability; cross-curricular concepts in cybersecurity modules and subjects in current qualifications, and the development of new focused cybersecurity qualifications. Programmes must be adapted to include new educational approaches including online courses and collaborative environments for cyber education. One of the reasons for the absence of formal qualifications at universities, is the lack of infrastructure and resources (teaching and research). Exchange programs for lecturers, researchers and students can enhance such capacity development and will support the development of these new degree and diploma programs in cybersecurity.

Business

There must be collaboration between industry, universities and government to build a sustainable knowledge-based workforce that support the needs of government, industry, and academia. The active engagement of businesses in research as part of the CCOI, will build a trusted relationship between them and higher education researchers that can solve their needs and, over time, enable ideas and techniques from the academic domain to be applied to industrially relevant problems in cybersecurity with the benefit of prompt exploitation of high quality cybersecurity research. Businesses can fund research projects in the CCOI, donate facilities to universities to accelerate innovation and support two-way secondments between university and academia.

The Network Emulation and Simulation Laboratory (NESL) is a simulation and emulation environment that is used for online emulation and simulation of networks and the testing of cybersecurity software and equipment developed by the CSIR. This platform can be used by companies to run cyber exercises for their cybersecurity employees. It is important that cybersecurity professionals from industry support these initiatives with examples of real-life scenarios that will ensure relevance and attractiveness of educational resources.

It is widely recognised that there is a need for a closer working relationship between academia and businesses in order to make educators aware of the developments in cybersecurity. Such collaboration will ensure that both undergraduate and postgraduate degrees meet business needs and help universities to develop programs that are directly linked to the knowledge and skills that cybersecurity jobs require. The courses should provide a strong foundation of cybersecurity knowledge but must also build hands-on skills [3]. Courses at TVET colleges can include first level technician programs for constant monitoring of a company's devices and systems to detect and deal with any security weaknesses.

Industry should support higher education institutions with curriculum development and other training processes (e.g. workshops), employers can get early access to promising technology graduates with the skills they want by engaging with potential recruits early in their degrees and potentially save on graduate recruitment costs. In addition, industry can support the development students' skills, knowledge and understanding of applications in the real world. Cybersecurity professionals can contribute ideas to lecturers about topics and activities to include in the curriculum.

Provision must also be made for bursaries, studentships and internships. The internships should be between 6 and 12 months in duration, and suitable either for undergraduates taking IT-related degrees, or for recent graduates. To make the most of internships, employers must have meaningful work for an intern to do, be willing to provide support such as a line manager.

4   Conclusion

This paper considers various actions required to build capability and capacity for cybersecurity in South Africa in addition to a discussion of the obstacles that have to be overcome to achieve this goal. The critical cybersecurity skills shortage is a global problem and South Africa is no exception. This paper considers measures for governments, business and academia to alleviate the shortage, and pay particular attention to the South African case.

To ensure a larger and more diverse cybersecurity workforce, countries need to develop critical technical skills, cultivate a more diverse workforce, and reform education and training programs. The results of the Global Cybersecurity Index imply that South Africa needs to enhance their commitment to cybersecurity capability development. There is a role for government, business and academia in the development of the required capabilities. Universities and colleges must be supported to initiate new cybersecurity qualifications. It is also important to enhance the role of businesses in capability building initiatives such as the participation in cybersecurity awareness in schools as well as be involvement in the career choices of young people. Businesses can support the development of curricula to also include information on the latest threats and attacks. The implementation of cybersecurity exercises gives opportunities of hand-on learning and can enhance interest in these careers. In addition, business can sponsor bursaries and support internships.

Cybersecurity is a complex career field with extraordinarily challenging problems, but with a diverse pool of experiences and ideas, we stand a much greater chance of successfully defending our assets.

References

1. Intel Security, in partnership with the Center for Strategic and International Studies. https://www.csis.org/programs/technology-policy-program/cybersecurity-and-warfare/other-projects-cybersecurity-0
2. HelpNetSecurity.   https://www.helpnetsecurity.com/2017/02/13/cyber-security-skills-gap-tips/
3. Media Planet future of Business and Tech. http://www.futureofbusinessandtech.com/online-and-mobile-safety/5-steps-to-closing-the-cybersecurity-skills-gap
4. CIO. https://www.cio.com/article/3005637/cyber-attacks-espionage/closing-the-cybersecurity-talent-gap-one-woman-at-a-time.html
5. TREND MICRO. https://blog.trendmicro.com/the-challenges-of-cyber-security-education-and-training-in-2015/

6. Ricci, M., Gulick, J.: Cybersecurity games: building tomorrow's workforce. J. Law Cyber Warfare **5**, 183 (2017)
7. ISACA. http://www.isaca.org/cyber/Documents/CSX-General-Awareness-Brochure_Bro_Eng_0816.pdf
8. http://fortifyexperts.com/employment-trends/cybersecurity-employment-trends/
9. https://winintelligence.org/wp-content/uploads/2017/07/FINAL-Cybersecurity-Skills-Gap-2017-Web-1.pdf
10. National Initiative for Cybersecurity Careers and Studies, Department of Homeland Security. https://niccs.us-cert.gov/nice-cybersecurity-workforce-framework-work-roles
11. Burning Glass Technologies. burning-glass.com/wp-content/uploads/Cybersecurity_Jobs_Report_2015.pdf
12. Harvard Business Review. https://hbr.org/2017/05/cybersecurity-has-a-serious-talent-shortage-heres-how-to-fix-it
13. NICE: Best Practices for Planning a Cybersecurity Workforce White Paper. In: Security, H. (ed.) (2014)
14. Katchy Consulting: Cybersecurity games: Building tomorrow's workforce. In: NIST (ed.) (2016)
15. International Telecommunications Union (ITU). https://www.itu.int/en/ITU-D/Cybersecurity/Documents/2017_Index_of_Indices.pdf
16. International Telecommunication Union. https://www.itu.int/dms_pub/itu-d/opb/str/D-STR-GCI.01-2017-PDF-E.pdf
17. ZDNeT. https://www.zdnet.com/article/australia-to-spend-au4-5m-on-cybersecurity-education-centres/
18. CIO. https://www.cio.com/article/3060813/it-skills-training/top-u-s-universities-failing-at-cybersecurity-education.html

Team Feedback Intervention and Team Learning in Virtual Teams: A Moderated Mediation Model of Team Cohesion and Personality

Jesús Sánchez[1] (iD), Ana Zornoza[1] (iD), Virginia Orengo[1] (iD),
Vicente Peñarroja[2] (iD), and Petros Chamakiotis[3](✉) (iD)

[1] Universitat de València, Avenida Blasco Ibáñez 21, 46010 Valencia, Spain
[2] Universitat Autònoma de Barcelona,
Campus de Bellaterra, 08193 Barcelona, Spain
[3] University of Sussex, Brighton BN1 9SL, UK
P.Chamakiotis@sussex.ac.uk

Abstract. Scholars and practitioners agree that virtual teams (VTs) have become commonplace in today's digital workplace. Relevant literature argues that learning constitutes a significant contributor to team member satisfaction and performance, and that, at least in face-to-face teams, team cohesion fosters team learning. Given the additional challenges VTs face, e.g. geographical dispersion, which are likely to have a negative influence on cohesion, in this paper we shed light on the relationship between team cohesion and team learning. We adopted a quantitative approach and studied 54 VTs in our quest to understand the role of feedback in mediating this relationship and, more specifically, the role of personality traits in moderating the indirect effect of team feedback and guided reflection intervention on team learning through team cohesion within the VT context. Our findings highlight the importance of considering aspects related to the team composition when devising intervention strategies for VTs, and provide empirical support for an interactionist model between personality and emergent states such as cohesion. Implications for theory and practice are also discussed.

Keywords: Virtual teams · Team cohesion · Team learning
Computer-mediated communication

1 Introduction

Today's organizations rely extensively on virtual teams (VTs) supported by rapid technological advancements and globalization [1]. These teams have become an essential mechanism in the creation of valuable knowledge and learning in modern organizations. In addition, learning is an important process that helps teams and organizations to adapt to the ever-changing environment and achieve their goals [2, 3]. Thus, the present study focuses on learning at the team level, and team learning (TL) is conceptualized as a process of adapting to change that leads to enhanced understanding

© IFIP International Federation for Information Processing 2018
Published by Springer Nature Switzerland AG 2018. All Rights Reserved
D. Kreps et al. (Eds.): HCC13 2018, IFIP AICT 537, pp. 136–148, 2018.
https://doi.org/10.1007/978-3-319-99605-9_10

or improved performance in teams [4]. Likewise, it helps team members to build and maintain a mutually shared cognition that increases perceived team performance [5]. Ortega et al. [6] highlighted that TL is a vital aspect in VTs, showing that it fosters satisfaction, team viability, and performance. TL is a social process that emerges through team members' interactions, which are influenced by beliefs about the team's interpersonal context [3]. In this context, the present study focuses on team cohesion, which has been found to foster TL in face-to-face teams "by increasing the motivation, trust, and cognitive familiarity for productive inquiry" [7].

VTs have some advantages, like the possibility to overcome geographical, temporal and organizational barriers, which facilitates the inclusion of members with diverse skills and knowledge [8]. However, VTs' characteristics pose several challenges to learning. For example, these teams might experience an increased difficulty to build a shared understanding [9], take longer time to reach an agreement [10], and experience difficulties in information processing [11]. Furthermore, some authors consider that in teams with high virtuality it might be difficult to develop ties between members, which can hinder the development of relational processes, emergent states, and negatively influence performance and collaboration [12]. Consequently, technological mediation has been found to have a negative impact on cohesiveness, affecting interpersonal and normative bonds in VTs [12]. Consequently, some authors point out that training interventions may be a viable strategy to overcome these challenges [13]. Following this logic, we developed a team feedback intervention which includes a period of reflection, to examine how to improve team cohesion and learning in virtual teams. In this intervention, after receiving process and results feedback, the teams engaged in a period of joint reflection. Furthermore, taking into consideration that team cohesion emerges from the social interactions between team members, it is necessary to ponder how the composition of the team, concretely deep-level composition characteristics like the personality of the team, can play a relevant role in this relationship [13–15].

In sum, the present study aims to investigate a moderated mediation model in which team personality moderates the indirect effect of team feedback on team learning through team cohesion in virtual teams.

1.1 Team Cohesion and Learning in Virtual Teams

Identifying the conditions that promote TL has been a significant area of study during the last decade, emphasizing the importance of several emergent states in the development of TL [4, 5]. Following Van den Bossche et al. [3] team cohesion is a relevant factor for team learning. Previous research has found that cohesive teams tend to display greater team mental model convergence and enhanced collaboration, communication, and trust, creating an environment that facilitates TL [2, 5]. In this study, team cohesion is conceptualized as team members' tendency to stay together because of positive relationships with other members and shared commitment to the team's task [15, 16].

However, despite the importance of team cohesion in facilitating TL, to our knowledge, research about this relationship in VTs is scarce [3]. In general, VTs face challenges that interfere with the creation of a positive social atmosphere and strong relationships among team members [1]. Following the Media Richnness Theory, computer-mediated communication (CMC) is less rich and hinders the development of relationships, group cohesion, and problem solving during the initial stages of the team [17]. In virtual settings, cohesion needs more time to develop [18], and is more difficult due to the lack of information [12]. However, VTs that receive training based on feedback and collective reflection have been found to display greater cohesion and collaborate in a more constructive way [19–21].

1.2   The Effect of a Team Feedback and Reflection-Based Intervention

Lacerenza and collaborators [13] stated that organizations can facilitate success in VTs through training, and called for research on training strategies in VT. The present paper proposes a training intervention based on feedback and guided reflection as a strategy to improve a VT's learning and cohesion [20, 22]. Team feedback consists of information provided by an external agent about previous actions, events, processes, and behaviors related to the task and the team's functioning [20]. Previous research suggests that providing feedback to teams has a positive impact on team cohesion [19]. Concretely, teams that receive feedback spend time discussing their reactions to the feedback and how to improve the team's functioning, and they work toward establishing the team's goals [19]. Furthermore, a period of guided collective reflection may help team members to change their teamwork by uncovering ways to improve and clarifying misunderstandings [20, 23].

Following the Social Information Processing theory, Burke and collaborators [17] found that cohesion in computer-mediated communication environments is lower than in face-to-face teams and develops over time. Moreover, they found that, as members share and discuss information and their opinions converge, they experience increased cohesion [17], which can be facilitated by feedback and guided reflection intervention. In this vein, Villado and Arthur [21] conducted a study comparing teams that carried out "After Action Reviews" (AAR) with teams that did not. Their results suggested that setting goals collaboratively, reviewing and discussing strategies and behaviors to improve performance, facilitated the emergence of team cohesion [21]. Furthermore, Gabelica and collaborators [20] pointed out that team feedback followed by guided group reflection helps teams to process the feedback, improving performance and learning in face-to-face teams. Therefore, based on the previous rationale, we propose the first hypothesis:

Hypothesis 1: Team feedback and guided reflection will have a positive indirect effect on TL via team cohesion in VTs.

1.3   The Role of Team Personality

Furthermore, the impact of interventions on team processes and emergent states might be influenced by the team's composition [13, 24]. Some authors highlight that the personality of team members can alter relational patterns during teamwork and the way the team adapts to changes [14]. This can modify the relationship between the team feedback and guided reflection intervention and team cohesion [25, 26]. However, the interactive effects of more profound team composition characteristics like personality on team processes have seldom been studied in VTs [1, 24, 27]. In the context of the present research, team personality is understood as the average team level of two relevant personality traits [15, 27, 28]. The question addressed in this study is how team personality traits influence the effect of a team feedback and guided reflection intervention on TL, via team cohesion, in VTs.

The present study focuses on two personality traits, openness to experience and agreeableness, which influence the development of team cohesion and TL on highly interactive tasks [29]. First, openness to experience is defined as the tendency to be open-minded, flexible, imaginative, and curious [30]. High openness to experience indicates a tendency to not avoid conflict and to try to solve problems collaboratively by seeking alternative solutions [27]. Furthermore, open individuals are more helpful when interacting in a team context, and they have positive attitudes toward minorities [27]. Therefore, teams with high scores on openness are considered more adaptable and open to experiencing new things and collaborating [31]. Openness also facilitates team adaptation and the generation of alternatives and testing of new ideas [14]. These characteristics might help to develop cohesion in teams that receive and review feedback collectively and collaboratively, whereas their absence could hinder this process. Second, agreeableness is defined as a tendency to be good-natured, friendly, cooperative, modest, and tolerant [30]. Individuals with high agreeableness often look for ways to achieve the team's goals, even if they are in conflict with their own goals [15]. In teams with high agreeableness, members try to engage in positive interpersonal processes, maintain social harmony, and reduce within-group competition [32]. By contrast, teams low in agreeableness tend to be argumentative, inflexible, uncooperative, intolerant, and disagreeable, thus displaying lower teamwork [32]. According to McGrath [33], when team members' opinions converge, they experience increased cohesion. Hence, when teams engage in a feedback review process, high agreeableness might help them to develop team cohesion through consensus and agreement.

Therefore, we propose a moderated mediation model where team personality traits (openness to experience and agreeableness) moderate the indirect effect of a team feedback and guided reflection intervention on TL through team cohesion, using a moderated mediational model, in VTs. Figure 1 presents the research model. Consequently, we propose the following two hypotheses:

Hypothesis 2: The indirect effect of team feedback with reflection on team learning via team cohesion will be moderated by openness to experience.

Hypothesis 3: The indirect effect of team feedback with reflection on team learning via team cohesion will be moderated by agreeableness.

2 Method

2.1 Sample

The sample was composed of 212 students enrolled in an Organizational Psychology course at a Spanish University. Gender distribution was 169 females and 43 males, with an average age of 23.91 years (SD = 4.38). Participants were randomly assigned

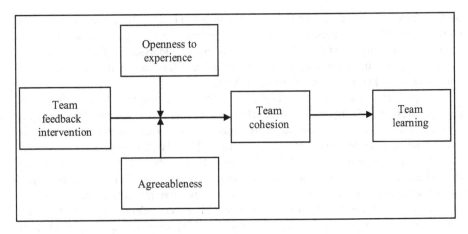

Fig. 1. Research model.

to teams of four members, taking into account the gender balance and maintaining the existing proportion of men to women among the population in the School of Psychology (there are three females and one male on each team). This process resulted in 54 participating teams. Participation in this experiment was voluntary, and it was an alternative way to complete the practical classes in the course.

2.2 Procedure

A laboratory experimental study was designed to test the hypotheses of this study. Teams were randomly assigned to either the experimental (twenty-eight teams) or control (twenty-six teams) condition. The two conditions were equal, except that the experimental teams received feedback. Each team attended the laboratory for three weeks, carrying out one work session each week. Participants attended an informative meeting where they signed a contract declaring their commitment to participating in the experiment, which included a norm stating that the participants were not allowed to meet their teammates outside the laboratory during the experiment. This was controlled by checking the chat logs created during the work sessions.

The tasks used were decision-making tasks and correspond to quadrant 2 of Argote and McGrath's [34] circumflex model, where the objective is to select a response proposed by the team, and the level of interdependence between team members is high. These tasks are suitable for delivering outcome and process feedback. The team feedback manipulation is described below.

During sessions 1 and 2, teams performed two decision-making tasks with a correct answer provided by experts (intellective tasks), "Lost at sea" [35] and "Wildfire" [36], making it possible to deliver team performance feedback.

During session 3, teams performed a decision task simulating a business environment, increasing the possibility of generalizing the results to real project teams. Teams had to select and arrange three human resources services from a pool of 12 possible services distributed among team members. After each session, participants completed an electronic questionnaire with the measures used in this study.

All teams worked in a virtual setting using synchronous CMC via Microsoft Groove 2007. In fact, each participant worked in a separate room at a workstation, and they were not informed of the team composition. This program features several tools (chat, whiteboard, notepad, shared workspace) that allow teams to work and share using the computer. During the informative meeting, all participants were briefly instructed in the use of this specific program for 15 min.

2.3 Team Feedback and Guided Reflection Intervention

A team feedback and guided reflection intervention was carried out in session 1 and session 2. It was based on the delivery of outcome and process feedback and a subsequent reflection period about it.

Teams received outcome feedback about the quality of the decision reached by each team and its members. The researcher acted as an instructor, guiding the team in understanding the feedback. The main requirements to solve these tasks consist of analyzing the situation, combining the individual contributions adequately, and developing an effective communication process.

In this vein, process feedback was based on individual and group perceptions of the interaction process developed while completing the tasks. These perceptions were collected through a checklist proposed in the studies by Warkentin and Beranek [37] and Beranek and Martz [38]. Team members rated several items on a 5-point scale. This information was summarized on a graph representing the levels of these perceptions. The core group processes included were: planning (e.g., "At the beginning of the team interaction, we defined the goals"), coordination (e.g., "We established a sequence to take turns speaking"), written communication strategies (e.g., "Team members used short, direct sentences to communicate"), information sharing management (e.g., "Team members shared their information and knowledge"), and socioemotional processes (e.g., "Team members relied on other team members to solve any problems arising during the interaction"). The instructor acted as a coach by helping the team to analyze its results.

Next, the instructor asked the team to discuss their strengths and weaknesses to design strategies to improve their efficacy in future sessions. Figure 2 shows the procedure for experimental and control teams.

2.4 Measures

Team personality traits were measured with items from Caprara, Barbaranelli and Borgogni [39], using a 5-point Likert scale from "Very low" (1) to "Very High" (5). Data were aggregated at the team level for each trait by calculating the mean for each team. Personality traits are not a shared property of the team, and team members' scores are not expected to coalesce; therefore, the calculation of aggregation indices and interrater agreement statistics is not necessary [28].

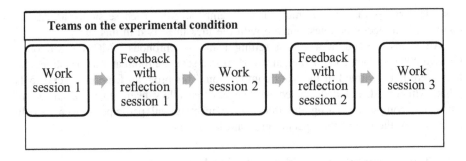

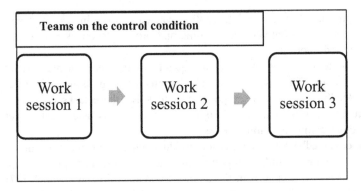

Fig. 2. Procedure for experimental and control teams.

Openness to experience: This variable was measured with 3 items. An example of an openness to experience item was "I am a person who always looks for new experiences". Cronbach's alpha for the aggregated scores was .70.

Agreeableness: This variable was measured using 5 items. An example of an agreeableness item was "I am convinced that I can obtain better results by cooperating with others rather than competing". Cronbach's alpha for the aggregated scores was .71.

Team cohesion: This variable was measured by 4 items taken from Karn et al. [40], after work session 2, once the team had received feedback. An example of an item was "To what extent are individuals in your project team helpful to you in getting your work done?". The items were measured on a 5-point Likert scale from "Not at all" (1) to "A lot" (5). Aggregation at the team level was justified, as we obtained the following results: the mean of the $AD_{M_{(j)}}$ was .43 (SD = .24); ICC (1) was .22; and the ANOVA was statistically significant (F(53, 158) = 2.10; p < .01). Furthermore, Cronbach's alpha for the aggregated scores was .83.

Team Learning: This variable was measured by five items taken from Edmondson [4], after working session 1 and session 3. An example of an item was: "This team regularly takes time to figure out ways to improve its work performance". The items were measured on a 5-point Likert scale from "I strongly disagree" (1) to "I strongly agree" (5). Data were aggregated at the team level. For session 1, aggregation was justified, as we obtained the following results: the mean of the $AD_{M_{(j)}}$ was .59

(SD = .30); ICC (1) was .15; and the ANOVA was statistically significant (F(53, 158) = 1.72; p < .01). Cronbach's alpha for the aggregated scores was .83. For session 3, aggregation was justified, as we obtained the following results: the mean of the $AD_{M_{(j)}}$ was .51 (SD = .25); ICC (1) was .21; and the ANOVA was statistically significant (F(53, 158) = 2.06; p < .01). Furthermore, Cronbach's alpha for the aggregated scores was .86.

3 Results

3.1 Preliminary Analyses

Descriptive statistics and correlations were calculated for all the variables in this study and shown in Table 1.

Table 1. Descriptive statistics and correlations.

Variable	M	SD	1	2	3	4	5
1. Openness to experience	3.28	.38	–				
2. Agreeableness	3.84	.36	.00	–			
3. Team cohesion S2	3.92	.39	.38**	−.14	–		
4. Team learning S1	2.86	.42	−.23	.07	.16	–	
5. Team learning S3	3.87	.42	.09	−.11	.39**	.14	–

**Correlation is significant at p < .05 level (bilateral)

The variables of this study showed moderate inter-correlations, and we conducted two confirmatory factor analyses to ascertain discriminant validity. Specifically, we compared the fit of a four-factor model (the items load in four correlated factors) to the fit of an alternative one-factor model (all the items load in one factor). We performed these analyses using MPLUS 6 [41] with the DIFFTEST option (279.61, d.f. = 6, p < .01); fit indices are shown in Table 2.

Table 2. Confirmatory factor analysis fit indices for one-factor and four-factor models.

Model	χ^2	d.f.	p	χ^2/d.f.	RMSEA	TLI	CFI
Four factors	134.34	98	.01	1.37	0.04	.97	.98
One factor	841.97	104	.00	8.10	0.18	.48	.55

3.2 Regression Analyses

The regression analyses were conducted with the PROCESS macro [42], which allows the use of bootstrapping when testing for mediation and conditional effects [43]. Aggregated scores of TL for session 1 are introduced as statistical control in further analyses. Moreover, as we used the same measurement method (e.g., questionnaire) to assess the mediator and dependent variables, it is likely that they share systematic covariation [44]. However, we tested the effect of the mediator on the dependent variable at different points in time, rather than concurrently, which minimizes the effect of common method bias. Hence, we tested the effect of team cohesion measured in session 2 on TL measured in session 3.

First, bootstrap analysis showed that the indirect effect of team feedback on TL via team cohesion was significantly different from zero (estimate of ab product term = .08; boot SE = .05; 95% confidence interval = .01 to .20). However, the direct effect of team feedback on TL was not significantly different from zero (estimate of c' = .13; boot SE = .11; 95% confidence interval = −.10 to .34). Thus, hypothesis 1 is supported.

Second, bootstrap analysis showed that openness to experience moderates the indirect effect of team feedback on TL via team cohesion, and the index of moderated mediation [42] is significantly different from zero, with an estimate of −.15 (boot SE = .10; 95% confidence interval = −.41 to −.02). Specifically, at low levels of openness to experience, the product term was significantly different from zero (estimate of ab product term = .13; boot SE = .06; 95% confidence interval = .03 to .30), whereas at high levels of openness to experience, it was not significantly different from zero (estimate of ab product term = .01; boot SE = .05; 95% confidence interval = −.08 to .11). Hence, hypothesis 2 is supported. Figure 3 shows the statistical diagram for hypothesis 2.

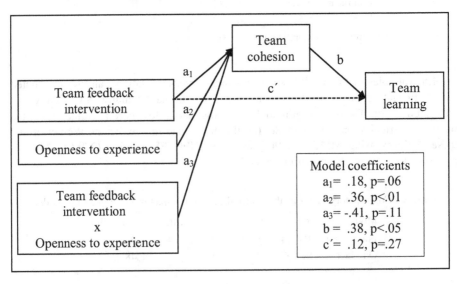

Fig. 3. Statistical diagram for hypothesis 2.

Third, bootstrap analysis showed that agreeableness does not moderate the indirect effect of team feedback on TL through team cohesion. The index of moderated mediation is not significantly different from zero, with an estimate of .12 (boot SE = .14; 95% confidence interval = −.01 to .48). Therefore, hypothesis 3 is not supported. Figure 4 shows the statistical diagram for hypothesis 3.

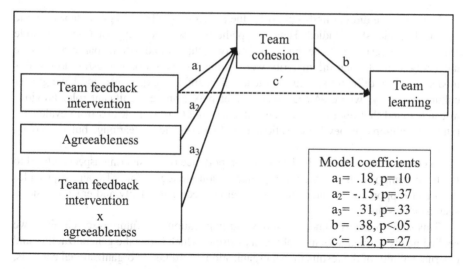

Fig. 4. Statistical diagram for hypothesis 3.

4   Discussion

The aim of this paper was to study the indirect effects of a team feedback with guided reflection intervention on TL through team cohesion, as well as the moderator role of team personality (openness to experience and agreeableness), in VTs.

We found that the team feedback intervention had a significant indirect effect on team learning via team cohesion in VTs. This result supports Hypothesis 1. Our findings highlight the importance of emergent states to develop TL in VTs. The proposed training intervention based on feedback and guided reflection encourages teams to discuss, share information, and set goals collaboratively. It becomes a team effort that requires the VT's members to jointly focus their attention on how to improve their teamwork and achieve their goals, favoring the emergence of team cohesion. Thus, team members develop feelings of closeness with other teammates and strengthen their commitment to the team's objectives [5]. These findings increase the understanding of how an intervention based on team feedback and guided reflection might improve TL in VTs. These findings support the positive effects of team training interventions in VTs [1]. Moreover, the effect of the intervention is mediated by team cohesion.

Past literature highlighted the need to study the effects that team composition might have on the effects of interventions [24]. Our results suggest that the mediated effect of team feedback and guided reflection on TL via team cohesion is negatively moderated by openness to experience. Thus, hypothesis 2 was supported. Specifically, teams with low openness to experience benefit more from the intervention than teams with a high level of openness. Less open-minded teams might have difficulties in considering new perspectives to solve problems and learn from others. Thus, helping them to reflect and discuss about the feedback might foster the emergence of cohesion and facilitate the members' engagement in team learning behaviors.

However, we did not find support for the moderating effect of agreeableness on the mediated relationship studied. Hence, hypothesis 3 was not supported. One possible reason for this result could be the homogeneity of the sample. All the participants were university students, and the majority were women. It would be interesting to test this moderation in a different setting with teams that differ in experience and have greater cultural diversity, where agreeableness might play a more significant role. Previous research found that high levels of agreeableness might prevent teams from evaluating different opinions or new information, thus hindering team learning, but improving cohesion [5].

In conclusion, this study highlights the importance of considering aspects related to the team composition when devising intervention strategies for VTs, and it provides empirical support for an interactionist model between personality and emergent states such as cohesion.

This study presents some limitations and implications for future research. First, we studied newly formed VTs in a laboratory setting, which limits the generalizability and external validity of the results to real organizational settings. In organizational contexts, VTs vary in their duration and purpose; therefore, it is also necessary to study the effectiveness of team feedback in already existing VTs [45]. Second, the present study does not analyze the effectiveness of this intervention on a long-term basis. Further research should address this by contemplating these long-term effects in real organizational environments. Finally, in this study all data were collected through self-report surveys, which raises the issue of common method variance as a potential problem [44]. However, several statistical analyses were successfully conducted to control this issue.

From a practical point of view, this study provides managers with some guidance about how to train VTs to improve TL. Encouraging the team to review its results and providing guidelines for processing feedback seem to be useful strategies for promoting team learning. The proposed intervention enhances team learning by fostering members' commitment to the team's goals and the creation of positive relationships. Furthermore, our results suggest that managers should consider that VTs with low openness to experience might benefit more from the proposed training intervention. This study is especially relevant for newly formed VTs with unacquainted members.

References

1. Gilson, L.L., Maynard, M.T., Young, N.C.J., Vartiainen, M., Hakonen, M.: Virtual teams research: 10 years, 10 themes, and 10 opportunities. J. Manag. **41**, 1313–1337 (2015)
2. Boon, A., Raes, E., Kyndt, E., Dochy, F.: Team learning beliefs and behaviours in response teams. Eur. J. Train. Dev. **37**, 357–379 (2013)
3. Van den Bossche, P., Gijselaers, W.H., Segers, M., Kirschner, P.A.: Social and cognitive factors driving teamwork in collaborative learning environments: team learning beliefs and behaviors. Small Group Res. **37**, 490–521 (2006)
4. Edmondson, A.C.: Psychological safety and learning behavior in work teams. Adm. Sci. Q. **44**, 350 (1999)

5. Bell, B.S., Kozlowski, S.W.J., Blawath, S.: Team learning: a theoretical integration and review (2012)

6. Ortega, A., Sánchez-Manzanares, M., Gil, F., Rico, R.: Team learning and effectiveness in virtual project teams: the role of beliefs about interpersonal context. Span. J. Psychol. **13**, 267–276 (2010)

7. Wong, S.-S.: Distal and local group learning: performance trade-offs and tensions. Organ. Sci. **15**, 645–656 (2004)

8. Tannenbaum, S.I., Mathieu, J.E., Salas, E., Cohen, D.: Teams are changing: are research and practice evolving fast enough? Ind. Organ. Psychol. **5**, 2–24 (2012)

9. Armstrong, D.J., Cole, P.: Managing distances and differences in geographically distributed work groups. In: Hinds, P., Kiesler, S. (eds.) New Ways of Working Across Distance Using Technology, pp. 167–189. MIT Press, Cambridge (2002)

10. Baltes, B.B., Dickson, M.W., Sherman, M.P., Bauer, C.C., LaGanke, J.S.: Computer-mediated communication and group decision making: a meta-analysis. Organ. Behav. Hum. Decis. Process. **87**, 156–179 (2002)

11. Curşeu, P.L., Schalk, R., Wessel, I.: How do virtual teams process information? A literature review and implications for management. J. Manag. Psychol. **23**, 628–652 (2008)

12. Driskell, J.E., Radtke, P.H., Salas, E.: Virtual teams: effects of technological mediation on team performance. Group Dyn. Theory Res. Pract. **7**, 297–323 (2003)

13. Lacerenza, C.N., Zajac, S., Savage, N., Salas, E.: Team training for global virtual teams: strategies for success. In: Wildman, J.L., Griffith, R.L. (eds.) Leading Global Teams, pp. 91–121. Springer, New York (2015). https://doi.org/10.1007/978-1-4939-2050-1_5

14. LePine, J.A.: Team adaptation and postchange performance: effects of team composition in terms of members' cognitive ability and personality. J. Appl. Psychol. **88**, 27–39 (2003)

15. van Vianen, A.E.M., De Dreu, C.K.W.: Personality in teams: its relationship to social cohesion, task cohesion, and team performance. Eur. J. Work Organ. Psychol. **10**, 97–120 (2001)

16. Tekleab, A.G., Quigley, N.R., Tesluk, P.E.: A longitudinal study of team conflict, conflict management, cohesion, and team effectiveness. Group Organ. Manag. **34**, 170–205 (2009)

17. Burke, K., Aytes, K., Chidambaram, L.: Media effects on the development of cohesion and process satisfaction in computer-supported workgroups - an analysis of results from two longitudinal studies. Inf. Technol. People **14**, 122–141 (2001)

18. Dennis, A.R., Garfield, M.J.: The adoption and use of GSS in project teams: toward more participative processes and outcomes. MIS Q. **27**, 289–323 (2003)

19. Gabelica, C., Van den Bossche, P., Segers, M., Gijselaers, W.: Feedback, a powerful lever in teams: a review. Educ. Res. Rev. **7**, 123–144 (2012)

20. Gabelica, C., Van den Bossche, P., Segers, M., Gijselaers, W.: Dynamics of team reflexivity after feedback. Frontline Learn. Res. **2**, 64–91 (2014)

21. Villado, A.J., Arthur, W.: The comparative effect of subjective and objective after-action reviews on team performance on a complex task. J. Appl. Psychol. **98**, 514–528 (2013)

22. Schippers, M.C., Homan, A.C., van Knippenberg, D.: To reflect or not to reflect: prior team performance as a boundary condition of the effects of reflexivity on learning and final team performance: boundary conditions of team reflexivity. J. Organ. Behav. **34**, 6–23 (2013)

23. Konradt, U., Otte, K.-P., Schippers, M.C., Steenfatt, C.: Reflexivity in teams: a review and new perspectives. J. Psychol. **150**, 153–174 (2016)

24. Salas, E., et al.: Does team training improve team performance? A meta-analysis. Hum. Factors **50**, 903–933 (2008)

25. Bell, B.S., Tannenbaum, S.I., Ford, J.K., Noe, R.A., Kraiger, K.: 100 years of training and development research: What we know and where we should go. J. Appl. Psychol. **102**, 305–323 (2017)

26. DeRue, D.S., Nahrgang, J.D., Hollenbeck, J.R., Workman, K.: A quasi-experimental study of after-event reviews and leadership development. J. Appl. Psychol. **97**, 997–1015 (2012)
27. Bradley, B.H., Klotz, A.C., Postlethwaite, B.E., Brown, K.G.: Ready to rumble: how team personality composition and task conflict interact to improve performance. J. Appl. Psychol. **98**, 385–392 (2013)
28. MacDonnell, R., O'Neill, T., Kline, T., Hambley, L.: Bringing group-level personality to the electronic realm: a comparison of face-to-face and virtual contexts. Psychol. Manag. J. **12**, 1–24 (2009)
29. Ellis, A.P.J., Hollenbeck, J.R., Ilgen, D.R., Porter, C.O.L.H., West, B.J., Moon, H.: Team learning: collectively connecting the dots. J. Appl. Psychol. **88**, 821–835 (2003)
30. Costa, P.T., McCrae, R.R.: Normal personality assessment in clinical practice: the NEO personality inventory. Psychol. Assess. **4**, 5–13 (1992)
31. McCrae, R.R.: Creativity, divergent thinking, and openness to experience. J. Pers. Soc. Psychol. **52**, 1258–1265 (1987)
32. Barrick, M.R., Mount, M.K., Judge, T.A.: Personality and performance at the beginning of the new millennium: what do we know and where do we go next? Int. J. Sel. Assess. **9**, 9–30 (2001)
33. McGrath, J.E.: Groups: Interaction and Performance. Prentice-Hall, Englewood Cliffs (1984)
34. Argote, L., McGrath, J.E.: Group processes in organizations: continuity and change. Int. Rev. Ind. Organ. Psychol. **8**, 333–389 (1993)
35. Gordon, J. (ed.): Pfeiffer's Classic Activities for Building Better Teams: The Most Enduring Effective, and Valuable Training Activities for Developing Teams. Jossey-Bass/Pfeiffer, San Francisco (2004)
36. Human Synergistics International: Bushfire Survival Situation: Leader's Guide. Human Synergistics International (2005)
37. Warkentin, M., Beranek, P.M.: Training to improve virtual team communication. Inf. Syst. J. **9**, 271–289 (1999)
38. Beranek, P.M., Martz, B.: Making virtual teams more effective: improving relational links. Team Perform. Manag. Int. J. **11**, 200–213 (2005)
39. Caprara, G.V., Barbaranelli, C., Borgogni, L.: BFQ Cuestionario "Big Five" (1998)
40. Karn, J.S., Syed-Abdullah, S., Cowling, A.J., Holcombe, M.: A study into the effects of personality type and methodology on cohesion in software engineering teams. Behav. Inf. Technol. **26**, 99–111 (2007)
41. Muthén, L.K., Muthén, B.O.: Mplus user's guide. In: Statistical Analysis with Latent Variables, vol. 3 (1998)
42. Hayes, A.F.: Introduction to Mediation, Moderation, and Conditional Process Analysis: A Regression-Based Approach. The Guilford Press, New York (2013)
43. Hayes, A.F.: Beyond Baron and Kenny: statistical mediation analysis in the new millennium. Commun. Monogr. **76**, 408–420 (2009)
44. Podsakoff, P.M., MacKenzie, S.B., Lee, J.-Y., Podsakoff, N.P.: Common method biases in behavioral research: a critical review of the literature and recommended remedies. J. Appl. Psychol. **88**, 879–903 (2003)
45. Geister, S., Konradt, U., Hertel, G.: Effects of process feedback on motivation, satisfaction, and performance in virtual teams. Small Group Res. **37**, 459–489 (2006)

ICTs and Sustainability

Exploring Sustainable HCI Research Dimensions Through the Inclusive Innovation Framework

Tobias Nyström$^{(\boxtimes)}$ (ID) and Moyen Mustaquim (ID)

Uppsala University, Uppsala, Sweden
`tobias.nystrom@im.uu.se`

Abstract. When frameworks and design principles for open innovation and open sustainability innovation (OSI) were established in earlier research, their foundations were originated from the expanded concepts of universal design (UD) from human-computer interaction (HCI) in a prescriptive form. This also was the basis of an inclusive innovation framework (IIF) aiming for a sustainable information system design. In this paper the IIF originating from the concept of combining UD and open innovation (OI) in promoting information technology enabling sustainability goals was analyzed together with OI and OSI frameworks. The role of OI in formulating the IIF was thereby strengthened, which in parallel helped recognizing the extended conceptions of sustainable HCI (SHCI) and its future research path through the use of IIF.

Keywords: Inclusive innovation framework · Open innovation
Open sustainability innovation · Sustainability · Sustainable HCI
Universal design

1 Introduction

The importance of sustainability has been acknowledged in academia, and different research fields contribute to the pursuit of a sustainable future. Research in computer science, information systems, and HCI directed towards sustainability has predominantly been focused on environmental sustainability with the goal of reducing the use of resources, e.g. saving electricity and water, and increasing recycling or lowering emissions of carbon dioxide [1]. These goals are esteemed ones, but a more potent solution could be attained by using a holistic perspective when moving society towards sustainability. To be able to do so, the system design should correspond to different sustainability goals. Keeping these in mind, IIF was proposed by Mustaquim and Nyström [2] for increasing sustainability goal achievement through the design of an IT system.

However, when considering a design process for system development it is vital to realize how the design process should be shaped and organized for the success

© IFIP International Federation for Information Processing 2018
Published by Springer Nature Switzerland AG 2018. All Rights Reserved
D. Kreps et al. (Eds.): HCC13 2018, IFIP AICT 537, pp. 151–165, 2018.
https://doi.org/10.1007/978-3-319-99605-9_11

of that process [3]. Many theoretical frameworks in the form of instructions have increased the problem of structuring a design process instead of appropriately guiding and helping the designers choose which process to follow and thereby gain a better design result. Consequently, this paper brings the IIF one step further forward in the attempt and exploration towards explaining the concept of SHCI. In this paper we have analyzed IIF using the reason-centric perspective of design, while two other preceding frameworks that work in parallel as a subset of IIF were analyzed using an action-centric perspective of design. The analysis showed that OI could successfully support IIF. The reason-centric properties of the IIF could successfully satisfy some of the new SHCI research trends, which confirmed that an IIF is apt for contributing in the system development on which SHCI is focused. To do so, six identified suggestions for SHCI research by Silberman et al. [4] were mapped with the reason-centric properties of IIF.

The paper is divided into six sections. The background section introduces the theoretical foundations on which the research of this paper was formulated. Section 2 presents the analysis of IIF, OI framework, and the OSI framework with the Function-Behavior-Structure (FBS) and the Sensemaking-Coevolution-Implementation (SCI) frameworks. Findings from the analysis are then compared to the context of SHCI research parameters, which are also presented in Sect. 3. In Sect. 4 the IIF is explored in depth based on the findings from the comparisons within the context of SHCI. Finally, discussion and future work possibilities are given in Sect. 5, followed by a conclusion in Sect. 6.

2   Background

2.1   The Inclusive Innovation Framework

The IIF (Fig. 1) was proposed to enhance the system development process by using four design principles taken from the UD concept that works to build the "inclusive innovation design space." By using the IIF system, designers will have a higher chance of reaching user satisfaction; the set sustainability goals will follow and finally system success can be achieved. The four design principles to follow in design are:

- **Simple intuitive use** gained when the information from the system is easily perceptible, and if the user can employ the system without much effort.
- **Perceptible information** will, by the system design, guarantee that information presented through the system be accurate, easily perceptible, and need little physical effort.
- **Low physical effort** denotes that the system design incorporates flexibility and accordingly needs less physical effort during use.
- **Flexible in use** signifies the system design allowing flexibility and being used intuitively.

Through the system supporting actions the probability to achieve set sustainability goals increases. Hence, the user satisfaction parameter is crucial and

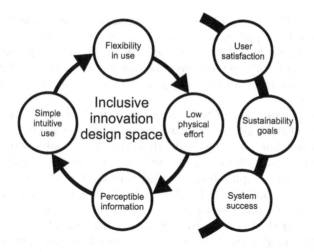

Fig. 1. IIF for sustainability (from [2])

should be manifested in the system's design strategy. To summarize the framework: by promoting the system designer's desired sustainability actions and/or goals, the system success phase should be reached if the system is easy to understand, remember, and learn, in addition to being simple and spontaneous. IIF is a holistic way of designing systems that tackle our dire situation concerning sustainability and increasing the possibility of reaching sustainability—a possible game changer.

2.2 Open Innovation and Open Sustainability Innovation

OI as a concept was introduced by Henry Chesbrough, but it is debated whether or not it is something genuinely new or simply a repackage of existing theories and practices in innovation strategies [5,6]. The different approaches and the lack of clear demarcations and definitions of innovation concepts like user innovation, OI, and crowdsourcing is apparent [2]. We see the strength and benefits of OI in its attempt to collect different innovation strategies, the emphasis on the importance to align innovation strategies with the overall business strategy, and its goal of bringing value and competitive advantage to a company. OI emphasizes the importance of external stakeholder involvement in the innovation process. This becomes crucial, especially when considering three identified important changes in "Research & Development" [7]:

- First, a shortening of the technology cycle. The cycles, including scientific and technological developments and the product life cycle, have been slowly shortening and thus forcing companies to work harder on product development, e.g. the mobile phone industry, which the product life cycle of a specific phone model has decreased from around 1–2 years in the early 1990s to now be around 6 months. OI could improve the link between research and development. Hence, new product innovations could become faster if external stakeholders like suppliers and consumers could be involved.

- Secondly, a technological explosion by around 90% of our present technical knowledge has been generated over the last 55 years. OI could improve the link with academic research through joint ventures, ideation, and new business incubator, etc.
- Thirdly, a globalization of technology and increased technological transfer in the form of strategic alliances and licensing has been noted by companies (especially in countries of the Pacific Rim) that have an ability to acquire and assimilate technology into new products, e.g. the creation in 2012 of a new company, "Japan Display Inc.," formed through the integration of Toshiba Mobile Display, Sony Mobile Display, and Hitachi Display. The company will carry out research and development in small and medium-sized displays [8]. OI implies that the business strategy incorporates the idea of an intellectual property (IP) market that makes it possible to sell, license, and acquire an IP to maximize the added value of both internal and external innovations. Hence designing a system that engages stakeholders by using OI strategies should increase the awareness and the possibility of reaching sustainability goals [9] and therefore the OI framework and OSI derives foundation from OI.

The OI framework consists of design principles that work in a logical sequence to achieve the overwhelming goal of increasing the stakeholder involvement that constitutes a prerequisite for OI and is therefore needed to accomplish a successful use of OI. The crucial components needed are: understanding of the importance of the business model, achieving extended user involvement, aiming for error reduction, and getting most users involved while eliminating restrictions [10]. OSI framework was constructed by using marketing theory that results in sustainable marketing and the basic buying decision that constitutes the purchase of a product. By using OI the end result could be a sustainability goal by a cyclic process that balances the customers' desired state and their requirements. Issues to be resolved are information presentation/communication, the gap between customers' desires and requirements, the convenience and support, and how to balance the added value compared to the cost [11].

2.3 Sustainable HCI

Academic sustainability research in HCI has burst in the recent years [1,12], which also can be seen in the increase of sustainability as subjects and/or tracks in computer science, information systems, and HCI conferences. This trend has also been noticed in other research fields. The use of sustainability is unfortunately somewhat arbitrary and dependent on the author and context, since no definitive definition exists, albeit the UN's Sustainability Development Goals having been argued in recent SHCI workshops [13]. The sustainable definition used in this paper was based on the declaration of the world commission on environment and development (WCED) regarding sustainable development as meeting the needs of the present, but not to compromise for the future generation to meet its needs [14]. Most research in SHCI is limited towards only dealing with environmental sustainability [1,15] and SHCI has previously been focused on reducing carbon dioxide emission, resource reduction by changing individuals' behavior towards consumption, and all these attempts through the design of systems [16]. Bates et al. [12] emphasized that broadening our understanding of how to redesign technology, systems, and society is of uttermost importance in a SHCI context. The essence of shaping the individual's behavior towards sustainability is critical and the design, thereby, plays an essential role in the transition to a sustainable society [17], although some argue a move beyond the individual to attain traction when considering sustainability [4,18].

The different frameworks developed by Mustaquim and Nyström could be used as philosophical guidelines to follow in order to increase the chance of reaching a set sustainability goal. A broader consideration of sustainability is also imperative due to the complexity and multidimensionality of sustainability, e.g. the triple bottom line (TBL) [19] that considers three components: the natural environment, society, and economic performance. Another viewpoint is given by the quadruple bottom line (QBL) [20], which states that sustainability is linked to personal needs, environmental needs, and social needs in which economical concern is a means to satisfying these needs. There are further frameworks to choose from. Which of these we prefer is not as vital a point as understanding the complexity and interconnection of variables that constitute sustainability. We need to consider a holistic view of sustainability when we design systems [21]. SHCI should therefore not be limited to only environmental concern if we want to achieve a truly sustainable system. Another consideration is the predominant focus on human needs and thereby omitting to give value and voice to other animals and living things. The designer of systems must be cautious when designing, since its influential power could give an unintentional and unconscious result [17].

3   Analysis, Comparison, and Findings

The designer should contribute new knowledge by answering questions relevant to human problems, by the creation of innovative artifacts which must be built and then evaluated [22–24]. The foundation of the design science paradigm can be found in engineering and the sciences of the artificial [3]. For analyzing the IIF an engineering design process theory titled "FBS framework" was selected. A representation of IIF with the FBS framework is shown in Fig. 2. The expected behavior of the structure is considered to yield "user satisfaction" and a predicted behavior of the structure is "system success." The expectations from the artifacts and their results are different sustainability goals, from which occasional transformation would occur with UD principles. Nonetheless, functional reformulations could occur between UD principles and sustainability goals while behavioral reformulation could occur between UD principles and user satisfaction in the form of transformation. User satisfaction and system success could be used for evaluation, e.g. in the form of a comparison or benchmarking of the designed system. Remy et al. [13] emphasized the need of SHCI to validate and showcase why a design solution works by thorough evaluations. Finally, the knowledge of UD principles could be transformed into the inclusive innovation design space.

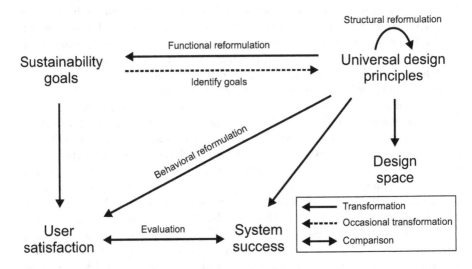

Fig. 2. A representation of IIF using the FBS framework (adapted from [25,26])

In the FBS framework the purpose of the design is perceived as the successful transformation of certain functions into a design description to facilitate the described artifact as able to produce the addressed functionalities [26,27]. The rationale behind selecting the FBS framework is that it reflects a reason-centric perspective of the system design. In reason-centric perspective the cognitivist view of human action is described as a sequence of different sets of action with some preconceived end [26,28] and a design could then be viewed as a plan-driven problem solved by triggering any replanning due to unanticipated conditions [26]. In the IIF the end design should reflect the addressed functionalities in the framework and each function could furthermore be viewed as a different set of actions with a desired end goal. Replanning could be necessary to implement successfully each of the functions from which each function implementation could be viewed as a plan-driven problem-solving strategy.

Alternatively, the OI and OSI frameworks were analyzed using the SCI framework adapted from Ralph [29], which emphasized the action-centric perspective of system design, as opposed to the rational decision-making, i.e. reason-centric perspective [26]. Social constructivism theorizes that social interaction constitutes what knowledge creation is based on and an action-centric perspective of the design. Therefore, the SCI framework could be viewed as a consistent reflection of a conversation between the designers and situation [26,29]. Both the OI and OSI frameworks from Mustaquim and Nyström [10,11] were based on the concept that improved design could be derived through interaction. Hence, it would be rational to use an action-centric perspective of design to analyze the OI and OSI frameworks. A representation of the SCI framework within the context of OI and OSI is shown in Fig. 3. The operations and concepts of the FBS and SCI frameworks were adapted from Ralph [26], and these two frameworks' corresponding meanings for the IIF (from [2]), OI framework (from [10]), and OSI framework (from [11]) were plotted and presented in Tables 1 and 2. Figures 2 and 3 were based on the operations and concepts of these two tables.

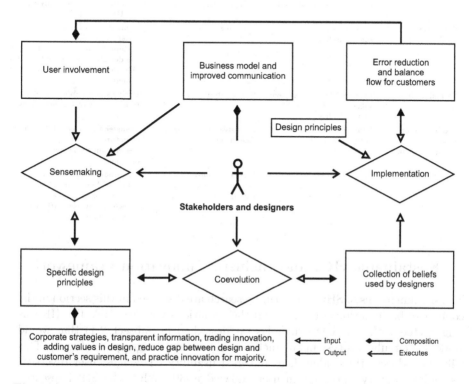

Fig. 3. A representation of OI and OSI frameworks using the SCI framework (adapted from [26])

A comparison between the reason- and action-centric perspectives of the three addressed frameworks, highlighted through the SHCI dimensions, were then generated and presented in Table 3. These dimensions of SHCI design issues were selected from the work of Silberman et al. [4]. The authors identified the selected six dimensions that address the next steps and efforts towards what SHCI research should aim at. Based on the factors listed in Table 3, conclusions were drawn. Thus SHCI, through the practice of IIF in system design, is explored and discussed in Sect. 4.

Table 1. Operations of the FBS framework and its corresponding meanings for the IIF

Operation	Inputs	Outputs	Meaning in inclusive innovation framework
Analysis	Inclusive innovation design space	Sustainable information system	The process of deriving the sustainability goals, user satisfaction, and system success
Catalog lookup	User satisfaction, system success and sustainability	Inclusive innovation design space	The appropriate design structure to successfully run the UD principles
Evaluation	User satisfaction and sustainability	System success	Comparison of user satisfaction and sustainability to determine if the design structure will be able to successfully use UD principles
Formulation	User satisfaction, system success, and sustainability	Sustainability	Derive sustainable behavior from the set of UD principles
Production of design documentation	Inclusive innovation design space	Inclusive innovation design framework	Transfer the selected design structure to a design description for system designers
Synthesis	Sustainability	Inclusive innovation design space and user satisfaction	Sustainability is used as expected behavior of the end system, based on the knowledge of user satisfaction with the system

4 Sustainable HCI and Inclusive Innovation Framework

The six dimensions of SHCI for future research are discussed in this section in the context of basic notions of SHCI and their relations with the IIF. The IIF was constructed with four UD principles (as described in Subsect. 2.1) that would work in a circular process in the inclusive innovation design space (Fig. 1). This will also address three identified universal usability challenges: user diversity, technology variety, and gaps in user knowledge [30]. While the SHCI research field has mainly been concerned with designing technology to change human behavior on environmental impacts [12,31] and designing technologies to reduce impact on the environment, an IIF for a system design process can contribute towards both of these dimensions of SHCI. By specifying and operationalizing certain goals through the design for sustainability, the dimensions of sustainability could be handled properly, since they exist independently. The IIF takes into account certain design goals and in that process look beyond the traditional way SHCI issues have previously been handled. The dimensions of sustainability are not independent themselves and therefore the definition of sustainability could vary depending on the situation and context. Hence, IIF in the design process could help in identifying the correct structured goal to define sustainability in the proper context of the problem.

The IIF could involve different stakeholders in the design process, since it is built within a design space of the OI. While much research has been conducted

Table 2. Different concepts of SCI framework and their meaning for OI and the OSI framework

Concept	Meaning for OI framework	Meaning in OSI framework
Constraints	Removing any restriction from the design objective of OI, by practicing it for the majority	Removing constraints to reduce the gap between customer's requirement and desire
Design agent	Selection of a group of entities for successful involvement of users in a wide-ranging perspective	Selection of a group of entities for making information presentation for the customer a less complicated task
Design object's environment	The totality of the wide range of user involvement and contact that is expanded through the academia	Make information presentation about a product for the customer an easy task
Design agent's environment	The totality of the whole business model involved in OI practice	The totality of the evaluation of product towards differing alternatives and enhancing better communication with customers
Design objects	The possibility of a reduced error objective, through the help of OI	Ensuring a balanced flow between different variables of customer cost for successful OSI practice
Goals	Realizing the corporate strategies properly for understanding the effect of a wide range of user involvement and thereby generating the proper business model	Provide transparent information to customers for the positive impact on their post-purchase behavior
Mental picture of context	Collection of design principles for system designers in OI design process and its designer's environment	Collection of design principles for sustainable innovation through OI
Mental picture of design object	Collection of beliefs used by the designers to improve the design principles concerning OI process	Collection of beliefs used by the designers to improve the design principles concerning OSI process
Primitives	Set of design principles for a successful user involvement initiation	Appropriate business model for the successful user involvement towards sustainable product development through innovation
Requirements	The ability to trade innovation for increased user involvement in the innovation process	Ability to add values into the product design for the convenience of the design process
Sense-making	Organizing the OI environment for creating or refining a new business model	OSI process planning through the simplicity in the design process
Coevolution	Refining the OI process using the mental picture of the extended business model	Provide error-free customer solutions for efficiency during the OSI process and update the mental picture of the designer for the innovation

in the domain of SHCI in a little over a decade, it is possible to notice a trend of predominantly scientific publications with frameworks and design principles for small-scale/specific problems and design issues. IIF showed that the design process could be iterative and cumulative over time by involving multiple stakeholders; therefore suitable to handle large-scale design problems associated with sustainability issues. Persuasions could be initiated and tackled by the introduction of the IIF in the design process. Also, very few of the SHCI research results are inevitable today and may be seen as end products for user behavior change for sustainability. A design process that is inclusive and based on UD principles aiming for sustainable outcomes with proper user satisfaction and system success would undoubtedly tend to contribute in designing products and services for end

Table 3. Comparison of two perspectives based on the SHCI dimensions

SHCI dimension	Reason-centric Perspective (IIF)	Action-centric Perspective (OI and OSI)
Specify and operationalize goals	The positivist approach using design principles outside the traditional way of looking into HCI for achieving sustainability through design	Design work in sustainability discourse outside HCI where the constructivist approach leads towards innovation
Longer timescale research	Long-term design process by involving different stakeholders triggering cumulative and iterative design process for improved sustainability achievement through design	Long-term social and economic process influencing OI and OSI method for improved sustainability address in practice
Building system for everyday use	Inclusive design process by making it possible to fit in everyday product or system design and evaluation, thereby building new knowledge in the SHCI domain	Direct influence of product design through the OI and OSI
Draw from and support work outside HCI	Expanding the traditional usability concept from HCI towards sustainability achievement by user satisfaction and system success	Gaining sustainability knowledge from business research, using the OI and OSI to produce new knowledge in SHCI
Diversifying sustainability issues	Bridging the gap between UD and sustainability by diversifying traditional sustainability issues under the shed of UD and its principles	Diversifying the SHCI scopes in new research domains through the creative practice of OI and OSI
Multi-scale, complex sustainability problems	Build new SHCI dimensions and actions based on the traditional sustainability issues for different artifact results and improved information processing capabilities	Escaping only the ecological sustainability issues by focusing on larger systems with different corporate strategies for practicing OI and OSI

users. The use of OI concept in the IIF design space influences this motivation towards truly designing products and services.

Several discussions have triggered the idea of using SHCI as a multi- and interdisciplinary research domain for collaborating with different research domains [1] (the roots of HCI are multidisciplinary [32]). Bringing external knowledge from other research domain and using it in the context of SHCI is interesting; the opposite is also necessary, i.e. to contribute other research domains from the SHCI perspective. Since sustainability is multidisciplinary in nature, the contribution from SHCI could be extensive in other research fields, which would extend HCI research possibilities together with contributions in other research domains. The traditional concept of usability engineering in HCI [32] could be expanded with IIF by looking into sustainability achievement through system success and user satisfaction, thus creating a completely new dimension of looking into sustainability through design). IIF is therefore highly promising and could probably contribute in the multidisciplinary research domain. Accordingly, SHCI research can see the sustainability problem as a more diversifying issue. The way SHCI looks into the sustainability problems (based upon the multidimensionality and many levels of analysis) have merely expanded its scope beyond academic publications. If the issues of sustainability are not diversified, then it might become trapped within its own loophole and make itself unsustainable. Diversification is therefore needed to perpetually define and redefine different sustainability problems. One such initiation of diversification could be started from a system design process to make the resulting design and the design process sustainable. IIF is designed to keep this in mind.

Creative practice of OI and OSI is expected within the design space of inclusive innovation, through which new knowledge about the sustainability problem could be identified and resolved. Finally, a complex view of sustainability would create the need and a demand to evolve design frameworks and design principles that are able to handle complex sustainability issues. Complex sustainability problems could be realized by practicing IIF during a design process. Considering large-scale system design and the involvement of different stakeholders in various social and political situations could lead the designers to realizing what sustainability is in that particular context. IIF could then contribute in achieving those sustainability goals. In conclusion, when discussing IIF and SHCI it could be said that the framework was revealed to be fitting for the purpose of SHCI research trends, as noticed from Table 3. The research trend parameters were discussed in this section in detail to argue that IIF in a design process could be applied to create systems that can be used for changing user behavior in complex sustainability issues, in long-term design problems, and to create products and services for daily use. In other words, the IIF could reflect SHCI design issues and requirements in a design process.

5   Discussions and Future Work

One of the primary goals of system design science is to shape and organize design processes. However, considerable design science research in academia is more prescriptive and not exploratory [26], which has initiated the idea of exploring the earlier proposed IIF under the shade of SHCI. Empirically, it was shown earlier that action-centric process theory is more successful in describing the shape of system design than with reason-centric perspective [26] which favors supports of the OI and OSI frameworks, which are a subset of the IIF analyzed within the context of reason-centric perspective. Ralph [33] did evaluate FSB and SCI through a multi-methodological approach and found SCI to represent more accurately represent software development practice. It did, however, neither prove SCI nor falsify FSB for development of software. It is important to realize that the IIF, OI framework, and OSI framework are not meant to produce any technological artifacts; instead, a virtual artifact, which is how the differentiation between classical design science research and system design research should be perceived in this paper. One of such virtual artifacts was selected to be a sustainability issue from the IIF, analyzed within the context of SHCI. In favor of descriptive and explanatory validity of IIF for SHCI, the existing framework could be seen as a process model whereby usually the abstract description of a proposed process is usually presented [34]. The analysis and results of this paper could then be seen as a process theory for which the outcome of the IIF as a process model appeared in a generalized way, within the context of SHCI.

On the other hand, the characteristic of the IIF in the context of SHCI also supports the genres and axes of SHCI identified by DiSalvo [1], when the authors raised and discussed issues like the requirement of application of the SHCI concept, thinking more than the traditional HCI concept; bigger, with large-scale and users' and group-design's problems.

Another aspect, called a "value-sensitive design approach," could be realized through the outcome of the results from this paper. Value-sensitive design is known to contribute to the foundation of different social issues in the HCI research [35]. Issues like sustainability could be an embodied value to incorporate in the design process for producing a good design outcome from the beginning and throughout a design process. Friedman et al. identified sustainability as one of the ethical principles to be used in value-sensitive design [36]. The IIF used four UD principles and the rationale was not philosophically grounded; rather, their selection was arbitrary. Therefore, by analyzing IIF using a reason-centric approach like FBS framework, it was grounded that a designer could be capable of controlling a design process, which is an information-processing metaphor supported by the reason-centric view, to satisfy a need like sustainability throughout the whole design process. However, as suggested by Ralph [26], a reason-centric perspective is a popular but questionable system design perspective. Action-centric perspective is more consistent and pragmatic. The IIF should therefore demand empirical verification. Nevertheless, the FBS framework was used only to analyze IIF and not to specify the development process. How pragmatic it would be to analyze IIF using an action-centric framework was not the topic of interest in this paper and therefore has not been discussed. Possibilities and scopes of further research work will now be discussed, for which some constraints of this research will be highlighted too.

The next step of this research could be viewed from three different perspectives. Firstly, empirical validation of the IIF for justifying the SHCI dimensions is central to see that the opinions formulated from the SCI and FBS frameworks are valid in a system development setup. At the same time, it would be interesting to be pragmatic and see how the SHCI dimensions could be realized by putting the IIF into practice in system development. This could be achieved by analyzing how a design process followed by the IIF could shape an organization. A system could be analyzed in the different phases of its development life cycle to determine whether IIF is successful in terms of realizing the new dimensions of SHCI. Secondly, since the SCI and FBS frameworks were initiated by the need of a different software development perspective, a system development could be analyzed in terms of programming and coding of the software by following the IIF and observing how well the addressed SHCI issues would behave in such a setup. Finally, to analyze existing systems by taking them as different sample cases could be another choice to add new scopes into this research. Case study analysis may find new parameters to be added into the SCI and FBS frameworks' concept and operation, which would extend or find new dimensions for SHCI.

6 Conclusions

In this paper the previously established IIF for sustainable system development was analyzed together with the OI and OSI frameworks by using two existing reason- and action-centric frameworks (FBS and SCI). The IIF could create a design space which would be based on OI and OSI, and this was the rationale behind analyzing these OI and OSI frameworks together with IIF. The reason- and action-centric properties from IIF together with OI and OSI frameworks were then compared with six SHCI dimensions, which were identified in previous research to be the most important impending issues for SHCI research. The analysis showed that IIF aiming for sustainable system development could be successful in mapping itself towards describing the different dimensions of SHCI. The action-centric perspective for comparison strengthened the fact that OI and OSI could work as a support for the IIF for effective realization of different sustainability characteristics of a system, while at the same time reflecting SHCI research prospects in a new dimension.

References

1. DiSalvo, C., Sengers, P., Brynjarsdóttir, H.: Mapping the landscape of sustainable HCI. In: Proceedings of the SIGCHI Conference on Human Factors in Computing Systems, CHI 2010, pp. 1975–1984. ACM, New York (2010). https://doi.org/10.1145/1753326.1753625
2. Mustaquim, M.M., Nyström, T.: Designing information systems for sustainability – the role of universal design and open innovation. In: Tremblay, M.C., VanderMeer, D., Rothenberger, M., Gupta, A., Yoon, V. (eds.) DESRIST 2014. LNCS, vol. 8463, pp. 1–16. Springer, Cham (2014). https://doi.org/10.1007/978-3-319-06701-8_1
3. Simon, H.A.: The Sciences of the Artificial. MIT press, Cambridge (1996)
4. Silberman, M.S., et al.: Next steps for sustainable HCI. Interactions **21**(5), 66–69 (2014). https://doi.org/10.1145/2651820
5. Trott, P., Hartmann, D.: Why 'open innovation' is old wine in new bottles. Int. J. Innov. Manag. **13**(04), 715–736 (2009). https://doi.org/10.1142/S1363919609002509
6. Trott, P., Hartmann, D.: Open innovation: old ideas in a fancy tuxedo remedy a false dichotomy. In: Open Innovation Research, Management and Practice, pp. 359–386. Imperial College Press (2013). https://doi.org/10.1142/9781783262816_0014. chap. 13
7. Rothwell, R., Zegveld, W.: Reindustrialization and technology. Longman, London (1985)
8. Japan Display Inc.: Message from the president (2014). http://www.j-display.com/english/company/index.html. Accessed 9 Sep 2014
9. Mustaquim, M.M., Nyström, T.: Designing sustainable IT system – from the perspective of universal design principles. In: Stephanidis, C., Antona, M. (eds.) UAHCI 2013. LNCS, vol. 8009, pp. 77–86. Springer, Heidelberg (2013). https://doi.org/10.1007/978-3-642-39188-0_9
10. Mustaquim, M.M., Nyström, T.: Design principles of open innovation concept – universal design viewpoint. In: Stephanidis, C., Antona, M. (eds.) UAHCI 2013. LNCS, vol. 8009, pp. 214–223. Springer, Heidelberg (2013). https://doi.org/10.1007/978-3-642-39188-0_23

11. Mustaquim, M.M., Nyström, T.: Open sustainability innovation—a pragmatic standpoint of sustainable HCI. In: Johansson, B., Andersson, B., Holmberg, N. (eds.) BIR 2014. LNBIP, vol. 194, pp. 101–112. Springer, Cham (2014). https://doi.org/10.1007/978-3-319-11370-8_8

12. Bates, O., Thomas, V., Remy, C.: Doing good in HCI: can we broaden our agenda? Interactions **24**(5), 80–82 (2017). https://doi.org/10.1145/3121386

13. Remy, C., Bates, O., Thomas, V., Huang, E.M.: The limits of evaluating sustainability. In: Proceedings of the 2017 Workshop on Computing Within Limits, LIMITS 2017, pp. 103–110. ACM, New York (2017). https://doi.org/10.1145/3080556.3080567

14. The World Commission on Environment and Development (WCED): Our common future. Oxford University Press (1987)

15. DiSalvo, C., Sengers, P., Brynjarsdóttir, H.: Navigating the terrain of sustainable HCI. Interactions **17**(4), 22–25 (2010). https://doi.org/10.1145/1806491.1806497

16. Dourish, P.: HCI and environmental sustainability: the politics of design and the design of politics. In: Proceedings of the 8th ACM Conference on Designing Interactive Systems, DIS 2010, pp. 1–10. ACM, New York (2010). https://doi.org/10.1145/1858171.1858173

17. Stegall, N.: Designing for sustainability: a philosophy for ecologically intentional design. Des. Issues **22**(2), 56–63 (2006). https://doi.org/10.1162/desi.2006.22.2.56

18. Knowles, B., Blair, L., Hazas, M., Walker, S.: Exploring sustainability research in computing: where we are and where we go next. In: Proceedings of the 2013 ACM International Joint Conference on Pervasive and Ubiquitous Computing, UbiComp 2013, pp. 305–314. ACM, New York (2013). https://doi.org/10.1145/2493432.2493474

19. Elkington, J.: Towards the sustainable corporation: win-win-win business strategies for sustainable development. Calif. Manag. Rev. **36**(2), 90–100 (1994). https://doi.org/10.2307/41165746

20. Walker, S.: The Spirit of Design: Objects, Environment and Meaning. Earthscan, London (2011)

21. Nyström, T., Mustaquim, M.: Sustainable information system design and the role of sustainable HCI. In: Proceedings of the 18th International Academic MindTrek Conference: Media Business, Management, Content & Services, AcademicMindTrek 2014, pp. 66–73. ACM, New York (2014). https://doi.org/10.1145/2676467.2676486

22. Hevner, A., Chatterjee, S.: Design science research in information systems. In: Design Research in Information Systems. Integrated Series in Information Systems, vol. 22, pp. 9–22. Springer, Boston (2010). https://doi.org/10.1007/978-1-4419-5653-8_2

23. Hevner, A.R., March, S.T., Park, J., Ram, S.: Design science in information systems research. MIS Q. **28**(1), 75–105 (2004)

24. March, S.T., Smith, G.F.: Design and natural science research on information technology. Decis. Support Syst. **15**(4), 251–266 (1995). https://doi.org/10.1016/0167-9236(94)00041-2

25. Kruchten, P.: Casting software design in the function-behavior-structure framework. IEEE Softw. **22**(2), 52–58 (2005). https://doi.org/10.1109/MS.2005.33

26. Ralph, P.: Comparing two software design process theories. In: Winter, R., Zhao, J.L., Aier, S. (eds.) DESRIST 2010. LNCS, vol. 6105, pp. 139–153. Springer, Heidelberg (2010). https://doi.org/10.1007/978-3-642-13335-0_10

27. Gero, J.S.: Design prototypes: a knowledge representation schema for design. AI Mag. **11**(4), 26–36 (1990). https://doi.org/10.1609/aimag.v11i4.854

28. Suchman, L.A.: Plans and Situated Actions: The Problem of Human-Machine Communication. Cambridge University Press, Cambridge (1987)
29. Ralph, P.: The sensemaking-coevolution-implementation theory of software design. Sci. Comput. Program. **101**, 21–41 (2015). https://doi.org/10.1016/j.scico.2014.11.007
30. Shneiderman, B.: Universal usability. Commun. ACM **43**(5), 84–91 (2000). https://doi.org/10.1145/332833.332843
31. Blevis, E.: Sustainable interaction design: invention & disposal, renewal & reuse. In: Proceedings of the SIGCHI Conference on Human Factors in Computing Systems, CHI 2007, pp. 503–512. ACM, New York (2007). https://doi.org/10.1145/1240624.1240705
32. Hartson, H.R.: Human-computer interaction: interdisciplinary roots and trends. J. Syst. Softw. **43**(2), 103–118 (1998). https://doi.org/10.1016/S0164-1212(98)10026-2
33. Ralph, P.: Software engineering process theory: a multi-method comparison of sensemaking-coevolution-implementation theory and function-behavior-structure theory. Inf. Softw. Technol. **70**, 232–250 (2016). https://doi.org/10.1016/j.infsof.2015.06.010
34. Curtis, B., Kellner, M.I., Over, J.: Process modeling. Commun. ACM **35**(9), 75–90 (1992). https://doi.org/10.1145/130994.130998
35. Fuchs, C., Obrist, M.: HCI and society: towards a typology of universal design principles. Int. J. Hum. Comput. Interact. **26**, 638–656 (2010). https://doi.org/10.1080/10447311003781334
36. Friedman, B., Kahn, P.H., Borning, A., Huldtgren, A.: Value sensitive design and information systems. In: Doorn, N., Schuurbiers, D., van de Poel, I., Gorman, M.E. (eds.) Early Engagement and New Technologies: Opening Up the Laboratory. PET, vol. 16, pp. 55–95. Springer, Dordrecht (2013). https://doi.org/10.1007/978-94-007-7844-3_4

ICT and Sustainability: Looking Beyond the Anthropocene

Maja van der Velden(✉) ⓘ

University of Oslo, Oslo, Norway
majava@ifi.uio.no

Abstract. This paper investigates the relation between information and communication technology and sustainability through two frameworks that promote sustainable development: the Sustainable Development Goals (SDGs) and Doughnut Economics. The instrumentalist technology perspective underlying the SDGs, guiding the perceived universality of ICT, presents ICT as a neutral tool. Doughnut Economics enables a more integrative approach, making the unsustainability of ICT itself visible. What these frameworks have in common is that they are located in the discourse of the Anthropocene. Feminist perspectives on this epoch by Donna Haraway and Anna Tsing focus the attention on different figures, rhythms, and futures made invisible by the centrality of the human species in the debates on the future of our planet. The idea that humans-with-technology will get us out the predicament of the Anthropocene needs urgent refinement and critical investigation.

Keywords: Doughnut economics · Feminist technoscience
Planetary boundaries · Technological anthropocene · Sustainability

1 Introduction

This paper presents a discussion of the relations between Information and Communication Technology (ICT) and sustainability through the perspective of two frameworks for sustainable development, the United Nations Sustainable Development Goals (SDGs) and Doughnut Economics [1]. The SDGs are a set of goals to "end poverty, protect the planet, and ensure prosperity for all as part of a new sustainable development agenda" [2]. Doughnut Economics is concerned with socially, environmentally, and economically sustainable development. Doughnut economics is presented by a doughnut-shaped visualization, in which the outer ring of the doughnut consists of nine planetary boundaries, which form the ecological ceiling for all life on our planet, and the inner ring as twelve key social and economic indicators, which form the social foundation for human life on the planet (see Fig. 1).

This discussion is situated within feminist perspectives on the Anthropocene. The Anthropocene is generally understood as a geological epoch in which the impacts of human activity dominate. Feminist technoscience problematize binaries that characterize the Anthropocene discourse, such as human/nonhuman and economy/ecology.

This paper is part of an international research project called Sustainable Market Actors for Responsible Trade (SMART). Within this project, I focus on a particular

Published by Springer Nature Switzerland AG 2018. All Rights Reserved
D. Kreps et al. (Eds.): HCC13 2018, IFIP AICT 537, pp. 166–180, 2018.
https://doi.org/10.1007/978-3-319-99605-9_12

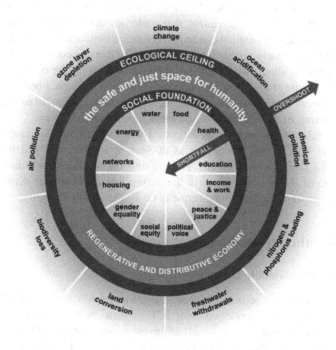

Fig. 1. The Doughnut [1]

ICT, the mobile phone. In our research we take a lifecycle approach, that means that we consider an ICT not only as a thing that is produced and consumed, but also as an ecology or assemblage of design (e.g., esthetics, functions, forms, uses), materials (e.g., minerals, metals, chemicals), humans (e.g., miners, workers, users), nonhumans (e.g., forests, fish, water, food, cattle, materials), values (e.g., just, fair, smart, green, fast, circular), politics (e.g., policies, laws), visions (e.g., good life, future), etc.

We actively use the doughnut-shaped visualization (see Fig. 1) to better understand the unsustainabilities found in the lifecycle of the mobile phone. We implemented in the SMART project a so-called hotspots analysis [3], a qualitative analysis, which resulted in the identification of environmental and social impacts in each of the mobile phone life cycle phases. We mapped these against the ecological foundation with the nine planetary boundaries (climate change, ocean acidification, chemical pollution, etc.) and against the social foundation, consisting of twelve key social and economic indicators (water, food, health, etc.). Through a weighing process we were able to find the most severe impacts on these boundaries and indicators, which we called hotspots.

As a socio-ecological system, the doughnut helped us to visualize the multiple ways in which humans and nonhumans interact in the mobile phone life cycle. At the same time, the doughnut, as 'The Safe and Just Space for Humanity', privileges humans. For example, Raworth asks: "Can we live in the doughnut?" [4][1]. In this paper I will explore the human-centeredness that underlies the Doughnut and the SDGs, while staying close to my original concern, the relation between ICT and sustainability.

The other binary made visible by the doughnut is that of economy versus ecology. The question here is about 'who' will sort out what is good for the ecology and what is good for the economy? I will problematize this question through a brief discussion of one of the hotspots found in our research, namely chemical pollution as a result of the informal recycling of mobile phones and other electronics in Ghana.

The remainder of the paper is as follows. I will explore the Sustainable Development Goals in Sect. 2 and the doughnut in Sect. 3. In Sect. 4 I will introduce the perspectives of Donna Haraway and Anna Tsing on the Anthropocene in order to question some of the binaries found in the sustainable development discourse. I will conclude this paper with some final remarks on ICT and sustainability.

2   The Sustainable Development Goals

2.1   ICT and Sustainable Development

Two lines of inquiry can be distinguished in research on ICT and sustainability. In the first one, and the most developed one, ICT is seen as an enabler of sustainable development, but is itself not an object of investigation. Since 1995, with the establishment of the United Nations Commission on Science and Technology for Development (UNCSTD) Working Group on IT and Development, ICT has been on the UN's development agenda. For example, ICT is perceived as a "catalyst for sustainable development" [6] or as having the capacity to "deliver the SDGs" [7]. The International Telecommunications Union (ITU) runs a campaign, ICT for a Sustainable World - #ICT4SDG - and has developed an ICT toolkit for every SDG [8]. Scholarly research into ICT and development increased significantly with the start of the 21st century, with the notion of ICT for sustainable development following soon after.

In the second line of inquiry, the sustainability of ICT itself is considered. This has not been a topic on the UN's development agenda and received initially less attention in scholarly circles. However, reports by civil society organisations on, for example, mining in conflict areas, working conditions in the electronics industry, and environmental degradation as a result of informal recycling practices, brought the unsustainability of ICTs to the foreground [9–13]. Our research in the SMART project is situated within this discourse.

The distinction between sustainable ICT and ICT for sustainability can also be found in the Sustainable Development Goals (SDGs) (see Fig. 2). The SDGs are a collection of 17 goals, with 169 associated targets and 304 indicators, set by the United Nations in 2015. The SDGs are perceived as global and universal, promoting sustainable development in all countries.

---

[1] Similarly, we can ask: Can we design for living in the doughnut [5]?

Fig. 2. United Nations Sustainable Development Goals

ICTs are seen as central to achieving the Sustainable Development Goals (SDGs) and are specifically mentioned in Goals 4, 5, 9, and 17 and their targets or indicators (see Table 1).

The second perspective, the need for ICT itself to be sustainable, is only indirectly mentioned in Sustainable development Goal 8 and 12 (see Table 2).

2.2   An Instrumental Understanding of ICT

There are several lines of critique developed around the SDGs. The main one is that the SDGs may promote increased growth, consumption, and production, while failing to address the limits of our planet:

> "Unfortunately, "sustainable development," as advocated by most natural, social, and environmental scientists, is an oxymoron. Continual population growth and economic development on a finite Earth are biophysically impossible. They violate the laws of physics, especially thermodynamics, and the fundamental principles of biology. Population growth requires the increased consumption of food, water, and other essentials for human life. Economic development requires the increased use of energy and material resources to provide goods, services, and information technology" [14].

If economic growth, as part of sustainable development, is "impossible", what are the consequences of this understanding for the responsible production and consumption of ICTs? For example, can we call it sustainable ICT, when we use it for green data centres (sustainable development), whose server capacity is used for accelerating unsustainable consumption? Can we call for slow and fair ICT [15], if we don't know if our planet can sustain any more ICT?

Table 1. ICTs and the sustainable development goals

Goal	Targets and Indicators
4. **Quality Education**: Ensure inclusive and equitable quality education and promote lifelong learning opportunities for all	Target 4.b. By 2020, substantially expand globally the number of scholarships available to developing countries, in particular least developed countries, small island developing States and African countries, for enrolment in higher education, including vocational training and **information and communications technology**, technical, engineering and scientific programmes, in developed countries and other developing countries Indicator 4.4.1. Proportion of youth and adults with information and communications technology (ICT) skills, by type of skill
5. **Gender Equality**: Achieve gender equality and empower all women and girls	Target 5.b. Enhance the use of enabling technology, in particular **information and communications technology**, to promote the empowerment of women
9. **Industry, Innovation, and Infrastructure**: Build resilient infrastructure, promote inclusive and sustainable industrialization and foster innovation	Target 9.c. Significantly increase access to **information and communications technology** and strive to provide universal and affordable access to the Internet in least developed countries by 2020
17. **Partnerships for the Goals**: Strengthen the means of implementation and revitalize the Global Partnership for Sustainable Development	Target 17.8. Fully operationalize the technology bank and science, technology and innovation capacity-building mechanism for least developed countries by 2017 and enhance the use of enabling technology, in particular **information and communication technology**

A critique more specific to ICTs is that the SDGs are based on an instrumental understanding of technology; ICT are presented as neutral, universal tools to achieve sustainable development. Feenberg [16] presents four characteristics of this instrumentalist perspective: (i) technology is indifferent to the ends to which it is employed; (ii) technology is indifferent to politics, which facilitates its transfer to other social contexts; (iii) technologies represent scientific ideas, which will be maintained in other social contexts; (iv) from the universality of technology follows that "the same standards of measures can be applied in different settings. Thus technology is routinely said to increase productivity in labour in different countries, different eras, and different civilizations" [16, pp. 6–7]. The perceived neutrality and universality of ICT in the SDGs suppress questions about the values and politics of ICT themselves, making their unsustainability invisible. A more integrative approach to ICT and sustainability is therefore warranted.

Table 2. Sustainability of ICTs

Goal	Target
8. **Decent Work and Economic Growth:** Promote sustained, inclusive, and sustainable economic growth, full and productive employment and decent work for all	Target 8.4. Improve progressively, through 2030, global resource efficiency in consumption and production and endeavour to decouple economic growth from environmental degradation, in accordance with the 10-Year Framework of Programmes on Sustainable Consumption and Production, with developed countries taking the lead
12. **Responsible Consumption and Production**	Target 12.2. By 2030, achieve the sustainable management and efficient use of natural resources Target 12.4. By 2020, achieve the environmentally sound management of chemicals and all wastes throughout their life cycle, in accordance with agreed international frameworks, and significantly reduce their release to air, water and soil in order to minimize their adverse impacts on human health and the environment Target 12.5. By 2030, substantially reduce waste generation through prevention, reduction, recycling and reuse

3 The Doughnut

3.1 Ecological Ceiling

In 2014, economist Kate Raworth, working at the time for the international organisation Oxfam, proposed the idea of 'Doughnut Economics' [17]. She was familiar with the Planetary Boundaries framework developed by Johan Rockström of the Stockholm Resilience Centre and Will Steffen of Australia National University [18, 19]. This framework is based on the idea of a finite planet. The nine planetary boundaries (see Fig. 1) are based on nine critical processes that together regulate the Earth's capacity to sustain the Holocene, the geological epoch starting about 12.000 years ago and which contains the growth and impact of all species. The Planetary Boundaries framework is the most developed scientific tool we have at the moment to benchmark the impact of human activity on the planet. The framework considers the planet as an integrated system. Changes in processes forming one boundary can have a knock on effect in processes forming another boundary. At the moment, four boundaries are crossed (overshoot): climate change, nitrogen and phosphorus loading, land conversion, and biodiversity.

3.2 Social Foundation

Raworth recognised the importance of the Planetary Boundaries framework, but argued that adding social and economic aspects could contribute to creating a more holistic perspective. She formed two rings, the outer ring representing the Planetary Boundaries, or what she calls the "Ecological Ceiling", and the inner ring the "Social Foundation"; the effect was that of a doughnut (see Fig. 1). The space within the two rings is the "safe and just space for humanity" as well as the "regenerative and distributed economy". In particular the "safe and just space for humanity" integrates the planetary boundaries and social foundation. At the moment, all twelve key social and economic indicators (see Fig. 1) fall short of providing the necessary social foundation to all humans. In other words, large parts of the world's population are still lacking access to clean drinking, food, education or live under the poverty line.

The current situation of shortfalls and overshoots in the Doughnut gives urgent direction to sustainability in the life cycle of ICTs. The Doughnut illustrates that ICTs must, at a minimum, ensure they are not contributing to the effects that are causing us to overshoot our planet's ecological ceiling or undermine the social foundations of human welfare. Thus, while not undermining the positive role ICT can play in the transformation to sustainable development, the Planetary Boundary framework and the Doughnut make also clear that the social and environmental sustainability of ICT cannot be ignored.

Raworth has mapped the Sustainable Development Goals on the Doughnut and found a large overlap [20]. The SDGs cover all of the dimensions of the social foundations in its goals; the only exception is the Doughnut's dimension of "Political Voice", which is only covered in some SDG targets. Also in terms of ambition, the SDGs aim to end human deprivation is comparable to the social foundation of the Doughnut. Raworth is less optimistic when it comes to the ecological ceiling. The SDGs don't cover all dimensions or they do it in an unclear manner:

> "Some are absolute and time-bound: end overfishing and halt deforestation by 2020. But two key ambitions – to halt biodiversity loss and combat climate change – lack target dates. And for others, the measure of success is unclear. What would it mean to 'significantly reduce' nutrient pollution by 2025? To 'minimize the release of' hazardous chemicals by 2030? Or to 'minimize the impacts of' ocean acidification (by no set date)?" [20].

3.3 ICT in a Socio-Ecological System

Raworth's Doughnut is a visualization of a planetary and global socio-ecological system. It provides us with a space in which the social and the ecological are entangled. These entanglements are defined by two systems, which are still perceived as separate: the nine planetary boundaries, a product of Earth Systems research, and the social foundation, a product of the Janeiro 20+ process, the process around the United Nations Conference on Sustainable Development, during which the process to develop the SDGs started. On the other hand, the Doughnut creates a space for integrative thinking and doing. This thinking and doing is no longer situated within one system or discipline or the other, but emerges from these two interrelated systems.

Nested within socio-ecological systems thinking, the Doughnut can strengthen integrative ways of thinking about ICT and sustainable development. Instrumentalist notions of ICT give way to critical and constructive understandings [16, 21, 22]. For example, that a mobile phone is produced in a way that uses child labor in the production of its materials or that has serious reproductive health consequences for the women workers assembling mobile phones, can not be cancelled out against the positive social or economic development mobile phones can provide.

A non-instrumentalist understanding of technology also opens up for inquiries that were buried down in ideas of universalism and neutrality, for example, who exactly will benefit from this safe and just space? Will only humans benefit from this safe and just space? In the next section I will explore these questions against the background of the notion of the Anthropocene.

4 Life in the Ruins of Capitalism

4.1 Anthropocene

The understandings of sustainability in the SDGs and the doughnut are firmly located in the discourse of the Anthropocene. This epoch, characterised by the dominant human influence on the planet, or the epoch in which human activities outcompete natural processes, is not yet formally accepted as a geological period. As a narrative, the Anthropocene has become an important marker for discussions around planetary boundaries, climate change, and sustainable development.

The term Anthropocene was popularised by Crutzen [23], who puts the start of the epoch at the end of the 18th century, a date coinciding with the invention of the steam engine. The Executive Committee of the International Union of Geological Sciences has not yet ratified the proposal to accept the Anthropocene as a formal unit in the geological timescale, but the latest research (January 2018) puts the start of the Anthropocene in the Fall of 1965, based on peak levels in radio-active elements in both Northern and Southern hemispheres as a result of nuclear weapon testing [24]. This period coincides with a renewed focus on the environment; for example, Rachel Carson's Silent Spring [25], warning us of the destructive power of DDT, was published in 1962. The notion of the Anthropocene is thus associated with human activities that include sophisticated technologies.

Critics of the term Anthropocene argue that the term hides more than it helps to make visible. Jason W. Moore proposed the term "Capitalocene" to replace the "Anthropocene's shallow historiciziation" [26]. Moore's critique includes the following elements:

- It is a-political in that it situates the start of the Anthropocene in 19th century Britain, with coal and steam as the main force: "Not class. Not capital. Not imperialism. Not even culture. But… […] humanity as an undifferentiated whole".
- It is based on a particular analytical logic that separates humanity of the web of life; humans are doing something to nature.

Other critique comes from Malm and Hornborg, who argue that the Anthropocene narrative, coming from the natural sciences, has entered the social sciences and humanities, naturalising social relations, such as inequality between the species. As such, they argue, this narrative makes things more invisible than visible, and it prevents rather than stimulate action: "If global warming is the outcome of the knowledge of how to light a fire, or some other property of the human species acquired in some distant stage of its evolution, how can we even imagine a dismantling of the fossil economy?" [27].

Setting up humans against other species makes the tremendous inequalities found within humanity as a whole invisible, as well as hides the situation that large groups, marginalised in the global economy, are bearing the brunt of the effects of climate change and other ecological transformations. The naturalisation of social relations also affects the range of solutions possible. Proposals to deal with the unwanted effects of the Anthropocene are often technical, rather than political and social. Climate manipulations, geo-engineering, and ICT are seen as fixes of natural processes.

Raworth mapped the SDGs on the Doughnut, showing that they don't deal comprehensively with the environmental challenges that result in the overshoot of the planetary boundaries [20]. But while the Doughnut offers a more integrative approach to inform the ICT and sustainable development discourse, it is still firmly set within the discourse of the Anthropocene. As a consequence, there is a strong risk is that the unwanted differentiation between the sustainability of ICT and ICT for sustainability will continue. The dominance given to humans, in combination with the human capacity to design and use tools, will strengthen the instrumentalist ICT for sustainable development narrative. New visions and solutions, focusing more on the social and political entanglements of sustainable development, including the sustainability of ICT, will remain invisible.

4.2 Staying with the Trouble in Multispecies Worlds

Donna Haraway's most recent book, "Staying with the Trouble: Making kin in the Chthulucene" [28], is motivated by the dualistic thinking found in climate change discourses. At the one hand a techno-optimism, informed by the unshakeable trust that science and technology will get us out of our predicament, while on the other hand a cynical pessimism, which declares it is too late to do anything. The book expresses similar critique of the concept of Anthropocene as mention above, stressing that the term neatly divides the world in humans and the rest, ignoring our mutual becoming.

Haraway's approach is to tell stories that move beyond narratives of techno-optimism and cynical pessimism, thus opening up a new space for more imaginary stories. These stories, about species entanglements in the 'Chthulucene', which are impossible in the Anthopocene's or Capitalocene's ontological certainties, open up for new possibilities:

> "In urgent times, many of us are tempted to address trouble in terms of making an imagined future safe, of stopping something from happening that looms in the future, of clearing away the present and the past in order to make futures for coming generations. Staying with the trouble does not require such a relationship to times called the future. In fact, staying with the trouble requires learning to be truly present, not as a vanishing pivot between awful or edenic pasts and

apocalyptic or salvific futures, but as mortal critters entwined in myriad unfinished configurations of places, times, matters, meanings" [28].

Haraway's stories of trouble involve mainly dogs [29], but also other critters, such trees, doves, and ants [28]. They are stories of making kin and multispecies. She shows how to "stay with the trouble" of ontological entanglements, that is, not to reduce this complexity to easy solutions, categories, and certainties. One of Haraway's concepts of trouble, the *cyborg*, which engages with ontological categories of gender, human, and technology, has been very productive as a story-telling and analytical device in ICT research [30–32].

Anna Tsing's latest book, "The Mushroom at the End of the World: On the Possibility of Life in Capitalist Ruins" presents a similar perspective as Haraway: "Making worlds is not limited to humans" [33]. Tsing starts her explorations in multispecies worlds with a similar critique on the notion of Anthropocene. She positions the timeline of the Anthropocene at the advent of modern capitalism, which "entangled us with ideas of progress and with the spread of the techniques of alienation that turned both humans and other beings into resources" [33].

Tsing describes how the notion of progress is embedded in how we understand what it means to be human: "[W]e learn over and over that humans are different from the rest of the world because we look forward" [33]. This means that nonhumans are also trapped in the temporal rhythm of progress, which Tsing calls the "driving beat" that drowns out other temporal rhythms [ibid.]. Tsing uses the musical term "polyphony" as a metaphor for how we can identify and listen to these individual temporal rhythms and at the same time experience their harmony and dissonance.

In her explorations of the polyphonic assemblage of human – mushroom relations, Tsing describes how people and mushrooms have found ways to survive on the margins and destructions of capitalism in the Anthropocene. While not offering a blueprint for collective survival, Tsing inspires us to listen better to the temporal rhythms of human and nonhuman actors in the ICT and sustainable development discourses and to find dissonance in harmony and harmony in dissonance.

4.3   Does This Change Anything?

Haraway invites us to move beyond narratives of techno-optimism and cynical pessimism and Tsing proposes that we listen more seriously to the temporal rhythms of human and nonhuman actors. In the context of the ICT and sustainability, the question is: Does this change anything?[2] In what follows I present a brief reflection on how feminist technoscience can contribute to exploring existing binaries and categories found ICT and sustainability discourses.

Meet Agbogbloshie, a large scrap metal yard in Accra, Ghana, where I implemented fieldwork on repair and recycling as part of my research on the life cycle of mobile phones. Agbogbloshie is the place where cars, machines, and condemned electronics, such as mobile phones, are recycled. Non-metals parts that cannot be

---

[2] Reference to the overall theme of the conference: "This changes everything".

recycled, remain behind as untreated waste or are used as 'fuel' for the burning of cables that contain copper.

In the Western media, Agbogbloshie is often presented as the world's largest e-waste dump and as an environmental disaster, e.g., [34–38]. In reality, Agbogbloshie occupies only about one square kilometer. The yard and its surroundings (a household waste dump, river, wetland) are thoroughly polluted and the men and women working here have dangerously high levels of toxins in their blood (see Fig. 3) [39, 40]. At the same time, the activities in and around the yard have created thousands of jobs [41]. Many of the young men doing the most strenuous low-paid work come from northern Ghana, who use this work as an entry point into the urban economy [42]. Climate change plays an important role in their migration to Accra [43]. The workers of Agbogbloshie produce spare parts for the repair of electronics, cars, bicycles, etc., thus extending their lifespan, and a large amount of the recycled metals are sold to national and international companies that re-use them.

The lenses offered by Haraway and Tsing provide a particular layer of analysis. While the Western media and scholars strengthen the driving beat of environmental destruction, more careful observations bring out what Tsing's calls a polyphonic assemblage: the daily rhythm of work, such as the ongoing 'banging' of tools on metal heard all over the yard and the cooking selling of food and water by women; the rhythm of the animals living of the debris, such as the birds in the river and cows and goats grazing on the plain of household waste next to the yard; the rhythms of obsolescence of consumer electronics in rich countries and the import of legal and illegal second-hand electronics in Ghana; the rhythms of international scrap metal prices, which regulate many of the activities in the yard; and not to forget the rhythm of the seasons that expose climate changes and bring new waves of young people to Agbogbloshie. Paying close attention to these individual rhythms and staying with the trouble of informal e-waste recycling may offer new insight in how to deal with e-waste in countries that have no sustainable e-waste recycling facilities.

Presenting Agbogbloshie's problems as the result of the illegal dumping of e-waste from rich countries creates a particular scenario in which only binaries are presented, such as the rich versus poor and exploiting versus exploited. Such stories often ignore Ghana's domestic ICT market, which played a central role in its economic development, and produce solutions, such as mechanization (cable-stripping machines, see Fig. 3) and industrialization, without considering global entanglements. For example, understanding why young men at Agbogbloshie still prefer burning the cables, while cable-stripping machines are available, is a complex story in which there are no clear perpetrators and victims.[3] Haraway thus warns against telling restrictive stories: "it matters what stories tell stories" [28]. Staying with the trouble is about "story-telling

---

[3] I talked with several of the young men burning cables. Their daily earnings are so low, depending on the price the middlemen are willing to pay, that they don't want to spend any money on electricity for running the machine. They als mention that operating the machine takes time; time they prefer to spend on collecting cables. Observing their work, I noticed they used plastic components from e-waste and isolation from old fridges as fuel for the fires. It takes about a minute to burn a kilo of cables. The thick smoke from the fires contains dangerous toxins, creating serious health risks.

Fig. 3. Cable stripping machine (left) and electronics recycling (right) in the Agbogbloshie scrap metal yard (Photos: SMART/Maja van der Velden)

for earthly survival", Haraway argues, stories that are situated in the now, stories of a thick ongoing presence, not an instantaneous presence [28, 44].

The purpose of this brief reflection on Agbogbloshie is to highlight that a more integrative approach can open up new ways of understanding the relation between ICT and sustainability. Tsing and Haraway remind us that ICT and sustainability is about the mutual becoming of humans and technology. Rather than promoting dualistic thinking, dividing the field into or ICT for sustainability and sustainable ICT, we can look for contact zones, spaces of dissonance within each and harmony between both. What we will find there are stories in which human, nonhumans, and earthly survival are collaboratively entangled. However, as long as we situated humans in the center of our stories, ICT will be understood as man's neutral tool that can be used for good or for bad. By bestowing man with ICT the agency for change, we remain caught in the predicament of the Anthropocene, literally and figuratively.

5 Concluding Remarks

The discourse on ICT and sustainable development is characterized by two divergent thoughts; ICT is perceived as both an enabler of sustainable development as well as a producer of unsustainability, because of the social and environmental impacts found in

178   M. van der Velden

the life cycles of ICTs. The notion of ICT as an enabler or facilitator is based on an instrumentalist understanding of technology, in which technology is perceived as a neutral tool, ready to be used by man for good or bad. This driving beat is strengthened by the human-centeredness underlying the sustainable development discourse as well as the human-centered narrative of the Anthropocene.

The example of electronics recycling in Ghana showed the entanglement of the two discourses. The work of feminist scholars, who invite us to both imagine different figurations and futures in the thick ongoing presence (Haraway) and to pay attention to local practices, often found in the margins of Anthropocene capitalism (Tsing), can help us to overcome telling restrictive stories. The resulting decentering of man and re-politicizing of ICT opens up for new ways of engaging with ICT and sustainability.

Lastly, the Anthropocene is more than a geological epoch based on measurements of human impact on the planet. We can also identify a technological Anthropocene, an epoch in which technology is understood as the facilitator of progress and growth. The dominant discourse or beat, that more technology will get us out of this predicament and will bring sustainable development, needs both refinement and critical investigation.

Acknowledgement. I would like to thank the two anonymous reviewers for their helpful comments; Anna Croon for asking about the nonhumans in the doughnut; Dr. Martin Oteng-Ababio, my SMART colleague in Ghana; and my fellow travelers to Ghana, Hanne Cecilie Geirbo and Alice Frantz Schneider. This paper is written as part of SMART, a Horizon2020-financed research project (grant agreement no. 693642).

References

1. Raworth, K.: A doughnut for the Anthropocene: humanity's compass in the 21st century. Lancet Planet Health **1**, e48–e49 (2017)
2. United Nations: Sustainable Development Goals. UN Sustainable Development Goals (2018). http://www.un.org/sustainabledevelopment/sustainable-development-goals/. Accessed 2 Feb 2018
3. van der Velden, M., Taylor, M.B.: Sustainability Hotspots Analysis of the Mobile Phone Lifecycle. University of Oslo, Oslo (2017). https://zenodo.org/record/1146844. Accessed 30 Nov 2017
4. Raworth, K.: A safe and just space for humanity: can we live within the doughnut. Oxfam Policy Pract. Clim. Change Resil. **8**, 1–26 (2012)
5. van der Velden, M.: Design for living in the doughnut. In: Proceedings of Relating Systems Thinking and Design (RSD6) 2017 Symposium, Oslo (2018). https://systemic-design.net/wp-content/uploads/2017/12/Maja-van-der-Velden-RSD6-working-paper.pdf. Accessed 30 Nov 2017
6. United Nations: ICTs as a catalyst for sustainable development: Sustainable Development Knowledge Platform (2016). https://sustainabledevelopment.un.org/index.php. Accessed 30 Jan 2018
7. SustainAbility: How ICT can deliver the SDGs . SustainAbility (2018). http://sustainability.com/our-work/case-studies/how-ict-can-deliver-the-sdgs/. Accessed 30 Jan 2018
8. ITU. ICTs for a sustainable world #ICT4SDG Toolkit (2018). http://www.itu.int:80/en/sustainable-world/Pages/toolkit.aspx. Accessed 30 Jan 2018

9. de Haan, E., Scheele, F., Kiezebrink, V.: Cobalt Blues: Environmental Pollution and Human Rights Violations in Katanga's Copper and Cobalt Mines. SOMO, Amsterdam (2016)
10. China Labour Watch, Future in Our Hands: Something's Not Right Here: Poor working conditions persist at Apple supplier Pegatron. Future in Our Hands, Oslo (2015)
11. Bafilemba, F., Lezhnev, S.: Congo's Conflict Gold Rush: Bringing Gold into the Legal Trade in the Democratic Republic of the Congo. Enough Project, Washington (2015)
12. Asia Monitor Resource Centre: Labour Rights in High Tech Electronics: Case Studies of Workers' Struggles in Samsung Electronics and its Asian Suppliers. AMRC, Hong Kong (2013)
13. Human Rights Watch: Precious Metal, Cheap Labor: Child Labor and Corporate Responsibility in Ghana's Artisanal Gold Mines. HRW, Washington (2015)
14. Brown, J.H.: The oxymoron of sustainable development. Bioscience **65**, 1027–1029 (2015)
15. Patrignani, N., Whitehouse, D.: Slow tech: a quest for good, clean and fair ICT. J. Inf. Commun. Ethics Soc. **12**, 78–92 (2014)
16. Feenberg, A.: Transforming Technology: A Critical Theory Revisited. Oxford University Press, Oxford (2002)
17. Raworth, K.: Doughnut Economics: Seven Ways to Think Like a 21st-Century Economist. Chelsea Green Publishing, London (2017)
18. Rockström, J., Steffen, W., Noone, K., et al.: Planetary boundaries: exploring the safe operating space for humanity. Ecol. Soc. **14**, 32 (2009)
19. Steffen, W., Richardson, K., Rockström, J., et al.: Planetary boundaries: guiding human development on a changing planet. Science **347**, 1259855 (2015)
20. Raworth, K.: Will these sustainable development goals get us into the doughnut (aka a safe and just space for humanity)? In: Poverty Power (2014). http://oxfamblogs.org/fp2p/will-these-sustainable-development-goals-get-us-into-the-doughnut-aka-a-safe-and-just-space-for-humanity-guest-post-from-kate-raworth/. Accessed 7 Sep 2016
21. Verbeek, P.-P.: Materializing morality design ethics and technological mediation. Sci. Technol. Hum. Values **31**, 361–380 (2006)
22. Akrich, M.: The description of technical objects. In: Bijker, W., Law, J. (eds.) Shaping Technology, pp. 205–224. MIT Press, Cambridge (1992)
23. Crutzen, P.J.: The "anthropocene". In: Ehlers, P.D.E., Krafft, D.T. (eds.) Earth System Science in the Anthropocene, pp. 13–18. Springer, Berlin Heidelberg (2006). https://doi.org/10.1007/3-540-26590-2_3
24. Turney, C.S.M., Palmer, J., Maslin, M.A., et al.: Global peak in atmospheric radiocarbon provides a potential definition for the onset of the anthropocene epoch in 1965. Sci. Rep. **8**, 3293 (2018)
25. Carson, R.: Silent Spring. Mariner Books, Boston (1962)
26. Moore, J.W.: The capitalocene, part I: on the nature and origins of our ecological crisis. J. Peasant Stud. **44**, 594–630 (2017)
27. Malm, A., Hornborg, A.: The geology of mankind? A critique of the Anthropocene narrative. Anthr. Rev. **1**, 62–69 (2014)
28. Haraway, D.: Staying with the Trouble: Making Kin in the Chthulucene. Duke Univ. Press, Durham (2016)
29. Haraway, D.: When Species Meet. University of Minnesota Press, Minneapolis (2008)
30. Markussen, R.: Politics of intervention in design: feminist reflections on the Scandinavian tradition. AI Soc. **10**, 127–141 (1996)
31. Ehrnberger, K., Broms, L., Katzeff, C.: Becoming the energy aware clock - revisiting the design process through a feminist gaze. Exp. Des. Res. **2013**, 5 (2013)

32. van der Velden, M.: What's love got to do with IT? On ethics and accountability in telling technology stories. In: Sixth International Conference on Cultural Attitudes towards Technology and Communication. University of Nîmes, Nîmes, France (2008)

33. Tsing, A.L.: The Mushroom at the End of the World: On the Possibility of Life in Capitalist Ruins. Princeton University Press, Princeton (2015)

34. Tue, N.M., Goto, A., Takahashi, S., et al.: Release of chlorinated, brominated and mixed halogenated dioxin-related compounds to soils from open burning of e-waste in Agbogbloshie (Accra, Ghana). J. Hazard. Mater. **302**, 151–157 (2016)

35. Chama, M.A., Amankwa, E.F., Oteng-Ababio, M.: Trace metal levels of the Odaw river sediments at the Agbogbloshie e-waste recycling site. J. Sci. Technol. Ghana **34**, 1–8 (2014)

36. BBC: Insider: Reggie Yates – A Week in a Toxic Waste Dump (2017). https://www.youtube.com/watch?v=3IPqgy2K8RI. Accessed 24 Feb 2018

37. Briefing RLT for B. Australian e-waste ending up in toxic African dump, torn apart by children. ABC News (2017). http://www.abc.net.au/news/2017-03-10/australian-e-waste-ending-up-in-toxic-african-dump/8339760. Accessed 29 Apr 2018

38. McElvaney, K.: Ghana's e-waste magnet. https://www.aljazeera.com/indepth/inpictures/2014/01/pictures-ghana-e-waste-mecca-2014130104740975223.html. Accessed 29 Apr 2018

39. Srigboh, R.K., Basu, N., Stephens, J., et al.: Multiple elemental exposures amongst workers at the Agbogbloshie electronic waste (e-waste) site in Ghana. Chemosphere **164**, 68–74 (2016). https://doi.org/10.1016/j.chemosphere.2016.08.089

40. Amankwaa, E.F., Tsikudo, K.A.A., Bowman, J.: 'Away' is a place: the impact of electronic waste recycling on blood lead levels in Ghana. Sci. Total Environ. **601**, 1566–1574 (2017). https://doi.org/10.1016/j.scitotenv.2017.05.283

41. Goldwater, S.: Regolith (2014). https://vimeo.com/107800720. Accessed 24 Feb 2018

42. Oteng-Ababio, M.M., Amankwaa, E.F.: The e-waste conundrum: balancing evidence from the North and on-the-ground developing countries' realities for improved management. Afr. Rev. Econ. Financ. **6**, 181–204 (2014)

43. Fielmua, N., Gordon, D., Mwingyine, D.T.: Migration as an adaptation strategy to climate change: influencing factors in North-Western Ghana. J. Sustain Dev. **10**, 155 (2017)

44. Yale University: Donna Haraway - "Making Oddkin: Story Telling for Earthly Survival." New Haven (2017). https://www.youtube.com/watch?v=z-iEnSztKu8. Accessed 24 Feb 2018

On the Complex Relationship Between ICT Systems and the Planet

Norberto Patrignani[1(✉)] and Iordanis Kavathatzopoulos[2]

[1] Politecnico of Torino, Turin, Italy
norberto.patrignani@polito.it
[2] Uppsala University, Uppsala, Sweden
iordanis.kavathatzopoulos@uu.se

Abstract. This paper addresses the challenges of designing sustainable Information and Communication Technology (ICT) systems. The complexity of ICT systems, the number of stakeholders involved (technology providers, policy makers, users, etc.), and the extension and global scale of ICT supply chain are the main challenges at the core of the complex relationship between ICT systems and the planet Earth. ICT offer an opportunity for an exchange between matter-energy and information: the better use of information offers the great opportunity for decreasing the environmental impact of human activities by decreasing the matter and energy consumption. But, on the other side, like any human activity, the design, production, use, and disposal of complex ICT systems, has as a consequence a growth in entropy. This intriguing dilemma is one of the most difficult challenges in front of designers, ICT companies, users, and policy makers. This paper concentrates on the designers, the engineers' dilemmas: what are the ethical competences, the skills, the methods for addressing these complex ethical dilemmas? Among the many ethical approaches, the "virtue/future ethics" is proposed as a core ethical competence for the designers and engineers of the future.

Keywords: Information and Communication Technology (ICT)
Entropy · Future ethics · Fairphone · Slow tech

1 Introduction

ICT systems are probably the most complex artifacts ever built by humans. Starting at chip level the number of fundamental electronic components (e.g. transistors) can easily reach the number of billions. Then these chips are inserted inside systems containing thousands of components at device level. These devices nowadays are interconnected with other billions of devices, etc. As a result we have a complexity that can easily reach the level of the human brain, the most complex result of natural evolution: 10^{11} neurons [1]. And this is just a rough estimation based only on the hardware side of ICT, if one includes also the software side, then complexity of the emerging systems is exponential.

Since their first realizations, in the 1950s, computers and ICT systems have been applied in a growing number of fields: from offices, to public authorities, to the general

© IFIP International Federation for Information Processing 2018
Published by Springer Nature Switzerland AG 2018. All Rights Reserved
D. Kreps et al. (Eds.): HCC13 2018, IFIP AICT 537, pp. 181–187, 2018.
https://doi.org/10.1007/978-3-319-99605-9_13

society. Today, many activities that once required a great amount of energy can be executed with the use of ICT systems. This implies a great amount of saving in energy consumption, pollution, and CO_2 release: for example a wise use of ICT can save, by 2030, 12.1 $GtonCO_2$, (1.8 in power generation, 3.6 in transports and mobility, 2.0 in agriculture, 2.0 in buildings and energy management, 2.7 in manufacturing [2]. On the other side, the power consumed during ICT use and application (all electronic systems are powered with electricity) generates an amount of CO_2 of about 1.25 $GtonCO_2$ (0.59 for powering end users devices, 0.3 for powering voice and data networks, and 0.36 for powering the data centers). As a result, the saving looks interesting: -10.85 $GtonCO_2$.

But there are other dimensions of the scenario: like any human activity, the design, production, use, and disposal of complex ICT systems, has as a lot of consequences in the material consumed in the design/production phase, and in a growing amount of e-waste at their end-of-life; in few words, ICT systems have, as a consequence, a growth in entropy. What is the balance of these opposite effects of ICT? How can designers and engineers face these challenges? What are the ethical competences needed? And how can these ethical competences be acquired?

2   ICT Entropy Balance

2.1   Material Consumption

Starting from the Personal Computing era, in 1980s, and further accelerating in the 1990s with the Web, the number of people using computers and the network have reached about 4.1 billions of people in 2018 [3]. Also, starting from January 2007, with the launch of the first smart-phone, a device connected to the network with a simple interface based on a touchscreen, about 7.5 billions of these "pocket" computers have been produced and distributed into the society [4]. Producing this number of devices required a huge amount of minerals and materials. For example, the highest "material intensity" in manufacturing is the one related to chips: producing one gram of a memory chip requires 850 grams of materials, fossil fuels, and chemicals; producing one gram of a microprocessor chip requires 3,440 grams of the same resources [5]. In particular it is important to underline that the most indispensable of these materials are the so called "rare-earths"; the seventeen rare-earth elements are Scandium (Sc), Yttrium (Y), plus the fifteen "Lanthanide": Lanthanum (La), Cerium (Ce), Praseody-mium (Pr), Neodymium (Nd), Promethium (Pm), Samarium (Sm), Europium (Eu), Gadolinium (Gd), Terbium (Tb), Dysprosium (Dy), Holmium (Ho), Erbium (Er), Thulium (Tm), Ytterbium (Yb), and Lutetium (Lu), they are dispersed throughout the earth's crust and they are difficult to mine. For example the Indium, one of the precious minerals essential for building displays, have been consumed in a total of 71 tons since the beginning of smart-phones era started in 2007; at the current rates of Indium extraction levels there are only 14 years of supply remaining [4]. Even more controversial is the origin of many of these minerals coming from war areas in Africa, like the so-called "conflict minerals" [6]. Can ICT be sustainable in the long-term at the current pace of material consumption?

2.2   Power Consumption

The dilemma about information-energy is one of the most debated in the history of science. It was James Clerk Maxwell that in 1867 triggered this discussion with the famous "Maxwell's demon" mental experiment where an high speed creature, able to discriminate between fast and slow molecules, as a consequence was creating a difference in temperature against the law of entropy: "... if we conceive of a being whose faculties are so sharpened that he can follow every molecule... He will thus, without expenditure of work, raise the temperature of B and lower that of A, in contradiction to the second law of thermodynamics..." (J.C. Maxwell, letter to P.G. Tait, 11 December 1867) [7]. But acquiring information requires an expenditure of energy, as physicist and inventor Leo Szilard demonstrated in 1929, and Leon Brillouin described in 1953: information does not come for free [8, 9]. Today it has even been calculated the amount of energy required for computing just 1 bit [10]:

$$W = K_b T \ln 2 \, (Joule)$$

where: $K_b = 1.38 \times 10^{-23}$ (J/°K), is the Boltzmann's constant, T = Temperature in °K = 273.15 + t (°C), and ln 2 = 0.69315 (logarithm in base e = 2.718). For example the minimum amount of energy required for computing 1 bit at the temperature t = 25° C (T = 298.15°K) is about 285.5×10^{-23} J, and the corresponding power consumed for computing 1 bit/sec is 285.5×10^{-23} W, 1 byte/sec is $2,284 \times 10^{-23}$ W, etc. Nowadays it is well known that the world energy consumption just for datacenters (where it is concentrated the computing power of the planet) has been about 416 TWh (TeraWatt-hours), just for reference, in 2016 the entire country of Italy consumed about 310 TWh of energy [11]. And this is just the 10% of the entire energy consumption of ICT. Other contributions are: 20% is due to networks, 45% to fixed lines access and 25% to mobile access. But just for smartphones the total energy consumption since their introduction in 2007 is about 968 TWh (73% for manufacturing, 19% for use, 6% distribution, and 2% for disposal). What will be, in the long term, the source of this growing power needed for running the ICT infrastructure?

2.3   e-Waste

The problem of e-waste (discarded electronic devices, because at their end-of-life or just for fashion reasons) is one of the most urgent issues for long-term ICT sustainability and its informal processing in developing countries leads to dangerous impact on human health and on the environment (since in all ICT devices are contained many hazardous substances). For example, in 2014, the United Nations University estimated that: roughly 42 million tons of e-waste was generated despite the value and the risk of related materials; smart-phones contributed for 3 million tons to this growing mountain of e-waste since it will reach 50 million metric tons in 2017 [12]. The first challenge is to investigate the destination of these devices at the end of their life, since they are sent to destinations where their management is very dangerous. The Blacksmith Institute and Green Cross Switzerland estimated that the most polluted place in the world is

Agbogbloshie, close to Accra in Ghana, a mountain of e-waste growing at a rate of 215,000 tons per year [13].

The entire ICT community and in particular the ICT industry and the designers and engineers of ICT systems should immediately start to face this challenge for the long-term ICT sustainability. Priority action is the recycling of ICT devices: for example, the cost of recycling gold from old computers is in the same order of the cost of mining the mineral [14]. However, the crucial step is in the hands of designers and engineers, it is in the choices made at design stage: ICT should be required to be recyclable-by-design (and repairable-by-design). Of course this would be facilitated if the interfaces of all modules are inter-operable and public, like in open software and open hardware [15]. In the long-term a more radical action could be a comprehensive industrial design and development ("regenerative design"), the industrial products should start to be seen as organisms with circulating materials creating waste-free systems [16].

3   The Ethical Competence of ICT Engineers

Indeed the challenges outlined in ICT are very difficult, not only because the stake-holders network of ICT is extended at global scale and complex. Or because the design challenges for ICT designers are still looking for practical solutions (e.g. recyclable-by-design, repairable-by-design, etc.). The examples of best-practices are till very rare and very few ICT companies have adopted these innovative and future-proof approaches. One well-known example is the little Dutch company designing the Fairphone [17]. Even the international advocacy organization Greenpeace has recently released a very intriguing report with a ranking among the seventeen world's leading ICT vendors with reference to their environmental impacts by evaluating energy use, resource consumption, and chemical elimination [18]. But there is a growing interest in a more deep question: is it enough to close the cycles? Or it is needed to slow down the ICT consumption cycles? [19]. From another point of view, it is emerging a new competence needed for engineers: an ethical competence. The main ethical approaches are consequentialism (focuses on the consequences of actions), deontology (focuses on actions themselves) and virtue ethics (focuses on the acting person and his/her character traits). Virtue ethics, even if formulated by Aristotle in 350 B.C., it is still relevant for engineers. Indeed facing the ICT long-term sustainability requires many virtues to engineers: expertise/professionalism, clear and informative communication, cooperation, willingness to make compromises, objectivity, being open to criticism, stamina, creativity, striving for quality, having an eye for details, and being in the habit of reporting on work carefully [20]. Also, virtue ethics involves also practical wisdom: the ability to make ethical judgments in complex situations, in a real context [21]. All in all, engineers need the skills to handle this multitude and complexity of the above issues, i.e. they need the virtue of phronesis [22]. The virtue of phronesis is the ability to think like a God, i.e. to run the process of thinking in the right way. Accordingly, focus of research and education in ICT ethics should be on thinking, developing the skills to think in the right way [23]. Long-term sustainability concerns the future of the planet and the future generations. One of the first thinkers concentrating on these issues was Hans Jonas: he proposed the need for appropriate technological choices with regard to the planet and future generations [24]. He proposed, probably for the first time in philosophy, to include also future generations in the ethical debate: the pace of ICT development is exactly at the center of this issue due to its exponential growth in power speed. Another ethical approach interesting in this context is the "future ethics". For the first time in our history, we start to imagine that, at the extreme, some consequences of our actions (not just of natural evolution) could bring us into a world without us. Can we imagine this scenario? And how does this future scenario influence our present behavior? And what kind of ethics are we going to use for deciding what is right and what is wrong? What could the norms that will steer us in the right direction be? What can designers and engineers learn from future ethics? A very good example is the so called "climate-change" issue: CO_2, as a by-product generated from combustion of fossil-fuels is considered the main component of greenhouse gases that, by increasing their concentration in the atmosphere, has led to an increase in the world's average temperature, the so called green-house effect [25]. As seen above, also ICT is contributing to this green-house effect. What do all these issues have in common? At least two characteristics are present: they are irreversible, and have serious consequences for future generations. So the only wise action is to start reducing the CO_2 emissions as soon as possible. A time dimension in our ethical analysis needs then to be addressed. But what are the new characteristics of our scenario when we think about time? For example, what does it mean to act quickly? Does that mean that time is running out? This is crucial for understanding possible future outcomes and for taking action now. The awareness (and knowledge) of the future become the background for taking action into the present. But what actions? In designing ICT systems this is the most critical issue. How can we introduce this time dimension in our ethical analysis? Jonas suggested to introduce "new stakeholders" in our philosophical and ethical debate: the planet and future generations. How are we responsible in front of them? This direction will bring us into a new outcomes-driven ethics (strongly linked with utilitarianism and consequentialism), very different from a rights-driven ethics. Our action is driven by some urgency, by some forecasted results. But how can designers balance the rights of living and future generations? Here starts the conflict between living in the present time and in the future time. This is the core problem of future ethics. What are the conditions that will convince ICT designers, policymakers (and ICT users) to take actions now, to change behaviors now, to steer technology developments now in a direction that is appropriate for taking into account these future risks? How do we face the actual risk, that people enter now into a kind of fatalism and refuse to think, to discuss, to understand and, finally, to change their behavior now? The tsunami of emerging technologies is overwhelming us at such a speed that project leaders, engineers, science and technology researchers (and policy makers) have many difficulties in recognizing social and ethical issues in new fields like ICT. Historically, we apply ethics to us and to relations among us, the human beings living in the present time. The problem with emerging ICT systems is that in many cases the consequences of their deployment are projected into a so distant future that we miss the direct interactions with the consequences of our actions (who care if in 2080 Indium is exhausted?). What if our actions will have an impact, not only on the next generations (our children and grandchildren, with which we will have some kind of interactions), but mostly to long-distant future generations? Until the last century the impact of human activities was mainly concentrated in terms of scope (the cities and their neigh-boroughs) and in terms of time (the present or next generation). Since few years this has changed. Indeed, new developments in some areas of ICT systems have the potentiality of impacting the entire planet and the future of many generations, the scope and time are at another scale, another order of magnitude. A good example of an impact on long-distant future generations is the nuclear waste management problem: even the best initiatives for addressing this issue (like Onkalo, the under construction long-term storage for all nuclear waste produced in Finland) have to accept that the nuclear waste will remain dangerous for more than 100,000 years: hundred millennia is a time that on the human scale is close to eternity, the saecula saeculorum [26]. Here a completely new urgency, not just for philosophers or ethicists, but for all researchers and in general for all of us emerges: how can we develop a new stage of ethics, an ethics that will drive our behavior and inform our decisions when the consequences of our acts are so distant in the future? [27].

4 Conclusions

Further studies and actions, for example education focused on supporting thinking in handling ICT ethics issues, are needed for developing the ethical competences for ICT designers and engineers. If these are the ethical competences needed by engineers, how can these ethical competences be acquired? Recently some of the world's most important academic institutions have recognized the need of introducing, as mandatory subject, foundations of ethics in computer science: the next generations of engineers need to be not just experts but also aware of the social and ethical impact of ICT [28]. In particular virtue ethics and future ethics are the most promising approaches for addressing the ethical issues of long-term sustainability of ICT and for understanding the complex relationships between ICT systems and the planet.

References

1. Herculano-Houiel, S.: The human brain in numbers: a linearly scaled-up primate brain. Front. Hum. Neurosci. **3**, 31 (2009). https://doi.org/10.3389/neuro.09.031.2009
2. GeSI: ICT Solutions for 21st Century Challenges, Global e-Sustainability Initiative. http://smarter2030.gesi.org/. Accessed 20 Jan 2018
3. Internetstats: Internet Usage Statistics, The Internet Big Picture, World Internet Users and 2017 Population Stats. www.internetworldstats.com/stats.htm. Accessed 20 Jan 2018
4. Greenpeace: From Smart to Senseless: The Global Impact of 10 Years of Smart-phones (2017)
5. SVTC: Silicon Valley Toxics Coalition, October 2007
6. Vazquez-Figueroa, A.: Coltan, Ediciones B (2010)
7. Leff, H., Rex, A.F.: Maxwell's Demon, Entropy, Information, Computing. CRC Press (1990)
8. Szilard, L.: On the reduction of entropy in a thermodynamic system by the intervention of intelligent beings. Zeitschrift für Physik. **53**(11–12), 840–856 (1929)
9. Brillouin, L.: Negentropy principle of information. J. Appl. Phys. **V24**(9) (1953)

10. Landauer, R.: Irreversibility and heat generation in the computing process. IBM J. Res. Dev. **5**, 183–191 (1961)
11. Ericsson: ICT and Power, Energy Performance Report 2016 (2016)
12. Baldé, C.P., Wang, F., Kuehr, R., Huisman, J.: The Global e-waste Monitor, United Nations University (2014)
13. Bernhardt, A., Gysi, N. (eds.): The Worlds Worst 2013: The Top Ten Toxic Threats, Blacksmith Institute, Green Cross Switzerland (2013)
14. Step: Solving the e-waste problem. www.step-initiative.org. Accessed 20 Jan 2018
15. Arduino: Arduino: an open source electronics platform. http://www.arduino.cc. Accessed 20 Jan 2018
16. Lovins, L.H.: Rethinking Production, State of the World 2008 - Innovations for a Sustainable World. The Worldwatch Institute, Washington, D.C. (2008)
17. Fairphone: The modular phone that's built to last. www.fairphone.com. Accessed 20 Jan 2018
18. Greenpeace:Guide to Greener Electronics 2017. http://www.greenpeace.org/greenerguide. org. Accessed 20 Jan 2018
19. Patrignani, N., Whitehouse, D.: Slow Tech and ICT. A Responsible, Sustainable and Ethical Approach, Palgrave-MacMillan (2018). ISBN 978-3-319-689449
20. Pritchard, M.S.: Responsible engineering. The importance of character and imagination. Sci. Eng. Ethics **7**(3), 391–402 (2001)
21. Van de Poel, I., Royakkers, L.: Ethics, Technology, and Engineering. An Introduction. Wyley-Blackwell, Oxford (2011)
22. Aristotle: Nicomachean Ethics, Papyros, Athens (1975)
23. Arendt, H.: Responsibility and Judgement. Schocken, New York (2003)
24. Jonas, H.: The Imperative of Responsibility. In Search of an Ethics for the Technological Age. University of Chicago Press, Chicago (1985)
25. Nova: Enhanced greenhouse effect - a hot international topic, Nova, Australian Academy of Science (2008)
26. Madsen, M.: Into Eternity: A Film for the Future. https://www.imdb.com/title/tt1194612/? ref_=nm_ov_bio_lk1. Accessed 20 Jan 2018
27. Birnbacher, D.: What motivates us to care for the (distant) future? Working Papers N° 04/2006. Iddri, 27 p. (2006). Conference by Dieter Birnbacher, Seminar on Sustainable Development, 21 February 2006
28. Singer, N.: Tech's Ethical 'Dark Side': Harvard, Stanford and Others Want to Address It, New York Times, 12 February 2018

Obsolescence in Information and Communication Technology: A Critical Discourse Analysis

Ines Junge[(⊠)] and Maja van der Velden

Department of Informatics, University of Oslo, Oslo, Norway
{inespj,majava}@ifi.uio.no

Abstract. Responsible production and consumption is one of the United Nations' Sustainable Development Goals. *Fast Tech*, resulting in premature obsolescence, is perceived as an important factor in unsustainable production and consumption patterns of information and communication technologies. In order to investigate societal perspectives on planned obsolescence and its root causes in Norway, we implemented a critical discourse analysis of the Norwegian written media. Technology discourses are often inspired by particular understandings of technology-society relations. We therefore mapped our findings on Andrew Feenberg's four theories of technology. All articles presented a critical perspective towards the phenomenon of obsolescence. The majority of articles expressed an instrumentalist understanding of technology as the cause of planned obsolescence, while the rest communicated technological determinism as the main worldview underlying planned obsolescence. Both instrumentalist and determinist understandings of technology are based on the understanding that technology is intrinsically neutral and can be used for good or bad ends. We argue that this *technology is neutral* perspective can undermine the development of policy and design interventions that can contribute to sustainable technology. A thorough engagement with the politics of technology is needed to reach the goal of responsible production and consumption.

Keywords: Norway · Planned obsolescence · Slow Tech
Theories of technology

1   Introduction

The term obsolescence means different things. Focussing on products, we can understand obsolescence as products breaking down prematurely, becoming out of date or just not used anymore. There are different forms of obsolescence [1, 2], but this paper is mainly concerned with planned obsolescence, the "deliberate curtailment of product life spans" [3], which is often discussed in the context of unsustainable production and consumption. *Responsible consumption and production* is one of the United Nations Sustainable Development Goals [4]. This goal aims, among others, at "doing more and better with less, increasing net welfare gains from economic activities by reducing resource use, degradation and pollution along the whole lifecycle, while increasing quality of life" [4]. Within this discourse, the planned obsolescence of ICT is based on

D. Kreps et al. (Eds.): HCC13 2018, IFIP AICT 537, pp. 188–201, 2018.
https://doi.org/10.1007/978-3-319-99605-9_14

a critical theory of technology, e.g. [5–7]; societal interventions to extend the lifespan of technology are perceived as both needed and possible.

According to Wyatt [8], technological determinism, rather than critical theory, is the dominant understanding of technology. In this perspective, society has no power over technological developments and their direction. In this paper, we will explore this apparent disparity between accounts of planned obsolescence and technological determinism by analysing texts on planned obsolescence in the Norwegian written media until the end of 2017. We will analyse these texts to bring out the main themes as well as the perspectives on technology underlying the discourse on planned obsolescence, in particular the relation between technology and society.

Feenberg's philosophy of technology forms the basis for understanding the relation or intersection between technology and society [9]. His approach identifies four dimensions of technology: autonomous (A) vs. human controlled (H) technology and neutral (N) vs. value-laden (V) technology[1,2] (see Fig. 1):

- Autonomous technology (A) has a unidirectional strong effect that is not or only minimally mediated by other factors (such as society)
- Humanly controlled technology (H), in which society has a unidirectional strong effect that is not or only minimally mediated by other factors (such as technology)
- Neutral technology (N) can be used for good or bad – there is no connection between means (technology) and ends (our goals)
- Value-laden technology (V), in which there is an intimate connection between means (technology) and ends (our goals).

The four dimensions intersect and form a 2 × 2-matrix with the couples AN - Determinism, AV - Substantivism, HN - Instrumentalism and HV - Critical Theory. Deterministic theories of technology "minimize our power to control technical development but consider technical means to be neutral" (see Footnote 2). Substantivist theories of technology share this "scepticism regarding human agency but deny the neutrality thesis" [ibid.]. Critical theories "affirm human agency while rejecting the neutrality of technology" [ibid.]. Instrumentalism asserts "both the possibility of human control and the neutrality of technology" [ibid.].

In this paper we will map discourses of obsolescence on these four theoretical frameworks. We envision that this will enable a better understanding of where planned obsolescence is located in the intersections of technology and society, thus contributing to future policy and design interventions that prolong the lifespan of ICTs and that can contribute to sustainable consumption and production.

---

[1] [10, p. 45].
[2] [11, p. 9].

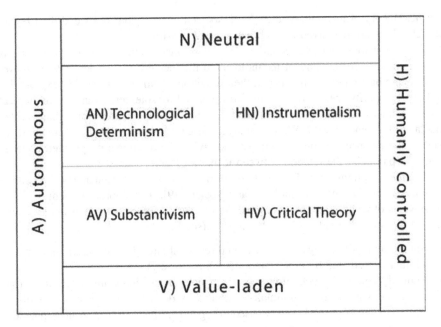

Fig. 1. Feenberg's model

2 Background and Methodology

In 2014, Patrignani and Whitehouse [12] called for the establishment of a Slow Tech movement. It was inspired by the Slow Food movement, founded in 1989 in Italy, a grassroots organisation, which proposed to reverse the effects of fast food[3]. In analogy to slow food, Slow Tech is not a "technology that is slow", but a concept that makes people "reflect, stand back, and consider" (ibid.). Patrignani and Whitehouse state that within computer ethics, a more proactive attitude has to be cultivated, which produces ICT that is good, clean and fair [12]. The approach is a holistic one, since it questions the complete value chain of ICT development and production [ibid.].

An example of today's "fast tech" is the smartphone, which is replaced on average every 18 months[4]. Such *fast consumption* is often based on a *fast pace of technological development*, which results in premature obsolescence [13]. Patrignani and Whitehouse emphasize that we "need to re-appropriate the pace of technological development and overcome the traditional view of "technological determinism" (Davies 1997)"[5]. The Slow Tech movement thus "signals a departure away from the traditional position of technology push and from the mantra that technology is driving the future"[6].

---

[3] [12, p. 82].

[4] [12, p. 84].

[5] [12, p. 89].

[6] [12, p. 81].

Patrignani and Whitehouse argue that "computer ethics have to become a tool to steer computing innovation constructively in a responsible way, and not simply a tool to compensate or fill a policy gap. This is a form of responsible innovation that places human beings, society, sustainability, the environment and planet as essential."[7]. They thus place the Slow Tech movement firmly in the Critical Theory quadrant of the theories of technology matrix. Their call for policy innovation is based on a perspective of technology as human-controlled and value-laden – thus opposing the technological determinist position.

2.1 Mapping Obsolescence Discourses

What types of understanding of the relationship between technology and society are underlying Norwegian public discourses on planned obsolescence? We employed a Critical Discourse Analysis (CDA) of written publications in the national media on planned obsolescence. Discourse analysis sees language as social practice; language or discourse is socially constitutive as well as socially conditioned [14]. CDA has a transformative component; by making the interconnectedness of things visible, CDA can be "a guide for human action", contributing to "producing both enlightenment and emancipation"[8]. The purpose of our analysis is to reveal the different discourse positions or ideological locations of these publications, in order to evaluate to what extent these positions do justice to Patrignani and Whitehouse's Slow Tech movement.

Inspired by the work of Sommervold [15], we selected *the critical discourse and dispositive analysis* method developed by Jäger [16]. This approach enabled us to identify the ideological discourse positions of the authors and their texts and to map these positions onto Feenberg's theories of technology matrix.

Our analysis is also inspired by Jaeger-Erben and Proske [17], who implemented a discourse analysis of planned obsolescence in German national and regional newspapers from the last 30 years. It revealed over 200 articles matching the terms "obsolescence" or "product lifetimes". They found that broad media coverage of obsolescence started in 2011, coinciding with the release of the film documentary "The Light Bulb Conspiracy"[9]. Jaeger-Erben and Proske present some first insights from their ongoing analysis, where they emphasize that consumers mainly attribute responsibility for, and power over, the lifetimes of products to product developers/producers and do not question their own practices of usage and disposal. Furthermore they show how products remain passive in their examined articles, appear as only objects for projections, whereas they would like to promote the materiality in the practices of consumption more. Jæger-Erben and Proske do not implement a form of mapping in their study, but their proposed design scenarios to stimulate longer lasting products form an important part of the overarching objectives of our research project.

---

[7] [12, pp. 81–82].

[8] [14, p. 10].

[9] [17, p. 182].

3   Critical Discourse Analysis

3.1   Method

In our study, discourse is the flow of the societal knowledge about "planned obso-lescence" gained and stored over time, determining individual and collective doing and/or formative action shaping society. Discourse exercises power[10], as it transports "knowledge on which the collective and individual consciousness feeds"[11]. In con-junction with our overarching research project, which is concerned with the transfor-mative change from designed obsolescence to sustainable technology design, the topic of obsolescence can serve as example for a dispositive. A dispositive, as Jäger (citing Foucault) calls it, is the interplay of the elements of discursive practices, non-discursive practices, and so-called manifestations/materializations (see Footnote 11). At the heart of this dispositive is the reconstruction of knowledge in the discursive practices, which builds the foundation for further investigation into "gaps" in the discourse, underlying non-discursive practices (unspoken, unwritten, embodied knowledge of doing), and underlying established or emerging manifestations (materialized knowledge, here designed technology and its lifecycle), that have to be reconstructed[12].

The data acquisition for the discourse analysis took place in *Retriever Atekst,* the Scandinavian media (newspaper, web, television, and radio) research database. A rough first search with "planlagt" and "foreldelse" or the English equivalents "planned" and "obsolescence" as key terms, gave a huge data set of mostly newspaper articles, which included articles that dealt with planned crimes and the legal limitation period (a valid meaning of the Norwegian equivalent for obsolescence). With the exact search phrase "planlagt foreldelse" (and/or "planned obsolescence"), these connota-tions where successfully excluded from the search result. We expanded the search with other compositions, including either "obsolescence" or "planned". Among them were "innebygd foreldelse" (build-in obsolescence) and "planlagt/kortere/forkortet levetid" (planned/shorter/shortened life-span). This resulted in a body of 70 articles.

A second round of filtering was implemented by a more superficial reading of the Norwegian articles, deciding if the phenomenon *planned obsolescence* (PO) was dis-cussed in depth or mentioned only once, but with (some of) its implications for society, economy, politics discussed. If the PO was just mentioned casually, or in a context that did not fit the above, the article was put aside. This second round resulted in 16 articles for further consideration in the actual discourse analysis.

We applied Jäger's set of analytical guidelines for processing the 16 articles[13]. The coding, in the form of a categorization strategy, was performed with the help of prepared tables for note-taking and comparison. Thus, each article was analysed in several categories: (1) institutional framework or context, including author and cause of the article; (2) text 'surface', including layout and structure of the article; (3) rhetorical

---

[10] [16, pp. 33–34].

[11] [16, p. 38].

[12] [16, pp. 59, 62].

[13] [16, pp. 55–57].

means, including argumentation strategy, players, references; (4) ideological statements, including perspectives on humans, technology, society and the future; (5) other striking issues; (6) summary; and (7) concluding interpretation. The following section is organized in the same manner (category 1 to 4), directly followed by the discussion of the results.

3.2   Results

Characterization of the Newspapers. The first step in processing the acquired data focussed on a general description of the media, which in this case is the national press in Norway, and its place in society. The newspapers included in the analysis are the major nationwide daily issued newspapers Aftenposten, Dagbladet, Klassekampen, VG (Verdens Gang) and the weekly published Morgenbladet (all with their headquarters located in Oslo), the regional newspapers Fædrelandsvennen, Fredriksstad Blad, Østlandets Blad, and the news magazines with certain thematic focus Norske Le Monde diplomatique (monthly international news magazine), Harvest (weekly nature/people/environment magazine) and Teknisk Ukeblad (monthly technology magazine). All newspapers define themselves as politically independent; since 2010, no Norwegian newspaper has been sympathising openly with a certain political party [18].

Institutional Framework or Context. The media coverage of planned obsolescence started in the early 2000s. At the time, the phenomenon was not yet called planned obsolescence, but was described through terms such as "short life-span". After two relevant articles in 2006, the term "planned obsolescence" started to surface with one article in 2010 ("Made to fall out of its hinges"), in 2011 ("Products that last"), and in 2012 ("A well-documented conspiracy"). The increase in media-coverage coincided with the broadcasting of the documentary film "Pyramids of Waste" (also called "The Lightbulb Conspiracy", by Cosima Dannoritzer) on Norwegian TV. In 2013 and 2014, several articles with headings like "Time for something new, you think?", "Breaks down as planned" as well as about the sharing economy, alternative economic models or the circular economy followed. In 2015, there was a noticeable low on media coverage of obsolescence, while 2016 was the year in which Apple was discussed in terms of product life-span, a new repair culture developed, and debates about smartphone swapping started. In 2017, alternative solutions, such as the circular economy, EU-regulations, and the repair culture in Norway gained attention.

Six of the selected articles were *written by* journalists employed by the newspaper. Three articles had no author mentioned and were obviously written by the editorial staff at the newspaper. Three had freelancer or regularly writing columnists employed for the article, among them was one philosophy professor; two articles were reader's letters by one writer/author and students; one article was written by an industrial designer, and one article was authored by a spokesperson of a political organisation (see Table 1).

Most of articles had a particular *cause* or reason why they were written. Seven of the 16 articles were published shortly after a documentary on planned obsolescence was broadcast on national TV, after a governmental/parliament press release, a report's publication, a sentence at court, or a company's marketing release. Others were

Table 1. List of newspaper articles used in the Discourse Analysis

Nr.	Title	Publication	Year	Author
1	Speculation in the warranty period	Fædrelands-vennen	2006	n/a
2	A mobile phone shall last for five years	Teknisk Ukeblad	2006	n/a
3	Made to fall out of its hinges	Klassekampen	2010	A. Thodok Eriksen
4	Products that last	Østlandets Blad	2011	C. F. Haugfos, B. A. Mong, O. Fosse, I. K. Kann
5	A well-documented conspiracy	Dagbladet	2012	Ø. Wyller
6	Time for something new, you think?	Fredriksstad Blad	2013	T. Skjeklesæther
7	Breaks down as planned	Aftenposten	2013	A. Mauren
8	Own or share?	(Norske) Le Monde diplomatique	2013	M. Denoun, G. Valadon
9	A radical idea	Klassekampen	2014	A. J. Vetlesen
10	Apple: Most people change their iPhone after three years	VG Nett	2016	Ø. Larsen-Vonstett, A. Støren Wedén
11	A new mobile phone every year?	Dagbladet	2016	L. Nøst
12	Will it be white Christmas again?	Harvest	2016	L. Julsen, K. Østli
13	A fix idea	Morgenbladet	2017	B. Stenvik, C. Belgaux, K. Hustad
14	This is how the EU wants to stop planned obsolescence of electronics	Teknisk Ukeblad	2017	n/a
15	Everything can be repaired	Aftenposten	2017	B. Stærk
16	Technology companies reprimanded for making things that need to be replaced often	Aftenposten	2017	K. Hanssen

inspired by a reflection over community events, meetings with experts, record-breaking technology, and the latest trends in European economy or climate change. Several of the articles appeared in the 'debate', 'reader's opinion', 'comment' or 'chronicle' section, while some were published in the economic, general news or culture section. The articles tended to be published on pages with a rather high page number, at the best page 3 or 4 was reached.

Text 'surface'. The *headlines* were often significant and promising and thus certainly a criterion for inclusion of the article into the analysis. If a headline was not promising on first sight, but amongst others discussed obsolescence, the article's plot was often embedded in a range of other discourse strands (see Rhetorical Means below). The articles' headlines can be grouped into a first category, showcasing obsolescence by using "break" (and synonyms/idioms of that) or "last" in the title (2, 3, 4, 7).

The second category applies the word "new" in conjunction with a question mark or some form for "exchange" in the title (6, 10, 11, 16). In the third category, terms such as speculation, conspiracy or planned obsolescence itself are used (1, 5, 14), and the last cluster exists around the term "fix/fixed", meaning repair or restoration (13, 15). The remaining headlines point to higher-level topics and/or give little hint, that the phenomenon obsolescence is discussed.

For the majority of articles, the *layout*, in terms of pictures and text-setting, was made up of a picture/illustration of some kind followed or surrounded by text in one or several columns. Nine of the articles showed realistic photographs of objects/scenes, the others illustrative comic-style or symbolic drawings, one a map and graphical sidebar information, and one used a photomontage to convey the message. The lightbulb was often used as a symbol for either short-lived products/a conspiracy image, or for energy/the earth/globe and in double meaning for an idea. At least five of the articles also pictured their author in a small portrait, next to the text.

The *themes* of the articles can be expressed in a wide range of key-words and -phrases, which can be clustered for to represent six bigger thematic blocks. Starting with the core theme-block about life-span of technology and related, the next block concerns break-down and disuse of technology and its different forms. These are followed by throw-away-mentality and overconsumption themes together with the block about environmental crisis and other consequences. The last two theme-blocks concern longevity of technology in its different forms and the themes economy/economic systems.

Rhetorical Means. As mentioned earlier, the main plot of some articles was embedded in a range of other discourse strands. This means that the main theme in the text, in our case planned obsolescence (PO), is described by addressing several themes and referring to other strands of discourse. These could concern a wide range of environmental issues, climate change, sustainable consumption in general, economical models or alternative work-life models. Less strong entanglement with other discourse strands was found in articles, which, for example, presented personal experiences with broken technologies.

The *argumentation* in the articles often had the same structure: one or more example(s) in the beginning, then PO would be explained, and the consequences, implications or counter-activities for individuals or societal structures elaborated. If obsolescence was presented in its larger context, first the whole scene was described and then the different aspects narrated and compared. Planned obsolescence or a similar phrase appeared most often only once in the first third or half of the text with a constricting effect on the argumentation.

In terms of *references*, the authors often drew on either none or a lot of different experts (interviewed for the purpose of the article) or sources of public/academic knowledge, one article had footnotes for an easier overview. Examples for experts/sources included are political scientists, philosophers, economists, marketing managers, industrial designers, technology researchers, and representatives of organizations like Greenpeace Norway, Future in our Hands, Restarters Oslo, Norwegian Consumer Counsel, Norwegian second hand store chain Fretex and Norwegian TV broadcaster NRK. One author (of a 2017 article) was included as an expert in a 2016 article, which highlights a new continuity in the discursive practice.

When reflecting about *implications and insinuations* across all articles, this can be summarized with the phrase "critique on PO is a matter of…", although not all articles expressed a clear critique. For some of the articles, critique of PO is a matter of (1) taking repair (ability) seriously or in one's own hands; (2) self-reflection, enlightenment and passive opposition/ignorance, (3) awakening from the magic aura around technology, (4) awakening from the addictive economy of innovation, (5) not giving in to profit-orientation, (6) implementation of longer-lasting products together with a change in societal attitude, (7) demanding longer-lasting products using consumers' purchasing power ("voting" with the wallet, market pull vs. technology push). In addition, critique is a matter of (8) reforming the/strengthen of regulation in the economic model or radical political uprising on a system (macro-) level, in which critique spreads out to overconsumption in general rather than a focus on PO.

In between these ways of thinking we would locate one article's implication, that (9) legislation and the judiciary in PO-cases showcase how wicked the problem and critique on PO can be, since success of regulatory efforts is restricted and (becomes) part of the problem. Yet another article has no take on critique towards PO, the implication there is, that consumers would have no stimulation to require any longer-lasting technology, for the simple reason that they (always) find themselves in the average group (3–4 years useful life of an iPhone for example) and are thus comforted.

Ideological Statements. The general *perspectives on humans* across the articles is complex: the consumer is regarded as a little naïve, either in need to be informed about, or not sure about, life-span/PO facts; humans are seen as basically good-natured, being lulled by "magical" technology, thus not acknowledging the facts about PO. Other articles state humans are certainly aware of the facts about PO (in electronics).

Another view on consumers and producers in the articles is that of being "homo economicus". On the one hand, producers are seen as profit-oriented and consumers are prompted to be more «homo economicus»-like and make use of the same weapon, i.e. their purchasing power. On the other hand, humans are seen as being different/diverse individuals, not «homo economicus», but rather «hard to read». Several articles reside between these two positions; humans are thus described as seeing themselves in good company with most of the other members of society, doing business-as-usual, being a bit prone to reject responsibility, and being not political enough.

The *perspectives on society* are often based on conflicting values between consumer and producer. When consumers and producers exercise their rights, in court for example, there are compromises found that show the power distribution between the corporate sector, the legislation/judiciary, and the user. Some articles perceive society as seemingly having control over technology/PO through consumer rights regulation, lawsuits and the like. This is particularly valid, when the members of society see themselves in good company with each other and agree on what "average" or "normal" means. Others regard society in more complex categories: ignorant (for example not so open in terms of providing information) or informed producers and ignorant (wasteful) or informed consumers. Others perceive society as a group of individuals, who do not (yet) act according to what they know/have insight in, or who are not "willing" to know. Several articles value the role of experts (for example professional repairers) as having a broader understanding of PO and the knowledge for intervention. Furthermore, in some articles, society is little valued in terms of being able to create a market pull (demand-side) against PO or in terms of result-oriented or executive political power.

The *perspectives on technology* vary across the articles. For a few, technology is a mere means to an end (tools, instruments for users) and is seen to have a "natural" degradation course. Others see technology as constantly innovated, pushed by business. Several articles transmit a view of technology as being unfortunately *the* outcome of the invisible hand of the economy and outside human control. They enumerate attributes like over-elaborated, "gadget"-like, stifling, marginal innovative, not adapted to the user or as automation taking people's jobs. In addition, the growing consumption of technology is related to a too low rate for proper recycling and to the high rate of energy, resources and work contained in consumer technologies.

Several articles convey the message that technology often is a black-box, though some notice it is easy (and not so magical) to repair in order to prolong the life-span. In these articles longer-lasting or even ever-lasting technology is mentioned as having been "out there", either from before the high-tech-age (mechanical) or since the high-tech-age began (just missing a market pull on the contrary to a technology push). Ever-lasting technology is also seen as existing in theory and its existence "in practice" is dependent on a society-level attitude change. In other articles the view on longer-lasting technology is a bit double edged, as authors wonder if it really is expedient to stick to "older" technology, not profiting from innovation and future efficiency gains.

The *future perspectives* in the articles can often be formulated as an if-else clause or an if-not-then phrase. Most of the articles draw a picture of the future as being dependent on a change in planned obsolescence and overconsumption, otherwise earth, as the living basis for humankind, would be severely compromised. So *if* everyone repairs/changes the attitude towards the old stuff, and/or *if* everyone awakens from the urge for the newest, and/or *if* we recognize the urgency for finding majorities/critical masses towards a change, and/or *if* the economic system can be changed substantially to zero-growth, *then* the living basis - the earth - is saved, and/or humankind was not too late to get up pace towards a critical mass, and/or crisis in form of negative growth will not take over.

On the other hand, there are several articles conveying a wait-and-see perspective or they leave it up to the reader what might happen afterwards. In these perspectives mostly the inner-societal competition between different stakeholders is considered key to whether and how to deal with the phenomenon PO. Hereunder fall the views that the future of PO might be a judiciary compromise, regulation might confine the product life-span/PO issues, or the future would be up to the consumers, using their purchasing power to counteract PO, while no urgency level is given other than that of the individual's ambition. A few would also let the reader decide whether appealing to the competitive instinct of companies, especially in Corporate Social and Environmental Responsibility, will do the trick towards sustainability.

4 Discussion

4.1 Mapping Technology Perspectives on Feenberg's Matrix

Figure 2 is a map of the different technology perspectives underlying the discussion of planned obsolescence in the 16 newspaper articles. The numbers refer to numbered articles in Table 1. The circles present the article's stance towards PO, while the hexagons represent the articles stance towards the root causes for PO. The map shows that the majority of articles express a critical perspective on PO. They express the need to change the current situation in which PO plays a dominant role in what has become the consumer society with its obsession for growth. These articles discuss several solutions to counter PO, such as using products as long as possible (lifespan), knowing the relative purchasing power and using it wisely; new regulation and active use of the Norwegian Consumer Act (warranty up to 5 years for electronics); change in business models (sharing instead of owning, lowering retail-prices for repair, circular economy); and product design that invites to a longer lifespan (repairable products, circular products).

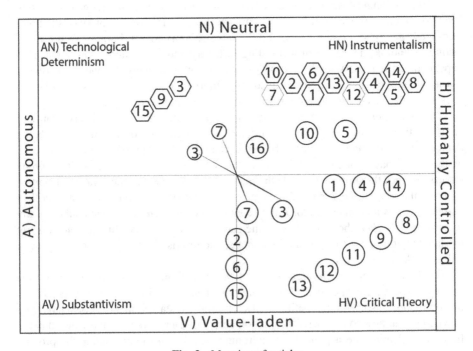

Fig. 2. Mapping of articles

Some of the articles (2, 6, and 15) can be found on the overlap between Critical Theory and Substantivism. This means that these articles reject PO, but don't see real possibilities for change, because technological development is only minimally mediated by society. In article 15 it is expressed as "frightening, that designers not only know to design for purchase but also for throw-away", where the author wishes back nostalgic mechanical rather than electrical products for to last another 50 years.

Three of the articles (5, 10, 16) express an instrumentalist perspective towards PO, arguing that this is business as usual: the technology push of PO is stronger than the market pull of products with a long lifespan. From article 5 the according mantra can be read "a satisfied consumer is not economically profitable".

Two articles (3, 7) overlap between Critical Theory and Technological Determinism. This means that these articles reject PO and at the same time keep being fascinated by technological development driving the future: In article 3 it reads "economy as is, needs growth, it is not stable because of its positive feedback-mechanism", whereas political reforms towards zero-growth are proposed later and contemporary critique on PO is denounced as "moral barking". Article 7 shares the opinion that "electronic consumer goods are about constant new products or technological functions, with cycles of <1 year it is then just logical not to make these long-lasting", whereas deploring that this same "greed culture" could "suffocate society".

In terms of mapping the root cause(s) for planned obsolescence, most articles are located in the Instrumentalism quadrant of the matrix. These articles describe these root causes as in terms of one of the characteristics of instrumental theory [9]. For example, "To always buy the latest model, even if the old one still functions, becomes an attractive proposal, when someone else will benefit" from the old mobile phone (article 11). Here technology is perceived as useful in any social context, they are not intertwined with local social arrangements. Article 9 mentions "the natural resource exploitation treadmill, which is based on the extreme idea of unlimited growth". Here is the idea of unlimited growth, through its metaphor of the treadmill, which underlies the root causes of PO. The universality of economic growth results in conceptions that it will perform in every context (country, era, civilization) in the same manner. A similar perspective is found in article 13: "to measure a society's success in economic activity". In these economic perspectives, technology is perceived a neutral product, "indifferent to the ends to which it can be employed to achieve"[14].

4.2   Options for Transformation and Emancipation

Through mapping our analysis of Norwegian newspaper articles on planned obsolescence on Feenberg's four main theories of technology, we showed that mainly critical perspectives in technology guide critiques of PO, while the root causes of PO are explained in instrumentalist terms, i.e., the products themselves are neutral, but human interventions created the PO. This outcome of our analysis is both a reason for optimism and for caution. Optimism, because there seems to be a real possibility for change: the majority perceives PO not as the characteristic of autonomous technology, but as the effect of societal intervention. Motivated by a strong belief in progress, almost all articles therefore discuss proposals to change the current state through other societal interventions. New regulation, repair, and consumers using their purchasing power wisely are often mentioned as future perspectives towards change.

There is, however, enough reason to be cautious about the options for change. Technological determinism, which perceives technology as an autonomous, neutral

---

[14] [9, p. 5].

force, which serves humanity's progress towards freedom and happiness [11], motivates several of the articles. What Instrumentalism and Technological Determinism have in common is the notion of neutral technology. As long as the dominant discourse on PO is informed by an understanding of technology as neutral, the values informing technologies remain invisible.

Our analysis points towards two conflicting positions contained in the articles, namely a critical perspective on PO and proposals that call for the transformation of technology and its industry on the one hand and an instrumental perspective when it comes to understanding the root causes for PO (and technology in general). Slow Tech, on the other hand, is based on the understanding of technology as the result of complex interactions with society, which is more in line with the critical theory perspective. Thinking of technology as a tool that can be used for good or bad is a powerful meme. We can therefore not speculate that the opponents of PO will embrace Slow Tech as a new meme.

5 Concluding Remarks

Critical Discourse Analysis is an important tool in understanding discourses on planned obsolescence. It enabled us to bring out societal perspectives on planned obsolescence and what are considered ways for challenging or opposing it. Combining this analysis with Feenberg's theories of technology framework added an extra layer of results and analysis. We found that the idea of neutral technology dominates the discourse on where planned obsolescence comes from or how it is maintained. None of the proposed measures to deal with planned obsolescence is situated in a critical understanding of technology as politics by other means. The critical stances towards PO found in the Norwegian media are thus a continuation of the liberal idea that we can control technology for more acceptable ends. This lack of deeper engagement with the politics of technology forms the main obstacle to the change that is needed to fulfill the goal of sustainable production and consumption.

References

1. Proske, M., Winzer, J., Marwede, M., Nissen, N.F., Lang, K.-D.: Obsolescence of electronics - the example of smartphones. In: Electronics Goes Green 2016+(EGG), pp. 1–8 (2016)
2. Butt, T.E., Camilleri, M., Paul, P., Jones, K.G.: Obsolescence types and the built environment – definitions and implications. Int. J. Environ. Sustain. Dev. 14(1), 20–39 (2015)
3. Cooper, T.: Inadequate Life? Evidence of consumer attitudes to product obsolescence. J. Consum. Policy 27(4), 421–449 (2004)
4. United Nations: Sustainable Development Goals, United Nations Sustainable Development (2018)
5. Pierce, A.J.: Aesthetic mediation and the politics of technology. Crit. Horiz. 15(1), 69–81 (2014)

6. Wieser, H.: Beyond planned obsolescence: product lifespans and the challenges to a circular economy. GAIA Ecol. Perspect. Sci. Soc. **25**(3), 156–160 (2016)
7. LeBel, S.: Fast machines, slow violence: ICTs, planned obsolescence, and e-waste. Globalizations **13**(3), 300–309 (2016)
8. Wyatt, S.: Technological determinism is dead; long live technological determinism. In: The Handbook of Science and Technology Studies, pp. 165–180. The MIT Press, Cambridge (2008)
9. Feenberg, A.: Transforming Technology: A Critical Theory Revisited. Oxford University Press, Oxford (2002)
10. Quan-Haase, A.: Theoretical perspectives on technology. In: Technology & Society : Social Networks, Power, and Inequality, Oxford University Press, Don Mills (2016)
11. Feenberg, A.: Questioning Technology. Routledge, New York (1999)
12. Patrignani, N., Whitehouse, D.: Slow Tech: a quest for good, clean and fair ICT. J. Inf. Commun. Ethics Soc. **12**(2), 78–92 (2014)
13. Longmuss, J., Poppe, E.: Planned obsolescence: who are those planners? In: Product Lifetimes and the Environment 2017 - Conference Proceedings, Delft, pp. 217–221 (2017)
14. Wodak, R.: Aspects of critical discourse analysis. Z. Für Angew. Linguist. ZfAL **36**, 5–31 (2002)
15. Sommervold, M.M.: 'Doctor Smartphone': a dispositive analysis of the Norwegian press's presentation of m-health applications. Int. J. Sociotechnol. Knowl. Dev. **8**(1), 1–16 (2016)
16. Jäger, S.: Discourse and knowledge: theoretical and methodological aspects of a critical discourse and dispositive analysis. In: Wodak, R., Meyer, M. (eds.) Methods of Critical Discourse Analysis. Introducing Qualitative Methods, 1st edn., pp. 32–62. SAGE Publications Ltd. (2001)
17. Jaeger-Erben, M., Proske, M.: What's hot what's not: the social construction of product obsolescence and its relevance for strategies to increase functionality. In: Bakker, C., Mugge, R. (eds.) PLATE: Product Lifetimes and the Environment: Conference Proceedings of PLATE 2017, Delft, The Netherlands, 8–10 November 2017, pp. 181–185. Delft University of Technology and IOS Press (2017)
18. Partiavis: Wikipedia, 07 March 2017

Aware but not in Control

A Qualitative Value Analysis of the Effects of New Technologies

Kathrin Bednar[(⊠)] and Sarah Spiekermann

Vienna University of Economics and Business, Vienna, Austria
kathrin.bednar@wu.ac.at

Abstract. The wide distribution of information and communication technologies (ICTs) has affected our lives in the working environment as well as in private and social contexts and has done so not only in a positive, but also threatening way. Researchers and scholars have therefore called for a sustainable and value-based design of technologies. However, in order to propose better designs, we first need to understand how ICTs affect users. While many studies have focused on the effects of the internet, smartphones, and social media, reported results suggest that the influences of these technologies are complex and often depend on contextual factors. This study aims to provide a starting point for future value-based designs of ICTs by offering insights on how students, as representatives for regular users of new technologies, experience the changes ICTs have brought to their lives. A qualitative content analysis of twelve in-depth, semi-structured interviews identifies values that flourish with ICTs but also discovers paradoxical effects: ICTs affect many of these values also in a negative way. Results indicate that users of ICTs are aware of negative effects, but lack the control to change their own behavior. Our findings point out that users need better protection and motivate the adoption of ethical design frameworks for ICTs.

Keywords: ICTs · Value-based design · Interview study · Awareness
Control

1 Introduction

The advent of the internet and the widespread dissemination of new information and communication technologies (ICTs) have changed our lives in the working environment as well as in private and social contexts. As ICTs are widely distributed and used, they affect not only individuals but society as a whole. Salehan and Negahban [1] discuss how excessive use of mobile applications can be harmful for society. They conclude that mobile application designers should think about features that prevent users from becoming addicted and point to the responsibility of governments and non-profit organizations. In recent years, researchers, scholars, designers, and human rights activists have called for a more sustainable and ethical design of ICTs [2–4], for example, by putting human values into the center of technological designs. But in order to design and produce sustainable technologies that protect human values and

© IFIP International Federation for Information Processing 2018
Published by Springer Nature Switzerland AG 2018. All Rights Reserved
D. Kreps et al. (Eds.): HCC13 2018, IFIP AICT 537, pp. 202–218, 2018.
https://doi.org/10.1007/978-3-319-99605-9_15

resources, we first have to understand what harms ICTs can cause. Only then can we consider "nonfunctional system requirements" such as the protection of values on top of functional requirements [4].

Existing research focuses on the negative effects of the internet [5–8], social media [1, 9–11] and cell phones [1, 12–14]. However, literature reviews have pointed out that reported results are contradictory as studies suggest harmful but also beneficial effects [15] and raise more questions than they can answer [16] because of methodological and theoretical shortcomings. Authors of review papers point to the "wealth of contradictory evidence suggesting both harmful and beneficial aspects of SMTs [social media technologies]" [15] and the need for further research to clear up these contradictions [17]. For example, contradictory results have been presented regarding the question whether internet access and use makes us happy [18] or decreases our level of happiness [9] and have also been discussed in the context of email and stress [19]. Often, results are difficult to compare and a holistic consistent insight into the true effects are missing. A recent literature review [17] summarizes the plethora of theoretical and conceptual frameworks that have been suggested for the adoption and use of social media. It discovered that previous studies used different constructs as antecedents, mediators, moderators, or outcomes of user behavior and its effects. The authors of the review article conclude that future research should address both positive and negative effects of ICTs. Others [20] stress that more research is needed that looks into users' motivations and their real life contexts. This is consistent with conclusions regarding prior research, namely that it "does not examine the drivers and outcomes of social-media use" [16]. Therefore, to better understand when internet use becomes pathological and what causes maladaptive internet use, we need to understand both the motivations for using ICTs [20] as well as the effects of ICTs.

Studies that have focused on the effects of ICTs rarely used values as their theoretical framework. However, if we want value sensitive [21] or value-based design [4] of ICTs, we have to identify the values that are fostered by ICTs as well as values that are harmed and could be protected by better designed technologies. In the empirical study we are presenting below, our goal was to better understand which values are fostered and undermined by ICTs used by students on a regular basis. More precisely, we interviewed 12 students on their use of smartphones and social media technologies and tried to elicit the value space that unfolds based on this use.

1.1 Effects of ICTs

A review of existing literature shows that the use of ICTs affects many value dimensions, including individuals' psychological and physiological wellbeing, the efficiency in their professional life as well as their freedom, which is reduced through online addiction. Furthermore, it presents factors that determine the effects of ICTs, such as the motivations of the users and the purpose and context of their use of ICTs.

Social media use has been associated with higher technostress, lower happiness, and worse performance [9]. Similar results have been observed for high cell phone use, which has been associated with worse academic performance as well as with higher anxiety and lower life satisfaction in college students [22]. These results were supported in subsequent studies of the same research group, which additionally found an association with poor sleep quality [13] and higher distress during leisure [12]. Stress has also been associated with email [19]. However, the association between stress and email cannot be explained by considering solely "material factors", e.g., the number of received emails and the workload they create. Rather, social norms that pressure individuals into keeping up with their e-mail load and being informed about new messages cause the perception of email as a symbol of stress [19].

Social factors play a role in the use of the internet and social media, too. For example, there seems to be a vicious cycle between internet addiction and loneliness [7]: excessive and unhealthy use of the internet increases feelings of loneliness over time, and loneliness then decreases offline social contacts – as people retreat. Therefore, the positive counter-effects of strong offline social contacts cannot unfold, and internet addiction continues to increase loneliness. The authors conclude that online contacts cannot replace offline contacts [7]. This claim is supported by other research [23], which discovered that the negative impact of online interactions on subjective well-being is greater than the positive impact of offline social networks. Correspondingly, it was found that smartphone use reduces the quality of face-to-face interactions and thus their positive impact on wellbeing [24].

It is not surprising then that social media use has been associated with decreased subjective wellbeing in a longitudinal study [23] and with depression in different age groups [5, 25]. In a study with young adults [26], those participants who used multiple social media platforms had substantially higher odds to experience symptoms of depression and anxiety. Thus, it is presumably the *number* of used social media platforms rather than the *time spent* on individual platforms that causes the association with these psychological symptoms.

There is growing research interest in framing excessive use of ICTs as a form of addiction in order to capture better its effects on the individual. However, theories propose different objects, causes, and consequences of addiction and set the level of pathology at different levels [8, 20, 27–32]. No general theory has been agreed on yet and it is not clear why people keep using the internet despite its negative effects [20]. This unclear theoretical grounding of empirical research makes it difficult to produce consistent findings. Therefore, researchers work on redefining the concept of addiction with regard to digital services and devices and reconsider the evaluation of the effects that using ICTs has on us.

In this context, arguments against the dismissal of excessive internet use as pathological are especially noteworthy. Researchers emphasize that the use of ICTs should not be considered in isolation. Rather, one needs to take into account several additional factors. For example, the outcomes of ICTs depend on the individual characteristics of users, such as "who they are, with whom they use the media, and for what purposes" [32]. Furthermore, it is important to look into users' motivations and the potential of online activities to compensate for psychosocial problems *before* framing user behavior as pathological [20]. Arguments in this direction stress that it is difficult to define objective criteria, as it is the individual user's subjective experiences, resources, and environments that determine whether internet use is healthy or unhealthy [31].

To summarize, whether ICTs exert positive or negative effects is often rather subjective than objective. It seems that in the end, it is the individual who determines whether he or she is using the internet in a healthy or pathological way [31]. We conclude that any research or design goals that considers effects on the users should take into account this subjective dimension, e.g., by including individual users in qualitative research and design studies.

1.2 Value-Based Approaches to a Sustainable and Ethical Design of Technologies

Values reflect "what a person or group of people consider important in life" [21]. They are "desirable transsituational goals, varying in importance, that serve as guiding principles in the life of a person or other social entity" [33]. Maslow [34] proposed physiological needs, safety needs, love needs, esteem needs, and the need for self-actualization in his theory of motivation. Spiekermann [4] aligns values identified in psychology and philosophy [35, 36] with Maslow's hierarchy of needs. The result is a structured arrangement of select values, which she then conceptually investigates for value sensitive design purposes (see Fig. 1).

Besides this work, many alternative lists of values relevant for ICTs have been proposed, e.g., by Friedman, Kahn, and Borning [21]. Yet, value lists can be misleading as values are contextually bound. The digital devices and services used by people in different situations bear the values that unfold [37]. And it is because of these individual predispositions that some values unfold more than others for a respective person, even if he or she uses the same technology as someone else [37]. This is what the research discussed above shows very well.

That said, there are certainly dispositions in the mentioned technologies that incentivize typical reactions on the side of the users. For instance, it has been suggested that today's digital technologies, such as smartphones and social media, are explicitly designed to foster addiction and hence undermine mental freedom [38, 39]. In the study presented below we identify and discuss a number of values that seem to be recurring among various users and hence may be triggered by the technological designs chosen.

ICTs do not only have an impact on values. There are certain preconditions that have to be met in order to allow for values to unfold. Maslow named freedom and cognitive capacities as preconditions for the satisfaction of basic needs [40]. We want to take up this differentiation and include preconditions here as "resources". In Davis' definition of healthy internet use[1] [31], time, cognitive wellbeing, behavioral wellbeing, and identity appear as individual psychological resources that can be affected by the use of ICTs. Psychological resources are linked to values, as without these resources, values cannot unfold. For instance, if someone is tired, the resources that are necessary to build friendship are missing. If someone is constantly distracted, it is hard

---

[1] "Healthy Internet refers to using the Internet for an expressed purpose in a reasonable amount of time without cognitive or behavioral discomfort. Healthy Internet users can separate Internet communication with real life communication. They employ the Internet as a helpful tool rather than a source of identity. There is no specific time limit, nor is there any behavioral benchmark."

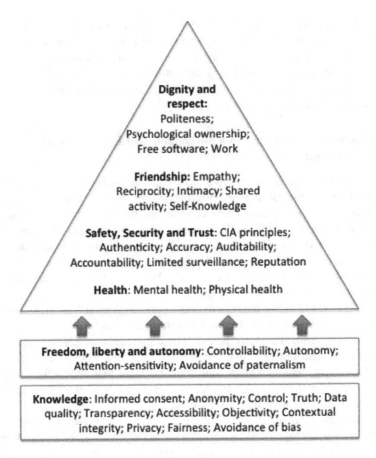

Fig. 1. A hierarchy of values relevant for ICTs (Source: Spiekermann [4], p. 150)

to build knowledge, etc. Therefore, we look into how ICTs affect not only human values that matter to users, but also their psychological resources.

1.3   Aim of This Study

This study takes a qualitative approach to explore the value space impacted by ICTs. Looking at prior research in the literature, we made two observations. On the one hand, high use of ICTs is often associated with addictive behavior, which explains observed negative effects with a lack of control. On the other hand, researchers neither agree on the specific effects of ICTs and their direction (positive or negative), nor the constructs of addiction and problematic use of ICTs.

Acknowledging the contextual sensitivity of values, Friedman et al. [21] suggest semi-structured interviews for the empirical investigation of values relevant for stakeholders. Specifically, they suggest probing the interview partners' reasoning and asking about values not only directly, but also indirectly – for example, by addressing a hypothetical situation or common events in the interview partners' everyday lives. In order to account for these considerations, the present study takes a qualitative approach to explore values in the context of ICTs. In the European Union, almost all (96%) young people and individuals with a higher level of education use the internet regularly [41]. Therefore, this study looks into how students, as representative users of new technologies, experience their use of ICTs. In doing so, this paper wants to add to existing literature by offering further insights on the users' subjective experience and perception of values.

The aim of this study is twofold. First, it aims to identify values that are currently fostered by ICTs as well as values that need to be better protected in future designs. Second, it takes into account that there is not yet a generally accepted theoretical framework that allows to differentiate pathological from non-pathological use of ICTs. Therefore, this study looks into two core factors that can help to better understand the current use of ICTs. On the one hand, it tries to find out to what extent users of ICTs are aware of their own usage and whether they are able to detect changes that have occurred because of it. On the other hand, it explores how psychological resources are affected by the use of ICTs. Finally, we want to understand to what extent students are still in control over their own resources and hence the value space that is accessible to them. To operationalize perceived control over ICTs, we explore which measures are proposed by students to meet negative influences of ICTs.

To summarize, this study tries to answer the following research questions:

- Which values are fostered by ICTs?
- Which values are undermined by ICTs?
- To what extent does use of ICTs affect psychological resources?
- Are users of ICTs aware of the effects of their usage behavior?
- Are users of ICTs in control of their usage behavior?

2   Method

Procedure. In-depth interviews were conducted at the Vienna University of Economics and Business in 2017. The sample was composed of five German native speakers and seven participants with a different native language. Therefore, the interviews were conducted in German or English, according to the personal preference of each participant. Interviews were audio-recorded and transcribed. Participants gave informed consent to their participation in the study, the recording of the interviews and the subsequent anonymized data analysis.

Sample. Participants (N = 12) were between 20 and 28 years old (M = 23.9, SD = 2.5). All of them were undergraduate students at the Vienna University of Economics and Business. The sample showed an equal distribution of gender, with six female and six male participants.

Interview Guide. We conducted semi-structured interviews, that is, interviews roughly followed prepared questions. At the beginning, we briefly introduced the participants to the topic and specific terms. They were instructed to think about ICTs as referring to new technologies and (social) media and we suggested the smartphone as a symbolic representation for these technologies. The first questions targeted costs and benefits or advantages and disadvantages of everyday use of ICTs. In case our interview partners found it difficult to come up with ideas, we suggested thinking of their daily routines and behaviors in different contexts. Subsequently we asked if they could think of anything that they would like to change about their own or other people's use of ICTs. Two scenarios were offered. We asked them what they would change if they were God, that is, an almighty power with the ability to change anything with immediate effect. In an alternative phrasing, we asked about the changes or measures they would suggest if they had to come up with a guideline for the following year as "Minister of Technology". We concluded by asking if they had any comments or wanted to share anything else.

Analyses. After the recorded interviews had been transcribed, we conducted a summarizing content analysis [42]. In this process, the qualitative data is subjected to several stages of analysis, which are described in the following section. The goal is to "reduce a large volume of material to a manageable level, but in so doing retaining the essential content" [42].

First, relevant units of analysis were identified. A text passage or expression was considered relevant if it hinted at a value or psychological resource that was fostered or harmed by ICTs. Measures and changes that were proposed or desired were also coded as relevant units. In a second step, all identified units were paraphrased, focusing only on relevant content within the unit ("Paraphrasing"). Text passages from German interviews were paraphrased in English. In a third step, a higher level of abstraction was obtained by summarizing the most important points expressed in the paraphrased text passages ("Generalization"). These generalized statements were then elected and the level of abstraction was further increased ("First reduction"). Through binding, integration and construction, general statements and expressions were formulated and finally arranged within a system of categories ("Second reduction").

Once the system of categories depicting the effects of ICTs had been established, each set of categories was associated with a value or psychological resource. Proposed measures and changes were considered separately.

3   Results

The following sections present a summary of the values and resources impacted by ICTs. The last section displays the measures and changes that were proposed or desired by our interview partners. Wherever a quote from the interviews is presented, an ID is given in squared brackets that identifies every interview partner with a character ("A" to "L"), followed by the number of the interviewee's statement in the interview analysis database.

3.1   Values Fostered by ICTs

When talking about positive effects of ICTs, study participants directly referred to smartphones, laptops, computers, internet, and mobile internet as specific technologies and devices in their examples. Next to general applications like a browser and email, they also mentioned the following applications in their interviews: Facebook, Facebook Messenger, Google Drive, Google Maps, Instagram, Apple's navigation app Maps, Microsoft Word, Nike sports app, Playtube, Qando (an Austrian public transportation app), Snapchat, Skype, Tinder, WhatsApp, and Youtube.

The following sections present and describe values fostered by ICTs in more detail, based on summaries of the expressions as well as exemplary statements from our interview partners. The core values fostered by ICTs go beyond convenience, efficiency, and information accessibility as they also include the unleashing of belongingness and joy.

Information Accessibility. ICTs are a source of information. Being equipped with a smartphone or laptop that has internet connection, students feel that they have easier, faster, and better access to information than it was ever possible before. Thinking especially about (social) media, students feel that they get information about everything in the world, all of the time. They also appreciate that they encounter new opportunities by chance as news or job possibilities pop up while browsing social media.

- [L #1] "Well, information is more available. We can find out whatever we want sooner than we were able to, I don't know, ten or fifteen years ago. So that would be the greatest advantage."

Belongingness. ICTs facilitate communication and connection to people. Many of the students' comments focused on how their smartphones, instant messaging, and social media applications allow them to feel constantly connected to their family, friends and colleagues. They like that they can share their experiences instantaneously, always reach people, and keep in touch with relatives or friends who live far away. They feel as if they can be everywhere, informed about everything, and therefore do not feel left out.

- [I #6] "...even if you're not there, you know everything, you feel like you're there, because, you know, you're kind of like - everywhere, you can be – everywhere".

Convenience and Efficiency. Perceived convenience comes from the perception that ICTs increase efficiency, help to structure everyday-life, and make everything easier. For example, ICTs allow organizing things last-minute, like buying concert tickets, and buying or booking stuff online. ICTs help to better structure and organize work and everyday-life. They save time as communication is faster, getting from one place to another can be organized easily and more efficiently, and information is better available. Apps that provide a timetable for public transport and offer navigation are especially appreciated in this context.

- [G #1] "I have to say I get lost incredibly easily, and I see with the mobile phone, it navigates me somewhere, where I don't know the place at all. So for me the navigation system on the mobile phone is one of the two things that I find fantastic."

Joy. ICTs are a source of entertainment and increase the joy when doing sports. They enable better access to music, movies, TV series and news. Several students especially appreciate that they can listen to music with their phones.

- [A #9] "One of the most important things regarding my phone... is music, I listen to a lot of music, also on the go".

One study participant was particularly fascinated by the advantages of smartphone apps for doing sports. He referred to an application that plays music and tracks you while running. It offers music with different paces that adapts to your personal speed and motivates you with cheers when you reach a specific milestone. GPS connection allows comparing personal results, which can then also be shared on social media and platforms.

3.2 Values Undermined by ICTs

Study participants named negative influences of ICTs on friendships and social relations as well as on knowledge and specific competences.

Friendship. ICTs digitalize friendships and reduce personal contact. Our interview partners feel that the role that ICTs play in their social lives noticeably impacts their personal relationships. They see the personal aspect reduced and communication altered through social networks and instant messages. First, students are bored by the many postings they see from their friends online. Second, when they meet with their friends in person – which they notice to happen less often as most of the interactions take place in the digital world – they often do not know what to talk about, as what they have experienced in the past days had already been discussed online. Third, they criticize that they cannot have normal conversations anymore as their conversation partners are distracted by their phones and do not listen.

- [D #6] "Real friendships suffer"
- [E #15] "The fun of just being with your friends is not enough anymore".

Knowledge. Dependence on ICTs causes loss of competences. Relating to the aforementioned benefits of efficient organization of everyday-life as well as navigation and public transport, students become aware of their dependence on technology. They realize that they lose the competence of getting along on their own by relying on having their smartphone and constant internet connection always. Without their smartphone, they feel as if a part of their body is missing. They feel incompetent, lonely, and are afraid of getting lost.

- [L #10] "When you lose your phone you feel useless and disconnected".

Also, they feel that we are all becoming "more stupid". In their opinion, we rely on technology too much, which is why our concentration and creativity decrease and our abilities, such as doing mental calculations or reading long texts, are lost. Moreover, we do not solve problems or find answers on our own anymore.

3.3 Psychological Resources Depleted by ICTs

Several psychological resources are negatively affected by ICTs. ICTs seem to impede control and autonomy by creating addiction, they cause stress and social pressure, are distracting, and waste time.

Loss of Control and Autonomy. Negative effects on individuals that came up repeatedly were symptoms of addiction combined with perceived loss of control. Participants felt that they spent too much time on their phones, watching TV series, engaging in online shopping or browsing social media platforms. Once they start, they find it very hard or even impossible to stop, which creates the feeling that they are not in control of their own behavior. They also spoke of habits that they cannot change, such as taking their laptop to bed with them or falling asleep and waking up with their smartphones.

- [E #13] "What I'm noticing with myself and with my friends is that… we cannot control it - that is the problem".

Reachability and Social Pressure. Students feel that they have to be reachable all of the time on a number of different channels and reply to messages within a short time. They fear that other people will worry or feel neglected if they are not reachable or do not reply, which gives them a bad feeling. But the vicious circle continues: they themselves do not want to miss out on anything that their friends post and start to worry or feel offended if their friends do not reply. These mutual expectations produce a social norm of reachability.

- [C #31] "People expect from you all of the time that you reply immediately, this is really, I find this very annoying".

Distraction. Students feel distracted by their smartphones and other devices with internet connection. At work, incoming emails disrupt their concentration. When their phone or somebody else's phone lights up or makes a noise when receiving a message or call, their attention is drawn towards it. Whatever allows them to connect with other people or to get to information easily and quickly also presents a source of distraction. Even the mere possibility of somebody trying to reach them makes them nervous. They want to check what messages they have received, sometimes because they do not want to miss out on anything, sometimes because they look for an excuse to stop working.

- [H #11] "For example, I'm writing my homework, I'm submitting my assignments and it's, yeah, then it's like I need to check my phone".

ICTs Waste Time. While ICTs are convenient to use and allow an efficient organization of everyday life, they can waste one's time, especially with social media and playing games.

- [C #27] "In the evening we don't work, we watch movies, videos, listen to music, we write for nothing, we chat".

3.4   Societal Resources Depleted by ICTs

Our resources cannot only be depleted at the individual level; some issues with ICTs directly play out at the societal level. The issues that came up in the interviews focus on the power imbalance between users and companies that produce, offer, and sell ICTs.

ICTs Create Issues Concerning Information Privacy. Students fear a lack of data protection and intrusion of digital privacy because big corporations gather a lot of information about their users. One issue they discussed is big data and how a whole profile can be built based on digital information about a person. Another issue are social platforms that share the data of the users and "spy" on them in instant messaging services.

- [F #5] "Facebook, for example, is a real data-collection and also data-selling machine, and this is something that I keep in mind".

ICTs Affect Users' Perception of Reality. Some students worry about the information distribution through ICTs. Social networks and media often create a restricted representation of the real world, leading to an ignorance of real world problems such as global warming and world hunger. As users become distributors of information, the reliability of information sources is often not easy to verify. Students criticize especially that social network platforms do not take the effects of the distribution of false information seriously enough.

- [A #26] "You make up your own realities by simply blocking out those things in the world, that are heading into a bad direction".

ICTs' Powerful Position Within Our Society. Some students reflected on the impact of ICTs on society as a whole, which they see critically.

- [E #21] "I think, if we continue using it this way, it will seriously do us more harm than good".

Their reflections mostly focused on the consequences of increasing automation and progress in the development of intelligent systems. Cyber-unemployment and self-driving cars were some of the phenomena they named next to a growing belief in the infallibility of technological systems and the attribution of a human status to new technological devices in homes. They stress that societal measures have to be taken, such as an adaptation of our tax systems and careful design considerations.

3.5 Desired Changes and Missed Activities

One aim of this paper was to identify whether users are aware of the effects of ICTs. The activities that our interview partners miss out on because of ICTs seem to hint at an unsuccessful anchoring of users in the real world that they are aware of and reflect upon when thinking about what they would like to change. Students express that through the widespread use of social media, the experience of a moment loses its value if it is not digitally shared. At the same time, they enlist a variety of activities that they could do if there was no internet connection or social media. These range from staying with their family to going outside to play, traveling, meeting friends in person, appreciating the moment, and resting and sleeping. Often, students nostalgically reported memories of their childhood or youth when they reflected on these missed activities.

- [D #6] "When I was kid we were going outside [sic] and we met outside without messaging ourselves or telling the time or date or day so basically we just went outside and we knew that some friends are waiting there and we could play or do whatever we wanted and because of the technology we are staying at home, playing PC games or internet and basically those bonds that people have had earlier are somehow losing themselves."

With these missed activities, we can identify rest and sleep, friendship, and being in nature as additional values that are harmed by ICTs.

3.6 Proposed Measures

We asked students what they would like to change about other people's behavior and to come up with measures that they would put forward as minister of technology. Some of the measures that they proposed or wished for were quite drastic. Students wanted to completely abolish and "delete" social media, the idea of smartphones, and any technology that would not let people think on their own. One person was especially concerned about the distribution of information on Facebook and wished to close down Facebook to protect its users from getting stuck in a filter bubble or being spied on.

The measure that was most often mentioned was the introduction of an age limit for the use of smartphones, the internet, social networks, and computer games. Age limits were set differently, ranging from 10 to 16 years. While some students allowed smartphones only after high school, they did not consider normal cell phones without internet connection as problematic.

Internet- or phone-free days or time periods were wished for by the students themselves as well as proposed from the imagined position of a minister of technology. These measures differed in their strictness, ranging from proposed guidelines for the population to restrictions of internet connection, e.g., in the evenings from 9 p.m. onwards. Often, students mentioned these measures in relation with the activities they feel to miss out on. For example, they hoped that internet-free periods of time would decrease the social pressure to reply immediately and increase the chances that they went outside to meet someone in person.

Some measures focused on better education and awareness in the population as part of school teaching, others specifically targeted adults who had not grown up with technologies and should be supported in their use of technologies. Next to specific IT trainings and awareness for the value of personal data, some students proposed that schoolchildren and adults should reflect about the role of technology within our society.

Especially those students who were concerned about the distribution of information and privacy wished for measures that specifically targeted social media platforms or networks. They wanted harder sanctions for data breaches by companies and better regulations for digital copyright violations. Companies offering messaging services should be closely examined to check for privacy violations and social networks should leave more control to the user, which also means less personalization.

4 Discussion

This study explored the motivations for using ICTs and identified values that are fostered by ICTs. Results of the summarizing content analysis present a paradoxical picture: ICTs also have a negative impact, not only by harming the same values they foster, but also by depleting psychological and societal resources that are necessary to perceive and appreciate values in the first place. Our findings indicate that the negative influences of ICTs on users have not yet been fully understood because of this complex interplay.

4.1   Paradoxical Effects of ICTs

While it is valuable to users to have better digital interconnectedness, ICTs act as technological mediators, which change the nature of friendships and move interactions to the digital world. Personal reunions decrease and real interactions are perceived as unsatisfactory. Moreover, being connected and reachable all of the time has the negative effects of inducing a fear of missing out, evoking addictive behaviors as well as stress.

A similar paradoxical effect can be observed for the values of information accessibility, efficiency and convenience. The beneficial functions of ICTs present a great potential to make users addicted [1]. It is this dependence on technology that is created, which, in turn, results in a loss of competences. As all information can be found on the internet, there is no need to remember facts anymore. Instead of solving problems or finding answers to questions on our own, we go back to support online. Any cell phone has a calculator, therefore we don't need to do mental calculations. And the constant stream of short social media entries, postings and instant messages causes impatience when confronted with longer texts. It seems that with ICTs, users trade long-term knowledge, creativity, and cognitive abilities with short-time information.

Time seems to present a third paradox in the context of ICTs. Our interview partners expressed that while technologies save our time, they also waste our time. This is interesting to consider, as time also plays an important factor in the consideration of internet addiction or problematic internet use. Problematic internet use is predicted by a deep absorption and engagement with online activities that causes an individual to lose track of time [43] and is associated with wasting time online without a purpose [31]. Therefore, saving time with online communication and information appears to lie close to wasting time because of a too deep absorption in online activities.

A paradox on a higher level is the fear of missing out, which is experienced in two ways. One reason for the addictive power of smartphones is the desire to be informed about what your friends are doing and to not be left out in any activities. This has been termed the "Fear of Missing Out" [44]. Interestingly, students do not only report a fear of missing out on the digital world. It seems that through their engagement in the digital world, a fear of missing out on the real world is created. This becomes apparent in the changes they desire. They miss being outside in nature, experiencing the moment, real interactions with their friends, as well as sleep and rest. The increasing importance of the digital seems to cause a desire for experiencing the real world again.

4.2   Loss of Resources and Control

It is interesting to see that our study participants mention activities and values they fear to miss out on in the real world because of their engagement in the digital world, but do not react by decreasing their use of ICTs. Spending a lot of time online and less time on other pleasurable activities, isolation from friends in favor of online friendships as well as a sense of guilt [31] are typical symptoms of internet addiction and seem to describe the experience of our interview partners. Other symptoms of internet addiction such as the loss of control and ongoing use in spite of negative effects [20] fit equally well to their reported experiences. Insights gained from the interviews suggest that with digital experiences and interactions a bubble is created. This bubble restrains users in their freedom and autonomy by causing distractions, addictive behaviors, and stress.

Our interview partners are fully aware of this going on, but feel incapable of reacting. They expressed the wish to stop, reduce, or change their use, but they do not feel in control of their own behavior and bring up other responsible entities with the legal and societal measures they propose. Looking at these measures, it is easy to see that students struggle with the amount of time they spend with new technologies (which is probably why they proposed technology-free periods of time). As they themselves find it very difficult to control their own behavior, they suggest other responsible entities, such as the government and schools. In some cases, the technologies themselves were held responsible, which is why students wanted to erase some of these technologies, such as social network platforms. They feel the need to regulate the use of ICTs at an early stage, targeting children and adolescents, and to raise awareness in the general population. As some students expressed in the interviews, early intervention and better awareness could prevent the development of addiction to ICTs.

Certain preconditions have to be met to enable human development: psychological as well as societal resources have to be protected by not allowing ICTs to put users into a situation in which they feel distracted, nervous, incompetent, and without control. These key human resources are indispensable for higher needs and values to flourish. However, findings of this study suggest that these resources are threatened.

4.3   Conclusion

We need to move towards a more critical and holistic view on technology and its role within our lives. We should be mindful of the trend that seems to become apparent with the ongoing widespread use of ICTs: human values that are dear to us are pushed into the background while at the same time important resources and preconditions for the perception of these values are depleted. New technologies do not only bring about beneficial changes. Therefore, we have to take into account potential negative effects on the individual, social, and societal level before products are launched. That is, we have to put more effort into the design phase. Design methods that focus on human values seem especially promising in that regard.

References

1. Salehan, M., Negahban, A.: Social networking on smartphones: when mobile phones become addictive. Comput. Hum. Behav. **29**, 2632–2639 (2013). https://doi.org/10.1016/j.chb.2013.07.003
2. ind.ie. https://ind.ie/ethical-design/
3. Patrignani, N., Whitehouse, D.: Slow Tech and ICT: A Responsible, Sustainable and Ethical Approach. Palgrave Macmillan, Cham (2018)
4. Spiekermann, S.: Ethical IT Innovation: A Value-Based System Design Approach. CRC Press, Boca Raton (2016)
5. Błachnio, A., Przepiórka, A., Pantic, I.: Internet use, Facebook intrusion, and depression: results of a cross-sectional study. Eur. Psychiatry **30**, 681–684 (2015). https://doi.org/10.1016/j.eurpsy.2015.04.002
6. Caplan, S.E.: Preference for online social interaction: a theory of Problematic Internet Use and psychosocial well-being. Commun. Res. **30**, 625–648 (2003). https://doi.org/10.1177/0093650203257842
7. Yao, M.Z., Zhong, Z.: Loneliness, social contacts and Internet addiction: a cross-lagged panel study. Comput. Hum. Behav. **30**, 164–170 (2014). https://doi.org/10.1016/j.chb.2013.08.007
8. Kuss, D.J., Griffiths, M.D., Binder, J.F.: Internet addiction in students: prevalence and risk factors. Comput. Hum. Behav. **29**, 959–966 (2013). https://doi.org/10.1016/j.chb.2012.12.024
9. Brooks, S.: Does personal social media usage affect efficiency and well-being? Comput. Hum. Behav. **46**, 26–37 (2015). https://doi.org/10.1016/j.chb.2014.12.053
10. Reid, G.G., Boyer, W.: Social network sites and young adolescent identity development. Child. Educ. **89**, 243–253 (2013). https://doi.org/10.1080/00094056.2013.815554
11. Barkhordari, R., Willemyns, M.: Young adults' construction of social identity on Facebook: a structural equation model. In: Proceedings of the 3rd European Conference on Social Media (2016)
12. Lepp, A., Li, J., Barkley, J.E., Salehi-Esfahani, S.: Exploring the relationships between college students' cell phone use, personality and leisure. Comput. Hum. Behav. **43**, 210–219 (2015). https://doi.org/10.1016/j.chb.2014.11.006
13. Li, J., Lepp, A., Barkley, J.E.: Locus of control and cell phone use: implications for sleep quality, academic performance, and subjective well-being. Comput. Hum. Behav. **52**, 450–452 (2015). https://doi.org/10.1016/j.chb.2015.06.021
14. Elhai, J.D., Levine, J.C., Dvorak, R.D., Hall, B.J.: Fear of missing out, need for touch, anxiety and depression are related to problematic smartphone use. Comput. Hum. Behav. **63**, 509–516 (2016). https://doi.org/10.1016/j.chb.2016.05.079
15. Best, P., Manktelow, R., Taylor, B.: Online communication, social media and adolescent wellbeing: a systematic narrative review. Child Youth Serv. Rev. **41**, 27–36 (2014). https://doi.org/10.1016/j.childyouth.2014.03.001
16. Bolton, R.N., et al.: Understanding Generation Y and their use of social media: a review and research agenda. J. Serv. Manag. **24**, 245–267 (2013). https://doi.org/10.1108/09564231311326987
17. Ngai, E.W.T., Tao, S.S.C., Moon, K.K.L.: Social media research: theories, constructs, and conceptual frameworks. Int. J. Inf. Manage. **35**, 33–44 (2015). https://doi.org/10.1016/j.ijinfomgt.2014.09.004
18. Pénard, T., Poussing, N., Suire, R.: Does the Internet make people happier? J. Soc. Econ. **46**, 105–116 (2013). https://doi.org/10.1016/j.socec.2013.08.004

19. Barley, S.R., Meyerson, D.E., Grodal, S.: E-mail as a source and symbol of stress. Organ. Sci. **22**, 887–906 (2011). https://doi.org/10.1287/orsc.1100.0573
20. Kardefelt-Winther, D.: A conceptual and methodological critique of internet addiction research: towards a model of compensatory internet use. Comput. Hum. Behav. **31**, 351–354 (2014). https://doi.org/10.1016/j.chb.2013.10.059
21. Friedman, B., Kahn Jr., P.H., Borning, A.: Value sensitive design and information systems. In: Zhang, P., Galletta, D. (eds.) Human-Computer Interaction and Management Information Systems: Foundations, pp. 348–372. M.E.Sharpe, Armonk (2006)
22. Lepp, A., Barkley, J.E., Karpinski, A.C.: The relationship between cell phone use, academic performance, anxiety, and Satisfaction with Life in college students. Comput. Hum. Behav. **31**, 343–350 (2014). https://doi.org/10.1016/j.chb.2013.10.049
23. Shakya, H.B., Christakis, N.A.: Association of Facebook use with compromised well-being: a longitudinal study. Am. J. Epidemiol. **185**, 203–211 (2017). https://doi.org/10.1093/aje/kww189
24. Rotondi, V., Stanca, L., Tomasuolo, M.: Connecting alone: smartphone use, quality of social interactions and well-being. J. Econ. Psychol. **63**, 17–26 (2017). https://doi.org/10.1016/j.joep.2017.09.001
25. Lin, L.Y., et al.: Association between social media use and depression among U.S. young adults. Depress. Anxiety **33**, 323–331 (2016). https://doi.org/10.1002/da.22466.Association
26. Primack, B.A., et al.: Use of multiple social media platforms and symptoms of depression and anxiety: a nationally-representative study among U.S. young adults. Comput. Hum. Behav. **69**, 1–9 (2017). https://doi.org/10.1016/j.chb.2016.11.013
27. Craparo, G.: Internet addiction, dissociation, and alexithymia. Proc. Soc. Behav. Sci. **30**, 1051–1056 (2011). https://doi.org/10.1016/j.sbspro.2011.10.205
28. Ko, C.-H., Yen, J.-Y., Chen, C.-C., Chen, S.-H., Yen, C.-F.: Proposed diagnostic criteria of Internet addiction for adolescents. J. Nerv. Ment. Dis. **193**, 728–733 (2005). https://doi.org/10.1097/01.nmd.0000185891.13719.54
29. Billieux, J., Maurage, P., Lopez-Fernandez, O., Kuss, D.J., Griffiths, M.D.: Can disordered mobile phone use be considered a behavioral addiction? An update on current evidence and a comprehensive model for future research. Curr. Addict. Rep. **2**, 156–162 (2015). https://doi.org/10.1007/s40429-015-0054-y
30. Kwon, M., et al.: Development and validation of a Smartphone Addiction Scale (SAS). PLoS ONE **8**, e56936 (2013). https://doi.org/10.1371/journal.pone.0056936
31. Davis, R.A.: Cognitive-behavioral model of pathological Internet use. Comput. Hum. Behav. **17**, 187–195 (2001). https://doi.org/10.1016/S0747-5632(00)00041-8
32. Shen, C., Williams, D.: Unpacking time online: connecting internet and massively multiplayer online game use with psychosocial well-being. Commun. Res. **38**, 123–149 (2011). https://doi.org/10.1177/0093650210377196
33. Schwartz, S.H.: Are there universal aspects in the structure and contents of human values? J. Soc. Issues **50**, 19–45 (1994). https://doi.org/10.1111/j.1540-4560.1994.tb01196.x
34. Maslow, A.H.: A theory of human motivation. Psychol. Rev. **50**, 370–396 (1943). https://doi.org/10.1037/h0054346
35. Krobath, H.T.: Werte: Ein Streifzug durch Philosophie und Wissenschaft. Königshausen & Neumann, Würzburg (2009)
36. Frankena, W.K.: Ethics. Prentice-Hall, Inc., Englewood Cliffs (1973)
37. Scheler, M.: Formalism in Ethics and Non-Formal Ethics of Values: A New Attempt Toward the Foundation of An Ethical Personalism. Northwestern University Press, Evanston (1973)
38. Alter, A.: How Technology Gets us Hooked (2017). https://www.theguardian.com/technology/2017/feb/28/how-technology-gets-us-hooked

39. Eyal, N., Hoover, R.: Hooked: How to Build Habit-Forming Products. Portfolio Penguin, London (2014)
40. Maslow, A.H.: Motivation and Personality. Harper & Row, New York (1970)
41. Eurostat: Internet Access and Use Statistics - Households and Individuals. http://ec.europa.eu/eurostat/statistics-explained/index.php/Internet_access_and_use_statistics_-_households_and_individuals
42. Mayring, P.: Qualitative content analysis: theoretical foundation, basic procedures and software solution (2014)
43. Mazzoni, E., Cannata, D., Baiocco, L.: Focused, not lost: the mediating role of temporal dissociation and focused immersion on problematic internet use. Behav. Inf. Technol. **36**, 11–20 (2017). https://doi.org/10.1080/0144929X.2016.1159249
44. Przybylski, A.K., Murayama, K., Dehaan, C.R., Gladwell, V.: Motivational, emotional, and behavioral correlates of Fear of Missing Out. Comput. Hum. Behav. **29**, 1841–1848 (2013). https://doi.org/10.1016/j.chb.2013.02.014

Gender

Feminist Technoscience as a Resource for Working with Science Practices, a Critical Approach, and Gender Equality in Swedish Higher IT Educations

Johanna Sefyrin[1]([✉]) [iD], Pirjo Elovaara[2], and Christina Mörtberg[3]

[1] Linköping University, 581 83 Linköping, Sweden
johanna.sefyrin@liu.se
[2] Blekinge Institute of Technology, 371 79 Karlskrona, Sweden
[3] Linnæus University, 351 95 Växjö, Sweden

Abstract. Science is according to the Swedish legislation for higher education (Högskoleförordningen) a central quality aim for higher educations. In the Swedish Higher Education Authority's (UKÄ) new quality assurance system, the integration of gender equality is one of several quality aspects that are being measured. This paper concerns a planned study with the aim to explore how feminist technoscience can contribute to challenging existing science practices, and a critical approach, while at the same time work as a theoretical resource for the integration of gender equality in Swedish higher IT educations. Feminist technoscience makes possible critical questions about scientific practices in both educational contexts and in work life, about researchers' positioning, about consequences, and about power issues. Posing such questions is central in IT educations, since we live in a society in which digital technologies increasingly constitute preconditions for a working reality, and both reproduce existing structures and form new patterns. In this reality it is central to ask whether current science practices are enough, and how feminist technoscience can make a difference, in those educations that produce the IT experts of the tomorrow. The study will be conducted as a qualitative field study with a focus on how teachers and students in Swedish higher IT educations practice science and a critical approach, and feminist technoscience in their educations.

Keywords: Science practices · Critical approach
Swedish higher IT education · Feminist technoscience

1 Introduction

This paper concerns a planned study in which we plan to explore how feminist technoscience can contribute to challenging existing science practices, and a critical approach, while at the same time work as a theoretical resource for the integration of gender equality in Swedish higher IT educations in a broad sense – information systems/informatics, engineering with a focus on computers and IT, and media and digital technologies programs. According to the Swedish Higher Education Ordinance

(Högskoleförordningen), science and a critical approach are central quality aims and an important part of the educational content on a higher educational level. Furthermore, in the Swedish Higher Education Authority's (UKÄ) new quality assurance system for higher education, gender equality is one of several quality aspects that are being measured. In the planned study we are interested in exploring questions of what science means in Swedish higher IT educations, how it is practiced, and if the current science practices in Swedish IT educations are enough to prepare the students for the challenges they will face as practitioners in a society which is increasingly digitalized in complex ways, and in which the digital and the social are increasingly, and intimately, entangled. In these explorations we will use feminist technoscience as a resource that can provide guidance for how to make a difference. A central concern in feminist technoscience is knowledge processes, in terms of the development of scientific knowledge, but also in terms of the design of technologies, and the implicit and explicit knowledge of organizational and social structures, practices and hierarchies that are inscribed into technologies [27, 49]. Researchers within the field have shown how the development of knowledge is intimately related to how the involved actors (researchers, designers, users etc.) are implicated in social and material relations, including those of gender, ethnicity, class and sexuality [18, 30, 42, 49, 52]. Feminist technoscience is inspired by constructionist approaches, and a central point of departure is that neither technology nor gender is understood as fixed or given. Rather, technology is understood as "contingently stabilized and contestable" [49, p. 8], and in a similar way gender is understood as a performance, or a social achievement [ibid.]. Feminist technoscience focus on gender equality – the social, economic and political relations between women and men in the production, design and use of technologies [ibid.], as well as the performance of gender. Gender and gender equality are related, and research in the field shows that femininity and masculinity are performed not only in relation to each other, but also in relation to technologies [ibid.]. Hence a central focus is on how gender and technology are mutually shaped in processes of development of scientific knowledge, and of design and use of technologies, in which neither are understood as fixed or given in advance [ibid.]. While the research field addresses a range of technologies, here we are interested in the technoscience processes that concerns digital technologies, both in terms of development of scientific knowledge, and processes of design and use.

Feminist science and technoscience scholars have been studying technoscience use, design and development practices, as well as the consequences of these practices during several decades [4, 10, 20, 23, 24], and have a lot to contribute with to more mainstream approaches, which have focused on other aspects of science practices, both in terms of how to understand and theorize these problems, but also for how they can be dealt with. Feminist technoscience constitutes a ground for posing critical questions about scientific practices, about researchers' positioning, about consequences of these practices for different actors, and about power issues related to knowledge making and scientific practices. A central point of departure for feminist technoscience is that science and technology are entangled with social interests, and that the involved researchers and knowledge developers must be understood as politically and ethically responsible for the practices and interventions that research may give rise to [52].

So, the aim with this study is to explore how feminist technoscience can contribute to challenging existing science practices, and a critical approach, while at the same time work as a theoretical resource for the integration of gender equality in Swedish higher IT educations in a broad sense. Exactly what the term science practices mean differs between disciplines, but our view of scientific practices is based on the use of this term in the research field of feminist technoscience, in which scientific practices are much more far reaching than those who take place in laboratories [26, 28]. The main research question is: How can feminist technoscience be a part of scientific practices and a critical approach in Swedish higher IT educations? This overarching question is broken down into three sub-questions: (1) Which are the scientific points of departure in Swedish higher IT educations? (2) Which are the possibilities or hindrances for an integration of gender equality in Swedish higher IT educations? And (3) How can feminist technoscience make a difference in the work with scientific practices and gender equality integration in Swedish higher IT educations?

2 Background

The background for our interest in gender equality and its relations to digital technologies is that these technologies are becoming more and more ubiquitous, and increasingly affect all the fine-grained parts of current societies and individuals' lives, and while they solve some of the existing problems, at the same time they give rise to new challenges [44, 45]. Some interpret this development as a fourth industrial revolution [46, 51], or as "a second machine age" [9], and then refer to how digital technologies such as 3D-printing, big data, artificial intelligence, robotics and automation, in combination with demographic changes, urbanization and globalization, are merged and amplify each other, and are expected to affect all parts of society in a disruptive way [45]. Be this a revolution or not, but it indicates a world of increasing complexity, in which digital technologies and relations play an important part, both in terms of constituting complexity, and in terms of expectations to contribute to solutions. Researchers have underscored that technologies are formative and do not only mirror an existing social order, but are designed in entangled relations of various agencies, and they reproduce the existing social, economic, cultural and political relations – including gender, ethnicity and class [7, 27, 48, 49]. Consequently technologies make possible some ways of acting, being, and living, and make other activities, and ways of being and living harder [29, 37, 49, 52], something which contributes to making some identities, positions and parts of the world visible, while some are made invisible [8, 29]. Hence digital technologies must be understood as inextricable from other relations, practices, and structures of societies [7, 49, 52].

The actors involved in designing and developing digital technologies do this in a world that is increasingly complex, and in which these technologies are more and more entangled with other parts of societies, including gender relations. Insights from research in feminist technoscience underscores that the processes of scientific knowledge, as well as design and development of technologies, are intimately intertwined with social issues – the social, the technological and the scientific are understood as knitted together in a seamless web of relations [49]. Researchers in the field also explore issues concerning consequences of technoscience practices, and argue that researchers, designers and developers must be understood as responsible – and accountable [3] – for the consequences of the technologies they contribute to shaping [52]. This requires that researchers and practitioners need to be prepared for this, in terms of for instance an ability to critically reflect on digital technologies' reproduction of problematic power relations and structures, their entanglement in power relations and their consequences for different actors – what the technologies do. These designers and developers – IT experts who often have a formal university degree of some sort, are shaped during their education. These higher IT educations prepare the students – who are the IT experts and decision makers of tomorrow – for professional practice. During higher education the disciplinary knowledge and traditions concerning which problems are interesting and possible to solve, what is doable, how the subject area is defined, and the view of what approaches and methods are useful in a specific situation, are communicated [6, 25, 36].

From the point of view of feminist technoscience, the design and production of science and technology cannot be distinguished from the networks, structures and practices in which it is enmeshed, so from this perspective, the issue of how to better prepare students in IT educations for their professional activities in an increasingly complex world, is all a matter of technoscience practices [4, 19, 20, 21, 26, 52]. It is a matter of how the design of technosciences are entangled in existing power relations, practices and structures, about the positioning of the researchers, and of the need for researchers to be aware of their responsibility of the possible consequences of technoscience practices and interventions. In this landscape of increasing digital complexity constituted of what Sørensen [45] discusses as combinations of digitalization, distribution and scale, we are faced with new challenges in the crossroads between disciplines. These questions concern issues of who is included and excluded in the design and use of digital technologies [14, 35], the unintended inscription of gender stereotypes into seemingly gender neutral digital technologies [34], computer ethics [1], care in technoscience practices [13], digital technologies in relation to environmental sustainability [31], and to the Anthropocene [46], just to name a few. This necessitates the possibility to ask questions that might require wider approaches than are currently possible within disciplinary boundaries, but that rather require multidisciplinary approaches [2, 45, 50]. In this situation we view feminist technoscience – with its focus on entangled practices in which humans are deeply and ontologically related with the social and material world, and on the gendered and ethical issues that arise in these practices [4, 41] – as a resource for asking complex but pressing questions.

3   Theoretical Framework

For the study we will take as our analytical point of departure feminist technoscience [20, 38, 49, 52]. Feminist technoscience can be understood as a knowledge field that is part of the larger field of feminist studies, and borrow theoretical inspiration from feminist science scholars such as Haraway [20, 22], Harding [23] and Barad [3]. Åsberg and Lykke [52, p. 299] write that

"Feminist technoscience studies is a relentlessly transdisciplinary field if research which emerged out of decades of feminist critiques. These critiques have revealed the ways in which gender, in its intersections with other sociocultural power differentials and identity markers, is entangled in natural, medical and technical sciences as well as in the sociotechnical networks and practices of a globalized world".

Feminist technoscience concerns the application of feminist science critique and analysis on scientific and other knowledge practices in order to explore the relations between feminism and science, and what they can learn from each other [52]. Moreover, technology and gender are viewed as mutually shaped, that is, technology is both a source and a consequence of gender relations [ibid.]. Latour's [27] statement that "technology is society made durable" underscores how existing sociopolitical hierarchies and relations are inscribed into technologies, which then contribute to the (re) production of for instance gender relations. An important point of departure is that also so called pure basic science is entangled in social interests, and that the involved researchers and knowledge developers must be understood as politically and ethically responsible for the practices and interventions that research may give rise to [52]. Feminist technoscience is a critical approach, and underscore that technosciences are often used in order to advance the interests of capitalist interests [ibid.], but an important focus is that it does not have to be this way. Feminist technoscience concerns both technological and scientific (technoscience) practices in general, and analyze the design and development of technological artefacts and systems in the same way as science practices are analyzed.

One central issue concerns how researchers' and other actors' situatedness affect their knowledge practices [19]. de la Bellacasa writes "That knowledge is situated means that knowing and thinking are inconceivable without a multitude of relations that also make possible the worlds we think with. The premise to my argument can therefore be formulated as follows: relations of thinking and knowing require care" [13, p. 198]. Another focus is how power relations affect who is included and who is not in technoscience practices [14, 24], how technosciences such as digital technologies contribute to both the reproduction of problematic social, economic and material structures, and to the destabilization of these [8, 27], problematic categorizations and representational practices [3, 8, 39], and power/knowledge in technoscience practices [17]. Feminist technosciences underscore that gender science is not only about relations between women and men, but also about understanding agency, bodies, rationality and the boundary making between e.g. nature and culture in technoscience practices [52].

The theoretical discussions in the field of feminist technoscience during the last years have centered on a number of 'turns' such as the posthumanist, materialist and ontological turn [52], and also the term Anthropocene is discussed [46]. These ideas have been used by a number of researchers in order to explore how gender and other aspects of reality are inscribed into information technology [5, 40], the accountability of designers, and strategies for designing without inscribing fixed or naturalized notions of gender into designs [47], entanglements of humans and machines [16, 41], sociomaterial relations in participatory design methods [15], gendered discourses in IT educations [12], and legal, ethical, and moral questions that surround security technologies [43]. These researchers focus on how, in design and use practices, humans are entangled with materialities (technological and other), how sociopolitical realities such as gender, ethnicity and class are inscribed into technologies which in turn reproduces these realities. These researchers explore how this takes place, the consequences of this, and on developing possible alternatives that are less problematic. The works of these researchers are often published in journals with an interdisciplinary scope, rather than in mainstream disciplinary journals, something which probably contributes to the fact that this knowledge is relatively unknown in related research fields such as in the more mainstream information systems (IS) field. In mainstream IS journals some of the ideas of feminist technoscience is discussed under the umbrella term of sociomaterialities [e.g. 11, 32, 33]. This research is based primarily on socio-technical systems theory, actor network theory, and practice theory [11], and less on feminist technoscience, but the works of Barad [3, 4] is nevertheless central. Consequently these discussions mostly go into the posthumanist ideas of feminist technoscience, and touch upon the consequences of this for information systems design, but do not go into the feminist concerns that are in focus in feminist technoscience. Here we argue that the feminist focus on who is involved in technoscience practices, and how the consequences of technoscience practices affect different bodies differently, would add important insights also in related disciplines.

For the planned research application we argue that the area of feminist techno-science is relevant for contributing to scientific practices and gender equality in IT educations, as digital technologies today constitute an increasingly integral part of society, both in terms of infrastructural preconditions for societal functions and services, and in terms of how social development is highly affected by the innovation and design of digital technologies. In several respects these technologies contribute to solving existing problems, and to a better life for many individuals, but they also reproduce problematic structures, and cause new problems and challenges. This points to the importance of working with issues of scientific practices concerning those issues that are in focus in feminist technoscience such as technological consequences, the responsibility and accountability of the designers of digital technologies, and of the relations of gender, sexuality, ethnicity and power in which design practices are entangled.

4   Methodological Approach

The planned study will be conducted as a qualitative field study, in which we study how teachers and students in Swedish higher IT educations understand and work with scientific practices and a critical approach, and how they work with gender issues – if this is done in terms of gender equality or if it is also done in terms of gender science as a ground for scientific practices, and if so, how this is done. The field study will be conducted through interviews, but also through the study of documents such as course syllabuses, course literature lists and other documents that describe how the teaching in those areas is planned and conducted. We have as our starting point for the practical implementation of the study the Swedish Information Systems Academy (SISA: http://sisa-net.se). We are also part of a recently initiated Swedish network for feminist technoscience, through which we will be able to find more colleagues with this kind of competence. These colleagues work with higher IT educations such as information systems/informatics, engineering with a focus on IT, and media and digital technologies programs, programs located at both philosophical and technical faculties.

Our plan is not to evaluate whether representatives of Swedish IT educations work with gender science as scientific practices, but rather to explore how this is currently done, ideas for how it can be done, and how feminist technoscience can make a difference compared to more mainstream approaches to science. This exploration of current competencies and practices in the area will be combined with the study of relevant research literature. Since the involved researchers work with feminist technoscience, this will constitute an analytical point of departure, with the aim of identifying different ways of working with feminist technoscience in higher IT educations, apart from working with gender equality and the recruitment of women to male dominated technical educations.

Our plan is to start the work by exploring how scientific practices and a critical approach is understood and practiced in Swedish higher IT educations, through collecting central policy documents – both national and local – and through interviewing teachers and students at some of these educations. Then we will proceed by mapping the Swedish higher IT educations which in some way work with gender and feminist technoscience, and interview teachers and students in those educations with a focus on how this is done and what it contributes with. Through this we will obtain information about how working with feminist technoscience in higher IT educations differ from, and might contribute to the work with scientific practices and a critical approach from a more traditional perspective (Table 1).

5 Expected Results and Contributions

We – the researchers who plan this study – position ourselves in the crossroads between feminist technoscience, informatics, information systems (IS), and media technology. As underscored by for instance Walsham [50], who work in the information systems (IS) field, this field has traditionally focused on helping organizations to use information and communication technologies more effectively, with the aim to improve organizational effectiveness in capitalist interests. Walsham [ibid.] argue that researchers in the IS field should focus more on how digital technologies can be developed and used in order to contribute to a better world, in a way that also serves other interests than those of efficiency and effectiveness. Ethical, as well as gender issues, related to information systems are not entirely absent to the IS field, but are nevertheless rather marginalized, as discussed by Adam [2]. Feminist technoscience is a research field that focus simultaneously on scientific practices and their embeddedness in social and political relations, and on the practical, political and ethical consequences of these practices [52]. In this application the significance and planned novelty concerns bringing into the related fields of informatics, information systems and media technology the insights of how gender and knowledge practices are related to both scientific and design practices, knowledge that can also be used in Swedish higher IT educations. These issues are relatively unknown in for instance the field of information systems, and would add significantly to the current discussion both on how the IS field should focus on contributing to a better world, rather than only focus on improving

Table 1. Project plan

Year	Activities/Tasks	Outcomes/Milestones
2019	a) Initial literature study. Duration: January - March	M1: Initial overview of relevant research
	b) Map Swedish higher IT educations Duration: March	M2: Overview of possible participants in study
	c) Take part of relevant national and local steering documents concerning scientific practices and a critical approach. Duration: Mid January – May	M1: Initial overview of how scientific practices is defined in documents
	d) Planning of the empirical studies and recruitment of participants Duration: June	M3: Acceptance to participate in the study
	d) Carry through a number of interviews. Duration: June – December	M4: Empirical material collected M5: Disseminate the follow-up to the project and acccounting administrator
	e) Project management : plan regular meetings, necessary reports, follow up budget, recruit a person for the transcriptions Duration: January - December	M6: Any requested reports have been turned in to the department and research council
2020	f) Transcribe and compile the gathered material Duration: January – March	M7: Digitalisation of the collected material
	h) Map IT educations which work with gender studies/feminist technoscience Duration: March	M8: Overview of possible participants
	i) Planning of the empirical studies and recruitment of participants Duration: March	M9: Acceptance to participate in the study
	j) Carry through interviews with a focus on how gender studies/feminist technoscience is practiced. Duration: April – October	M10: Empirical material collected
	k) Transcribe and compile the gathered material Duration: mid January – April	M11: Digitalisation of the collected material
	l) Project management: necessary reports to department and the research council, follow up budget Duration: January – December	M12: Disseminate the follow-up to the project and accounting administrator at the department M13: Any requested reports have been turned in
2021	m) Analysis and synthesis of research material Duration: January – June	M13: Conceptualisation scientific practices and a critical approach in combination with FTS
	n) Dissemination: na) To scholars: Journals and conference papers Duration: June – December	M14: Journals: Information, Technology & People, and/or Science, Technology & Human Values, NORA – Nordic Journal of Feminist and Gender Research, International Journal of Feminist Technoscience
	nb) To research participants and organisations nc) To teachers: Knowledge support Duration: May – August	M16: Popular scientific publication
	o) Project management: plan and facilitate reporting Duration: January – December	M17: The report of the project sent to the research council, report to the department

efficiency and effectiveness in capitalist interests [see 50], and the discussion about "sociomaterialities" [e.g. 11, 32, 33] which has introduced the posthumanist ideas embraced by feminist technoscience into the IS field, but which mostly bypasses the feminist concerns. We argue that this discussion would benefit significantly from acknowledging the research that over the years has been done in the field of feminist technoscience, albeit in interdisciplinary journals and conferences rather than in mainstream IS journals, and also acknowledging the full meaning and relevance of the posthumanist ideas now being discussed in the mainstream IS field, that is, of how the entanglement of the social and the material include also the entanglement of sociopolitical relations such as gender, ethnicity and class in the design and use of information systems.

6 Discussion

This short paper has presented a planned study with the aim we aim to explore how gender science can contribute to science practices and a critical approach, while at the same time work as a theoretical resource for the integration of gender equality, in Swedish higher IT educations in a broad sense – information systems/informatics, engineering with a focus on computers and IT, and media and digital technologies programs. The most expected result of the study is foremost to bring into the related areas of information systems, informatics, and media technology the insights of feminist technoscience, of how an analytical focus on gendered bodies matter in technoscience practices.

Acknowledgements. We would like to thank the reviewers for their constructive feedback and suggestions for how to improve the paper.

References

1. Adam, A.: Gender, Ethics and Information Technology. Palgrave Macmillan, Basingstoke (2005)
2. Adam, A.: IS and its agenda. J. Inf. Technol. **27**(2), 102 (2012)
3. Barad, K.: Posthumanist performativity: toward an understanding of how matter comes to matter. Signs J. Women Cult. Soc. **28**(3), 801–831 (2003)
4. Barad, K.: Meeting the Universe Halfway: Quantum Physics and the Entanglement of Matter and Meaning. Duke University Press, Princeton (2007)
5. Bath, C.: Searching for methodology. In: Ernst, W., Horwath, I. (eds.) Gender in Science and Technology, Interdisciplinary Approaches, pp. 57–78 (2013)
6. Berner, B.: Perpetuum mobile? Teknikens utmaningar och historiens gång. Arkiv Förlag, Lund (1999)
7. Bijker, W.E.: How is technology made?—That is the question! Camb. J. Econ. **34**(1), 63–76 (2009)
8. Bowker, G., Star, S.L.: Sorting Things Out. Classification and Its Consequences. The MIT Press, Cambridge and London (1999)

9. Brynjolfsson, E., McAfee, A.: The Second Machine Age: Work, Progress, and Prosperity in a Time of Brilliant Technologies. WW Norton & Company, New York (2014)
10. Butler, J.: Bodies That Matter. On the Discursive Limits of "Sex". Routledge, New York and London (1993)
11. Cecez-Kecmanovic, D., Galliers, R.D., Henfridsson, O., Newell, S., Vidgen, R.: The sociomateriality of information systems: current status, future directions. MIS Q. **38**(3), 809–830 (2014)
12. Corneliussen, H.: Diskursens makt–individets frihet: Kjønnede posisjoner i diskursen om data (The power of discourse–the freedom of individuals: Gendered positions in the discourse of computing) (Doctoral dissertation, thesis, Dep. of humanistic informatics, University of Bergen) (2002)
13. de la Bellacasa, M.P.: Matters of care in technoscience: assembling neglected things. Soc. Stud. Sci. **41**(1), 85–106 (2011)
14. Elovaara, P., Igira, F.T., Mörtberg, C.: Whose participation? Whose knowledge? Exploring PD in Tanzania-Zanzibar and Sweden. In: Jacucci, G., Kensing, F. (eds.) Proceedings of the Ninth Participatory Design Conference. ACM (2006)
15. Elovaara, P., Mörtberg, C.: Carthographic mappings: participative methods. In: Proceedings of the 11th Biennial Participatory Design Conference, pp. 171–174. ACM (2010)
16. Ernst, W.: Emancipatory interferences with machines? Int. J. Gend., Sci. Technol. **9**(2), 178–196 (2017)
17. Finken, S.: Methods as technologies for producing knowledge. An encounter with cultural practices – reflections from a field study in a high-tech company. Doctoral dissertation, Roskilde University (2005)
18. Hackett, E.J., Amsterdamska, O., Lynch, M., Wajcman, J.: The Handbook of Science and Technology Studies. The MIT Press, Cambridge (2008)
19. Haraway, D.: Situated knowledges: the science question in feminism and the privilege of partial perspective. In: Haraway, D. (ed.) Simians, Cyborgs, and Women. The Reinvention of Nature, pp. 183–201. Routledge, New York (1991)
20. Haraway, D.: Modest_Witness@Second_Millennium. FemaleMan©_Meets_OncoMouse™. Feminism and Technoscience. Routledge, New York and London (1997)
21. Haraway, D. (ed.): The Haraway Reader, pp. 321–342. Routledge, New York (2004)
22. Haraway, D.J.: When Species Meet, vol. 224. University of Minnesota Press, Minneapolis (2008)
23. Harding, S.G.: The Science Question in Feminism. Cornell University Press, Ithaca (1986)
24. Harding, S.: Whose Science? Whose Knowledge? Thinking From Women's Lives. Cornell University Press, Ithaca (1991)
25. Huber, L.: Disciplinary cultures and social reproduction. Eur. J. Educ. **1990**, 241–261 (1990)
26. Latour, B.: Science in Action: How to Follow Scientists and Engineers Through Society. Harvard University Press, Harvard (1987)
27. Latour, B.: Technology is society made durable. Sociol. Rev. **38**(1_suppl), 103–131 (1990)
28. Law, J.: After Method: Mess in Social Science Research. Routledge, London and New York (2004)
29. Löwgren, J., Stolterman, E.: Thoughtful Interaction Design: A Design Perspective on Information Technology. MIT Press, Cambridge (2004)
30. McNeil, M., Roberts, C.: Feminist science and technology studies. In: Theories and Methodologies in Postgraduate Feminist Research: Researching Differently, pp. 29–42 (2011)
31. Melville, N.P.: Information systems innovation for environmental sustainability. MIS Q **34**(1), 1–21 (2010)

32. Niemimaa, M.: Sociomateriality and information systems research: quantum radicals and cartesian conservatives. ACM SIGMIS Database DATABASE Adv. Inf. Syst. **47**(4), 45–59 (2016)

33. Orlikowski, W.J., Scott, S.V.: Sociomateriality: challenging the separation of technology, work and organization. Acad. Manag. Ann. **2**(1), 433–474 (2008)

34. Oudshoorn, N., Rommes, E., Stienstra, M.: Configuring the user as everybody: gender and design cultures in information and communication technologies. Sci. Technol. Hum. Values **29**(1), 30–63 (2004)

35. Robinson, L., et al.: Digital inequalities and why they matter. Inf. Commun. Soc. **18**(5), 569–582 (2015)

36. Salminen-Karlsson, M.: Bringing women into computer engineering: curriculum reform processes at Two Institutes of Technology. Linkoping Studies in Education and Psychology Dissertations, No. 60 (1999)

37. Scott, S.V., Orlikowski, W.J.: Entanglements in practice: performing anonymity through social media. MISQ **38**(3), 873–893 (2014)

38. Sefyrin, J., Mörtberg, C.: "We do not talk about this": problematical silences in eGovernment. Electron. J. E-Gov. **7**(3), 259–270 (2009)

39. Sefyrin, J., Gidlund, K.L., Öberg, K.D., Ekelin, A.: Representational practices in demands driven development of public sector. In: Wimmer, M.A., Janssen, M., Scholl, H.J. (eds.) EGOV 2013. LNCS, vol. 8074, pp. 200–211. Springer, Heidelberg (2013). https://doi.org/10.1007/978-3-642-40358-3_17

40. Sommervold, M.M., van der Velden, M.: Visions of illness, disease, and sickness in mobile health applications. Societies **7**(4), 28 (2017)

41. Suchman, L.: Human-Machine Reconfigurations: Plans and Situated Actions. Cambridge University Press, New York (2007)

42. Suchman, L.: Feminist STS and the sciences of the artificial. In: Hackett, E., Amsterdamska, O., Lynch, M., Wajcman, J. (eds.) The Handbook of Science and Technology Studie, 3rd edn, pp. 139–164. MIT Press, Cambridge (2008)

43. Suchman, L., Follis, K., Weber, J.: Tracking and targeting: sociotechnologies of (In) security. Sci. Technol. Hum. Values **2**(6), 983–1002 (2017)

44. Swedish Government Official Reports 2015:65: Om Sverige i framtiden. En antologi om digitaliseringens möjligheter. [About Sweden in the future. An anthology about the possibilities with digitalization] (2015)

45. Sørensen, C.: The curse of the smart machine? Digitalisation and the children of the mainframe. Scand. J. Inf. Syst. **28**(2), 57–68 (2016)

46. Tsing, A.L., Swanson, H.A., Gan, E., Bubandt, N.: Arts of Living on a Damaged Planet: Ghosts and Monsters of the Anthropocene. University of Minnesota Press, Minneapolis (2017)

47. Van der Velden, M., Mörtberg, C.: Between need and desire: exploring strategies for gendering design. Sci. Technol. Hum. Values **37**(6), 663–683 (2012)

48. Wajcman, J.: From women and technology to gendered technoscience. Inf. Community Soc. **10**(3), 287–298 (2007)

49. Wajcman, J.: Feminist theories of technology. Camb. J. Econ. **34**(1), 143–152 (2010)

50. Walsham, G.: Are we making a better world with ICTs? Reflections on a future agenda for the IS field. J. Inf. Technol. **27**(2), 87–93 (2012)

51. World Economic Forum: The Future of Jobs. Employment, Skills and Workforce Strategy for the Fourth Industrial Revolution. Global Challenge Insight Report (2016)

52. Åsberg, C., Lykke, N.: Feminist technoscience studies. Eur. J. Women's Stud. **17**(4), 299–305 (2010)

Mind the Gap Gender and Computer Science Conferences

Sytze Van Herck$^{(\boxtimes)}$ (iD) and Antonio Maria Fiscarelli$^{(\boxtimes)}$ (iD)

University of Luxembourg,
11, Porte des Sciences, 4366 Esch-sur-Alzette, Luxembourg
{sytze.vanherck,antonio.fiscarelli}@uni.lu

Abstract. Computer science research areas are often arbitrarily defined by researchers themselves based on their own opinions or conference rankings. First, we aim to classify conferences in computer science in an automated and objective way based on topic modelling. We then study the topic relatedness of research areas to identify isolated disciplinary silos and clusters that display more interdisciplinarity and collaboration. Furthermore, we compare career length, publication growth rate and collaboration patterns for men and women in these research areas.

Keywords: Gender · Bibliometrics · Topic modelling

1 Introduction

Diane Jackaki described the feeling of most Digital Humanists in her keynote "Jack of all trades, master of One" at the Digital Humanities Summer School of 2017 in Oxford [1]. Even in interdisciplinary areas of research, people still cling to their disciplinary backgrounds. In our title "Mind the Gap" we refer to the continuing split between disciplinary areas, even when interdisciplinarity is actively encouraged in many fields. We also discuss the gender gap and the consistently low number of female researchers in computer science. An example of the disciplinary schism can be found in cryptography where researchers attend and publish at conferences such as the International Cryptology Conference (CRYPTO). A title such as "New and Improved Key-Homomorphic Pseudorandom Functions" [2] already suggests that cryptography research can be very specific. Our aim is to identify disciplinary areas in Computer Science (CS) through topic modelling and study the interdisciplinary overlap between these research 'silos'. Furthermore we look into collaboration patterns and in particular

S. Van Herck—Supported by the Luxembourg National Research Fund (FNR) DTU-DHH, C2DH.

A. M. Fiscarelli—Supported by the Luxembourg National Research Fund (FNR) DTU-DHH, C2DH, CSC-ILIAS.

gender distribution for each research area [3]. The example from cryptography illustrates our assumption that conference papers published throughout the years can be grouped to represent a CS area.

2 Topic Modelling

The main idea is to define a topic (or CS area) as a set of conferences and each conference as the set of all papers that have been published. A paper is defined as the set of keywords contained in its title. In the next step, similar conferences are grouped together in CS areas using text mining. Other examples of automated topic modelling are provided in [4,5] where a probabilistic model for topic modelling is proposed. On the other hand, Biryukov and Dong [6] arbitrarily define fourteen different CS subareas based on top ranked conferences, while in [7] the CS areas are defined according to experts' opinion and the conferences' impact ratings.

2.1 Dataset

The dataset is publicly available at https://data.mendeley.com/datasets/ 3p9w84t5mr/1 and contains 148512 papers published at 81 different CS conferences since 1960 [8]. We limited the data subset to papers published between 2000 and 2015 since the DBLP bibliographic library had a narrow focus at the start which broadened over the years to include most CS conferences [9]. By 2005 DBLP covered 65% of conferences from the aggregated list Reitz and Hoffmann created [9]. As a result of our selection the conferences CCC, Digital Libraries, EuroCOLT, ISTCS, MFDBS and PDIS were excluded either because they changed names or ended before 2000, leaving us with 104680 papers and 75 conferences.

2.2 Data Retrieval

The dataset contains the URL associated to each paper instead of the full title. Therefore we used a scraping tool to retrieve the title of a paper based on the URL and the associated xpath selector. About 19% of the papers did not contain any URL and we simply removed them. We discovered that all the other papers were published on 4 main websites: the AAAI conference website (https:// www.aaai.org/ocs/), the Springer website (https://link.springer.com), the Computer Science Digital Library of the IEEE Society https://www.computer.org/ csdl and the ACM Digital Library https://dl.acm.org/. Making use of the R package "rvest" we were able to scrape the Springer website and the Computer Science Digital Library of the IEEE Society, collecting data for about 50% of the papers and 51 conferences. Unfortunately, the AAAI conference website and the ACM library make use of dynamic content that rendered the scraping process impossible. These two websites contain the remaining 50% of papers and 24 conferences. ACM kindly provided us with a collection of all proceedings published in their digital library. The collection consists of XML files related to a specific conference proceeding of a certain year and contain information about the conference itself and all papers published afterwards. The title of each paper can be easily retrieved using its XML tag. Considering only conferences held between 2000 and 2015, we were able to collect data related to 23 conferences. The ACM library did not contain any proceedings for the IEEE International Conference on Computer Communications (INFOCOM). In the end we were able to retrieve data for 74 conferences.

2.3   Text Mining

The corpus contains a document for each conference, and a document lists the keywords of all papers published at the conference. We used text mining methods to process the data and extract CS areas, but only after cleaning up the data. For example, we converted each letter to lower case, removed numbers, punctuation, stopwords (words that do not contain any significance such as articles and prepositions) and performed stemming by reducing the words to roots. The R package "tm" provides all these functionalities and a collection of stopwords for the English language. At the end of this phase, the corpus contained 73 documents with 21158 distinct terms. We then built a term frequency-inverse document frequency (tf-idf) matrix, where the number or rows is equal to the number of documents in the corpus and the number of columns is equal to the number of terms in the corpus. Each entry of the matrix is computed as follows:

$$w_{ij} = tf_i \times \log \frac{N}{df_i} \tag{1}$$

where tf_i is the frequency of term j in document i, N is the number of documents in the corpus and df_i is the number of documents that contain the term j. Each row entry of the tf-idf matrix represents a document in the corpus, where each element represents the relevance of a certain word in the document.

2.4   The Clustering Algorithm

We used a clustering algorithm to group conferences and define CS areas [10]. This specific algorithm requires a similarity matrix. Therefore we used the cosine measure to compare documents, defined as follows:

$$sim(d_i, d_j) = \frac{\sum_{k=1}^{n} w_{ik} w_{jk}}{\sqrt{\sum_{k=1}^{n} w_{ik}^2} \sqrt{\sum_{k=1}^{n} w_{jk}^2}} \tag{2}$$

Based on this measure we can define a similarity matrix S, a square matrix whose number of rows and columns are equal to the number of documents in the corpus. Each entry of the matrix defines how similar two documents are, where $S_{ij} = 0$ indicates that the documents do not have any term in common and $S_{ij} = 1$ indicates that the two documents consist of the same set of terms.

After creating the similarity matrix, we can introduce a clustering algorithm. We selected the Degenerate Agglomerative Hierarchical Clustering Algorithm (DAHCA) for several reasons. First it is hierarchical and agglomerative, meaning that it can recognize hierarchies of clusters from a large number of very specific clusters to a small number of generic clusters. In addition, unlike other hierarchical clustering algorithms, it allows the merging and formation of clusters of different sizes.

2.5 Computer Science Areas

As a result of the DAHCA, we ended up with a four-level hierarchy containing 34, 19, 8 or 3 clusters. The first level of 34 clusters was too specific, while the last level of 3 clusters was too generic. In the end we decided to visualise the third level containing 8 clusters because it would be most readable and meaningful. A part of the hierarchy is shown in Table 2, where we assigned a meaningful name to the eight clusters chosen from the second level. Based on the conference titles and keywords, the clusters were named: Databases and Information Systems (DBIS), Knowledge Engineering (KE), Software Engineering (SE), Artificial Intelligence (AI), Interdisciplinary/Networks/Web (I/N/W), Cryptography (CRYPTO), Theoretical Computer Science/Concurrency (TCS/C), and Algorithmic Theory (ALGO). Table 1 contains the most relevant words for each CS area. More specifically, SE includes conferences on software engineering, software maintenance and code analysis. AI falls into four categories: learning theory, machine learning, optimisation and computer vision. I/N/W includes interdisciplinary conferences on human computer interaction, computational

Table 1. Top ten most relevant keywords in each CS area

CS Area	Keywords
DBIS	"retriev", "entiti", "topic", "xml", "recommend", "relev", "queri", "learn", "databas", "text"
KE	"conceptu", "prefac", "ontolog", "schema", "busi", "uml", "olap", "warehous", "xml", "semant"
SE	"softwar", "mainten", "workshop", "engin", "refactor", "revers", "reengin", "evolut", "legaci", "comprehens"
AI	"imag", "stereo", "recognit", "scene", "motion", "pose", "segment", "camera", "face", "video"
I/N/W	"poster", "genom", "gene", "protein", "wireless", "transcript", "demo", "regulatori", "acl", "ancestr"
CRYPTO	"cryptanalysi", "cipher", "encrypt", "attack", "secur", "signatur", "rsa", "multiacparti", "zeroacknowledg", "relatedackey"
TCS/C	"announc", "brief", "logic", "automata", "bisimul", "firstacord", "azaiaalqcalculus", "quantum", "schedul", "concurr"
ALGO	"automata", "approxim", "planar", "problem", "quantum", "bound", "algorithm", "game", "graph", "minimum"

biology and computational linguistics, as well as conferences on networks and the web. CRYPTO focuses on cryptography and software encryption. TCS/S treats logic, theoretical computer science, and concurrent and parallel systems. Finally, ALGO contains algorithms and theoretical computer science. In Table 2, the CRYPTO cluster is identified at the first level and remains separate at the next levels, demonstrating how particular and specific cryptography conferences are. Furthermore, the cluster I/N/W contains very diverging topics ranging from human-computer interaction to world wide web, but these topics might be grouped because of a similar application or theoretical foundation.

Table 2. List of conferences included in each cluster. The outer left column contains the eight cluster names and the central column contains the conferences included in each cluster. The outer right column contains the same conferences but they are listed in different rows that represents the cluster in the previous (more specific) level for a total of 19 clusters.

Cluster	Conferences	Conferences (specific)
DBIS	ADBIS CIKM SIGMOD	ADBIS CIKM SIGMOD
	DASFAA ICDE	DASFAA ICDE
	DBPL	DBPL
	ICDT	ICDT
	PODS	PODS
	EDBT SSDBM	EDBT SSDBM
KE	CoopIS ER	CoopIS ER
	KDD UIST	KDD UIST
	RIDE DOLAP	RIDE DOLAP
SE	CSMR ICSM ASE WCRE	CSMR ICSM ASE WCRE
	FASE ICSE	FASE ICSE
	ICPC SCAM MSR	ICPC SCAM
		MSR
AI	ALT COLT ICML	ALT COLT ICML
	CADE PLDI POPL	CADE PLDI POPL
	IPCO SOCG	IPCO SOCG
	SIGMETRICS SOSP STOC	SIGMETRICS SOSP STOC
	CVPR ICCV SIGCOMM	CVPR ICCV SIGCOMM
	LFCS DISC/WDAG ISSAC	LFCS DISC/WDAG ISSAC
I/N/W	CHI	
	IGPCE RECOMB MOBICOM OSDI	CHI
	IJCAI WWW	IGPCE RECOMB MOBICOM OSDI
	PODC SIGIR VLDB NSDI	IJCAI WWW
	AAAIDEA ACL	PODC SIGIR VLDB NSDI
	WIDM	
		AAAIDEA ACL
		WIDM
CRYPTO	CRYPTO EUROCRYPT FSE	CRYPTO EUROCRYPT FSE
TCS/C	CONCUR LICS	CONCUR LICS
	FSTTCS SP SPAA	FSTTCS SP SPAA
	SWAT WADS	SWAT WADS
ALGO	ESA ICALP ISAAC SODA FOCS MFCS	ESA ICALP ISAAC SODA
	LATIN STACS	FOCS MFCS
		LATIN STACS

3   Visualisations

After outlining the creation of the eight clusters, we will interpret some of our results in this section. Several visualisations serve both as a tool for analysis and as a communication method. First of all, we study topic relatedness to understand the interdisciplinarity and overlap between different research areas based on a visualisation created in R. Secondly, we create several more visualisations to analyse gender in relation to career length, publication growth and collaboration. For these visualisations we generated the data source through SQL queries executed per cluster. We ran all queries using Python 3's pymysql library to connect to the MySQL database and combined the results of each cluster in a single csv file. The final visualisations were created in Tableau and allow interactions such as details-on-demand and filtering.

3.1   Topic Relatedness

Authors do not always publish at the same conference and especially in interdisciplinary areas of CS, authors tend to collaborate more often and publish in different conferences. Figure 1 displays how different areas of CS relate to each other and to what degree authors publish in different CS areas. We first built a topic relatedness graph where each node represents a CS area and edges represent how related they are to each other. The node size indicates the number of papers published and different shades of gray indicate the average number of authors per paper. Light shades of gray represent a high number of authors,

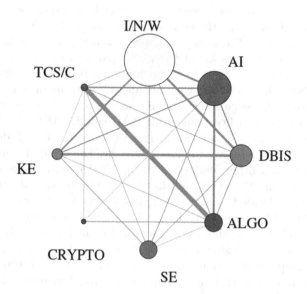

Fig. 1. Topic relatedness graph for eight conference clusters linked based on the percentage of authors who published in both research areas.

while dark shades of gray indicate a low number of authors. The edge thickness is based on the percentage of authors that have published at least one paper in two linked CS areas. Even though all areas are connected, when an edge is not visible this indicates a very loose connection.

As you can deduce from the visualisation, CRYPTO contains the lowest number of papers and the lowest average number of authors per paper. The CRYPTO cluster therefore represents a niche area where researchers are less inclined to collaborate, probably because their research is very specific as we assumed initially. TCS/C and ALGO also show similar results. As a complete opposite, I/N/W contains a much higher number of papers and average number of authors per paper than any other area. In fact, it contains conferences about human-computer interaction, bioinformatics and computational linguistics; all areas which promote collaboration between researchers. If you then look at the relatedness of different areas, CRYPTO is the least related to other CS areas. This isolation of CRYPTO indicates that researchers specialised in cryptography do not publish in any other research area. SE is also rather isolated, yet it closely links to six other research areas, whereas CRYPTO only shows some links to three other areas. ALGO has the highest general relatedness, probably because algorithmic theory is the foundation of many CS areas. The areas that show the highest relatedness and share the highest numbers of authors are TCS/C and ALGO, followed by KE and DBIS.

3.2   Career Length

We should first define gender and explain how this information was generated in the dataset. Gender as a psychological and sociological term originated in the United States and refers to "the state of being male or female as expressed by social or cultural distinctions and differences, rather than biological ones; the collective attributes of traits associated with a particular sex: or determined as a result of one's sex" [11]. Even in this definition a binaristic understanding of gender is implied, where a person can only identify as being male or female. The same binary distinction occurs in the dataset we use. The gender of an author was determined based on their first name using the Genderize API [12] which returns either "Male, Female or NA" for 'not assigned' based on a list of identified first names, returning a confidence score for each result. The Genderize API performs relatively better than other methods inferring gender from names on the web, yet this approach mostly works well for western industrialized countries [13]. Agarwal et al. also decided to assign "NA" to any author name with a confidence score below 60% [14]. In general, the gender was not determined for 14,2% of authors, while 69,1% of authors were identified as male, and only 16,7% were identified as female [14]. Science careers often show the trend of a leaky pipeline, where people drop out at various segments of their career and women drop out more often than men as their career progresses [15]. Based on this finding in literature we decided to compare the career length for men and women within the different clusters. The career length represents the period between the first and last year that an author published at a conference included in the dataset.

Career Length

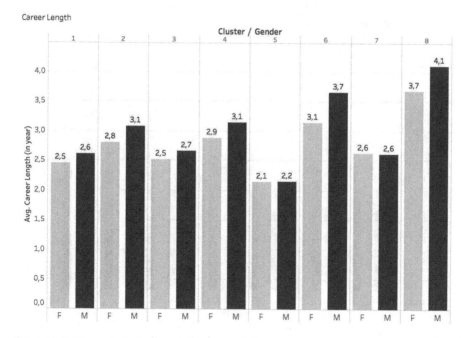

Fig. 2. Average career length of female and male authors in years for each cluster. The clusters are numbered as follows: (1) DBIS, (2) AI, (3) I/N/W, (4) TCS/C, (5) KE, (6) CRYPTO, (7) SE and (8) ALGO.

Figure 2 represents the average career length of men and women in the eight fields of research we defined earlier. In general the average career length for women is lower than for men, which confirms the leaky pipeline issue even for the brief span of fifteen years. The biggest difference in career length between men and women can be found in CRYPTO, the research area with the second lowest average percentage of female authors (at just 12,6%). On the other hand there is almost no difference in the career length of male and female researchers for the KE and SE research areas, which is generally shorter than in other research areas. We assume that this short career length is related to the rapidly changing nature of these research areas. The longest career length occurs in the ALGO cluster, probably because this is a research discipline that remains fairly stable and discipline specific.

3.3 Publication Growth Rate

The publication growth rate (PGR) indicates the growing or diminishing popularity of a research area for each cluster over the course of sixteen years. We look into both the absolute and the relative publication growth for male and female authored papers in each cluster to assess whether publications authored by women grew at a faster rate than those of men. Finally, we compare

Publication Growth Rate

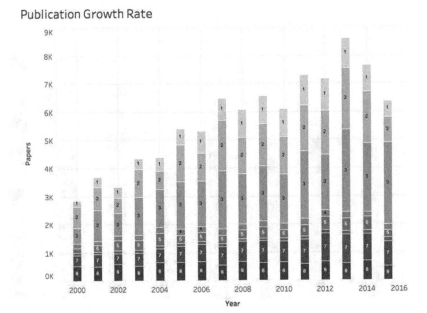

Fig. 3. Publication growth rate per year for each cluster. The clusters are numbered as follows: (1) DBIS, (2) AI, (3) I/N/W, (4) TCS/C, (5) KE, (6) CRYPTO, (7) SE and (8) ALGO.

publication growth of two theoretical and disciplinary research areas (TCS/C and ALGO) to the PGR of rather interdisciplinary clusters (DBIS, I/N/W and KE).

In Fig. 3 the largest research area in terms of the number of publications is the I/N/W cluster, whereas CRYPTO contains the lowest number of publications overall. Table 2 shows that CRYPTO only contains three conferences in a single cluster. That same explanation does not hold true for I/N/W because this research area contains fourteen conferences, compared to seventeen conferences in the AI cluster. When we study the I/N/W cluster in detail however, it becomes clear that the Computer-Human Interaction (CHI) conference causes the high number of publications for this research area (see Fig. 6).

In order to compare relative growth rates, we calculated the growth rate comparing the number of papers in 2014 to the number of papers in 2000. Since the dataset uses a snapshot from the DBLP Dataset on September 15th of 2015, we decided to calculate the growth rate based on the last full year contained in the dataset.

$$PubGrowRate_{i,y2,y1} = \frac{P_{i,y2} - P_{i,y1}}{P_{i,y2} + P_{i,y1}} \tag{3}$$

where $P_{i,y}$ is the number of papers published during the year y.

In Fig. 4 we decided to study the publication growth for each research area split by gender. We simply counted the number of papers written by either female

Publication Growth Rate (gender)

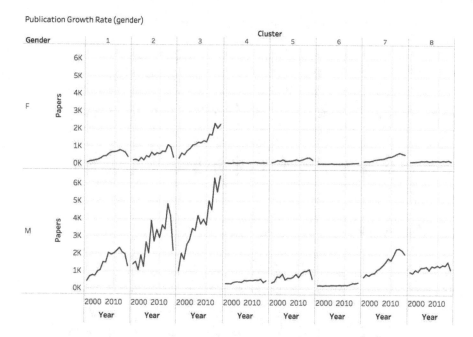

Fig. 4. Publication growth rate for female and male authors per year for each cluster. The clusters are numbered as follows: (1) DBIS, (2) AI, (3) I/N/W, (4) TCS/C, (5) KE, (6) CRYPTO, (7) SE and (8) ALGO.

or male authors and left out the unidentified authors entirely. Some papers were counted twice in case they were written by a man and a woman so the total number of papers does not equal the sum of male and female authored papers. The I/N/W cluster has the highest number of both male- and female-authored papers, with 2322 papers authored by women in 2013 compared to 6452 papers authored by men in 2015. The lowest number of male- and female-authored papers on the other hand can be found in CRYPTO with only 20 papers written by women in 2003, and 168 papers written by men in 2002. Even though the highest and lowest number of papers can be found in the same clusters, women consistently authored fewer papers than their male counterparts in the dataset. When we look at the relative PGR however, the rise in the number of female-authored publications is higher for all clusters. The largest difference in PGR for men and women can be found in the DBIS research area where female-authored papers grew by 78,6% and male-authored papers by only 64,1%. In ALGO on the other hand the difference in PGR for men and women was lowest, with 23,6% for women and 22,7% for men. The rather interdisciplinary clusters such as DBIS, I/N/W and KE showed the highest relative PGR with 62,5%, 63,3% and 49,9% respectively. The theoretical and disciplinary conference clusters such as TCS/C (0,3%) and ALGO (14%) on the other hand showed the lowest relative PGR. The smallest growth rate of 0,3% for TCS/C might be due to a strict limitation of the number of papers accepted for conferences in this CS research area.

4. Theoretical Computer Science / Concurrency

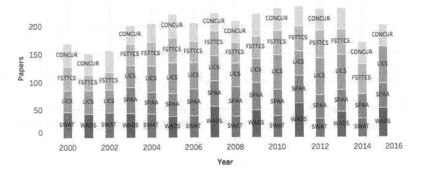

8. Algorithms

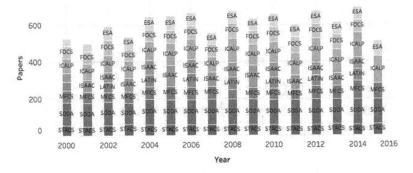

Fig. 5. Comparison of the publication growth rate per year of TCS/C and ALGO.

Figure 5 displays two theoretical clusters (TCS/C and ALGO) on conference level. Both TCS/C and ALGO show little variation in the number of papers accepted for each single conference. Even so, some conferences are considerably more popular (in terms of PGR) than others. In the TCS/C cluster for example, the International Conference on Concurrency Theory Symposium on Logic in Computer Science (LICS) has a PGR of 22,8% between 2000 and 2013, whereas the Scandinavian Symposium and Workshops on Algorithm Theory (SWAT) dropped 16,5% in PGR between 2000 and 2014. In the ALGO research area the International Colloquium on Automata, Languages, and Programming (ICALP) gained 27,8% of publications, compared to an increase of only 1,5% in publications for the IEEE Symposium on Foundations of Computer Science (FOCS). In addition, conferences in these research areas publish a relatively low number of papers varying between 28 and 66 papers in the TCS/C cluster, and 40 to 139 publications in the ALGO cluster.

The interdisciplinary research areas of clusters such as DBIS, I/N/W and KE displayed in Fig. 6 all contain at least one conference with a steep publication growth rate: from 66,7% for the Conference on Information and Knowledge

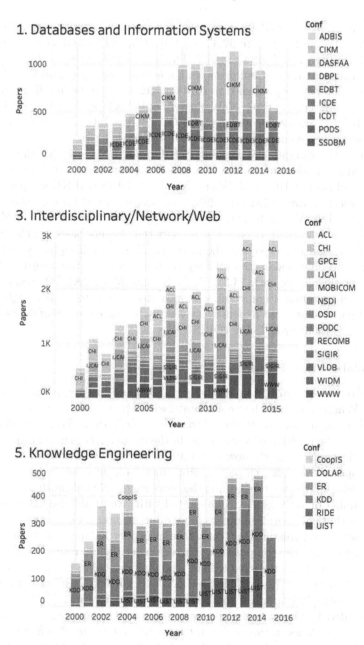

Fig. 6. Comparison of the publication growth rate per year of DBIS, I/N/W and KE.

Management (CIKM) in DBIS, over 69,9% for Mobile Computing and Networking (MOBICOM) in I/N/W, to 62,3% for the ACM User Interface Software and Technology Symposium (UIST) in KE. The conferences with the highest number of publications are the Conference on Knowledge Discovery and Data Mining (KDD) with 296 papers published in 2014 for KE, 1028 papers published in 2013 for the CHI conference in the I/N/W cluster, and CIKM with 520 papers in 2012 within DBIS. In spite of the overall high PGR in these interdisciplinary research areas, some annual conferences ended before 2015.

Although the disciplinary clusters TCS/C and ALGO display the smallest difference in PGR based on gender, the opposite is not entirely true for the interdisciplinary clusters DBIS, I/N/W and KE. Both DBIS and KE are part of the top three research areas where the difference between PGR for men and women is highest, yet I/N/W finished third to last with a difference of only 3,8% PGR between men and women. However, if we sort the clusters based on the relative PGR for female-authored papers, the distinction between disciplinary and interdisciplinary becomes clear. Disciplinary conferences have the lowest PGR for female-authored papers with 14,3% (TCS/S) and 23,6% (ALGO) respectively, whereas interdisciplinary conferences show a clear trend towards a higher percentage of female-authored papers every year including increases of 63,4% (KE), 72,6% (I/N/W) and even 78,6% (DBIS).

3.4   Collaboration Patterns

Academic researchers are often evaluated, funded and hired based on their publications. Whether or not they collaborate with other researchers makes a difference in the value that is attributed to their contributions. Furthermore, when co-authoring, the position of a researcher in the list of authors is often considered a good indication of exactly how much of the work they performed. Given the limited scope of this research paper, we cannot look into the author's position but we do have information regarding the percentage of female authors per paper and the number of authors they collaborated with. We would also like to test our assumption that collaboration occurs more often at interdisciplinary conferences and whether or not this makes a difference in gender balance for single papers. Conferences present the composition of an academic field of research on an international level and form the ideal case to study gender balance. This distribution of men and women in research institutions and specific areas of research has become increasingly important to obtain government funding.

We decided to visualize the gender balance within the larger clusters and at specific conferences in the tree map format introduced by Ben Schneiderman [16]. Tree maps convey information through both area and colour, which allows researchers to locate outliers and identify cause-effect relationships [17]. Because we wanted to display as many variables as possible in a limited space, we decided to use tree map visualisations. In order to interpret tree maps correctly, we will first explain the variables assigned to area size, color and clustering. In Fig. 7 the larger groupings represent the clusters, whereas the divisions within the cluster visualize a specific year. The size of each rectangle represents the number of

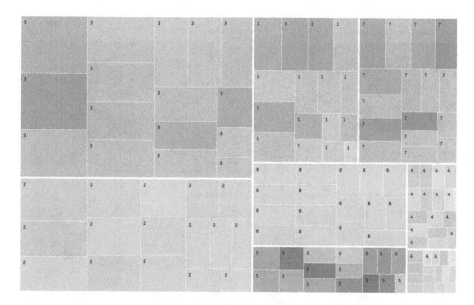

Fig. 7. Average percentage of female authors per paper grouped by cluster and split by years. The clusters are numbered as follows: (1) DBIS, (2) AI, (3) I/N/W, (4) TCS/C, (5) KE, (6) CRYPTO, (7) SE and (8) ALGO.

papers in a given year. The clusters are ordered left to right and top to bottom starting from the largest to the smallest number of papers and within a cluster the years are ordered in the same way. The color represents the percentage of female authors and varies from 7,9% to 21,5% yet to allow comparison with Fig. 8 the color scale ranges between 0% and 35% from light to dark gray. The tree map comparing the conferences with the highest and lowest percentage of female authors are structured in the same way, but the highest clustering represents a single research area and at the second level each conference is grouped together, split into specific conference years. Tableau also enables details-on-demand, so when you hover over a single data entry, the conference acronym, conference year, percentage of female authors and total number of papers are displayed.

In Fig. 7 the fifth conference cluster (middle cluster at the bottom) represents KE and contains the highest percentage of female authors overall. CRYPTO (bottom right cluster) on the other hand shows the lowest percentage of female authors. The larger the number of papers in a cluster, the higher the percentage of female authors (with the exception of KE). The clusters we labeled interdisciplinary in our previous sections (DBIS, I/N/W, KE) and SE all contain a higher percentage of female contributors, whereas the disciplinary clusters (TCS/C, ALGO) and AI have fewer female authors overall. In KE the years with the highest participation of women with more than 20% female-authored papers include 2001 (20,3%), 2006 (20,1%), 2009 (21,1%), 2013 (20,8%) and 2015 (21,5%). The CRYPTO research area contains fewer than 10% female authors in conference

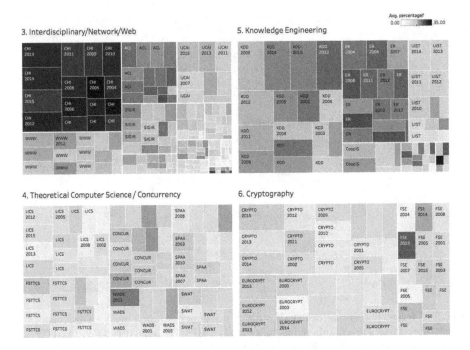

Fig. 8. Comparison of the gender distribution in four research areas split into single conferences. Top: I/N/W and KE with the highest average percentage of female authors per paper. Bottom: TCS/C and CRYPTO with the lowest average percentage of female authors per paper.

years 2003 (8,9%), 2006 (7,9%) and 2007 (9,97%) and is the only conference cluster including fewer than 10% female authors. Higher percentages of female authors did therefore not necessarily occur at the end of the period studied here. In order to gain more insight into the gender balance at disciplinary and interdisciplinary conference clusters, we will now compare the interdisciplinary I/N/W and KE to the disciplinary TCS/C and CRYPTO in Fig. 8.

If we look at Fig. 8 certain conferences have a higher percentage of female authors than others even within the same research area. The highest percentage of female authors overall can be found at the CHI conference with over 30% of female-authored papers for four years, including 2001 (30,0%), 2002 (31,6%), 2005 (32,21%) and 2006 (30,7%). Besides the Association for Computational Linguistics (ACL) and WIDM conference, very few other conferences within I/N/W contain more than 20% of female-authored publications. Within KE both the ACM User Interface Software and Technology Symposium (UIST) and CoopIS conference contain fewer than 20% female authors for most years, with the exception of 20,6% female authors at UIST in 2002, and 20,07% of female-authored papers at CoopIS in 2003. In the disciplinary clusters the lowest percentage of female authors can be found in the CRYPTO cluster at EUROCRYPT in 2003 (4,6%) and at FSE in 2006 (4,4%) although FSE also contains the highest percentage of female authors within CRYPTO in 2013 (24,7%). In TCS/C the WADS conference in 2011 has an exceptionally high percentage of female authors at 22,4%. This comparison demonstrates that the gender balance for an entire cluster does not account for high differences in female authorship at the conference level. Although the CHI conference in the I/N/W research area contains the highest percentage of female authors, not all other I/N/W conferences have such a high level of female participation. On the other hand, the disciplinary research areas also showcase some outliers where they reach the 20% female-authored publications threshold. One explanation for a higher female collaboration rate in interdisciplinary fields could stem from the assertion that women are more attracted to research areas that emphasise social issues, which perhaps appear more often in interdisciplinary research [18].

4 Conclusion

In literature on bibliometrics such as [6,7] we discovered manual categorisation of conferences in clusters. In order to avoid this rather subjective approach, we decided to first define conferences based on the text mining of paper titles, secondly we grouped conferences using a clustering algorithm and thirdly we manually assigned names to the clusters based on the conference titles. The algorithm provided four levels of clustering and we decided to use a grouping of eight clusters at the basis of our visualisations.

The topic relatedness graph illustrated the isolation of CRYPTO and lower levels of collaboration in CS areas such as CRYPTO, TCS/C and ALGO. In I/N/W on the other hand we discovered more collaboration between authors. In general the career length for women was lower than for men, illustrating the leaky pipeline. In both engineering clusters (KE and SE) authors had a shorter career length in comparison to the longest career length in ALGO, probably because ALGO remains more stable whereas KE and SE depend on rapidly changing technology. Studying the publication growth rate we found that interdisciplinary research areas such as DBIS, I/N/W and KE had a faster publication growth than disciplinary research areas such as TCS/C and ALGO. Furthermore, the publication growth rate for female authors is positively correlated with the interdisciplinarity of a research area, whereas the difference between male and female publication growth rate is less indicative. When we then look at collaboration patterns, all interdisciplinary clusters mentioned previously as well as SE contain a higher percentage of female authors than the disciplinary clusters. However, the breakdown of clusters into individual conferences shows that in some cases the higher percentage of female authors was caused by a single conference (such as CHI). Overall the definition of a research area as disciplinary or interdisciplinary lies at 20% female authors.

First of all, we would like to point out that the overall percentage of female authors is low in computer science. The percentage of female PhD students in CS lies at a similar percentage with 22,1% in 2004 and a decrease to 20,8% in 2014 [19]. When we split research areas into disciplinary and interdisciplinary fields, we do find that female authors are mostly concentrated in interdisciplinary research areas. This begs two related but contradictory questions: Why are women more attracted to interdisciplinary fields of research? Or, why do interdisciplinary conferences publish more female-authored papers? Although we cannot answer these questions here, we do think it is in every conference organisers best interest to encourage both female authors and collaboration. Janet Abbate points out that women should receive the same respect, mentoring and help with research, grants and publications as their male peers [20]. Furthermore, conference organisers should provide accommodations such as childcare at conferences [20]. Most importantly, women should not be isolated or marginalized, but rather included and represented as keynote speakers, editorial board members and conference organisers [20].

References

1. Jakacki, D.: Jack of all trades, master of one: the promise of inter methodological collaboration (2017). https://player.fm/series/digital-humanities-at-oxford-summer-school/2017-opening-keynote-jack-of-all-trades-master-of-one-the-promise-of-intermethodological-collaboration. Accessed 11 Jan 2018

2. Banerjee, A., Peikert, C.: New and improved key-homomorphic pseudorandom functions. In: Garay, J.A., Gennaro, R. (eds.) CRYPTO 2014. LNCS, vol. 8616, pp. 353–370. Springer, Heidelberg (2014). https://doi.org/10.1007/978-3-662-44371-2_20

3. Van Herck, S.: Visualising gender balance: ten computer science conferences and the digital humanities conference compared (2017)

4. Paul, M., Girju, R.: Topic modeling of research fields: an interdisciplinary perspective. In: Proceedings of the International Conference RANLP-2009, pp. 337–342 (2009)

5. Daud, A., Li, J., Zhou, L., Muhammad, F.: Conference mining via generalized topic modeling. In: Buntine, W., Grobelnik, M., Mladenić, D., Shawe-Taylor, J. (eds.) ECML PKDD 2009. LNCS (LNAI), vol. 5781, pp. 244–259. Springer, Heidelberg (2009). https://doi.org/10.1007/978-3-642-04180-8_33

6. Biryukov, M., Dong, C.: Analysis of computer science communities based on DBLP. In: Lalmas, M., Jose, J., Rauber, A., Sebastiani, F., Frommholz, I. (eds.) ECDL 2010. LNCS, vol. 6273, pp. 228–235. Springer, Heidelberg (2010). https://doi.org/10.1007/978-3-642-15464-5_24

7. Bird, C., Devanbu, P., Barr, E., Filkov, V., Nash, A., Su, Z.: Structure and dynamics of research collaboration in computer science. In: Proceedings of the 2009 SIAM International Conference on Data Mining, SIAM, pp. 826–837 (2009)

8. Swati, A., Ashish, S., Nitish, M., Rohan, K., Denzil, C.: DBLP records and entries for key computer science conferences (2017). https://data.mendeley.com/datasets/3p9w84t5mr/. Accessed 11 Jan 2018

9. Reitz, F., Hoffmann, O.: An analysis of the evolving coverage of computer science sub-fields in the DBLP digital library. In: Lalmas, M., Jose, J., Rauber, A., Sebastiani, F., Frommholz, I. (eds.) ECDL 2010. LNCS, vol. 6273, pp. 216–227. Springer, Heidelberg (2010). https://doi.org/10.1007/978-3-642-15464-5_23

10. Fiscarelli, A.M., Beliakov, A., Konchenko, S., Bouvry, P.: A degenerate agglomerative hierarchical clustering algorithm for community detection. In: Nguyen, N.T., Hoang, D.H., Hong, T.-P., Pham, H., Trawiński, B. (eds.) ACIIDS 2018. LNCS (LNAI), vol. 10751, pp. 234–242. Springer, Cham (2018). https://doi.org/10.1007/978-3-319-75417-8_22

11. Gender, N.: OED Online. Oxford English Dictionary (2011). Accessed 24 Jan 2018

12. GenderizeAPI. https://genderize.io. Accessed 24 Jan 2018

13. Karimi, F., Wagner, C., Lemmerich, F., Jadidi, M., Strohmaier, M.: Inferring gender from names on the web: a comparative evaluation of gender detection methods. CoRR abs/1603.04322 (2016)

14. Agarwal, S., Mittal, N., Katyal, R., Sureka, A., Correa, D.: Women in computer science research: what is the bibliography data telling us? ACM SIGCAS Comput. Soc. **46**(1), 7–19 (2016)

15. Sonnert, G., Holton, G.: Who Succeeds in Science?: The Gender Dimension. Rutgers University Press, New Brunswick (1995)

16. Shneiderman, B.: Tree visualization with tree-maps: 2-D space-filling approach. ACM Trans. Graph. **11**(1), 92–99 (1992)

17. Asahi, T., Turo, D., Shneiderman, B.: Visual decision-making: using treemaps for the analytic hierarchy process. In: Conference Companion on Human Factors in Computing Systems, CHI 1995, pp. 405–406. ACM, New York (1995)

18. Henwood, F., Miller, N., Senker, P., Wyatt, S.: Technology and In/equality: Questioning the Information Society. Taylor & Francis (2002)

19. Foundation, N.S.: Women, minorities, and persons with disabilities in science and engineering. field of degree: Women. https://www.nsf.gov/statistics/2017/nsf17310/digest/fod-women/computer-sciences.cfm. Accessed 24 Jan 2018

20. Abbate, J.: Recoding Gender: Women's Changing Participation in Computing. History of Computing. MIT Press, Cambridge (2012)

ICT Changes Everything! But Who Changes ICT?

Hilde G. Corneliussen[1]([✉]), Clem Herman[2], and Radhika Gajjala[3]

[1] Western Norway Research Institute, Sogndal, Norway
hgc@vestforsk.no
[2] Open University, Milton Keynes, UK
[3] Bowling Green State University, Bowling Green, OH, USA

Abstract. Information and communication technology (ICT) has a changing power and digitalization is gradually changing society in all aspects of life. Across the western world, men are in majority in the ICT industry, thus, the computer programs that change "everything" are most often made by men. Unless questioned, this male dominance can be perceived as a "norm" and becomes invisible. Against this background, this paper will provide three examples of how a feminist gaze can contribute to raise important questions and produce an awareness of how exclusion mechanisms have produce a highly homosocial tendency in design of ICT systems in the western world.

The three cases illustrate how a feminist gaze leading to feminist interventions can make a difference in various ways. The first author presents a case study of a pilot for involving programming in public education in secondary schools in Norway, where a complete lack of gender awareness makes this an offer for boys in most schools. Author two presents a case study comparing the situation in the IT business in the UK and India, finding challenges not only to the situation in the western world, but also to white western feminism. Author three discusses alternative ways of involving women in ICT work, through practices of feminist pedagogy, emphasizing hands-on work.

Keywords: Feminist theories · ICT competence · Feminist pedagogy
Global perspectives

1 Introduction

ICT and digitalization envelop our everyday lives – in most societies worldwide, digital infrastructures shape basic everyday tasks in the household and at work. Digitalization has gradually changed society in all aspects of life, from our private life, including leisure activities [25], who we communicate with [12], which interest groups we associate with [24], to education [18] and working life. Online shopping, banking, public services etc., have transformed our work experiences as well as relationships between companies and their customers. Where previously a person responded to our wishes and requests, there might now be a computer program providing the options, guidance and help to make choices. This means that a lot of our everyday life activities are shaped by the design and infrastructure of the digital gadgets and software that

D. Kreps et al. (Eds.): HCC13 2018, IFIP AICT 537, pp. 250–257, 2018.
https://doi.org/10.1007/978-3-319-99605-9_18

surround us. While the consumer base of ICTs globally is diverse and keeps increasing, those that work in the software industry and who shape the design and accessibility of these technologies are unrepresentative of the wider population. For instance, the gendered nature of the ICT labor force is a global concern. It is well known that women software developers are both marginalized and intimidated in Silicon Valley and other contexts [19] and that only 10% of Wikipedia editors are women. For instance, Wikipedia has about 24 million articles written collaboratively by volunteers globally, but 90% of these volunteers are men. Initiatives to increase women's participation in the editing of Wikipedia thus are themselves feminist interventions and can be found in diverse geographical location such as urban USA as well as in rural India. Thus, we ask the following question – ICT might change everything, but who changes ICT? The computer programs that change "everything" are – often quite literally – *man*-made, in an ICT industry where about 4 in 5 are men in many Western countries. The already low number of women in the ICT industry is even declining, according to Deloitte's predictions.[1]

In this paper, the three co-authors examine the under-representation of women in ICT from three distinct contexts. In doing so we each take up particular intersections as feminist researchers to explore how more women can be included in the ICT workforce internationally. We argue for a feminist approach to examining the issue of gender inclusion and diversity in ICT labor. In doing so we bring into conversation three distinctly different contexts – one from Norway, one from India and one from Mid-western USA. Each of these contexts has specific feminist histories and socio-economic conditions that lend themselves to unique situations of inclusion of women in the IT workforce. Thus theoretically, no single feminist theoretical frame/gaze can be applied unproblematically. The description of these three contexts will allow us to raise questions in relation to feminist solutions to the problems in each context. In one instance we see the issue of state feminism and an overall well-being in women's material condition (Norway) but there is a lack of attention to recruiting and retaining women in the IT workforce; in the second instance, a case study from India, the larger socio-economic and cultural contexts of women's empowerment are mixed – however the participation of women in the IT sector is much higher in this context than in the other two examples, challenging assumptions of universal explanations for ICT inclusion and exclusion. The third context discussed is a university general education classroom context in a Midwestern university in USA where a significant portion of the classroom population are technology users but have little understanding of the coding and infrastructural issues around the technologies they use. As some interviewees in this latter project noted – they could be seen as technology dependent but not tech-nology savvy. The three case studies thus illustrate how a feminist gaze can help to reveal how a particular gendering of ICT might be reproduced in different cultural contexts that intersect with other diversities of socio-economic and technological access.

---

[1] https://www2.deloitte.com/global/en/pages/technology-media-and-telecommunications/arti-cles/tmt-pred16-tech-women-in-it-jobs.html.

2   5 Mill NOK per Year for a Gender-Blind Pilot for Programming in Secondary School

Norway is generally good at gender equality, scoring high on the World Economic Forum's Global Gender Gap Index. The unitary school has been important in Norway for at least two centuries, with an emphasis on providing all children and youth with the same educational opportunities in elementary school. And still we are not entirely successful in doing this.

The "Nordic Paradox" has been suggested as a description of a similar high degree of gender equality, combined with poor results when it comes to recruiting women to computing education and, consequently, the computing business [3, 7] found across the Nordic countries. While there are more women choosing computing fields associated with humanities, arts, and design, programming is worst off, reflected in the latest statistics for higher education, where women made up between 5 and 10% in applicants for programmes and courses in programming in higher education.[2]

If ICT is vital for society, competence about ICT is important, and, in particular, knowledge about controlling the technology that ends up controlling us by deciding our actions and choices. Thus, programming and creating the algorithms that control technology have appeared as increasingly important, and have also been at the centre for recent attention to how algorithms involve social bias and can cause social, economic and political harm [21]. In other words, the skill of programming has appeared as increasingly important to learn, quite contrary to what we believed in the 1990s, when the focus was on making computer applications easier to use, to eliminate any need for more advanced technical skills. But, simplification often also means less control, and less knowledge about the applications means less understanding of the choices that the technology makes for us. Or rather: the tech people, those who make the programs and thus also define the choices.

Recently, a growing choir of voices claim the importance of learning to code, or program, like Rushkoff, who suggests that it is a matter of Program or Be Programmed [23]. Even young children are invited to learn programming, in school and in after-school clubs. Making programming available for more people is not a new wish. Grace Murray Hopper, pioneer in developing programming languages, was concerned with making computers available for more people [17]. Women made up a considerable proportion of programmers in the US software industry in the 1950s and 1960s – up to 30% [13] – that is, in a period when gender inequality was expected in working life, there were more women in software and programming than in the top scoring "gender equal" countries in 2018. The historical facts around this negative development in the Western world have gradually been revealed since the 1980s, showing that the masculinization of ICT and programming in particular, is a historical and cultural construction, made by an increasing professionalization of both education and the profession. In this process, women seem to have lost the position they had formerly filled [13]: one where they felt welcome and appreciated, and where they even though they were a better fit than men. "It really amazed me that these men were programmers,

---

[2] Statistics from The Norwegian Universities and Colleges Admission Service, April 2018.

because I thought it was women's work!" said one of the women who worked as a programmer in the 1950s in the US [1]. In the process of gendering computing as a male field, a particular type of person was increasingly preferred, creating a circular logic that this type of person was the one needed for computing and gradually this increased the masculinization of the field [13].

Let us make a jump to 2016 and Norway. The masculinization of computing has been going on for decades, and the continually low proportion of women in computing has made it expected and thus invisible. When code club instructors and parents were interviewed in Norway, they illustrated how they were aware that there were less girls than boys. However, because this simply mirrors what people are used to finding in most computing contexts, they accepted it without questioning it [10]. It appeared as "natural" and not something that they could or should fix.

This is the cultural context of the national project introducing programming in secondary schools in Norway, as a pilot running between 2016 and 2019. The pilot material contains a "trial curriculum", not very detailed, and with nothing about gender or inclusion [11]. A survey of the 140 pilot schools spread across the country showed that a total of 18% girls participated the first year, however only 15% the second year of the pilot. More than five schools had failed to recruit girls at all! None of the schools had failed to recruit boys. And more than 100 single classes had no girls, only boys. Again, apart from single classes with one or two pupils, there were no larger groups of girls in classes without boys. The lack of an inclusion strategy in the pilot represents a sad example of how gendered structures tend to be reinforced when a gender-blind strategy is employed. Perhaps the "Nordic paradox" should not be considered a paradox at all in this particular case, as the low proportion of girls rather can be tied to the choice of introducing programming without any awareness of the strongly gendered patterns already recognized in this field.

Even though there is a general awareness in society about the low proportion of girls and women choosing a career in ICT, the pilot illustrates that this awareness does not automatically translate into activity or interventions to change the situation. This suggests that what is missing is not an awareness of the low proportion of girls and women, but rather awareness of how this is a result of social and cultural constructions. It is a result of choices that were made, and different choices could produce different results.

3 Gender Disrupted in a Global System of IT Work

The Norwegian case is in stark contrast to the situation in our second case study. The feminist gaze is often criticized as being a white western perspective – while this is not a new argument it has found renewed voice as a result of the perceived narrow focus of the recent high profile women's marches and other new feminist movements [9]. Thus we should question first of all what we mean by feminist and how we can use that term in an inclusive way that incorporates the experiences of women of color and women from the global south more generally. While gender disparities and 'programming' cultures are no doubt reproducing male dominance within ICT especially as led by the major IT companies in Silicon Valley, and feminist critiques are important in addressing highly sexist and hostile cultures, such experiences are by no means a universal experience.

The poor participation rates of women in ICT are not reflected in a number of other countries in particular the so-called BRIC countries such as Brazil, Russia, India and China [26], where women are much more highly represented. As Charles and Bradley have noted "International variability is striking even if we consider only engineering, the most sex-segregated field. [...] If anything, these results suggest a tendency for fields to be more segregated in highly affluent societies" [8].

In a recent project comparing gender in ICT in India and the UK, some common assumptions made in the Western feminist research literature about technology and masculinity have been challenged. Figures show that women form more than 35% of entry level programmers and technical staff in IT in India [22]. Companies in India, keen to (a) retain talented and trained staff and (b) to be seen as 'modern' and cutting edge, consciously portray themselves to be women friendly, and offer policies and benefits that attract women – one example is free transportation to and from work (essential in some Indian cities where sexual harassment on public transport is common), plus generous maternity leave over and above any statutory entitlements (which have only become enshrined in law recently). This is understood by women and men alike who perceive working in IT as a highly desirable career, regardless of gender. All over Bangalore there are visible posters and billboards that show positive role models of women working in IT and even popular soap operas feature women software engineers. Thus working in IT is not considered gender incongruent as it has been characterized in the West. Nor is engineering considered a masculine area of study – figures for women in Indian Higher Education Institutions show much higher percentages of women in technical subject areas than elsewhere [20].

So gender, we could say, is disrupted in this global system of IT work. However, we may still need to question to what extent neo-colonial power structures and inequalities continue to be reproduced across multiple sites of IT work. In this case does ICT change everything, or continue to reinforce and shape existing global inequalities?

4   Making a Difference with Feminist Pedagogy in Rural Ohio (USA)

Feminist pedagogy and hands-on work within digital environments can be one way to counteract the issues raised in the above two sections [2]. The final case study, provides a personal account of being an educator with the potential for using ICT as an agent of change.

In my classes I have developed assignments around Wikipedia editing, curating of social media and even the use of mobile phone texting apps like snapchat. These are comparatively "low" end tools and make the technology and any soft coding associated with them very accessible [6]. Students feel a sudden surge of empowerment in using such tools and develop a sense of ownership of the knowledge they create and share [5]. In working with undergraduate students in the NW Ohio, USA, I have found that young women and students of color and diverse backgrounds use the opportunity to turn the gaze back on to the mainstream narratives of technology as they insert themselves into the narrative through Wikipedia editing assignments, curating of social media feeds using Instagram and twitter and in developing digital humanities oral history archiving projects collaboratively [4]. These assignments make technology user-friendly by demystifying the process of editing Wikipedia for instance. Exploration and discussion in such courses – following the assignments and during the process of doing the assignments – often pushes students towards a rethinking of their abilities.

In such exploration and thinking through of the use of digital tools in a hands-on manner is supported by basic underlying feminist pedagogy of doing and engaging and returns us to the last 20 years of work by cyberfeminist [16] and other critical pedagogues who learn from participatory frameworks developed by fan communities and others - "crowd sourcing" in their organic everyday in efforts to negotiate the use of these technologies [15]. This allows us to simultaneously gain a close involved understanding and a critical thoughtful distance in relation to multiple entry points into these environments. Women in these classes tend to be participants in such communities through their leisure activities and are exciting to realize that they already come with technology skills that can further them in the business world or gain them entry into even the technology sector for employment.

Here the techniques of teaching serve to highlight the context of corporeality and subjectivity through pedagogic exercises that serve to highlight the technology in renewed and different ways from their assumed everyday leisure or work use. As the students engage these contexts through an engagement with the process of building, co-creating and living in online spaces, it is possible for them to understand the production of selves as within gendered and raced hierarchies through technospatial praxis. This problematizes their self perception as technologically savvy digital natives while also reveals to them different ways in which the design of the technologies are limited and in need for further development while thinking about access and inclusion in multi-dimensional ways.

5　Conclusion: The Feminist Gaze Changes Everything

This conference theme focuses on challenges caused by the Anthropocene. As we have illustrated here, we cannot ask such questions without also involving a perspective of gender, as well as other social categories that are producing social differences today, to ensure that we are aiming for a better future for everybody.

Understanding mechanisms producing exclusion from digital cultures is imperative for developing advice for local, national and international authorities, policymakers, and educators aiming to reduce excluding forces.

Strategies of inclusion are not simply mechanisms of exclusion reversed, as suggested by Faulkner and Lie:

"While the development of inclusion strategies should be informed about the nature of the exclusion processes that one tries to overcome, inclusion activities should not just be directed at curbing exclusion mechanisms. In addition, and this is very important, inclusion strategies need to have outspoken positive measures. To stop exclusion is not the same as achieving inclusion; in fact, too strong a focus on exclusion mechanisms may make inclusion seem impossible" [14].

The feminist gazes we have presented here include a reworking of embedded discourses of ICT production that are based on Western experiences of gendered exclusion but also a critical understanding of the potential for transnational globalised IT workers to address global challenges from the perspective of those most immediately affected. We propose an immersive feminist epistemological engagement with technology. We argue for the feminist gaze to open new ways of perception that are vital in preparing for the enormous disruptions that are to come with the acceleration of technological change including artificial intelligence, robotics and so on. We must educate the programmers and ICT workers of our future to adopt a critical and informed understanding of societal challenges, not just teach them "how to code".

References

1. Abbate, J.: Recoding Gender. Women's Changing Participation in Computing. MIT Press, Cambridge, London (2012)
2. Belenky, M.F., Clinchy, B.M., Goldberger, N.R., Tarule, J.M.: Women's Ways of Knowing: The Development of Self, Voice, and Mind. Basic Books, New York (1986)
3. Bergman, S., Rustad, L.M.: The Nordic Region-A Step Closer to Gender Balance in Research? Joint Nordic Strategies and Measures to Promote Gender Balance Among Researchers in Academia. Nordic Council of Ministers, Copenhagen (2013)
4. Bomberger, A.M.: Ranting about race: crushed eggshells in computer-mediated communication. Comput. Compos. 21(2), 197–216 (2004)
5. Boyd, D.: It's Complicated: The Social Lives of Networked Teens. Yale University Press, New Haven (2014)
6. Bruns, A.: From prosumer to produser: understanding user-led content creation (2009)
7. Charles, M., Bradley, K.: A matter of degrees: female underrepresentation in computer science programs cross-nationally. In: Cohoon, J.M., Aspray, W. (eds.) Women and Information Technology. Research on Underrepresentation, pp. 183–203. MIT Press, Cambridge, London (2006)
8. Charles, M., Bradley, K.: Indulging our gendered selves? Sex segregation by field of study in 44 countries. Am. J. Sociol. 114(4), 924–976 (2009)
9. Collins, P.H.: Black Feminist Thought: Knowledge, Consciousness, and the Politics of Empowerment. Routledge, New York (2002)
10. Corneliussen, H.G., Prøitz, L.: Kids Code in a rural village in Norway: could code clubs be a new arena for increasing girls' digital interest and competence? Inf. Commun. Soc. 19(1) (2016). Special Issue: Understanding Global Digital Cultures
11. Corneliussen, H.G., Tveranger, F.: Programming in secondary schools in Norway – a wasted opportunity for inclusion. In: Proceedings of Gender&IT 2018, Heilbronn, Germany, May 2018 (Gender&IT 2018), pp. 172–182. ACM, New York (2018)
12. Dralega, C.A., Mainsah, H.: Ethnic minority youth participation in the production and consumption of social media in Norway. Vestlandsforsking-rapport nr. 4/2014 (2014)
13. Ensmenger, N.: Making programming masculine. In: Misa, T.J. (ed.) Gender Codes: Why Women are Leaving Computing, pp. 115–141. IEEE Computer Society and Wiley, Hoboken (2010)
14. Faulkner, W., Lie, M.: Gender in the information society: strategies of inclusion. Gend. Technol. Dev. 11(2), 157–177 (2007)

15. Gajjala, R., Altman, M.: Producing cyber-selves through technospatial praxis: Studying through doing. In: Liamputtong, P. (ed.) Health Research in Cyberspace, pp. 67–84. Hauppauge, NY, Nova Publishers (2006)

16. Gajjala, R., Oh, Y.J.: Cyberfeminism 2.0: where have all the cyberfeminists gone? Cyberfeminism **2**, 1–9 (2012)

17. Gürer, D.W.: Pioneering women in computer science. Commun. ACM **38**(1), 45–54 (1995)

18. Kortuem, G., Bandara, A., Smith, N., Richards, M., Petre, M.: Educating the Internet-of-Things generation. Comput. Educ. **46**(2), 53–61 (2013)

19. Massanari, A.: # Gamergate and the Fappening: How Reddit's algorithm, governance, and culture support toxic technocultures. New Media Soc. **19**(3), 329–346 (2017)

20. Ministry of Human Resource Development: All India Survey on Higher Education (AISHE) 2014–2015, Ministry of Human Resource Development - Department of Higher Education (2016)

21. Pasquale, F.: The Black Box Society: The Secret Algorithms that Control Money and Information. Harvard University Press, Cambridge (2015)

22. Sondhi, G., Raghuram, P., Herman, C.: Skilled migration and IT sector: a gendered analysis. In: Rajan, S.I. (ed.) India Migration Report, 2018, New Delhi, India, Routledge (2018 forthcoming)

23. Rushkoff, D.: Program or Be Programmed: Ten Commands for a Digital Age, Soft Skull Press, Berkeley (2011)

24. Shirky, C.: Here Comes Everybody: The Power of Organizing without Organizations. Penguin Press, New York (2008)

25. Taylor, T.L.: Multiple pleasures: women and online gaming. Convergence **9**(1), 21–46 (2003)

26. World Bank: Labor force participation rate, female (2015). http://data.worldbank.org/indicator/SL.TLF.CACT.FE.ZS/countries/1W?display=default. Accessed 28 Jan 2017

Becoming-with in Participatory Design

Sisse Finken[1(✉)], Christina Mörtberg[2] , and Pirjo Elovaara[3]

[1] TiP Group, Department of Business IT, IT University of Copenhagen,
Copenhagen, Denmark
sisf@itu.dk
[2] Department of Informatics, Linnaeus University, Kalmar Växjö, Sweden
christina.mortberg@lnu.se
[3] Department of Technology and Aesthetics, Blekinge Institute of Technology,
Karlshamn, Sweden
pirjo.elovaara@bth.se

Abstract. We draw on feminist technoscience to analyze actions and activities performed between participants in a Participatory Design workshop that unfolds in a realm of e-government. Stepping into this empirical site we want to show how participants (invited persons, researchers, methods, artifacts, gender stereotypes) become with each other. With such take on research endeavors we feed into current discussion in feminist research by illustrating how theory and practice intertwine and create realities.

Keywords: Feminist technoscience · Participatory design · Ontology

1 Introduction

"Staying with the trouble requires making oddkin; that is, we require each other in unexpected collaborations and combinations, in hot compost piles. We become-with each other or not at all. That kind of material semiotics is always situated, someplace and noplace, entangled and worldly" [1][1].

The opening quote is from Haraway's book [1] in which she seeks to: "cut the bonds of the Anthroposcene and Capitalocene"[2] in that they carry with them logics of "techno-apocalypses" and "game over attitudes"[3]. Such logics, Haraway argues, prevents us from staying with the troubles, which "is both more serious and more lively"[4]. As an alternative to the Anthroposcene and Capitalocene, Haraway introduces the Chthulucene, which includes the "dynamic ongoing sym-chthonic forces and powers of which people are part, within which ongoingness is at stake" [2][5].

In drawing on Feminist theorizing – especially with concerns to 'become-with´, 'situated', and 'ongoingness' as put forward in the above – we enter a reading of a Participatory Design (PD) workshop [3] and show how the inclusion of subjects and

---

[1] p. 4.
[2] p. 4–5.
[3] p. 3.
[4] p. 4.
[5] p. 160.

© IFIP International Federation for Information Processing 2018
Published by Springer Nature Switzerland AG 2018. All Rights Reserved
D. Kreps et al. (Eds.): HCC13 2018, IFIP AICT 537, pp. 258–268, 2018.
https://doi.org/10.1007/978-3-319-99605-9_19

objects can fruitfully be read as material semiotic practices[6] in which participants (invited persons, researchers, methods, artifacts, gender stereotypes) become-with each other and how they, rather than sitting still, are constituted in encounters. Thus, with the re-visit to the PD workshop our focus is on how entities are becoming with in boundary-making practices that unfold at the workshop. In line with this, [6] remind us that design is always situated. Being situated is also what [7] pleads for as a funda-mental part of PD. They state: "[In fact, as we shall see,] the origination of participatory design as a design approach is not primarily designers engaging in use, but people (as collectives) engaging designers in their practice"[7].

In this paper, we find inspiration in feminist technoscience strands in general and especially in Agential realism when engaging in a reading of the workshop, which we situate as an ongoing ontology [5]. That is to say that we acknowledge that boundaries between 'nature and culture', 'social and material', 'human and nonhuman' are not always obvious. Thus, with agential realism we are provided a possibility to understand how meaning and matter are constituted in material-discursive practices or material semiotic practices, or, as something that emerges from "intra-actions" [5].

The paper is structured in the following way: first we coin our aim with reference to feminist technoscience and agential realism. We then move on to a short delineation of PD, especially focusing on previous work concerning feminism and PD. Next, we enter the empirical case, which is analyzed and discussed from a position of agential realism with explicit focus on bringing in ongoing ontology to participative endeavors. Lastly, we conclude the paper emphasizing how participants (methods, gender stereotypes, researchers, paper, pen, cars, civil servants, etc.) are becoming, and, thusly, that paying attention to the performance between (them) is important.

2   Theoretical Orientation

When entering the workshop below, we are concerned about the actions and activities that take place between the involved participants and their making of each other in ongoing and evolving endeavors. But first, we introduce more carefully the theoretical concepts used.

'Intra-action' [5], is one central concept in agential realism, which illustrates that subjects and objects are not separate, but rather entangled. Højgaard et al. [8] say it the following way: "Everything is always engaging something else, in specific ways designated by concepts: intra-activity, i.e. matter and meaning, object and subject, nature and culture are mutually articulated and mutually entangled"[8]. Another central concept is that of 'apparatuses' [5]. In bringing in apparatuses we do not mean to

---

[6] Haraway [4] uses material semiotic practices to grapple with entanglements of subjects and objects and Barad [5] uses material-discursive pratices. We treat these concepts as synonyms.

[7] p. 162.

[8] p. 68.

highlight the ensemble of human and nonhumans, rather, we find it fruitful to emphasize that: "apparatuses are specific material reconfiguration of the world" [5][9]. This means that apparatuses structure how we see, yet, at the same time they are not outside other orders (such as culture) that constitute what we see. This again means that apparatuses are part in the ongoing becoming of reality, of meaning and matter [9, 10].

Apparatuses also enact cuts that: "produce "objects" of particular knowledge practices…" [5][10] and "boundaries, properties, and meanings"[11]. It is the cuts that separate what will be called objects and subjects[12]. The objects and subjects do not pre-exist but their meanings emerge through agential cuts. The cuts are thereby not drawn once for all; but breaks ongoing activities due to the specific context where the intra-actions take place, e.g. in a design process. The very design process is the enactment of agential cuts in which subjects, objects, properties, and boundaries unfold. The cuts are enacted in ongoing activities in a design process, but they also raise ethical issues, as any cut, even an agential cut, can hurt. While interaction builds on a principle of separation, intra-action represents two ontologically inseparable entities. The intra-actions continue until a break is enacted. We make use of the concept agential cut in our reading of a PD workshop to understand each iteration in design as the enactment of a cut – a break in ongoing activities; a becoming-with each other.

In this article we bring in Barad's orientation to apparatuses by way of relating it to research methods. Such methods, which we bring along to the field and/or to the desk when engaging in research efforts - be it anthropological work or PD endeavors - have a bearing on our orientations in the world and what comes to matter in ongoing 'intra-actions' (e.g. [5, 11, 12]).

In line with this, we could say that research and design methods are part of the worlds becoming. Photography, for example, is something more than a way to document, or representing, reality; it is an apparatus (beyond the camera or video recorder) that enacts and re-configures different realities through in- and exclusions. Such in- and exclusions could be focused/blurred areas on a photo, the very cut of the world (what is outside the frame of the photo?, who is behind the camera?), and/or the very framing of a scenery and/or creation of e.g. otherness, eternal sunshine, good looks in line with a given time's beauty codex [13]. Similarly, the design method used at the present workshop, "mapping practices" [3] becomes one way of meeting, sensing, and looking into [14] whether the endeavor is audio recorded, videoed, or jotted down on paper. This also goes for the different material brought along to the workshop (such as pens, paper, images, glue, etc.), and it goes for the questions we ask, the interviews we perform, and the observations we make. They are ways of conduct that have onto-logical consequences. Accordingly, PD methods are modes of doing that draw out different boundaries, and such boundary-making in- and excludes. This again influences what comes about in 'intra-action' [5]. Barad reminds us that it is necessary to draw boundaries to create meaning, and that these boundaries have "material-

---

[9] p. 142.

[10] p. 147.

[11] p. 340.

[12] p. 333.

consequences" [15][13]. Thus, boundary-making is not taken for granted since it is not innocent; it has "ontological implications" [9][14]. Similarly, the methods brought along to PD sites have ontological implications. And the (so called) outcome from these PD sessions – be it service designs, reports, information technologies, or scientific texts (like this one) – draws out different boundaries and should, accordingly, be seen as ongoing re-configurations of the world, rather than representations of encountered practices. PD efforts and the involved participants (e.g. methods, materials, discourses, identities), per se, are not definite static entities that interact – they are becomings of this world.

With this, we wish to make a feminist technoscientific intervention that concerns a caring for the very actions and activities that are performed between participants.

3 Participatory Design

PD centers its ideology and practices on involvement of participants in design endeavors. The early formation of PD took its offspring in the 1970:ies in cooperation with Scandinavian labor unions as an effort to empower workers through development of workplace information technology [16]. 'Democracy', 'critical', and 'participant driven' are terms to be used when describing PD. Further, PD can be described as a design approach that builds on visions concerned with involving multiple voices in design processes [17]. PD centers on participative methods and democratic practices, it inspires mutual learning, and it advocates for locating and situating practices and actions in the contexts of the participants involved [17]. Such guiding principles concern accountability and its importance for PD and its praxis. Within PD various methods and techniques - e.g. mock-ups, prototyping, workshops, scenarios, interviews - are used to establish grounds for communication and mutual learning in the design processes.

For the purpose of the present paper, we leave aside the more general descriptions of PD and engage work that has been concerned with bringing in gender or feminist perspectives into PD.

Markussen [18] discusses experience and how both users and designers are implicated in the design process. The image of an invisible designer is contested by asserting his/hers presence as co-creator and accountable in the creation of realities or mattering in PD processes (see also [19]).

Another example is found in Sefyrin [20] who discusses design as sociomaterial practices in which participation, gender, power, and knowledge are intertwined. Sefyrin builds her discussion on an ethnographic study of an eGovernment project performed in a Swedish government agency. To expand design to be sociomaterial includes both human and nonhuman actors. Methods, visions, organizational boundaries, innovation practices, gendered practices are examples of the latter. The administrative officers – all women - were central actors in the entire project depending on their knowledge and

---

[13] p. 187.

[14] p. 73.

experiences of the work practices. Sefyrin illustrates how sociomaterial encounters (e.g. the business process analysis method, gendered division of labor, organizational boundaries, and changed project objective), intersect with human actors that reconfigured the administrative officers from being core knowers to becoming marginalized knowers with restricted agency. Sefyrin concludes her work stating that participation: "comes into being in situated practices. With this view participation is fluid and shifting; the result of the ongoing intra-actions of gender, power, knowledge, and various sociomaterial practices"[15].

Hence, feminist scholars have focused on PD, both as a design practice and from more theoretical angles. Bath [21] can be positioned in the latter when she scrutinizes a number of design approaches with the intention to develop an approach she calls the degendering of technology. Bath argues, that PD can contest the inscription of gender in design, but she emphasizes that the approach is also open to certain objections. One such is that PD implies a taken-for-granted-ness in terms of the possibility of inscribing emancipatory ideas into technology. Another tendency of feminist PD researchers is to re-essentialize gender when they pay attention to skills and competences aiming at making also women's work visible [21]. Although feminist researchers have explored PD as a gendered process, Bath asserts that it is necessary to explore PD further. We intend to follow Bath's remark.

PD is a value-centered approach that is both political and ethical motivated. An exploration of whose values that intervene in a PD process has resulted in a reconfiguration of the designer from being invisible and everywhere to becoming positioned somewhere and accountable [18, 22, 23]. Accountability is a key concept in PD. It is viewed by [24] as an expression of PD's ethical stand, they write: "an accountability of design to the worlds it creates and the lives of those who inhabit them"[16].

However, it is not only values that emerge in PD projects; rather, all entities included in the design process are co-constituted. In borrowing from Barad's work [5], we understand each intra-action in PD projects as the enactment of a cut, in which subjects and objects emerge. Thus, to understand PD as becoming means that it depends on what is included and what is excluded. The design process that takes place in the present workshop is the enactment of cuts in which entities get their meanings. With this, it is our desire to discuss PD-based design practices as an ongoing becoming-with each other [1].

4   Realities Emerge

The workshop was held in 2005 within the research project 'From government to e-government: gender, skills, technology and learning'. The project was conducted as a joint research and design activity between two of the authors and a number of female public-sector employees from five south-Swedish municipalities. The intention with the project was to bring everyday practices, which are absent in governmental policies, into

---

[15] p. 118.

[16] p. 5.

the design of digital services. Within the project we organized several workshops based on the design ideology of participation both of the design researcher and practitioners [3]. Our concern was to work with design methods, which were easy to transport and easy to use, and not demanding preparations or too much investment in time.

In entering intra-actions in the workshop, we are reminded of Barad's [5] words that boundary-making is necessary, it is not innocent, and it in- and excludes. That is, e.g., happiness came into being in the meeting between the director of the city-planning department (Kerstin) and us (two researchers) when she welcomed us. Kerstin introduced two other civil servants (the urban planners Maria and Nina) and a conference room to be used for the workshop.

At the workshop, the encounter between images, hands, glue and white sheet a first way to present themselves (Kerstin, Maria and Nina) emerged. Within this, the researchers and their method also came into being. This first encounter initiated a conversation with comments such as "she is like I" or "this woman reminds me of the leading politician in this municipality". The intra-activities continued in the encounter between Kerstin, Maria, Nina, the two researchers, pictures of furniture cut out from magazines, and the technical equipment. New encounters emerged when images were glued on to a big white sheet in an effort to create a narrative of the civil servants' work and workplace. Simultaneously, with these mapping activities, the civil servants and researchers talked and discussed. In the design process – at the workshop - the enactments of cuts got their meaning from the included entities. Cuts, e.g., were performed when the civil servants explained why and what they pasted on to the sheets. That is, the entanglements were reconfigured and the boundaries between the entities became obvious. At other times the researchers' questions, clarifications, or other entities created cuts.

The enrolled audio recorder also participated and recorded the experiences at the workshop. In this way, we could say, a reality of "practice" does not exist as a fixed one; rather it comes into being between our actions, materials, the methods, and the discourses we include [25]. When listening to the documentation afterwards, the recorder prompted us to more carefully pay attention to a specific situation in which a picture of a car was requested. That is, at a certain point during the workshop Maria suddenly expressed a need for a car. This request interrupted the ongoing activities of gluing and conversing. I.e., a cut is enacted when Maria uttered: "I need a car" and "I can't find any". In response to her request, she was suggested to "draw a car". This little request and the responding suggestion we hardly paid attention to during the event of workshop, but it became apparent later on via the audio recorder. I.e., during the mapping, Maria articulated a need for including other materials than the ones brought along to the workshop site by the researchers. The cut reconfigured the involved participants and made obvious that in previous intra-actions (in the event of preparation for the workshop) neither cars nor mobility had been included. This cut reconfigured the researchers' knowing about the civil servant as an indoor urban planner; she was also working outdoor and being mobile. Within this, Maria's visits to and travels between her office and e.g. construction projects or construction enterprises unfolded by this very cut. We read this as a 'becoming-with' that was made apparent by the audio recorder.

In addition, Maria's need highlighted how boundaries drawn in previous enactments – not including a car or mobility – came to have ontological implications in later iterative intra-actions [9]. Barad [5] writes: "[indeed], intra-actions iteratively reconfigures what is possible at a given moment and what is impossible – possibilities do not sit still"[17]. In a new intra-action it is possible to include what was excluded in a previous one. At the workshop, the sketched car came into being in an encounter between the participants, a hand, a pen, and a paper. This reconfigured the civil servant – she became a mobile subject (urban planner) between their devices or materiality in form of the sheet, images, pens, lines, colleagues and their relationships.

Further, this situation can be read as an example of another kind of configuration in that the civil servants are reconfigured from participants in and users of material (brought along to the workshop) to designers and facilitators of such. And, in turn, we can read this as an example in which the two researchers *are* constituted as researchers in the very encounter between their documented research material, the participative workshop, Barad's theories, enacted cuts, new materials, and knowing.

Another encounter documented by the recorder was the entanglements of governing principles. We should mention here that a municipality is governed by various policies and principles decided by politicians, which are then translated and implemented by the civil servants. In this example from the workshop Maria and Nina included two dominating governance principles: "What does the plan tell us?" and "Is this proposal aesthetically acceptable?". The boundaries were drawn differently with respect to how they previously had been drawn at the workshop. Both the city-plans and aesthetic issues co-emerged. Problems or different views on how to construct the roof of a new planned building - cheep, simple, functional opposed to aesthetics, also came into existence when relationships were entangled. In this way, we could say, agency not only relates to humans; rather, it is something that is performed in actions. In an interview, Barad explains that agency is neither limited to humans nor to something one possesses; Rather it "is an enactment, a matter of possibilities for reconfiguring entanglements" [26][18]. The entanglements were changed including new possibilities that reconfigured the participants, the maps or the world that came into being through the actions and doings with the inclusion of external and internal relationships. Hence, this illustrates how agency is situated and continues in research practices - in its "ongoingness" [1].

At the workshop, narratives unfolded in intra-actions between the sheet, people, and technologies. The stories also included accounts about how Maria and Nina are greeted when in contact with construction enterprises, agencies, politicians, and citizens. Maria and Nina said: "It is the "old boys" and "we are the young blondes". They told about how their looks, age and gender are commented on, how they reflect upon these meetings with anger, and, at the same time, determined professionalism. Nina and Maria touched the male dominated Swedish construction sector in their extension of their practices and doings. Age, gender, and professionalism are constituted or becoming-with their touches. Thus, the urban planners "play in the intertwined

---

[17] p. 234.
[18] p. 54.

practices of knowing and becoming" [12][19] when they become "the young blondes" vis-a-vis construction enterprises and other external partners who become "the old boys". Although asymmetrical power relations (old boys – blondes) are constituted in this entanglement it became reconfigured when one of the researchers said: "You possess power". Maria and Nina responded: "yes, we are able to say no" since the permission to build is approved by the urban planners.

Gradually the urban planners and the city-planning department's day-to-day activities unfolded in a co-emergence with a range of entities. The material semiotic reality was intertwined in the workshop – in the mappings or civil servants "grapples with the ordinary" [27][20]. Thus, realities were created between actions and doings. This became obvious, for example, in the start of the workshop when various images were discussed and explained before the civil servants chose and pasted one image of themselves on to the sheet.

Here we leave the city-planning department, Kerstin, Maria, Nina, and everybody else present at the workshop and continue with a discussion of the workshop in terms of bringing in ongoing ontology to participative endeavors.

5 Coming into Being

At the workshop, participants 'become-with' in 'ongoingness' [1]. That is, the different images, pens, scissors, post-it-notes, paper sheet, tables, whiteboard, words, methods, tape recorder, cuts, blonde planners, expert planners, old boys, local politicians, citizens, business contacts, researchers are "reconfigured and reconfiguring" [5][21] in "ongoing process[es] of (re-)production over time and across sites." [28][22]. This we encountered at the workshop where some participants were present from the very beginning, others were constituted through new entanglements, and yet others again through listening to the audio recordings.

Thus, what we have aimed at, with this reading of the workshop, is to make a feminist technoscientific intervention that shows how meaning and matter come into being between, rather than in-between clearly defined empirical entities. Specifically, Barad explains in an interview that she is concerned with actions between constituents: "[…] intra-action conceptualizes that it is the action *between* (and not *in*-between) that matters" [26][23]. In our reading, thus, meaning and matter emerge out of entanglements through which new possibilities become. Bringing such understanding along to participative efforts reflects what goes on in these research sites – they become, with other words, "critical sites" [28][24]. Such understanding is important when entering processes

---

[19] p. 812.

[20] p. 3.

[21] p. 235.

[22] p. 278.

[23] p. 14.

[24] p. 267.

of research efforts on which realizations of future technologies/services, and/or scholarly accounts are based.

At the workshop a range of participants became-with each other in the mapping practice. In this way, neither the civil servants nor the researchers were "outside observers of the world" [5][25]; but, we could say, they came into existence in the intra-actions that took place at the workshop. An example of such is the situation with the car that was included and which came to reconfigure knowing and being of both researchers and civil servants. In this way, entanglements of meaning and matter matters in the processes that took place. Various realities were created depending on what was included and excluded in the practices of the different participants present. Further, the inclusion of e.g. a car illustrates how new possibilities emerge when subjects and objects meet.

At the workshop, other participants, than those of humans, paper, scissors, images, gender stereotypes, and identities were present. These others are by another name called 'methods' (or 'apparatuses'). They are created and included with the purpose of achieving something like participative practices; but, at the same time, these methods are not outside; they are part in constituting our very performance. Along these lines, design methods are something more that tools produced and used by humans; they have a bearing on our 'becoming-with', and what comes to matter. In this way, design methods (workshops, mapping practices) and other research methods (interviews, observations) are also modes of doing, which have ontological implications [5, 11, 12, 25].

With this we mean to highlight that they iteratively configures and reconfigures our world and give it particular material form [5].

6 Conclusions

In our call for a feminist technoscientific intervention we sat out on a route delineating issues of concern within Participative Design. We then entered a workshop where a range of participants (methods, gender stereotypes, researchers, cars, civil servants, etc.) met and came into being in ongoing entanglements. In the analysis we considered actions between participants; i.e. that which intra-acts in practices. This paper, thus, is concerned with reflecting the becoming-with in participative research endeavors. Along these lines, we want to emphasize PD's central concern for accountability, which entails strong ethical attentiveness towards design practices as situated and locally bound, and towards design outcomes, which are considered with respect to the consequences they may have for those practices.

With our concern for encounters and emergencies that come about in activities, we have wanted to show the fruitfulness of being concerned about 'become-with', the 'situated', and 'ongoingness' [1] in everyday and research practices. With this we gesture to Science and Technology Studies and Feminist Technoscience, e.g. [5, 29–31], and ask: who participates in the research processes; what do these participants do; with what effects, for whom? And how are such participants accounted for in design

---

[25] p. 182.

practices? What kind of ontological implications do boundary-making practices have with their in- and exclusions?

In an effort of keeping the accountable heart of PD alive, we ask for new questions that are related to ontological understandings precisely because they have consequences for design practices and outcomes. By way of inviting feminist technoscience into PD we hope to bring about fresh strands that can contribute to PD-based design practices as situated and becoming-with in its ongoingness.

Acknowledgement. This paper is 'becoming-with'. It would not have been the same without the participating civil servants, research methods, materials, discourses, comments from previous reviewers, Helena Karasti, two HCC13 reviewers, theories, email, internet, etc. We thank you all.

References

1. Haraway, D.J.: Staying with the Trouble: Making Kin in the Chtulucene. Duke University Press, Durham (2016)
2. Haraway, D.J.: Anthropocene, Capitalocene, Plantationocene, Chthulucene: Making Kin. Environ. Hum. **6**, 159–165 (2015)
3. Elovaara, P., Mörtberg, C.: Cartographic mappings – participative methods. In: Bødker, K., Brattetei, T., Loi, D., Robertson, T. (eds.) Proceedings of PDC 2010, Sydney, Australia, pp. 171–174 (2010)
4. Haraway, D.J.: Modest_witness@second_millenium. Female man©_meets_oncomouse™: Feminism and Technoscience. Routledge, New York and London (1997)
5. Barad, K.: Meeting the Universe Halfway: Quantum Physics and the Entanglement of Matter and Meaning. Duke University Press, Durham (2007)
6. Suchman, L., Trigg, R., Blomberg, J.: Working artefacts: ethnometods of the prototype. Br. J. Sociol. **53**(2), 163–179 (2002)
7. Telier, A.: Design Things. MIT Press, Cambridge (2011). (By Binder, T., De Michelis, G., Ehn, P., Jacucci, G., Linde, P., Wagner, I.)
8. Højgaard, L., Juelskær, M., Søndergaard, D.M.: The "WHAT OF" and the "WHAT IF" of agential realism – the search of the gendering subject. Kvinder, Køn og Forskning, NR **1–2**, 67–68 (2012)
9. Hekman, S: The Material of Knowledge: Feminist Disclosures. Indiana University Press, Bloomington (2010)
10. Irni, S.: Indeterminate matter. NORA Nord. J. Feminist Gend. Res. **18**(1), 52–56 (2010)
11. Foucault, M.: On the genealogy of ethics: an overview of work in progress. In: Dreyfus, H.L., Rabinow, P. (eds.) Michel Foucault: Beyond Structuralism and Hermeneutics, pp. 229–252. The University of Chicago Press (1983)
12. Barad, K.: Post-humanist performativity: toward an understanding of how matter comes to matter. Signs J. Women Cult. Soc. **28**(3), 801–831 (2003)
13. Crang, M., Cook, I.: Doing Ethnographies. Sage Publications, London (2007)
14. Barad, K.: On touching—the inhuman that therefore I am. Differ. J. Feminist Cult. Stud. **25**(3), 206–223 (2012)
15. Barad, K.: Meeting the universe halfway: realism and social constructivism without contradictions. In: Nelson, L.H., Nelson, J. (eds.) Feminism, Science, and the Philosophy of Science, pp. 161–194. Kluwer Academic, Dordrecht (1996)
16. Finken, S.: Discursive Conditions of Knowledge Production within Cooperative Design. SJIS **15**, 57–72 (2003)

17. Kensing, F., Greenbaum, J.: Heritage having a say. In: Simonsen, J., Robertson, T. (eds.) Routlegde International Handbook of Participatory Design, pp. 21–36. Routledge, New York (2012)
18. Markussen, R.: Politics of intervention in design: feminist reflections on the scandinavian tradition. AI Soc. **10**(2), 127–141 (1996)
19. Vehviläinen, M.: Gender, expertise and information technology. University of Tampere, Department of Computer Science, Tampere (1997)
20. Sefyrin, J.: Entanglements of participation, gender, power and knowledge in IT design. In: Bødker, K., Bratteteig, T., Loi, D., Robinson, T. (eds.) Proceedings of PDC, pp. 111–120. ACM Press, Sydney (2010)
21. Bath, C.: Searching for methodology: feminist technology design in computer science. In: 5th European Symposium on Gender & ICT, Digital Cultures: Participation - Empowerment – Diversity, 5–7 March 2009. University of Bremen (2009)
22. Suchman, L.: Located accountability in technology production. SJIS **14**(2), 91–105 (2002)
23. van Der Velden, M., Mörtberg, C.: Participatory design and design for values. In: van den Hoven, J., Vermaas, P., van de Poel, I. (eds.) Handbook of Ethics, Values, and Technological Design: Sources, Theory, Values and Application Domains, pp. 41–66. Springer, Dordrecht (2015). https://doi.org/10.1007/978-94-007-6994-6_33-1
24. Robertson, T., Simonsen, J.: Participatory design: an introduction. In: Simonsen, J., Robertson, T. (eds.) Routledge International Handbook of Participatory Design, pp. 1–17. Routledge, New York (2012)
25. Hekman, S.: Constructing the ballast: an ontology for feminism. In: Alaimo, S., Hekman, S. (eds.) Material Feminism. Indiana University Press (2008)
26. Dolphijn, R., van der Tuin, I.: New Materialism: Interviews & Cartographies. Open Humanities Press, Ann Arbor (2012)
27. Haraway, D.J.: When Species Meet. University of Minnesota Press, Minneapolis (2008)
28. Suchman, L.: Human-Machine Reconfigurations: Plans and Situated Actions. Cambridge University Press, Cambridge (2007)
29. Foucault, M.: The History of Sexuality. Volume 1: An Introduction. Vintage Books, Auflage (1990)
30. Latour, B.: On recalling ANT. In: Law, J., Hassard, J. (eds.) Actor Network Theory and After, pp. 15–25. Blackwell Publishers (1999)
31. Mol, A.: The Logic of Care: Health and the Problem of Patient Choice. Routledge, London (2008)

Ethical and Legal Considerations

Three Views to a School Information System: Wilma from a Sociotechnical Perspective

Olli I. Heimo[✉], Minna M. Rantanen, and Kai K. Kimppa

Turku School of Economics, University of Turku, Turku, Finland
{olli.heimo, minna.m.rantanen, kai.kimppa}@utu.fi

Abstract. Visma Wilma has become a standard in Finnish school system as the de facto school information system for teachers, parents and students to use. Whereas the digitalisation of the school system seems inevitable there have been some issues in the information system design to promote practices and values that are suboptimal – or even substandard for a school as an entity.

In this paper we analyse the Wilma system from sociotechnical perspective with three different viewpoints: students', parents', and teachers' and bring out requirements and recommendations on how Wilma should be constructed in accordance of the aforementioned practices and values in mind.

Keywords: School information systems · Information systems
Ethics · Sociotechnical perspective

1 Introduction

Digitalisation is an on-going process in our information age and the school system is not an exception. As both the public and private sectors have pursued to ease up the communication and information processing with new information system solutions, the school system has also been inundated with changes: blackboards are now smartboards, Moodle and other electronic platforms are turning to be a preferred way to return homework, students get email addresses from the schools etc. It would be surprising if there would not be systems for the students' timetables or possibility to contact teachers via the internet.

The Finnish school information system Visma Wilma (formerly StarSoft Wilma) is the interface part of Visma's school information system package (with Visma Primus and Visma Kurre) developed to ease communication and sharing information within schools, between schools, and between students and their guardians (henceforth parents). With the system students, teachers, and parents can share information and view timetables [1]. It is usually seen as "a school journal", a notebook traditionally used for communication between school and home, but it extends to a be-all-end-all system for storing information about school activities [2].

The digitalisation however does come with a price tag. The analogue systems were not subject to digital divide or hacking, nor were they so pervasive to the social structure of schools and homes. Still it is clear that digitalisation also brings utility for the easiness of both communication and acquiring needed information. However, the

D. Kreps et al. (Eds.): HCC13 2018, IFIP AICT 537, pp. 271–281, 2018.
https://doi.org/10.1007/978-3-319-99605-9_20

new digital information systems bring unintended consequences some of which could have been mitigated and some clearly come unforeseen.

In this paper, we analyse the Wilma system from a sociotechnical perspective, a lens and a viewpoint from which one can reflect the world, by analysing the main interest groups: teachers, parents, and students to understand where these unintended consequences can be mitigated with the current knowledge. Note that in this case, sociotechnical theory is used as a perspective, not as a theory per se. We discuss the analysis and present proposals on how Wilma and similar systems should be used and how future systems should be constructed to better support the co-operation between these interest groups.

2   Sociotechnical Perspective

The term sociotechnical system was coined in the coal mine study conducted by Trist and Bamford to describe the relationship between human beings and technology in 1950's [3]. Sociotechnical theory was a counter reaction to 1950s Taylorism. Taylorism was created on the idea that a system could be optimized with standardisation of work and by making working more efficient with technology [4].

Trist and Bamford [5] acknowledged that machinery that was supposed to make coal mining more efficient actually caused problems and dangerous situations. They argued that this was due to neglecting the miners when designing new solutions. Later, similar studies were conducted with similar results: both technical and social systems should be taken into consideration when designing a system that works optimally [3]. Thus, instead of focusing only on technical system, one should also consider aspects such as work tasks and people doing the work so that the system would be as effective as possible and to avoid undesirable side-effects.

Since 1950s sociotechnical theory has inspired people to design more democratic information systems, but it has also faced a lot of resistance, mainly because it was considered to be time consuming and leading to ineffective processes in manufacturing. However, work in general has transformed from manufacturing to being more and more knowledge work [6]. Change in the characteristics of work highlight the importance of human beings in the information system design, thus making sociotechnical perspective a fruitful framework to analyse modern information systems.

From sociotechnical perspective an organization is a system that has social and technical subsystems. The social system (human beings) uses the technical system to produce something to clients that are outside of the organisation. Thus, these systems are in constant interaction with each other and the environment. The social system contains human beings, their traits and relations to each other and to the organisation that they are a part of [7].

Since people are the core of the social system, the quality of the social system can be observed only by taking into consideration subjective experiences of the individuals in that system. Their interpretation about their relation to their work tells how the social system is working [6, 8]. Thus, when designing or researching a sociotechnical system, one should aim to the participation of people who are using or connected to the technical system [7].

The technical system that the social system is using can be considered to contain both tasks and technologies [9]. Thus, the technical system is much more than technology. As Mumford [10] states, technology is much more than an artefact since it almost always contains some kind of processes that have specific phases and a target. These processes are conducted by people, so there is a constant dependency between technology and human beings using that technology [10].

Thus, a sociotechnical system can be seen as a whole that contains both social and technical systems which are inseparable from each other due to the constant interaction in the social environment. This constant interaction can have unexpected consequences [6]. This challenges the idea that one can achieve predictable consequences with technology [4]. To avoid unexpected negative consequences and to achieve as optimal a system as possible, one should analyse the sociotechnical system as whole [6].

From this perspective, an information system itself is a sociotechnical system that contains both a social and technical systems that are used in certain environments. The technical aspect of the information system is the electronic information system and the social system is the users. So that the whole system would work in the best possible way, it should be taken into consideration what the users want and need in relation to the technical system [11, 12].

It should also be kept in mind that since the interaction between the social and technical systems is continuous and the environment that they are placed in is rarely static, information system development should be a dynamic process from use to development, not vice versa [13].

The technical system in this case is Wilma and the tasks that are connected to it. Due to the nature of this system, there are different social systems that are connected to this technical system: teachers, students and parents. In the forthcoming chapters we analyse the system itself and these three interest groups with focus on the undesired and unpredictable consequences that could have been foreseen with careful analysis beforehand and still could be corrected to create an optimal system for schools, students and parents.

3 Wilma

Wilma is a technical system with multiple functions for multiple stakeholders. To teachers it is a tool for evaluation, marking absences, and communicating with the parents. To parents it allows the monitoring of students' school activities and communication with teachers. To older students it can be used as a messaging forum with private and group communications, course feedback, questionnaires, electrical application forms, formal decisions, the history of grading and "much more". Information is delivered immediately to the parents (via the system itself and through email) and can be used with all common browsers, and iOS and Android apps [1].

Wilma was implemented during the 2000s to large amount of Finnish schools and is used in most of the Finnish municipalities as one of the primary tools in teaching. Some teachers claim that one cannot get employed without skills to use Wilma [14]. One indication of the dominating market position is that no teacher allowed themselves to be interviewed for this study without anonymization. Some parents feel that the system is frustrating and it is not clear what the point of Wilma in general is [15, 16]. Many also view the system often as a "student criminal record" [17–20].

Evaluation is essential in schools, but Wilma has turned the evaluation of the students and their behaviour, rather than their achievements, easy and constant. Although Wilma has been intended to be used as a conduit for constructive feedback [see e.g. 21], many entries are merely critiques or notions about behaviour. Although Wilma entries are not meant to be personal critique towards the students and their developing identities, they can be interpreted as such by the students [2].

Oinas et al. [22] noticed that both negative and positive feedback is given but boys receive more negative feedback than girls and the feedback is also distributed unevenly among students so that negative feedback is concentrated to relatively small number of pupils. They argue that for more equal treatment of pupils and to prevent harmful effects of constant negative feedback specific guidelines are needed.

The owner and developer of Wilma, Visma [21] admits that electronic communication can easily be misunderstood. They claim that the reason for this is partly that sometimes less attention is paid to communication when it happens in electronic form than when communicating face to face or in phone [21]. Written communication is indeed more easily misunderstood since it lacks the non-verbal cues such as tones of voice or facial and bodily expressions that are quite essential to human communication.

Furman [21] also notes that the Wilma system is not adjusted to work in schools in a way teachers and parents would want it to work. For these reasons, they have published a guidebook about communicating through Wilma. This guidebook represents the ideal way of communicating through Wilma, but only concentrates on how teachers should communicate to parents. In brief the guidelines for teacher's interaction are (1) tell how you wish that the student would act and what are the benefits of desired behaviour, (2) create faith in possibility of success, and (3) show that you consider the guardian to be the expert of their child [21].

Many of these guidelines refer to situations where there is something negative about the behaviour of a student. The guidebook highlights also the role of positive feedback and represents ways to give positive feedback through a third person, collectively, and in problematic situations [21]. However, the guidelines do not give tools on how to give positive feedback about student's behaviour directly to the students, but only to their parents.

Furman [21] also acknowledges that communication might raise some negative emotions even though messages are not intended to critique parents. However, it is obvious that current guidelines do not give students or children an active role, but rather are aimed to keep the parents calm and informed about their child's (wrong) doings. Wilma seems to feed the idea that no feedback is good feedback, although also positive feedback would probably be appreciated by both the parents and the students.

Wilma in reality is not all about negative feedback, since it allows teachers also to praise good behaviour [22]. Alas, maybe due to the aforementioned "no feedback is good feedback" attitude, negative feedback options are overrepresented in the system. There has been discussion about Wilma having 8 negative feedback categories and only 2 positive ones. A teacher that raised this issue to discussion in Facebook felt that there should be more options for the students to gain positive feedback [2].

The information reported to Wilma is private but yet it is delivered to the parents of the child. Hence it seems that the privacy of the child's day is no longer guarded but is reported to the parents piece by piece, thus enforcing a new type of Panopticon to the child. Moreover, Visma company acknowledges that there are no proper guidelines or practices on how to use this new technology and hence the end decision whom to report and on what is a decision made by the teacher. Heimo, Rantanen and Kimppa [2] state that it "*is relative both to the student and the teacher alike what actions from the day are reported – or is anything reported at all. Thereby equal treatment of subjects – the adolescent – is nearly impossible.*"

The system seems to be a substitute for an adolescent 'criminal record', but with the exception of fair treatment: the markings come with no trial or other method that guarantees the 'convict' a fair possibility to defend oneself. Yet these markings may stay there for an eternity because this criminal record is not administered by the central government but the IT-supports of the city governance and the practices on how this information is stored is not public. Thus the information can be stored and accessed much later – and possibly by those not permitted to do so to be used against the citizens [2].

4   Teachers

The role of the teacher is manifold. Whereas the title implies that the person with the title teaches there is more to it: foremost the teacher is a pedagogue with a responsibility to be the guide to adult world in all matters academic and in some matters social. The teacher is a referee, a guide, a substitute parent and the police, judge, and executioner – the foremost authority – during the school day. The task is not easy. Although the teachers are limited with their power they might still appear omnipotent and omniscient – at least to the smallest of the kids – but not to the parents. To the parents the teachers should represent themselves as specialists and experts of their specific field and the information systems should support that.

Yet it seems that systems like Wilma make the teachers represent themselves as mere informants of the children's daily activities during schooldays who outsource the keeping of the order in the classroom to the parents. The parents – kids of the yesteryear – assume (rightly?) that the teacher keeps the order and teaches their offspring to read and write, whereas the school has evolved from those years. The teachers are for example not allowed to use physical or even emotional punishments against the kids and that leaves them without the options of the teachers of the parents' times.

The balance of power due to the modern child-protective legislation has turned in favour of the students who are more and more aware of their rights and therefore these new tools to "punish" the kids boil down to complaining about them to their parents and then hoping that the parents guide the children. If that does not help, the teacher at least has a good set of information to turn in the kid (and the family) to the child protective services. Wilma is a solution for this problem – at least in part. It delivers the teachers' notes to the school district, to parents, and to the (older) students.

But there is of course a snake in the paradise. Wilma is meant to be a tool for the teachers and with this tool the teachers' work is predetermined. It is supposed to support the actual work tasks – teaching and pedagogy – by easing up and saving time for this purpose. Instead of different possibilities for communication teachers are forced to use this system as the main means of communication and information processing – even if they do not have enough information on how to use the system or feel that the use of the system is in contradiction with the idea that they see as proper pedagogical practice. In addition they are encouraged – sometimes strongly – to do (even daily) minor reports on the students [14]. Even more, as the information processing has been made easy, the requirement of the amount of information is raised to meet the possibilities of mining the information.

The Wilma activities of the teacher can also be monitored. The amount of feedback can be used as a measurement of the teacher's activity and efficiency and the feedback given can also be used against the teacher. And since the tool is there to be used, the teacher is also recommended to use it as a tool to keep order in the classroom. Sadly though, there are not that much of "best practices" for the teachers to deal with these reports and thus they tend to be small, 5 to 10 word comments (with bad grammar!), not describing the situation well enough (due to lack of time to report), and vague enough not to get the teacher prosecuted. This of course leads to unintended consequences and thus to additional problems. Even with small additions to the Wilma system, writing them for each (or at least most) of the kids still takes its own time, which is either extra unpaid work or away from other, more constructive work such as planning classes or grading exams [14].

The system also supports situations in which the teacher can misuse the system to punish a student, even for an act which they have not committed. This can include situations where the teacher has ended up in a disagreement with the parents or because of a quality, trait or feature of a student that the teacher for one reason or another disagrees with. The feature can be used by writing a report to the system and by marking and using those markings as a proof and stigmatisations thus justifying a harsher punishment. Yet, peer influence of other teachers can lead to situations in which teachers are more likely to write more positive comments or not to write negative comments due to the amount of positive reports done by their colleagues [2]. For example Oinas et al. [22] have stated that especially negative feedback seems to accumulate to certain pupils.

5   Students

The main role for the students in the Wilma system is to be targets of the use. Whereas the teachers produce the material and the parents (ought to) read and act accordingly, the students are rather passive targets with only little direct contact to Wilma system. Pupils (grades 1–9, under 16 years) are rarely the users of this system whereas older underage students can have their own accounts to use these systems aside of their parents.

The students can roughly be divided to two groups: children (age between 6 and 11) and adolescents, i.e. the age between childhood and young adulthood (ages 12 to 16). This division is used by the Finnish school system and thus the adolescent get more privileges and more responsibility in the school life and their teaching is moved from single-teacher classrooms to specialised teacher classrooms. In the latter they participate in more course-like school experience with specialised teachers teaching their subjects rather than one teacher teaching every subject for their own students. Thus, the adolescent also are able to access their own Wilma account and see the feedback themselves whereas the children usually cannot.

Whereas the children require more constant care and attention, and require more limits and control, the adolescents are slowly starting to become adults. Teenagers are going through a set of physical, psychological, and social changes, and are in process of turning into adults which is why they are in the midst of developing their cognitive skills, identities, morals etc. and this is something the school supports (or at least should support). Hence the Wilma system should have two different goals: for the children and those working with them the system should support different set of values than for the adolescents and those working with them. In this chapter, the adolescent are more in the focus, but the children are not forgotten.

It must be kept in mind that the system should exist only to promote the students' learning and welfare – because the school exists for that reason (and for the reason to keep the kids occupied during daytime). Therefore, a system which does not support this goal is not a proper system for this task [see e.g. 23]. Moreover the system should follow the values of the organisation [24].

The Wilma system should promote the values of the school system. None the less it seems that the Panopticon system of Wilma turns the students into subjects of an Orwellian society: it teaches them that their actions are recorded and can be used against them– and that it is normal.

Therefore the feedback given is in a major role on how the adolescents keep on the "positive track". Whereas the role of the adolescent is turned to a passive role of avoiding bad feedback instead of learning about the balance of good and bad feedback, the actions of those adolescents will change. As mentioned earlier, in Wilma the attitude seems to be "no feedback is good feedback". Whereas the narrative should be guiding towards good, now it seems only to be guiding away from the "bad" or "unwanted" and when the proper feedback is lacking the feedback might deem the adolescent as "bad" themselves.

It is important to remember that the children and the adolescents talk about Wilma and compare the feedback amongst them. Where some teachers are eager to give feedback through Wilma, others are not. Other students tend to gather more feedback from all of them and it is not always all of their own accord thus they might feel unjustly deemed as 'criminals'. Moreover, the problem comes with the parents. As some parents use the Wilma function of getting every report in their email instantly, others visit the system once a week or even rarer just to sign the reports. This difference in attitude also reflects to the students as where some parents take these notifications seriously – or even by overreacting – others have more laid back attitude towards any of them. Hence other students are quite afraid of getting any negative feedback others just don't simply care and therefore using these notifications as means to punish or keep order seems somewhat unfair [14].

Reference withheld [2] introduce a rebellious movement – one of the aforementioned defence mechanisms – in teenagers: the Wilma ruined my life Facebook group. In this group, the negative feedback gained is turned into positive. As the intent of getting the adolescent humiliated, they publish these notions and seek positive attention from their peers. In Wilma ruined my life group negative feedbacks are often seen as humoristic and even competed against each other for the best feedbacks [2]. More current phenomenon is an Instagram group where teenagers share their life with Wilma reports [25, 26].

As the whole teacher-student-parent relationship seems to be problematic and Wilma or similar systems are not going away, more research on this effect to the students should be done as soon as possible to understand the change in the mechanics on teacher-student-parent relations due to digitalisation.

6 Parents

One of the key issues is to notice the parents' role in this information system. Whereas they are the factual guardians of the students, they have also a role of verifier. When raising a child it is not sufficient to keep up boundaries and check that the future taxpayer will do as told and as required, it also requires defending and protecting the kid from harms and abuse.

The system however has changed the process from face-to-face or phone discussions to stored digital discourse where the teacher's role is to inform the parents of the malpractices their offspring have conducted. This leads to two problems:

1. Most of the feedback is negative.
2. It is not discourse, only informing.

As most of the feedback is negative and – as mentioned before – in very short form, it may trigger a defensive reaction from the parent. Surely some of the parents think of their kids to be perfect and never to be able to conduct malicious deeds, but most of the parents should be able to understand this. Moreover, the acceptance of the level of negative feedback (especially with the lack of comparative data) might affect the parent-child relation or parent-teacher relation – most likely both.

If the discourse is lacking, the only two options for the parent is to accept (and sign) the students' wrongdoings or fight back. Neither of these options is actually discussing and therefore "the battle lines have been drawn". This usually leads to *user resistance*, where the users rebel against the system – actively or passively. Whereas Ali et al. [27] define user resistance manifestation as *"[it] may manifest itself in a visible and overt fashion (such as sabotage or direct opposition), or in a less obvious and covert action (such as inertia) to stall and ultimately kill a project."* In addition, it can manifest itself to an already implemented system which is an organisational change to the users that are included in it – that is the parents – who see the change from the point of their days in school. This resistance should be minimised in accordance to acquire effective and functional use of the system [27].

One problem with Wilma is that the information flowing from the school is almost constant even though it does not require any action from the parent. This constant information flow might cause "information overload". The messages (when used with the mobile app) may interrupt the parents too often and if they are checked only once per week, there is a problem of "a fair trial".

If the parent uses the system rarely, other problems arise. Most critically some important or urgent information might be lost (e.g. permission to participate to a field trip). Secondly, the information is targeted to separate sections of the day (e.g. Tuesday morning 8–10 a.m.) and if discussed about with the child Friday afternoon, the kid might not have any recollection of the event. Therefore, the instant feedback the kid should get from the "wrongdoings" and the possibility for the child to defend oneself against those "digital accusations" is limited – at the best. Moreover, the learning from the "wrongdoing" is lost and all that is left is an overall bad feeling with a hint of inadequacy. This will affect the child's sense of self and most likely the child's sense of justice.

Therefore, the problem of what is important to intervene with when rising a child is outsourced from the teachers to the parents – who do not have the full picture but merely a dozen ten-word descriptions and a forgetful child. Moreover, the parents interpret the messages differently and the kids can have different consequences from the parents with similar track records since there is no guidelines on how the teachers should write these and how should parents react to these reports thus more affecting to the sense of justice and self.

7 Discussion

As shown above Wilma and its use has an impact on how the communication between the home and school is done and is hugely dependant on the personalities of those using it. It is also clear that the feedback given should be done in different manner to counter the inevitable misunderstandings. Moreover, the use of this information system leaves a lot of open questions about how the responsibility between the school and home about the child's behaviour in and out of the school should be distributed.

While it is important to notice that digitalised systems such as Wilma ease up the day-to-day life both in school and at home and that information can easily be derived for the stakeholders to analyse and utilise, there still are problems to be dealt with. First and foremost, it can be argued that the effects of the chosen methods – e.g. the Panopticon-style reporting of children's daily activities and giving mainly negative feedback – are not studied enough to be used within the pedagogical environment in this scale without taking a huge risk on what kind of future citizens we are rising.

Yet again the increase in the workload of the teachers as well as the change in their work routines can lead to diminished results in teaching. Whereas a teacher could use the time spent with Wilma to focus on teaching, some of that time is now used on reports of minor annoyances the teacher has encountered. Moreover, if the teacher is required to focus on these annoyances it might turn the teaching event towards more classroom discipline oriented event.

As the parents react to Wilma in different manner, the effects of the reports may be actually be undesired by the teacher or the school. While other parents try to coach their offspring not to get these markings, others will rebel against the system, start defending the child against the system or just stop caring about the reports at all. This of course affects the students' view of the reports as punishment as well.

As the students may deem the system to be unfair it also implements reactions of its' own. As some might suffer from the feeling of being "bad" or "unwanted" due to negative feedback, others try to manage with it by making fun about it. None the less the effect can easily be an undesired one – again.

Whereas the consequences seem to differ according to the user (or the target of use), one thing seems clear: the system – as used now – can clearly increase confrontation between school and home, teachers and students, teachers and parents, and parents and children. Whereas the school environment should be constructed to be co-operation between these stakeholders, a constant flow of short and negative messages are not likely to promote it.

From the sociotechnical perspective, it is crucial that the work is meaningful. As discussed earlier, there are various parts in which the meaningfulness in using this information system can be arguably questioned. To improve the Wilma system, one must focus on the factors that not only promote the functions and the data gathering of the system, but also make the system to be a credible, functioning tool which makes the users feel that time spent with the system is profitable – meaningful.

As a solution, the use of this system – and every other school information system – should promote the values the school should aim towards: openness, fairness, reasoned dialogue, and co-operation in meaningful way. If the system is designed – or even used – with these values in mind, the system should improve the day-to-day school-life.

References

1. Visma: Wilma (2017). https://www.visma.fi/inschool/wilma/
2. Heimo, O.I., Rantanen, M.M., Kimppa, K.K.: Wilma ruined my life: how an educational system became the criminal record for the adolescents. SIGCAS Comput. Soc. **45**(3), 138–146 (2016). https://doi.org/10.1145/2874239.2874259
3. Herbst, P.G.: Sociotechnical Design: Strategies in Multidisciplinary Research. Tavistock, London (1974)
4. Leavitt, H., Whisler, T.L.: Management in the 1980's. Harvard Bus. Rev. **36**(6), 41–48 (1958)
5. Trist, E.L., Bamfort, K.W.: Some social and psychological consequences of the longwall method of goal getting. Hum. Relat. **4**(1), 3–38 (1951)
6. Mumford, E.: The story of socio-technical design: reflections on its successes, failures and potential. Inf. Syst. J. **16**(3), 317–342 (2006)
7. Munkvold, B.E.: Tracing the roots: the influence of socio-technical principles on modern organisational change practices. In: Coakes, E., Willis, D., Lloyd-Jones, R. (eds.) The New SosioTech - Graffitti on the Long Wall, pp. 13–25. Springer, London (2000). https://doi.org/10.1007/978-1-4471-0411-7_2
8. Martel, J.-P., Dupuis, G.: Quality of work life: theoretical and methodological problems, and presentation of a new model and measuring instrument. Soc. Indic. Res. **77**(2), 333–368 (2006)
9. O'Hara, M.T., Kavan, B.K., Watson, R.T.: Information systems implementation and organisational change: a socio-technical systems approach. In: Coakes, E., Willis, D., Lloyd-Jones, R. (eds.) The New SosioTech - Graffitti on the Long Wall, pp. 149–159. Springer, London (2000). https://doi.org/10.1007/978-1-4471-0411-7_14

10. Mumford, E.: Technology and freedom. In: Coakes, E., Willis, D., Lloyd-Jones, R. (eds.) The New SosioTech - Graffitti on the Long Wall, pp. 29–38. Springer, London (2000). https://doi.org/10.1007/978-1-4471-0411-7_3

11. Hirschheim, R., Klein, H.: Paradigmatic influences on information systems development methodologies: evolution and conceptual advances. Adv. Comput. **34**, 293–392 (1992)

12. Mumford, E.: Designing Human Systems for Health Care - The ETHICS Method. Eight Associates, England (1993)

13. Nurminen, M.I., Forsman, U.: Reversed quality life cycle model. In: Human Factors in Organizational Design and Management-IV: Development, Introduction and Use of New Technology - Challenges for Human Organization and Human Resource Development in a Changing World, Stockholm, Sweden, 29 May–2 June 1994 (1994)

14. Heimo, O.I and Rantanen, M.M.: Source withheld for anonymity. Discussion with a teacher about Wilma, November 2017

15. Junttila, J.: Koulujen Wilma-merkinnät ahdistavat niin oppilaita, opettajia kuin vanhempiakin – Merkinnöissä kannustus kasautuu yksille oppilaille ja nuhteet toisille. Helsingin Sanomat, 14 August 2017. https://www.hs.fi/tiede/art-2000005322915.html?share= 12c127a4e43128bdb7dd2fec3a6ca88d

16. Helsingin Sanomat (Producer): Wilma herättää rajuja mielipiteitä: "Opettajien oksennusastia", 30 November 2015. https://www.hs.fi/hstv/uutiset/art-2000002945817.html?share= 1e5e5c1dacc64a837b6f5308c5ed119c

17. Koivisto, K.: Lehtori: Wilma on yliinnokkaan opettajan ylläpitämä rikosrekisteri. EteläSuomen Sanomat, 27 February 2011. http://www.ess.fi/uutiset/kotimaa/2011/02/27/lehtoriwilmaon- yli-innokkaan-opettajan-yllapitama-rikosrekisteri

18. Ilta-Sanomat: Suomen koululaisten uusi villitys huolestuttaa: "Lasten rikosrekisteri" leviää kaikkien nähtäväksi, 19 April 2013. https://www.is.fi/perhe/art-2000000609504.html

19. Tirkkonen, K.: Koululaiset: Wilma on rikosrekisteri. YLE, 13 May 2009. http://yle.fi/uutiset/ koululaiset_wilma_on_rikosrekisteri/5250971

20. Helin, S.: Sari Helin: Wilma pilaa kodin ja koulun loputkin välit. YLE, 4 February 2015. http://yle.fi/uutiset/sari_helin_wilma_pilaa_kodin_ja_koulun_loputkin_valit/7780204

21. Furman, B.: Viesti Wilmalla viisaasti. Opettajan opas kodin ja koulun väliseen sähköiseen viestintään. Visma Company (2017)

22. Oinas, S., Vainikainen, M.-P., Hotulainen, R.: Technology-enhanced feedback for pupils and parents in Finnish basic education. Comput. Educ. **108**, 59–70 (2017). https://doi.org/10. 1016/j.compedu.2017.01.012

23. Nurminen, M.I.: People or Computers: Three Ways of Looking at Information Systems. Studentlitteratur, Lund (1988)

24. Heimo, O.I., Kimppa, K.K., Nurminen, M.I.: Ethics and the inseparability postulate. In: ETHICOMP 2014. Pierre & Marie Curie University, Paris (2014)

25. Ilta-Sanomat: Opettajien väitetysti kirjoittamat Wilma-viestit keränneet jo 60 000 seuraajaa Instagramissa, aitoudesta ei varmuutta – "Uhkasi tappaa äitinsä ja heittää käsikranaatin", 21 November 2017. https://www.is.fi/kotimaa/art-2000005458865.html

26. Määttänen, J.: Instagram-suosikkitili julkaisee oppilaiden saamat pahimmat Wilmahuomautukset – Soitimme Wilma-viestien asiantuntijalle ja kysyimme, pitääkö tästä olla huolissaan, 21 November 2017. https://www.hs.fi/nyt/art-2000005458111.html?share= 326754db1e84b888e75e5b311f61e579

27. Ali, M., Zhou, L., Miller, L., Ieromonachou, P.: User resistance in IT: a literature review. Int. J. Inf. Manag. **36**(1), 35–43 (2016). https://doi.org/10.1016/j.ijinfomgt.2015.09.007

Do Honest People Pull the Short Straw?

The Paradox of Openness

Kiyoshi Murata[1]([✉]) [iD], Yohko Orito[2] [iD], and Miha Takubo[3] [iD]

[1] Meiji University, 1-1 Kanda Surugadai, Chiyoda, Tokyo 101-8301, Japan
kmurata@meiji.ac.jp
[2] Ehime University, 3 Bunkyo-cho, Matsuyama, Ehime 790-8577, Japan
orito.yohko.mm@ehime-u.ac.jp
[3] Osaka International University,
6-21-57 Tohda-cho, Moriguchi, Osaka 570-8555, Japan
mihachi@oiu.ac.jp

Abstract. Widespread acceptance of the value of the culture of openness and honesty in cyberspace, due to the proliferation of (in many cases, ostensibly free) online services such as social media, paradoxically encourages 'clever' or 'crafty' people to use those services in a closed or controlled fashion to their own advantage. Online services that would motivate such people to exploit 'honest' or 'innocent' users undermining the open and honest culture have been provided. This situation will lead to social issues, such as the spread of online behaviour that treats others as only a means, the distortion of digital as well as real identities of a wide range of individuals, and human alienation. Nobody except social media platform companies seems to get the benefit from people's social media usage in the longer term. In this paper, the nature of these issues is examined with referring to actual cases, and measures to address them, such as the establishment of the right to be translucent and the notion of co-ownership of digital objects, are proposed.

Keywords: Social media · Openness · Online honesty · Strategic use
Identity

1 Introduction

The development and permeation of social media have spawned a new phase in personal information and privacy protection. Before the advent of social media, online services for individuals like online shopping and search services encouraged users to disclose their own personal information including their interests and concerns, and access to such personal information disclosed online was restricted exclusively to the online service providers and distribution of it was controlled by them; this is still the case for most of online services other than social media. On the other hand, social media are designed so that individual users are encouraged to reveal and disclose their own personal information, and that of others (usually friends and acquaintances), because the open sharing of personal information on a social media platform is integral to ensuring the profitability of its business. In this respect, social media pose a unique

D. Kreps et al. (Eds.): HCC13 2018, IFIP AICT 537, pp. 282–292, 2018.
https://doi.org/10.1007/978-3-319-99605-9_21

privacy issue. As Lucas [1] points out, "[e]ven if your privacy settings are super-high, it's always possible one of those 'friends' will rat you out".

The more individual Internet users disclose and share personal information about themselves and others on a social media platform, the more the economic value of the platform is enhanced. Accordingly, social media platform companies desire to build and maintain the open and honest culture online. The 'friends of friends are friends' structure, which is exemplified in Facebook's 'like' and 'share' functions and in Twitter's official and unofficial retweet functions, is embedded in social media platforms to provide the users with opportunities to observe the attributes, status, thought and/or behaviour of friends of their online friends for this reason. In fact, social media platforms such as Facebook, Twitter, Instagram and YouTube have attempted to enhance Internet users' open and honest communication with their friends, friends of friends, and friends of friends of friends, as well as with an unspecified number of other people, by revealing personal information not only pertaining to themselves, but also to these others through various modalities of expression, including text, sound, pictures and moving images. Consequently, personal information revealed by oneself and others is accumulated on the Internet and in the databases of social media companies in a state of being ready to be processed, used and shared, and hardly any ordinary person can control this accumulation, or the access to and use of such information.

Regardless of whether they are conscious or unconscious of the values embedded in a service, those who enjoy using it accept these values to a certain extent. When a user considers Google search results to be appropriate or acceptable for them, or that they need to register on Facebook under their own names, they substantively affirm the values underlying the technological schemes of such online services. In fact, social networking services (SNSs) have been accepted by the majority of Internet users, with no or little resistance against the default user environment settings of the services, as a tool to expand their communicative ability, deepen their human interactions, and enrich their lives in real space. In Japan, Facebook became the dominant SNS, overtaking 'mixi', the local Japanese SNS, in October 2011. Interestingly, whereas almost all users enjoyed using the mixi SNS under pseudonyms, most of the same people did not hesitate to register on Facebook under their own names because they believed that the platform required them to do so. Contrary to the findings of boyd and Hargittai [2], these users seemed not to care about their privacy settings on the site.

Whereas people use various social media services for different purposes, many of those services are federated with each other. Instagram and LINE, an instant messaging service similar to WhatsApp, are other popular social media platforms, and provide their users with a social sign-in capability; that is, those users who accept this can access the services by using their Facebook login information, and give Instagram and LINE permission to use other types of Facebook information of them, such as their 'friend lists'. The linkage function of Twitter enables its users to automatically upload their tweets on Facebook. Many social media services encourage users to share their smartphone directories with the media platform companies to enhance the connectivity with their friends in real space. In fact, the social media-driven culture of openness has seemed to be accepted among a wide range of people.

However, any technological service is an object of interpretation. Once a service starts to be used, its users are free to find and create their own ways of engaging with it, possibly departing from the developer's original intentions. The value and culture of openness that many social media platforms support is not necessarily accepted by the users; rather, this is at the users' discretion. While there are many 'honest' or 'innocent' social media users who, consciously or unconsciously, affirm the value and culture of openness by using the default user environment settings of social media platforms and by casually posting personal information pertaining to themselves and others on social media sites, 'clever' or 'crafty' users can engage with social media strategically, as a tool to benefit themselves by exploiting honest users who, to such individuals, have only instrumental value. Given the potentially significant benefit to clever users of using social media in this way, they may be strongly motivated to covertly control the personal information of themselves and others that they and others reveal. In fact, individuals who use social media in this manner have already been observed. The widespread acceptance of the value and culture of openness in cyberspace, which owes to the proliferation of social media, paradoxically encourages 'clever' people to use social media in a closed or controlled fashion, to their own advantage. This is expected to lead to social issues, such as widespread online behaviour that treats others only as a means, the distortion of digital as well as real identities of a wide range of individuals, and human alienation, which would be serious especially for people in young adulthood. Nobody except social media platform companies seems to get the benefit from social media usage in the longer term. This study, as a basically conceptual one, deals with these issues through investigating the nature of them and attempts to propose policies to address the issues, based on the previous work of two of the authors [3]. The work has been extended through investigating actual online services which seem to foment the clever or crafty use of social media.

2   The Age of Openness?

2.1   The Open and Honest Culture Advocated by Facebook

As described in its original mission "Give people the power to share, and to render the world more open and connected" [4], Facebook appears to be aiming for an informationally open, transparent society in which everyone actively reveals everything about him/herself. Kirkpatrick [5] described how Mark Zuckerberg, the founder of Facebook, believes that people should have just one identity and that having two or more identities showed a lack of integrity[1]; that in a more open and transparent world people would be held to the consequences of their actions and be more likely to behave responsibly[2]; and that more transparency should make for a more tolerant society in which people accept that everybody does 'bad' or embarrassing things sometimes[3]. Zuckerberg also said that transparency increases integrity, by essentially saying the same thing to everyone [6][4]. Zuckerberg's insistence marks a sharp contrast with the

---

[1] p. 199.

[2] p. 200.

[3] pp. 210–211.

[4] p. 175.

account of the value of privacy Rachels [7] provided. According to him, privacy is important if we are to ensure our ability to create and maintain different sorts of social relationships with different people, and the idea that different standards of conduct with different people is a sign of dishonesty is wrong. Zuckerberg seems to disregard the value of privacy, and the characteristics of the services and functions that Facebook provide seemingly reflect Zuckerberg's belief in open and transparent society even after they changed their mission statement in June 2017 – "Give people the power to build community and bring the world closer together". They are also consistent with the principles and logic underpinning a digitised market economy in which money and personal information are circulated as currency. Individual users enjoy a variety of 'charge-free' online services that are paid for with personal information.

Although strong criticism of Facebook's adherence to openness has been expressed by many people who consider that the company's attitude poses a significant threat to the right to privacy, Jarvis [6] supports the culture of informational openness or 'publicness', represented by the widespread use of various kinds of social media, and highlights the benefits of disclosing personal information, including sensitive information. Showing empathy for Facebook's exploitation of people's desire to connect with each other[5], and for Zuckerberg's perspective that Facebook enhances humanity[6], Jarvis points out the various benefits of publicness and states that publicness represents an ethic of sharing[7] and should be balanced with privacy as an ethic of knowing – the importance of which, according to Jervis, has been overstressed. However, to gain an appreciation of the benefits of informational transparency for individual social media users, we need to recognise the asymmetry in this transparency between individuals and organisations, which may have a harmful effect on a wide range of people: whereas the transparency of social media users is becoming very pronounced, the transparency of social media platform companies, with respect to the ways in which they handle personal information, remains low.

In the context of surveillance studies, Lyon [8] insists that organisations that engage in personal information processing should accept accountability for ensuring transparency, to safeguard the dignity of users, considering the disparity in power between individuals and organisations[8]. However, most social media platform companies do not satisfy this requirement for accountability with respect to their handling of personal information, and many people blindly accept pseudo-personalised services that they can enjoy in exchange for revealing their personal information online.

As an advocate of an open and honest culture, Facebook requires its users to register under their own names, provide their real information and not to provide any false personal information on the site [9] – and the majority of them do so – although it is also true that a significant number of users are pseudonymous or effectively anonymous.

---

[5] p. 2.

[6] p. 22.

[7] p. 110.

[8] p. 187.

2.2 Online Services that Undermine the Open and Honest Culture

Despite Facebook's and other social media platform companies' persistent effort to build an open and honest culture, online services which could undermine this effort, or which would abet clever users in embellishing themselves online, have been launched. For example, Klout – a website and mobile application launched in 2008 – measures its users' online social influence via 'Klout Score' through analysing their postings on social media sites including Facebook, Twitter and Instagram [10, 11]. This controversial service [12] may encourage its user to embellish him/herself online to get a higher Klout Score, if he/she expects the score relates to his/her interests or reputation. Reppify – a San Francisco based company – provides recruiters and human resource departments with a job applicant's 'job fit score' calculated based on his/her personal information put on social media sites [13]. If this service becomes widely used, those who want to find good jobs would substantively be forced to reveal their personal information online – or, they are almost non-existence as job seekers – and to control what they publish online so that they can receive high job fit scores. They are compelled to internalise expectations of their potential employers. Actually, it has become usual that employers or potential employers investigate a job seeker's social media postings to judge whether he/she is eligible to be employed or not [1].

VALU is a Japanese online service released in May 2017, which would undermine the open and honest online culture. On the VALU site, an individual user accredited by VALU Inc. can issue virtual stock called VALU for a commission of JPY 500. The upper limit of the initial offering price of a user's share is calculated in bitcoin based on his/her social media presence including the numbers of Facebook friends and Twitter followers. The total number of authorised shares of a user is decided also based on his/her social media presence, and the issuance of additional VALU is not permitted. Stockholders, or VALUERs, of a user's VALU can receive benefits such as exclusive information or novelty goods from him/her, and can freely transfer their stock to other users. This service would provide an incentive for potential VALU issuers to strategically embellish themselves online to enhance the economic value of their VALU as well as for VALUERs of VALU a user issues to support him/her not because they are fans of him/her but because they desire to get a gain in share dealings, although VALUERs are described as fans of issuers of their stocks in the term of use of VALU [14]. From the viewpoint of VALUERs, VALU issuers could be just devices whereby to make money and VALU issuer governance becomes a matter.

In September 2017, Metaps Inc., a Japanese data analytics company, launched their online time trading pit service called Timebank, which enable an individual to benefit from an expert consultation online [15]. The certification as an expert and his/her consultancy fees are determined based on his/her online influence measured by, for example, the number of Twitter followers. This service could motivate people to pretend online influencer. In fact, that number can easily be increased by buying fake followers [16].

Instagram faces a similar situation. This photo sharing application and service is popular, and Instagram influencers are now regarded as effective advertising tools – photos, for example, of their wearing dresses uploaded on Instagram are expected to promote the sale of those dresses. However, a US marketing company Mediakix [17] demonstrated that an Instagram influencer can be created through purchasing fake followers and engagement at small cost. This means that anyone can impersonate an Instagram influencer. In Japan, on the other hand, many Instagram users compete to post "Instagrammable" or "Insta-genic" photos on the photo sharing site to show their fulfilling real or offline life. Family Romance Inc. based in Tokyo launched its business to support these people. The company dispatches professional staff who play customers' parents, siblings, friends or acquaintances and are taken photos with customers for fabricating their fulfilling real life [18].

Such strategic online behaviour, i.e. of being dishonest on social media platforms, illustrates the existence of another form of online informational transparency asymmetry: the asymmetry between those who, consciously or unconsciously, commit to informational openness and those who consciously attempt to control their identity (or at least, their digital identity) in cyberspace. To enhance the strategic value of their digital identity, the latter group or clever people have an incentive to exploit the former group or innocents. Whereas clever people are motivated to consciously control what information about them is opened up online by them or others, they have an incentive to reveal innocents' information for their own benefit, and hope innocents to keep to behave honestly online in order to maintain their edge against innocents. At the same time, however, those who proactively engage in online self-commodification may be subject to the distortion of their digital identity or diremption between their identity and self-awareness.

Some questions that raise, therefore, are: "Is online openness and honesty a virtue in the current Internet environment?"; and "Is the pretence of openness and honesty online a wise act?"

3   Risks Entailed in an Open and Honest Culture

3.1   Diremption Between Self and Identity

Kierkegaard [19] describes the nature of one's self as "a relation that relates to itself" or "the relation's relating itself to itself in the relation"[9]. In the current eco-environment (or human habitat), which is composed not only of nature but also of "technological conjunction" [20], this can be interpreted in terms of one's self-image that is determined by relationships with others including creatures, organisations, communities and artefacts, and is actively and/or passively constructed – and/or deconstructed – in a repeating fashion according to these relations. Based on his studies of phenomenological psychopathology, Kimura [21, 22] points out that one's self-image is repeatedly generated, or emerges, through one's own mental processes, not those of others, that differentiate the self from non-self in an individualised, personal context. In this regard, Kimura states that the self is subjective, dynamic and relational, as Kierkegaard suggested, and temporal, as Heidegger [23] noted, and, from the viewpoint of time, one's current self or relation is developed according to on one's past self or relation, through differentiation processes.

---

[9] p. 13.

An individual's identity is also developed relationally and dynamically. According to Goffman [24], both the social and personal identity of an individual are part of other people's concerns and definitions of that individual[10]. The personal identity of an individual is composed of positive marks, or 'identity pegs', and

> "the unique combination of life history items that come to be attached to the individual with the help of these pegs form his identity. Personal identity, then, has to do with the assumption that the individual can be differentiated from all others, and that through this means of differentiation a single continuous record of social facts can be attached, entangled, [...] becoming then the sticky substance to which still other biographical facts can be attached. [...] personal identity can and does play a structured, routine, standardised role in social organisation just because of its one-of-a-kind quality"[11].

In the current socio-economic and technological climate, the fact that people use social media in their own ways to consciously or unconsciously construct relationships with others – through mutually revealing personal information about themselves and/or others at various levels of accuracy and detail – will inevitably affect the development of their identity. If an individual uses social media as a tool for writing his/her online biography according to his/her own preferences; if it is possible for him/her to select a specific audience for a specific post online at will; and if he/she can completely control what personal information is revealed to others, he/she does not need to worry about the negative impact of social media on the development of his/her identity. Of course, none of these conditions are fulfilled suggesting that, today, an individual's digital identity can take on a life of its own such that they may be compelled to play a part in creating their own distorted digital identity, as defined in certain contexts. Those who realise that they are compelled in this direction would suffer serious diremption between their identity, defined in a heteronomous fashion, and self; as a result, they would also suffer dysfunction with respect to the mental processes involved in generation of the self.

3.2 Strategic Creation of a Digital Identity: Is It Really Advantageous?

For clever Internet users, social media may seem to be an expedient tool for subtle self-promotion. Such users understand the nature of social media, for example that profile information uploaded to social media websites is propagated much more widely than might be expected, and that they have a wider audience on social media platforms than could ever be imagined before; therefore, these individuals carefully evaluate the target audience that their online postings reach. They craft articles and regularly post them on social media sites at the right moment to convince their target audience that they are admirable and acceptable people. To do this, these users need cognisance of the decoding capacity of their audience [24][12]. Also, they never forget to check their online friends' and acquaintances' postings, to ascertain which of these postings could aid their own self-promotion, as well as those that are obstacles to it, on a regular basis.

---

[10] p. 105.

[11] p. 57.

[12] p. 51.

If they identify any of the latter type of postings, they endeavour to erase them as quickly as possible. Those who desire to strategically control their digital identity should give their full attention to the management of potentially stigmatising information pertaining to themselves that others can disclose, or pass around online [24][13], although such management is extremely difficult in the current Internet environment. In addition, they should attempt to encourage others to post positive things about them online and discourage the posting of negative things.

Do these activities really enrich their lives? Are these clever people truly wise and prudent? In a certain sense, they are controlled by the architecture of social media. Although, for example, they can successfully embellish their digital identity and, as a result, obtain good jobs, this does not mean their lives are successful; on the contrary, they would be forced to continue to wear the mask created by their clever online activities. When the gap between the virtual identity created by their strategic social media use and actual identity is recognised by others in real space, they would suffer stigma, as Goffman [24] suggests[14].

However, those users whose activities on social media sites are manipulated openly and covertly by the clever people are exploited by them and alienated, in many cases unconsciously. It is easy to call such exploited users unwise. However, considering that the majority of Internet users are non-technical users, and that the technological architecture of social media is reviewed and upgraded on a regular basis, effective measures to make them more prudent should be adopted urgently.

4 Towards a Richer and More Tolerant Information Society

Under the current circumstances, where the boundary between real space and cyberspace is being dissolved, many people have experienced the phenomenon of 'disappearing bodies' [25], and identity is composed of digital and real space components. The two types of informational transparency asymmetry, between individuals and organisations and between honest people and clever people, suggest that we may now live in a world where open and honest people can only make fools of themselves. The Internet economy and digital network society have seemingly rendered honesty as no longer a virtue. In an informationally transparent society, where it is very hard for anyone to prevent another from revealing and accessing his/her personal information, are the wise people those who are adept in crafting or counterfeiting their digital identity to their own advantage without anyone knowing? As discussed above, the answer is no.

A paradoxical situation now exists in which various kinds of online services for individual users, which encourage openness with respect to their own and others' personal information, provide clever users with an incentive to strategically hold back and/or counterfeit their personal information, which has in turn made it difficult for many people to control their identity in a favourable manner. Froomkin [26] suggested

---

[13] p. 42.

[14] p. 2.

that "the most effective way of controlling information about oneself is not to share it" and "the easiest way to control databases is [...] to keep information to oneself"[15]. However, those who practice such behaviour would suffer from social exclusion [27] and would be at an economic disadvantage. Additionally, the counterfeiting of personal information revealed online can distort the digital identity of the subject of the information, and this distortion may in turn cause serious distortion of his/her identity in real space, affecting quality of life for a lengthy period, because any information posted on the Internet may remain accessible indefinitely and stigmatising information tends to spread rapidly and widely due to rampant online vigilantism.

Thus, as Rachels [7] pointed out, it is still important for us to safeguard our ability to autonomously construct relationships with different people through selectively providing them with personal information, which contradicts Mark Zuckerberg's belief. To do so, while maintaining quality of life at a satisfactory level in the present, we need to use the various services available on the Internet, including social media, very prudently. To ensure prudence, in addition to the full accountability of service providers regarding the transparency of their personal information handling, it is necessary for us to establish the 'right to be translucent', which relates to our capacity to control the selective disclosure of our personal information and therefore can be executed on others' activities regarding the revealing of our personal information. Both complete informational transparency and informational opaqueness would be harmful to individuals as well as to society; the 'right to be translucent' guarantees people the ability to autonomously set the level of informational translucence in different contexts. It is noteworthy that this right never justifies clever people's embellishing themselves and exploiting others online to make themselves look good. This right encourages people to prudently maintain their honesty online.

We also need to develop the notion of the 'co-ownership of digital objects' so that we can, to a certain extent, claim ownership of digital objects stored in organisational databases or owned by other individuals that contain our personal information (e.g. digital photos of us taken by others using their own cameras). The right to be translucent and to take co-ownership of digital objects should be implemented within the architecture of Internet services, including social media. Considering that most Internet users do not read the privacy policies that online businesses almost always post on their websites [28–30], such implementation is extremely important.

Establishing a system of a 'privacy premium' would be one of the most useful ways of striking a balance between people favourably controlling their identity and maintaining the prosperity of the digital economy. The majority of existing Internet businesses that provide charge-free services force their customers to 'purchase' the services by providing personal information, or to otherwise decide against using them. Under that system, people are required to choose whether to partake of a commercial service by paying with personal information or with money.

Moreover, as suggested in the previous section, an effective education system to cultivate prudent Internet use should be established as a matter of urgency. Instead of instilling existing rules and norms for Internet usage, a wide range of non-technical

---

[15] p. 1464.

users have to be encouraged to understand important human values such as individual dignity, freedom and autonomy as well as the core values underpinning ICT professionalism, including an ethical code of conduct for ICT professionals, to cultivate their prudence, because the online environment is always changing.

5 Conclusions

In the current paradoxical Internet environment, in which various kinds of online services encourage individual users to share the personal information of themselves and others honestly, and which provides clever users with an incentive to strategically hold back and/or counterfeit their personal information, many people experience difficulties maintaining favourable control of their identities. Consequently, social issues, such as the spread of online behaviour that treats others as only a means, the distortion of the digital identities of a wide range of people, and human alienation, will occur. To address such issues, it is essential to establish (a) the right to be translucent, (b) the notion of co-ownership of digital objects, (c) a system for a privacy premium, (d) an effective education system to cultivate prudent non-technical Internet users, and (e) the implementation of important human values into the system architecture of Internet services.

References

1. Lucas, S.: Job hunting? Take a close look at your Facebook page. MoneyWatch (2014). https://www.cbsnews.com/news/job-hunting-take-a-close-look-at-your-facebook-page/. Accessed 6 Jan 2018
2. boyd, d., Hargittai, E.: Facebook privacy settings: Who cares?. First Monday **15**(8) (2010). http://firstmonday.org/ojs/index.php/fm/article/view/3086/2589. Accessed 6 Jan 2018
3. Murata, K., Orito, Y.: The paradox of openness: is an honest person rewarded? In: Proceedings of CEPE 2013, pp. 221–231 (2013)
4. Johnson, K.: Facebook gives up on making the world more open and connected, now wants to bring the world closer together. VentureBeat (2017). https://venturebeat.com/2017/06/22/facebook-gives-up-on-making-the-world-more-open-and-connected-now-wants-to-bring-the-world-closer-together/. Accessed 6 Jan 2018
5. Kirkpatrick, D.: The Facebook Effect: The Real Inside Story of Mark Zuckerberg and the World's Fastest-Growing Company. Virgin Books, London (2011)
6. Jarvis, J.: Public Parts: How Sharing in the Digital Age Improves the Way We Work and Live. Simon & Schuster, New York (2011)
7. Rachels, J.: Why privacy is important. Philos. Public Aff. **4**(4), 323–333 (1975)
8. Lyon, D.: Surveillance Studies: An Overview. Polity Press, Malden (2007)
9. Facebook statement of rights and responsibilities. https://www.facebook.com/legal/terms. Accessed 6 Jan 2018
10. Parr, B.: Klout now measures your influence on Facebook. MashableAsia (2010). http://mashable.com/2010/10/14/facebook-klout/#OXKYBVbB0GqW. Accessed 6 Jan 2018
11. Ha, A.: Klout users can now add Bing to their account and include Instagram in their score. TechCrunch (2013). https://techcrunch.com/2013/03/28/klout-instagram-bing/. Accessed 6 Jan 2018

12. Miller, R.J.: Delete your Klout profile now!. SocialMediaToday (2011). http://www.socialmediatoday.com/content/delete-your-klout-profile-now. Accessed 6 Jan 2018
13. Garling, C.: Didn't get that new job? You need a better Facebook score. Wired (2011). https://www.wired.com/2011/11/reppify-identified-facebook-linkedin. Accessed 6 Jan 2018
14. VALU terms of use. https://valu.is/terms. Accessed 6 Jan 2018
15. Timebank website. https://timebank.jp/. Accessed 16 Apr 2018. (in Japanese)
16. Nihon Keizai Shimbun: Widespread trade of "Like!". Nihon Keizai Shimbun (2018). https://www.nikkei.com/article/DGXMZO29361450T10C18A4CC1000/. Accessed 16 Apr 2018. (in Japanese)
17. Meidakix: Are fake Instagram influencers deceiving brands? Mediakix (2017). http://mediakix.com/2017/08/fake-instagram-influencers-followers-bots-study/. Accessed 6 Jan 2018
18. Family Romance. http://family-romance.com/service/realappeal.html. Accessed 6 Jan 2018. (in Japanese)
19. Kierkegaard, S.: The Sickness Unto Death: A Christian Psychological Exposition for Upbuilding and Awakening. Princeton University Press, Princeton (1980). (Edited and translated by Hong, H.V., Hong, E.H.)
20. Imamichi, T.: Eco-ethica. Kodansha, Tokyo (1990). (in Japanese)
21. Kimura, B.: Time and the Self. Chuokoron-Shinsha, Tokyo (1982). (in Japanese)
22. Kimura, B.: The Self as Relations. Misuzu Shobo, Tokyo (2005). (in Japanese)
23. Heidegger, M.: Being and Time. Harper & Row, New York (1962). (Translated by Macquarrie, J., Robinson, E.)
24. Goffman, E.: Stigma: Notes on the Management of Spoiled Identity. Simon & Schuster, New York (1963)
25. Lyon, D.: Surveillance Society: Monitoring Everyday Life. Open University Press, Buckingham (2001)
26. Froomkin, A.M.: The death of privacy? Stanford Law Rev. 52(5), 1461–1543 (2000)
27. Allmer, T.: A critical contribution to theoretical foundations of privacy studies. J. Inf. Commun. Ethics Soc. 9(2), 83–101 (2011)
28. Acquisti, A., Gross, R.: Imagined communities: awareness, information sharing, and privacy on the Facebook. In: Danezis, G., Golle, P. (eds.) PET 2006. LNCS, vol. 4258, pp. 36–58. Springer, Heidelberg (2006). https://doi.org/10.1007/11957454_3
29. Murata, K., Orito, Y., Fukuta, Y.: Social attitudes of young people in Japan towards online privacy. J. Law Inf. Sci. 23(1), 137–157 (2014)
30. Orito, Y., Fukuta, Y., Murata, K.: I will continue to use this nonetheless: social media survive users' privacy concerns. Int. J. Virtual Worlds Hum. Comput. Interact. 2, 92–107 (2014)

Philosophy as the Road to Good ICT

Iordanis Kavathatzopoulos$^{(\boxtimes)}$ ⓘ and Ryoko Asai$^{(\boxtimes)}$ ⓘ

Uppsala University, Uppsala, Sweden
{iordanis,ryoko.asai}@it.uu.se

Abstract. Handling satisfactorily ICT ethics issues in the design as well as in the use of systems, demands continuous adjustment to relevant values. In privacy, robotics and sustainability, this can be achieved through the development of personal thinking skills and the establishment and running of suitable group processes. In ethical decision making it is important to make a distinction between thinking as a process, and value-content as the result of this process. By focusing on the process, i.e. philosophizing, the philosophical method of deliberative thinking, we can construct and apply tools to support ethical decision making during the development and the use of ICT systems.

Keywords: Ethics · ICT · Method · Moral · Philosophizing · Privacy
Robots · Sustainability · Tools

1 Introduction

ICT affects our lives in an almost total way. Artificial intelligence and autonomous agents are both welcome and scaring. Our privacy is threatened while ICT gives us access to the information we need about other people. New technology may help us save the environment but at the same time it consumes huge amounts of energy and valuable minerals.

Although urgent, it is very difficult or impossible to find optimal solutions to the above issues. Conflicting interests and values decide what has to be done; not only between different groups but also inside the same person standing in front of a choice about ICT. Every thinkable answer contains both risks and possibilities. In our effort to find solutions we have always to negotiate and make compromises. Issues of robots, privacy and environment are difficult and contradicting, and they cannot be solved by making laws or rules based on wishful thinking about a perfect world. Conflicting conditions force us to choose different pathways to solutions than focusing on answers. Working with processes like regulating and shaping the process of finding definitions and answers seems to be the right approach. In that case, the focus is on tools, methods and skills to run a process of continuous creation and revision.

A dialectic process is necessary in ICT issues in order to identify significant interests and values, and to formulate principles and policies. Handling robot, environment and privacy issues, and working for secure ICT systems demand continuous adjustment to relevant values as well as the necessary personal skills and suitable group processes. Focusing on the method and making sure that the right way of proceeding has been adopted is the way to get satisfactory answers to the problems of ICT security

D. Kreps et al. (Eds.): HCC13 2018, IFIP AICT 537, pp. 293–298, 2018.
https://doi.org/10.1007/978-3-319-99605-9_22

and privacy. The philosophical method of deliberative thinking, i.e. philosophizing, has to be the ground on which to build such methods and tools.

2   Autonomous Agents and Robots

The development of so called independent systems and robots that are capable of processing information and acting independently of their human operators, has been accelerated as well as the hopes, and the fears, of the impact of those artifacts on environment, market, society, and human life generally. Many ethical issues are raised because of these systems being today, or in the future, capable of independent decision making and acting. Will these IT systems or robots decide and act in the right way, or will they cause harm?

In situations where humans have difficulties perceiving and processing information, or making decisions and implementing actions, because of the quantity, variation and complexity of information, independent agents can be of great help to achieve goals and obtain optimal solutions to problems. One example of this is financial transactions where the speed and volume of information makes it impossible for human decision makers to take the right measures, for example in the case of an economic crisis. Another example is dangerous and risky situations, like natural disasters or battles in war, where the use of drones and military robots may help to avoid soldier injuries and deaths. A third example comes from human social and emotional needs, for example in elderly care where robots may play an important role providing necessary care as well as to be a companion to lonely elderly people.

It is clear that such ICT systems have to make decisions and act to achieve the goals for which they had been built in the first place. Will they make the right decisions and act in a proper way? Can we guarantee this by designing them in a suitable way? But if it is possible, do we really want such machines given the fact that their main advantage is their increasing independence and autonomy, and hence we do not want to constrain them too much?

There are many questions around this, most of which converge on the issue of moral or ethical decision making. The definition of what we mean by ethical or moral decision making or ethical/moral agency is a very much significant precondition for the design of proper ICT decision systems. Given that we have a clear definition we will be able to judge whether an ICT system is, (1) capable of making ethical decisions, and (2) able to make these decisions independently and autonomously.

3   Privacy

Focus on the process of thinking and decision making is also valid regarding the issue of privacy. Privacy appears to be a very important issue today when ICT permeates more and more aspects of our life. Mainly this is understood as a risk of breaching the privacy of persons, and possibly the privacy of groups, organizations, corporations and states.

If we make an effort to describe the nature of privacy we can easily and rather fast come to the conclusion that privacy is not only something that has to be protected. Although this is important, underlined by both lines of definitions, it seems that privacy sometimes has to be diminished or intervened in order to satisfy important interests and values (see for example Tavani [10]). One is to create a bond to another person, group or organization. To achieve this one has to give access to private information, or even to give up a part or all limitations toward this special person or organization. It is a matter of trust between each other.

The other situation, which is the most common one, is that a person, group or organization, which we may call a separate entity, has always another important interest added to the interest of protecting its own privacy: To breach, diminish or intervene the privacy of any other entity that is a prospective or actual partner in any sense. It is very important for any entity to acquire access to the information about any other entity that is of some interest. The reason for that is the need for correct information. Every separate entity, with its privacy protected, releases only the information it wants the others to have. By that it wants to affect the other's decision making toward a preferred direction. On the other hand, the other entity's interest is to make the right decision and to achieve it access to correct information is a necessary condition. A right decision cannot be based solely on information controlled and supplied by the other entity.

If we now go back to the ways of approaching the issue of privacy, and look upon them through the glasses of our observations of its nature we may have good arguments to maintain that a process-focused approach is more helpful and fruitful. Given the controversial nature of privacy (protect it and breach it at the same time) and the clashes arising constantly between all entities in a social interaction, the focus cannot be on normative solutions which even if they work are always limited to a certain situation, but on the ways skills, methods and tools we use in order to create, revise and apply policies, guidelines, rules and principles to manage the issues of privacy.

4 Environment and Sustainability

ICT has undoubtedly a heavy impact on environment. It may cause large environmental catastrophes or it may contribute positively to the protection of the environment. For example, building computer hardware demands a great amount of many different and special resources, running the systems consumes increasing amounts of energy, and disposing of computers pollutes the environment.

Raw materials used in manufacturing computer hardware are very rare in nature and they can only be found on certain limited places on earth. Besides the risk of them drying up sooner rather than later, there is also a political risk. Production of necessary computer parts is conditional on the political will of foreign governments or on the actions of opposition groups or guerillas. If they hinder or stop mining and transportation of rare earths, production of computer hardware will suffer. Another sustainability risk, related to the above political risk, may also appear. It is about work environment conditions. Factories manufacturing computer hardware are established in countries where worker rights are not upheld properly and work environment is not protected enough. Producing computers in this way implies serious sustainability risks. Sooner or later there will be conflicts and protests will take place, or there will be radical restructures and relocations of production, leading to supply shortages of necessary hardware parts.

Once the hardware has been assembled to produce a whole computer machine and the software installed, the system will start to be used. But its use demands plenty of energy. And this energy has to be produced in some way, which in itself may be dangerous for the environment if it is of the sort called "dirty energy", i.e. use of fossil materials with a high content of carbon dioxide and pollutants. More, the need for energy to power the running of ICT systems is increasing, implying that more energy has to be produced in the future. It is not difficult to see that a big risk pertaining to the sustainability of ICT use emerges. But alongside the risk there is a possibility. The hope that ICT can be used as a tool to achieve reduced levels of energy consumption, for example, by allowing and supporting energy saving actions like teleconferencing or by using the power of ICT to calculate and coordinate better ways of organizing energy use or designing energy-saving technology. However, in the case of cloud computing and in spite of many optimistic plans and hopes, because of synergies of concentrating data storage and treatment, we see a clear increase in energy consumption.

Computers do not live forever. After some time they break down or become obsolete and they are replaced by new ones. Furthermore, the accelerating pace of technology development results in an accelerating pace of computer replacement. Old computers become waste and they need to be taken care of. This is in itself a big challenge causing significant environmental and human health concerns. However, the way this is handled causes more concern. Often computer waste is sent to developing countries which lack regulation, experience, resources, or the political will to take care of computer waste in a professional way. All this creates a really nasty situation for the environment and the people who handle this waste.

There is no generally accepted truth about issues of ICT, environment and sustainability. In general terms most of us do agree on what should be done to sustain our environment or our way of life. But when we move closer to concrete projects like road construction, location of production plants and the like, conflicting opinions or dilemmas take over. Often most of the arguments are based on very good sustainability grounds although they are not compatible with each other. Eventually we will stand in front of the same problem as the one in ICT, i.e., to find a solution that works with the concrete project at hand and which may differ to the solution belonging to another project. All of this points to the significance of the method or of the process involved in finding answers and solutions.

5   The Power of Philosophy

The distinction between content and process is important in the effort to define ethical or moral decision making. In common sense, ethics and morals are dependent on the concrete decision or the action itself. Understanding a decision or an action being ethical/moral or unethical/immoral is based mainly on a judgment of its normative qualities. The focus on values and their normative aspects is the basis of the common sense definition of ethics.

Despite its dominance, this way of thinking causes some difficulties. We may note that bad or good things follow not only from the decisions of people but also from natural phenomena. Usually sunny weather is considered a good thing, while rainy weather is not. Of course this is not perceived as something related to morality. But why not? What is the difference between humans and nature acting in certain ways? The answer is obvious: Option, choice. Although common sense does realize that, people's attachment to the normative aspects is so strong that it is not possible for them to accept that ethics is an issue of choice and option. If there is no choice, or ability of making a choice, then there is no issue of ethics.

Now if ethics is connected to choice then the interesting aspect is how the choice is made, or not made; whether it is made in a bad or in a good way. The focus here is on how, not on what; on the process not on the content or the answer. Indeed, regarding the effort to make the right decision, philosophy and psychology point to the significance of focusing on the process of ethical decision making rather on the normative content of the decision.

Starting from one of the most important contributions, the Socratic dialog, we see that *aporía* is the goal rather than the achievement of a solution to the problem investigated. Reaching a state of no knowledge, that is, throwing aside false ideas, opens up for the right solution. The issue here for the philosopher is not to provide a ready answer but to help the other person in the dialog to think in the right way. It is about a skill [6]. Ability to think in the right way is not easy and apparently has been supposed to be the privilege of the few able ones [7–9]. For that, certain skills are necessary, such as Aristoteles's *phrónesis* [2]. When humans are free from false illusions and have the necessary skills they can use the right method to think in order to be able to find the right solution to their moral problems [1]. This is the autonomous way of thinking according to Kant [3].

This philosophical position has been applied in psychological research on ethical decision making. Focusing on the process of ethical decision making psychological research has shown that people use different ways to handle moral problems. According to Piaget [5] and Kohlberg [4], when people are confronted with moral problems they think in a way which can be described as a position on the heteronomy-autonomy dimension. ICT systems have many advantages that can be used to stimulate autonomous thinking during a process of ethical decision making, for example in designing systems adapted to important values.

References

1. Arendt, H.: Responsibility and Judgement. Shocken, New York (2003)
2. Aristoteles: Nicomachean Ethics. Papyros, Athens (1975)
3. Kant, I.: Grundläggning av sedernas metafysik, trans. Daidalos, Stockholm (2006)
4. Kohlberg, L.: The Just Community: Approach to moral education in theory and practice. In: Berkowitz, M., Oser, F. (eds.) Moral Education: Theory and Application, pp. 27–87. Lawrence Erlbaum Associates, Hillsdale (1985)

5. Piaget, J.: The Moral Judgment of the Child. Routledge and Kegan Paul, London (1932)
6. Platon.: Protagoras. I. Zacharopoulos, Athens (1981a)
7. Platon.: Theaitetos. I. Zacharopoulos, Athens (1981b)
8. Platon.: Apologia. Sokratoys. Kaktos, Athens (1982)
9. Platon.: Politeia. Kaktos, Athens (1992)
10. Tavani, H.T.: Philosophical theories of privacy: implications for an adequate online privacy policy. Metaphilosophy **38**, 1–22 (2007)

Discussing Ethical Impacts in Research and Innovation: The Ethics Canvas

Wessel Reijers[1]([✉]), Kevin Koidl[2], David Lewis[2],
Harshvardhan J. Pandit[2], and Bert Gordijn[3]

[1] ADAPT Centre, School of Computing, Dublin City University, Dublin, Ireland
wreijers@adaptcentre.ie
[2] ADAPT Centre, School of Computer Science and Statistics, Trinity College
Dublin, Dublin, Ireland
{kevin.koidl,dave.lewis,harshvardhan.pandit}
@adaptcentre.ie
[3] Institute of Ethics, Dublin City University, Dublin, Ireland
bert.gordijn@dcu.ie

Abstract. Technologies are increasingly intertwined with people's daily lives. Consequently, there is an increasing need to consider the ethical impacts that research and innovation (R&I) processes, both in commercial and non-commercial contexts, bring about. However, current methods that offer tools for practicing ethics in R&I inadequately allow for non-ethicists such as engineers and computer scientists to practise ethics in a way that fits the character of their work. As a response, we propose a tool for identifying ethical impacts of R&I that is inspired by a method for the generation of business models, the Business Model Canvas. This tool, the Ethics Canvas, enables researchers to engage with the ethical impacts of their R&I activities in a collaborative manner by discussing different building blocks that together constitute a comprehensive ethical interpretation of a technology. To assess the perceived usefulness of the Ethics Canvas, a classroom experiment was conducted, followed-up by a questionnaire. The results suggest that the Ethics Canvas (1) is perceived as useful for identifying relevant stakeholders and potential ethical impacts and (2) potentially triggers reconsiderations of technology designs or business models.

Keywords: Ethics Canvas · Applied ethics
Responsible research and innovation · Practising ethics

1 Introduction

Due to the increasing pervasiveness of technologies in people's everyday lives (e.g. social media, artificial intelligence, genomics, communication and transportation technologies), it becomes increasingly important to reflect on the ethical impacts of research and innovation (R&I) processes and their outcomes. In academic R&I settings, ethical considerations are typically mediated by professional codes of conduct and more or less bureaucratic "ethics clearance" procedures. In commercial R&I settings, ethical considerations are far less systemised and are often predominantly taken into

D. Kreps et al. (Eds.): HCC13 2018, IFIP AICT 537, pp. 299–313, 2018.
https://doi.org/10.1007/978-3-319-99605-9_23

account through legal requirements (e.g. in the general data protection regulation). Both in and outside academia R&I, practices show considerable shortcomings because they are usually reactive, not suitable for anticipating potential ethical impacts and not in accordance with the notion of ethics as a reflective activity. Consequently, there is a need for developing new methods and tools to guide the practice of ethics in R&I processes, which has led to a burgeoning literature on practising ethics in R&I.

This paper proposes a novel tool for discussing ethical impacts in the process of R&I. We conceptualise the R&I process as consisting of four distinct stages: (1) the formation of (scientific) knowledge and concepts that can be operationalized for technological applications, (2) the translation of this knowledge into a technology design, (3) the prototyping and testing of this design and (4) the introduction of the R&I outcomes into society [1]. Each of these stages of the R&I process can bring about distinct ethical impacts. However, existing methods that offer tools for practicing ethics in R&I do not adequately facilitate the discussion of these impacts amongst R&I practitioners[1]. Below, we identify an important shortcoming in existing methods for practicing ethics in R&I. In order to improve the way ethics is currently dealt with in R&I processes we then propose a novel tool that enables R&I practitioners to engage with the ethical impacts of their R&I activities.

To achieve this, we searched for an extensively adopted tool that facilitates accessible and clear processes of discussion and reflection amongst non-experts. Consequently, we transformed a business-modelling tool that is widely used in business development practices, the Business Model Canvas (BMC) [2], into the "Ethics Canvas". The Ethics Canvas is a collaborative brainstorming tool that has two distinct aims: (1) to have R&I practitioners come up with and discuss possible ethical impacts of the technologies they develop, and (2) to have R&I practitioners consider pivots in their technology design or business model to avoid or mitigate the negative ethical impacts. The overall aim of this tool is to foster ethically informed technology design by improving the engagement of R&I practitioners with the ethical impacts of their R&I activities. We assessed the perceived usefulness of the Ethics Canvas by putting it into practice in a classroom situation of business & IT students who were developing novel technological applications. A follow-up questionnaire that the students filled in provided some initial suggestions with regards to the usefulness of the Ethics Canvas for practising ethics in R&I.[2]

In what follows, we first shortly discuss existing methods that offer tools for practicing ethics in R&I and discuss an important shortcoming of these methods. Second, we discuss methods used to create business models that can offer tools for overcome this shortcoming. Third, we propose the design of the Ethics Canvas that is inspired by the Business Model Canvas approach in business modelling research. Fourth, we explore the merits of the Ethics Canvas in a practical setting by evaluating the outcomes of a questionnaire that students filled in after having engaged in the Ethics Canvas exercise that related to a technological application they were working on.

---

[1] With "practicing ethics" we refer to any way of doing ethics R&I processes in the broadest sense.

[2] This study has been approved by the Trinity College Dublin Research Ethics Committee.

2 Challenges for Practicing Ethics in R&I

In recent years, there has been a strong increase in discussions about responsible R&I [3], responsible technology design [4] and responsible approaches to instructional technology research [5]. This tendency is due to growing concerns about ethical impacts that technological innovations can have on our society, intensifying public debate and mounting concerns about unsustainable technological developments (pollution, climate change, etc.). Policy makers reinforce the move towards responsible R&I, for instance by incorporating ethics assessment practices in funding mechanisms, as is the case in the framework programmes of the European Union [3]. According to Stilgoe et al. [6], literature on responsible research and innovation generally focuses on four dimensions of the assessment of R&I practices: (1) the anticipation of future societal impacts of technology design, (2) reflection on the values that are implied in technology design, (3) inclusion of stakeholders in the design process and (4) responsiveness of technology design to societal changes. Ethical impacts of technologies form an important consideration in this context of responsible research and innovation, since all of these four dimensions consider aspects of human-technology interactions or relations that have a strong normative significance.

Resonating with at least the first three dimensions of responsible R&I, methods for practising ethics in R&I are (1) dealing with uncertainty of technological change, such as anticipatory technology ethics [7], (2) enabling, organising and ensuring ethical technology design, such as ethical impact assessment [8] (3) identifying, analysing and resolving ethical impacts, such as the ethical matrix [9] and (4) enabling, organising and ensuring appropriate stakeholder participation, such as value sensitive design [10, 11]. Not each method for practising ethics falls neatly into one of these categories of use, but these categories nonetheless provide a useful overview of the core aspects of practising ethics in R&I that should be taken into account. In this paper, we will restrict our investigations predominantly to the aspect of enabling, organising and ensuring technology design.

One critical shortcoming of current methods is that they insufficiently manage to offer tools to integrate ethics in the day-to-day work of R&I practitioners [11]. Many of the methods for practising ethics in R&I offer tools that are targeted at ethicists and that presuppose special ethics expertise, which causes difficulties for R&I practitioners in adopting those tools in their everyday activities. As a result, for instance, an R&I practitioner cannot simply engage in value sensitive design by following the proposed steps in the respective literature. Similarly, an ethical impact assessment needs the involvement of people that manage the assessment process and offers little grounds for R&I practitioners to assess their day-to-day work.

Yet, the engagement of R&I practitioners in practising ethics is crucial for achieving ethical technology design. In the overall process of practising ethics, Brey [12] distinguishes a disclosure level, at which ethical impacts are explored and identified, a theoretical level, at which theoretical frameworks are developed and employed to evaluate these impacts and the application level, at which moral deliberation takes place as the basis for overcoming the negative ethical impacts in the R&I process. According to Brey, the disclosure level is aimed at revealing, or rather identifying the potential ethical impacts of a technological application. He accentuates the role of R&I practitioners in dealing with ethics in R&I at this level, arguing that they play a vital role in disclosing ethical issues of emerging technologies and in making sure that technology design choices are informed by considerations of these ethical issues [12]. Brey argues that researchers, designers and innovators are important actors at the disclosure level, because they have an understanding of the technology that many ethicists and policy-makers lack. Hence, we have good reasons to look for a novel tool that overcomes the shortcomings of tools offered by existing methods and facilitates engagement of R&I practitioners with ethics in their day-to-day work[3].

Resulting from the foregoing considerations, we propose two requirements that such a tool should satisfy. First, it should be accessible to non-ethicists, or people without a substantial background in ethics. This argument is reinforced by the Council for Big Data, Ethics and Society, which argues that ethics engagement should happen in "hybrid spaces" in which people with different roles in the R&I process collaborate [14]. Second, it should enable people with different roles and backgrounds to work together in identifying ethical impacts. The different interpretations people have of potential ethical impacts of technologies can be brought to the table by means of a collaborative process in which multiple people involved in an R&I process express their expectations of potential ethical impacts in the form of narratives (i.e. for this group of stakeholders, such-and-such feature of our technology can have such-and-such ethical implications). As we will see later, this requirement fits with theories in Science and Technology Studies (STS) that explain how our understanding of technologies results from an interaction between different interpretations of technologies for different people [15].

In line with these two requirements, we have to make sure that the threshold for using our tool should be low and that it should be possible to use it without thorough background knowledge of ethical theories or conceptual discussions of values. Additionally, the tool should facilitate an open-ended process of interpretation in a collaborative fashion to identify potential ethical impacts of an R&I process and its outcomes. At the moment, methods in the fields of applied ethics and ethics of technology offer no tools that adequately fulfil these two requirements. For this reason, we decided to look at fields that are unrelated to academic ethics, but that do focus on creating low-entry tools for collaborative processes of discussion and interpretation; focusing on a specific use case. This brought us to the field of business development, and notably the field of business model development.

3 Turn to the Business Model Canvas

In the field of business model development, some discussions of responsible research and innovation have already emerged. For instance, Henriksen et al. discuss business models that promote sustainable ways of production, or "green business model

---

[3] For our current purposes and the scope of this paper it is not feasible to propose a full-fledged method. However, the Ethics Canvas tool fits with a newly developed method that introduces a narrative approach in ethics of technology [13].

innovation" [16]. In a similar vein, Bocken et al. explain how a re-definition of the notion of "value" in business models can help rendering businesses more sustainable, for instance by focusing on the entire supply-chain [17]. However, these approaches primarily focus on the design of the business case (in terms of resources, customers, etc.) and not on technologies that are developed in R&I processes. To change this focus, we will investigate how we can transform existing business model development approaches to align them with our aim of constructing a tool for disclosing the ethical impacts in R&I processes in which technologies play a crucial role.

Before we do so, however, we have to address the question of to what extent tools in business model development methods incorporate the two requirements we introduced in the previous section: (1) engaging non-ethicists with the disclosure of ethical impacts and (2) facilitating this as a collaborative process of interpretation. We can observe how business models are defined in the literature. As pointed out by Zott et al. [18], a business model can be understood as an "architecture", a "heuristic logic", a "concise representation" and also a collection of "stories", aimed at describing and explaining how a particular enterprise functions or operates. A spectrum of business models can be identified, with on the one hand business models that are meant to offer a strict representation of both internal and external processes of an existing corporation, and on the other hand models that use stories to give an account of these processes – possibly of businesses that do not already exist (i.e. a model for a start-up). The latter type of business modelling approaches is particularly interesting for our purposes, since it appears to focus on an understanding of business processes in terms of narratives that are constructed through social interaction.

Lucassen et al. [19] use two indicators that capture the two aspects of the above-mentioned spectrum (between models that are strictly representational and those that are the result of people's interpretations) to review and compare different visual business modelling approaches. They use the notion of "capturing" to indicate to what extent a business modelling method accurately represents a business process, and the notion of "communicating" to indicate to what extent a business-modelling tool is accessible and generates understandable outcomes. They argue that the so-called Business Model Canvas (BMC) is most successful with regards to the indicator of "communicating", compared to two other established models[4] "because it effectively models explicit information of both tangible and intangible aspects of a business and communicates this information in a highly accessible manner to parties unfamiliar with the modelling technique" [19]. As Kuparinen argues, the BMC can be classified as a "narrative business model" [20], because it enables "participant narratives" [21]. The BMC provides a visual-linguistic tool (see Fig. 1) that can be used in a collaborative process in which participants generate ideas by offering and discussing certain narratives that are related to the thematic boxes displayed on the canvas.

Thus, we argue that of the existing business modelling approaches, the BMC fulfils the two requirements we formulated. First, as Lucassen et al. [19] argue, it is highly accessible and understandable to people without specific knowledge of the field. If the

---

[4] The two traditional business model approaches that the business model canvas was compared with are the "software ecosystem model" approach and the "board of innovation" approach [19].

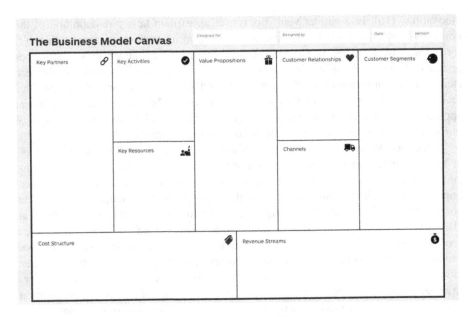

Fig. 1. The BMC [2].

structure of the BMC can be incorporated in a tool for disclosing ethical issues, it would be an answer to Brey's [12] concern regarding the disclosure level for it allows researchers to engage with ethical reflection in an accessible manner without them having to have thorough knowledge of the field of applied ethics. Second, since the BMC relies on the collaborative generation of participant narratives, it seems to satisfy the second demand to a large extent. It enables participants to engage in a collaborative process of interpreting and discussing business processes. Considering the foregoing arguments, turning towards the BMC to find a novel tool for disclosing ethical impacts in R&I processes is justified. However, we need to transform the BMC, which is clearly focused on discussing business processes and has little to do with ethics, into a tool that can be used in the context of practicing ethics in R&I.

4   Designing the Ethics Canvas

To explain the process of designing the Ethics Canvas, we first briefly describe the BMC and discuss its aims and the way in which it is used in a collaborative setting. The BMC was developed by business theorists Osterwalder and Pigneur [2] as a visual-textual plane that is divided up into nine "building blocks" through which a business model can be described in a holistic manner. It is argued that a business model can be defined as a model that "describes the rationale of how an organisation creates, delivers, and captures value" [2], and that this definition can be captured by participants discussing all the "building blocks" of a business model. By engaging in a collaborative discussion about the different building blocks of a business model, such as 'key partners', 'channels' and 'revenue streams', participants working with the BMC are able to arrive at a comprehensive understanding of the way in which their organisation is supposed to create, deliver and capture value.

In its original form, the BMC is printed on paper and used as the core instrument for a collaborative workshop. In addition to the canvas, Osterwalder and Pigneur provide for a handbook that provides guidance for the workshop participants in understanding the meaning of the different building blocks and presents use-cases of the canvas as well as techniques for designing better business models. The printed canvas is used as the focal point of a collaborative workshop, with participants discussing and writing down ideas for each of the building blocks. Next to the original BMC, online applications have been developed that offer digital versions[5] of the canvas, through which teams of different sizes can create multiple business models and save them on their accounts. The BMC has experienced widespread adoption in the business modelling of start-ups. Its ease of use in capturing and communication a business model lends itself well to the identification and resolution of uncertainties typically facing teams developing a start business model. Blank [22] describes how BMC is widely used in the teaching of start-up business modelling to research and innovation across universities in the United States. In this capacity, the BMC is used as an easily updated 'scorecard' for documenting the development of pivots in a business model when following Blank's own iterative, evidence-driven Customer Development methodology [23] combined with Reis' agile approach to start-up development [24]. Osterwalder et al. [25] have elaborated how the value proposition and customer segments elements of the BMC can be further categorised in the detailed modelling and testing of product market fit. These developments indicate that the form of the BMC has proven adaptable both to integration into independently developed methodologies as well as for methodological elaboration in critical areas.

Taking the business model canvas as a starting point, we aimed to transform it in a way that would enable its users to discuss how a technology might bring about ethical impacts for different stakeholders instead of discussing a business model. To achieve this, we considered different building blocks that could amount to a holistic ethical analysis of a certain technological application. The building blocks were constructed in a two-way process: by considering literature in Science, Technology and Society studies (STS) and philosophy of technology, and simultaneously engaging in a trial-and-error exercise of using the Ethics Canvas to improve its user-friendliness. Each building block consists of a central term and a number of core questions that can guide the discussion concerning a term.

We consulted literature that provides accounts of different aspects of impacts of technologies on individuals, groups and society as a whole. We need to stress that this consultation was mostly aimed at pragmatically gathering different vantage points to consider ethical impacts of technology, and not at providing a coherent theoretical framework underpinning the Ethics Canvas. The STS literature offers useful accounts of the ways in which technologies are embedded in relationships between different "relevant social groups" [15], which can be types of individuals (e.g. producers,

---

[5] See for instance https://strategyzer.com/ and https://canvanizer.com/new/business-model-canvas.

technology users, women, elderly) or institutional, collective actors (e.g. government, companies, labour unions). Akrich [26] discusses the Actor-Network Theory (ANT) approach and shows how technologies can have impacts on actors that are not directly connected to its design, production or use such as non-users but also non-humans (understood as e.g. the impact of a mobile phone on a supply chain for raw materials). She argues that technologies can politicise social and material relations, which can for instance be made explicit by considering how non-users of social media applications can become marginalised.

In order to subsequently understand how technologies impact relevant individuals or groups, we turn to writings in philosophy and technology. Ihde [27] and Verbeek [28] show how individuals can change their behaviour or relationships by engaging with technologies. For instance, Verbeek shows how the ultrasound technology has transformed the relationship between parents and their unborn child [28], and how technologies, such as traffic lights and speed bumps, mediate the behaviour of car drivers [28]. These scholars accentuate that "ethical impacts" are not simply consequences of technological change, but should be understood as impactful relations between human beings and technologies. Feenberg [29] goes beyond this focus on the technological mediation at the level of the individual, by arguing how technologies can impact relations between people and collectives, for instance between workers and their companies, between governments and labour unions. In line with this, he shows how technologies can impact the public sphere, in which "everyday communicative interactions" take place [29], in which ideologies are formed and social struggles arise. To consider ethical impacts that are more directly related to the material aspect of technologies, we consulted scholars discussing "constructive technology assessment". These show that technology assessment should take impacts of technologies on the environment and production processes into account [30]. Finally, to provide a bridging step in the move from description (i.e. what are the ethical impacts?) to prescription (i.e. what should be done?), we turn once more to value sensitive design and included the notion of technical choices driven by value considerations [10] as the logical end-point of the Ethics Canvas. However, we broadened up the choices to be considered, asking participations to think beyond the technical by also considering organisational changes or changes in policies.

Although we did not provide a full-fledged and exhaustive review of literature dealing with the impacts of technologies on humans, groups, and society as a whole, our discussion does give us an adequate picture of what the building blocks of the Ethics Canvas could look like. To summarise, we can infer the following characterisations of technology impacts from the literature:

- Ethical impacts occur as relations between technologies and different types of actors, which can be types of individuals and types of collectives, or groups.
- Technologies can mediate the behaviour of individuals, but also the relations that people have with one-another.
- Technologies can mediate the worldviews of social groups and can bring about social conflicts between social groups.

- A technology impacts the material network in which it is designed, produced and used, including for instance the supply chain it constitutes and the natural resources it needs.

While taking the abovementioned characterisations of technology impacts as a guideline, we entered into a trial-and-error design process of the Ethics Canvas. This design process was aimed at making sure that the rationale of the Ethics Canvas design would not only be grounded in the relevant literature, but that it would also be user-friendly and intuitive. Based on the literature, we designed nine different versions of the Ethics Canvas, all with different building blocks and layouts. These designs were iterated through a series analysis exercises conducted by the Ethics Canvas design team, which consisted of the authors of this paper and other researchers who collectively possessed expertise in applied ethics, personalisation in digital applications, knowledge engineering, software engineering and innovation methodologies. In addition, versions of the Ethics Canvas were trialled in teaching and training settings with over 260 undergraduate and postgraduate students in computer science, engineering, business studies and working on groups on pre-assigned digital application designs. This provided a further source of design insight into improving the usability of the Ethics Canvas design. The criteria for success we used during these meetings were that participants (1) should be able to complete the entire canvas within a reasonable amount of time (a maximum of 1,5 h) and (2) should be able to address each building block without having to consult any external source.

As a result of this trial-and-error exercise, some important changes were made concerning the wordings of each box, because some terms use in the consulted literature (e.g. actor, human-technology-world relations, ideology) were not intuitive for the users and needed to be translated into concepts that are more easily usable (e.g. group, behaviour, worldview). The table below (Table 1) provides an overview of the conceptual framework of the Ethics Canvas, displaying sources in the academic literature and the corresponding approaches that each building block is based on and explicating what changes in terminology were applied to ensure the usability of the Ethics Canvas.

Eventually, the design process brought us to the current design of the Ethics Canvas (Fig. 2). The Ethics Canvas is organised according to nine thematic blocks that are grouped together according to four different stages of completing the canvas. The first stage (blocks 1 and 2) challenges the participants to consider which types of individuals and groups might be relevant stakeholders when considering a specific technology. The second stage (blocks 3 to 6) asks the participants to consider potential ethical impacts, considering the different stakeholders that were identified. The third stage (blocks 7 and 8) asks the participants to consider potential ethical impacts that are not stakeholder specific, pertaining to product or service failure or any problematic use of resources. The fourth stage (block 9) challenges participants to think beyond the potential ethical impacts they discussed and discuss some initial ideas for overcoming these ethical impacts. To complete the Ethics Canvas exercise in a physical space, participants can write down their ideas on a printed Ethics Canvas, and consult the Ethics Canvas

Table 1. Overview of (1) the central questions of the Ethics Canvas, (2) authors consulted to address these, (3) the approaches used by these authors, (4) the changes in wordings applied during the trial-and-error sessions and (5) the final boxes for the Ethics Canvas.

Central question	Literature consulted	Approach	Change in wording	Boxes
Who are affected?	Pinch and Bijker [15], Akrich [26]	Actor Network Theory	Relevant social group/actor/actant => individual/group	(1) Individuals affected
				(2) Groups affected
How are stakeholders affected?	Ihde [27], Verbeek [28]	Postphenomenology	"Human-technology-world" relation => behaviour/relations	(3) Behaviour
				(4) Relations
	Feenberg [29]	Critical Theory of Technology	Ideology => worldviews Struggles => social conflicts	(5) Worldviews
				(6) Social Conflicts
	Schot and Rip [30]	Constructive Technology Assessment	Risks of products and processes => product or service failure Environmental aspects => Problematic use of resources	(7) Product or service failure
				(8) Problematic use of resources
What can be done?	Friedman, Kahn, and Borning [10]	Value Sensitive Design	Technical choices driven by value-considerations => What can we do?	(9) What can we do?

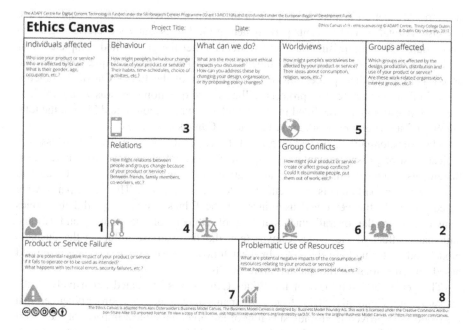

Fig. 2. The Ethics Canvas, version 1.9.

Manual [31] that provides guidance on how to conduct the exercise. An online version of the Ethics Canvas[6] has also been developed. On this platform, people can collaborate to complete a particular Ethics Canvas online while being in different physical places.

5 Assessing the Usefulness of the Ethics Canvas

The BMC is a widely used tool for business model development and has been positively assessed [19]. We wanted to similarly assess the Ethics Canvas and its usefulness as a tool that supports practising ethics in R&I settings. Comparing the Ethics Canvas with other tools for practising ethics in R&I is not possible due to lack of similar tools that are used in day-to-day activities of R&I practitioners. Therefore, we assessed the Ethics Canvas through evaluating its perceived usefulness amongst its users and its anticipated effects related to follow-up activities.

We organised an Ethics Canvas pilot with students who were required to create a new ICT application as part of their coursework. The students attended a one-hour lecture at which the content of the Ethics Canvas Manual was presented. After this, the students were given the assignment to complete the Ethics Canvas in groups, using the online version for their particular R&I project in approximately one hour. Students

---

[6] https://ethicscanvas.org/index.html.

were free to meet up in a physical space or to hold a conference call for completing the exercise. A total of 109 students participated in the Ethics Canvas exercise, organised into groups, each comprising of 3 or 4 students. After the groups had completed their Ethics Canvasses, all participating students were asked to fill in a questionnaire that asked them about their perception of the usefulness of the Ethics Canvas to practise ethics in their respective R&I projects. Filling in the questionnaire was voluntary. The feedback questionnaire was filled in by 31 students, which represented 28% of the total number of students who worked on the Ethics Canvas exercise.

The questionnaire followed a 5-point Likert scale, with a 1-point assessment indicating strong disagreement and a 5-points assessment indicating strong agreement. Statements were formulated in the affirmative mode and as negations to be able to assess whether participants paid attention to the statements. The participants were asked about (1) the perceived usefulness of the Ethics Canvas (e.g. did the Ethics Canvas add to the overall understanding of ethical considerations?) and (2) the anticipated effect of the Ethics Canvas (e.g. did the exercise influence the business model and or technology design?). In what follows, these two aspects are discussed based on reflections on the questionnaire results.

The perceived usefulness of the Ethics Canvas was evaluated extensively in the questionnaire. Generally, 56% of the participants agreed and 28% strongly agreed that the exercise improved their understanding of the potential ethical impacts of their R&I projects. Participants were asked whether the Ethics Canvas exercise widened their understanding of different individuals or groups affected by their project, to which 44% of the participants replied that they agreed and 29% that they strongly agreed. On being asked whether the exercise helped them create a broad overview of potential ethical impacts of their project, 42% of the participants stated to agree and 35% to strongly agree. To further the scope of the assessment, the participants were asked whether the ethical impacts they discussed in the task sufficiently fitted the structure of the Ethics Canvas. 40% of the participants agreed that it sufficiently fitted and 21% strongly agreed. To assess the value of the Ethics Canvas in stimulating productive discussions, participants were asked whether they considered any ethical impacts that were not known to them or unclear beforehand. Only 21% of the participants disagreed or disagreed strongly with this question, indicating that the majority of the participants discussed ethical impacts that were new to them. This suggests that the Ethics Canvas can be a useful tool to guide participants into discussing ethical impacts that group members didn't know or didn't clearly think about beforehand.

The second theme of the survey focused on the assessing the anticipated effect the Ethics Canvas has the business model and technology design of the ICT application that the students are working on. First the participants were asked whether the exercise would have any impact on their project's technology design, resulting in 32% of the participants agreeing and 16% strongly agreeing. A similar question was asked in relation to the impact of the canvas on the business model. 52% of the participants agreed that the Ethics Canvas led them to reconsider their business models and 5% strongly agreed. Finally, the participants were asked whether the exercise was useful in promoting the group's ethical behaviour. 35% of the participants agreed that the exercise promoted ethical behaviour and 40% even strongly agreed. Even though these outcomes do not directly indicate that follow-up actions have been taken or will be taken, they at least indicate an intention amongst the students to use the outcomes of the Ethics Canvas exercise to adjust their business models or technology designs.

Overall, the results suggest that it is reasonable to state that the Ethics Canvas is perceived as a useful tool to guide participants in discussing a broad range of ethical impacts as well as the identification of relevant stakeholders. Moreover, the results indicate that it is reasonable to assume that the Ethics Canvas can lead to the intention of participants to reconsider their business models or technology designs. Nevertheless, results also indicate that the structure of the Ethics Canvas will need to be improved to be more inclusive of potential ethical impacts. Moreover, our study is limited due to the limited participation rate (28% of all the students who worked on the Ethics Canvas exercise). This might possible have led to biased results, because the cohort of students that voluntarily filled in the questionnaire could have coincided with the cohort of students that was most positively engaged during the Ethics Canvas exercise. Hence, even though these initial results positively suggest that the Ethics Canvas is a useful tool for practising ethics in R&I, further development of the Ethics Canvas and additional ways of assessing its usefulness will be needed for future studies.

6   Conclusion

In this paper, we presented a novel tool for the discussion of ethical impacts in R&I settings. The Ethics Canvas responds to shortcomings in the current methods that offer tools for practicing ethics in R&I, concerning the lack of ways in which R&I practitioners can engage in practising ethics in their day-to-day work. We argued for two requirements for constructing a suitable tool for addressing the disclosure stage: that it should be accessible and clear to R&I practitioners and that it should facilitate a collaborative process in which people can discuss different interpretations of impacts of technologies. Since no existing tool in the field of ethics of technology seemed to address this need in an adequate way, we turned to the field of business model development instead. In this field, we assessed the BMC as a suitable tool because it is highly accessible to different types of people, and structures a collaborative effort to discuss issues surrounding a central goal. We designed the Ethics Canvas by redirecting the focus of the canvas format from business modelling to a comprehensive identification of ethical issues of an R&I process. Utilising established theories in philosophy of technology and STS that are aimed at understanding ways in which technologies can impact the behaviour and relations of individuals and collectives, and engaging in a trial-and-error design process, we formulated different building blocks of the Ethics Canvas. Finally, we put the Ethics Canvas to the test in a classroom setting, which resulted in initial positive results, which suggest that the Ethics Canvas is perceived as a useful tool for discussing relevant stakeholders and potential ethical impacts in R&I projects and for triggering anticipations of pivots in business models or technology designs. However, more studies will need to be done to further develop the Ethics Canvas and assess its usefulness in multiple ways.

Finally, we should reflect on two limitations of the Ethics Canvas that could prompt future research. First, even though the exercise can provide R&I teams with a much better overview and understanding of ethical impacts of their R&I activities it does not yet provide a way to evaluate these impacts. That is, is does not provide a way to evaluate whether a certain ethical impact is to be considered positive or negative or whether it is to be considered severe or non-severe. Additional tools will thus have to be developed to enable this, which will probably have to draw strongly from theories in normative ethics (i.e. consequentialism, deontology, virtue ethics) that offer the best intellectual resources for shaping evaluation practices. Second, the Ethics Canvas draws from conceptual work in academic literature, but does not yet offer a way to translate engagement with the Canvas in practice to revisit its conceptual roots. Potentially, multiple Ethics Canvas exercises could for instance be used as empirical input for revisiting and refining the actor network theory. Future work could therefore focus on the translation of concrete and numerous outcomes of Ethics Canvas exercises into changes in the conceptual framework that guide our thinking about R&I activities.

Acknowledgements. The ADAPT Centre for Digital Content Technology is funded under the SFI Research Centres Programme (Grant 13/RC/2106) and is co-funded under the European Regional Development Fund. In addition, this paper has received funding from the European Union's Horizon 2020 research and innovation programme under grant agreement No. 700540.

References

1. Roberts, E.B.: Managing invention and innovation. Res. Technol. Manage. **50**(1), 35–54 (2007)
2. Osterwalder, A., Pigneur, Y.: Business Model Generation: A Handbook for Visionaries, Game Changers, and Challengers (2010). https://www.businessmodelgeneration.com. Accessed 2 Dec 2017
3. Owen, R., Macnaghten, P., Stilgoe, J.: Responsible research and innovation: from science in society to science for society, with society. Sci. Public Policy **39**(6), 751–760 (2012)
4. Tromp, N., Hekkert, P., Verbeek, P.-P.: Design for socially responsible behavior: a classification of influence based on intended user experience. Des. Issues **27**(3), 3–19 (2011)
5. Reeves, T., Herrington, J., Oliver, R.: Design research: a socially responsible approach to instructional technology research in higher education. J. Comput. High. Educ. **16**(2), 97–116 (2005)
6. Stilgoe, J., Owen, R., Macnaghten, P.: Developing a framework for responsible innovation. Res. Policy **42**(9), 1568–1580 (2013)
7. Brey, P.: Anticipatory ethics for emerging technologies. NanoEthics **6**(1), 1–13 (2012)
8. Wright, D.: Ethical impact assessment. Ethics, Sci. Technol. Eng. **163**(c), 163–167 (2014)
9. Forsberg, E.: The ethical matrix — a tool for ethical assessments of biotechnology. Global Bioethics **17**(1) (2004)
10. Friedman, B., Kahn Jr., P.H., Borning, A.: Value sensitive design and information systems. In: Himma, K.E., Tavani, H.T. (eds.) Human-Computer Interaction and Management Information Systems: Foundations, pp. 1–27. Wiley, Hoboken (2006)
11. Reijers, W., Wright, D., Brey, P., Weber, K., Rodrigues, R., O'Sullivan, D., Gordijn, B.: Methods for Practising Ethics in Research and Innovation: A Literature Review, Critical Analysis and Recommendations. Science and Engineering Ethics (2017)
12. Brey, P.: Disclosive computer ethics: the exposure and evaluation of embedded normativity in computer technology. Comput. Soc. **30**(4), 10–16 (2000)

13. Reijers, W., Gordijn, B., O'Sullivan, D.: Narrative ethics of personalisation technologies. In: Kreps, D., Fletcher, G., Griffiths, M. (eds.) HCC 2016. IAICT, vol. 474, pp. 130–140. Springer, Cham (2016). https://doi.org/10.1007/978-3-319-44805-3_11

14. Metcalf, J., Keller, E.F., Boyd, D.: Perspectives on big data, ethics, and society. The Council for Big Data, Ethics, and Society (2006). http://bdes.datasociety.net/council-output/perspectives-on-big-data-ethics-and-society/. Accessed 1 Dec 2017

15. Pinch, T.J., Bijker, W.E.: The social construction of facts and artifacts: or how the sociology of science and the sociology of technology might benefit each other. Soc. Stud. Sci. **14**(3), 221–232 (1984)

16. Henriksen, K., Bjerre, M., Bisgaard, T., Høgenhaven, C., Almasi, A., Grann, E.: Green Business Model Innovation: Empirical and Literature Studies. Nordic Innovation Report. Nordic Innovation, Oslo (2012)

17. Bocken, N., Short, S., Rana, P., Evans, S.: A value mapping tool for sustainable business modelling. Corp. Governance Int. J. Effective Board Perform. **13**(5), 482–497 (2013)

18. Zott, C., Amit, R., Massa, L.: The business model: recent developments and future research. J. Manage. **37**(4), 1019–1042 (2011)

19. Lucassen, G., Brinkkemper, S., Jansen, S., Handoyo, E.: Comparison of visual business modeling techniques for software companies. In: Cusumano, M., Iyer, B., Venkatraman, N. (eds.) Software Business: Third International Conference, ICSOB 2012, p. 14. Cambridge, MA, USA, 18–20 June 2012, Proceedings (2012)

20. Kuparinen, P.: Business model renewal and its networking aspects in a telecom service company. Master thesis, Tampere University of Technology, Tampere (2012)

21. Oliveira, M., Ferreira, J.: Book review: business model generation: a handbook for visionaries, game changers and challengers. Afr. J. Bus. Manage. **5**(7) (2011)

22. Blank, S.: Why the lean start-up changes everything. Harvard Bus. Rev. **91**(5), 63–72 (2013)

23. Blank, S.: The Four Steps to the Epiphany: Successful Strategies for Products that Win. BookBaby, Pennsauken (2013)

24. Reis, E.: The Lean Startup. Crown Publishing, Lake Arbor (2011)

25. Osterwalder, A., Pigneur, Y., Bernarda, G., Smaith, J.: Value Proposition Design. Wiley, Hoboken (2014)

26. Akrich, M.: The De-scription of Technical Objects. In: Bijker, W., Law, J. (eds.) Shaping Technology, Building Society. MIT Press, Cambridge (1992)

27. Ihde, D.: Postphenomenology and Technoscience. Sunny Press, New York (2009)

28. Verbeek, P.-P.: What Things Do; Philosophical Reflections on Technology, Agency, and Design. Pennsylvania University Press, Pennsylvania (2005)

29. Feenberg, A.: Questioning Technology. Routledge, New York (1999)

30. Schot, J., Rip, A.: The past and future of constructive technology assessment. Technol. Forecast. Soc. Change **54**, 251–268 (1997)

31. Lewis, D., Reijers, W., Pandit, H.: Ethics Canvas Manual (2017). https://ethicscanvas.org/download/handbook.pdf. Accessed 20 Dec 2017

The Ethics of Inherent Trust in Care Robots for the Elderly

Adam Poulsen[1]([✉]) [iD], Oliver K. Burmeister[1] [iD], and David Kreps[2] [iD]

[1] Charles Sturt University, Bathurst, NSW, Australia
apouls02@postoffice.csu.edu.au
[2] Salford University, Greater Manchester, UK
d.g.kreps@salford.ac.uk

Abstract. The way elderly care is delivered is changing. Attempts are being made to accommodate the increasing number of elderly, and the decline in the number of people available to care for them, with care robots. This change introduces ethical issues into robotics and healthcare. The two-part study (heuristic evaluation and survey) reported here examines a phenomenon which is a result of that change. The phenomenon rises out of a contradiction. All but 2 (who were undecided) of the 12 elderly survey respondents, out of the total of 102 respondents, wanted to be able to change how the presented care robot made decisions and 7 of those 12 elderly wanted to be able to examine its decision making process so as to ensure the care provided is personalized. However, at the same time, 34% of the elderly participants said they were willing to trust the care robot inherently, compared to only 16% of the participants who were under fifty. Additionally, 66% of the elderly respondents said they were very likely or likely to accept and use such a care robot in their everyday lives. The contradiction of inherent trust and simultaneous wariness about control gives rise to the phenomenon: elderly in need want control over their care to ensure it is personalized, but many may desperately take any help they can get. The possible causes, and ethical implications, of this phenomenon are the focus of this paper.

Keywords: Robotics · Value sensitive design · Artificial intelligence
Healthcare

1 Introduction

Elderly care robot technology is going through what Moor calls a technological revolution [1]. Such a revolution is the moment at which a technological development, prompted by a technological paradigm evolution or major device improvement, causes enormous social impact [1]. Care robot technologies are fundamentally changing elderly care. Still in its infancy, the technological revolution of elderly care robots needs nurturing to ensure ethical care is delivered to the increasing number of elderly [2–10].

Researchers at Florida state university "surveyed 445 people between the ages of 80 and 93 and found that most of the adults over 80 are using technological gadget[s]

D. Kreps et al. (Eds.): HCC13 2018, IFIP AICT 537, pp. 314–328, 2018.
https://doi.org/10.1007/978-3-319-99605-9_24

daily" [11]. Although ethical considerations in relation to technology-based care of the elderly have been the subject of numerous studies [12–17], relatively little has been considered regarding care robots [18, 19] and the integration of complex robots into care for the elderly. One particular month long social robot study revealed that the acceptance care robots depends on factors from social and psychological usage context, one of the former being trust [20]. That study glanced over the phenomenon presented here. In their results, the researchers stated that the "trustworthiness of the robot was a serious issue for most participants, it seemed more important [than] privacy. Yet, most participants did trust the robot and its messages or they did not even think about questioning the integrity of the robot" [20]. The care robot used in that study was constructed and tested, as opposed to the care robot framework presented in this paper. While a small number care robot studies have been conducted with tested care robots with a focus on the ethical considerations, none attempt to comprehensively explore the phenomenon presented here. Moreover, none have found the phenomenon with an untested care robot. What are the ethical implications of the elderly giving their trust to an untested care robot? It is the hope that this paper will provide an initial discussion which will further encourage more debate and study to comprehensively answer that question.

As a result of long-term demographic changes many elderly people find themselves forced by circumstances to accept whatever care is on offer. Compounding the already apparent problem of impersonal care in many establishments, care robots could open up social care for the elderly to further abuse. However, the care robot technological revolution might, by contrast, present an opportunity for empowerment of the elderly in care, and an improvement upon current provision. This paper outlines a study undertaken which revealed these issues.

The paper begins by describing the design approach used to envision the hypothetical elderly care robot used in the study, then the hypothetical framework itself, followed by a brief summary of the study. We then present the results of the study, and a discussion on the background and ethical implications of the phenomenon of inherent trust in care robots.

2 Values in Motion Design and Dynamic Value Trade-Offs in Run-Time

Values in Motion Design (VMD), formerly the design process of the 'attentive framework,' is a care robot design approach that intends to not only help overcome the lack of carers, but provide better care without human error or ill intent [21]. The approach stems from Value Sensitive Design (VSD) [22, 23] but since VSD "lacks a complimentary or explicit ethical theory for dealing with value trade-offs" [24], it rejects the notion that value trade-off decisions should be made exclusively by designers and user sample groups. Further justification for this rejection is linked to care ethics. In care ethics, good care is "determinative in practice" [25]. Which is to say that good care isn't standardized 'elderly care management' derived from following a normative ethical theory, instead it is determined during the act of caring by carers within the carer-patient relationship [9, 26–29]. VMD rises from the rejection of all value trade-offs being made during the design process and the need for good care ethics in care robot technology; it provides a way to deal with shortcomings of VSD.

VMD asserts that each care patient has unique values and value priorities, and that some values and priorities are open to constant changes. Thus, VMD suggests that care robot technology should be able to identify those values, priorities, and changes, and then adapt to them using dynamic value trade-offs in run-time in order to provide good, customized care. VMD doesn't suggest that all values should be customisable due to safety issues, it makes a distinction between intrinsic and extrinsic patient care values. Intrinsic values are the end goal of care, such values include wellbeing and safety. Extrinsic values are those that help to reach intrinsic ones. Extrinsic values, and the priority of them, are personal; each individual's values are different. Privacy, independence, and other such extrinsic values are those that care robot technology should adapt to. In distinguishing intrinsic and extrinsic values, one acknowledges that there are value trade-off decisions that are unsafe for users to make and instead designers should make them, as is the case for intrinsic values. Moreover, there are those value trade-offs (extrinsic) that could and should be made by users to provide good, customised care.

To follow the VMD approach, designers need tools. They need a design tool to identify all values and to design intrinsic value elements (AI safety and physical component control systems, as well as physical robot components themselves). Additionally, they need a computational dynamic value trade-offs in run-time method (AI value customizer system) to use so it can customise extrinsic values to users. The VMD approach recommends using care-centered value sensitive design (CCVSD) [19] for the former, and extrinsic value ordering embedded in an AI system for the latter. These recommendations form a care robot design package called the attentive framework.

3   The Attentive Framework

For the study within this paper, the conceptual AI system used to embed extrinsic value ordering in was the learning intelligent distribution agent (LIDA) model of computational consciousness [30, 31] was used. Both CCVSD and the LIDA model have their limitations, but are nonetheless useful for the purposes for constructing a framework that adheres to the VMD approach. The attentive framework is a theoretical framework of highly sophisticated care robots (attentos), using a type of computational 'consciousness' to relate to the elderly individuals in their care, and make ethical decisions by design. As a thought experiment the attento proves very useful for gleaning what attitudes to future care robots might be, and what problems might arise. Value sensitive design (VSD), as argued elsewhere [12], needs to take better account of social power, and adopt some normative positions concerning which values the framework itself values most highly. The notion of computational 'consciousness,' like so many terms in the world of computing (e.g. 'information', 'memory,' – see Checkland's critique [32], and arguments made elsewhere [33]) anthropomorphizes what is perhaps better understood as a detailed computational model of agent perception. Whilst such an agent perception model fails to address the 'hard' problem [34] of the 'I' of consciousness experiencing the decision trees of perception, and could perhaps be improved with better accounting for the 'enactive approach' [35] locating perception between the agent and the perceived, rather than merely within the perceiver, it nonetheless offers a substantive computational model for the problems inherent in getting robots to make decisions related to their context. Attentos would also support a patient customization function: the 'conscious' ordering of extrinsic patient care values (such as autonomy and privacy), thus being able to make dynamic value trade-offs in run-time, so as to provide good, customized patient care.

The attentive framework takes the VMD approach in designing an AI value customizer system and physical robot elements. The AI value customizer system is somewhat hypothetical, due to the 'hard' problem of consciousness [34]. In the framework, an attento focuses on ensuring that extrinsic patient care values are upheld. It allocates decisions that are safe to make (extrinsic value ordering) to the attento's interpretation of the patient's care values. It sets a patient value priority list for each unique patient and attempts to match it to that patient. An attento performs dynamic value trade-offs in run-time, via extrinsic value ordering – 'consciously' interpreting and adjusting the list in practice to provide customized patient care. The value priority list, which an attento has for each patient, aids the attento in customized action selection during care. The ordering of the list dictates the way the attento looks after the patient; the highest priority values are considered first in each possible action selection. An attento does this with computational 'consciousness' and an 'affirmation of values' function. Computational consciousness provides: situation observation and evaluation; reactionary responsiveness; external stimuli perception; internal modelling of situations, patients, and patient values and their expression of values; and attentiveness. Additionally, the framework posits a 'subjective experience' and internal 'moral' dialogue taking place within computational 'consciousness,' which it provides as key in making the care robot something that the patient can have a good care experience with. Finally, the affirmation function affirms what a patient values in their care, by asking them or their guardian/s, by listening to what a patient or their guardian(s) explicitly tells them about the patient's values, by conferring with other carers, and by performing a self-check of what they have interpreted and now understand to be a patient's values. Affirming a patient's values updates the value priority list of that patient, thus ensuring the actions which the attento chooses are customized.

The physical robot elements, which includes the AI safety and physical component control systems, as well as physical robot components themselves, is CCVSD inspired [19]. It focuses on ensuring that intrinsic patient care values (such as safety) are upheld. It places decisions that are unsafe for patients to make in the hands of designers. Designers are to develop a robot that suits the safety requirements of the patients and environment. The CCVSD process should be well informed by professional codes of ethics [36–39], healthcare regulations, and with stakeholders involved. The 'AI safety and physical component control systems' and 'AI value customizer system' are two distinct elements of the AI. The former regards intrinsic values and the latter is concerned with extrinsic values. The distinction recognises that there are some elements of the complete AI system that must include intrinsic value trade-offs made by the designer, such as control mechanism governance like the speed at which a limb is articulated. The speed should be set at the time of design, not changed dynamically during run-time, just like any intrinsic value considerations.

While the attentive framework is the recommended toolkit for VMD, designers are not limited to only using CCVSD and extrinsic value ordering supported by the LIDA model. Any other tools that can provide a way to identify values and design for intrinsic values, as well as a AI system to provide dynamic value trade-offs in run-time for extrinsic values, could be used in the VMD approach.

4   Method

In 2017, a study was undertaken to test the validity of the attentive framework. The study employed a social constructionist, interpretivist methodology. Data was gathered in two phases. The first was a heuristic, expert evaluation. The second an online survey. Both focused on a specifically designed attento, the 'elderly care medicine delivery attento', as well as scenarios involving care robot-patient interactions. The two phases and overall results have been addressed in another paper [21]. Further details can also be found in the thesis titled 'Dynamic Value Trade-offs in Run-time to Provide Good, Customised Patient Care with Robots' published here: https://researchoutput.csu.edu. au/en/publications/dynamic-value-trade-offs-in-run-time-to-provide-good-customised-p. In this paper the focus is on the survey results, comparing the responses of elderly respondents to younger age groups.

Participants were presented with the medicine delivery attento's design (functionality, competencies, and components) and the concept of dynamic value trade-offs in run-time. Moreover, participants were shown two scenarios in which the attento encountered a situation where values should be considered, at which point it examined the relevant patient's value priority list, evaluated the situation, revealed relevant extrinsic values, and made a decision based on the situation variables and value priority list. Participants were asked to put themselves in the shoes of the elderly person in the scenario and then at the end of each scenario they were asked: *"Would you trust your care robot's decision in this scenario?"* and *"Do you feel the care robot has respected the way you want to be treated and behaved appropriately?"* After answering, they were presented with the same scenario setup but the person's value priority list had changed so that the person's highest value was now different, thus the robot's actions were different in order to respect that highest value instead. They were then asked the same questions. The highest value changed 3 times over 2 scenarios, with each change the same questions were asked. The online survey used Survey Monkey. Scaled and multiple-choice questions were asked, each followed by open-ended questions. The scaled and multiple-choice questions were asked to help participants identify and categorize open-ended responses, and to stay engaged. The scaled question queried the acceptability and usability of the attentive framework by asking how likely they were to accept and use it in their everyday lives. Scenario questions addressed the trustworthiness of the attento in the scenarios, and dynamic value trade-offs in practice. The survey study was conducted from August to September 2017, with 102 random international participants. Table 1 shows the complete set of demographic data for survey participants. Participant sampling was random and international in the hopes to

Table 1. Survey participant demographics

	Survey participants (rounded)
Age group	
Under 50	63%
Didn't answer	21.5%
Over 50	15.5%
Country	
Australia	33%
Didn't answer	25%
United States of America	15%
United Kingdom	9%
Canada	3%
Germany	2%
Japan	2%
New Zealand	2%
Austria	1%
Brazil	1%
Cyprus	1%
Denmark	1%
Estonia	1%
Norway	1%
Pakistan	1%
Sweden	1%
United Arab Emirates	1%
Gender	
Male	42%
Female	35%
Didn't answer	21%
Other/Prefer not to answer	2%
Type of location	
Urban (city)	38%
Didn't answer	21%
Rural	6%
Regional (town)	3%
Highest level of education	
Bachelor Degree	25%
Didn't answer	21%
Year 12 or equivalent	14%
Postgraduate Degree	13%
Certificate III or IV	10%
Graduate Diploma or Graduate Certificate	7%
Advanced Diploma or Diploma	6%
Junior High School	2%
Year 10 or equivalent	2%

get cross-culture and fairer set of data. Participants were recruited randomly using social media websites.

Approval to conduct the study was given by the University Human Research Ethics Committee. This study aimed to gather end-user perspectives on whether a particular care robot designed according to the attentive framework, an elderly care medicine delivery attento, that is capable of delivering quality, customized care (defined as being determinative in practice) is value sensitive, acceptable, and usable.

5   Results

This paper focuses on the phenomenon that the elderly were willing to inherently trust a care robot even though they wanted more control over its decisions. Thus, only those results relevant to this phenomenon are presented and discussed.

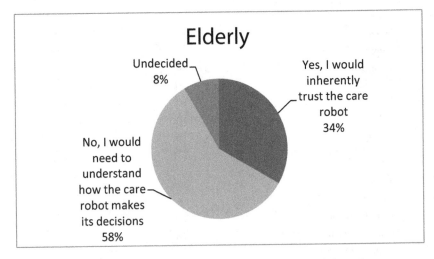

Fig. 1. Elderly participant distribution to the question: Would you inherently trust your care robot or would you need to understand how it makes its decisions?

As seen in Fig. 1, 34% of the elderly participants indicated they would inherently trust the attento, whilst only 16% of those under 50 years of age were willing (as seen in Fig. 2). Regarding the desire for control, all but 2 (who were undecided) of the elderly participants said yes to the following question: *"Would you want the ability to change how your care robot makes its decisions?"* It is from this we can see the contradiction of inherent trust in something one wishes to control and change, and thus the resulting phenomenon.

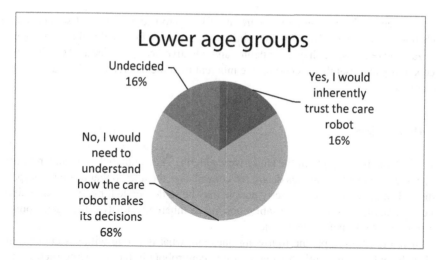

Fig. 2. Lower age group participant distribution to the question: Would you inherently trust your care robot or would you need to understand how it makes its decisions?

The phenomenon is further evident in the results shown in Fig. 3, which indicates that the elderly participants of the study were more likely to accept and use the attento in their everyday lives than the lower age groups. The elderly distribution is more focused towards the 'likely' side whilst the lower age group distribution is further spread. Moreover, the elderly participants dominate the 'very likely' category. As indicated by Fig. 3 the greater percentage of all participants were willing to accept and

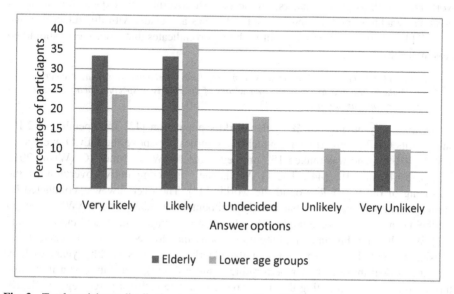

Fig. 3. Total participant distribution to the question: How likely are you to accept and use your care robot in your everyday life?

use the attento. Since those over 50 are more likely to use a care robot sooner, this is both positive and negative. Positive since it encourages further development of customizable care robots such as the attento, and negative because it indicates uninformed acceptability and usability – echoing the inherent trust the elderly were found to have in the attento.

6 Discussion

Twelve of the participants in the study were elderly. The contradiction of inherent trust in the attento and simultaneous desire for control over the attento that those participants indicated suggests that some elderly people may be so desperate for care that they deem a new technology acceptable, usable, and more inherently trustworthy than younger generations would before seeing it.

Such a result prompts the following question, what is wrong with current care that makes the elderly inherently trust an untested care robot? In the following sections this phenomenon is explored from an international perspective.

6.1 Finnish Policy

A case study to demonstrate the desire for personalized care and the failure to deliver it is the current state of elderly care in Finland. The Finnish healthcare sector strongly encourages good elderly care insofar that it even has a national quality framework for care of the elderly; it is one of the few OECD countries to do so [40]. Finland's National Advisory Board on Health Care Ethics (ETENE) published a report on the elderly and ethics of care [41]. The report aimed to advise social and healthcare workers, as well as policy makers, on the Finnish government's expectation of care – particularly addressing the "sensitive ethical issues associated with this [elderly] stage of life" [41]. The main position point in the report indicates that elderly care should be personalized:

> "Treating elderly persons as individuals forms the basis of ethically sustainable eldercare. Care should be tailored to the needs and wishes of the elderly, respecting their values and taking their opinions into account" [41].

Despite only having 0.07% of the world's population [42] and spending a 2.1% share of its GDP on elderly care, which is "significantly above the OECD average of 1.6%" [40], Finland was ranked 15th on the Global AgeWatch Index (GAWI) in 2013 [43] and 14th in 2015 [44]. The GAWI is the "first comparative overview of the wellbeing of older people around the world" [43]. The overview was conducted by HelpAge International, a global elderly wellbeing watchdog. The GAWI measured wellbeing in terms of "income, health, education and employment, and environment" [43]. What brought Finland's ranking down, other than low educational levels and low pension for elderly women, was that the elderly have "less healthy years to look forward to than those in better performing countries" [43]. The future is a more disturbing prospect when noting that it's expected that the national percentage of elderly will jump from 27.2% (in 2015) to 32.4% by 2050 [44].

In the case of Finland, one can see high expectations of personalized elderly care but the failings to provide it. In a country with highly funded public and universally accessible elderly care [45], as well as a small population [42], which focuses primarily on value-based personalized elderly care [41] and thus recognizing the desire for it, it still fails to implement good, personalized care due to lack of resources and staffing [46].

Although the Finnish government has the right idea and the right funding, they fail to implement policy. As a result, access to the right care is a problem, and a cause for the phenomenon. A lack of resources has existed in Finland since the end of the 1990's [9], since then "there has been a rapidly growing shortage of medical doctors and dentists in health centers, especially in remote rural areas" [9]. Without carers to implement policy, there is no access to personalized care.

The lofty aims set out by national policy create high public expectation. That expectation, the aging population, and low availability of clinicians threatens cost of, and access to, personalized elderly care for the Finnish people [45]. A lack of carers is in itself another cause of the phenomenon.

6.2   Less Carers and Ill-Intent in Current Care in Canada and Australia

In western countries the number of elderly is rising and the current system cannot accommodate this [47, 48]. Not only is the number of professional carers entering the field falling, but more current carers are leaving the field [49, 50]. To add to the numbers crisis, there are more cases coming to light of carer ill-intent. In June 2017, Elizabeth Wettlaufer, Canadian elderly care nurse, was convicted of eight murder charges against patients in her care [51]. Megan Haines was convicted of murdering two elderly ladies whilst caring for them in the Ballina, New South Wales (NSW) nursing home where she worked as a nurse in 2016 [52]. Newcastle, NSW nursing home team leader Garry Davis was found guilty of murdering two patients in 2016 [53]. Roger Dean, elderly care nurse, killed eleven patients after maliciously setting the nursing home where he worked alight; Dean was sentenced in 2013 [54]. There are many more cases [55], but the point is: human carers are capable of ill-intent. Given the elderly numbers crisis and possible human ill-intent, it could be concluded that the best solution is care robots capable of providing quality and 'conscious' human-level care. The attentive framework described in this paper was designed to do just that.

Perhaps elderly people are coming to the same conclusion. That a care robot could give them a carer if they don't have one, or it could replace one that has shown ill-intent. If they come to this conclusion than that could be a cause for the phenomenon. Possible causes of the phenomenon aside, the next section explores the following question, what is the ethical implications of the phenomenon?

6.3   It's an Opportunity to Capitalize on, with Substandard Care Robots

It isn't unusual for unethical technology bureaucrats to take advantage of people. In the following cases agencies and companies have capitalized, or attempted to capitalize, on other technological revolutions.

1. In 2017, the Federal Communications Commission (FCC) attempted to consolidate power over internet distribution and control and give it to the US government [56]. The FCC's attack on net neutrality could lead to internet filtering and usage throttling. For the government to create a monopoly of the internet within the US is a clear attempt at capitalizing on users who are not equip to fight back.

2. Google was found to be abusing "its market dominance as a search engine by promoting its own comparison shopping service in its search results, and demoting those of competitors" [57]. Users searching Google for online products were directed towards Google's prices while rival prices were unfairly relegated. Google's abuse of their monopoly on internet searches lead to a £2.14bn fine for this unethical practice.

3. John Deere tractors are proprietary in the sense that only John Deere dealerships and authorized repairs shops can work on their tractors with embedded software [58]. A license agreement forbids users from nearly all repairs and modifications to farming equipment [58]. It "prevents farmers from suing for "crop loss, lost profits, loss of goodwill, loss of use of equipment … arising from the performance or non-performance of any aspect of the software" [58]. Deere & Company are abusing the application of embedded software to prevent users from making their own repairs to their purchases, and instead forcing them to make further payments to Deere & Company through authorized repair avenues.

4. Apple practiced "planned obsolescence" [59]. Although the practice is a fact, the motive is unclear. The theory is that to encourage users to upgrade their iPhone, Apple was throttling the performance of their phones as a new iPhone was about to be released [59]. Purposefully making a gadget obsolete, regardless of the motive, is an unethical practice and a successful case of capitalizing on a technology revolution.

5. Digital Rights Management (DRM) technologies, such as those used by digital distribution companies like Valve (which uses Steam, an online game distribution platform), allows users to buy software or gadgets but not allow them the freedom to use them as they wish [60]. Companies use DRM technologies to unethically maintain rights over the products they distribute, capitalizing on digital distribution platforms.

Capitalizing on the care robot technology revolution with substandard products is possible. Related to the phenomenon, the bureaucrats could be care robot designers, ethicists, policy makers, builders, and producers; elderly care institution owners and operators; assistive home care businesses; etc. The fear is that any of those people involved with care robots could abuse the phenomenon for gain but with no intention of actually improving care. It could also happen to be that such unethical behaviour is unintentional, however the result is this the same – their 'bandwagon' products provide poor quality care.

Care robot companies may enter the market with no ethical guidance for care robot design, construction, maintenance, etc. and/or with purposefully substandard care robots. They may find the same phenomenon, as found in the study described, and attempt to capitalize on it. In the current global consumer economy this is an entirely possible scenario. In that likely case, the elderly will be cared for in a way that may be misguided and unethical, much like other users were treated in the cases mentioned.

7 Conclusion

A particularly disturbing part of the phenomenon, as found in the study, was that the inherent trust was evident even when the participants lacked a technological understanding of the attento's ethical decision making. It is generally accepted that a product, such as a refrigerator or a car, is inherently trustworthy based on the assumption that the producers conducted safety tests and performed lengthy and careful design processes. However, it is strange that a theoretical framework (the attentive framework), inspired that trust. Furthermore, participants of the study were informed that the attento was 'conscious', that its model for ethical decision making was extrinsic value ordering, and that both of these features are mostly untested. The LIDA model (the computational consciousness model used for the attentive framework in the case of this study) has been subjected to some testing, where a 'conscious' AI was used by the LIDA model designers - Baars' and Franklin - to assign naval tasks for sailors [30]. These tests were far from the complex and theoretical claims of 'consciousness' (subjectivity and moral dialogue) made for the attentos in this study. Yet in a personal communication with the lead author, Wendell Wallach (a consultant, ethicist, scholar, and author of papers on the LIDA model), Wallach stated that as "far as consciousness goes, your claims for CC [computational consciousness] are valid" [61].

Perhaps it is the case, with futuristic concepts such as autonomous cars and androids in the news, care robots are not such a hi-tech notion to the general public. Even so, the inherent trust in this case is clearly unfounded. Care robots, especially those that fully replace the function of a carer (like the medicine delivery attento in the study) are still in their infancy. One as complex as the attento in this study is theoretical, with unproven capabilities.

Finally, another contribution of this study has been to the area of care ethics. Through the analysis of the phenomenon one can see that it is both an ethical implication of the care robot technological revolution, and an ethical issue of current care. As for the resolution of both points, we maintain the assumption that by resolving the first - by implementing ethical care robots capable of good, customised care - then the second will also be resolved. When such care robots will be capable of crossing the threshold of the 'hard' problem of consciousness, and evidencing subjectivity and moral dialogue, remains to be seen.

References

1. Moor, J.: Why we need better ethics for emerging technologies. Ethics Inf. Technol. **7**(3), 111–119 (2005)
2. Draper, H., Sorell, T.: Ethical values and social care robots for older people: an international qualitative study. Ethics Inf. Technol. **19**(1), 49–68 (2017)
3. Sharkey, A., Sharkey, N.: Granny and the robots: ethical issues in robot care for the elderly. Ethics Inf. Technol. **14**(1), 27–40 (2012)
4. Sharkey, A., Sharkey, N.: The eldercare factory. Gerontology **58**(3), 282–288 (2011)
5. Sparrow, R., Sparrow, L.: In the hands of machines? The future of aged care. Mind. Mach. **16**(2), 141–161 (2006)

6. Tokunaga, S., et al.: VirtualCareGiver: personalized smart elderly care. Int. J. Softw. Innov. **5**(1), 30–43 (2017)

7. Garner, T.A., Powell, W.A., Carr, V.: Virtual carers for the elderly: a case study review of ethical responsibilities. Digital Health **2**, 1–14 (2016)

8. Landau, R.: Ambient intelligence for the elderly: hope to age respectfully? Aging Health **9** (6), 593–600 (2013)

9. Vallor, S.: Carebots and caregivers: sustaining the ethical ideal of care in the twenty-first century. Philos. Technol. **24**(3), 251–268 (2011)

10. Burmeister, O.K.: The development of assistive dementia technology that accounts for the values of those affected by its use. Ethics Inf. Technol. **18**(3), 185–198 (2016)

11. Bhupinder, C., Rachna, K.: Role of Technology in Management of Health Care of Elderly. J. Gerontol. Geriatr. Res. **6**(1), 1–3 (2017)

12. Burmeister, O.K., Kreps, D.: Power influences upon technology design for age-related cognitive decline using the VSD framework. Ethics Inf. Technol. (2018). https://doi.org/10. 1007/s10676-018-9460-x

13. Burmeister, O.K., et al.: Enhancing connectedness through peer training for community-dwelling older people: a person centred approach. Issues Mental Health Nurs. **37**(6), 406–411 (2016). https://doi.org/10.3109/01612840.2016.1142623

14. Sayago, S., Blat, J.: Telling the story of older people e-mailing: an ethnographical study. Int. J. Hum Comput Stud. **68**(1–2), 105–120 (2010)

15. Burmeister, O.K.: Websites for seniors: cognitive accessibility. Int. J. Emerg. Technol. Soc. **8**(2), 99–113 (2010)

16. Seals, C.D., et al.: Life long learning: seniors in second life continuum. J. Comput. Sci. **4** (12), 1064–1070 (2008)

17. Moreno, T.: http://www.usabilitysciences.com/respect-your-elders-web-accessibility-for-seniors. Accessed 24 Apr 2011

18. van Wynsberghe, A.: Healthcare Robots: Ethics, Design and Implementation. Ashgate Publishing Ltd., Farnham (2015)

19. van Wynsberghe, A.: Designing robots for care: care centered value-sensitive design. Sci. Eng. Ethics **19**(2), 407–433 (2013)

20. de Graaf, M.M.A., Allouch, S.B., Klamer, T.: Sharing a life with Harvey: exploring the acceptance of and relationship-building with a social robot. Comput. Hum. Behav. **43**, 1–14 (2015)

21. Poulsen, A., Burmeister, O.K.: Overcoming carer shortages with carebots: dynamic value trade-offs in run-time. Australas. J. Inf. Syst. **22** (2018)

22. Friedman, B., Kahn, P.H.J., Borning, A.: Value sensitive design and information systems. In: Zhang, P., Galletta, D. (eds.) Human-Computer Interaction and Management Information Systems: Foundations, pp. 348–372. M. E. Sharpe, New York (2006)

23. Friedman, B.: Value-sensitive design. Interactions **3**(6), 17–23 (1996)

24. Manders-Huits, N.: What values in design? The challenge of incorporating moral values into design. Sci. Eng. Ethics **17**(2), 271–287 (2011)

25. Beauchamp, T.L.: Does ethical theory have a future in bioethics? J. Law Med. Ethics **32**(2), 209–217 (2004)

26. Upton, H.: Moral theory and theorizing in health care ethics. Ethical Theor. Moral Pract. **14** (4), 431 (2011)

27. Tronto, J.C.: Creating caring institutions: politics, plurality, and purpose. Ethics Soc. Welfare **4**(2), 158–171 (2010)

28. Gámez, G.G.: The nurse-patient relationship as a caring relationship. Nurs. Sci. Q. **22**(2), 126–127 (2009)

29. Vanlaere, L., Gastmans, C.: A personalist approach to care ethics. Nurs. Ethics **18**(2), 161–173 (2011)
30. Baars, B.J., Franklin, S.: An architectural model of conscious and unconscious brain functions: Global workspace theory and IDA. Neural Netw. **20**(9), 955–961 (2007)
31. Baars, B.J., Franklin, S.: Consciousness is computational: the LIDA model of global workspace theory. Int. J. Mach. Conscious. **01**(01), 23–32 (2009)
32. Checkland, P.: Information systems and systems thinking: time to unite? Int. J. Inf. Manage. **8**, 239–248 (1988)
33. Kreps, D.: Matter and memory and deep learning. In: Hirai, Y., Fujita, H., Abiko, S. (eds.) Berukuson Busshitsu to Kioku wo Shindan suru: Jikan Keiken no Tetsugaku, Ishiki no Kagaku, Bigaku, Rinrigaku eno Tenkai (Diagnoses of Bergson's Matter and Memory: Developments Towards the Philosophy of Temporal Experience, Sciences of Consciousness, Aesthetics, and Ethics), pp. 196–225 (2017)
34. Chalmers, D.J.: The Conscious Mind. Oxford University Press, Oxford (1996)
35. Noë, A.: Action in Perception. MIT Press, London (2006)
36. Burmeister, O.K.: Professional ethics in the information age. J. Inf. Commun. Ethics Soc. **15**(2), 348–356 (2017)
37. Burmeister, O.K.: Achieving the goal of a global computing code of ethics through an international-localisation hybrid. Ethical Space Int. J. Commun. Ethics **10**(4), 25–32 (2013)
38. Bowern, M., et al.: ICT integrity: bringing the ACS code of ethics up to date. Australas. J. Inf. Syst. **13**(2), 168–181 (2006)
39. Burmeister, O.K., Weckert, J.: Applying the new software engineering code of ethics to usability engineering: a study of 4 cases. J. Inf. Commun. Ethics Soc. **3**(3), 119–132 (2003)
40. Organisation for Economic Co-operation and Development (OECD) Homepage. https://www.oecd.org/els/health-systems/Finland-OECD-EC-Good-Time-in-Old-Age.pdf. Accessed 10 Jan 2018
41. The National Advisory Board on Health Care Ethics (ETENE). Old Age and Ethics of Care (2008). http://etene.fi/en/publications
42. Statistics Finland Homepage. http://www.stat.fi/til/vamuu/2017/09/vamuu_2017_09_2017-10-24_tie_001_en.html. Accessed 10 Jan 2018
43. Yle Uutiset Homepage. https://yle.fi/uutiset/osasto/news/finland_lags_in_seniors_wellbeing/6858107. Accessed 11 Jan 2017
44. Global AgeWatch Index Homepage. http://www.helpage.org/global-agewatch/population-ageing-data/country-ageing-data/?country=Finland. Accessed 11 Jan 2017
45. Teperi, J. et al.: The Finnish health care system: a value-based perspective. http://www.hbs.edu/faculty/Publication%20Files/Finnish_Health_Care_System_SITRA2009_78584c8b-10c4-4206-9f9a-441bf8be1a2c.pdf
46. News Now Finland Homepage. http://newsnowfinland.fi/editors-pick/finlands-elderly-care-crisis. Accessed 11 Jan 2018
47. Koldrack, P., et al.: Cognitive assistance to support social integration in Alzheimer's disease. Geriatr. Mental Health Care **1**, 39–45 (2013)
48. Australian Bureau of Statistics Homepage. http://www.abs.gov.au/ausstats/abs%40.nsf/Latestproducts/4430.0Main%20Features302015?issue=2015&num=&opendocument=&prodno=4430.0&tabname=Summary&view=. Accessed 12 Jan 2018
49. Bernoth, M., Dietsch, E., Davies, C.: Forced into exile: the traumatic impact of rural aged care service inaccessibility. Rural Remote Health **12**(1294), 1–8 (2012)
50. Bernoth, M., et al.: The impact of a participatory care model on work satisfaction of care workers and the functionality, connectedness and mental health of community-dwelling older people. Issues Mental Health Nurs. **37**(6), 429–435 (2016)

51. British Broadcasting Corporation Homepage. http://www.bbc.com/news/world-us-canada-40412080. Accessed 12 Jan 2018

52. Australian Broadcasting Corporation Homepage (a). http://www.abc.net.au/news/2016-12-16/megan-haines-sentenced-for-murder-of-two-elderly-women/8126418. Accessed 12 Jan 2018

53. Australian Broadcasting Corporation Homepage (b). http://www.abc.net.au/news/2016-09-28/nursing-home-employee-garry-davis-found-guilty-of-murder/7883704. Accessed 12 Jan 2018

54. Daily Mail. http://www.dailymail.co.uk/news/article-3225332/Convicted-murderer-Roger-Dean-appeals-life-sentences-received-lighting-fire-nursing-home-resulted-death-14-elderly-people.html. Accessed 12 Jan 2018

55. Bernoth, M., et al.: Information management in aged care: cases of confidentiality and elder abuse. J. Bus. Ethics **122**, 453–460 (2014)

56. Internet Society Homepage. https://www.internetsociety.org/blog/2017/12/net-neutrality-fccs-december-14-vote/. Accessed 29 Jan 2018

57. Telegraph Homepage. http://www.telegraph.co.uk/technology/2017/06/27/eu-hits-google-record-21bn-fine-abusing-internet-search-monopoly/. Accessed 29 Jan 2018

58. Vice Homepage. https://motherboard.vice.com/en_us/article/xykkkd/why-american-farmers-are-hacking-their-tractors-with-ukrainian-firmware. Accessed 29 Jan 2018

59. Business Insider Homepage. http://www.businessinsider.com/apple-battery-throttling-gives-customers-reason-to-distrust-2017-12. Accessed 29 Jan 2018

60. Electronic Frontier Foundation Homepage. https://www.eff.org/issues/drm. Accessed 29 Jan 2018

61. Wallach, W.: Personal Communication (2017)

The Legitimacy of Cross-Border Searches Through the Internet for Criminal Investigations

Taro Komukai[1(✉)] and Aimi Ozaki[2]

[1] College of Risk Management, Nihon University, Tokyo, Japan
komukai.taro@nihon-u.ac.jp
[2] KDDI Research, Inc., Tokyo, Japan

Abstract. On the Internet, information is transmitted instantaneously across borders. Enormous volumes of information are collected and stored throughout the world. Information on the Internet can also be subject to criminal investigations. The increasing problem for criminal justice authorities is that the information they seek to access is often stored in other States and is, therefore, outside their jurisdiction. Exercising a state power over data stored inside another State's territory could be a violation of sovereignty.

Discussing cross-border data investigation needs to consider both the sovereignty of the State in which the data are stored and human rights of the investigation subject. These issues are closely related to each other and, thus, likely to be confused. Regarding data collection for investigatory purposes, if there is no infringement of the investigation subject's human rights, concerns are rarely raised regarding sovereignty infringement. However, the existence of two types of investigation subjects, data subjects and data controllers, complicates the issue.

This paper provides an approach to improve cross-border data investigations, with due consideration of human rights and international law, by analyzing current international discussions in this field.

Keywords: Criminal investigation · Privacy · Personal data · International law
Sovereignty

1 Criminal Investigation into Data Stored in Other States

1.1 Necessity for Overseas Search

On the Internet, information is transmitted instantaneously across borders. Criminals naturally use e-mails and various other services on the Internet. Sensors installed in smartphones and various Internet of Things (IoT) technologies enable the collection and storage of enormous volumes of information. Information on the Internet can also be subject to criminal investigations. However, because information is often stored outside the State of the investigating authorities, it is increasingly necessary for them to access data stored in other States.

© IFIP International Federation for Information Processing 2018
Published by Springer Nature Switzerland AG 2018. All Rights Reserved
D. Kreps et al. (Eds.): HCC13 2018, IFIP AICT 537, pp. 329–337, 2018.
https://doi.org/10.1007/978-3-319-99605-9_25

Server computers providing cloud services via the Internet are scattered throughout the world. The user is not usually aware of where their data are located. For criminal justice authorities, being able to access computer data is often indispensable for a successful investigation. In the future, investigations into computer data will further increase. Criminals must not be allowed to evade justice by placing data in foreign servers.

Conversely, a state is traditionally limited to exercising power within its own territory. Thus, while criminal justice authorities can compel suspects and network service providers to cooperate with investigations inside their own territorial jurisdiction, they cannot forcibly access data in other States. It is not clear whether a criminal justice authority can access data abroad through the computers of investigation subjects in its own territory.

For law enforcement authorities' cross-border investigations, there are schemes for mutual legal assistance. However, especially in relation to cyberspace, many of the problems with mutual legal assistance have been widely recognized. In the United States, the scheme based on mutual legal assistance treaties (MLATs) [1] is deemed time-consuming and cumbersome; moreover, there are no formal tools for sourcing assistance in conducting law enforcement searches in countries that have not signed an MLAT [2]. The Council of Europe has been promoting mutual legal assistance based on the Cybercrime Convention. However, the Cybercrime Convention Committee admits that, in some situations, this does not provide a realistic means to obtain information through investigation assistance, since this can take from six to 24 months [3]. Criminal justice authorities are increasingly demanding the ability to directly access data stored abroad, especially in emergency situations. In some cases, they also find it difficult to identify which State has jurisdiction over the data.

1.2   Interest to Be Protected

Sovereignty is guaranteed as a fundamental principle of international law [4]. It is also considered as "[i]ndependence in regard to a portion of the globe" giving "the right to exercise therein, to the exclusion of any other State, the function of a State" [5]. If a State's criminal justice authority exercises state power over the people and organizations based in other States, this infringes sovereignty [6]. Thus, the acquisition of data using state power is not allowed where this would threaten the independence of the State where the data exists.

There is also the issue of the investigation subject's human rights. For example, the Fourth Amendment of the Constitution of the United States, Article 8 of the European Convention on Human Rights, and Article 35 of the Constitution of Japan all require due process of law and adherence to statutory procedures in criminal investigations with compulsory measures. In this regard, access to data is only proper when it satisfies the following requirements: (1) the criminal justice authority accesses the data in accordance with lawful legal procedure; and (2) the legal procedure does not violate higher-level norms, such as international law and the constitution of the investigating State.

1.3   Scenarios to Be Discussed

Criminal justice authorities are not allowed to investigate people and organizations based in another State without the latter's consent or other specific allocation of authority under international law, since such investigations are considered as the conduct of state power [7].

Conversely, in conducting investigations, criminal justice authorities are generally allowed to access data stored in other States that is publicly available via the Internet, since such data can be considered publicly available also in the authorities' own State [6]. The Council of Europe's Cybercrime Convention affirms this in Article 32, paragraph 1.

When a criminal justice authority conducts a compulsory investigation of a computer in its own State, it faces the dilemma of whether it can order the submission of data in other States that are available through that computer. They have to consider both the sovereignty of the State where the data are stored and the investigation subjects' human rights. Investigation subjects include not only suspects or other related people, data subjects, but also data controllers such as internet service providers (ISPs), cloud service providers, etc. Data subjects are the people identified by the data, while data controllers are the people or organizations that determine the purpose and means of processing personal data [8].

For situations in which criminal justice authorities directly contact private foreign service providers to request the voluntary provision of extraterritorial data, there are two principal conflicting views:

- Since the information that the service provider holds is not publicly available, gaining access to it requires either a specific allocation of authority under international law or the consent of the State enjoying enforcement jurisdiction over the data sought.
- A mere State request made directly to a private entity and unaccompanied by compulsion to comply does not interfere with the exclusive right of the other State to exercise enforcement jurisdiction within its territory [6].

Table 1. Problems in each scenario.

Interest to be protected type of investigation	Sovereignty	Rights of Data Subject	Rights of data controller
Compulsory investigations of data subjects	Infringement of target state's sovereignty	Search or seizure without due process of law	No infringement of any interest
Compulsory investigations of data controllers	Infringement of target state's sovereignty	Search or seizure without due process of law	Search or seizure without due process of law
Request for cooperation to data controllers	Controversial	Invasion of privacy and data protection	No infringement of any interest

Regarding this issue, the Cybercrime Convention Committee proposes an international agreement to clarify in which cases direct cooperation may be obtained regardless of mutual legal assistance.

Based on the above, the scenarios in which criminal justice authorities face problems in accessing data stored in other States are summarized in Table 1.

2 Cases

2.1 Microsoft Corp. v. United States, 829 F.3d 197 (2016)

The United States Department of Justice suspected that a mail account of the Web e-mail service provided by Microsoft was being used to promote the drug trade. Therefore, through a search and seizure warrant under the Stored Communications Act (SCA: 18 U.S.C. §§2701–2712 (2012)), the Department of Justice requested to Microsoft to disclose information relating to the mail account. Microsoft disclosed all the target information stored in the U.S. but refused to disclose information stored in a data center in Dublin, Ireland, in relation to which it filed a motion to quash.

The District Court dismissed Microsoft's motion, and imposed a civil contempt order against Microsoft for failing to comply with the warrant. On Microsoft's appeal, the Second Circuit Court reversed the District Court's denial of the motion to quash, vacated the order holding Microsoft in civil contempt, and remanded the matter to the District Court.

In upholding the Microsoft's appeal, the Second Circuit Court ruled that the SCA warrant is effective only within the U.S. The court explained that congressional legislation is assumed to apply only within the territorial jurisdiction of the U.S. unless a contrary intent is clearly shown with an affirmative indication; the SCA's provisions contain no such indication. The court also mentioned that the SCA and the warrant rule in the Federal Rules of Criminal Procedure should be interpreted to reflect their original purposes of protecting privacy.

The execution of the warrant was then determined by the Second Circuit Court to be extraterritorial law enforcement, because privacy was infringed in the location from which the data were to be obtained. This case once reached the U.S. Supreme Court, but was vacated because of enactment of the Clarifying Lawful Overseas Use of Data Act (CLOUD Act).

2.2 In Re Search Warrant 232 F.Supp.3d 708

Prior to the Second Circuit Court's decision in the Microsoft case, Google's policy was to disclose information about customers' communication content stored in foreign countries in response to SCA warrants from criminal justice authorities.

However, after that decision, Google decided to reject SCA warrant requests for disclosure of information located in foreign countries. Consequently, the FBI sued Google to seek disclosure of such information. The United States District Court for Eastern District of Pennsylvania reaffirmed that SCA warrants are only effective within the United States. However, the court decided that the FBI could use the warrant to order Google to transfer information from a foreign server to Google's server in

California, which would then become disclosable. The court reasoned that this transfer would not infringe any access or possessory interest of the customer, so it could not be considered as "seizure" to request the transfer of information for disclosure.

2.3   Unpublished Judgment of Tokyo Koto Saibansho [Tokyo High. Court], December 7, 2016 (Japan)

Through a revision to the Criminal Procedure Act in 2011 (Article 218, paragraph 2), Japan introduced a procedure to seize electronic data on the server to which a seized computer is connected via the Internet. In this case, having seized the suspect's PC under a warrant, the police obtained data from a Gmail account used by the suspect. As the Gmail mail server appeared to be located outside Japan, it was questioned whether the police could legally access the mail server.

The Yokohama District Court expressed concern that investigating information stored on a server in another State could be a violation of sovereignty. Given the high possibility that the server was located in a foreign country, and the law enforcement agency's awareness of this, the court held that the agency should not have accessed the Gmail data (Yokohama Chiho Saibansho [Yokohama Dist. Ct.], March 17, 2016, LEX/DB25542385 (Japan)).

The Tokyo High Court upheld the decision and ruled that the law enforcement agency should have conducted mutual legal assistance because the server was most likely located in a foreign country.

3   Discussion

3.1   Sovereignty

The U.S. courts act on the assumption that laws established in the U.S. can only be applied within the State's territorial jurisdiction [9]. U.S. law could only apply to a foreign jurisdiction when the U.S. Congress has clearly demonstrated such intention. It thus appears that U.S. laws are established with consideration for other States' sovereignty, though Congress reserves the right to enact laws with extraterritorial application. It also seems permissible for criminal justice authorities to order people or entities within the territorial jurisdiction of the U.S. to disclose information stored in foreign States, pursuant to a lawful subpoena [2]. The rationale may be that this compulsory investigation concerns people or entities within the United States' territorial jurisdiction, rather than the information itself.

Academic discussions on this issue in the U.S. offer conflicting views. Jack L. Goldsmith insists that "territorial sovereignty" is a concept without clear definition and has never had definitive content; instead, it changes "in response to changed international circumstances, including changed technological circumstances." Goldsmith argues that "such searches are not prohibited by norms of territorial sovereignty, and are not without precedent." [10] Conversely, Patricia L. Bellia insists that although the searching State may view its actions as "merely advancing a claimed power to regulate extraterritorial conduct causing harmful effects within its own borders," the target State "may view a remote cross-border search itself as extra- territorial, conduct with harmful local effects." [11] Recently, two opposing views have been raised: the first contends that accessing data held overseas does not infringe the sovereignty of other States provided the Fourth Amendment is properly respected, [12] whereas the second insists that the Fourth Amendment should limit the government's authority, necessitating a new international framework that considers other States' sovereignty in determining the application of a U.S. warrant [13]. It is not disputed that the U.S. Congress can enact laws of extraterritorial application by clearly demonstrating this intention unless this draws international condemnation.

Conversely, Japanese courts deny criminal justice authorities the right to access data stored overseas, believing that, as an exercise of state power, this could constitute an infringement of another State's sovereignty. Japanese academics also suggest that data held overseas should only be accessed in accordance with Article 32 of the Cybercrime Convention: this requires a criminal justice authority to obtain lawful and voluntary consent from the State in which non-public data are stored [14–16].

However, Article 32 of the Cybercrime Convention was not intended to limit cross-border investigations only to the situation it details. The "Explanatory Report" of the Cybercrime Convention provides a detailed account of this article:

> The issue of when a Party is permitted to unilaterally access computer data stored in another Party without seeking mutual assistance was a question that the drafters of the Convention discussed at length. There was detailed consideration of instances in which it may be acceptable for States to act unilaterally and those in which it may not. The drafters ultimately determined that it was not yet possible to prepare a comprehensive, legally binding regime regulating this area. In part, this was due to a lack of concrete experience with such situations to date; and, in part, this was due to an understanding that the proper solution often turned on the precise circumstances of the individual case, thereby making it difficult to formulate general rules. Ultimately, the drafters decided to only set forth in Article 32 of the Convention situations in which all agreed that unilateral action is permissible. They agreed not to regulate other situations until such time as further experience has been gathered and further discussions may be held in light thereof. In this regard, Article 39, paragraph 3 provides that other situations are neither authorized, nor precluded [17].

The Council of Europe's Cybercrime Convention Committee explored solutions for accessing evidence in the cloud for criminal justice purposes. They identified the necessity for criminal justice authorities to access overseas data without complying with Article 32, and found that this had already occurred. In particular, such a need arises where criminal justice authorities must preserve evidence, in cases of emergency, and, in some cases, where the authorities are empowered within their own State, subject to defined procedures and safeguards. The committee, therefore, recommended adding such a provision to the convention [3].

In 2008, NATO established the Cooperative Cyber Defense Centre of Excellence. Its international group of experts conducted a scientific study on applying international law to cyber conflicts and cyberwar. Its second report, called "Tallinn Manual 2.0 on the International Law Applicable to Cyber Operations," was published in 2017. It proposed the following rule for extraterritorial law enforcement by a State:

Rule 11-Extraterritorial enforcement jurisdiction

A State may only exercise extraterritorial enforcement jurisdiction in relation to persons, objects, and cyber activities on the basis of:

(a) a specific allocation of authority under international law; or
(b) valid consent by a foreign government to exercise jurisdiction on its territory [7].

In its explanation of this rule, Tallinn Manual 2.0 indicates that a criminal justice authority is allowed to exercise jurisdiction over an entity domiciled in its own State and require the entity to provide access to data stored in another State:

> Consider a situation involving a private entity domiciled in State A that stores its data in State B. State C, as part of its law enforcement activities wants to access that data. The Experts agreed that the consent of State A is insufficient to permit remote access by State C to the data in State B. Remotely accessing the data would be an exercise of enforcement jurisdiction by State C in State B that necessitates a specific allocation of authority under international law or State B's consent. However, the Experts likewise emphasized that State A may exercise its jurisdiction over the entity and, for example, require it to provide the respective data to State C [6].

3.2 Rights of Investigation Subject

Investigation subjects' human rights must be protected in accordance with the due process of law guaranteed by each State's constitution. Human rights are also closely connected to sovereignty infringement. When the human rights of people or entities in a given State's territory are infringed by another State, the independence of the former State is also often infringed. In fact, the U.S. courts consider infringement of the investigation subject's human rights when judging whether sovereignty has been infringed.

In the Microsoft case, the Second Circuit Court emphasized that the SCA is intended to protect users' right to privacy in the content of their communications; consequently, it considered that compulsory investigation of data held outside the jurisdiction of the U.S. infringed that right. Conversely, in the Google case, the District Court asserted that, with respect to human rights infringement, an order to transfer data from a foreign server to a computer in the U.S. does not differ form an order to transfer data from a server within the U.S. It should be noted that both these U.S. cases concerned the investigation of data controllers, rather than data subjects.

When a subject is directly investigated, they can refuse to provide the information and the criminal justice authority must comply with any applicable statutory procedure. PCs or other devices belonging to the suspect must not be compulsorily investigated without a warrant or subpoena limited in both subject and scope, and the suspect may lodge an objection against the warrant or subpoena. The right to privacy applies regardless of whether the data are stored in the investigating State or in another State.

On the contrary, when the investigation is conducted into data controllers, such as ISPs or cloud service providers, the data subject – whether a suspect or other relevant person – is not usually involved. Moreover, as a user of the network services, the data subject is often not even aware of what kind of data has been saved in computer servers. Consequently, information that users would not expect to be collected is stored without their awareness. Such an investigation could also be conducted without the awareness of the State in which the data are stored [18].

The European Union adopted a directive on data protection associated with criminal investigation, prevention, etc., in 2016 (Directive (EU) 2016/680). Its preamble states:

> Where personal data move across borders it may put at increased risk the ability of natural persons to exercise data protection rights to protect themselves from the unlawful use or disclosure of those data. At the same time, supervisory authorities may find that they are unable to pursue complaints or conduct investigations relating to the activities outside their borders. Their efforts to work together in the cross-border context may also be hampered by insufficient preventative or remedial powers and inconsistent legal regimes. Therefore, there is a need to promote closer cooperation among data protection supervisory authorities to help them exchange information with their foreign counterparts [19].

This means that natural persons, as data subjects, should be protected and that safeguards for data protection are also necessary in international cooperation between criminal justice authorities.

4   Conclusion

The need for investigation into computer data will continue to increase in the future. As the computers that provide networked services spread throughout the world, criminal justice authorities will increasingly need to investigate data stored in other States.

When a criminal justice authority directly investigates on the suspects or other related people, certain procedural guarantees apply regardless of whether the data is stored inside or outside the investigating State. Conversely, when an investigation targets a data controller, information that users do not expect to have been collected may be disclosed. This may pose more serious problems with respect to the data subject's data protection and privacy and the sovereignty of the Stata in which the data are stored. In particular, when a criminal justice authority requests data controllers to provide information voluntarily, the data subject is not involved and both statutory procedures and territorial sovereignty may be ignored.

From the above, and to advance the upholding of law and order in the world, discussions of cross-border data investigations from the viewpoint of international law and human rights protection should be based on the following understanding:

1. Subject to compliance with statutory procedures in its own territory, a criminal justice authority should be allowed to investigate data stored in another State when accessed via the computers or other devices through which the data subject, such as the suspect or other related person, was accessing the data, without any specific allocation of authority under international law.
2. A criminal justice authority should not be allowed to investigate data stored in another States pursuant to an investigation into a data controller without the consent of the State where the data are stored or a new and specific allocation of authority under international law, including the requirement to provide ex-post notification to the sovereign State where the data are located.

This work was supported by JSPS KAKENHI Grant Number JP18K01393.

References

1. Mutual Legal Assistance Treaties (2013) 7 FAM § 962.1. http://fam.state.gov/FAM/07FAM/07FAM0960.html
2. Microsoft, 829 F.3d 197 (2016)
3. Council of Europe Cybercrime Convention Committee (2016) Criminal justice access to electronic evidence in the cloud: Recommendations for consideration by the T-CY, 9, pp 44–46
4. Jennings, R,, Watts, A,: Oppenheim's International Law. 9th edn, 564 (1993)
5. United Nations: Island of Palmas arbitral award, 838 (1928)
6. Schmitt, M.N.: Tallinn Manual 2.0, pp 66–71. Cambridge University Press (2017)
7. Lotus, S.S. (Fr v Turk): PCIJ (ser A) No 10 (Sept 7), 18 (1927)
8. European Union: Regulation 2016/679 of the European Parliament and of the Council of 27 April 2016 on the protection of natural persons with regard to the processing of personal data and on the free movement of such data, and repealing Directive 95/46/EC (2016)
9. Morrison, V. National Australia Bank Ltd. 561 US 247 (2010)
10. Goldsmith, J.L.: The Internet and the Legitimacy of Remote Cross-Border Searches Frontiers of Jurisdiction. 2001 U Chi Legal F 103: 109–117 (2001)
11. Bellia, P.L.: Chasing Bits across Borders. 2001 U Chi Legal F: 35, 42 (2001)
12. Kerr, O.S.: The fourth amendment and the global internet. Stan. Law. Rev. 67(285), 329 (2015)
13. Daskal, J.: The un-territoriality of data. Yale LJ 125(326), 332–334 (2015)
14. Sugiyama, T., Yoshida, M.: An explanatory note about the revision of Penal code and Criminal Procedure Act to cope with the development of information processing. Hoso-Jiho 64(4), 101 (2012)
15. Yasutomi, K.: Criminal Procedure Act, Sanseido. 2nd edn., 218 (2017)
16. Taguchi, M.: Criminal Procedure Act, Koubindou. 7th edn., 119 (2017)
17. Council of Europe: Convention on Cybercrime - Explanatory Report - [2001] COETSER 8 (2001)
18. Komukai, T.: Legal issues on Criminal Justice Access to data in the Cloud. ISPJ SIG Technical Report Vol. 2018-EIP-79 No.6: 5 (2018)
19. European Union: Directive 2016/680 of the European Parliament and of the Council of 27 April 2016 on the protection of natural persons with regard to the processing of personal data by competent authorities for the purposes of the prevention, investigation, detection or prosecution of criminal offences or the execution of criminal penalties, and on the free movement of such data, and repealing Council Framework Decision 2008/977/JHA (2016)

Discussions on the Right to Data Portability from Legal Perspectives

Kaori Ishii[(✉)]

Faculty of Library, Information and Media Science,
University of Tsukuba, Tsukuba, Japan
kaoriish@slis.tsukuba.ac.jp

Abstract. This study discusses the legal issues pertaining to data portability from the perspectives of both personal data protection and antitrust laws. Since legal challenges arise from the differences between antitrust law and data protection law, there is a need to define the legal position of data portability. My analysis is based on a review of these three topics: Is the right to data portability in the EU General Data Protection Regulation (GDPR) effective? (2) Should the right to data portability be legally regulated? and (3) Can the right be regulated from an antitrust perspective?

What are indicated from the above discussions are: (1) the right to data portability in the GDPR is the first promising provision which has given rise to several issues—in particular the scope of the data, IT costs imposed on SMEs, and theoretical boundaries and enforcements based between data protection and antitrust laws—that warrant further examination; (2) if the controller-controller portability is called for, antitrust perspective broadly encompass the scope of data is preferred than data protection regulation; (3) combining data protection and antitrust perspectives into a single law would be difficult due to the differences of them; (4) when it comes to establish data portability scheme from antitrust perspective, data portability should be obliged depending on the kinds of platform.

Keywords: Data portability · Privacy · Personal data · Antitrust

1 Introduction

This article discusses legal issues on the right to data portability both from personal data protection and antitrust perspectives, and provides some policy recommendations for formulating the right to data portability.

The EU General Data Protection Regulation (GDPR) [1] introduced a new right to data portability. One of its intentions is addressing data monopolization by "GAFA."[1] The European Commission (EU Commission) acknowledges the possible advantages of the right from a competition perspective because start-ups and smaller companies will be able to access data markets dominated by digital giants and attract more consumers with privacy-friendly solutions, increasing competitiveness in the economy [2].

---

[1] GAFA is a buzzword meaning Google, Apple, Facebook, and Amazon.

D. Kreps et al. (Eds.): HCC13 2018, IFIP AICT 537, pp. 338–355, 2018.
https://doi.org/10.1007/978-3-319-99605-9_26

This right primarily empowers the control of personal data by a data subject, while simultaneously preventing vendor lock-in. The Article 29 Data Protection Working Party (WP29)[2] states that the data portability right facilitates data subjects' ability "to move, copy or transmit personal data easily from one IT environment to another," and also fosters competition between controllers in the context of the Digital Single Market strategy [3].[3]

Conversely, large and strong online platforms have already been established by giant U.S. internet companies, creating a need to question the framing of the right and identifying legal challenges.

The data portability right has been managed on a country basis. For instance, the French Digital Republic Act (une République numérique) enacted on October 7, 2016, introduced the right to data portability. The midata program launched in 2011 and backed by the UK government facilitates consumers' access to their personal data in a portable, electronic format. The Obama Administration launched a series of My Data initiatives in 2010. Comparing the right to data portability in the EU and efforts in other countries is helpful for devising policy recommendations and ensuring an objective discussion.

Legal challenges stem from the differences between the approach of antitrust law and data protection law. The former aims for fair and free competition by prohibiting private monopolization, unreasonable restraint of trade, and unfair trade practices. From this perspective, facilitating switching between IT providers may be preferable. The latter law aims at protecting personal data by granting the rights to data subjects. Data transactions are thus permitted only when the data subject's control is warranted. These differences lead to conflicts between enforcement agencies. Under certain conditions, a data protection authority may impose some restrictions against personal data transactions, but a regulatory agency in competition law may insist on personal data sharing among competitors. Thus, defining the legal positioning of data portability becomes important.

2 The Right to Data Portability

2.1 General Data Protection Regulation

The Right to Data Portability. Article 20(1) of the GDPR defines the right to data portability, granting the data subject the right to receive his/her personal data provided to a controller, in a structured, commonly used, and machine-readable format, and the right to transmit those data to another controller without hindrance from the current

---

[2] WP29 is composed of respective representatives of the supervisory authority (ies) designated by each EU country, the authority (ies) established for the EU institutions and bodies, and the EU Commission.

[3] Digital Single Market is "one in which the free movement of goods, persons, services and capital is ensured and where individuals and businesses can seamlessly access and exercise online activities under conditions of fair competition, and a high level of consumer and personal data protection, irrespective of their nationality or place of residence" [3].

controller [1]. Article 20(2) grants the data subject the right to have his/her personal data transmitted directly from one controller to another, where technically feasible. This right is close to the right of access already protected in the Data Protection Directive in 1995 [4], but it expands the right of access to direct transmission between controllers.

WP29 published Guidelines on the Right to Data Portability (last revised and adopted on April 05, 2017) [5]. It aims at clarifying the scope, conditions under which the right applies, and the scope of "personal data provided by the data subject." A directory of a data subject's contacts created by a webmail service, titles of books purchased online, or bank transactions to a service that manages budget are examples of data included in the scope of the right. WP29 notes that "the right to data portability is not limited to personal data that are useful and [is] relevant for similar services provided by competitors of the data controller[4].

Although WP 29 indicates that the term "provided by the data subject" must be interpreted broadly, "inferred data" and "derived data" such as the outcome of an assessment of user health or a profile created for risk management and financial regulations (e.g., to assign a credit score or comply with anti-money laundering rules) are excluded from this scope[5]. The term "provided by" includes personal data related to the data subject activity or results from the observation of an individual's behavior, but does not include data resulting from subsequent analysis of that behavior[6]. Personal data created by a personalization or recommendation process, by user categorization or profiling are derived or inferred data, resulting in the exclusion from the right[7].

WP29 interprets "hindrance," as it "can be characterized as any legal, technical or financial obstacles placed by data controller in order to refrain or slow down access, transmission or reuse by the data subject or by another data controller"[8]. For instance, fees for delivering data and excessive delay fall under "hindrance"[9].

WP29 considers that "technical feasibility" should be assessed on a case-by-case basis. As Recital 68 of the GDPR does not oblige creating processing systems that are technically compatible, WP29 follows this by interpreting "portability aims to produce interoperable systems, not compatible systems"[10]. While WP29 does not identify the specific format, it strongly encourages cooperation between industry stakeholders and trade associations to devise a common set of interoperable standards and formats.

WP29 recognizes that the right will enhance competition between data controllers; but does not assure that the right will limit portable data to data necessary or useful for switching services[11].

---

[4] [5, p. 6].

[5] [5, p. 10].

[6] [5, p. 10].

[7] [5, pp. 10–11].

[8] [5, p. 15].

[9] [5, p. 15].

[10] [5, p. 17].

[11] [5, p. 4].

2.2 Efforts in Member Countries

French Digital Republic Act. The French Digital Republic Act (une République numérique) enacted on October 7, introduces the definition of "digital platform" and the right of data portability [6]. Article 48 of the Act (Article 224-42 of the Consumer Protection Code) requires any online public communication service provider to recover the following data for the consumer for free: all the files stored online by the consumer; all the data from using the consumer's user account and online account that is retrieved in an open standard, and is easily reusable and exploitable by an automated processing system; and other types of data associated with the user's online account that facilitate change of service providers. The last type of data takes into account the economic importance of the services concerned, the intensity of the competition between the suppliers, the utility for the consumer, the frequency, and the financial stakes of the use of these services.

SelfData Initiatives. WP29 offers midata in the United Kingdom and MesInfos/SelfData by FING in France as examples of experimental applications in Europe.

The midata program was launched in 2011 with the support of the Department for Businesses, Innovation and Skills. According to the midata website, a midata file is a record of up to 12 months of transaction history of the customer's personal current accounts (PCA). On downloading their midata file, the customer can submit it to comparison providers, who analyze the data in the file and provide customized information. This may help identify possible account switching options [7]. The midata Innovation Lab (miL) was set up to promote the midata program in 2011; the areas of the project originally covered education, transport, and health [8]. Currently, the midata initiative focuses on banking data. GoCompare.com is the first comparison provider launched in March 2015 to offer customers current bank account switching, whose efforts are expected to promote the midata program [9].

MesInfos/SelfData project, launched in 2012, is a pilot project that collects, uses, and shares personal data by and for individuals, under their complete control and is designed to fulfil their needs and aspirations. In 2017, the project will take actions to make experiments into reality by providing a personal cloud with 3,000 testers; transmitting data on these testers to each personal cloud of several organizations including insurance, energy, and telecom providers; and adding more data by testers on their personal cloud to gain use value from their data [10].

2.3 Experiences in the United States

The United States. The Obama Administration launched a series of My Data initiatives in 2010 [11] that aim to provide all Americans easy and secure access to their own personal data, such as Blue Button for health data, Green button for electric utility data, and My Student Data for Federal student data. "Data portability" in this sense refers to enhancing "the ability to download the information that a service stores for or about an individual" [12]. However, unlike the GDPR, the term does not allow direct switching of providers.

The Obama administration asked for comments from stakeholders on issues including benefits and drawbacks, the need for governmental regulation, and health data in September 2016. The administration published comment summary in January 2017 and stated that "portability should be incentivized but not mandated." This means that additional government regulation is not necessary, since the market should not be regulated in a manner that is inefficient, ineffective, and not suitable to context-specific data portability needs, as they would move overseas to avoid overly burdensome regulations and new regulations would be premature for rapidly developing industries [13]. U.S. data portability is underlined by clear and transparent communication, thereby building individuals' trust.

3   Antitrust Laws and "Essential Facilities" Doctrine

3.1   The United States

Sherman Act. The right to data portability can be analyzed from the antitrust law perspective, as undertakings that refuse to move data to another undertaking may constitute a "refusal of deal." The U.S. first discussed this issue. Before the enactment of the Sherman Act in 1890, some court decisions had imposed "duty to deal" on public businesses such as a railway company or a shipping company [14].

Article 1 of the Sherman Act punishes any contract in restraint of trade or commerce; and Article 2 punishes monopolization, attempt to monopolize, and conspiracy to monopolize (15 U.S.C. §§ 1, 2). Refusal of a deal by a large online platform or platforms may contradict these provisions; however, this is deemed unlawful in exceptional circumstances. The U.S. Supreme Court, in the United States v. Colgate & Co. (1919), held that "in the absence of any purpose to create or maintain a monopoly, the act does not restrict the long recognized right of trader or manufacturer engaged in an entirely private business, freely to exercise his own independent discretion as to parties with whom he will deal" [15]. This ruling was followed by the Trinko decision in 2004. Contrary to the Aspen decision in 1985 that indicated a refusal to cooperate with rivals as a violation of Article 2 [16], the Supreme Court in Trinko held that "we have been very cautious in recognizing such exceptions, because of the uncertain virtue of forced sharing and the difficulty of identifying and remedying anticompetitive conduct by a single firm", "the few existing exceptions from the proposition that there is no duty to aid competitors"[12]. Opposing this ruling, the Department of Justice and the Federal Trade Commission (FTC) jointly argued that "if such a refusal involves a sacrifice of profits or business advantage that makes economic sense only because it eliminates or lessens competition, it is exclusionary and potentially unlawful," citing the Aspen decision [18]. Thus, "refusal of deal" remains controversial. If following the

---

[12] [17, pp. 408, 411].

ruling in Trinko, a refusal of data portability by a single dominant may not be deemed unlawful.

Refusal of data access has been disputed in some cases[13]. In LiveUniverse v. MySpace (2007), LiveUniverse alleged that MySpace prevented users from watching vidiLife videos that they or other users previously had loaded onto their MySpace webpage, violating Article 2. The District Court dismissed the claims as a company generally has a right to deal, or refuse to deal, with whomever it likes, as defined in the Trinko decision [20]. The District Court's dismissal was affirmed by the U.S. Court of Appeals. In Facebook v. Power Ventures Inc., Facebook alleged that Power accessed the Facebook website to extract all kinds of social networking contacts of users from its platform in violation of its terms of use, and when Facebook attempted to stop Power's unauthorized access, Power circumvented Facebook's technical barriers. The district court dismissed Power's claim that Facebook maintained monopoly power by threatening potential new entrants to the social networking market [21]. In PeopleBrowsr v. Twitter, PeopleBrowsr asked Twitter to grant it (full firehose) access to Twitter data to be able to offer analytics services and was denied this request. The parties resolved the case, and PeopleBrowsr was given firehose access through the end of 2013 [22, 23]. Vanberg and Ünver comment that US antitrust law and principles took a divergent path from mandatory access obligations, particularly after Trinko decision [19]. They argue that "proving the 'indispensability' or 'essentiality' of the requested input often poses the main difficulty for the plaintiffs to overcome" [19, para. 3.3.2].

Essential Facilities Doctrine. Information monopolization raises concerns about the "Essential Facilities" doctrine, which was developed in the 1970s. The theoretical background supporting the doctrine include the bottleneck theory facilitated by Neale [24], and the "public utility" facilitated by Sullivan [25].[14]

This principle derives from the Terminal R. Association ruling in 1912 [26], in which nonmembers of the defendant's joint company were refused access to railway terminal facilities. The ruling held that the building unified system of terminals violated Articles 1 and 2 of the Sherman Act, said to be the first leading case applied by the essential facilities doctrine. The doctrine was reaffirmed in other decisions [27]. While this doctrine typically encompasses physical facilities, the Sherman Act applies to the refusal of access to electronic network systems [28].

The first court case explicitly acknowledged the "essential facilities" doctrine was the Hetcht case [29]. The District of Columbia Circuit defined the doctrine by citing Neale's article, stating that "where facilities cannot practicably be duplicated by would-be competitors, those in possession of them must allow them to be shared on fair terms. It is illegal restraint of trade to foreclose the scarce facility"[15]. However, the Trinko

---

[13] [19, para. 3.3.2].

[14] "[I]f a group of competitors, acting in concert, operate a common facility and if due to natural advantage, custom, or restrictions of scale, it is not feasible for excluded competitors to duplicate the facility, the competitors who operate the facility must give access to the excluded competitors on reasonable, non-discriminatory terms," Sullivan [25, § 48, at 131].

[15] [24, p. 67].

decision refused to apply the doctrine stating that it had never recognized nor intended to recognize it[16].

3.2 The European Commission

Treaty on the Functioning of the European Union. The EU has a history of antitrust law that is less intensive than the U.S. Article 101 of the Treaty on the Functioning of the European Union (TFEU) [30] prohibits agreements, decisions, and concerned practices that may affect trade between Member States and prevent competitions. Article 102 prohibits abuse by one or more undertakings in a dominant position. Articles 101 and 102 succeeded Articles 81 (ex-81) and 82 (ex-86) of EC Treaty (Treaty of Rome) in 1957 with the conclusion of the Lisbon Treaty in 2009.

The dominant position was clarified in the Hoffmann case in 1979 [31]. The European Court of Justice (ECJ) defined abuse is an objective concept relating to the behavior of an undertaking in a dominant position that influences market structure in a manner that weakens the degree of competition and hinders the maintenance of the degree of competition still existing in the market or the growth of that competition [31, para 91]. The judgment in the European Court (fifth chamber) in another case interpreted an abuse as occurring when without any objective necessity, an undertaking holding a dominant position on a particular market reserves to itself an ancillary activity that could have been carried out by another undertaking as part of its activities on a neighboring but separate market, which could potentially eliminate all competition from such undertaking[17]. The refusal to enable data portability by a dominant firm is seen as "a form of exclusionary abuse as it might drive its competitors out of a specific relevant market and increase market concentration"[18].

Essential Facilities Doctrine in the EU. The EU has adopted the essential facilities doctrine from the U.S. Sherman Act. If a monopolist refuses "to provide other firms with access to something that is vitally important to competitive viability in a particular market," it constitutes a violation of Article 1 and 2 of the Sherman Act.[19] Renowned scholar Dr. Temple Lang notes a fundamental view to establish responsibility for refusal of access under the doctrine. He states the following: (1) competition law does not require companies to give their competitors access to their assets, net-works, or intellectual property; (2) this is same under both Articles 101 and 102 of the EC Treaty, under the "essential facilities" principle; (3) "this principle applies only if the refusal to give access has serious anticompetitive effects, if access is essential to enable competitors to compete, and if there is no legitimate business justification for the refusal"[20]. He further elaborates by stating, "The principle applies only where the facility cannot be duplicated at all by competitors, even if acting together, for legal, economic or

---

[16] [17, pp. 410–411].

[17] [32, para 27].

[18] [19, para 3.2].

[19] [33, p. 87] .

[20] [34, S117–118].

geographical or other physical reasons, and where the refusal to contract would eliminate competition in a downstream market for which access to the facility is necessary, and not merely advantageous"[21]. As the U.S. Supreme Court cautiously limits the scope of the doctrine, interpretations in the EU also appear restrictive.

In Commercial Solvents, the ECJ first found the denial of deal owing to abuse of dominant position according to Article 86 (currently 102). Commercial Solvents was a monopolist manufacturer of chemical raw materials who refused to supply material to a regular customer and competitor on the downstream market, thereby risking all competition on the part of this customer. Other court cases have also developed this doctrine through denial of access [36].

The European Commission expressly declared the criteria for an "essential facility" in B&I Line v. Sealink case (1992). The European Commission held that "a dominant undertaking which both owns or controls and itself uses an essential facility, i.e., a facility or infrastructure without access to which competitors cannot provide services to their customers, and which refuses its competitors access to that facility or grants access to competitors only on terms less favorable than those which it gives its own services, thereby placing the competitors at a competitive disadvantage, infringes Article 86, if the other conditions of that article are met"[22].

In the Magill case, three Irish broadcasting companies refused to share weekly listings of TV programs to the Magill TV Guide. The ECJ in 1995 held that this refusal prevented constitutes an abuse under Article 86 (current 102)[23]. Similar to U.S. courts, this decision implicates that intangible obstacles can impediment new entries to the market.

In IMS Health (2015), the ECJ presented restrictive conditions to ensure that a refusal to deal is treated as abuse: (1) the refusal relates to a product or service that is indispensable for carrying on a particular business; (2) the refusal prevents the emergence of a new product with a potential consumer demand; (3) it is unjustified and aims to exclude any competition in a secondary market[24,25]. Inge Graef et al. noted that similar to the U.S. antitrust law, dominant undertakings can decide freely with whom they wish to deal under the abuse of the dominance regime of European competition law. Only in exceptional circumstances can an obligation to contract be imposed based on the essential facilities doctrine[26].

The ECJ held in Microsoft (2007) that "non-Microsoft work group server operating systems must be capable of interoperating with the Windows domain architecture on an equal footing with Windows work group server operating systems if they were to be marketed viably on the market"[27]. This was a specific case of Microsoft almost holding a dominant position in the relevant market, and a considerable legal burden had to be

---

[21] [35, p. 21].

[22] [37, para 41].

[23] [38, para 53–54].

[24] [39, para 38].

[25] This ruling is confirmed in Microsoft case [41, para 332].

[26] [40, p. 382].

[27] [41, para 421].

met particularly with regard to proving the indispensability of the data to which access is sought[28]. Regarding this, Lang strongly distinguishes the position of Microsoft and Google on the account of the nature of the product or service, the essentiality of the product or service, the burden of switching cost, and the existence of network effects. He defines a "platform" as "a combination of hardware and software on the basis of which other companies (software vendors in the Microsoft case, and advertisers in the Google case) offer products and services to end customers in competition with one another." He identified Windows as Microsoft's platform and the Internet as that of Google. The contrasts between Microsoft's Windows and Google's Internet are: Microsoft charges users and Google offers free services; software developers must be available on Windows, while publishers can reach consumers through a variety of services other than Google; switching cost is high in the case of Microsoft and it is negligible in the case of Google; there were important network effects in Microsoft case, while there do not seem to be any network effects for search activities[29,30]. His argument clearly denies Google's dominant position and thereby rejects that it is an essential facility.

3.3 Merger Cases Bridging Privacy and Anti Competition

Some merger cases take into account privacy affects. In re Google-DoubleClick (2007), both the European Commission [42] and the FTC [43] referred to the effects on privacy. While the European Commission separated the merger decision and legal obligations in the 1995 Data Protection Directive [4] etc., it permitted internet service providers to track all the online behavior of their users and stated that large internet service providers could team up with advertisement companies to utilize such data within the confines of privacy rules, but that with customers' consent, they could use such data, for instance, in exchange for lower prices[31]. Though the FTC also approved the merger, two members expressed privacy concerns raised owing to the production of highly sophisticated targeting data by combining both companies [44, 45]. In re Microsoft-LinkedIn (2016), the European Commission acknowledged that data privacy was an important parameter of competition in the SNS service market. It stated that privacy-related concerns could be considered in competition assessment "to the extent that consumers see it as a significant factor of quality, and the merging parties compete with each other on this factor" [46]. A privacy concern would arise if both undertakings' user databases are integrated, as this could shut out LinkedIn's competitors from accessing Microsoft's API, which they need to access user data stored in the Microsoft cloud [46].

---

[28] [41, pp. 382–383].

[29] [35, pp. 7–9].

[30] Google case seems to be related to the case that the European Commission fined Google €2.42 billion for abusing dominance as search engine by giving illegal advantage to own comparison shopping service, on June 27th, 2017.

[31] [42, para 271].

Facebook's misleading practice caused the European Commission in 2017 to fine it €110 million for providing incorrect or misleading information during the Commission's investigation under the EU Merger Regulation [47]. Facebook made a commitment in 2014 that it would not establish reliable automated matching between Facebook and WhatsApp users' accounts [48]. However, in 2016, WhatsApp announced updates to its terms of service and privacy policy, contradicting the said Facebook commitment.

The European Commission fined Google €2.42 billion for breaching EU antitrust rules in 2017. Google was found to have abused its market dominance as a search engine by promoting its own comparison shopping service in its search results, and demoting those of competitors, thereby depriving consumers of genuine choice of services. The Commission held that search engine markets in all EEA countries had been monopolized by Google, which had high market shares exceeding 90% in most countries since 2011. The more consumers use a search engine, the more attractive it becomes to advertisers, resulting in attracting even more consumers and improving results. This creates high barriers for entering the market [49]. The European Commission also noted two preliminary findings in 2016 with respect to the Android operating system and AdSense that Google had abused its dominant position [50, 51].

4 Discussion

4.1 Issues for Discussion

The above discussion identifies the following issues: (1) Is the right to data portability in the GDPR effective? (2) Should the right to data portability be legally regulated?; (3) Can the right be regulated from an antitrust perspective?

4.2 Is the Right to Data Portability in the GDPR Effective?

While the right to data portability is already provided in the GDPR, the right has not strongly influenced countries' legislations other than the EU member states. This right is critically reviewed by Vanberg and Ünver[32]. They list six issues: (a) limitations on data generated by the data controller; (b) privacy rights of third parties; (c) technical feasibility of data transfer; (d) disproportionate costs and efforts; (e) transfer of data may compromise valuable proprietary information and intellectual privacy; (f) enforcement issues pertaining to the right to data portability; and (g) privacy and data security risks.

Authors argue regarding Issue (a) that an auction website such as eBay allows users to only move their personal data and not their ratings and reputation to another auction site, as the latter is provided by the service provider[33]. Issue (b) is illustrated in a

---

[32] [19, para. 2.1].

[33] The authors referred to Inge Graef et al. [40].

photograph on Facebook in which several people appear; one data subject cannot import it to another social networking platform, as others appear in the picture[34]. Collaboration among market players is suggested to address Issue (c). Regarding Issue (d), many small- and medium-sized companies (SMEs) do not have the resources to be aware of the GDPR overall compliance, and write a corresponding software to move data to another provider. Not only is data portability costly, but also IT costs on SMEs will be significantly increased by the EU data protection reform[35]. Issue (g) pertains to the burden imposed on SMEs. In Issue (e), authors illustrate a case impeding a business model of an online digital service that helps users of online clothing retailers. If such a service provider is required to move data including detailed personal data specific to its services, this will clearly have a stifling effect on competition and innovative solutions. To address Issue (f), authors question legal and theoretical boundaries between the right and other laws, as well as enforcements. According to their analyses, the GDPR data portability is ineffective.

Swire and Lagos made a critical approach to the right to data portability [52]. They analyzed this right in the GDPR draft stage under antitrust or competition law, data protection, and privacy perspective, and pointed out several flaws as below.

The right to data portability is far broader than competition law as the right is considerably over broad and reduces consumer welfare. Despite the difficulty of demonstrating exclusionary practices including refusal to apply, denial of access to an essential facility, or a tying violation under European law, the right to data portability ignores arguments about substantial efficiency. The differences between the right to data portability and competition law are elaborated as follows: "[f]irst, the RDP [the right to data portability] does not require a showing of market power and applies equally to monopolies and to small and medium enterprises. Second, the RDP uses a per se approach that does not compare the precompetitive efficiencies against the harms to competition. Third, failure to write EIM [export–import module] software does not fit under the traditional categories of exclusionary conduct prohibited by current competition law"[36]. Ensuring interoperability is considerably hard to achieve even with Open Document Formats. The right to portability would impose substantial costs on suppliers of software and apps, which would then be passed on to consumers[37]. Competition law does not require the first service provider to write the EIM, as the exclusionary practices trigger sanctions only when there is a particularized showing in a specific market of harm to consumers, and the legal rule establishes high thresholds for the application of the essential facilities doctrine[38].

The authors also raised legal challenges to the right to data portability from the perspectives of data protection and privacy. They argued that the right is not well established, no jurisdiction has experimented with anything resembling the right, and the right appears to essentially be normal legislation and regulation rather than part of

---

[34] This case is illustrated by Barbara Engels [55] as below referenced.

[35] This issue has been intensively discussed in Swire and Lagos [52].

[36] [52, pp. 350–351].

[37] [52, pp. 354–356].

[38] [52, pp. 360–365].

the constitutional process despite the human right or the fundamental right argument in the EU[39]. In particular, the serious risk that the right would pose to security must be noted among their arguments. They assert that "one-time access to a site, such as by a hacker, can turn into a lifetime's download of data from that site. Defining the RDP, therefore, should be done with full awareness of risks to the right to data security"[40].

WP29 has partially responded to the above concerns. The guidelines allow controllers to transmit the entire directory of incoming and outgoing e-mails when switching a webmail service, or to move both the account holder and the remitters' information when transmitting bank account information. Collaboration among market players to overcome technical feasibility of data transfer is agreed by WP29 guidelines. WP29 indicates some authentication such as a shared secret, a onetime password, or suspending or freezing the transmission in addition to general risk mitigation measures. However, these measures are already implied in Article 5(1) (f) of the GDPR. It does not condition specific security measures on transmitting data[41].

Contrary to the narrow interpretation of the scope of the data, the European Commission expressed its concern over the overly broad interpretation of EU privacy regulators, because including observed data and raw data extend beyond what has been agreed upon in the legislative process. Observed data was one of the most controversial aspects of the guidelines.

4.3 Should the Right to Data Portability Be Legally Regulated?

Legally regulating the right to data portability gives rise to three options. The first is to limit personal data by stipulating the right in an act to protect personal data, the second is to encompass a broad range of data by stipulating the right in an act to anti-competition. The third is to enact a new law incorporating both perspectives.

The GDPR preceded an anti-competition act. Although the right to data portability in the GDPR has led to controversial issues, this new incorporation is very promising, as it significantly empowered the data subject. Other countries have encouraged voluntary efforts. The United States resorts to voluntary efforts, as it considers that portability should be incentivized but not mandated. The U.K. and France have also engaged in self-data approaches, some of which are backed by governmental agencies. It should be noted that they aim to help consumers access and use data collected about them by service providers, and not to directly switch data between undertakings.

Vanberg and Ünver emphasize the importance of controller–controller data transfer and request clear guidelines from the WP29, such as "what is meant by technically feasible, what is meant by data provided by the data subject himself/herself, as well as clarifying the delimitations of the right to data portability" [19, para. 5]. My argument is that controller–controller portability cannot be obliged from data protection perspective, as such obligation excessively impedes the economic rights of data controllers and imposes unnecessary legal burden on them. GDPR included "technically feasible"

---

[39] [52, pp. 365–373].

[40] [52, p. 373].

[41] [5, pp. 11, 18–19].

in controller–controller portability to address the above concerns. Moreover, the purpose of data protection is to protect individual's right, and not to foster competitive environment. If data portability is based on data protection, the structure of the right has to be established under the control of an individual, in addition to the scope of data being limited to personal data.

This article does not necessarily encourage legislative proposal on data portability, but it considers legal obligations from antitrust perspective might be needed if controller–controller portability should be achieved. Concerning the third pattern of regulation, the Digital Republic Act in France is a leading example. This act can include non-personal data portability, as it takes into account the economic importance of the services concerned, and the right includes "all the files stored online by the consumer." The European Commission encourages introducing a general right to data portability for non-personal data, considering that the right "could be seen as a possible means to enhance competition, stimulate data sharing and avoid vendor lock-in".[42]

As some merger cases pertain to privacy concerns, there are possibilities of bridging privacy and anti-competition, even as discrepancies exist between them. For instance, if a dominant online platformer seeking to combine customer data with another company contradicts its previous statements, it may be fined. Regarding personal data, enforcement policies by a competitive regulator and a data protection authority must be considered. In principle, rejection of access to personal data is not usually deemed illegal as the basic concept of an act on protecting personal data restricts disclosure of personal data from a business entity to a third party. A dominant company will be liable to the violation of access refusal against an antitrust law only when there is no issue from the personal data protection perspective, since individuals have provided their consent to the disclosure. In other words, when a company holds a dominant power in a certain market, data collected through business activities in the market play an indispensable role in businesses, and obtaining alternative data is technically and economically difficult, then unreasonable rejection to data access request by others may violate an antitrust law[43].

However, Swire et al. point out "important aspects of ICT industries suggest that a rule that mandates interoperability will often reduce innovation"[44]. As MySpace replaced Friendster and later Facebook took the MySpace dominant position, successive dynamic competition in the technology space comes from Joseph Shumpeter's "creative destruction"[45]. As a result, obligatory data portability based on the anti-competitive perspective is not a simple solution.

---

[42] [53, pp. 46–49].

[43] This issue was discussed in the expert committee in the Fair Trade Commission of Japan [54].

[44] [52, p. 358].

[45] [52, p. 358].

4.4   Can the Right Be Regulated from an Antitrust Perspective?

Considering antitrust laws and discussions of the essential facilities doctrine, a "duty to deal" cannot be easily granted to a competitor, as the principle of freedom of trade poses high legal barriers.

Barbara Engels analyzed the right to data portability from a competition policy [55]. She argued that "it is recommendable or at least not harmful to competition to make data portability obligatory when platforms offer complementary services. Furthermore, data portability can be recommendable when market players offer substitute products and one player is dominant due to anticompetitive conduct"[46]. For platforms offering essentially the same products (substitutes), data portability is desirable if market dominance is abused, as portability reduces the risk of customer lock-in. By contrast, data portability is harmful if there is no abusive anticompetitive conduct, since SMEs would be precluded from gaining returns on investments. Enforcements through competition law are preferable[47]. For platforms offering complementary services (e.g., a trading and a payment platform), data portability obligatory is recommendable or not harmful when platforms offer complementary services. Further, when market players offer substitute products and one player is dominant due to anticompetitive conduct, data portability can be recommendable. Conversely, where there is no anticompetitive conduct resulting in market dominance, data portability should not be obligatory but rather enforced through competition law if necessary. However, these conclusions need to be interpreted[48] in a nuanced fashion on the timeframe and on the type of innovation.

Engels researched anti-competitive behaviors in online markets by mapping the category of platform markets and economical aspects including network effects economics of scale, differentiation, congestion, switching costs, and market concentration. In search engine markets, positive direct network effects are low, positive indirect network effects are high, and economics of scale are also high, the degree of differentiation is low, congestion is low, and switching costs are medium. What should be noted is that the market concentration is high, which increases the risk of dominance abuse. Therefore, search engines should focus on a data portability regulation. In the case of trading platforms and social network markets, data portability should be obligatory only when they are particularly large and offer complementary or substitute products. The author remarks that contrary to the ex-ante regulation of the right to data portability, ex-post enforcements based on competition law are also possible. According to her, the right to data portability should be interpreted in a tailored manner as well as be dependent on the type of platform[49].

---

[46] [55, pp. 9, 13].

[47] [55, pp. 7, 10, 13].

[48] [55, pp. 9–10].

[49] [55, pp. 13–14].

5 Conclusion

Data portability is a right crossing data protection and competitive perspectives. As the right to data portability in the GDPR is explained based on the fundamental human rights, WP 29 does not clearly state the effects of the right on fostering competition. As Engels pointed out, "Data portability could significantly strengthen innovation by making data more available - but it could also hamper innovation by making data too available. A clear correlation is not detectable and thus should also not be suggested by the GDPR"[50].

According to the above analyses by Vanberg and Ünver, and Swire and Lagos, the current GDPR provision seems to be ineffective. If the right to data portability intends to adjust to anti-competitive perspective, the obligations must not be equally applied to large platformers and SMEs, rigid authentication methods have to be explored, and intensive examinations on the inter-operative format should be elaborated.

Engels proposes that data portability should be interpreted in a tailored manner as well as dependent on the type of platform. Though there is not an established definition on how "platformers" can be defined, Lang's definition is informative as a general term.

This article does not necessarily criticize the obligatory right to data portability, but proactive efforts to overcome the above issues are imperative. In particular, the possibility of controller–controller portability should be pursued. In terms of personal data protection, data portability must be analyzed on the basis of each individual; thereby the scope of the discussion is inevitably narrowed. By contrast, competitive perspective does not limit the range of data, and it can encompass the obligatory controller–controller portability. When it comes to examining such a right to portability, ensuring that data would not be gathered by large enterprises and clarifying legal conditions on imposing sanctions should be considered essential.

In sum, what are indicated from the above discussions are: (1) the right to data portability in the GDPR is the first promising provision which has arisen a lot of discussions issues, in particular the scope of the data, IT costs imposed on SMEs, and theoretical boundaries and enforcements based between data protection and antitrust laws, need to be further examined; (2) if the controller–controller portability is called for, antitrust perspective broadly encompass the scope of data is preferred than data protection regulation; (3) combining data protection and antitrust perspectives into a single law would be difficult due to the differences of them; (4) when it comes to establish data portability scheme from antitrust perspective, data portability should be obliged depending on the kinds of platform.

To achieve effective data portability, controller–controller transfer is preferable, and by following certain conditions, an antitrust regulatory scheme can be implemented. While this right does not overcome the monopoly owned by digital giants, it is expected to foster sound data flow using existing data platforms.

---

[50] [55, p. 13].

Acknowledgements. I would like to thank Ms. Mika Nakashima for assisting me with this study by providing useful information. This work was supported by JSPS KAKENHI Grant Number 15K03237.

References

1. European Union: Regulation (EU) 2016/679 of the European Parliament and of the Council of 27 April 2016 on the protection of natural persons with regard to the processing of personal data and on the free movement of such data, and repealing Directive 95/46/EC (General Data Protection Regulation). Off. J. L. **119**, 1–88 (2016)
2. European Commission. http://europa.eu/rapid/press-release_MEMO-15-6385_en.htm
3. European Commission. http://eur-lex.europa.eu/legal-con-tent/EN/TXT/?qid=1447773803386&uri=CELEX:52015DC0192
4. European Union: Directive 95/46/EC of the European Parliament and of the Council of 24 October 1995 on the protection of individuals with regard to the pro-cessing of personal data and on the free movement of such data. Off. J. L. **281**, 31–50 (1995)
5. Article 29 Data Protection Working Party (2017) Guidelines on the right to data portability. Retrieved from http://ec.europa.eu/newsroom/just/item-de-tail.cfm?item_id=50083
6. The Law Number 2016-1321, The Digital Republic Act of October 7, 2016 (1). https://www.legifrance.gouv.fr/af-fichTexte.do?cidTexte=JORFTEXT000033202746&categorieLien=id
7. PCA midata. http://www.pcamidata.co.uk/
8. Department for Business Innovation & Skills. https://www.gov.uk/government/up-loads/system/uploads/attachment_data/file/262271/bis-13-1314-the_midata-inno-vation-opportunity-v2.pdf
9. GoCompare. http://www.gocompare.com/money/midata/
10. MESINFOS. http://mesinfos.fing.org/
11. White House: My Data: Empowering All Americans with Personal Data Access (2016). https://obamawhitehouse.archives.gov/blog/2016/03/15/my-data-empower-ing-all-americans-personal-data-access
12. White House: Exploring Data Portability (2016). https://obamawhitehouse.ar-chives.gov/blog/2016/09/30/exploring-data-portability
13. White House: Summary of Comments Received Regarding Data Portability (2017). https://obamawhitehouse.archives.gov/blog/2017/01/10/summary-comments-re-ceived-regarding-data-portability
14. State v. Hartford & New Haven R.R. Co., 29 Conn. 538 (1861), Texas Express Co. v. Texas & Pacific Ry. Co., 6 F. 426 (C.C.N.D. Tex. 1881), Southern Express Co. v. Memphis, etc. R. Co., 8 F. 799 (C.C.E.D. Ark. 1881)
15. United States v. Colgate & Co., 250 U.S. 300, 307 (1919)
16. Aspen Skiing Co. v. Aspen Highlands Skiing Corp. 472 U.S. 585 (1985)
17. Verizon Communications, Inc. v. Law Office of Curtis v. Trinko, LLP, 540 U.S. 398 (2004)
18. The Statement Made by the Department of Justice and Federal Trade Commission in Trinko Case. http://supreme.findlaw.com/supreme_court/briefs/02-682/02-682-mer-ami-usa.html
19. Vanberg, A.D., Ünver, M.B.: The right to data portability in the GDPR and EU competition law: odd couple or dynamic duo?. Eur. J. Law Technol. **8**(1) (2017)
20. LiveUniverse, Inc. v. MySpace, Inc., (C.D. Cal. June 4, 2007), affirmed by 304 Fed. Appx. 554 (9th Cir. December 22, 2008)
21. Facebook Inc., Plaintiff, v. Power Ventures, Inc., et al.: U.S. Dist. LEXIS 93517 (N.D. Cal. July 20, 2010) (2010)

22. PeopleBrowsr.   http://blog.peoplebrowsr.com/2012/11/peoplebrowsr-wins-tempo-rary-restraining-order-compelling-twitter-to-provide-firehose-access/

23. PeopleBrowsr: PeopleBrowsr and Twitter settle Firehose dispute (2013). http://blog.peoplebrowsr.com/2013/04/peoplebrowsr-and-twitter-settle-firehose-dispute/

24. Neale, A.D.: The Antitrust Laws of the United States of America, 2nd edn. (1970)

25. Sullivan, L.A.: Handbook of the Law of Antitrust (Hornbook series) (1977)

26. United States v. Terminal Railroad Association, 224 U.S. 383 (1912)

27. Associated Press v. the United States, 326 U.S.1 (1945)

28. Otter Tail Power Co. v. United States, 410 U.S. 366 (1973)

29. Hetcht v. Pro-Football Inc., 570 F.2d 982 (1977)

30. Consolidated versions of the Treaty on European Union and the Treaty on the Functioning of the European Union. Off. J. C 326: 1–390 (2007)

31. Case 85/76 Hoffmann-La Roche & Co. AG v Commission of the European Com-munities. ECR 461 (1979)

32. Case 311/84 CBEM v. CLT and IPB. ECR 3261 (1985)

33. OECD: The Essential Facilities Concept (1996). http://www.oecd.org/competi-tion/abuse/1920021.pdf

34. Lang, J.T.: Competition Law and Regulation Law from an EC perspective. Fordham Int. Law J. 23(6), S116–S121 (1999)

35. Lang, J.T.: Comparing microsoft and Google: the concept of exclusionary abuse. World Compet. 39(1), 5–28 (2016)

36. Istituto Chemioterapico Italiano S.p.A. and Commercial Solvents Corporation v Commission of the European Communities. ECR 223 (1974)

37. Commission Decision of 11 June 1992 relating to a proceeding under Article 86 of the EEC Treaty (IV/34.174-Sealink/B&I-Holyhead: Interim measures). http://ec.europa.eu/competition/antitrust/cases/dec_docs/34174/34174_2_2.pdf

38. Joined Cases C-241/91 and C-242/91 Radio Telefis Eireann (RTE) and Independ-ent Television Publications Ltd (ITP) v. Commission of the European Communities (1995) ECR I-743

39. Case C-418/01 IMS Health GmbH & Co. OHG v NDC Health GmbH & Co. KG (2004). ECLI:EU:C:2004:257

40. Graef, I., Wahyuningtyas, S.Y., Valcke, P.: Assessing data access issues in online platforms, 39 Telecommunications Policy, pp. 375–387 (2015). http://dx.doi.org/10.1016/j.telpol.2014.12.001

41. Case T-201/04 Microsoft Corp. v Commission of the European Communities (2007). http://curia.europa.eu/juris/liste.jsf?num=T-201/04

42. Case COMP/M.4731 Merger Case on Google and DoubleClick (2007). http://ec.europa.eu/competition/mergers/cases/deci-sions/m4731_20080311_20682_en.pdf

43. Statement of Federal Trade Commission Concerning Google/DoubleClick (2007). https://www.ftc.gov/system/files/documents/public_state-ments/418081/071220googledc-commstmt.pdf

44. In the matter of Google/DoubleClick Dissenting Statement of Commissioner Pam-ela Jones Harbour (2007). https://www.ftc.gov/sites/default/files/documents/public_statements/statement-matter-google/doubleclick/071220harbour_0.pdf

45. Concurring Statement of Commissioner Jon Leibowitz Google/DoubleClick (2007). https://www.ftc.gov/sites/default/files/documents/public_statements/concurring-state-ment-commissioner-jon-leibowitz-google/doubleclick-matter/071220leib_0.pdf

46. European Commission: Mergers: Commission approves acquisition of LinkedIn by Microsoft, subject to conditions (2016). http://europa.eu/rapid/press-re-lease_IP-16-4284_en.htm

47. European Commission: Mergers: Commission fines Facebook €110 million for providing misleading information about WhatsApp takeover (2017). http://eu-ropa.eu/rapid/press-release_IP-17-1369_en.htm

48. European Commission: Mergers: Commission approves acquisition of WhatsApp by Facebook (2014). http://europa.eu/rapid/press-release_IP-14-1088_en.htm

49. European Commission: Antitrust: Commission fines Google €2.42 billion for abusing dominance as search engine by giving illegal advantage to own comparison shopping service (2017). http://europa.eu/rapid/press-release_IP-17-1784_en.htm

50. European Commission: Antitrust: Commission sends Statement of Objections to Google on Android operating system and applications (2016). http://eu-ropa.eu/rapid/press-release_IP-16-1492_en.htm

51. Antitrust: Commission takes further steps in investigations alleging Google's com-parison shopping and advertising-related practices breach EU rules http://eu-ropa.eu/rapid/press-release_IP-16-2532_en.htm

52. Swire, P., Lagos, Y.: Why the right to data portability likely reduces consumer welfare: antitrust and privacy critique. Md. Law Rev. **72**(2), 335–380 (2013)

53. European Commission: Staff Working Document on the free flow of data and emerging issues on the European data economy (2017). https://ec.europa.eu/digital-single-market/en/news/staff-working-document-free-flow-data-and-emerging-issues-european-data-economy

54. Fair Trade Commission: Expert Committee Report on Data and Competition Policy (2017). http://www.jftc.go.jp/cprc/conference/index.files/170606data01.pdf (in Japanese)

55. Engels, B.: Internet Policy Review 4 (2016). http://policyreview.info/articles/analy-sis/data-portability-among-online-platforms

Philosophy

Artificial Intelligence Does Not Exist: Lessons from Shared Cognition and the Opposition to the Nature/Nurture Divide

Vassilis Galanos[(⊠)] [ID]

Science, Technology and Innovation Studies Subject Group,
School of Social and Political Science,
University of Edinburgh, Old Surgeons' Hall, Edinburgh EH1 1LZ, UK
Vassilis.Galanos@ed.ac.uk

Abstract. By changing everything we know about artificial intelligence (AI),
the ways in which AI changes everything will be more plausible to explore.
Arguments concerning AI as a potential threat are based on two taken-for-
granted assumptions, namely, that AI exists as a separate category of intelligence, different to "natural" intelligence, and that intelligence is an inherent
property of separable entities, such as humans or robots. Such arguments have
given rise to ethical debates and media commentary concerned with AI, often
quite extrapolating, followed by catastrophic scenarios. However, several discussions in the philosophy of social science (as well as in theoretical approaches
to synthetic biology and cybernetics) have suggested (a) that the distinctions
between "natural"/"human" and "artificial"/"nonhuman" are fallible, and (b) that
intelligence should most likely be conceived as an environmental/systemic
property or phenomenon – a shared cognition. In an attempt to import these
discussions within the context of the socio-ethical implications of AI, this paper
deconstructs the components of the term AI by focusing firstly on the invali-
dation of the term "artificial" and secondly on "intelligence." By paraphrasing
Lacan's dictum that "the woman does not exist" as in relation to the man, this
paper proposes that AI does not exist as in relation to a natural intelligence or in
relation to non-intelligent entities. By this double, apparently simple, lesson
learned from a re-examination of AI's characteristics, a number of questions are
raised, concerning the co-production of morality in meshed human/robotic
societies, as well as a tentative agenda for future empirical investigations.

Keywords: Artificial intelligence · Shared cognition · Ecology of mind
Nature-Nurture divide · Roboethics · Philosophy of social science

1 Introduction

"Sociology may know about class, or about gender. But how much does it know about spe-
ciesism - the systematic practice of discrimination against other species? And how much does it
know or care about machines?" [35]

Arguments about ultraintelligence [22], superintelligence [4, 8], or technological
singularity [63, 64], are based on the assumption that artificial intelligence (AI) exists

D. Kreps et al. (Eds.): HCC13 2018, IFIP AICT 537, pp. 359–373, 2018.
https://doi.org/10.1007/978-3-319-99605-9_27

as a separate entity which competes with human, natural, or otherwise named conventional types of intelligence. The present paper is an attempt to challenge the fixity and consistency of the term AI from a social ontology perspective, as a means to support a non-dichotomous argument of ontological and mental continuity between humans and machines. Instead of being alarmed by how AI might change everything and impose an existential threat, it should be useful to think of alternative ways to conceive AI and change everything about how we face it. As humans become more mechanized [2, 23] and machines become more humanized [21, 32, 42, 46] it will gradually make little or no sense to distinguish between artificial and non-artificial intelligence [18]. However, a general eschatological climate of fear and skepticism towards intelligent machines is indicated, a stance which is further sustained and perpetuated by a recent hype in the press, associated with prestigious figures of science and business (yet, interestingly non-AI specialists like Stephen Hawking or industrialists like Elon Musk) who warn about the end of humankind by AI through media of mass appeal or, in other cases, through philosophical inquiry [7, 13–17, 20, 24–26, 60]. This controversy brings forth a number of ethical questions (in the emerging field of roboethics [37]), difficult to be tackled according to our current criteria, contradicting the human-machine continuum suggested by other authors (and defended in the present article). Meanwhile, it has been suggested that this form of dogmatic apprehension of "singularitarianism" (i.e. the belief that autonomous supra-human AI entities will outperform and even dominate humans) is on the one hand in lack of evidential and realistic basis, and on the other might impose great ethical and technical difficulties in AI R&D [18, 19].

In this brief conceptual investigation, I propose that emphasis on human responsibility with regard to AI can be fostered through the minimal requirement of abolishing the artificiality of AI and the outdated notion that intelligence is a separate component belonging to individual entities. To sustain the argument, I will examine separately the two parts of the phrase, namely "artificial" and "intelligence," applying arguments stemming from the philosophy of social science (PSS) concerning (a) the opposition to the nature/nurture and nature/culture divides [59], and (b) the holistic (non-individualist) theories of shared cognition, treating intelligence as a phenomenon occurring within systems or collectives and not as an individual unit's property [38]. Through this terminological challenge, I do not propose a new definition of AI; instead, I recommend that AI is indefinable enough outside research contexts, so that humans should think more of the social impact upon AI, instead of AI's impact upon humanity.

The everyday understanding of AI (very often pronounced simply as/eɪ aɪ/, alienated from the acronym's meaning) is loaded with taken for granted assumptions adhering binary conceptualizations of the given/constructed or the singular/plural cognition. However, this was not the case in the early foundations of the field. According to McCarthy, Minsky, Rochester, and Shannon's 1955 classic definition, AI is the "conjecture that every aspect of learning or any other feature of intelligence can in principle be so precisely described that a machine can be made to simulate it" [44]. Advanced AI, thus, should prove that our celebrated human intelligence is totally replaceable. According to Paul Edwards' historical accounts,

"AI established a fully symmetrical relation between biological and artificial minds through its concept of 'physical symbol systems' [...] In symbolic processing the AI theorists believed they had found the key to understanding knowledge and intelligence. Now they could study these phenomena and construct truly *formal-mechanical* models, achieving the kind of overarching vantage point on both machines and organisms" ([10] original emphasis).

On the contrary, examples of the public (mis)understanding of AI and its clear-cut discrimination from human intelligence can be found in recent newspaper articles, when AI and human intelligence are equally responsible for various accidents, but AI is mainly accused – chess and Go players compete and machines impose threats, beauty judging algorithms are accused for racial discrimination, toddlers are bruised accidentally by patrolling robots, job losses to novel AI software, are only but a few of recent newspaper stories [27, 36, 45, 46, 51, 55, 66, 67]. From all this, it is inferred that artificial and human intelligences do exist, and moreover, they do exist as separate items. All of the cases above were phenomena which involved a symmetrical amount of human and machine, organic and inorganic intelligence; however, due to the novelty (and perhaps the "catchy-ness") of the technology, the blame falls upon AI, highlighting the need for a sociological investigation of the human-AI relationship. More specifically, such empirical accounts of human-machine interaction raise profound ontological questions, concerned with the location of intelligence and the difference between given and constructed. Such questions have been investigated through the PSS and other related disciplines, but so far, the philosophy of computer science and AI has left to a great extent underexplored.

A pure sociology of AI is still lacking, at least since its early announcement by John Law. According to him, machines are discriminated by sociologists as inferior actors imposing some determinism upon society, yet, controlled by humans: "Most sociologists treat machines (if they see them at all) as second class citizens. They have few rights. They are not allowed to speak. And their actions are derivative, dependent on the operations of human beings" [35]. As shown above, humans and machines are widely understood as binary opposites, even by advocates of human-machine equality, like Turing ("one could not send the creature to school without the other children making excessive fun of it" [61]) or Sloman:

"History suggests that the invention of such robots will be followed by their exploitation and slavery, or at the very least racial discrimination against them. Will young robots, thirsty for knowledge, be admitted to our schools and universities? Will we let them vote? Will they have equal employment opportunities? Probably not. Either they will be forcibly suppressed, or, perhaps worse, their minds will be designed to have limits" [54]

By challenging the ontological foundation of AI, I aim to blur the sharp boundary separating machine from human intelligence, building a framework of open potentialities where intelligence is a shared processual phenomenon with no primacy of value in its natural or artificial traits. The theme of this paper is inspired by the non-binarization between female and male, as expressed by psychoanalyst Jacques Lacan. He defended femaleness by the non-negation of a missing sexual organ, exclaiming provocatively that "*la femme n'existe pas*" ("the woman does not exist," [31]), but affirmatively has vagina, so is not heteronomously determined by the man (the constitutive phallus). With the danger of oversimplification, his argument means that the binarization is futile as long as it is based on a dominating, privileged constitutive agent (the male), whereas this formal difference does not make any difference at all (hence, the man does not exist either). I suggest that a similar movement should be made with artificial and human intelligence, however, without the reference to psychoanalysis (and ghosts inside the machines hylomorphist arguments), but through the pathway of understanding intelligence as a primary phenomenon with humans and machines as its agents.

2 Artificial: Nature-Nurture, Nature-Culture, and the Convergence of *Physis* and *Techne*

"Try to imagine the world not tomorrow or next year, but next century, or next millennium: a divorce between *physis* and *techne* would be utterly disastrous both for our welfare and for the wellbeing of our habitat" [14]

Are behavioral characteristics learned or inherited? Are entities and phenomena natural outcomes or are they products of sociocultural manipulation? These two questions synopsize two very common themes in the PSS (as well as biology and general philosophy), known as the nature/nurture and the nature/culture debate[1] [38, 40, 58]. Are machines products of a long-term evolutionary process, inscribed in natural randomness, or are they the outcomes of human intention? Does their intelligence depend on human intelligence or is it simply intelligence?

According to Longino, "[w]hen confronting a social phenomenon, [...] we frequently ask whether the behavior is a result of nature or nurture, of our (inherited) biological makeup or of our social environment. Another contrast used to mark roughly the same distinction is that between innate and learned" [38]. Longino's stance rejects the dichotomy as misleading, referring to "methodological reductionism," that is, a strategy of reducing the analyzed phenomenon to its constituents and therefore speak of different scales of impact affecting the generated phenomenon. In such a way, for example, socioeconomic factors (nurture) can explain behavior (nature), but also psychological behavior can explain social phenomena, which in turn can be reduced to molecular levels of analysis, and so on. This assertion reflects a general tendency towards the abandonment of the dichotomy and the recognition of an interactionism between them. As Sherry points out: "There is no longer any question among most developmental psychologists, cognitive scientists, neuroscientists, and biologists that nature interacts with nurture to determine human behavior" [53]. Based on this axiom, we are left with two main options: (a) either the concepts of nature and nurture exist but only as long as they are in interaction (the biologist view):

---

[1] The two debates basically differ in their disciplines of reference, that is, the former is usually associated with biology and the second with anthropology and sociology. For the purpose of this paper, I treat them – as well as the concept of artificiality – in tentative synonymy with reference to their common meaning: "Culture derives from the Latin word for tilling or plowing, *colere*, whose past participle, *cultus* (plowed), is the direct ancestor of the modern term. It means to raise, nurture, or develop. In this sense, at least, culture literally cannot exist without nature, since tilling requires land" [56].

"We have moved beyond *versus*. Whether it is medical traits like clinical depression, behavioral traits like criminality, or cognitive traits like intelligence, it is now widely recognized that 'nature versus nurture' does not apply. [...] Rather, it is a truism that these complex human traits arise from both nature and nurture, and differences in those traits arise from both differences in nature and differences in nurture" (original emphasis[2] [58])

Or, (b) the very concept of nature versus culture can be criticized precisely as a cultural construct (MacCormack in [40]) and hence the entire existence of nature and culture can be doubted. "There is no culture, in the sense of the cumulative works of man [*sic*], and no nature to be tamed and made productive" (Strathern in [40]). When we speak about culture, however, as long as no reference to biology is given, we consider it as opposable to nature:

"In general, cultus is clearly the artificial, learned, and to some degree arbitrary aspect of human existence, as opposed to those aspects that we are born with or to (natus). This makes it the opposite of nature not only in the nature/culture debate, but in the old nature/nurture dichotomy as well. However, it is equally clear that culture, like nature, harbors paradox. Those who would reject nature as an unclear concept but still accept culture as a given need to look more carefully at both" [56]

Similarly, for Bruno Latour's principle of symmetry, nature and culture simply do not exist, but different groups of humans in different times have constituted different sets of what is natural and what is cultural (or societal) [34]. What constitutes culture and nature, also constitutes a set of paradoxes, for example nature can be the enemy to be tamed, the extra human disaster, but also it can be the reference to the norm, as when one acts according to natural reason. "The solution appears along with the dissolution of the artifact of cultures. All natures-cultures are similar in that they simultaneously construct humans, divinities and nonhumans" [34]. The social inconsistency of terming "nature" and the "natural" has been consistently explored in contexts of genomics and synthetic biology, where the importance of inheritance, innate characteristics, and environmental factors are of significant value [33, 48]. As Calvert puts it, "[a]n important aspect of how we understand 'natural' rests on what we oppose to it," in our case, the artificial (in tentative synonymy with "synthetic"), the social and the invented [6]. The debate is reaching a peak with Fausto-Sterling's connectionist approach on dynamic biological systems, concluding that "we are always 100 percent nature and 100 percent nurture" [12]. I do not see why these arguments stemming from synthetic biology could not be imported in the social studying of AI, given the similarity of binary oppositions researchers face[3].

The question concerning human intelligence as an innate characteristic or as an externally attached nourishment, can be posed with respect to the AI machine. What differentiates human from machine intelligence in such a dramatic way that allows the former to label the latter's intelligence as artificial? To my knowledge, there has been only one – and indeed very recent – related approach to AI, by Jordi Vallverdú when

---

[2] While space does not allow for further analysis, it is useful to suggest the relevance of this mention to "behavioral traits like criminality" when one thinks of AI applications assisting risk assessment in court systems, or other ethical dilemmas emerging from natural versus artificial forms of intelligence [37].

[3] Also, given that recent advances in synthetic biology are increasing making use of AI technologies.

introducing his article writes in the context of the forthcoming Singularity: "I will refer to both [humans and artificial devices] as kinds of 'entities', rejecting the distinction between 'natural' and 'artificial' as outmoded and just plain wrong" [62]. I sympathize, but simultaneously suggest that the outmodedness of the distinction is worth explored before being totally rejected, and furthermore, and highlight the difficulty in having done with the dichotomy, at least in language (something which is proven in the rest of his paper, despite his promise). To sum up:

Taking a physicalist/naturalist point of view, everything that exists in the universe (or multiverse) is natural. As Alfred North Whitehead puts it in his classic work "The Concept of Nature," "[f]or natural philosophy everything perceived is in nature. We may not pick and choose" [65]. If AI exists, it is natural – therefore, the "A" in "AI" is fallacious. If a flower, a dolphin, or a robot exhibits intelligence, it is intelligence despite its nonhumanity. It becomes obvious, then, that AI is by all means partaking in *physis* (nature) as much as in *techne* (craft, manipulation of nature). Natural kinds, by definition, do not exclude mechanic or constructed kinds; the only condition for the establishment of a natural kind is the common appearance of "certain necessary relations" of individuals of a given kind towards other kinds [9]. In this sense, AI entities might differ from human entities, but this does not allow for the label of artificiality to be given to any of the two kinds.

Taking a social constructionist point of view [3], everything which we perceive and verbalize is a cultural product. Hence, nothing is a natural given, but anything we observe, manipulate, and produce is modified by our social shaping and personal interests. If we perceive AI, it is the result of social manipulation – therefore, the "A" in AI is redundant. It is nonsensical to admit that a form of intelligence is artificial to the extent that everything we intelligently perceive is an artificial interpretation. It becomes obvious, then, that AI is by all means partaking in *techne* (craftsmanship). However, this *techne* is nothing else than the cultural value that we attribute to all givens:

> "Culture is *nomos* as well as *techne*, that is, subsumes society as well as culture in the marked sense. Nature is equally human nature and the non-social environment. To these images of the 'real' world we attach a string of evaluations – so that one is active, the other passive; one is subject, the other object; one creation, the other resource; one energizes, the other limits" (Strathern in [40])

Strathern, in her deconstruction of the nature-culture dichotomy, further refers to other taken-for-granted binaries as "innate/artificial" and "individual/society" (in [40]). Hence, this common treatment of all similar dipoles acts here as a smooth passage to the second part of the argument which analyses the singular/shared intelligence as well as the intelligence/non-intelligence. To recapitulate, AI can be seen both as an innate characteristic of a mechanism which satisfies a number of technical conditions in some sense as well as a constructed attribute dependent on its cultural contexts in some other sense.

3 Intelligence: Distributed Cognitive Agency and Giant Steps to an Ecology of Mind

"It would not, I imagine, be very bold to maintain that there are not any more or less intelligent beings, but a scattered, general intelligence, a sort of universal fluid that penetrates diversely the organisms which it encounters, according as they are good or bad conductors of the understanding" [41]

"But, surely, the interesting question is what entitles us to attribute intentionality to non-machines in the first place? What makes our description of human intentionality other than metaphorical?" (Woolgar, in [35])

Does a decision-making intelligent machine act as a single entity or as in relation to a group? Does its intelligence (natural, artificial, or otherwise) exist inside it, or is it the outcome of collective processes? These are questions which PSS tackles when addressing themes of individuals versus populations, and two main strands, individualism and collectivism, have been developed in order to methodologically explain phenomena either "in terms of individuals and their intentional states" or through other means when this method is found insufficient [59]. Tollefsen thoroughly overviews the different approaches, and while the question is admittedly related to the nature-nurture debate, however, the individual-population question is mostly a matter of method and not of ontological metaphysics of belief. There are many intermediate approaches, so, in a sense, the aforementioned "interaction" was there since the beginning. With AI, due to its permanent networked condition, it becomes almost imperative that we adhere to the collectivist approach. There is no precise ontological or epistemological limit separating a human's actions from their AI (or other) tools, as, given a particular case, all agents function as functions of each other; the calculations of an online buying recommendation system are the result of my interaction with the system which reflects at the same time my personal behaviour but also other customers' behavior, and so on. The distribution of intelligence and agency boundaryless and expanding and AI applications provide good evidence for this. However, this discussion is older than AI's recent resurgence, and the most relevant authors for the present theme examined here are Bratman, Pettit, Hutchins, and Epstein (with his references to Tuomela and Searle).

Michael Bratman speaks of shared cooperative activity (SCA) a concept of collective involvement for the achievement of a given goal with the following three requirements: (i) Mutual responsiveness, (ii) commitment to the joint activity, and (iii) commitment to mutual support [5]. Bratman's account is seminal, yet weak from a collectivist perspective, since as he admits, not all characteristics are found in the examined cases, and most importantly, SCA "is broadly individualistic in spirit; for it tries to understand what is distinctive about SCA in terms of the attitudes and actions of the individuals involved" [5]. With AI, we may assume only after some extrapolation, that responsiveness exists in the sense of a higher ethical motivation (however, ethical inscription in robotics is underway, [37]). If we make a distinction between responsiveness as a feature of value-driven decisions, and responsivity as an entity's ability to respond, at the current stage of AI development, we may speak of responsivity, but not of responsiveness. Similarly, algorithmically programmed commitment is – at least to our human eyes – no commitment at all. This is debatable, for example, if we consider a nihilistic approach to ethics, which negates the existence of values as driving forces, or the human mind as a well-advanced algorithmic process, or algorithmic commitment as an extension of human commitment, and so on. The clear-cut differentiation between human and machine is again blurred. In any event, the following discussion might help revising the SCA concept.

Philip Pettit's seminal book The Common Mind [49, 50] explores what constitutes human intentional thinking agents, and after sharply defining his terms concludes to his theory of the common or manifest mind, which is the necessity of interaction between individuals. Like Bratman, however, he also privileges the individual over the collective as the underlying force of this common decision. In his later article, he seems to withdraw this prioritization by referring to the interaction as the very prerequisite for one's autonomy. If an individual is not within a society, she cannot comprehend her individuality. While people are autonomous in one sense, "[t]hey may depend on one another for attaining the basic prerequisite of their individual autonomy; they may be able to realize that autonomy only in one another's company" [49, 50]. Again, this model can be applied to AI only via extrapolation. Since AI does not manifest its ontology by individuation, as it does by networking, the rule of verifying one's individualist value through their dependency with the group is not very convenient. However, it is quite reasonable to suggest that since the robot's "purpose" is to help humans, and since humans build robots to help them, the more the two are in interaction, the more the verification of the human-machine positive synergy will be.

Edwin Hutchins has been a pioneer both in contributing to the group mind hypotheses [28, 29, 59], as well as monitoring and reviewing relevant theories [30]. Constantly revisiting his terminology, in 1991 he modelled his connectionist distributed cognition framework in his theory of the "constraint satisfaction network." Such networks are composed of units whose connections represent constraints, whose frequency and density, in turn, determine the judgement of the network [59]. The units can be sub-network of a hierarchically higher network, so humans can be the units of a group, but also the inner complications of a human body may act as a constraint satisfaction network for a person. Hutchins generalizes his theory as such:

> "A system composed of a person in interaction with a cognitive artifact has different cognitive properties than those of the person alone [...] A group of persons may have cognitive properties that are different from those of any person in the group [...] A central claim of the distributed cognition framework is that the proper unit of analysis for cognition should not be set a priori, but should be responsive to the nature of the phenomena under study" [29]

In another article from the same year, he places his own theory among the pantheon of shared cognition frameworks which he denotes as "cognitive ecology" and defines as "the study of cognitive phenomena in context" [30]. Hutchins reviews the history and the differences between the approaches – namely, "Gibson's ecological psychology, Bateson's ecology of mind, and Soviet cultural-historical activity theory" [30]. Based on the simple premise that "[e]verything is connected to everything else" but "not all connectivity is equally dense" [30], cognitive ecology understands intelligence as a phenomenon and not as logical process, distributed beyond the human cranium, reaching multiple exo-human elements. While, like all previously analyzed theories of shared mind, Hutchins' theory takes human as the standard unit of interest, his repeated references to the work of Gregory Bateson offer a significant advantage with regard to AI's placement in the group mind theorizations. As Bateson straightforwardly refers to his notion of the ecology of mind (EoM), *"the mental characteristics of the system are immanent, not in some part, but in the system as a whole"* ([1], original emphasis). An example of an EoM follows:

> "Consider a man [*sic*] felling a tree with an axe. Each stroke of the axe is modified or corrected, according to the shape of the cut face of the tree left by the previous stroke. This self-corrective (i.e. mental) process is brought about by a total system, tree-eyes-brain-muscles-axe-stroke-tree; and it is this total system that has the characteristics of immanent mind" [1]

Interestingly, Bateson's ideas were shaped after his engagement with cybernetics and systems theory, the building blocks of AI, so that, in a sense, this paper comes now full circle. Within an EoM, or a cognitive ecology, or a not-necessarily-human constraint satisfaction network, intelligence exists despite the ontological nature of the units within the system. Paraphrasing Bateson, we may consider an ecology of human-smartphone-wireless connection-AI algorithm-food, and so on. Edwards speaks of such environments generated by new technologies as "closed worlds," pretty much echoing the same cyberneticist systems symmetry. Simply put (and similar to Hutchins' constrain networks), the restriction of a closed world opens up the possibilities for interconnections between the participants and for maximization of actions according to the rules: "Everything in the closed world becomes a system, an organized unit composed of subsystems and integrated into supersystems" [10]. Of great interest, is the sociologist and systems theorist Niklas Luhmann's contribution to legal frameworks – something which is yet to be related to recent discussions about robotic legal personhood [37]. Luhmann states that "a person is a unity formed only for purposes of communication, merely a point of allocation and address," reducing personhood to a temporary, partially self-contained, and self-aware unity ("which does not exclude the possibility of its imagining that it is a person") related to other similar unities [39].

Before concluding, I should mention my intentional avoidance in mentioning Raimo Tuomela and John Searle's theories of shared intention, who emphasize on collective intention as the primary decision-making driving force [59]. The reason of avoidance is twofold and is explicated in Brian Epstein's recent work on social objects without intention: on the one hand, various sub-groups constituting a phenomenon in question have different intentional [11]. On the other, when a fact or an object fails in fulfilling the role of its collective acceptance, this does not imply its failure as an institutional entity [11]. In fact, drawing from lessons in anthropology, he reminds us that several implied and unseen factors are generating social objects, so that a theory of collective intention does not hold (66–67). Among AI specialists, Searle's general disbelief towards the potentialities of AI and a machine's capability to think is well-known through his Chinese Room argument [52]. It is verified that these theories prioritize the individual human over the group, despite their holist-labels; in a sense, we can refer to them as crypto-individualist. Beata Stawarska emphasizes upon the enhancement of the I-You relationship and the decomposing of egocentrism through the advent of AI and robotics, leaving an open potentiality for equal communication with robots [57], but nonetheless does not explicitly expand the notion to human-AI symbiosis.

To conclude, intelligence, according to shared cognition approaches can be viewed as a phenomenon taking place in the context of a given ecology and not as an organism's intrinsic property. No organism can be imagined without a context, and therefore, intelligence is not owned by individuals but happens only within interaction. The fallacy of the letter "I" in AI is now sustained, since intelligence is not restrained within certain boundaries, and therefore it makes no sense to attribute this feature to a natural or artificial entity.

4 Conclusions–Objections–Future Work: AI Does Not Exist

A recurring problem (or perhaps advantage) in AI and robotics research is that the very term "AI" is relationally defined [21, 26, 36, 42, 43]. Sometimes an AI can mean a particular self-contained device, in the same way an automobile means a specific vehicle used for transportation. To a certain extent, this proposition is wrong, because one may argue that learning robots such as iCub or OpenCogBot [21, 43] make use of AI software, but they are not AIs themselves. Some other times, AI can mean the precise the software, which is enables after the coexistence of applications, physical supports, and goals, in the same way that transportation is the function of vehicles, infrastructure and operations of transport. To a certain extent, this proposition is also wrong, since claiming that IBM Watson or applications of advanced microcircuitry [32, 42] are themselves AIs is of little or no meaning given that they are only enabled to perform as parts of greater systems. (In that sense, any computer application or even a simple pocket calculator is an AI, and indeed this was the basic assumption for the early conceptions of this terminology, that is, the replication of any mental act [44, 52].) In most of the times both propositions are simultaneously right and wrong, depending on the context they are used. The problem occurs when the terms are used in non-research language, as in the press [27, 36, 55, 66]. In such cases, and after the present paper's analysis of terminology, it appears that propositions about AI are neither right or wrong; they are meaningless. While space limitations do not allow for an elaborate discussion of the topic, it seems that there is a need for AI and robotics researchers to act as brokers and intermediaries for the improvement of the public understanding of their respective fields. Science and Technology Studies (STS) scholars have often raised the important issue of such understandings, when "institutional hybrids," cases of scientific and technological artefacts or terms do not match exactly the criteria of multiple overlapping arenas such as law, policy, mass media, science fiction, and thus causing confusion (for example, in the case of "cybrids" and xenotransplantation where STS and other scholars collaborated to provide with analytical taxonomies of terminology, while also pointing out the difficulties of precise definition [23]).

As in certain cases of nonhuman transplants to humans and vice versa (not human-enough to be human, not animal-enough to be animal), the subject-referents of AI (for instance, autonomous robots), are, like humans, neither natural nor artificial, neither intelligent nor unintelligent, or else they are both. Consciousness, awareness, and intentionality are developing assemblages of contingencies, networks, and families of relationships, linked together by scales of context – according to the purposes of every researcher. On the one hand, AI exists, and in that sense is as natural (and as restricted by nature) as anything else which agreeably "exists." On the other, like any other notion, it is artificial, constructed and in continuous interplay with other machines, with humans, and the environment. Therefore, to the extent that our current human categorizations of what constitutes natural and artificial, or intelligence and non-intelligence, are vastly contingent and context-based concepts, we may proclaim: AI does not exist. Following Edwards, who suggests that AI and robots are historical constructs [10], AI is a historical convention as much as the notion of the human is – which, if human judgement is taken out of the loop, also does not exist.

If, however, it is proved that AI has no meaningful reason of being an ontological category – and proved it is as societies exist in networks of meshed human and nonhuman intelligence – then what accounts for justifying contemporary AI R&D and its ethics? The collapse of both nature/culture and human/nonhuman intelligence divides, leaves open the question of responsibility and action. As Vicky Kirby puts it in her forward to the recent volume What if Culture was Nature All Along:

"This reversal from natural to cultural explanations brings a sense of dynamism and political possibility – in short, no need for despair if we can change things. Yet such interventions also carry the message that nature/biology/*physis* is, indeed, the 'other' of culture, the static and primordial benchmark against which human be-ing and its agential imagination secures its exceptional status. But if the capacity to think stretches across an entire ecological landscape, what then? If nature is plastic, agential and inventive, then need we equate biologism and naturalism with a conservative agenda, a return to prescription and the resignation of political quietism?" [33]

No. At least, as far as AI is concerned, I suggest that the question left open by the present investigation is thoroughly socio-political. Among the basic priorities for future investigation of social studies of AI, after this paper's heretical conceptualization, are:

(a) attempts at more precise definitions and analytical taxonomies of various applications of AI according to experts,

(b) tentative (yet rigorous) demarcation of expertise especially in the cases of prestigious figures in mass media associating themselves with AI, and

(c) empirical investigation through qualitative means of the impact of current AI hypes and/or disillusionments in the public sphere on AI R&D and policymaking[4]

The overall feeling left by mainstream social commentary about AI is that the technology will change society. However, social studies should aim at highlighting how societal factors are impacting the conceptions of AI, and possibly, from an ethical scope, how should we change AI conceptually towards the greatest benefit (instead of proposing technologically deterministic responses of ethics to AI's impact).

If we change everything we take for granted about AI, we can see how AI and (not "in") society might change everything – as an act of co-production. Can there be a

---

[4] Exploring further details of issues of AI-related expertise and policymaking would exceed the scope of this paper; however, such studies should take into account the present paper's recommendations for the impreciseness of the term AI.

politics of decentralized and simultaneous 100 percent natural and 100 percent artificial cognition? As mentioned earlier, the emerging field of roboethics deals with the inscription of ethical drives into robots [19], [37]. Given empirical cases of perpetuation of biases based on the input of partial data (such as the AI-based beauty contest, [36]), one is tempted to ask: what is the normative morality "taught" to machines by humans? Moreover, if nature, nurture, human intelligence and AI do not exist, does "morality" exist? An increasing number of cybernetic devices becomes attached to human bodies or acts together with human brains for decision making, and an increasing number of human features and functions are inscribed to machines. Therefore, the line between the two traditionally assumed kinds blurs – in a similar manner with the blurrification that took place between the online and the offline, giving birth to the onlife condition [47]. Dichotomies are dangerous, and humans have been learning this the hard way (divisions according to gender, race, class, species have been infiltrated into institutional and social frameworks, leaving little or no room for nuances). Their social and legal implications are tremendous and difficult to modify after their lock-in. Policymaking and public portrayals of AI should adhere to the pragmatism of a human-machine continuum, and taken for granted dichotomies be taken with a pinch of salt. These questions verify the need of further exploration of networked and dynamic human-AI societies and admixed organic and inorganic features for future research.

Acknowledgements. The present paper has been greatly benefitted from the kind comments on earlier drafts by Richard Freeman. I would also like to express my gratitude to the two anonymous referees for providing suggestions for the improvement of this chapter.

References

1. Bateson, G.: Steps to an Ecology of Mind: Collected Essays in Anthropology, Psychiatry, Evolution, and Epistemology. University of Chicago Press, Chicago (1972)
2. Bedard, S., Tack, D., Pageau, G., Ricard, B., Rittenhouse, M.: Initial Evaluation of the Dermoskeleton Concept: Application of Biomechatronics and Artificial Intelligence to Address the Soldiers Overload Challenge. Defence Research and Development Canada Valcartier (QUEBEC) (2011). [online report, unclassified]. http://cradpdf.drdc-rddc.gc.ca/PDFS/unc121/p537035_A1b.pdf
3. Berger, P.L., Luckmann, T.: The Social Construction of Reality: A Treatise in the Sociology of Knowledge. Penguin, London (1991). Originally published: 1966
4. Bostrom, N.: Superintelligence: Paths, Dangers, Strategies. Oxford University Press, Oxford (2014)
5. Bratman, M.E.: Shared cooperative activity. Philos. Rev. **101**(2), 327–341 (1992)
6. Calvert, J.: Synthetic biology: constructing nature? Sociol. Rev. **58**(s1), 95–112 (2010)
7. Cellan-Jones, R.: Stephen Hawking warns artificial intelligence could end mankind. BBC News (2014). http://www.bbc.com/news/technology-30290540. Accessed 05 Dec 2015
8. Chalmers, D.: The singularity: a philosophical analysis. J. Conscious. Stud. **17**(9–1), 7–65 (2010)

9. Collier, J.: On the necessity of natural kinds. In: Riggs, Peter (ed.) Natural Kinds, Laws of Nature and Scientific Methodology, pp. 1–10. Kluwer Academic Publishers, Dordrecht, Boston, London (1996)

10. Edwards, P.N.: The Closed World: Computers and the Politics of Discourse in Cold War America. MIT Press, Cambridge (1997)

11. Epstein, B.: Social objects without intentions. In: Konzelmann Ziv, A., Schmid, H. (eds.) Institutions. Emotions, and Group Agents, pp. 53–68. Springer, Dordrecht (2014). https://doi.org/10.1007/978-94-007-6934-2_4

12. Fausto-Sterling, A.: The bare bones of sex: Part 1—sex and gender. Signs: J. Women Cult. Soc. **30**(2), 1491–1527 (2005)

13. Floridi, L.: Philosophy and Computing: An Introduction. Routledge, London (1999)

14. Floridi, L.: Information: A Very Short Introduction. Oxford University Press, Oxford (2010)

15. Floridi, L.: The Philosophy of Information. Oxford University Press, Oxford (2011)

16. Floridi, L.: The Fourth Revolution: How the Infosphere is Reshaping Human Reality. Oxford University Press, Oxford (2014)

17. Floridi, L.: Singularitarians, Altheists, and Why the Problem with Artificial Intelligence is H. A.L. (Humanity At Large), not HAL. In: Sullins, J. (ed.). Philosophy and Computers, vol. **14** (2), pp. 8–11 (2015)

18. Flusser, V.: Into Immaterial Culture. Metaflux Publishing, São Paulo (2015)

19. Galanos, V.: Singularitarianism and Schizophrenia. AI Soc. **32**(4), 573–590 (2016)

20. Gibbs, S.: Elon Musk: artificial intelligence is our biggest existential threat. The Guardian, October 27 2014. https://www.theguardian.com/technology/2014/oct/27/elon-musk-artificial-intelligence-ai-biggest-existential-threat. Accessed 25 Nov 2014

21. Goertzel, B., et al.: OpenCogBot: Achieving generally intelligent virtual agent control and humanoid robotics via cognitive synergy. In: Proceedings of ICAI 2010 (Editors and place unspecified) (2010). https://pdfs.semanticscholar.org/8b1e/37b11af2c25181569a1815767737bdd691cb.pdf

22. Good, I.J.: Speculations concerning the first ultraintelligent machine. Adv. Comput. **6**, 31–88 (1965)

23. Haddow, G., Bruce, A., Calvert, J., Harmon, S.H., Marsden, W.: Not "human" enough to be human but not "animal" enough to be animal–the case of the HFEA, cybrids and xenotransplantation in the UK. New Genet. Soc. **29**(1), 3–17 (2010)

24. Hawking, S., Russell, S., Tegmark, M., Wilczek, F.: Stephen Hawking: 'Transcendence looks at the implications of artificial intelligence-but are we taking AI seriously enough?'. Independent, 2014(05–01), 9313474 (2014). http://www.independent.co.uk/news/science/stephen-hawking-transcendence-looks-at-the-implications-of-artificial-intelligence-but-are-we-taking-9313474.html. Accessed 05 Dec 2015

25. Hern, A.: Elon Musk says he invested in DeepMind over 'Terminator' fears. Guardian, 18 June 2014. https://www.theguardian.com/technology/2014/jun/18/elon-musk-deepmind-ai-tesla-motors. Accessed 30 July 2014

26. Hern, A.: China Censored Google's AlphaGo Match Against World's Best Go Player. Guardian, 24 May 2017. https://www.theguardian.com/technology/2017/may/24/china-censored-googles-alphago-match-against-worlds-best-go-player. Accessed 25 May 2017

27. Hooton, C.: A robot has passed a self-awareness test. Independent, 20 July 2015. http://www.independent.co.uk/life-style/gadgets-and-tech/news/a-robot-has-passed-the-self-awareness-test-10395895.html. Accessed 25 July 2015

28. Hutchins, E.: The social organization of distributed cognition. In: Resnick, L.B., Levine, J. M., Teasley, S.D. (eds.) Perspectives on Socially Shared Cognition, pp. 283–307. American Psychological Association, Washington, DC (1991)

29. Hutchins, E.: Enaction: Towards a New Paradigm for Cognitive Science. MIT Press, Massachusetts (2010)
30. Hutchins, E.: Cognitive ecology. Top. Cogn. Sci. **2**(4), 705–715 (2010)
31. Johnston, A.: Non-existence and sexual identity: some brief remarks on Meinong and Lacan. In: Lacanian Ink: The Symptom, no. 3, Fall/Winter (2002). http://www.lacan.com/nonexist. htm. Accessed 30 Mar 2017
32. Keller, I., Lohan, K.S.: Analysis of illumination robustness in long-term object learning. In: Okita, S.Y., Mutlu, B., Shibata, T. (eds.) 2016 25th IEEE International Symposium on Robot and Human Interactive Communication (RO-MAN), pp. 240–245. IEEE, August 2016
33. Kirby, V.: Foreword. In: Kirby, V. (ed.) What if Culture was Nature All Along?. Edinburgh University Press, Edinburgh (2017)
34. Latour, B.: We Have Never Been Modern. Harvester Wheatsheaf, Hertfordshire (1993)
35. Law, J.: Introduction: monsters, machines and sociotechnical relations. In: Law, J. (ed.) A Sociology of Monsters: Essays on Power, Technology and Domination. Routledge, London, London (1991)
36. Levin, S.: A beauty contest was judged by AI and the Robots didn't like Dark Skin. Guardian, 08 September 2016. https://www.theguardian.com/technology/2016/sep/08/ artificial-intelligence-beauty-contest-doesnt-like-black-people. Accessed 15 Sept 2016
37. Lin, P., Abney, K., Bekey, G. (eds.): Robot Ethics: The Ethical and Social Implications of Robotics. MIT Press, Cambridge, Massachusetts, London (2012)
38. Longino, H.: Individuals or populations? In: Cartwright, N., Montuschi, E. (eds.) Philosophy of Social Science: An Introduction, pp. 102–120. Oxford University Press, Oxford (2014)
39. Luhmann, N.: Closure and openness: on reality in the world of law. In: Teubner, G. (ed.) Autopoietic Law: A New Approach to Law and Society, pp. 335–348. Walter de Gruyter, Berlin (1988)
40. MacCormack, C.P., Strathern, M.: Nature, Culture and Gender. Cambridge University Press, Cambridge (1980)
41. Maeterlinck, M.: The Intelligence of the Flowers. The University Press, Cambridge (1907)
42. Markram, H., et al.: Reconstruction and simulation of neocortical microcircuitry. Cell **163** (2), 456–492 (2015)
43. Metta, G., Sandini, G., Vernon, D., Natale, L., Nori, F.: The iCub humanoid robot: an open platform for research in embodied cognition. In: Madhavan, R., Messina, E. (eds.) Proceedings of the 8th Workshop on Performance Metrics for Intelligent Systems, pp. 50–56. ACM, August 2008
44. McCarthy, J., et al.: A proposal for the Dartmouth summer research project on artificial intelligence, August 31, 1955. AI Mag. **27**(4) (2006). http://www.aaai.org/ojs/index.php/ aimagazine/article/view/1904/1802. Accessed 02 Feb 2016
45. McGoogan, C.: Robot Security Guard Knocks Over Toddler at Shopping Centre. The Telegraph, 13 July 2016. http://www.telegraph.co.uk/technology/2016/07/13/robot-security-guard-knocks-over-toddler-at-shopping-centre/. Accessed 20 Sept 2017
46. Murgia, M.: Humans versus robots: how a Google computer beat a world champion at this board game – and what it means for the future. Telegraph, 14 May 2016. http://s.telegraph. co.uk/graphics/projects/go-google-computer-game/index.html. Accessed 20 Sept 2016
47. Onlife Initiative: The Onlife Manifesto. In: Floridi, L. (ed.). The Onlife Manifesto: Being Human in a Hyperconnected Era, pp. 7–13. Springer International (2015). https://doi.org/10. 1007/978-3-319-04093-6_2
48. Parry, S., Dupré, J.: Introducing nature after the genome. Sociol. Rev. **58**(s1), 3–16 (2010)
49. Pettit, P.: The Common Mind: An Essay on Psychology, Society, and Politics. Oxford University Press, Oxford (1996)
50. Pettit, P.: Defining and defending social holism. Philos. Explor. **1**(3), 169–184 (1998)

51. Rajan, N.: Robot Kills Volkswagen Factory Worker. The Huffington Post, 02 July 2015. http://www.huffingtonpost.co.uk/2015/07/02/robot-kills-man-at-volkswagen-factory_n_7711462.html. Accessed 20 Feb 2017
52. Searle, J.R.: Is the brain's mind a computer program? Sci. Am. **262**(1), 26–31 (1990)
53. Sherry, J.L.: Media effects theory and the nature/nurture debate: a historical overview and directions for future research. Media Psychol. **6**(1), 83–109 (2004)
54. Sloman, A.: The Computer Revolution in Philosophy: Philosophy, Science and Models of Mind. The Harvester Press, Sussex (1978)
55. Solon, O.: Oh the Humanity! Poker Computer Trounces Humans in Big Step for AI. The Guardian, 30 January 2017. https://www.theguardian.com/technology/2017/jan/30/libratus-poker-artificial-intelligence-professional-human-players-competition. Accessed 01 Feb 2017
56. Sorvig, K.: Nature/culture/words/landscapes. Landsc. J. **21**(2), 1–14 (2002)
57. Stawarska, B.: Primacy of I–you connectedness revisited: some implications for AI and robotics. In: AI & Society (2017). https://link.springer.com/article/10.1007/s00146-017-0695-6
58. Tabery, J.: Beyond Versus: The Struggle to Understand the Interaction of Nature and Nurture. MIT Press, Massachusetts (2014)
59. Tollefsen, D.: Social ontology. In: Cartwright, N., Montuschi, E. (eds.) Philosophy of Social Science: An Introduction, pp. 85–101. Oxford University Press, Oxford (2014)
60. Treblin, N.: Robots could be the worst thing ever for humanity, warns Stephen Hawking. RT, 22 October 2016. https://www.rt.com/uk/363502-artificial-intelligence-stephen-hawking/. Accessed 01 Nov 2016
61. Turing, A.M.: Computing machinery and intelligence. Mind **59**(236), 433–460 (1950)
62. Vallverdú, J.: The emotional nature of post-cognitive singularities. In: Callaghan, V., et al. (eds.) The Technological Singularity, The Frontiers Collection, pp. 193–208. GmbH Germany: Springer-Verlag, Heidelberg (2017). https://doi.org/10.1007/978-3-662-54033-6_11
63. Vinge, V. (1993). The Coming technological singularity. Balley, S., Landis, G.A., Nichols, L.D., Ziegfeld, R., Chen, J., Hassett, V. (eds) VISION-21 Symposium, NASA Lewis Research Center and Ohio Aerospace Institute, 30–31 March 1993. https://ntrs.nasa.gov/archive/nasa/casi.ntrs.nasa.gov/19940022856.pdf
64. Vinge, V.: Signs of the Singularity. IEEE Spectrum **45**(6) (2008)
65. Whitehead, A.N.: The Concept of Nature. Cambridge University Press, Cambridge (1920 [2015])
66. Williams, O.: A Japanese Insurance Firm is Replacing Its Workers With Artificial Intelligence. The Huffington Post, 05 January 2017a. http://www.huffingtonpost.co.uk/entry/japanese-insurance-firm-artificial-intelligence_uk_586e5d39e4b0c1c826fa8cc8. Accessed 06 Jan 2017
67. Williams, O.: Robot Convinces Google's 'I'm Not A Robot' Tool That It's Not A Robot, Internet Implodes. The Huffington Post, 17 January 2017b. http://www.huffingtonpost.co.uk/entry/robot-google-bot-detection-tool_uk_588b6f35e4b0302743196b39. Accessed 28 Jan 2017

PHR, We've Had a Problem Here

Minna M. Rantanen[✉] and Jani Koskinen[✉]

Information Systems Science, Turku School of Economics,
University of Turku, Turku, Finland
{minna.m.rantanen, jasiko}@utu.fi

Abstract. Personal health records (PHRs) have been a global trend in recent decade. It has been seen as a concept and tool that could help patients maintaining health, improving their well-being, and supporting communication with healthcare professional etc. Despite the great amount of research about PHR there is no consensus what a PHR actually means in academic literature or other arenas. There are multiple terms in use and multiple definitions which set challenges for rational discourse between citizens/patient, healthcare providers, system developers and policy makers. Especially, when citizens—as key stakeholder—should also be able to understand what those systems are we need clear and understandable definition for PHR's. In the paper, we conduct a brief survey for different definitions and show the problems that arise with the incoherent use of the term "PHR".

Keywords: Personal health record · PHR · Definition · Rational discourse
Quasi-rational discourse

1 Introduction

Rantanen and Heimo [1] state in their article about definition of term patient information system (PIS): "To have a discussion with one another we require a common set of terms understood by everyone. To develop complex multidisciplinary information systems we need a possibility for discussion. To enhance our level of healthcare we require complex multidisciplinary information systems. Thus, the further development of terminology in the subject is not only recommended but required."

The same statement applies to all terms in field of health related informatics[1]. The need for clearing the terminology of health informatics and health information technology is pointed out by several authors [2]. Besides PIS, terms like eHealth, electronic medical record (EMR) and electronic health record (EHR) have had their share of critique about vagueness and multiple meanings [3–5]. Also definition of personal health record (PHR)—or lack of it—has been noted before [6–9]. However, there is still no consensus about what does the term PHR mean or what separates it from several similar terms used to describe information systems for health information management.

---

[1] Medical informatics, nursing informatics, health informatics, etc. Note that field(s) itself has not been able to create the common name for the research area.

D. Kreps et al. (Eds.): HCC13 2018, IFIP AICT 537, pp. 374–383, 2018.
https://doi.org/10.1007/978-3-319-99605-9_28

Although many scholars seem to agree, that there indeed is a problem with terminology in health informatics, not all share this view. For example, Coiera [10, p. 113] states that "With such a wide variation in the functions that could be expected from an EMR, it is probably unwise to try to define the EMR in any formal way. It is more fruitful to observe that there are a range of clinical activities that use and communicate information, and that some of these can be supported through the introduction of technology".

However, there are several problems if we accept situation where term are not properly defined. By accepting unclear terms we lack of common ground for discussion, face problems of interpreting the current literature etc. We will focus those problems in more detail later in this paper. However, we want to note it shortly here: to solve problems we need to have a discussion, and to have meaningful discussion participants need to have the same understanding about the used terms—in this case about the term PHR. It seems that based on confusing use of terms in academic literature we have ended up in situation where understating about PHR is obscured: our academic discourse/understanding is blurred and political communication can be even claimed to be infertile.

In this paper, we focus on the definition of PHR and problems that lack of definition creates. In the second section, we will give insight to background of PHRs and role of those in the healthcare and health(care) informatics. In the third section, we present the state of incoherence in the PHR term use and present some variation of the term[2]. In the fourth section, we present examples of problems that these several conceptualizations and vague definitions of PHR create for public discussion and academic research. In the fifth section, we are using Habermas [11, 12] as source for our consideration for needed discourse and to highlight the need for consensus about terms and their definitions. In the final chapter, we draw the conclusions and shed light on our future research.

2 Background of PHRs

In today's society, healthcare is changing from doctor centered to consumer centered service, where individuals are authorities of their own health instead of being mere passive patients [13]. Thus, the patients are more and more seen as customers that must be served. This has set the need for information systems used in healthcare and PHR is getting more and more attention as it has this personal aspect build in [14, 15]. Shared decision-making and PHRs as part of it is seen as promising approach in healthcare even it has not achieve the expectations [16]. Therefore, PHR can be reasonably seen as central technology and concept for patient/customer/citizen -oriented healthcare in this patient-centered and even individualist era of healthcare.

Simultaneously, paradigm of healthcare is moving—or at least it should be—from sickness centered care towards preventive care where the aim is to support the health of individual and hence help them to achieve personal plans [17–20]. Thus, in modern

---

[2] Even the claim that those terms are variation of PHR is actually inconsistent with spirit of this paper that seeks the clear terminological coherence of life.

society individuals are seen more and more as experts of their own health and as the ones, who should be the ones taking care of their well-being in sickness and in health— although they still may need support from medical professionals.

Internet and web-based services have allowed people access vast amount of information about well-being, that traditionally has been a privilege of medical professionals. It has been argued that also people's perception of health has shifted toward more holistic view, and that they are actually more interested in gathering information about their health. [18, 21, 22] Simultaneously, technological development has made it also easier to track and measure one's health. An extreme example of this is the rise of the bio-hacker culture [23].

More modest example is the popularity of personal health records (PHRs) among healthcare service providers. Many countries, researcher and healthcare organizations seem to believe, that PHRs are the solution to the sustainability gap of public healthcare system [22–24]. However, lack of inter-operationality between EHRs and PHRs still exists, even though the first notions of PHRs can be traced back to the late 1970s [25]. Likewise, even though there has been effort to increase the use of PHRs the adoption rate has been low [26].

Nevertheless, healthcare is under pressure to become more efficient due to aging of the population, which is assumed to decrease available funding as well as increase demand of healthcare services [20]. PHRs are seen as solutions that offer several benefits that can help to achieve more sustainable healthcare [7]. In theory, users of PHRs can get more accurate health information, monitor their own health and communicate easier with healthcare professionals [22, 27, 28].

These theoretical benefits are seen as gateway to more efficient and sustainable healthcare, since it is assumed that by focusing on more preventive measures and by providing people self-treatment instructions the demand of healthcare will decrease [29]. Some studies have shown that use of PHRs may be a key component when designing new models of healthcare. It has been shown that in case of chronically ill patients, PHRs have provided better coordination of care, communication and patient empowerment as well as decreased need for consulting a doctor [22, 27, 29].

Besides effects that will rise from more autonomous patients, wider utilizing of PHRs is seen as an action that will benefit also healthcare professionals. In theory, if patients use PHRs, healthcare professional will get more accurate information to work on and thus, the quality of treatment will improve. [6, 29] Thus, PHRs are often represented as a simple (technical) solution to a major problem facing healthcare. However, as we can see from the past, problems with efficiency in healthcare have rarely been solved by simple implementation of an information system [30–33]. In healthcare, careless attempts to change the healthcare system by implementing a technical system, have in the worst-case scenarios led to loss of human lives—such as in case of London Ambulance service [34].

It must be remembered, that this example is extreme and more often the consequences are less severe. For instance, it has been studied that promoted benefits of electronic medical records (EMR) such as efficiency and cost savings are rarely met, because these systems are not designed to support the processes of healthcare professionals, but rather to full-fill the idea of new and efficient process [30, 32, 35].

Thus, it could be beneficial to conduct more user-centered design and development of these kinds of systems to acknowledge social dimension.

In case of PHRs, majority of users are not medical professionals but individuals that have varying knowledge, motivations and goals when using these systems. User groups can vary from individuals that live specific chronic condition to whole nations [33]. This makes the users of PHRs more heterogeneous group than for instance the users of EMRs and thus, conducting a user-centered design and development more challenging.

Since many countries are currently developing their public healthcare with implementation of PHRs [33], we argue that it should be possible to develop these systems based on public discussion. This discussion should allow willing citizens to participate on development of governmental PHRs, so that these systems would serve them in the best possible way and make it possible to reach more sustainable healthcare that is seen as goal of national PHR development.

3 Different Terms and Various Meanings

The wide use of term PHR's is evident and intuitively it can seems to be quite straightforward term to use. However, the PHR is concept that is neither unambiguous or generally defined but instead has long and changeable history. [13] Although PHRs have been lately discussed as something new and innovative, in reality the concept has been first used in the late 1960s. During the 1970s and 1980s term PHR was used in the literature referring the paper-based document that was carried by individual. During these decades cases research was focusing to some group of people—as young female students in Japan—or some social concerns as maternal and child health [13].

We claim that the 1990s was a decade when it really started to be noted and new millennium is time when it popped up to be a mainstream term of healthcare (IS) research. In the 1990s the PHR was used also as "patient-held health record" and this idea of patient-held approach has been trend in literature even there was also other derivatives of term PHR [13]. Nowadays it seems that term PHR is stabilized to mean personal health records.

The problem is same for the whole area of healthcare information system research we do not have common definition for acronyms that are used in research [1, 5, 6]. In other words, it seems that field do not have common understanding about the terms. In most cases articles using terms—as PHR, EHR etc. —are not using any clear definition. However, there are some occasionally, but not systematically, used definitions of PHR. In addition that we have different meanings for term PHR there found different variants/modification for it such as:

- interactive preventive health record (IPHR) [36]
- electronic personal health record (ePHR) [37]
- personally controlled health management systems (PCHMS) [38]
- mobile personal health records (mPHR) [15]
- personal health record application (PHA) [39]
- self-management mobile personal health record (SmPHR) [40]
- personal electronic health records (P-EHR) [41]

Likewise, there are commonly used two categories for PHR's: Tethered PHR's that are part of EHR or at least connected to it and Stand-alone ones that are independent records even the categories can overlap [6]. There exists somewhat known and used definitions for PHRs even those still cannot seen that they have established position or recognition in the field of Health informatics. For instance, definitions from Markle Foundation are to some extend used in scientific literature.

Markle foundation: "A PHR is an Internet-based set of tools that allows people to access and coordinate their lifelong health information and make appropriate parts of it available to those who need it" [42] and "an electronic application through which individuals can access, manage and share their health information, and that of others for whom they are authorized, in a private, secure, and confidential environment." [43].

There are, however, some problems with these definitions. These definitions [42, 43] suggest, that PHR cannot be anything else than an electronic system. This is problematic, since individuals can, and probably do, also store information about their health on paper [44]. Thus, defining PHR as "internet-based" or as "an electronic application" is too narrow to grasp the full spectrum of PHRs, which have been and still can be also analogical systems.

First definition of Markle Foundation [42], also suggests that in order to a system be a PHR, the information should cover the whole life of individual. This is rather optimistic idea since some PHRs can be linked to local patient information systems, and thus, information can be limited to specific time that individual has lived in that area. Even if PHR is not limited to certain area, it is not likely that an individual would use the same system their whole life, since people are keen to try new systems in order to find one that fits their needs [23].

Markle Foundation's second definition [43] does also suggest, that a PHR is a PHR only if it is in "private, secure, and confidential environment". Since, health information is private information, these attributes should be noted when designing a PHR. Nevertheless, it cannot be stated that a PHR is not a PHR, when it is a target of hacking or its environment is otherwise compromised. Thus, private, secure and confidential environment is only a preferable characteristic of PHR, not one that defines it.

For instance, International Organization for Standardization (ISO) has also made an effort to form a definition for PHR. Although earlier definitions share the problems of being limited to electronic PHRs and desirable features [22], the updated version from 2014 avoids these problems.

ISO definition: "PHR representation of information regarding or relevant to the health, including wellness, development, and welfare of a subject of care, which may be stand-alone or integrating health information from multiple sources, and for which the individual, or their authorized representative, manages and controls the PHR content and grants permissions for access by and/or sharing with other parties" [45].

This definition of ISO does not limit PHRs to electronic systems, does not assume that a PHR contains lifelong information, and it does not mix preferable characteristics with fundamental aspects. However, this particular version from 2014 has been rarely used in the scientific papers. It could serve as a good ground definition to PHR—if it would be used. However, there is still need to analyze this definition and its relation to other terms used, since it might not sufficient to cover them all.

4 Problems and Challenges

The aforementioned heterogeneous use of term will harm research on PHR's as we lack the common agreement or understanding what PHRs actually are. In some articles PHR can mean the extension for EHR so that patient has possibility to see their patient information and in some occasions manage their information. However, in another article PHR is seen as stand-alone system for collecting information about one's health. Thus, despite the efforts made in defining this term, there is a conceptual vacuum that can create misunderstandings and other problems.

Besides there being many different definitions in scientific writings there is also a problem of not defining what is meant by PHR [13, 46, 47]. This, we argue, is more severe problem than using any of the existing definitions or creating a yet another definition. This is a major problem due to variety of different definitions and inter-pretations that people can have. Hence, when definition is not given, readers can interpret the term PHR in different way that the writers would have assumed. Misin-terpretations can lead to misinterpretation of the whole written work and thus, undermine its purpose.

This also creates a problem of comparability, since without knowing the implicit interpretation about PHR that different authors have, we cannot compare the results [1, 48]. For example, if one author claims that PHRs have been beneficial in certain situ-ation and other claims opposite and both have neglected defining the PHR, can we trust that they are talking about same kind of PHR? On the other hand, also use of different definitions and variety similar terms makes it hard to compare and combine results in whole research area. This causes unnecessary fragmentation of research, that could be solved with consensus about terms and definitions used in literature. As mentioned, some definitions have gained more popularity than others in scientific community, but there are major differences between them.

It could be also claimed, that many of these definitions fail to capture some fun-damental aspects of PHRs or, on the contrary, focus on irrelevant aspects that are not fundamental as noted earlier. On the other hand, the definition by ISO [45]—which seems to grasp the basic idea of PHR—has not been taken into use. Instead, there is an unfortunate habit of not stating what is meant by the term PHR. Existence of multiple definitions, lack of definitions and variety of interpretations force us down to con-ceptual analysis of the essence of PHR—a laborious task that should be conducted in another paper.

These problems do not limit to the scientific community alone. If scientific com-munity has disagreements and contradictory interpretations about the definition of PHR, it can be assumed that laymen have no better understanding what is meant by this concept. Since PHRs are affecting and will be affecting large masses of people in the future, there should be a possibility to understand these systems that will handle their private health information.

Development of national PHRs highlights the need for clear and commonly understood definition of PHR. As said, PHRs affect and will affect many people in the future and to develop them we should be able to discuss about them not only among professionals, but also with people that are or will be ones to use them [33]. The lack of definition or the lack of consensus about the meaning of PHR is a barrier of having a meaningful discourse, since people having the conversation could have very different interpretation about what is a PHR in the first place.

5 Rational vs Quasi-Rational Discourse

As basis for meaningful discourse we are using the rational discourse by Habermas where all subjects of legislation have possibility to take part in discourse [11]. The Habermasian rational discourse is based on arguments which are evaluated by rationality and plausibility. Those arguments can be based on logic, ethics, or other justified basis. The condition for rational discourse is that no strategic games are allowed in it. A strategic game is a way of using power against others by using something other than a better argument as bargain, and this is not allowed. Like Lyytinen and Hirschheim [49] shows, the Habermas's rational discourse is promising approach for understanding social aspects of IS. Especially important is the idea that norms should be formed through discourse in which every stakeholder is given a possibility to be involved [11].

Thus, the rational discourse is way to act where agreement can be forged. Discourse has four criteria to be described as rational one. Those are clarity, truthfulness, correctness and appropriateness. In addition for those criteria, there certain ground rules. First, actor have possibility to participate discourse and express their arguments. Secondly, all actors need to accept the better and thus more rational argument over inferior one [11]. These four criteria are used as basis of rationality and thus can be used to analyze current discourse about PHRs in the public sphere [12] and also in the academic literature.

However, even Habermasian discourse is just an ideal state and may not be ever reached, it does not mean that we should abandon idea. If we not even try to reach this rationality, we are prisoners of quasi-rational discourse. By Quasi-rationality we are referring to discourse that can by first view seem to be rational one but actually is based on nonsense, jargon and in best scenario; bad interpretation of evidence [50].

In case of national PHRs it we argue, that it is not recommended, but required to make discussion possible especially in democratic countries. However, this task cannot be left solely too governmental officials, who too often have no experience in the field of information systems and tend to make definitions that do not grasp the full nature of an information system [33]. Instead the political discussion is in many cases based on jargon, nonsense and quasi-rationality [50].

6 Conclusion

As shown before we can state that healthcare is evolving together with—or because—technological development. However, it seems that high expectations laid upon information technologies as solution for challenges of healthcare are not met. Especially, PHRs are seen as solutions that have momentum to make people more active, informed and at the end healthy.

The problem is that we do not even know what we are referring with the term PHR. When literature of health informatics is missing common terminology it means that it is actually impossible make comparison between conducted research as focus of those can be on different kind of systems even terms as similar. This has consequences as research findings can be contradictory. If one research sees PHR as stand-alone memo made by individual and other sees it as extension of EHR (used by healthcare professionals) where patient access to see part of their medical information, the conclusion most likely will differ. Using different terms as synonyms is not helpful either.

Thus, we have a problem here. The terms used in field of health informatics should be carefully analyzed and clearly defined so that we can discuss these matters. We should find a consensus about meaning of the term PHR, so that we could develop these systems to be better and to do so, we should also make it possible to the users to participate in the meaningful discussion.

This means that we need to review the terms and definitions used in literature systemically. In future research we are aiming to conduct systematic review of main terms like PHR and EHR. The long term goal is to create ontology of health informatics terminology based on these reviews. In addition to that, there is need to persuade the researchers of the field to start use those defined terms that ontology offers and also engage those researchers to develop that ontology in future in a meaningful way.

References

1. Rantanen, M., Heimo, O.I.: Problem in patient information system acquirement in Finland: translation and terminology. In: Kimppa, K., Whitehouse, D., Kuusela, T., Phahlamohlaka, J. (eds.) HCC 2014. IAICT, vol. 431, pp. 362–375. Springer, Heidelberg (2014). https://doi.org/10.1007/978-3-662-44208-1_29

2. Hersh, W.: A stimulus to define informatics and health information technology. BMC Med. Inform. Decis. Mak. **9**(1), 24 (2009)

3. Garets, D., Davies, M.: Electronic patient records EMRs and EHRs concepts as different as apples and oranges at least deserve separate names. Healthcare Informatics online, October 2005

4. Oh, H., Rizo, C., Enkin, M., Jadad, A.: What is eHealth (3): a systematic review of published definitions. J. Med. Internet Res. **7**(1), e1 (2005)

5. Häyrinen, K., Saranto, K., Nykänen, P.: Definition, structure, content, use and impacts of electronic health records: a review of the research literature. Int. J. Med. Inf. **77**(5), 291–304 (2008)

6. Tang, P.C., Ash, J.S., Bates, D.W., Overhage, J.M., Sands, D.Z.: Personal health records: definitions, benefits, and strategies for overcoming barriers to adoption. J. Am. Med. Inform. Assoc. **13**(2), 121–126 (2006)

7. Kaelber, D.C., Jha, A.K., Johnston, D., Middleton, B., Bates, D.W.: A research agenda for personal health records (PHRs). J. Am. Med. Inform. Assoc. **15**(6), 729–736 (2008)

8. Reti, S.R., Feldman, H.J., Safran, C.: Governance for personal health records. J. Am. Med. Inform. Assoc. **16**(1), 14–17 (2009)

9. Thompson, M.J., Reilly, J.D., Valdez, R.S.: Work system barriers to patient, provider, and caregiver use of personal health records: a systematic review. Appl. Ergon. **54**, 218–242 (2016)

10. Coiera, E.: Guide to Health Informatics, 2nd edn. Hodder Arnold, London (2003)

11. Habermas, J.: Between Facts and Norms: Contributions to a Discourse Theory of Law and Democracy. MIT Press, Cambridge (1996)

12. Habermas, J.: The Public Sphere: An Encyclopedia Article. Media and Cultural Studies: Keyworks, pp. 102–107 (2001)

13. Kim, J., Jung, H., Bates, D.W.: History and trends of "personal health record" research in pubmed. Healthc. Inform. Res. **17**(1), 3–17 (2011)

14. Lahtiranta, J., Koskinen, J.S.S., Knaapi-Junnila, S., Nurminen, M.: Sensemaking in the personal health space. Inf. Technol. People **28**(4), 790–805 (2015)

15. Lee, G., Joong, Y.P., Soo-Yong, S., Jong, S.H., Hyeon, J.R., Jae, H.L., Bates, D.W.: Which users should be the focus of mobile personal health records? Analysis of user characteristics influencing usage of a tethered mobile personal health record. Telemedicine e-Health **22**, 419–428 (2016)

16. Davis, S., Roudsari, A., Raworth, R., Courtney, K.L., MacKay, L.: Shared decision-making using personal health record technology: a scoping review at the crossroads. J. Am. Med. Inform. Assoc. **24**(4), 857–866 (2017)

17. Antonovsky, A.: The salutogenic model as a theory to guide health promotion. Health Promot. Int. **11**(1), 11–18 (1996)

18. Lahtiranta, J.: Current challenges of personal health information management. J. Syst. Inf. Technol. **11**(3), 230–243 (2009)

19. Akter, S., D'Ambra, J., Ray, P.: Development and validation of an instrument to measure user perceived service quality of mHealth. Inf. Manag. **50**(4), 181–195 (2013)

20. Demiris, G.: New era for the consumer health informatics research agenda. Health Syst. **1**(1), 13–16 (2012)

21. Piras, E.M., Zanutto, A.: "One day it will be you who tells us doctors what to do!". Exploring the "personal" of PHR in pediatric diabetes management. Inf. Technol. People **27** (4), 421–439 (2014)

22. Caligtan, C.A., Dykes, P.C.: Electronic health records and personal health records. Semin. Oncol. Nurs. **27**(3), 218–228 (2011). Patient-Centered Technologies: Enhancing Communication and Self-Care for Patients and Caregivers

23. Holopainen, A.: Mobiiliteknologia ja terveyssovellukset, mitä ne ovat? Duodecim **131**(13), 1285–1290 (2015)

24. Househ, M.S., Borycki, E.M., Rohrer, W.M., Kushniruk, A.W.: Developing a framework for meaningful use of personal health records (PHRs). Health Policy Technol. **3**(4), 272–280 (2014)

25. Heart, T., Ben-Assuli, O., Shabtai, I.: A review of PHR, EMR and EHR integration: a more personalized healthcare and public health policy. Health Policy Technol. **6**(1), 20–25 (2017)

26. Ozok, A.A., Wu, H., Gurses, A.P.: Exploring patients' use intention of personal health record systems: implications for design. Int. J. Hum.-Comput. Interact. **33**(4), 265–279 (2017)

27. Dullabh, P., Sondheimer, N.K.E., Evans, M.A.: How patients can improve the accuracy of their medical records. eGEMs **2**(3) (2014)

28. Bonander, J., Gates, S.: Public health in an era of personal health records: opportunities for innovation and new partnerships. J. Med. Internet Res. **12**(3), e33 (2010)

29. Genitsaridi, I., Kondylakis, H., Koumakis, L., Marias, K., Tsiknakis, M.: Evaluation of personal health record systems through the lenses of EC research projects. Comput. Biol. Med. **59**, 175–185 (2015)

30. Weis, J.M., Levy, P.C.: Copy, paste, and cloned notes in electronic health records. Chest **145** (3), 632–638 (2014)

31. Chao, C.A.: The impact of electronic health records on collaborative work routines: a narrative network analysis. Int. J. Med. Inf. **94**, 100–111 (2016)

32. Bushelle-Edghill, J., Brown, J.L., Dong, S.: An examination of EHR implementation impacts on patient-flow. Health Policy Technol. 6(1), 114–120 (2017)
33. Rantanen, M.M.: Terveydenhuollon digitalisaatio sosioteknisestä näkökulmasta. Master's thesis, Turku School of Economics (2017)
34. Dobson, J.: Understanding failure: The London Ambulance Service Disaster. In: Dewsbury, G., Dobson, J. (eds.) Responsibility and Dependable Systems, pp. 130–161. Springer, London (2007)
35. Chaudhry, B., Wang, J., Wu, S., et al.: Systematic review: impact of health information technology on quality, efficiency, and costs of medical care. Ann. Intern. Med. 144(10), 742–752 (2006)
36. Kerns, J.W., Krist, A.H., Longo, D.R., Kuzel, A.J., Woolf, S.H.: How patients want to engage with their personal health record: a qualitative study. BMJ Open 3(7) (2013)
37. Kogut, S.J., Goldstein, E., Charbonneau, C., Jackson, A., Patry, G.: Improving medication management after a hospitalization with pharmacist home visits and electronic personal health records: an observational study. Drug Healthc. Patient Saf. 6, 1–6 (2014)
38. Lau, A., Dunn, A., Mortimer, N., Proudfoot, J., Andrews, A., Liaw, S., Crimmins, J., Arguel, A., Coiera, E.: Consumers' online social network topologies and health behaviours. In: Lehmann, C., Ammenwerth, E., Nøhr, C. (eds.) MEDINFO 2013. Volume 192 of Studies in Health Technology and Informatics, Netherlands, pp. 77–81. IOS Press (2013)
39. Massoudi, B.L., Olmsted, M.G., Zhang, Y., Carpenter, R.A., Barlow, C.E., Huber, R.: A web-based intervention to support increased physical activity among at-risk adults. J. Biomed. Inf. 43(5, Supplement), S41–S45 (2010). Project HealthDesign
40. Park, H.S., Cho, H., Kim, H.S.: Development of a multi-agent m-health application based on various protocols for chronic disease self-management. J. Med. Syst. 40(1), 1–14 (2016)
41. Santos, C., Pedrosa, T., Costa, C., Oliveira, J.L.: Concepts for a personal health record. Stud. Health Technol. Inf. 180, 636–640 (2012)
42. Markle Foundation: The personal health working group final report (2003). http://www.providersedge.com/ehdocs/ehr_articles/The_Personal_Health_Working_Group_Final_Report.pdf
43. Markle Foundation: Connecting Americans to their health care: A common framework for networked personal health information (2006). http://www.markle.org/sites/default/files/CF-Consumers-Full.pdf
44. Davidson, E.J., Østerlund, C.S., Flaherty, M.G.: Drift and shift in the organizing vision career for personal health records: an investigation of innovation discourse dynamics. Inf. Organ. 25(4), 191–221 (2015)
45. International Organization for Standardization: ISO/TR 14639-2:2014(en) (2014). https://www.iso.org/obp/ui/#iso:std:iso:tr:18638:ed-1:v1:en:te
46. Tang, P.C., Lansky, D.: The missing link: bridging the patient-provider health information gap. Health Aff. 24(5), 1290–1295 (2005)
47. Arens-Volland, A.G., Spassova, L., Bohn, T.: Promising approaches of computer supported dietary assessment and management—current research status and available applications. Int. J. Med. Inf. 84(12), 997–1008 (2015)
48. Valta, M.: Sähköisen potilastietojärjestelmän sosiotekninen käyttöönotto: seitsemän vuoden seurantatutkimus odotuksista omaksumiseen. Ph.D. thesis, University of Eastern Finland, Faculty of Social Sciences and Business/Department of Health and Social Management (2013)
49. Lyytinen, K., Hirschheim, R.: Information systems as rational discourse: an application of Habermas's theory of communicative action. Scand. J. Manag. 4(1), 19–30 (1988)
50. Koskinen, J., Rantanen, M.M.: Discourse about governmental eHealth information systems —jargon, non-sense and quasi-rationality. In: Ethicomp 2018 (2018 in print)

An Exploration of Opportunities for a Theory of Information Inadequacy

Miranda Kajtazi[1]([⊠]) and Darek Haftor[2]

[1] Lund University, 223 62 Lund, Sweden
miranda.kajtazi@ics.lu.se
[2] Uppsala University, 751 20 Uppsala, Sweden
darek.haftor@im.uu.se

Abstract. Our everyday experiences show that the lack of needed information in various human affairs may give rise to consequences that we would like to avoid – e.g. the 2004 Tsunami in Southeast Asia. However, we still do not have a coherent theoretical body that addresses such experiences of information inadequacy as this changes everything in respect to the current conception of the information society, where technology plays a central role. To this end, we provide an initial exploration of opportunities for such a theory: when needed information is not available in human affairs, for any reason. We start with diagnoses of five existing central theoretical bodies that constitute promising candidates to account for instances of information inadequacy. The results show though that these do not offer a comprehensive account for situations where needed information is missing. Secondly, an empirical investigation was conducted, utilizing grounded theory approach, where fifty cases of information inadequacy were analysed. This revealed a number of patterns of plausible causes of information inadequacies in human affairs, which offer a preliminary foundation for a future theory of information inadequacy. This result suggests that information inadequacies may be understood as various instances of information-lack and information-overflow. These two, in turn, include numerous factors that cause information inadequacies, ranging from political and cultural structures, through human individual capabilities, and ending with procedural set-ups and technological artefacts. We advocate that further research should be conducted to explore various instances of information inadequacy aimed to the formulation of a coherent theory.

Keywords: Information management · Information needs
Information overload · Information lack · Information inadequacy

1 Introduction

Some fundamental questions of our contemporary debates are concerned with phenomena that relate to information problems, predominantly experienced with difficulties in human, social and industrial affairs. Such are the dramatic situations of e.g. the Lehman Brothers bankruptcy in 2008, the tsunami in Indonesia in 2004, the Space Shuttle Challenger destruction in 1986 or the release of the atomic bomb in 1945. Situations like these are concerned with decision-making processes and require a

D. Kreps et al. (Eds.): HCC13 2018, IFIP AICT 537, pp. 384–394, 2018.
https://doi.org/10.1007/978-3-319-99605-9_29

rational behavior to process information related to them [17]. Philosophers, scientists and industrialists hypothesize about information problems and intend to develop theories or solutions that are partially helpful [1, 2, 8].

Information has a deep impact on personal well-being, decision-making processes, innovation and production [7, 12]. But, the failure to achieve balance between the surging volumes of information we access (mostly affected by electronic information) and its obverse, the information underload [20], allow conceptualizing that the information-related problems are fairly typical. Our everyday experiences manifest numerous instances in which information is the key that generates various consequences, many of which are experienced as failures and fatalities in human, social and industrial affairs. Therefore, in this paper a core phenomenon is explored: the lack of needed information in human, social and industrial affairs. The lack of needed information is understood as a composition of different behavioral aspects of human agents that implicate how the production, the transfer or the use of information is performed based on intrusive manners. Although related topics have tackled similar phenomena for some decades now [6, 7, 12, 18, 20], there is little we understand about it. Indeed, there is no comprehensive understanding that has tackled such a phenomenon at length.

The objective of this paper is to give an understanding of the phenomenon of the lack of needed information by developing a model of why and how the lack of needed information contributes to unwanted consequences in human, social and industrial affairs. Empirically, the exploration of this phenomenon is based on grounded theory approach as originated by Glaser and Strauss [11], but has been further developed by Orlikowski [19], Sarker et al. [22], and Charmaz [5].

The paper is organized as follows. First, a literature review on five information behavior theories is presented. Then, an overview of grounded theory approach is provided. Furthermore, the application of grounded theory approach (coding process) and a model derived from data analysis are presented. Finally, the paper gives some practical and theoretical implications that may advance studies with focus on the lack of needed information and its impact in organizations and societies.

1.1 Do Information Behavior Theories Account for Information Inadequacy?

Five theories have been of particular interest to investigate the phenomenon in context, selected during a careful literature search on aspects of information overflow and information lack: Social Network Theory; Social Cognitive Theory; Theory of Information Asymmetry; Information Theory; and Social Construction of Technology Theory. Conceptually, these five theories are examined in terms of their use in developing information behavior theories, which are intended to understand information practices (information need and seeking, information-seeking behavior, cognitive information retrieval, etc.). Information behavior theories are well established and focus on information-related phenomena, which mostly tend to address human cognitive behavior in relation to using information in its physical or digital form[1]. These

---

[1] [10] p. 3 xix.

theories represent an interdisciplinary approach that refers to various aspects of information behavior, and are therefore thought to be useful in addressing the phenomenon of the lack of needed information. The selection of these five theories is based on the need to investigate their potentials in addressing the phenomenon of the lack of needed information. Selected theories are based on characteristics that profoundly influence problem-solving activities that are specifically focused on trying to understand human motivational states when people are involved in various information practices. Below, a short introduction to each of these theories is given, in order to understand their benefits, limitations and implications for the phenomenon of the lack of needed information.

Social Network Theory was first coined by Barnes [3]. This theory intends to specify the role of an individual in a social group. The use of this theory in information behavior theories is based on the idea that human information behavior is shaped by and shapes individuals, social networks, situations and contexts where information practices take place. This theory is widely used in understanding information needs, information construction, and actions based on available information – all focusing on information problems that concern individuals in a social group. In summary, social network theory is mainly used in determining the perception of the need for information in relation to its availability to satisfy the need of an individual. Searching for an understanding of the lack of needed information, the benefit of this particular theory is in its focus on "information need". However, this theory only partially helps to determine the information needs of an individual in dramatic situations, because dramatic situations always happen unexpectedly, and therefore the availability of and the need for information in a particular situation is unexpected when needed for edgy decisions.

Social Cognitive Theory originated from Bandura [2]. This theory is used to develop information behavior theories to show how individuals operate with information based on their cognitive activities. It examines how individuals influence behavior change and developments in social groups, when they are engaged in different forms of social experiences by determining the meaning of information and its exchange in social interactions [25]. This theory is interesting for elaborating on human thought and action in a particular situation. Nevertheless, its limitation for understanding the lack of needed information in dramatic situations is that it only focuses on individual's behavior in information-seeking processes, mostly for their own needs, and not on their needs that are determined by the situation itself.

The Theory of Information Asymmetry was first introduced by Akerlof [1]. This theory is used to explain the role of asymmetric information in economic transactions. It focuses on human behavioral aspects when engaged in economic transaction, specifically focusing on "dishonesty" in economic markets. The theory explains how individuals are prone to influence the inclusion of imperfect information in economic transactions of personal interest [1]. This theory is helpful for understanding how the meaning of information is affected in situations where an individual influences the meaning for personal benefit. Yet, in general and in dramatic situations where the meaning of information is rather unexpected and not necessarily influenced by another individual, this theory can only partially account for individuals' needs for a decision making process.

Information Theory has flourished since Shannon's model of a mathematical theory of communication [23]. This theory is mostly used to understand how information messages can be transmitted in a linear engineering form, using two entities: sender and receiver. Information theory was further developed and used to construct new information behavior theories that also focus on human-related information messages. Among its uses in many engineering disciplines, information theory is also used in communication theory to advance the study of information retrieval processes. This theory is steadily advancing, but in practice such advancements still remain entangled in the field of engineering. In dramatic situations it is impractical to use automated processes for information retrieval where information needs cannot be always fulfilled by means of technology. This is because the lack of needed information appears in diverse situations and contexts, where technology may still be inaccessible.

The Social Construction of Technology Theory focuses on the development of technologies influenced by human needs. The most influential scholars that advocate the social construction of technology are Pinch and Bijker [21]. This theory is interesting in that it presents an interplay between social, economic, political and environmental factors in the process of developing technology. Thus, social construction is characterized by the needs of individuals that influence innovation and development of technology to fulfil human needs. The theory then suggests that the phenomenon of the lack of needed information may be manageable in the future as technology develops at a rapid pace, mostly focusing on optimizing information flows for human needs. However, this still remains challenging, considering that in many situations technology is not always helpful for timely provision of information and in uncertain developments of situations.

From the above introduction, it is evident that such theories derive from different disciplines. Their intention is to specify how people need, seek, manage, give and use information in different contexts. This suggests that information behavior theories call for an interdisciplinary approach to investigate the phenomenon of the lack of needed information. This review suggests that although such theories account for the phenomenon of the lack of needed information, their focus is rather implicit and their benefit is only partial in trying to understand and remedy situations where the needed information is lacking. Analytically, what is addressed with these theories is rather the behavior of humans or machines that produce, transfer and receive information, as a chain of events, by not specifying what really happens with the production of information, when it happens and how to make sure that timely information can be produced and transferred to meet the human needs in critical situations.

Communication theory was used from the beginning as a guide to understand the addressed theoretical bodies in terms of three roles: the information sender (source), the information mediator, and the information receiver. The analysis showed that the addressed theoretical bodies are significant for partial understanding of what happens with information at the information receiver (the process of information consumption), but are weak in accounting for information transfer, and they do not address information production, which is central for understanding the lack of needed information. An illustration of this is given in Fig. 1:

Information Behaviour Theories	Sender (Source) Information Production	Mediator Information Transfer	Receiver Information Consumption
- Social Network Theory	?	?	O
- Social Cognitive Theory	?	?	O
- Theory of Information Asymmetry	?	?	O
- Information Theory	?	☐	O
- Social Construction of Technology Theory	?	☐	?

? - not addressed   ☐ - vague   O - central

Fig. 1. Information behavior theories and their impact on sender (source), mediator and receiver of information.

Implications of this literature review have led to the understanding that the phenomenon of the lack of needed information remains unexplored and requires thorough investigations. Thus, there is no comprehensive a priori theory to be used for the design of an empirical investigation. An empirical investigation of various instances of information inadequacy was therefore conducted and is presented in the following.

2   Empirical Investigation: A Grounded Theory Approach

A number of authors have developed theories that postulate how problems with information in human affairs arise in different circumstances [1, 7, 9, 15]. These problems may be caused by different factors, among which are the management factor, the political factor or the ethical factor (e.g. [7, 20]). In practice, information is considered as an invaluable asset of three core competent organizational processes engaged in communication: (a) information production; (b) information exchange; and (c) information recipient [16].

Communication in organizational processes is often followed by unprecedented difficulties that result in failure in successful management of information-related practices [13, 20]. There is substantial relevant research that investigates problems with information mirrored in communication theory with the focus on information practices [4, 7, 18]. Recent investigations, especially those of the last two decades, have documented different information-related problems that occur in an unexpected fashion [18]. Theoreticians and practitioners argue that societal, political and economic movements have become more contagious with information problems than ever predicted [14]. This paper intends to give an understanding of information-related problems by analyzing data derived from dramatic situations (e.g. natural disasters, financial failures, etc.) and by systematically applying grounded theory approach in order to find an answer that explains how the phenomenon of the lack of needed information arises in human, social and industrial affairs.

2.1 A Summary of Selected Empirical Cases

In this study, data collection and analysis are based on secondary sources. The collection resulted in fifty empirical cases. The data analysis is conducted using open coding, axial coding and selective coding, which are adapted for the purpose of this research, according to procedural aspects illustrated by Strauss and Corbin [24], enhanced by Orlikowski [19], Sarker et al. [22] and Charmaz [5].

Fifty empirical cases comprise of different dramatic situations that are selected for the purpose of emphasizing the phenomenon of the lack of needed information. More concretely, the selected number of situations are grouped as follows: Natural Disasters (9); Environmental Disasters (6); Financial Failures (7); Health Failures (6); Political Scandals (6); Conflict Situations (3); Engineering and Technological Failures (8); Nuclear and Chemical Disasters (5). The fifty cases identified are analyzed further on with grounded theory approach. They are categorized in an a priori manner, solely for the purpose of facilitating the reader's understanding of what situations are taken into consideration.

However, this does not have any influence on the empirical analysis.

3 Data Analysis and Results

Data analysis emerged iteratively, starting with early open-ended research, primarily line-by-line text analysis, and continued with more strategic selection of emerging concepts and categories [19]. The benefit of the iterative processes is that the initial phase of exploration followed a flexible path in understanding and collecting data, while the later phase of conceptualization followed a more strictly organized path with strategic planning of analysis.

The coding process as formulated by grounded theory approach is employed more formally in data analysis after all the data have been collected, selected and refined. The analyses were based on three types of coding presented by Strauss and Corbin [24], which are: open coding, axial coding, and selective coding.

The initial result of open coding analysis followed with 182 codes. Each code was associated with the representative text as derived from the description of each case. The codes that emerged were needed to give an initial and an informal understanding of what causes the phenomenon of the lack of needed information in human, social and industrial affairs.

The actual conceptualization and interpretation of the phenomenon of the lack of needed information became clear in the early phase of data analysis. The conceptualization of fifty cases developed on the basis of analyzing each case deriving characteristics that could show what causes the lack of needed information. The results of such a conceptualization were mainly dependent on several induced codes that were identified as recurring in many situations. For instance, codes such as "did not alert" or "warning system(s)" were crucial for interpreting the phenomenon in context. The use of the majority of codes clearly presented significant similarities in all the situations, resulting in an early, yet a crucial interpretation of the phenomenon in context.

Axial coding continued with constant comparative analysis through data. Codes found in the data became more meaningful when they continued to be merged, changed, and even eliminated. The codes that were merged represented a type of code used to show a key input for the purpose of generating categories. The codes that were changed were adapted to other similar codes, which may have reduced redundancy. The eliminated codes were primarily redundant (it is important to point that the categorization is not only interpretive but also the data spoke for the categorization itself). With axial coding, the analysis process led, firstly, to refining of the identified codes and induction of concepts. Of 182 initial codes, 35 codes were engaged intensively by formulating one group of concepts (17) and two groups of codes: substantive codes (13) and theoretical codes (5). The concepts (17) were successfully used for categorization. The theoretical codes (5) were successfully used for presenting the main causes that justified the identification of (13) substantive codes. Furthermore, the concepts (17) were used to interlink the theoretical codes and substantive codes by showing strong dependency. Detailed overview of these results is presented in Fig. 2.

The axial coding analysis that acted based on classifications and comparative analysis resulted in the identification of 8 sub-categories. As a result, the comparative analysis showed two main differences between the 8 identified sub-categories. The differences resulted in grouping the sub-categories by introducing two main axial categories, i.e. information lack and information overflow, and their interrelations with sub-categories, concepts and codes. Therefore, the classification of 35 codes (17 concepts, 13 substantive codes and 5 theoretical codes) into 8 sub-categories and grouped in two main categories is based on the following definitions:

Information Lack

(1) *Information is non-existent.* – is characterized by failure to communicate information in situations when actions are unforeseen and the responsible body for transmitting information is unaware of such a need, usually due to mismanagement.

(2) *Information is insufficient.* – is characterized by failure to communicate ontime information as a result of pre-planning of circumstances that may cause unwanted results in a specific situation. Unawareness, mismanagement and difficulty in understanding represent failure to act in a timely fashion.

(3) *Information is censored.* – is characterized by serious violation of information. Such information is usually hindered intentionally, secretly and illegally for the purpose of suppressing original information that is intended for the public and that may be significant for their needs. Fraud is one of the key acts that reflect the censoring of information.

(4) *Information is undelivered.* – is characterized by incompetent acts of humans, with a dual outcome. The act is either done intentionally by prohibiting the use of information or the undelivered information is caused by unawareness.

Information Overflow

(5) *Information is ambiguous.* – is characterized by lack of control of information. It is usually accompanied by miscalculations and lack of accurate evidence that misleads important decision-making processes.

(6) *Information is redundant.* – is characterized by duplication or even multiplication of the same information (repetition of information's message in synonyms or with the same excessive expression) due to lack of control or unawareness.

(7) *Information is irrelevant.* – is characterized by types of information that have no validity and are shared by unknown sources. Such information holds misinterpretations.

(8) *Information is undervalued.* – is characterized by mismanagement that may cause misinterpretation of information, possibly by lack of awareness or unawareness.

A significant number of codes, both substantive and theoretical, that are ultimately used in generating the 8 sub-categories have been recurrent within one or more of the sub-categories, as presented in Fig. 2.

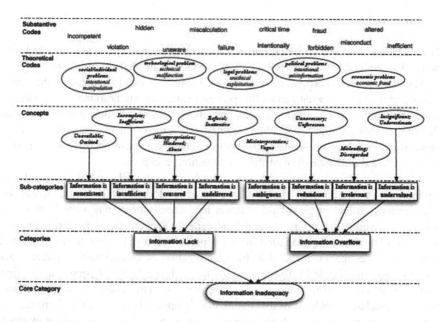

Fig. 2. Information behavior theories and their impact on sender (source), mediator and receiver of information.

Selective coding is employed as the final step required to generate the core category, ultimately to generate a middle-range theory [5]. The data analysis has developed the core category by verifying that the phenomenon of the lack of needed information is evident in practical senses. Thus, the core category as a result of analysis is named in this study "information inadequacy". With the core category at hand, the aim is to integrate all analysis into one formulated comprehensive outline that could portray the phenomenon of the lack of needed information in human, social and industrial affairs.

The analysis performed generated new and interesting results that are used to formulate an explicit meaning of what is characterized as "information inadequacy", defined as follows: "dramatic situations (many of which happen on a daily basis) that encounter information as the key resource in different situations and circumstances, manifest various consequences, many of which are experienced as failures and fatalities in human, social and industrial affairs".

It is justifiable, as well as moderate, to state that information inadequacy as such is not taken as seriously as a problem in our current information society, which is usually accompanied by unwanted consequences.

4   Conclusion

This study has proposed an initial outline of information inadequacy that resulted from the need to understand the phenomenon of the lack of needed information.

The theoretical investigation was initiated with the need to identify theoretical bodies that may clarify what causes this phenomenon. This study found that theoretical bodies that implicitly claim to handle this phenomenon, i.e. Information Behavior Theories, cannot account for, explain, or suggest a remedy for the dramatic situations where there is a lack of needed information. These can only account for a partial, hence, a limited understanding of the phenomenon in context.

A need for empirical investigations thus became crucial, and it triggered new explorations in interpreting what is changing about today's information access and what remains critical in global information landscapes (these may vary from social, political, economic or environmental landscapes). The empirical investigation was based on a constructivist grounded theory approach on a collection of fifty empirical cases. This investigation resulted in the identification of characteristics, patterns and causes of how the needed information fails to reach the intended person at the right time and place, causing unwanted consequences. The analysis suggested that information-related problems of that nature mainly appear because of problems that are caused by information source (sender) and information mediator – human or machine. The results of this investigation have developed an initial outline of information inadequacy that could possibly guide the development of a future theory of information inadequacy.

In practice, the proposed outline of information inadequacy addresses all humans who are concerned with information in everyday practices and intend to enhance their time by carefully managing information. More importantly, information inadequacy can be a diagnosis tool that allows industrialists, technology developers, environmentalists and others to think for enhancing information communication in the future.

Given the results of the empirical investigation conducted here, the identified factors portray how hindrances to information provision may be utilized as guidelines for the diagnosis and re-design of information provision processes. In short, this would imply that each pattern of information inadequacy identified, might be used to direct new and innovative diagnostic and re-design teams that focus on information management and on more careful planning of information flows that are present and important in dramatic situations that happen in everyday basis. Such an understanding may possibly guide further development of a future theory of information inadequacy that can be instrumental in developing more efficient information systems for organizations and societies for an operational use of information.

References

1. Akerlof, G.: The market for 'Lemons': quality uncertainty and the market mechanism. Q. J. Econ. **84**(3), 488–500 (1970)
2. Bandura, A.: Self-efficacy: toward a unifying theory of behavioral change. Psychol. Rev. **84** (2), 191–215 (1977)
3. Barnes, J.A.: Class and committees in a Norwegian island parish. Hum. Relat. **7**, 39–58 (1954)
4. Bawden, D., Robinson, L.: Training for information literacy: diverse approaches. In: Proceedings of the International Online Information Meeting, pp. 87–90. Learned Information Europe Ltd, Oxford (2001)
5. Charmaz, K.: Constructing Grounded Theory: A Practical Guide Through Qualitative Analysis. Sage Publications, Thousand Oaks (2006)
6. Creese, G.: Information scarcity to information overload. Inf. Manage. Mag. 20–22 (2007)
7. Dean, D., Webb, C.: Recovering from information overload. McKinsey Quarterly (2011) https://www.mckinseyquarterly.com/Recovering_from_information_overload_273. Accessed 25 Apr 2018
8. Ennals, R., Stratton, L., Moujahid, N., Kovela, S.: Global information technology and global citizenship education. AI Soc. **23**, 61–68 (2009)
9. Eppler, M.J., Mengis, J.: The concept of information overload: a review of literature from organization science, accounting, marketing, mis, and related disciplines. Inf. Soc. **20**, 325–344 (2004)
10. Fisher, E.K., Erdelez, S., McKechnie, L.: Theories of Information Behavior, 2nd edn. American Society for Information Science and Technology, New Jersey (2006)
11. Glaser, B., Strauss, A.L.: The discovery of grounded theory: strategies for qualitative research. Aldine, Chicago (1967)
12. Hemp, P.: Death by information overload. Harvard Bus. Rev. **87**(9), 82–89 (2009) http://hbr. org/2009/09/death-by-information-overload/ar/1. Accessed 25 Apr 2018
13. Hwang, M.I., Lin, J.W.: Information dimension, information overload and decision quality. J. Inf. Sci. **25**(3), 213–219 (1999)
14. Krotoski, A.: The information revolution. Undergraduate Lecture Series. Oxford Internet Institute (2010). http://alekskrotoski.com/post/oxford-internet-institute-the-informationrevolution. Accessed 25 Apr 2018
15. Mingers, J.C.: Information and meaning: foundations for an intersubjective account. Inf. Syst. J. **5**(4), 285–306 (1995)

16. Mortensen, C.D.: Communication Theory. 2nd edn. Transaction Publishers, New Jersey (2009)
17. Newell, A., Simon, H.A.: Human Problem Solving. Prentice-Hall, Englewood Cliffs (1972)
18. Ojala, M.: Transforming information quality. Online **33**(4) (2009)
19. Orlikowski, W.J.: CASE tools as organizational change: investigating incremental and radical changes in systems development. MIS Q. **17**(3), 309–340 (1993)
20. O'Reilly, Ch.A: Individuals and information overload in organizations: is more necessarily better? Acad. Manage. J. **23**(4), 684–696 (1980)
21. Pinch, T.J., Bijker, W.E.: Science, relativism and the new sociology of technology: reply to Russell. Soc. Stud. Sci. **16**(May), 347–360 (1986)
22. Sarker, S., Lau, F., Sahay, S.: Using an adapted grounded theory approach for inductive theory building about virtual team development. Database Adv. Inf. Syst. **32**(1), 38–56 (2001)
23. Shannon, C.E.A.: Mathematical theory of communication. Bell Syst. Tech. J. **27**, 379–423 (1948)
24. Strauss, A., Corbin, J.: Basics of Qualitative Research. Sage Publications, California (1990)
25. Wilson, T.: Information-seeking behaviour: designing information systems to meet our client's needs. In: 25th International Conference of the Association of Caribbean University, Research and Institutional Libraries, San Juan (1995)

Author Index

Printed in the United States
By Bookmasters